REASONS TO DOUBT

OXFORD MONOGRAPHS ON CRIMINAL LAW AND JUSTICE

Series Editor:
Andrew Ashworth CBE QC, Emeritus Vinerian Professor
of English Law, All Souls College, Oxford

This series aims to cover all aspects of criminal law and procedure including
criminal evidence. The scope of this series is wide, encompassing both practical
and theoretical works.

Reasons to Doubt

Wrongful Convictions and the Criminal Cases Review Commission

CAROLYN HOYLE
and
MAI SATO

OXFORD
UNIVERSITY PRESS

Great Clarendon Street, Oxford, OX2 6DP,
United Kingdom

Oxford University Press is a department of the University of Oxford.
It furthers the University's objective of excellence in research, scholarship,
and education by publishing worldwide. Oxford is a registered trade mark of
Oxford University Press in the UK and in certain other countries

Published in the United States of America by Oxford University Press
198 Madison Avenue, New York, NY 10016, United States of America

British Library Cataloguing in Publication Data
Data available

Library of Congress Control Number: 2018952418

ISBN 978–0–19–879457–8

Printed and bound by
CPI Group (UK) Ltd, Croydon, CR0 4YY

For David Rose and Thomas Sato-Tapmeier

General Editor's Preface

In this searching examination of an important—some would say, world-leading—institution of criminal justice, Carolyn Hoyle and Mai Sato assess the Criminal Cases Review Commission of England and Wales both on its own terms and in its broader social and legal contexts. The authors' emphasis is on understanding by what means and to what extent the Commission contributes to the remedying of wrongful convictions. This involves an exploration of the working principles and practices of individuals at different levels in the Commission, with particular reference to the initial filtering of applications, and also an exploration of the Commission's relationship to other agencies such as the police, the Crown Prosecution Service, and the Court of Appeal. Indeed, it is the relationship with the Court of Appeal that underlies the whole operation of the Commission, since it may only refer a case if it believes there is a 'real possibility' that the Court will quash the conviction. This narrow gateway casts the Commission as a predictor of the Court's decisions, and raises the question whether the Commission should go no further than a defensive/predictive approach or should push boldly at the boundaries in an attempt to loosen the Court's approach. Hoyle and Sato base their assessment of the Commission's work on a strong sample of cases and extensive interviews of those employed by the Commission, set against the background of a criminal justice system struggling to cope with swingeing cuts to legal aid, widespread non-disclosure of evidence, and declining trust in forensic science evidence. The result is a compelling monograph on the quality of criminal justice in England and Wales, a quarter of a century after the report of the Royal Commission on Criminal Justice.

Andrew Ashworth

Preface

In September 2010, at a two-day seminar on wrongful convictions at the National Institute of Justice, Washington DC, the first author witnessed an impassioned critique of the Criminal Cases Review Commission ('the Commission') that sowed the seeds for this book. With only forty or so participants, most of them US academics, criminal justice practitioners, and staff at the Department of Justice, it was a restrained event, with several presentations and time for discussion. Given the primary focus on the US, contributions from the Chair of the Commission and a lay member of its sister Commission in Scotland were a welcome counterpart to debates about the efficacy of innocence projects across the US. But while most talks were met with polite questions and comments, the presentation by the Chair of the Commission, elicited an astonishing onslaught from the only other English academic present.

The Commission's Chair, Richard Foster, had explained to those present that it reviews possible wrongful convictions in England, Wales, and Northern Ireland and refers back to the Court of Appeal ('the Court')[1] cases in which it considers there to be a 'real possibility' that the Court will deem the conviction to be unsafe. While the talk was informative, it was also unremarkable: a description of the aims of the Commission and a summary of the numbers of cases received and the proportion referred for fresh appeals. The critic's impassioned outburst claimed that for some applicants at least, the Commission was a failing and unaccountable body that should not be the model for reform elsewhere. He attacked its rationale and remit, and claimed that there was an unacceptably low proportion of deserving cases referred back to the Court. His most intriguing point was the reason he adduced for this alleged failing: an accusation that the Commission simply did not care about innocence. Later, as experts from New Zealand and Canada told of their countries' interest in the Commission as a model for reform of their own post-conviction review procedures, he took further opportunities to diminish the Commission's apparent strengths.

The heat of his argument aroused the first author's curiosity. What was it about this organization, of which she had learnt little since its inception thirteen years prior, that had incited such ire? Why was he so certain that an organization which, on the face of it, seemed to offer greater opportunities for reversing wrongful convictions than its counterparts in the US or other common law jurisdictions was a failure, so early in its life? And which, if any, of his many criticisms were fair?

Seven years later, as we were writing this book, the Commission reached its twentieth anniversary, and *The Justice Gap*, an online magazine focusing on law and justice, ran a series of articles to mark this milestone. Most concluded that while the Commission was an improvement on its predecessor, a small bureaucratic unit within the Home Office, its record, 'like the curate's egg', was 'partly excellent, partly abysmal'; and that while there were examples of cases that showed 'exemplary' investigation, in others, investigations had been poor (Robins, 2017). Seven years of criticisms, but none founded on empirical research, for there was no such research in existence. Filling this lacuna is the task we set for this book.

Thus, this monograph presents the findings of a thorough, four-year empirical study of decision-making and the use of discretion within the Commission—the first of its

---

[1] Typically, the Court of Appeal Criminal Division, but in cases tried at the magistrates' courts, a referral is back to the Crown Court.

kind. It reveals what happens to applications for post-conviction review made to the Commission by those in England and Wales who consider themselves to have been wrongfully convicted. It explores how Commission staff exercise their discretionary powers in identifying and investigating possible wrongful convictions for consideration by the Court. Our research comprised qualitative and quantitative analysis of case files and aggregate data, as well as interviews with decision-makers, a survey of staff, and close analysis of the internal guidance that informs decision-making in all cases, guidance not publicly available. It therefore attempts to grasp the workings of the Commission from a sociological perspective, and to understand how discretion operates within it at both the individual and institutional level.

The use of discretion is central to this investigation because while the law has created the Commission's decision-making structures, and while the Commission guides its staff by way of producing detailed 'Casework Guidance Notes' for all types of cases and different stages of each investigation, both the hard and soft law leaves considerable room for discretion as to how these structures operate. Hence, we examine the structural and cultural factors that shape the Commission's discretion in key functions: in its selection of just a proportion of cases for thorough investigation (from about 1,400 applications a year); in its decision-making while investigating cases; and in its choices about whether there is fresh argument or evidence that would present a 'real possibility' that the Court would quash the case where the Commission is persuaded that there are reasons to doubt the safety of the conviction.

As we report above, and demonstrate in Chapter 2, the Commission has been subject to considerable criticism of its remit and efficacy in performing these functions. Its critics focus particularly on its referral rate, on its decisions as to which cases to devote its limited investigative resources to, and on its relationship with the Court. While we are interested in matters of efficacy, this is not simply a 'does it work?' study. The Commission cannot only be understood by reference to the number or types of cases it refers to the Court, nor by the proportion of those convictions which the Court then overturns. It must also be judged by its methods in choosing which cases to focus on, by how it decides what an investigation should include, and by when and how it decides to conduct those investigations. Also significant is an examination of its place within the wider criminal justice process: how it manages its relations with other criminal justice institutions and its clients and stakeholders—applicants, their legal representatives, and those from whom it seeks to gather evidence.

In laying bare these issues, we scrutinize the Commission's day-to-day working practices, its working rules and assumptions, and how these influence and give meaning to its understanding of the 'real possibility test'—what evidence it considers is likely to persuade the Court to quash a conviction. In this sense, we try to describe the Commission not simply as a legal body, but as a cultural institution, and to expose the social meaning and significance of its rituals and techniques (Garland, 2001). However, we do not attempt to establish one overarching theory of how the Commission works. Instead, we seek to explore it from various angles, in order to produce a compound picture that reveals its complexities, and its multi-faceted and sometimes apparently contradictory nature. We do this mainly in Chapters 5–13, with Chapters 1–4 setting the scene for the research and providing information to help our readers to make sense of our data.

Chapter 1 introduces the reader to the Commission, charting its origins and remit, and providing, by way of comparison, information on other jurisdictions' post-conviction review procedures. Chapter 2 seeks to understand the nature of criticisms about the Commission, before describing the aims of this study and the methods adopted to realize them. Chapter 3 presents the theoretical framework that shaped our empirical research, and helped us to make sense of the data we gathered. In Chapter 4, we describe what happens to each application received by the Commission and present a framework from organizational theory within which we consider how the Commission makes crucial decisions throughout its investigatory process.

Chapters 5–13 focus on our empirical study, taking the reader through the decisions made by the Commission on applications it receives. These applications present to the Commission a range of potential flaws: in investigations by police and prosecutors; in trials; and in first appeals following conviction. To help the reader understand the range of possible misconduct and legal, scientific, or human error that might lead to an applicant being wrongfully convicted, or to believing themselves to be so, Chapter 5 situates the types of applications received by the Commission within the extant literature on the sources of wrongful conviction. Chapter 6 then considers how the Commission makes sense of approximately 1,400 applications it receives each year, and how it decides which of these to subject to full investigation, while screening out others early through a 'triage' process, when it considers they present no obvious basis for a review.

Chapter 7 reviews the issues presented by cases that turn on forensic and expert evidence—the largest category in our sample. It considers how the Commission investigates such applications and makes its decisions. The Commission's approach to sexual offence cases that tend to present evidence pertaining to the credibility of the complainant is considered in Chapter 8, while Chapter 9 looks at those cases that raise concerns about breaches of due process or malpractice by the police, and Chapter 10 focuses on applicants' claims of incompetence by their legal representatives at trial.

The legislation that established the Commission—the Criminal Appeal Act 1995—requires the Commission to work with other parts of the criminal justice system in some of its reviews. Section 15 of the Criminal Appeal Act 1995 allows the Court to direct the Commission to investigate a discrete issue on the Court's behalf, which means that the Commission might find itself investigating cases during first instance appeals or during applications for leave to appeal. The Commission has the power to progress this Court-directed investigation in the manner it deems most appropriate, and to investigate related matters too, as long as it keeps the Court informed about its investigations. Chapter 11 considers such investigations and also analyses those rare cases where the Commission uses its powers—under section 19 of the Criminal Appeal Act 1995—to appoint an investigating officer to carry out enquiries to assist in the exercise of any of its functions.

Chapter 12 considers how the Commission balances its aim to be thorough in each investigation with its requirement to be efficient, ever mindful of the long queue of applicants waiting for their case to be reviewed. It reflects on apparent variations in how Commission staff conduct their investigations: when, for example, they seek expert evidence on a case; when they choose to interview an applicant; and when they consider it sufficient to study the case file and the relevant law without conducting any further investigation.

In Chapter 13, we look at what happens in cases when the Commission has decided there are no grounds for referral but where the applicant comes back with further information or a new application to try to persuade the Commission that it was wrong. In considering its response to 'further submissions' or 'reapplications', we reflect on the Commission's relationship with applicants over the course of an investigation, and consider the extent to which the increasing threat of judicial review of both the investigation and the application's outcome may influence the Commission's willingness to revisit its own, earlier decisions.

The concluding chapter (Chapter 14) reflects on the key findings from our empirical study and describes the main cultural and structural influences on decision-making. It also considers the place of the Commission within the wider state machinery, and its relationship with the police, the Crown Prosecution Service, legal representatives, the media, and miscarriage of justice campaigners, bearing in mind the wider political landscape in which these organizations operate. But its principal focus is on the vital relationship between the Commission and the Court, reflecting on criticisms that the Commission is too 'deferential' to the Court when it comes to making decisions about which cases meet the 'real possibility test'.

Acknowledgements

This book is based on years of empirical research on the Criminal Cases Review Commission ('the Commission'). We are indebted to the Chair, commissioners, case review managers, and all other staff at the Commission for giving us permission to study their handling of cases over more than four years. They have tolerated our presence, critical questioning, and demands on their time with good grace. They have, furthermore, provided us access to data and resources, and their coffee machine. We had not anticipated how long it would take to record detailed information on the progress of each of our cases. Casefiles are not only exhaustive in their detail, but complex in their substance. Many require a reasonable working knowledge of criminal or procedural law, of forensic science, of police and prosecution practice, and of the workings of various other public and private bodies. It took us some time to acquire this level of knowledge and a lot of patience from Commission staff who we quizzed when we were unsure or confused. The legal advisers were particularly generous with their time and tolerant of our sometimes naïve questions.

Key personnel at the Commission have read each of the chapters that follow in order to check that we have not breached our agreement to keep our data anonymous (see Chapter 2). In doing so, they were also able to check that we had made no errors in our discussion of their approach to cases. While some Commission staff may not agree with our analysis in each and every page that follows, we are confident that there are no errors of fact about the organization.

We have also benefited from the expertise of those who have been previously employed at the Commission and who generously gave their time to be interviewed. We do not name them here as we quote from them within the book and wish to preserve their anonymity.

We appreciate the time that applicants' legal representatives have spent talking to us about the cases they are investigating. Their insights into the experiences of their clients as well as their views on the Commission were invaluable.

We are grateful to our Advisory Group, which comprised an experienced criminal barrister, Henry Blaxland QC; a knowledgeable criminal appeal solicitor, Matt Foot; the then Chair of the Commission, Richard Foster, and two members of the Centre for Criminal Appeals (Emily Bolton and Sophie Walker), a charity that investigates potential wrongful convictions on a pro bono basis. Each of these has been a useful contact and source of information at various stages of the project.

We have been supported in our work by generous funding. Carolyn Hoyle conducted a scoping study of the Commission during 2010 and, following that, an extensive pilot study in 2011–13, both partly funded by the University of Oxford John Fell Fund.[2] From 2013 to 2015, the Leverhulme Trust funded an in-depth, two-year study of discretion and decision-making at the Commission.[3] This allowed Carolyn Hoyle, the Principal Investigator, to employ a part-time research officer (Mai Sato) to collaborate on the project. And the University of Oxford John Fell Fund funded research assistance during our fourth year of study.[4] This funding allowed us to employ two research assistants, Naomi-Ellen Speechley, who helped us to collect some of our data, and Laura Tilt, who provided valuable office-based research assistance. We are

---

[2] 103/926 2011 & 122/684 2013.   [3] RPG-2013-170.   [4] 141/073 2015.

grateful to the Leverhulme Trust and the John Fell Fund for their generous support of our research.

We have drawn on other research assistance at the University of Oxford for reviews of the literature and media, and transcriptions of some of our interviews, and are thankful to Emma Burtt, Gabrielle Watson, and Popy Begum. All interviews that contained confidential data were transcribed by Alison McPherson of Premier Typing Transcription Services. Sincere thanks are due to Paul Almond, University of Reading, whose advice on legal decision-making and criminal law was invaluable. Finally, we thank David Rose for his comments on earlier drafts of our chapters.

Carolyn Hoyle, University of Oxford
Mai Sato, University of Reading
April 2018

Contents

List of Figures, Tables, and Boxes

Figures

Tables

Boxes

1

Responding to Wrongful Convictions

Introduction

Concerns about wrongful convictions were not new to the closing decades of the twentieth century, as the infamous cases of *Timothy Evans*[1] and *Derek Bentley*[2] demonstrate. However, they did not provoke official consideration of the need for systemic reform. This began with the major enquiry into the criminal justice process triggered by the wrongful conviction of three men for the murder of Maxwell Confait in 1972.[3] The *Confait* case—based as it was on confession evidence—demonstrated the risk of false self-incrimination by vulnerable suspects, particularly those with learning difficulties. After these convictions were overturned by the Court of Appeal ('the Court') in 1975, the government launched a judicial enquiry into the *Confait* case (Fisher, 1977). This enquiry led to the establishment the Royal Commission on Criminal Procedure, under the chairmanship of Lord Philips (Royal Commission on Criminal Procedure, 1981).

Its report, published in 1981, led to the establishment of a new Crown Prosecution Service[4] as well as the introduction of the Police and Criminal Evidence Act 1984 ('PACE'), which provides a framework for the use of police powers such as arrest, detention, and interrogation, and aims to balance these with the rights of the public.[5] Though few would say that the changes brought about by the Royal Commission on Criminal Procedure were ineffective, they did not cure all the ills of the criminal justice system. Indeed, early research on the impact of PACE showed that there was 'clearly some way to go before we can be confident that the risk of further miscarriages of justice has been minimised' (Coleman et al., 1993:31). Furthermore, the changes came too late for many of those already imprisoned following corrupt investigations by the police and flawed trial and appeal processes. These included the *Guildford Four*, the *Maguire Seven*, the *Birmingham Six*, and *Judith Ward*, all convicted of terrorist Irish Republican Army ('IRA') bombings in England during the Northern Irish 'troubles' (Kee, 1986; Mullin, 1990; Rose, 1992).

The implicit complacency about the general reliability of police investigations and the safety of convictions was shaken to the core by this series of 'catalytic cases' (Ashworth,

---

[1] Timothy Evans was convicted of murdering his wife and daughter in 1950, and sentenced to death. Another man was convicted of this murder three years after Evans' execution.

[2] Derek Bentley was convicted of being a party to murdering a policeman in 1952, and sentenced to death. Bentley's conviction was based on police evidence: three officers told the court they had heard him encourage the co-defendant to shoot by shouting 'let him have it'. Bentley's defence claimed he was under arrest at the time the shots were fired and was simply urging the co-defendant to give up his gun. Bentley's conviction was finally quashed in 1998.

[3] In 1972, Ronald Leighton and Colin Lattimore were convicted of murder and manslaughter, respectively, following the death in a fire of Maxwell Confait. Just three years later their convictions were quashed by the Court of Appeal. Lord Fisher's review of the convictions concluded that the confessions relied on by the prosecution could not have been made by the boys and that the Judges' Rules that at the time laid out the correct procedures for criminal investigations had been breached.

[4] The new Crown Prosecution Service was established by the Prosecution of Offences Act 1985.

[5] The accompanying Codes of Practice should be followed by police officers when carrying out their work.

Reasons to Doubt: Wrongful Convictions and the Criminal Cases Review Commission. © Carolyn Hoyle and Mai Sato 2019. Published 2019 by Oxford University Press.

1998:11), which began to come to light with the 1989 release of the *Guildford Four* after fifteen years' wrongful imprisonment.[6] As he heard their second appeal, and the Crown's presentation of new evidence demonstrating that their confessions had been fabricated by detectives, Lord Lane commented: 'The officers must have lied' (Lord Lane cited in Rose, 1992:1). While formerly he may have believed that individual officers might lie under oath, it was clear from his comment that he had never imagined that systematic, orchestrated group perjury was possible in the justice system of the United Kingdom. Indeed, Lord Lane, along with his fellow judges, had adamantly resisted the idea that miscarriages of justice could be anything other than wholly exceptional (Rose, 1992). With those epochal words, and the widespread upheaval which followed them, came a general acceptance that the criminal process lacked integrity and that a fairer and more easily accessible method for remedying alleged miscarriages of justice was essential.

A Royal Commission on Criminal Justice ('the Runciman Commission') was announced in 1991 by the then Home Secretary on the day that the Court quashed the convictions of the *Birmingham Six* (Royal Commission on Criminal Justice, 1993). The Runciman Commission investigated whether changes where necessary in the following areas: the conduct of police investigations; the role of the prosecutor in gathering evidence and deciding whether to prosecute; the role of experts in criminal proceedings; the rights of the accused to a proper defence; the balance of powers of the courts in proceedings; the role of the Court in considering new evidence on appeal; and the arrangements for considering and investigating allegations of miscarriages of justice when appeal rights have been exhausted (Royal Commission on Criminal Justice, 1993:i–ii). It commissioned and published twenty-two research studies by criminologists and lawyers, took oral and written evidence from various organizations[7] and individuals working within the system, held seminars to discuss the main issues under consideration, surveyed other jurisdictions, and made visits to criminal justice institutions (Royal Commission on Criminal Justice, 1993). It also drew on the work of journalists and academics whose outputs focused on particular cases and on wrongful convictions more generally (see Walker, 1993:6–13 for a review of outputs).

As the Runciman Commission was gathering evidence, further cases were quashed by the Court, suggesting a system in crisis (McConville and Bridges, 1994). These included a series of cases arising from investigations by the West Midlands Serious Crime Squad, which was disbanded in 1989 following the publication of evidence of police beatings, fabrication of evidence, and denial of access to lawyers. Other cases occasioning public and political disquiet included the *Tottenham Three*,[8] whose appeals were heard in 1991, and the conviction of a vulnerable defendant, Stefan Kiszko,[9] quashed in 1992.[10] Shortly before the Runciman Report was published, the conviction of the *Cardiff Three* for the murder of a prostitute was overturned in December 1992,

---

[6] The *Guildford Four* were convicted in 1975 of bombings carried out in public houses in Guildford, Surrey, by the Provisional IRA.

[7] JUSTICE—an all-party law reform and human rights organization—produced a report in 1989, estimating that up to fifteen defendants each year may be wrongfully convicted (JUSTICE, 1989).

[8] Three men imprisoned in 1987 for the murder of a policeman during violent clashes on the Broadwater Farm housing estate in London (see further, Rose, 1992).

[9] Kiszko was released from prison after medical evidence showed that he would have been unable to produce the sperm which had been the key inculpatory evidence leading to his conviction for the sexual murder of Lesley Molseed.

[10] The medical evidence that exonerated Kizsko had been collated before the trial, but had not been disclosed.

with the Court expressing revulsion at the evidence before it of oppression by the police officers who investigated the case. The Runciman Commission could therefore have been in no doubt that it was reviewing a criminal justice system that was in many ways deeply flawed and unacceptably prone to error:

The widely publicised miscarriages of justice which have occurred in recent years have created a need to restore public confidence in the criminal justice system. That need has not diminished since we were appointed. (Royal Commission on Criminal Justice, 1993:6)

In 1993, it made 352 recommendations to increase the chances of the conviction of guilty persons *and* to reduce the risks of unsafe convictions through enhanced protections of suspects *and* increased powers for criminal justice agencies (Royal Commission on Criminal Justice, 1993). The Report was criticized for 'being many things to many people, with something to please and annoy everyone' (Young and Sanders, 1994:436). It was argued that the aim of ensuring the efficient conviction of the guilty—for example by endorsing the extension of police powers—had taken precedence over the Commission's purported aim of preventing wrongful convictions (e.g. McConville and Bridges, 1994).

Most academic studies focused critical attention on the consequences of changes to the police and prosecution services (see Sanders et al., 2010 for a review). Less attention was paid to the Runciman Commission's recommendation no. 331 to set up a new authority to correct possible miscarriages of justice, as it was then too early to assess its potential efficacy. This recommendation led to the establishment of the Criminal Cases Review Commission ('the Commission') for England, Wales, and Northern Ireland in 1997 by Article 8 of the Criminal Appeal Act 1995. This new authority was set up to review a sentence or conviction following the exhaustion of first instance appeals. The Commission is the focus of this book. Its foundation represented the apparent fulfilment of a demand which had been made with increasing intensity since the time of the *Confait* case by criminal defence lawyers, liberal politicians, campaigners, and those who claimed they had been wrongfully convicted. Remarkably, perhaps, with the fulfilment of the demand, its performance, as we stated in our introduction, has been subject to almost no empirical scrutiny.

Finding a Solution? The Criminal Cases Review Commission

To make sense of the Commission, we must appreciate what it replaced. The first system of regular appeals against criminal conviction was introduced in England and Wales by the Criminal Appeal Act 1907, which created the Court of Criminal Appeal—the forerunner of today's Court (Criminal Division) established in 1966. Since 1908, the only further recourse for people convicted of criminal offences, who had been refused leave to appeal or whose appeals had been dismissed, was to apply to the Home Secretary for executive intervention.[11] A small unit, known as the Criminal Case Unit of the C3 (Criminal Policy) Division of the Home Office, was established within central government to review applications and ask the Home Secretary to refer meritorious

---

[11] The only other option was to ask the Home Secretary to recommend that the Queen exercise the royal prerogative of mercy; however, this provided little solace to those who believed themselves to be innocent as it started from the premise that the person was guilty.

cases where there was fresh evidence back to the Court.[12] C3 had the power to order investigations of alleged miscarriages of justice and refer appropriate cases back to the Court for reconsideration. In 1994, there were 12 case workers and two and a half senior staff posts committed to working on applications for post-conviction review and yet the department received hundreds of petitions a year, few with legal represen-tation (Pattenden, 1996:348–53; Taylor with Mansfield, 1999:231–3). Given that C3 was under-resourced, and those civil servants assessing the petitions were not legally trained, the quality of investigations was inevitably poor. Furthermore, in some cases, C3 would ask for investigations to be conducted by the police, the very organization responsible for many if not most of the wrongful convictions under consideration.[13] It was, according to Michael Zander QC, who served on the Runciman Commission, 'a pathetic little organisation' (Zander cited in Robins, 2017), a view shared by others in a debate on the Royal Commission Report in the House of Lords where C3 was de-scribed as 'tardy in its response, reluctant to be open in communicating fresh informa-tion and … [starting] from the presumption that a conviction is well-founded' (Lord Alexander of Weeden cited in House of Lords, 1993:793).[14]

In the final years of C3's existence, the Home Secretary received between 700 and 800 representations of wrongful convictions a year—some for fairly trivial summary convictions, some for sentencing only, but most concerned appeals against convictions for serious offences in the Crown Court that had resulted in long prison sentences (May, 2017). There had been a sharp upturn during 1989–90, possibly as a result of the exposure of those high-profile miscarriages of justice connected with IRA bomb-ings discussed above, but the rising trend could be traced back to the early 1980s when the number of representations received was lower than 500. In this era, subsequent appeals by referral were rare; just a handful each year,[15] while C3 was notoriously slow (Home Affairs Committee, 1982). Paul May, a miscarriages of justice campaigner, dealt with C3 on a few of the cases he investigated and has summed up the unit as:

[P]oorly staffed … none legally qualified. Its processes were opaque and unaccountable. Officials mostly saw their job as rebutting evidence uncovered by prisoners, lawyers, journalists and cam-paigners. Cases dragged on for years frequently culminating in curt, inexplicable dismissals. (May, 2017)

At the time, the English criminal justice system clearly valued the notion of fi-nality (Malleson, 1994). Indeed, at the start of the twentieth century, when there was mounting pressure on the government to establish an appeal court, opposition to this notion centred on the risks posed to the finality of convictions, with critics citing the dangers posed by frivolous applications, limited judicial resources and, particularly, the inappropriateness of judges revising a jury's verdict without hearing the actual wit-nesses themselves (Nobles and Schiff, 1995:311). The Criminal Appeal Act 1968 was understood to embrace the principle of finality of litigation and interpreted as requiring that only a single appeal against conviction was permitted, even when fresh evidence

---

[12] Many have suggested that successive Home Secretaries were reluctant to do this in part because the statutory power was thought to impinge on the separation of powers: 'The executive was under-standably cautious before acting in a way which might be seen to interfere with the administration of justice. As such it was a power to be exercised rarely' (Lord Burnett of Maldon, 2017:para:10).

[13] Criminal Appeal Act 1968, section 17. The Home Office had no formal powers to direct the police but it was rare for a force to be uncooperative (Pattenden, 1996:350; Taylor with Mansfield, 1999:231–3).

[14] Hansard Debate 26, October 1993, vol. 549 cc777–842 at 793.

[15] C3 contributed to an annual average of five cases being quashed by the Court between 1980 and 1992 and before the 1980s references were even fewer (Pattenden, 1996:363).

came to light after an appeal had been dismissed, as was confirmed in *R v Pinfold*.[16] Though C3 could refer cases back to the Court—indeed it was the only option for those who had already appealed—over the years that it operated, successive Home Secretaries expressed themselves extremely reluctant to disturb jury verdicts, and the Court certainly expressed no appetite for hearing more cases. Hence, the Runciman Commission was keen to establish an independent institution to review cases where the Court had not provided relief, and the consensus among even the Commission's harshest critics, is that whatever its faults, it has undoubtedly out-performed C3. The Runciman Commission had argued for:

[T]he establishment of a new *independent* body to consider allegations of miscarriage of justice, to arrange for their investigation where appropriate, and, where that investigation reveals matters that ought to be considered further by the courts, to refer the cases concerned to the Court of Appeal. (Royal Commission on Criminal Justice, 1993:180; emphasis added)

However, while the Commission was expected to be independent of the executive and the courts (Home Office, 1994), there are limits to its independence. It is unable to quash convictions itself, having the power only to refer cases back to the Court for their consideration (though once referred, the Court is then obliged to hear the appeal). Furthermore, while it is a non-governmental body (sometimes referred to as a 'quango'), it is reliant on the Ministry of Justice for its funding, and on the legislature for its powers. These ties to the Court have led some critics to argue that the Commission is consigned to a subordinate role, which will ensure deference to the Court's current and evolving approach to what constitutes an 'unsafe' guilty verdict (see Chapter 2).

In giving the Commission power to refer cases to the Court,[17] Parliament set the parameters of the legislative test that was to be applied, the 'real possibility test' (Criminal Appeal Act 1995, section 13(1)(a)). Under this test, the Commission must be satisfied there is a real possibility that the Court will quash the trial verdict. As the Commission is required to consider how the Court will respond to a referral, its decision-making is inextricably linked to the test subsequently applied by the Court. Set out in section 2 of the Criminal Appeal Act 1968, this test is simply whether or not the conviction is 'unsafe'; the Court does not need to be satisfied that the applicant is innocent. These principles were stated perhaps most explicitly in the case of *Hickey* in 1997, the year the Commission was established:

This court is not concerned with guilt or innocence of the appellants, but only with the safety of their convictions. This may, at first sight, appear an unsatisfactory state of affairs, until it is remembered that the integrity of the criminal process is the most important consideration for the courts which have to hear appeals against conviction. Both the innocent and the guilty are entitled to fair trials. If the trial process is not fair, if it is distracted by deceit or by material breaches of the rules of evidence or procedure, then the liberties of all are threatened. (per Roch U, *R v Hickey*[18])

In practice, a real possibility is established when there are new arguments or evidence that have not previously been considered by the trial or appeal courts (Criminal Appeal Act 1995, section 13(1)(b)). In theory, the Commission can refer a case back

---

[16] [1988] B.B. 462.
[17] The jurisdiction of the Commission extends to the magistrates' court, for which a referral would be to the Crown Court, though most of its applications relate to convictions from the Crown Court, which are referred back to the Court.
[18] [1997] EWCA Crim. 2028.

to the Court even when there is nothing new based on the principle of 'lurking doubt'
(*R v Pope*[19]). However, it has never used this power. Zander (2015) has argued that
this is because in most cases where the Commission is persuaded that there has been a
wrongful conviction, it will manage to find something new to justify a referral, in the
knowledge that the Court is extremely reluctant to overturn jury verdicts *unless* there
is something new (see Chapter 14).

The Commission will commit considerable resources to searching for fresh arguments or evidence when it is thought that there are reasons to doubt the safety of the
conviction. It draws on resources which, while they can vary from year to year, currently include thirty case review managers (full-time equivalent), five group leaders,
one legal and one investigations adviser, about twelve commissioners (because some
work part time they are the equivalent of eight full-time commissioners). There is
also administrative and executive support, comprising around thirty-three employees
(Criminal Cases Review Commission, 2017b:3). The Criminal Appeal Act 1995 fur-
nishes it with various powers and responsibilities; it can require disclosure of evidence
from public (article 17) and private bodies (article 18a),[20] instruct police forces to carry
out investigations of cases prosecuted by other police forces (article 19), and it must
carry out investigations for the Court when, for example, there is evidence of some jury
impropriety (article 15).

Since the Commission started work in 1997, when it inherited over 200 cases
from C3, it has received 22,141 applications from people, often prisoners, who believe themselves to be wrongfully convicted and/or sentenced (Criminal Cases Review
Commission, n.d.).[21] While applications to the Commission were typically fewer than
1,000 a year, since the launch of a simplified application form in 2012 and a concurrent increase in prison visits by the Commission, that figure has risen to a 'new normal'
of approximately 1,400 a year (Criminal Cases Review Commission, 2013a, 2014a,
2015a, 2016a, 2017a). The Commission has so far referred 3 per cent of cases (636
cases) back to the appeal courts; 629 cases have been heard by the appeal courts and of
these, appeals were allowed in 421 cases (Criminal Cases Review Commission, n.d.).[22]
Given that most referrals are for serious offences,[23] the release from a conviction, and
often a prison sentence for hundreds of people over the lifetime of the Commission is
to be commended. However, with a typical 3–4 per cent referral rate—which dropped
to a remarkably low 0.8 per cent in 2016/17 (Criminal Cases Review Commission,
2017a:14)—most of those who apply to the Commission do not find relief.

Post-conviction Review Around the World

The UK is not unique. In all Western democracies, appeals processes may fail to identify
wrongful convictions: appeals solicitors do not have adequate resources to investigate
cases; judges fail to recognize when the system has erred; or at the time of direct appeal
forensic science was insufficiently developed to be of probative value. Thus, elsewhere

[19] [2012] EWCA Crim. 2241.
[20] Section 18a was added to the Criminal Appeal Act 1995 by the Criminal Cases Review
Commission (Information) Act 2016.
[21] This figure refers to applications received between April 1997 and December 2017 (retrieved
from the Commission's website on 7 March 2018).
[22] These figures were retrieved from the Commission's website on 7 March 2018.
[23] Approximately 22 per cent for homicide; 18 per cent for sexual offences; 12 per cent for robberies
and other serious, mostly indictable-only offences (Criminal Cases Review Commission, 2017a).

procedures have been established to review cases which have failed to find relief at the appeal court. Some such jurisdictions have looked to the English Commission as a model to emulate, while others prefer to rely on innocence projects or on the executive. Before we continue with our examination of the English Commission, we consider briefly post-conviction review elsewhere to provide the reader with some comparative context.

Scotland, Norway, and North Carolina: modelled on the English Commission

The Scottish Criminal Cases Review Commission was established in 1999 by the Crime and Punishment (Scotland) Act 1997.[24] In many ways, it is very much like the English Commission. It has extensive powers to compel other parties to provide information concerning wrongful convictions. It can refer a conviction and/or sentence back to the appeal court if it believes 'a miscarriage of justice may have occurred' (article 25(1), 194C(a)) and if it believes 'it is in the interests of justice that a reference should be made' (article 25(1), 194C(b)). Therefore, the notion of miscarriage of justice is a legal one and does not require evidence of factual innocence. Though the wording is different, most legal commentators see it as essentially the same test as that used by the English Commission (e.g. Duff, 2009).

The setup of the Scottish Commission is also similar to that of the English Commission. Decisions on cases are made by eight board members (equivalent of commissioners) of whom a third must be solicitors or advocates, and legal officers (equivalent of case review managers, though in Scotland all are legally qualified).[25] The Scottish Commission does not receive anywhere near the approximately 1,400 applications a year that reach the English Commission: in 2016/17 it received just 150 applications, up two on the previous year, and almost three quarters were 'solemn' offences.[26] It has usually had a slightly higher referral rate than the English Commission, though more of its referrals are on a sentence only basis: by the end of March 2017, when it had concluded investigation of 2,264 cases, it had referred 130 to the appeal court; a referral rate of 6 per cent.[27] These comprise a wide range of offences; some are relatively minor, though most are serious (Leverick et al., 2009). However, like its English sister, its referral rate has declined in recent years: from an average of 4 per cent to 0.9 per cent (Scottish Criminal Cases Review Commission, 2017:22).[28]

In addition to the number of total applications, the main difference between the English and Scottish Commissions concerns the power to refer a case back to the appeal court. In Scotland, the decision to refer a case is made by *all* board members, whereas in the English Commission only three commissioners make this decision (Duff, 2009). This greater collective accountability, the Scottish team argue, provides

---

[24] Crime and Punishment (Scotland) Act 1997, section 24.

[25] Recently, it has introduced senior legal officers to take on the more complicated cases and to provide guidance and assistance to the legal officers; a similar role to the group leaders introduced into the English Commission structure a few years ago (Interview with members of the Scottish Criminal Cases Review Commission, May 2015).

[26] Of applications received from 1999 to 2017, 20 per cent were for murder, 13 per cent for rape, 15 per cent for other sexual offences, and 14 per cent for assaults (Scottish Criminal Cases Review Commission, 2017).

[27] 4.2 per cent in the case of conviction referrals.

[28] As noted above, the rate at the English Commission had declined during the same period from a 3.3 per cent long term average to 0.8 per cent (Criminal Cases Review Commission, 2017a:14).

a stronger element of quality control (#84).[29] It is certainly true that the Scottish Commission has been the subject of far less criticism than the English Commission. Indeed, a report following a ten-year review of the Scottish Commission found that while stakeholders felt there had been some teething problems at its inception, they considered that its reputation was good and saw it as an essential feature of an effective Scottish justice system (Leverick et al., 2009).

The Norwegian Criminal Cases Review Commission was established in 2004 following an infamous miscarriage of justice (the *Liland* case).[30] Modelled on, and with the same powers and remit as the English and Scottish Commissions, it enjoys fewer resources than the English Commission,[31] given its much smaller caseload (barely over 100 cases a year) (Grøndahl and Stridbeck, 2016). It conducts full investigations of about 40 per cent of the cases it receives, and it has a higher referral rate. A review of the Norwegian Commission by the University of Oslo in 2012 found that it works well, but recommended, among other things, more transparency and a reduction in the number of 'minor' cases that the Commission reviews (the vast majority of its applications are from those with sentences of less than six months in prison, some who received non-custodial sentences (Grøndahl and Stridbeck, 2016), as well as older cases (more than ten years since the conviction) (Stridbeck and Magnussen, 2012b).

In America, most states have nothing more than volunteer-led innocence projects to provide post-conviction support to indigent defendants who can demonstrate that they are innocent. The only institution that is comparable to the English and Scottish Commissions is the North Carolina Innocence Inquiry Commission ('NCIIC'), which receives applications from those who have been convicted of a felony in a North Carolina State Court. Established in 2006 as a state agency, and staffed by eight commissioners,[32] it has considerable investigatory powers that volunteer-led innocence projects lack; for example, it can compel testimony and issue subpoenas. That said, although it was modelled on the English Commission, it has a mandate restricted to claims of proven factual innocence, with evidence not previously heard at trial or appeal (Wolitz, 2010). The appeal court also requires a more stringent test to quash a conviction; unlike the UK appeal courts, which require only that the conviction be unsafe, the three superior court judges appointed by the Chief Justice of the North Carolina Supreme Court to hear a NCIIC case must be unanimous in their judgment that there is convincing evidence of the applicant's *innocence*. As both the three-judge panel and the NCIIC operate within such a stringent test,[33] it should not be surprising that few cases are successful (Roach, 2015).

---

[29] All our interviewees are given an interview code (e.g. '#1'). See Chapter 2 for a description of our data collection.

[30] Per Liland was convicted of a double murder in 1970 and refused a retrial in 1976. Released in 1993, he petitioned for the reopening of his case and was finally acquitted in 1994 on the grounds of fresh evidence. He was compensated, though he died just two years later (Stridbeck and Magnussen, 2012b:1387).

[31] The Norwegian Criminal Cases Review Commission has five voting members, including the chairperson, three legally trained members and two lay members, as well as an administrative staff of eleven persons, including legally and police-trained investigators (Stridbeck and Magnussen, 2012a).

[32] To include a judge, a prosecutor, a defence attorney, a victim advocate, a sheriff, and at least one lay person.

[33] The NCIIC's remit is set by the North Carolina General Statutes.

Use of executive power: Canada

There has been the right to review convictions in Canada since 1923, though the process was not formalized until 1993, when the Criminal Conviction Review Group (a small group of lawyers who report directly to the Minister of Justice) was established for the review of convictions for offences under a federal law or regulation (Campbell and Denov, 2012). Following criticisms over delays and failures of accountability, its remit was changed in 2002 to give it more investigative powers. It is now more like the English Commission, in that applicants must have exhausted their normal avenues of appeal and the application must present 'new and significant' information not previously before the courts of sufficient probative value to present a realistic prospect that the conviction will be overturned. In other words, evidence must be provided that might reasonably be expected to have affected the verdict if it been presented to the original trial court (Canadian Department of Justice, 2016).

Both the Canadian and English systems focus on the safety of the conviction, with the appeal courts not requiring evidence of proven innocence (Roach, 2012b:1497). However, they differ in their mechanisms for having a case referred back to the appeal courts. The English Commission can refer a case back to the Court, which it is obliged to hear, whereas in Canada an elected politician has responsibility for reversing a wrongful conviction. The Canadian body reports on their investigation to the Minister, whose decision it is to decide if the case should be referred back or not, and the Minister can also order a new trial (see further Campbell and Denov, 2012). This has led to criticism that it lacks transparency and independence (Saguil, 2007).

A further difference between the two institutions can be found in the number of applications and number of cases referred. Whereas the English Commission receives about 1,400 applications each year, the Canadian body receives only about twenty. It is not possible to provide direct comparisons between their referral rates—due to different recording systems—but they are probably not too dissimilar. That said, according to Kent Roach who has compared both systems, the extremely high success rate in the appeal courts of Canada, as compared to England and Wales and Northern Ireland, suggests that the Minister of Justice there may be more risk averse, referring only those cases certain to persuade the appeal court to quash the conviction (Roach, 2012b:1499). Even after the 2002 reform, the Canadian procedure has attracted similar criticisms to the English Commission, being seen as 'cumbersome, onerous and lengthy' and 'ultimately ineffective for most wrongfully convicted individuals' (Roach, 2012b:1500; see also Walker and Campbell, 2010).

Various public enquiries—including the 'Milgaard Commission'[34]—recommended the establishment of a more independent body modelled on the English Commission; to date, without success (Roach, 2012a). Kent Roach, who has conducted extensive comparative research on post-conviction review procedures, has argued that the Canadian system should be replaced with a Canadian Criminal Cases Review Commission 'to ensure that those claiming wrongful convictions can in appropriate cases use state powers and resources to discover and obtain new evidence that could lead to convictions being reversed' (Roach, 2015:420). That said, he has credited the Canadian system for being more generous and flexible than the US post-conviction review process and more willing to consider new evidence on its merits. Unlike the US system, the Canadian and English systems define wrongful convictions more broadly to include procedural unfairness and evidence that casts doubt on the safety of the

---

[34] David Milgaard was exonerated in 1997 by the results of DNA testing (Roach, 2012b:283).

verdict, and do not require the defendant to establish actual innocence as a precondition for relief (Roach, 2013).

Proposals to establish a Commission: Australia and New Zealand

While only a handful of jurisdictions have established post-conviction review groups, others, particularly some American states (Schehr and Weathered, 2004), as well as Australia and New Zealand, have contemplated establishing commissions (Dioso-Villa, 2014:374). The South Australian Criminal Cases Review Commission Bill 2010 sought to provide a mechanism for relief for convicted persons whose rights of appeal had been exhausted (whose only option was petition to the governor for a pardon in the exercise of the prerogative of mercy). If enacted, the Bill would have established a commission much like the English Commission, with similar terms of reference and powers of investigation. In 2012, the Parliament of South Australia Legislative Review Committee reported on its enquiry into the Bill (Parliament of South Australia Legislative Review Committee, 2012), recommending that such a commission not be established in South Australia and that the Attorney General not pursue the establishment of a commission at a national level because of the importance of the principal of finality. Instead, the Committee recommended that the law be amended to provide that a person may be allowed at any time to appeal against a conviction for serious offences if the court is satisfied that the conviction is tainted, and where there is fresh and compelling evidence in relation to the offence which may cast reasonable doubt on the guilt of the convicted person (South Australian Legislative Review Committee, 2012).

In 2013, South Australia introduced such legislation to allow a second or subsequent appeal on the basis that the Full Court is satisfied that there is fresh and compelling evidence that should be considered or if the Full Court thinks that there was a substantial miscarriage of justice (similar legislation was enacted in Tasmania in 2015). However, there is no assistance for the convicted person, as there is in England (Roach, 2015:415–19), and as Hamer and Edmond have pointed out:

How is a wrongfully convicted defendant, in prison and with few resources or skills, going to discharge this burden? ... it is difficult to see this reform giving much hope to the wrongfully convicted. (Hamer and Edmond, 2013)

Not surprisingly, in the two years following this legislation, there were only two convictions overturned and in both cases the Full Court ordered that a new trial be held following the quashing of the original convictions (Roach, 2015:417).

In New Zealand, a Royal Prerogative of Mercy process includes very little investigation of the conviction. Officials at the Justice Ministry consider the case and make a recommendation to the Governor General who can issue a pardon, though most applications are declined. There is no independent, dedicated unit to consider cases, with decisions being made by the executive, on advice from bureaucrats without expertise. In recent years, concerns over police malpractice and faulty police investigations leading to miscarriages of justice have dented public confidence in the justice system and persuaded a lobby group to call for the introduction of an English-style Commission (Birdling, 2011; New Zealand Law Society, 2016). Sir Thomas Thorp established a review in 2003–4 to compare New Zealand's system with those of Scotland and England, recommending that New Zealand establish a commission based on Scottish and English Commissions (Taylor, 2013). He studied the Scottish system again in 2010 and concluded that Scottish procedures had succeeded in identifying and correcting many more miscarriages than would be possible under the New Zealand system. He has made clear that fears in New Zealand that an independent commission would overwhelm the courts have not been borne out in Scotland (Taylor, 2013). Birdling, who compared the New Zealand Royal Prerogative of Mercy system with England's Commission, found that the current New Zealand procedures are 'manifestly deficient and that many of the features that have made the [English Commission] successful in this regard could be adopted in New Zealand even if an independent body was not established' (Birdling, 2011:227). Indeed, Birdling has argued that New Zealand should adopt a similar independent commission so that decisions about whether to refer a case back to the appeal court are made by an impartial body, not by the executive, in a transparent process in order to restore public confidence (Birdling, cited in Snow, 2013).[35]

The English Commission—a relatively young organization, born of necessity during a climate of fear and scepticism about the efficacy and safety of the criminal process—has become something of a model for post-conviction review for other western democracies. Though it undoubtedly refers back to the Court many more cases than its predecessor, and while the discussion above suggests it may be considered superior to other mechanisms established elsewhere, it is criticized for missing 'clear cases' of innocence and some argue that it has evolved into a different institution than was imagined by the Runciman Commission almost twenty-five years ago. Chapter 2 will consider these criticisms, which first provided the impetus for this study.

[35] In September 2018, New Zealand introduced the Criminal Cases Review Commission Bill which intends to establish a Commission similar to the English model by the summer of 2019 (New Zealand Law Society, news 27 September 2018, Criminal Cases Review Commission Bill introduced at https://www.lawsociety.org.nz/news-and-communications/latest-news/news/criminal-cases-review-commission-bill-introduced.

2

A Commission under Scrutiny

Introduction

As the world's first statutory, publicly funded body charged with the task of reviewing alleged miscarriages of justice (McGuinness, 2016), the Criminal Cases Review Commission ('the Commission') makes decisions within a changing political and fiscal climate. It has not escaped public sector cuts (House of Commons Justice Committee, 2014), and its decision-making process is regularly subject to critical scrutiny from campaigners, journalists, and academic commentators. For example, some have claimed that the Commission does not adequately review potential miscarriages of justice and that its legislation precludes the discovery and referral of *innocent* applicants.[1] Often, critics focus their attention on a particular applicant whom they consider to be innocent, but whose case has not been referred by the Commission.[2] Most criticisms have come in the past five to ten years. In its first decade, there was far less known about how the Commission operated,[3] but at that time it was generally seen as an improvement on its predecessor (Nobles and Schiff, 2001; Walker and McCartney, 2008). Recent criticisms have coincided with—though are not likely wholly generated by—a decline in the referral rate over the past seven to eight years. As noted in Chapter 1, from a relatively consistent rate of referrals over the history of the organization, the referral rate has reduced from 3.5 per cent in 2009/10 to 1.8 per cent in 2015/16 and 0.8 per cent in 2016/17, representing the referral of twelve cases back to the Court of Appeal ('the Court').[4] Indeed, most critics have not focused on the proportion of cases referred, but on what can be implied from selected cases that have come to the attention of the media through the efforts of campaigners. We sought therefore to better understand concerns about the Commission through analysis of media coverage.

A review of media reports on the Commission in two national newspapers (*The Guardian* and *The Times*) between 1995 and 2013 generated 239 articles. The clear majority of articles (74 per cent) were neutral in their tone and content; 13 per cent were positive, praising the Commission for thorough investigations—typically following the referral of a reasonably high-profile case; 8 per cent were critical; with 5 per cent having elements of both criticism and positive commentary.[5] Hence, only

---

[1] See, for example, the various contributions to Robins ed. (2012).

[2] For example, Woffinden (2010) has written that the Commission's failure to refer the case of Susan May to the Court of Appeal for a second time is evidence of a failing Commission 'characterized by pusillanimity and procrastination'.

[3] According to David Calvert Smith, the Commission is still not well known: 'there are lots of people who apply for parole, and who claim to be innocent, but do not know about the Commission or that they may be eligible to apply' (Notes from the Commission's twentieth Anniversary Conference, November 2017).

[4] The Commission's self-reported long-term referral rate is 3.3 per cent (Criminal Cases Review Commission, 2017a). The rate started to decline in 2011/12 when it was 2.5 per cent, dropping further to 1.6 per cent in 2012/13, 2.7 per cent in 2013/14, and 2.2 per cent in 2014/15 (Criminal Cases Review Commission, 2016a). Nonetheless most of the criticisms of the Commission discussed in this chapter predate this recent decline.

[5] We identified 239 articles that included the term 'Criminal Cases Review Commission' in *The Times* and *The Guardian*.

Reasons to Doubt: Wrongful Convictions and the Criminal Cases Review Commission. © Carolyn Hoyle and Mai Sato 2019. Published 2019 by Oxford University Press.

a small minority of the articles identified by our search were explicitly critical of the Commission. In most of these, the Commission was criticized for being inefficient or slow (Woffinden, 2010), though some of these criticisms were offered in the context of an appreciation that the Commission was a victim of budget cuts and had limited resources (e.g. Hopkins, 2012). While there was no clear relationship between the tone of the article and the year of publication, there were a few more critical articles published in the final few years of our survey, between 2010 and 2013. This might be explained by academics, practising lawyers, and campaigners bringing their concerns about the Commission into the public domain through print media, social media, and academic and practitioner publications, particularly in relation to cases that the Commission has refused to refer back to the Court which campaigners believe to be meritorious.[6]

An early indication of growing concern among 'lawyers and campaigners' came on the Commission's fifteenth anniversary in 2012, when a campaign was launched by the Innocence Network UK, now disbanded[7] but led at the time by the Bristol academic Michael Naughton. At the launch conference, it was argued that people with a 'plausible claim of innocence' had not had their convictions referred by the Commission, that the Commission was too deferential to the Court, and that it was no longer 'fit for purpose'[8] (for a further discussion of these criticisms, see Heaton (2015:6)).

The literature on the Commission has focused inter alia on its restrictive definition of a wrongful conviction; its reluctance to receive new expert evidence; its failure to make full use of its powers to review and obtain police and prosecution files; its tendency to misunderstand or overlook the circumstances in which the Court will exercise its discretion to receive evidence; poor communication between the Commission and applicants and their solicitors; inconsistencies in the investigations, attitudes, and thoroughness of the work among different members of staff; and the validity of its supposed 'success' rate of quashed convictions (see various chapters in Naughton ed. (2009) and Naughton with Tan (2010)). Above all, the limiting nature and application of the 'real possibility test' in investigating and referring potential wrongful conviction cases has been subject to wide-ranging critique (Malone, 2009; Newby, 2009; Nobles and Schiff, 2009:158). Furthermore, some who wrote favourably about the Commission in the early days, seeing it as a clear improvement on its predecessor (Nobles and Schiff, 2001), have more recently criticized its claims to success (Nobles and Schiff, 2009).

It is noteworthy, however, that the numerous criticisms levelled at the Commission—though they may be *prima facie* compelling—have little empirical basis (Heaton, 2013:97). Few critics have ever visited the institution, let alone subjected it to empirical scrutiny.[9] Of course, some criticisms can be made without ever stepping a foot

---

[6] *The Guardian's* 'Justice on Trial' series is of particular relevance here; e.g. 'Miscarriages of justice? Cases that campaigners want CCRC to reconsider' 27 March 2012, https://www.theguardian.com/law/2012/mar/27/criminal-cases-review-commission-case-studies.

[7] For a discussion of the recent demise of 'Innocence Network UK', and the continuing efforts of a handful of university innocence projects, see Robins (2016).

[8] A meeting of academics, solicitors, and journalists held at the House of Commons on 30 November 2010, was entitled 'Is the Commission fit for purpose?' and various newspapers followed this up with critical pieces on the Commission (Doward, 2011; Laville, 2012; Robins, 2011; Woffinden, 2010). See also various essays in Naughton (2009).

[9] While there have been a few empirical studies of the Commission (Heaton, 2013; Hodgson and Horne, 2009; O'Brian, 2011), according to various commissioners we interviewed, most critics who have written about the Commission have done no research there and most have not even attended seminars or other 'stakeholder' events hosted by the Commission.

inside the Commission. For example, legal representatives of Commission applicants can legitimately point to the time to review applications or to the preparedness of the Commission to maintain effective communication with applicants. Critics can also publish persuasive commentaries on the restrictions imposed by the real possibility test and on the Court's safety test without empirical enquiry. However, other criticisms require empirical evidence to support them. Hence, it became clear to us that the time was right for the first major independent and empirical assessment of decision-making and discretion within the Commission.

The aim of this book is to *understand* how the Commission operates. To what extent does the organization tasked with remedying wrongful convictions fulfil its public function and realize its stated values? If it falls short, how might we explain the gaps between the ambitions of the Royal Commission on Criminal Justice ('the Runciman Commission') and the day-to-day policies and practices of the Commission? How does the Commission predict the Court's response and how does this influence the nature and style of its investigations? Does the Commission challenge the Court with cases in an attempt to clarify or develop case law?

As a point of preliminary enquiry, we consider some of the key criticisms of the Commission in greater detail. We begin by setting out the structural failings of the Commission itself as perceived by critics external to the institution, before we move on to articulate our key research aims and describe the methods we employed to realize our goals.

Key Criticisms

Relationship with the Court of Appeal

The statutory grounds for referral which govern the operation of the Commission 'provide strong *prima facie* evidence of an essentially dependent position' (Duff, 2009:701). The statutory test, laid out in section 13(1) of the Criminal Appeal Act 1995, requires that the Commission considers, before making a referral, that there is a real possibility that the Court will quash the conviction. The real possibility must derive from an argument or evidence that was not raised in the original proceedings. While the phrase 'real possibility' is not defined in the Criminal Appeal Act 1995, the assumption is that the test prescribed in section 13(1)(a), although imprecise, denotes a contingency which must be 'more than an outside chance or a bare possibility, but which may be less than a probability or a likelihood' that the Court will find the conviction to be unsafe.[10] Criticisms arise because the test requires the Commission to consider before making a referral to the Court if the case has a real possibility of being overturned by the Court (discussed further in Chapter 4), a test that ex-commissioner, David Jessel (2012:17) has referred to as 'the wicked fairy at the christening of the CCRC ... a baptismal curse'.[11]

Critics argue that the centrality of the real possibility test to the Commission's work compromises its claim to independence, indeed makes it deferential to the Court.[12]

---

[10] See further Lord Bingham's judicial interpretation of the real possibility test in *R v Criminal Cases Review Commission (ex parte Pearson)* [1999] 3 All ER 498.

[11] Notably, however, this criticism is neither new nor intrinsic to the Commission. The Commission's predecessor—the Home Secretary and C3 Division—was also conceptualized in these terms (Nobles and Schiff, 1995:315).

[12] The boldness of this claim should not be underestimated, given that the *raison d'être* of the Commission is to be independent. The Commission was created following the failures of its

Some have argued that the Commission is circumscribed not only by the law, and a lack of statutory independence from the Court (e.g. Naughton, 2012:21),[13] but by a concern to please the Court. On these points, some critics are more forceful than others. We return to the issue of the relationship between the Commission and the Court in Chapter 14, but here we consider some of the more critical views on this matter.

The Commission can be viewed as acting as a filter to the Court (James, 2000).[14] Hence, for Kerrigan (2009:174) 'accusations that the CCRC is ... subordinate to the [Court] are truisms. That is the way that the system has been designed by Parliament'. Nobles and Schiff (1995) see it as inevitable that the Commission would have developed this relationship even in the absence of a statutory restriction on its powers. Given that the Commission has no independent power to quash convictions—but can only refer cases to the Court—it is deterred from making referrals that, in view of the Court's practices, would only fail (Nobles and Schiff, 2005). Hence, the real possibility test simply implies that the Commission is always in the realm of 'second-guessing' (Bunting, 2014) how the Court may assess a case following a referral, and anticipating how readily the Court will accept its new arguments (e.g. Nobles, 2012; Price, 2016). Not surprisingly, the judiciary tends not to criticize the Commission's filtering process. Indeed, the then Chair of the Sentencing Council, Lord Justice Treacy, noted at a Commission stakeholder conference, in 2014, that 'in making references, the Commission focuses with a degree of realism on the points which can properly be argued' (Lord Justice Treacy cited in Curtis, 2015).

For Naughton (2013), however, the Commission's subordination to the criteria of the Court carries further implications. His view is that the test assists 'the factually guilty to have convictions overturned on points of law and breaches of due process' (Naughton, 2013:166). By extension, he argues, rather than instilling our confidence in the criminal justice system, the Commission's approach might undermine confidence if:

[T]he 'real possibility test' means that the factually innocent may be procedurally barred from having their convictions referred to the [Court], while the convictions of the factually guilty will be referred by the [Commission] and overturned if they are believed to fulfil the test. (Naughton, 2013:166–7)[15]

In short, it is argued that by focusing on the real possibility test, the Commission cannot refer cases to the Court in the interests of 'justice', or 'innocence', as understood

---

predecessor, the Home Secretary and C3 Division, which had been attributed to its constitutional relationship to the courts. As part of the executive, the Home Secretary and C3 Division could not be seen to challenge the independence of the senior judiciary at the Court of Appeal (Nobles and Schiff, 2001).

[13] Peter Duff, a legal academic who was once a commissioner at the Scottish Commission, argues that while heavily constrained by the law and a legal world view, the Scottish Commission is more independent of the legal system than some commentators would suggest (Duff, 2009).

[14] The following quotation, which appears on the Commission's website, implies that the Commission is subordinate to the Court:

We cannot perform a 're-run' of a trial just because the evidence of the defence was not accepted by the jury and the evidence of the prosecution was. We have to be able to present to the appeal court a new piece of evidence or new legal argument, not identified at the time of the trial, that might have changed the whole outcome of the trial if the jury had been given a chance to consider it. (Criminal Cases Review Commission, n.d.)

[15] See also, Roberts and Weathered (2008), cf. MacGregor (2012).

in public and political discourse, for example (e.g. James, 2000).[16] As such, it is argued, some individuals may receive more valuable assistance from university innocence projects and civil society advocacy groups (Green, 2016; Naughton, 2014; cf. Foster, 2016b) though of course any appeal—no matter the provenance—will need to satisfy the real possibility test if it reaches the Court.

As the Court must only decide if a conviction is 'unsafe', not if the appellant is innocent, and as the Commission must anticipate the Court's approach to cases in order to justify a referral, the Commission's decision-making draws on a legal rather than an innocence-based understanding of wrongful convictions. For some time, the Commission stated on its website that it was not concerned with guilt or innocence but with the safety of convictions: after some criticism for this, the comment was recognized as unhelpful, and removed (Jessel, 2012:18).

Naughton (2012:20–3) has argued that the Commission should focus on innocence in the way that innocence projects across the US have, as well as their younger sisters in the UK. Such bodies typically reject cases where they are not persuaded that the applicant is innocent, even if they can demonstrate breaches of their due process rights to a fair trial. Similarly, Sam Poyser (2012:50) has argued that 'legal restrictions mean that the CCRC is often unable to conduct the kind of investigations that can get to the truth of claims of innocence'. However, Commission staff recognize that it is almost impossible to know when an applicant is innocent or guilty:

I don't think innocence plays any significant part at all. I think individual case reviewers and commissioners form their own view about whether somebody might or might not be innocent. But it is the safety of the conviction that we're looking at and a lot of cases you could probably not say, hand on heart, 'This man was innocent.' But you could say 'This man didn't have a fair trial, the system let him down, he shouldn't have been convicted, this new evidence should have been considered.' And that's what the statute requires the Court of Appeal to do and requires us to predict that the Court of Appeal will do. So, I think the vast majority of us have put notions of innocence to one side and we really do focus on our statutory test and whether or not the system's got it right because somebody that the system has let down is in some ways every much an innocent victim as somebody who really didn't commit the offence. (#17)[17]

The Commission is therefore firmly of the view that cases that can demonstrate significant breaches of procedural safeguards are rightly within its purview, not least as in such cases there will inevitably be a greater chance that an innocent person has been convicted. As Quirk (2012:31) rightly argues, 'the test of unsafety is more widely protective than a test of innocence'.[18] Furthermore, a former commissioner, Alastair MacGregor, has challenged the suggestion that the Commission does not care about innocence:

Of course the commission cares about factual innocence. Nothing is more likely to lead to a commission referral than compelling new evidence of factual innocence. Evidence of that type is, however, rarely discoverable and in its absence the Commission ... works to overturn not

---

[16] Cf. the approach of the Scottish Commission, which claims to refer cases on the basis of its belief that a miscarriage of justice has occurred, and that it is in the public interest to return it to the Court for review (see Chapter 1).

[17] All our interviewees are given an interview code (e.g. '#1'). See below for a discussion of our methods for data collection.

[18] See also Hoyle (2016) and McCartney and Roberts (2012).

only the wrongful convictions of those who others believe to be innocent, but also the wrongful convictions of those who only might be innocent (though others doubt it) and even, indeed, of those who, whatever the evidence of their guilt, have been convicted only after substantial systemic error or wrongdoing. (MacGregor, 2012:12)

Given that the test of the Court, and therefore the Commission, is one of safety, and not innocence, there is an inherent tension between the operational remit of the Commission, as working within the constraints of the Criminal Appeal Act 1995, and public and political discourse on wrongful conviction that routinely goes unremarked. Indeed, the conceptual confusion in the use of the term 'fit for purpose' among campaigners, journalists, and academic commentators alike arises in part from competing notions of what the purpose of the Commission is or should be, most notably whether it should be about *innocence* or *safety*. This tension is also apparent in considering the real possibility test, which many argue is the 'wrong test' and should be removed (Naughton, 2012:22, though see Malone (2012:23) for a counter-argument). The test was not devised by the Commission, but established by Parliament to require the Commission to consider carefully before making a referral if the Court would have good reason to doubt the safety of the conviction. Given that it requires the Commission to anticipate the Court's likely response to both the weight and the nature of the fresh evidence, it will inevitably guide the Commission in its review and its decision about whether a case satisfies the real possibility test. As one of our interviewees argued:

[For our critics], the issue that the debate is coalescing around at the moment is 'Is the test right?' which in part, if not in whole, is code for 'We don't like what the Court of Appeal does' because ... at one level, since the Court of Appeal decides, you could have any test, any old test you wanted as the basis for referral, but the only rules that will count will be the rules around safety that the Court applies. So, if you don't like the real possibility test, you're saying I don't like what the Court of Appeal does ... it's a sort of oblique way of criticizing the Court, in my judgement. (#9)

MacGregor (2012) has explored this argument further asking what purpose would be served by the Commission referring cases that it considers not to meet the test. He concludes that the only compelling answer is that the Commission should have the power to make 'contrarian' references on occasion to 'oblige the court publicly to confront and address the concerns that exist in relation to a case and/or to look again at some issue or principle on which it has already expressed a concluded view' (MacGregor, 2012:13).

MacGregor's point can be used to address concerns about the 'low' referral rate. There seems to be consensus among critics and friends of the Commission that, in practice—despite referring more cases than its predecessor—it is overly cautious (House of Commons Justice Committee, 2014). Although, according to Graham Zellick (2005)—who, at the time of his writing, was the Chair of the Commission—the low referral rate should not necessarily be a cause for concern. Rather, the public should be reassured by the low referral rate as this means that the prosecution and the courts are performing well (Zellick, 2005:950). The current Chair, Richard Foster, reiterated this point over a decade later, stating that a decision not to refer is 'not a failed review' but confirmation that 'the conviction is securely based thereby helping maintain confidence in the system', a sign, in other words of 'a well-functioning system' (Foster cited in Robins, 2017).

The allocation of finite resources

The Commission is a 'casework organisation' (House of Commons Justice Committee, 2015:para:30). Enquiring deeply into a case requires *investigation*, the purpose of which is to establish whether there is fresh evidence that was not available before the trial or the appeal courts (Zander, 2012). With some 1,400 applications a year, the Commission must employ its limited resources judiciously in order to review each case thoroughly but also efficiently; otherwise, the queues of those waiting for their cases to be attended to will increase exponentially. This is no easy task and, perhaps not surprisingly, the Commission is sometimes criticized for misjudging the balance between thoroughness and efficiency (discussed in Chapter 12).

As a non-departmental public body, the Commission is funded by the Ministry of Justice through a grant-in-aid. Between 2009/10 and 2014/15, funding to the Commission fell from £6.5 million to £5.3 million, which amounts to a 30 per cent cut when adjusted for inflation (House of Commons Justice Committee, 2015:para:31). The Chair of the Commission has confirmed that for every £10 that his predecessor spent on a case ten years ago, he now has just £4, which he has described as 'the biggest cut that has taken place anywhere in the criminal justice system' (House of Commons Justice Committee, 2015:para:31). At the Commission's twentieth Anniversary conference in November 2017, he returned to this theme, describing the Commission as 'strained' and explaining that in broad terms, the Commission's budget had not increased for over a decade, during which time applications had increased by about 50 per cent (Fieldwork notes).

However, the Commission has for a long time claimed to be inadequately resourced. While a former commissioner suggests that it was 'generously funded in the early years', before becoming regulated 'from a spirit of underlying hostility' (Elks, 2008:335), at its inaugural press conference, the founding Chair, Sir Frederick Crawford, complained that funding was 'several hundred thousand pounds' short of what was needed. There is certainly evidence from the Annual Report at its tenth anniversary, that the then Chair, Graham Zellick, was concerned about cuts of £300,000 a year and felt the limited resources were leaving his staff 'frustrated … angry and dispirited' (Zellick cited in Robins, 2017).

While the Commission has faced its budgetary challenges under austerity with patience and dedication to seeing its duty fulfilled (McGourlay et al., 2016), critics contend that inadequate funding nonetheless compromises the quality of the work that the Commission conducts (House of Commons Justice Committee, 2015; Robins, 2016). The Commission must operate with a budget that enables it, in each year, to dispose of at least the same number of cases it receives in a year. This has become more difficult since 2012, when the Commission, in line with its commitment to improve access to justice, introduced a simplified ('easy read') application form—alongside other outreach work to ensure greater access to its services—which resulted in an unprecedented increase in the number of applications to the Commission (House of Commons Justice Committee, 2015).[19]

While some critics claim that the Commission does not refer *enough* cases,[20] others express concern that it uses some of its finite resources on appeals against sentence

---

[19] Efforts by the Commission to ensure greater access to their services led to a 74 per cent increase in the number of applications to the Commission from 933 in 2010–11 to 1625 in 2012–13 (House of Commons Justice Committee, 2015:para:31).

[20] For a discussion of such criticisms, see Quirk (2012:31).

and on reviewing relatively *trivial* cases, such as road traffic offences (e.g. Naughton, 2013:186), and applications involving the wrongful conviction of refugees and asylum seekers for unlawful entry to the United Kingdom (Bucks, 2016; Gilligan, 2016; Scott, 2016). The implication being that the Commission is wasting its time on these un-deserving cases instead of focusing solely on the serious convictions that the Runciman Commission envisaged when it recommended the establishment of an independent review body.

Given that the Commission is committed to reviewing all eligible applications, and not rejecting those that others deem to be trivial, and given the recent increase in applications, it is not surprising that there has been considerable concern about the length of time it takes to review a case. While timescales are immaterial for some com-mentators (e.g. House of Commons Justice Committee, 2014),[21] others insist that the Commission too often defaults on its promise to process applications expeditiously: in other words, that it is simply too slow (May, 2014; Price, 2016). This criticism was repeated by veteran miscarriages of justice campaigner, Chris Mullin, at the twentieth Anniversary conference of the Commission in November 2017: 'It's working pretty well but it's too slow' (Fieldwork notes). The Commission itself has conceded that its lengthy waiting times are a source of concern, with each Annual Report over the past few years stating their determination to reduce the queues. With this in mind, in 2015, the Commission published plans to make changes to its screening practice (Criminal Cases Review Commission, 2015a; see also Chapter 6) and the 2016/17 Annual Report suggests that these changes are beginning to reduce the time applicants wait until their case is considered. That said, changes at the start of the process seem to have contributed to the overall lengthening of average review times. This is perhaps not surprising given the continuing high numbers of applications, almost 1,400 in the year 2016/17 (Criminal Cases Review Commission, 2017a:5–14). Until the relatively recent rise in applications, waiting times had been 'significantly reduced' (#24) but since then the organization has struggled. As one interviewee told us:

We simply didn't have enough commissioner resources to deal with the upsurge in applications we got when we introduced the easy-read application form. We went from 900 cases a year to 1,500 cases a year, roughly. And, at the same time, we were getting less and less commissioner resource than we had, and we were falling further and further behind in terms of cases awaiting screening by commissioners, cases where commissioners had done an initial bit of screening and then said we need this in and that in and so on. And there were lots of cases that were taking six months, a year, or more, to come through that screening process before they could then get into a queue. (#64)

There are two distinct issues. The first is the time that an applicant must wait before the Commission begins its review of his or her case; the second is the length of time it takes to complete a review and arrive at a decision.[22] Both can prove burdensome. The

---

[21] '[The Commission's] obsession with the speed with which it deals with applications is an un-helpful distraction. In my experience, no Applicant that I have ever dealt with is in the slightest bit interested in the time scale for the CCRC to consider his or her case. He doesn't mind whether it will take 6 months or a year or two, what he is interested in is that the investigation and/or review will establish he has been wrongly convicted and that his case will be referred back to the [Court] so that the Court can then quash his conviction' (Maddocks cited in House of Commons Justice Committee, 2014:22).

[22] See Annual Report 2015/16, Key Performance Indicators on 'time from receipt to allocation', 'duration of review', and 'time to decision from application' (Criminal Cases Review Commission, 2016a); see also Chapter 4.

Commission's position is that if complex work is to be done satisfactorily, it will take time to unravel:

How long a case then takes once it's under review can vary from a very short period indeed, because it's relatively straightforward, or very straightforward, to months or, or years depending on the nature both of the investigation, the prosecution, what the, the issues are. (#24)

While most have been sympathetic to the Commission's dilemma of reviewing thoroughly an increased caseload with reduced resources, some have argued that speed often comes at the expense of thoroughness or vice versa (e.g. James, 2000). It has been suggested that those applicants serving shorter sentences are likely to have completed their sentences before a comprehensive review can take place, thus discouraging others from applying in the first place, with those serving long sentences 'hav[ing] no prospect of early consideration' (James, 2000:146).[23] However, most criticisms have focused on the lack of thoroughness of the review procedure.

A case review can include analysis of all relevant documentation and law, or it may require a case review manager ('CRM') to instruct experts, contact lawyers, witnesses, and even jurors. In other words, in some cases, the review necessitates no more than a 'desktop' analysis of the relevant documents, whereas in others further investigations are thought to be necessary.

It has been suggested that the Commission's investigations are 'increasingly under-resourced', with 'a slower, more superficial "paperwork approach" to cases, rather than one that utilizes its extensive investigative powers' (Poyser, 2012:49). In other words, that it carries out too many 'desktop' reviews, conducting 'thorough' investigations infrequently (Naughton, 2012:21). Indeed, Naughton (2009) has described the Commission's reviews as mere safety checks on the lawfulness or otherwise of criminal convictions, as opposed to detailed inquisitorial investigations (examined in Chapter 12).

There are clearly different ideas about how successful the Commission has been. For some, such as Michael Zander, who was a member of the Runciman Commission, the Commission is an 'efficient, competent, responsible body' (Zander, 2015:74), a 'major step in the right direction' though still 'not working perfectly because of a lack of resources and a lack of imagination' (Zander, 2017). And, for most, it is widely accepted to be an improvement on its predecessor (James, 2000) and should be praised for those occasions when it has expertly identified cases, and has been determined and expeditious in its investigation of them (Rose, 2011). However, the prevailing view, as we have discussed above,[24] is that the Commission does not function as the 'safety net'[25] of the criminal justice system as originally envisaged, and potential victims of wrongful convictions are left unsupported.

The Commission is criticized for being a bureaucratic organization, with a restrictive culture firmly embedded in—rather than distinct from—the criminal

---

[23] Furthermore, any refusal to admit guilt is likely to have broader implications for the prisoner too in terms of his or her parole options or prison categorization (Naughton, 2004). And those whose convictions are eventually quashed may therefore have experienced longer periods of wrongful imprisonment than they would had they pled guilty and served the 'discounted' sentence (Evans, 2012).

[24] Exceptions to this view include Hannah Quirk, who has worked as a CRM at the Commission and has a nuanced and sensitive understanding of the work conducted there; Michael Zander, who fully understands the legal constraints within which the Commission must operate; and Jackie Hodgson, who has conducted research on the influence of legal representation on applications to the Commission.

[25] *R (on the application of Nunn) v Chief Constable of Suffolk Constabulary and another* [2014] UKSC 37, para:39.

justice infrastructure (House of Commons Justice Committee, 2014). Woffinden (2015) has even argued that the Commission has 'institutionalised' miscarriages of justice, since its creation has served to allay what might otherwise have been serious administrative concerns about a 'demonstrably defective' criminal justice system. As we make clear in Chapter 1, some valid criticisms can be made without recourse to empirical data, others less so. This book therefore subjects some of these criticisms to rigorous empirical enquiry. In particular, it considers the criticisms that the Commission is too deferential to the Court, that it is overly cautious in interpreting the real possibility test; that it does not get the balance right between thoroughness and efficiency in its use of its finite resources; that it is inconsistent in its response; and that it sometimes does not communicate adequately with applicants and their legal representatives. The following section describes how it approaches these tasks.

Aims of the Book

Given its undeniably limited resources, the Commission has insufficient capacity to conduct in-depth reviews of *all* applications it receives. Therefore, just as hospital emergency departments operate a 'triage' system for deciding which patients should be seen immediately, which can wait, and, importantly which need extensive medical investigations, the Commission operates a case screening process and has a high rate of attrition. It refers back to the Court[26] between 1 and 4 per cent of its approximately 1,400 applications a year, and subjects just over a half to full and thorough investigation. It can exercise considerable discretion in deciding which cases to review thoroughly; and what types of investigations to conduct.

As with all institutions that have considerable discretionary powers and that are publicly funded, there should be critical scrutiny of how the Commission exercises these discretionary powers, and how it defends its decisions to refer some cases back to the Court, but not others. This research subjects the application of the real possibility test to in-depth socio-legal analysis, drawing on the extant literature on discretion, particularly on the exercise of institutional discretion and the application of legal tests, as well as the broader literature on the sociology of organizations (see Chapters 3 and 4). And it does so throughout the whole investigation and decision-making process from screening, through substantive investigations, to the decision whether to refer cases to the Court. The aims of this book can be articulated as a series of related research questions:

1) What influences the early identification of potentially unsafe convictions within a huge caseload (the 'triage' process)? Is there variation within the Commission on how many cases decision-makers 'screen in' or 'screen out'; are some decision-makers more risk averse than others? These questions are examined in Chapter 6.

2) Once an application is subject to a full review, how far do CRMs and commissioners delve into a case on matters that give them reasons to doubt the safety of the conviction? For example, when do they seek forensic tests or expert opinion?

---

[26] A small proportion of applications to the Commission are for convictions secured in the magistrates' court. However, as most cases in this study related to Crown Court convictions, we refer to the Court of Appeal.

What informs the choice of experts and the weight given to their opinions? What is the response when there is divergence in forensic evidence or where expert opinion is changing? What influences the Commission's predictions of what weight the Court will give to forensic or expert evidence? How does the Commission investigate claims of police malpractice or defence incompetence and how do they respond to the sensitive matter of victim reliability, particularly in cases involving convictions for sexual offences? These questions are examined in Chapters 7–10.

3) At what stage in the substantive review of a case is it thought that the real possibility threshold has been met? How do decision-makers express their interpretation of the real possibility test and construct their 'case' in the Statement of Reasons, to justify their decisions both to the applicant and—in cases that are referred—to the Court? To what extent is decision-making understood as an interactive, dynamic process, and to what extent is it framed in legal terminology? How do Commission staff defend their decisions and variability across similar cases? These questions inform Chapters 6–13 and are returned to in our concluding chapter (Chapter 14).

4) How does the Commission communicate with other criminal justice institutions and applicants and their legal representatives? To what extent is the Commission dependent on other institutions—e.g. the police and public and private bodies—in investigating cases? In cases where the Commission makes a provisional decision not to refer a case back to the Court, what impact, if any, do applicants and their legal representatives have in reversing the Commission's provisional decision? These questions are examined in Chapters 11–13.

5) In most chapters, we subject the main criticisms directed at the Commission to empirical scrutiny, focusing in particular on the balance between efficiency and thoroughness in Chapter 12.

6) While it is explicitly not our aim to consider decision-making at the Court, we do reflect on the influence of Court judgments as a crucial factor in Commission decision-making in Chapters 6–13, returning again to this issue in the concluding chapter.

Realizing the aims of our research has taken us many years: time spent immersing ourselves in the Commission; identifying a robust sample; analysing voluminous case files, including Court judgments; interviewing CRMs, commissioners, and others working on our selected sample of cases; carrying out quantitative analysis of working practices; and reading Commission policy and internal guidelines, with most internal guidelines not publicly available and therefore revealed here for the first time.[27] Over this time, we have seen most of our 'live' cases reach their conclusion, and changes to personnel and practices at the Commission, creating something of a moving target for analysis. The final section of this chapter describes the methods we employed in seeking to understand the work of the Commission.

[27] The main body of our research was funded by a grant from the Leverhulme Trust. Our pilot study and our study of the asylum cases (discussed below) were both funded by two separate grants from the University of Oxford John Fell Fund.

Methodological Approach

A matter of definition

Titles of popular literature on wrongful convictions—works by John Grisham or Scott Turrow, for example—often employ the concept of innocence to direct the reader's attention to the plight of one person who has been wrongfully convicted, and for whom the account reveals unequivocal evidence of innocence. While trials start from a presumption of innocence, once the defendant has been convicted, the system need only concern itself with the safety of that conviction, and indeed the Supreme Court has made clear, in its recent refusal of compensation claims by *Adams*[28] and *George*[29] that innocence is not restored when the Court quashes an unsafe conviction (Hoyle, 2016).

The Commission, somewhat inevitably, adopts the Court's focus on safety. Given that our attention here is on the Commission, and to a lesser extent the Court, we too shy away from explicit concern with innocence. While American academics often refer explicitly to innocence (see Garrett, 2011; Scheck et al., 2003), those in the UK have taken various approaches to defining and problematizing their terminology. Some have concerned themselves with 'innocence' while using the terminology of 'miscarriages of justice' (e.g. Roberts, 2004) and, on the other end of the spectrum, others have adopted a definition so broad that it includes convictions overturned at first appeal (Naughton, 2004), which most would consider to be the system working as it should. We do not have the space to offer a more thorough review of the landscape of disputed terminology, but we found the work by Nobles and Schiff (2000) to be most helpful here. Hence, we adopt the term 'wrongful conviction', to describe cases which display at least one of two features: those innocent of the offence of which they were convicted, and those whose convictions are flawed by significant breaches of due process (Nobles and Schiff, 2000). There is, needless to say, an overlap between these categories.

Identifying our sample of wrongful convictions

The first author began this research in 2011 with a scoping study, carrying out interviews with the Commission management team, and with a sample of commissioners and CRMs, aimed at identifying initial research parameters. This was followed by a pilot study (2011–12), during which time the aims and objectives of the research were refined, and the sample of cases chosen. During this pilot phase, we adopted a purposive sampling method to identify the categories of cases, and within those categories the cases that would best illustrate decision-making processes within the Commission. These decisions were based on studying 'live cases' on the database; consultation with the Case Categorization Team and the legal advisers; and our discussions during 'scoping interviews' with commissioners and CRMs. We sought to collect a mixture of mostly 'closed' and some 'live' cases. Closed cases are those for which the Commission has made the final decision whether to refer the application back to the Court. Live cases refer to those that were ongoing during the fieldwork and therefore allowed us to observe decision-making and to conduct interviews as the case unfolded. All cases were selected from applications received since 2000.

---

[28] *R v Adams* [2007] 1 Cr App R 34, [2007] EWCA Crim 1.
[29] *R v George (Barry)* [2007] EWCA Crim 2722.

We gathered information on 146 cases from applications received since 2000. Some applicants apply to the Commission more than once so the number of cases in our purposive sample is not equal to the number of applicants. Our purposeful sample consists of six categories:

1. historical institutional abuse cases (17 cases; 15 applicants; the main focus of Chapter 8);[30]

2. contemporary sexual offence cases (17 cases; 15 applicants; the main focus of Chapter 8);

3. forensic and expert evidence cases (61 cases; 42 applicants; the main focus of Chapter 7);

4. police investigation cases (Criminal Appeal Act 1995, section 19)[31] (14 cases; 10 applicants; discussed in Chapter 11);

5. Court directed investigations (Criminal Appeal Act 1995, section15)[32] (14 cases; 9 applicants; discussed in Chapter 11); and

6. asylum cases (migrants and asylum seekers convicted of immigration violations) (23 cases; 23 applicants; discussed in Chapter 10).[33]

Our Appendix provides basic anonymized details of each of our sample cases, including the year the application was received, the offences the applicant was convicted for and which the applicant considers to be unsafe, the decision of the Commission (whether to refer or not) and—in cases of a referral—the Court's decision (whether the conviction was quashed or upheld).

In our view, our six categories of cases comprise the bulk of the work at the Commission and, between them, demonstrate the different sources of wrongful conviction, different types of investigation, and the range of operational challenges faced by the Commission. This method of 'criterion sampling' does not reflect *offence* types, but *approaches* to investigation. We selected for each of our categories clusters of cases upon which the Commission had built institutional knowledge and working practices. We over-sampled referred cases, and therefore the reader should not generalize the likelihood of cases resulting in a referral from our sample of cases.

These categories of cases pose specific challenges for the Commission. For example, historical institutional abuse cases are difficult to investigate due to time delays and atypical policing methods (including 'trawling'). Contemporary sexual offences must be approached within the context of advances in forensic gynaecological evidence or the difficulties of establishing whether victims are reliable. Expert evidence cases inevitably require understanding of the latest forensic science: for example, low copy DNA. Hence our samples provide ample variation to allow for a rich understanding of how the Commission operates on a day-to-day basis, something that would be missed by a focus only on those high-profile murder cases that tend to make newspaper headlines. While Chapter 8 focuses mainly on those cases collected under our categories of 'historical institutional abuse cases' and 'contemporary sexual offence cases', and

---

[30] Chapters 9 and 10 also draw on those cases discussed in Chapters 7 and 8.

[31] These cases are where the Commission appoints a police force to carry out specific Commission-directed investigations.

[32] These cases often concern allegations of jury impropriety.

[33] We included cases concerning the wrongful conviction of refugees and asylum seekers who entered the UK without the appropriate documents even though most were convicted in the magistrates' courts, as the Commission had experienced a significant rise in such applications and they produced a much higher referral rate than for other groups of cases.

Chapter 7 draws mainly on the cases collected under the category of 'forensic and expert evidence cases', we do not use these cases exclusively. Hence, some contemporary sexual offence cases are discussed in the chapter focusing on forensic and expert evidence, and some 'forensic and expert evidence cases' are discussed in Chapter 8 which deals with convictions for sexual offences. Chapter 11, however, focuses exclusively on those cases collected as 'police investigation cases' and 'court-directed enquiries'.

We excluded Northern Irish cases for three reasons: the characteristics of these cases are quite distinct and we were not confident we had a sufficiently sound knowledge of the context within which most of these applications arose ('The Troubles').[34] Most are old, pose challenges in terms of the probable involvement of the army, and raise issues of national security, presenting the Commission with particular investigative challenges and costs (Elks, 2008:288; Quirk, 2013:977). Furthermore, these cases are referred to the Northern Ireland Court of Appeal and there is evidence to suggest that Court interprets its real possibility test differently to the English Court.[35] It is for these reasons that these cases are dealt with primarily by one Northern Ireland expert at the Commission, though some have questioned whether the Commission itself 'lacks a detailed understanding of the political and historical context of these cases' (Quirk, 2013:976).[36]

Collecting qualitative and quantitative data

As noted above, our qualitative data are made up of 146 cases. For each case, we reviewed: application; case record; case plan; both the provisional (where applicable) and the final Statement of Reasons (a document outlining the justification for referring or deciding not to refer a case to the Court); correspondence with legal representatives, expert witnesses, the applicant, etc.; and internal correspondence and minutes of committee meetings.[37] We interviewed both current and former members of staff including CRMs, commissioners, legal and investigations advisers, administrative team, and management about cases and the working practice and culture of the Commission. We also interviewed staff at the Scottish Commission and four lawyers with considerable experience of Commission applications. In total, we conducted ninety interviews. In addition, we analysed all of the Commission's Casework Guidance Notes—internal policy guidelines that prescribe how individual commissioners and case review managers should proceed at each stage in various different types of cases or situations. For each case we considered the extent to which the guidelines had shaped the casework approach and what other factors influenced decision-making or led Commission staff to disregard the advice in these internal policy documents.

Overall, we spent more than four years visiting the Commission studying case files and interviewing members of the Commission. During our fieldwork, we observed several changes to organizational procedure and practice (discussed in Chapter 6).

---

[34] Most applications from Northern Ireland relate to 'the troubles' and some have argued that applications 'can serve as an informal truth recovery mechanism to explore all the wrongdoings that went on in the barracks and police stations' or as a 'one-sided, paramilitary-focused exploration of the past by the Historical Enquiries Team' (Quirk, 2013:951).

[35] Not only have applications from Northern Ireland been referred to the appeal courts at about three times the rate for all Commission applications, but about 90 per cent of the convictions referred have been quashed (compared to around 70 per cent of cases overall) (Quirk, 2013:952).

[36] Section 8(6) of the Criminal Appeal Act 1995 requires only that at least one of the Commissioners has 'knowledge or experience of any aspect of the criminal justice system in Northern Ireland'.

[37] In a few cases, we observed case committee meetings on 'live cases'.

Though not part of our research design, our time at the Commission facilitated informal ethnography; 'hot-desking' among CRMs and chatting over coffee and lunch with staff about the changing organizational landscape, and observing reactions to news media, Court decisions, or Ministry of Justice statements.

Our quantitative data included: a small pilot dataset to explore initial decision-making across a wider sample of cases; a large micro-level administrative dataset; and a questionnaire-based survey of CRMs to explore the types of investigations they carry out on cases. At the start of our research, we constructed the pilot database to explore factors associated with the outcome of screening; that is, whether a case is screened out by a screening commissioner at the first hurdle, or passed onto for a full review.[38] Analysis of these data suggested that the identity of the screening commissioner was most strongly associated with the outcome of screening. The Commission provided us with their administrative data between January 2005 and December 2014 consisting of 11,289 cases. This included variables that allowed us to examine screening behaviour of commissioners, in relation to case review and case outcome (see Chapters 6, 11, and 13).

Given the criticism of the length of time taken by the Commission to investigate cases, we were keen to understand to what extent the Commission was frustrated in its efforts to conduct its reviews in a timely fashion by factors beyond their control. Some commissioners spoke to us about the frustrations of waiting for other criminal justice organizations to provide relevant data on their applicants or on other aspects of their cases, or of investigations being delayed by expert witnesses failing to meet the deadlines for data or reports imposed by the Commission. Two of the main ways that the Commission works with others outside of the organization are by its use of the powers granted by sections 17 and 19 of the Criminal Appeal Act 1995. Section 17 gives the Commission the power to preserve and obtain documents and other relevant material held by public bodies (and since we completed our fieldwork, by private bodies). Section 19 provides the power to require the appointment of an investigating officer—typically a police officer from a public police force—to carry out inquiries to assist the Commission in the exercise of any of its functions. As such, the Commission must manage relationships with people from other professional bodies from whom they need assistance. They must ensure that the data is reliable, complete, and provided in a timely fashion.

Given that the use of section 17 powers speaks to both the thoroughness and the efficiency of the Commission's investigations, we analysed the Commission's use of this power through micro-level administrative data collected by the Commission between January 2011 and December 2013. Regarding section 17 requests, we analysed data on: the type of public body (e.g. Courts, local authorities, National Health Service agencies, police, probation); the type of notice served (preservation or request); the date the notice was served; the date when a response was received; what this response was; and the outcome of the case. For all section 19 requests, we analysed how frequently the Commission delegated its investigation to a police force, and whether there was an external police force or the original police force at trial.

---

[38] Data gathered included information about the applicant (e.g. sex, date of birth, at liberty or in prison); the case (e.g. date of conviction, type of offence, type of sentence, previous applications to the Commission); the screening process (e.g. the name of the screening commissioner, time spent on screening, case-specific issues identified); and other factors (e.g. whether it was a high-profile case, whether the applicant had the support of a legal representative or an innocence project).

The survey of CRMs' investigative practices was a potentially sensitive issue. As noted above, the Commission has been criticized for conducting only 'desk-based' reviews of materials submitted by applicants and their legal representatives, without engaging in 'real' investigatory work, such as exploring forensic evidence or interviewing key actors in the case. In some of the Commission's cases, investigations can be successfully completed by thorough review of the materials submitted by applicants and their legal representatives, and by consideration of case law, legislation, and precedents set by the Court. However, sometimes it will be necessary to go beyond the paperwork and conduct more 'empirical' investigative work. With this in mind, we conducted an anonymous online survey of CRMs to measure how much investigation beyond the case files and legal analysis they typically conducted, and what factors militate against such investigations in cases that have been screened and accepted for review. We defined empirical investigative work—for the purpose of this survey—as any contact with outside agencies or individuals beyond the Commission for the purpose of gathering data to help CRMs make decisions about how to proceed with a case (see Chapter 12 for more detail on the methodology).

Ensuring anonymity

To ensure anonymity for applicants and their representatives, and Commission staff,[39] we avoid naming the applicant in our cases, even when their convictions have been quashed by the Court and much information about their case is in the public domain. We do not name individual Commission staff or applicants' representatives to avoid making connections that might identify others. As a few of our cases are high profile, and have been subject to media attention, we have at times altered the details of the case slightly to avoid identifying the applicant. As noted above, our Appendix assigns each case with an identifier (e.g. case HIA1). All our interviewees are given an interview code (e.g. '#1') and for the most part we do not distinguish commissioners, CRMs, group leaders, and management staff, referring to all as 'interviewees'. These years of scrutiny of an organization and its decision-making processes have produced considerable empirical data. Before we present those data, we turn to our theoretical research to provide a framework for making sense of our findings.

---

[39] We received security clearance from the Ministry of Justice to gain access to case files (ref: 299962) and 'in house' Commission training on using the databases and on handling sensitive data. We agreed to sign a confidentiality agreement between the University of Oxford and the Commission, committing us to make every effort to avoid identifying applicants or Commission personnel in any publications. The project was approved by the University of Oxford's Research Ethics Committee (ref: SSD/CUREC1A/11-235).

3

Making Sense of Decision-making

Introduction

This book starts from the premise that the legal framework for decision-making at the Criminal Cases Review Commission ('the Commission')—the 'real possibility test' (Criminal Appeal Act 1995, section 13(1)(a))—the probability of a case being likely to succeed at the Court of Appeal ('the Court')—is a relatively fluid concept to be determined in each case. Interpreting how persuasive fresh evidence or argument might be to the Court, the Commission needs to be mindful of the Court's response in recent past cases, as the Court's jurisprudence presents something of a moving target.

While the real possibility test is a legal test, with decisions about process and outcome influenced by internal guidelines—Formal Memoranda and Casework Guidance Notes—as well as case law, decisions can be shaped by factors beyond the law. The different professional backgrounds and even personalities of Commission staff may influence investigations, as might legal representatives, campaigners, and the media. Furthermore, the Commission's investigatory process is potentially open-ended. There is considerable scope for discretion, for thorough examination of all possible avenues, or for choosing a more superficial consideration of the case.

In deciding if there are reasons to doubt the safety of the conviction, and what particular grounds there might be for an appeal, case review managers ('CRMs') and commissioners may consider both the 'construction' of the original case for the prosecution, including any procedural irregularities or ignored evidence (e.g. McConville et al., 1991); the case at trial (e.g. Baldwin and McConville, 1979; see also Chapters 4, 6, 7, and 12 in Hunter et al., 2016); and any further evidence that has come to light since the trial, such as new forensic evidence. It can also commission new forensic tests or call new expert witnesses, follow up new lines of enquiry, and order police investigations. In consequence, there may be some variability across cases, and over time.

This study subjects decision-making at the Commission to socio-legal analysis, considering in particular, the application of the real possibility test at screening, investigation, and referral back to the Court. In this chapter, we introduce the theoretical framework for the analysis of discretion and decision-making that we further develop in Chapter 4, and draw on in subsequent chapters that examine the response of the Commission to our sample of cases.

We consider the rich legal and socio-legal literature on discretion, reflecting on the key features of discretionary behaviour, as well as how it is facilitated and constrained in practice. We find a 'naturalistic' approach to understanding decision-making most helpful for case-based analysis, drawing heavily on Keith Hawkins' (2002) framework of legal decision-making, developed in *Law as a Last Resort: Prosecution Decision-Making in a Regulatory Agency*. Looking beyond the Commission's responses to specific cases, Chapter 4 considers the wider processes and structures embedded within the Commission as they impact on the progress of applications through the organization. There, we draw on a particular contribution to the literature on the sociology of organizations which focuses on institutional decision-making, 'the knowing organization'

Reasons to Doubt: Wrongful Convictions and the Criminal Cases Review Commission. © Carolyn Hoyle and Mai Sato 2019. Published 2019 by Oxford University Press.

(Choo, 2006). We use Choo's framework to describe the key stages of decision-making from the receipt of an application to the Commission's decision whether to refer a case back to the Court. First, we must say something more about the law that guides the Commission's decision-making and demonstrate the gap it leaves for discretion.

The Real Possibility Test

In deciding which cases fit the criteria for a referral back to the Court, the Commission must work within both the 1968 (section 23) and the 1995 (section 13) Criminal Appeal Acts. Section 13 of the 1995 Act sets out the conditions for making a reference: most notably, that there is 'new' evidence or argument—for example, on a point of law—not previously raised at trial or appeal, that raises a *real possibility* that the Court will quash the conviction (though the Commission can refer a case without new evidence under 'exceptional circumstances'). Given that section 2(1) of the 1968 Act provides that the Court shall allow an appeal against conviction only if it thinks that the conviction is unsafe, meeting the real possibility test requires the Commission to assess whether the Court is likely to find the conviction to be unsafe when presented with new argument or new evidence.

The Court must consider that it is 'necessary or expedient in the interests of justice' to receive the new evidence within the criteria set out in section 23 of the 1968 Act: the evidence must be capable of belief, capable of forming a ground for allowing the appeal, and there must be a reasonable explanation for the failure to adduce the evidence at trial if the evidence had been available to the defence at the time (section 2d). In the oft cited case of *Steven Jones*, the Court clarified the application of section 23, warning against the presentation of better expert witnesses at appeal whose evidence could have been given at trial:

[The appellant] is not entitled to hold evidence in reserve and then seek to introduce it on appeal following conviction. While failure to give a reasonable explanation for failure to adduce the evidence before a jury is not a bar to reception of the evidence on appeal, it is a matter which the Court is obliged to consider in deciding whether to receive the evidence or not ... Expert witnesses, although inevitably varying in standing and experience, are interchangeable in a way in which factual witnesses are not. It would clearly subvert the trial process if a defendant, convicted at trial, were to be generally free to mount on appeal an expert case which, if sound, could and should have been advanced before the jury. (*Steven Jones*[1])

That said, the Court has since demonstrated *some* flexibility on this matter. In *R v Soloman*[2] the fact that the evidence had been available and could have been raised at trial did not prove fatal to the appeal as the evidence was particularly strong.

Hence, in deciding whether there is new evidence and whether that evidence gives rise to a real possibility that the Court will find the conviction to be unsafe, the Commission must consider not only the legislation, but subsequent guidance from the Court, as well as the Administrative Court and the House of Lords and, since 2009, the Supreme Court. This guidance—provided by judgments and occasional reprimands from the Court[3]—is regularly reviewed by the Commission and reproduced with

---

[1] [1997] 1 Cr App R 86.   [2] [2007] EWCA Crim 2633.
[3] For example, the Court has sought to place limitations on the Commission in relation to referrals on 'lurking doubt', where there is no new evidence, and very old cases. Furthermore, it has reprimanded the Commission for certain referrals based on a change of law or on assertions of legal incompetence (1982).

analysis in Casework Guidance Notes, in memos on Court judgments, in Statements of Reasons prepared for applicants and the Court, in presentations to the Commission, and in informal communication between Commission staff. These are the routine ways in which decision-makers make sense of evolving interpretations of the law (Hawkins, 2002:50–1).

While much of this institutional knowledge is driven by decisions made by the Court on cases referred by the Commission, as well as on direct appeal judgments, decisions made by the Administrative Court in judicial reviews of the Commission's decisions *not* to refer can also be instructive. The first challenge to the Commission's decision not to refer a conviction to the Court (in the case of *Pearson*[4]) led to an important judgment by Lord Bingham which elucidated the Commission's role in deciding whether any particular case meets the real possibility test, having a lasting impact on the Commission's decision-making:

The real possibility test prescribed in section 13(1)(a) of the 1995 Act as the threshold which the Commission must judge to be crossed before a conviction may be referred to the Court of Appeal is imprecise but plainly denotes a contingency which, in the Commission's judgement, is more than an outside chance or a bare possibility but which may be less than a probability or a likelihood or a racing certainty ... The Commission is entrusted with the power and the duty to judge which cases cross the threshold and which do not ... In a conviction case depending on the reception of fresh evidence, the Commission must ask itself a double question: do we consider that if the reference is made there is a real possibility that the Court of Appeal will receive the fresh evidence? If so, do we consider that there is a real possibility that the Court of Appeal will not uphold the conviction? The Commission would not in such a case refer unless it gave an affirmative answer to both questions.

Bringing the focus back to the case in hand—*Pearson*, Lord Bingham continued:

The Commission had, bearing in mind the statutory threshold, to try to predict the response of the Court of Appeal if the case were referred and application to adduce the evidence were made. It could only make that prediction by paying attention to what the Court of Appeal had said and done in similar cases on earlier occasions. It could not rationally predict the response of the Court of Appeal without making its own assessment, with specific reference to the material in this case, of the considerations to which the Court of Appeal would be obliged to have regard and of how it would be likely to exercise is discretion. (Lord Bingham, *R v Criminal Cases Review Commission ex p Pearson*[5])

Hence, the Administrative Court refused the application from Pearson, reluctant to usurp the function which Parliament had, deliberately accorded to the judgement of the Commission.

With *Pearson* in mind, the Commission's internal guidance—Casework Guidance Note—on the real possibility test makes clear that commissioners should take a robust but sensible approach and give each case proper scrutiny before deciding whether the test is met (Criminal Cases Review Commission, 2011o). It reproduces Lord Bingham's words, noting that there must be more than an outside chance of success but that there does not have to be a probability; that referrals must be more than threadbare, but success need not be assured. It also makes clear that the Commission, in second-guessing the Court, must be cognisant of the Court's decisions in previous cases. Hence the Commission regularly conducts careful analysis of the Court's response to its referrals to better predict its responses to future cases.

---

[4] *R v Criminal Cases Review Commission ex p Pearson* [1999] 3 All ER 498.
[5] [1999] 3 All ER 498.

Pendleton[6] too is often referred to in Commission deliberations. Both the Court in its judgments, and the Commission in its Statements of Reasons, draw heavily on this House of Lords' judgment. Following a referral by the Commission, Pendleton's conviction had been upheld by the Court, which asserted that the criminal justice system requires trial by jury and not a second trial by judges in the Court (on jury deference, see Chapters 11 and 14). Notwithstanding, the Lords subsequently quashed the conviction. Drawing on prior case law, they argued that in making a judgment on whether a conviction is unsafe, the Court should test its provisional view by asking whether the evidence if given at trial might reasonably have affected the decision of the jury to convict. If it might, the conviction must be thought to be unsafe. While the House of Lords in *Pendleton* did not change the law, it reminded the Court that in difficult cases it should consider what doubts the jury might have had.

Since *Pendleton* the Commission, in deciding its cases, has asked itself whether the new evidence takes the case into the realms of 'difficulty' as discussed by Lord Bingham, and not assumed that the prosecution at trial had made out an incontrovertible case. In other words, the Commission is guided by anticipation of how the judges might consider what a jury would have made of any new evidence, what the jury might have thought is sufficient to quash a conviction or order a retrial.

That said, as Laurie Elks (2008:69) in his authoritative account of Commission referrals makes clear, the majority decision in *Pendleton* is not the last word on the subject. Other cases since have taken a less liberal approach and the Commission has found itself on the receiving end of sharp rebukes by the Court for its weaker referrals. The Court, like any other decision-making body, can make somewhat inconsistent decisions and at times shut the door to what previously had seemed to be promising routes to overturning convictions. Post-*Pendleton* jurisprudence appears to set the bar somewhat higher for the Commission and, as a result, commissioners may have become more 'timid' in deciding which cases meet the test for a referral 'without [the Commission] adopting an explicit policy to that effect or even necessarily appreciating that its approach has been changing' (Elks, 2008:71). Clearly, the legal framework of statute and evolving case law leave some room for discretion, for different approaches to cases, and for bolder or more cautious decisions on referring cases back to the Court. We turn now to the socio-legal literature on discretion to help us to make sense of the Commission's decision-making within this legal framework.

On Discretion

Organizing ideas: the need for socio-legal analysis

Nearly half a century ago, Davis (1969:233) called for a new jurisprudence that would draw back from a narrow understanding of law to a wider appreciation of the various influences on discretionary decision-making. Since then, the concept of discretion has been explored from two somewhat distinct disciplinary perspectives: law and sociology. Apart from the positivist approach to discretion, where lawyers and sociologists have converged, it is clear that lawyers[7] and sociologists[8] have tended to pose different

---

[6] *R v Pendleton* [2001] UKHL 66 [2002 1 WLR 72 (HL); see further Chapter 7.
[7] See e.g. Galligan (1986) and Pattenden (1982).
[8] See e.g. Bottomley (1973) and McBarnet (1981), who offers a persuasive account of the function of discretion.

questions of discretion. However, it is interesting also that members of the same discipline can perceive discretion differently and pursue disparate lines of enquiry (see various contributors in Hawkins ed. (1992b)).

Broadly, and somewhat crudely, the legal approach assumes that the most important and effective constraints on discretionary decision-making are to be conceived in legal terms. For example, this may be through statutes, case law, duties to provide reasons for a particular decision, or other influences discernible in the policy statements of legal bureaucracies—what could be described as soft law (for a discussion of this approach, see Hawkins, 2002). Hence, legal philosophers and lawyers focus on 'discretion as a quality of rules' (Lempert, 1992).[9] A legalistic perspective tends to define its terrain in unduly narrow terms. It may prove restrictive, ineffectual, or unsuited to certain contexts; it may lead to a manner of thinking about the issue requiring discretion that may in itself prejudge the matter (Hawkins, 1992a).

The sociological treatment of discretion is broader in scope. While it too appreciates the role of law in legal decision-making, it emphasizes the 'many other forces that work upon a legal decision-maker compelling or constraining action which reside in matters normative, economic, political and organizational' (Hawkins, 1992a:18). Indeed, legal rules, procedures, and institutions are merely one set of factors that operate at the individual and organizational level, which must necessarily be supplemented by other sets of factors. This line of thought also recognizes that decision-making takes place within an organizational context that imposes a particular set of objectives and introduces new constraints upon those responsible for decision-making (Hawkins, 1992a). Sociologists have tended to approach their subject through empirical as well as theoretical enquiry (e.g. Lempert, 1992; Pepinsky, 1984; Skolnick, 1966).

Hence, while both sociologists and most legal scholars who study discretion appreciate the role of the law yet recognize that it does not alone explain all decisions made, their approaches vary. Sociologists often adopt a broad frame of analysis. They consider the various cultural and structural factors that might influence discretion, while oftentimes focusing empirically on a specific part of the criminal process or a specific organization, such as the police, or in Hawkins (2002) case, prosecutors in a regulatory agency. Legal scholars, who tend not to conduct empirical research, often focus on judicial decision-making, and engage in rather abstract consideration of whether or how the law leaves space for discretion.

We are inclined to concur with Lacey (1992), who claims that these somewhat different approaches to discretion from law and sociology are best considered together—or viewed as interdependent. For Lacey (1992), conventional legal approaches to discretion must be modified in light of the methods and insights of the wider social sciences (see also Bell, 1992; Campbell, 1999; Walton, 2015:236). Adopting a similar line of thought to Lacey (1992), Hawkins (1992a) is receptive to both the legal and the sociological when making sense of discretionary decision-making. He suggests that discretion might be regarded as 'the space … between legal rules where legal actors must exercise choice' (Hawkins, 1992a:11). This is certainly our understanding of the use of discretion at the Commission.

There is, in our view, no prospect of explaining decision-making at the Commission without understanding how commissioners and CRMs interpret evidence in each case in light of the real possibility test; nor, for example, are their responses to claims of procedural irregularities comprehensible without appreciation of what the law permits.

---

[9] See also Greenawalt (1975) and Barak (1989).

We argue that at the Commission, the practice of discretion, so defined, is pervasively influential. Given its status as an independent, non-governmental body—and, in particular, having been afforded special legal powers and statutory responsibilities (Criminal Cases Review Commission, 2016b)—it is an example, we suggest, of an organization that merits a socio-legal approach to understanding discretion. Such an approach needs to take seriously the role of the law in structuring decision-making but appreciate that sociological factors will also influence the exercise of discretion. Our review of the literature and analysis of decision-making in casework proceeds on this basis.

Legal approaches to discretion

Most legal scholars who write about discretion accept it is inevitable, but tend to assume a proper legal strategy can keep it in check and reduce its potential for harm (see Galligan, 1986 for a discussion of this body of work). Legal scholars, such as Schneider (1992), have explored why discretion might be preferred to strict adherence to rules; for example, to allow agencies to develop rules gradually over time.

There are a number of potential theoretical starting points for a discussion of discretion from a legal perspective. The first is the work of legal philosophers such as Dworkin (1977)—a fierce critic of legal positivism—who have principally been concerned with clarifying the concept of discretion as it applies to the formal adjudicative process.[10] The second is the influential work of Davis (1969), which considers the problems posed by discretion in the broader public law context, where he examines the advantages of rules versus discretion as a mechanism for developing agency policy.

In responding to Hart's classic text, *The Concept of Law* (1961), Dworkin attempted to distinguish between 'weak' and 'strong' discretion; the latter, he asserted, was the focus of legal positivism, and referred to discretion to make a decision when there are no standards set by authority. For Dworkin (1977), law has a solution to most problems. When decision-makers, such as judges, have no discretion in the strong sense, they simply make decisions by applying the relevant rules and laws. However, in hard cases, Dworkin (1977:75–83) argued, when there are no clear rules to apply, or where a rule is ambiguous, the judge is not obliged to make a particular decision. In the absence of rules, Dworkin (1977:17) asserted, judges (or other decision-makers) must appeal to principles.

[I]f someone's case is not clearly covered by such a rule ... then that case cannot be decided by 'applying the law'. It must be decided by some official, like a judge, 'exercising his discretion', which means reaching beyond the law for some other sort of standard to guide him in manufacturing a fresh legal rule or supplementing an old one.

In such a situation, Dworkin (1977) found a place for morals in the law, as well as individual rights, and it was this contribution to legal scholarship that has ensured his continued relevance today.

Legal positivists had argued that in the absence of a guiding statute or case law, judges responded to difficult cases by exercising discretion and finding a solution that seemed to be the most appropriate. This suggests that the judge makes the law in such cases. However, Dworkin (1977) favoured an interpretive understanding of judicial

---

[10] See Dworkin's (1963) critique of H.L.A. Hart's (1961) theory of legal positivism. For a helpful analysis of Dworkin's critique of Hart's positivism, and the rebuttals offered by Hart and his supporters, see Shapiro (2007).

decision-making; though interpreting legal materials, judges reflect and promulgate the moral values and principles of the society. In this sense, the judge does not go beyond the law to find subjective judgments; rather, he or she finds the morality within the legal framework. For Dworkin (1977) therefore, the law and morals should not be separated. Of course, if a valid rule exists, it should be applied. If not, principles must be employed, principles that describe rights, and the judge's job in such cases is to weigh up the various principles to select the right one, and thereby uphold the moral norms of society (Dworkin, 1963:637). 'Hard' legal positivists have sought to identify 'pedigrees' in such principles that could be termed 'judicial custom', or to argue that judges are under a legal obligation to apply extra-legal standards, and hence, there is no real discretion here.[11] Of course, most legal positivists do not take this line, but have sought instead to reject Dworkin's characterization of positivism.[12]

Davis (1969:50–1) started from the premise that there is considerable discretion in the criminal process, exposed the various injustices that it has the capacity to engender and, furthermore, argued that it should be structured, confined, and ultimately controlled. Without legal limits, Davis suggested, decisions are made on the basis of individual, arbitrary, or intuitive standards (Davis, 1969:50–1).[13] Hence, he confronted the basic question of how to reduce the improper use of discretionary power from a political perspective. Davis' work has attracted criticism, for example, with regards to its narrowly legalistic perspective and mechanical view of decision-making, its adherence to the idea and ideal of the rule of law, and its normatively idealistic understanding of a rule-based approach to decision-making and its practical potential (Baldwin, 1995; Lacey, 1992).

A jurisprudential contribution from Bell (1992) contrasts two views as to the nature of law in the context of discretionary decision-making. One is the notion of 'ruled justice', where law is viewed as a set of 'normative directions' (Bell, 1992:110) of greater or lesser specificity, designed to guide and control the behaviour of citizens. The other is a more sociological approach in which law, in its terminology and values, is seen as a resource for legal actors, with which they engage, often instead of, and in preference to, reference to formal legal machinery. This perspective recognizes a more complex relationship between legal norms and individual conduct and is more helpful for our purpose here (Bell, 1992; Campbell, 1999). Unlike Dworkin (1963), we see discretion in the interpretation of the law in all cases, not just 'hard cases', and unlike Davis (1969), we do not assume that in the absence of legal limits, discretion will be unconstrained and unstructured and inevitably a bad thing.

It was always our aim to consider how the law frames and structures decision-making at the Commission: to see law not as determining decision-making but as shaping it, as a resource for decision-makers to draw on, but only one among many resources. We are interested not only in 'hard law', the legislation that sets parameters for the referral of cases from the Commission to the Court, but also in 'soft law', the formal policies and internal guidelines that guide the processing of applications. However, we were determined to understand how various extra-legal, sociological factors also shape discretion and decision-making. We do not intend to view these as additional factors to take into consideration, but as means by which decision-makers can make

---

[11] See Shapiro, 2007:22–6.

[12] For a discussion of their responses to Dworkin (1963), see Shapiro (2007).

[13] For a discussion of Davis' (1969) approach, see Gifford (1983) and Campbell (1999). For a study of 'inclusive legal positivism' that develops Hart's (1961) thesis in *The Concept of Law*, see Waluchow (1994).

sense of and act upon the laws, policies, and guidelines of the Commission, as well as guiding behaviour in the gaps left by the soft and hard law. In other words, just as the sociologist, Max Weber (1968) thought that legal ideas and legal reasoning should be a central concern of sociology (see also Schluchter (2003)), we see legal scholarship and sociological understanding of law as inseparable. We are, that is, in agreement with Roger Cotterrell on the importance of interpreting law 'systematically and empirically as a social phenomenon' (Cotterrell, 1998:183). This is not to reduce legal ideas to something 'other than law', but to express 'their social meaning as law in its rich complexity' (Cotterrell, 1998:181). Hence, we turn to more sociological understandings of discretion to see how they might guide our approach.

Sociological approaches to discretion

Sociology, like legal scholarship, has not produced a cohesive approach to the law. At one end, we find the rather uncompromising theory of autopoietic systems, developed by Niklas Luhmann (1985). While there has been much debate about what autopoiesis[14] means, it assumes a self-referential and closed system, with the law functioning independently of other social systems. Hence there is a circular relation between legal decisions and normative rules:

Decisions are legally valid only on the basis of normative rules because normative rules are valid only when implemented by decisions. (Luhmann, 1986:115)

Rather less opaquely, Teubner (1984:295) explains:

A self-referential structure emerges only when a decision resolving a conflict refers to another such decision and develops criteria for deciding out of the relation between them. This self-referential structure becomes an autopoietic organization to the degree that references to external factors, e.g. politics or religion, are replaced by references to legal rules (stemming from court decisions, doctrinal inventions, or legislative acts).

While there has been considerable criticism of autopoiesis (e.g. Bradney, 1992), Michael King (1993) attempts to provide a robust defence. However, he concedes that it is hard not to dismiss this unpronounceable theory as an attempt to aggrandize legal theory and defend and perpetuate its traditional hegemony:

What are we to make of a theory which apparently sees the legal system as firmly closed to all external influences and which refuses even to accept the obvious fact that 'people make decisions'? (King, 1993:218)

What indeed? We dismiss this approach rather quickly as having little to offer our analysis of the Commission.

Unpronounceable theories aside, other sociological approaches to law and legal decision-making may be more helpful. Within criminology and criminal justice, many studies of policing have adopted a sociological approach. Subcultural studies of policing highlighted the importance of detailed observation, documenting the occupational milieu of police work by describing the norms, values, and working practices of police officers (Holdaway, 1983, 1996), all of which are relevant to our study of decision-makers in the Commission. However, the law, the police organization, its policies, and senior management remained unexamined. More environmental models of

---

[14] 'Auto' refers to the 'self', while 'poiesis' means 'creation or production'. An autopoietic system therefore would be one that is capable of reproducing and maintaining itself.

policing took into account the basic environmental features of the organization, such as its management, organizational structure, and processes, as well as the constraints of the law (Grimshaw and Jefferson, 1987)[15] and are more helpful for our purpose.

Relatedly, Grimshaw and Jefferson (1987) considered the extent to which the police are permitted and, indeed, required actively to shape their general role, concluding that the police are provided with considerable latitude. Specifically, they note a 'structuring of discretion according to informal working rules developed by the police' (McConville et al., 1991:22–3).[16] Indeed, while there may be compelling logistical and moral reasons for uniformity in pursuit of the singular virtue of general order, the police retain a high level of discretion in the performance of their function (Grimshaw and Jefferson, 1987; Jefferson and Grimshaw, 1984).[17]

Most sociological approaches to discretion in the criminal justice system do not reject the importance of law, but see law as just one of many structures that shape decision-making (Schneider, 1992). Once it is recognized that there are various non-legal variables informing decision-making and guiding actors in making sense of the law, Davis' concerns about discretion being unfettered dissipate somewhat. Sociologists' work on discretion has made apparent the importance of context in appreciating decision-making, and led to an interpretive approach to understanding the:

'Operational ideologies', 'frames of reference' or 'assumptive worlds'—systems of values and beliefs which allow agents to make sense of, to impose explanations on, and to order events in the world in which they are operating. (Lacey, 1992:364)

Hence, Lacey (1992:380) argues that lawyers should modify their approach in light of these sociological insights 'if the dangers of the legal paradigm are to be averted'.

In the sociological literature, an analytic distinction can be made between positivist and naturalistic ways of theorizing discretionary decision-making.[18] On this understanding, positivist or rational choice forms of enquiry, which at one time were the more common approaches, are popularly advanced in legal settings and adopt a restrictive, mechanistic and instrumental view of the decision-making process. The positivistic approach sees legal decisions as guided solely by the law and legal rule, with informed legal actors thoughtfully and rationally weighing up the issues within a legal framework and adjudicating the case accordingly (Campbell, 1999).

What distinguishes this approach from a hard legal positivist position is that sociologists allow for policies to be included in 'the law', accepting the influence of both hard and soft law. However, the idea that a discrete case is adjudicated by an actor who weighs up the matter from a broad legal perspective is shared by certain sociologists and lawyers. For our purpose, this approach would require us to look only at how the Commission decides cases based on the statute, case law, and the policies and guidelines of the Commission (Formal Memoranda and Casework Guidance Notes). To some extent, commissioners and CRMs have a positivist assumption about their own decision-making. They see themselves as guided and restricted by the legislation, notably the real possibility test, as well as decisions made by the Court in previous similar cases:

---

[15] See also Bowling (1999).   [16] See also Hoyle (1998).
[17] See also Loader and Walker (2008).
[18] For a discussion of positivism and naturalism, and the key differences between them, see Keat (1971).

[W]e have to look at each case distinguished on its own facts, and obviously, we need to read what's coming out of the Court of Appeal so we understand their thinking [if] there's a real possibility. (#74)

They also recognize that they are influenced in their decision-making by policies imposed by the Commission in the form of Casework Guidance Notes and Formal Memoranda and in other institutional directives aimed at helping staff to recognize and review appropriately those cases which may meet the real possibility test. In other words, Commission staff assume that the decision whether to refer a case back to the Court is made simply on the merits of the case, that two separate CRMs or commissioners would likely come to the same conclusion if presented with the same evidence. As one interviewee told us, 'when you refer a case ... You try and decide it on its merits' (#40). However, as David Nelken (1998:407–8) reminds us, 'legal actors often have little grasp of the factors which shape "inputs" and "outcomes" of their decisions'.

A positivistic approach, we believe, would provide only a partial picture. It has no place for the sense-making and interpretation that inform decisions and that we have witnessed in each and every case we have analysed. It allows no role for politics, resources—such as a limited budget or temporal constraints, or for the internal culture of the organization. Nor can it accommodate the influences of differences in experience, expertise or personality, all of which we anticipated would likely inform decision-making. A naturalistic approach goes much further, and, drawing heavily on Keith Hawkins' *Law as a Last Resort* (2002), we adopt this approach in our analysis of the Commission. In accordance with the naturalistic perspective, we argue that decision outcomes should not be viewed in a self-evident way: what is 'merited' is context-sensitive and open to interpretation in each case. This might explain why there will sometimes be different approaches and outcomes in apparently similar cases. Indeed, Hawkins (2002:31) questions what it might mean to consider a case 'on its merits'. What merits self-evidently determine outcomes, and how are they determined?

Naturalistic forms of enquiry are derived from interpretive sociology, involve descriptive analysis, and acknowledge the context and social world in which these decisions take place (Hawkins, 1986, 2002). The aim is to consider:

[t]he various contexts within which decisions are made and the conditions that lead to certain legally consequential outcomes (rather than others), which in turn need to be identified and explained. (Hawkins, 2002:30)

It is recognized that decision-makers ascribe meaning to salient features in a particular case (Hawkins, 2002:31):

Decisions are treated as interpretive practices. Thus, although it is commonly said that decisions are made 'on their merits', a naturalistic approach takes the position that there is nothing self-evident or taken for granted about a decision, and that what is regarded as 'merited' is not only open to interpretation in each case, but only makes sense in the context of each decision.

The framing of information, connoting the structure of knowledge, experience, and values that a decision-maker relies on when approaching a case, is an important aspect of a decision-making process (Hawkins, 2002:31). In this way, the naturalistic approach—unlike those of both legal and sociological positivists—understands decision-making as an interpretive practice (Hawkins, 2002:31). This fits with our understanding of how Commission staff make their decisions. Indeed, some of those we interviewed at the Commission were a little more reflective than certain colleagues about their role and about what it means to interpret evidence and to develop a 'case' in light of the statutory test and other structural and cultural variables, as this excerpt from an interview with a member of staff in a managerial role suggests:

I had a conversation with a case review manager that went roughly along these lines.... Me: 'So, tell me how you approach reviewing your cases ...' They said, 'Em, well, it's easy, isn't it—you just work out if there's a real possibility.' 'Okay, can you break that down for me—how do you go about doing that?' 'Well, it's obvious most of them have done it so there isn't ... ' [Laughing] 'Okay, so how do you ... ?!' 'Yes, yeah, and that was ... that was it? You just weigh it up and you work out whether you think they've done it or not', and that was his approach to case review. It was [laughing], 'right, we're going to have to change this, aren't we?!' (#63)

In *Law as Last Resort: Prosecution Decision-Making in a Regulatory Agency* (Hawkins, 2002), as well as in other leading contributions (Hawkins, 1992a, 2003), Hawkins suggests that to gain an understanding of the nature of discretionary decision-making, a connection ought to be made between a range of factors in the decision-making environment and the decision-making processes in which individuals engage. Hawkins' (2002) typology of 'surround', decision 'fields', and decision 'frames' allows this connection to be made. With occasional references to the work of Lacey (1992), Baumgartner (1992), Emerson and Paley (1992), and Feldman (1992), all included in a collection of essays edited by Hawkins (1992b), we draw on *Law as a Last Resort* to provide the main theoretical framework for understanding discretion at the Commission; an explicitly naturalistic socio-legal approach.

Focusing for a moment on the process of decision-making that takes place at the Commission—from receipt of an application to the final decision whether or not to refer a case back to the Court—Hawkins' (2002) theoretical framework makes clear that it is unhelpful to see the final reference as encompassing 'the legal decision' in the case. Of course, it is the decision that needs to be justified within a legal framework (the real possibility test) but it is by no means the only one. All the sense-making activities that precede this final decision in each and every case, some made over a period of years, provide multiple points of discretion and decision-making, all of which need to be fully understood. His work also makes explicit the negotiations that can take place when groups are expected to make decisions, groups comprising individuals with somewhat different biographies and approaches:

In resolving differences about what a particular decision outcome should be, matters such as expertise, experience, status, and personal charisma frequently influences choices made. (Hawkins, 2002:33)

Hawkins further notes that at times what can seem like a final 'decision' is in fact little more than ratification of an earlier series of decisions, all leading in that direction. Hence a status of legal certainty about a case can be the product of a series of judgments and decisions that might have been influenced by various factors beyond the law, hard or soft. He explains the process of 'typification', where decision-makers develop understandings of what 'normal' cases are, or 'normal' ways of deciding on cases (Hawkins, 2002:35) that can lead to routine approaches, and that repetitive decision-making can result in 'organizational precedent' that shapes behaviour. As we explore in the chapters that follow, certain routine activities and approaches at the Commission did develop the status of organizational precedent, to be considered alongside legal precedent, the influence of which Commission staff are fully aware of. We explore these issues further in Chapter 4, but here we turn to Hawkins' (2002) notion of 'surround', 'field', and 'frame' to better understand sense-making for:

To focus on a single decision point ... risks excluding the social context that surrounds legal decision-making, the field in which the decision is set and viewed, as well as the interpretive and classificatory processes of individual decision-makers. (Hawkins, 2002:30)

These three concepts will help us to organize theorizing on decision-making in the following chapters.

The Surround, Decision Fields, and Decision Frames

While it may be correct to point out, in the context of the Commission, that certain factors might influence decision-making, whether they be an internal policy, a specific recent judgment by the Court, budget cuts, or the background of the decision-maker (e.g. defence law or journalism), this does not tell us how these different possible influences might play out, how they interact with one another and if one is likely to be more powerful than another.

To understand the nature of decision-making fully, some connection needs to be forged between these forces ... and the processes that individuals engage in when deciding about a particular matter ... Decisions about legal standards and their enforcement, like other legal decisions, are made, then, in a much broader setting (their 'surround') and within a context, or 'field', defined by the legal and organizational mandate. Decision 'frames', the interpretive and classificatory devices operating in particular instances, are influenced by both surround and field. (Hawkins, 2002:47–8)

Surround

Hawkins' notion of the surround refers to the social, economic, and political environments which condition discretionary decision-making (Hawkins, 2002:48–50). Surrounds are rarely unchanging, and a shifting landscape can impact on the organization, as it chooses or is forced to respond to external changes. Changes in the surround of the Commission that we have witnessed during our research have included evolving forensic science, evolving Court jurisprudence, and a dramatic rise in applications to the Commission and reduction in the budget. If we take a moment to consider how a reduction in the budget allocated to the Commission by the Ministry of Justice might change behaviour, it becomes apparent that those working under budgetary constraints might not always recognize their own response. Most of our interviewees told us that resources did not dictate their investigations:

We [like to say] we don't concern ourselves with money [laughing], although we do! But not in terms of investigation—there is no limit on the amount of money we'll spend on an investigation, if it's the proper thing to do. The question is always 'Is it right to get this work done?' not 'And how much will it cost?' We ask that later, once we've made the decision whether we'll do it, which is, I think, the right way to do it. (#5)

They did though concede that resources impacted on the queues; with fewer people to investigate cases, applicants waited longer before having their application considered: 'We all find it intensely frustrating that we can't get rid of the backlog because we don't have the resources' (#17). Mindful of the queues, and of the Commission's reputation for being too slow, there was unease within the Commission about limited resources. While we were persuaded by the statements that they would not refuse to conduct a forensic test if it was likely to prove to be exculpatory, we did nonetheless perceive the influence of queues on their behaviour. Hence some staff referred to the pressure to 'screen' out applications that did not appear to be strong, without more than superficial consideration, a concern we return to in Chapter 6:

> I am never conscious of deciding not to pursue something [because it] is too expensive. But obviously, equally, you are thinking, 'Well, one might do this in a perfect world but, you know, one has to respect the fact one's spending public money.' [we screen out weaker cases] . . . because otherwise the backlog was going to become so great. So, the reducing resources make it harder, but I think they will, inevitably, just mean that the backlog will get longer and longer. (#27)

Surround in this context could also refer to pressure put on the organization from those outside its walls. These might include politicians, criminal justice professionals, innocence projects, or journalists criticizing the institutional approach of the Commission in general.

Field

The decision field refers to the defined setting in which decisions are made. It is, primarily, the law—including, statutes guiding the Commission's remit—and the policies and guidance issued by the organization to guide its decision-making. The field of the Commission comprises organizational imperatives found within Casework Guidance Notes and Formal Memoranda ('sets of ideas about how its ends are to be pursued' (Hawkins, 2002:50) which operate at the formal level), as well as 'working rules', expectations, and assumptions. These informal, cultural, influences inform staff about how different cases should be approached and how decisions should be made and accounted for both at the institutional and at the individual level. Hence the formal and informal 'field' provide 'general guidance on . . . sources you can approach for advice on certain things' (#29). In other words, the field is 'something defined by and acted on by the organization' (Hawkins, 2002:50). The guidance also aims to reduce variability in the responses to cases. As one interviewee put it, 'the casework guidance, I think, means that we will, to some extent, have standardized our approach to certain things' (#8).

Unlike the surround, the field tends to be fairly constant, 'anchored by fixed occupational roles and tasks sanctioned by the legal bureaucracy, and the routine ways in which people make sense of what they encounter' (Hawkins, 2002:51). However, a change in procedure can shift the field. Hence, in Chapter 6 we show how a change in the organizational structure of the Commission, with the introduction of 'group leaders' and their assistance in the 'triage' process, led to subtle shifts in screening practice.

Hawkins (2002) also discusses extensively the role and value of formal legal rules in discretionary decision-making. For example, he notes that systems of formal rules, despite their appearance of precision and specificity, tend to operate in imprecise ways. Importantly, precision and consistency are not necessarily achieved by the drafting of more elaborate schemes of rules. The question of whether and how a particular rule applies in a particular case is inevitably reserved for the discretion of the legal actor concerned. More generally, we might understand the operation of formal legal rules in relation to a legal system that is not necessarily neatly organized; rather, it is comprised of a loosely related set of subsystems, which are prone to internal flaws and inefficiencies. In this way, in such a highly discretionary system, we might envisage the formal legal rules 'as a series of markers towards desirable standards around which are zones of tolerance' (Hawkins, 2002:427).

Emerson and Paley's (1992) work, in which they invoke the analogy of the 'organizational horizon', shows how organizations condition the way in which decisions are made. This connotes the idea that discretionary decision-making ought to be understood in broad and general terms. Emerson and Paley note that while organizational horizons can and do shift, they nonetheless provide a framework within which discretionary decisions are made. Within these organizational horizons, decision-makers are expected to have a working knowledge of how other cases of the same nature would be approached, as well as the implications of allowing the case to proceed to the next stage of the relevant administrative or bureaucratic process (Emerson and Paley, 1992). In this sense, the surround may directly impact on the field. Hence, case law from the Court is part of the surround—and so beyond the control of the Commission—but once the Commission reacts to evolving Court jurisprudence, by including discussion of those cases in its formal guidance to staff, cases become an integral part of the decision field.

Our fieldwork provided many examples of decisions which explicitly referenced other similar cases, and drew on the decision-making processes involved in those cases. We saw this in our sample of cases where the applicant had been prosecuted for entering the United Kingdom without the appropriate documentation—for example a valid passport—and without proper legal advice that they had a defence under domestic and international law. Developing organizational knowledge about the causes of such wrongful convictions, and the most likely mechanism for justifying a referral to the Court, resulted in an expeditious response to applications as well as more consistent decision-making. Rather quickly, these asylum cases were viewed as a distinct category, where particular expertise was developing in the organization and staff explicitly drew on other cases to make decisions about process and outcomes (see Chapter 10; further Sato et al., 2017).

Frame

For Hawkins, the legal rules and even the substantive law might be viewed as a statement of aspiration, as a referent, a shaper of practice or as a realistic target for actual practice. How the law is conceptualized in a given situation depends in part on bureaucratic policy but is formed more substantially by the framing practices of individual decision-makers. Hence, the real possibility test must be applied by individual decision-makers slightly differently for each and every case in the context of both formal policy, substantive law, and a set of ever-shifting understandings of how persuasive certain evidence might be in that particular context at that particular time. This is inevitably influenced by past judgments handed down by the Court as well as by the Commission's interpretation of the factors that influenced those judgments. This speaks to Hawkins' notion of a decision frame.

A frame is 'a structure of knowledge, experience, values, and meanings' that Commission staff employ in deciding when there are reasons to doubt the safety of a conviction and how to proceed with analysis of a case. It addresses the question 'What is going on here?' (Hawkins, 2002:52). Bourdieu's (1990) insights could be relevant here. He suggests that actors are shaped inevitably by the practice of which they are a part and often, unreflectively, acquire and internalize a cultural habitus (socialized norms or tendencies that determine behaviour and thinking), thus shaping their everyday practices. Habitus is neither the result of free will, nor determined by structures, but generated as a result of interplay between the two; thus, creating and conditioning individual dispositions (Bourdieu, 1990). To the extent that actors draw regularly on the linguistic resources and traditions of their practice, they tend to act in a relatively unreflective manner. However, they retain an innate capacity for self-observation and reflexivity, which allows them to adapt their practices to suit particular circumstances (Bourdieu, 1990). Though Bourdieu's habitus speaks to the cultural milieu of the Commission, we find Hawkins' notion of frames more helpful to our understanding of how this environment can shape the behaviour of decision-makers within the Commission.

According to Hawkins (2002), frames are employed by individual decision-makers to make sense of what they encounter, to impose meaning upon it. Frames could be seen as 'working rules' or 'assumptions' that guide understanding of what has happened, or is happening, and of how information can be made sense of. They help people to interpret and to classify the world around them. In the Commission, frames help to organize the content and meaning of applications, at receipt of the application and all the way through the review process, as further data become available. As Hawkins explains, the facts of the case are not synonymous with the frame. A frame is applied to a case in order to identify the 'relevant' or 'helpful' facts and discard those that do not help the decision-maker's analysis. At the same time, as 'facts and frames are reflexive' (Hawkins, 2002:53), facts can narrow the potential frame.

Frames are influenced by the culture of the organization but also by individual biographies. Hence, a commissioner with a prosecution background might interpret an application through a somewhat different frame to a commissioner from a civil service background or one from a regulatory background. As one interviewee explained:

Commissioners ... are very individual. And when you get to meet them and to work with them, you very quickly see the threads from where they've come from. So, for example, X comes from a defence solicitor background, you see that in the way that they approach work ... very keen to get hold of defence papers, very keen to look at issues where an applicant might be criticizing the police. One of the commissioners is [an experienced barrister], and the way in which they work, clearly used to being able to delegate work to people, not have to necessarily do all the groundwork themself. (sic) But wants to read absolutely everything, so that they know that case inside out, and nothing's missed ... And you see that through each of them. (#26)

Personality types and different cultural values and predispositions among commissioners may also account for variation in methodological approaches to evaluating and making sense of the data presented to them by the CRM. For example, one of our interviewees who had many years of experience working with commissioners explained:

[D]ifferent commissioners have different styles. X likes to read it and agree it [instantly]. Y likes to read it and maybe have a meeting and to make lots of amendments. Z likes to have a meeting just to make sure he's clear the basis of the decision that he's making. But it's different styles ... (#5)

Similarly, different framing behaviour will likely influence distinct approaches from legal advisers, investigations advisers (who tend to be from policing backgrounds), and even throughout hierarchical structures—with a young, inexperienced CRM likely to adopt a different frame to an established commissioner.

Individual CRMs' experience, cognitive styles, and preferences will inevitably influence the manner in which information is sought, processed, and utilized (Choo, 2006:46). It takes confidence to know when there is sufficient information for a decision, or to persuade a group of peers that an initial decision is valid. Hence, cautious decision-makers might require more data before a decision is made, while more confident CRMs may feel able to make a decision with less information or more equivocal data. Hence, information needs should be understood both in terms of a decision-maker's cognitive needs (gaps or deficiencies in their understanding or knowledge) and in terms of their affective or emotional needs.

Lack of information impacts on people differently. For some, uncertainty will create anxiety, apprehension, frustration, and a lack of confidence. To manage stress caused by uncertainty, some will seek ever larger amounts of information, while others suffer greater arousal at information overload. Consequently, some CRMs may seek data that closes down the possibilities in the case, whereas others may explore more and ever varied sources. The risk with the former is that a decision is made prematurely without all available relevant information, whereas the risk of the latter is that an investigation takes many more months or years than might be necessary, causing distress to the applicant and impacting on resources at the Commission.

Our interviews with CRMs and commissioners suggested that there was variability in their propensity to seek further information, either from experts or from their own colleagues. One explained to us, in relation to seeking advice from investigations advisers:

I think some people differ.... I like taking advice and I like bouncing ideas off and I like being able to ask what I think might be a stupid question. I don't necessarily go to see an Advisor with a specific query in mind. I'll quite often go and see them to say, 'Can I just talk this through with you? I'm thinking of doing this—what do you reckon?' that sort of thing. So, I'm one of those that uses them quite a lot, almost as much as a sounding board as anything else, and to check my own judgement occasionally. (#1)

Others sought information or advice by sending emails to all staff:

We're not a huge organization, so it's not difficult to ask somebody, and that's what happens a lot: an email will come round saying 'Does anyone have a case that was like X?' (#8)

Even with guidance from Formal Memoranda and Casework Guidance Notes, and with supervision, CRMs can differ considerably in their approach to investigations. One interviewee spoke about some CRMs 'getting enthusiasms about cases and just going away on endless frolics' but then went on to say that:

some commissioners are ... slightly too inclined to want to commission yet further work, because they're reluctant to take a decision until they've explored every avenue ... [It] is sometimes a pretext for ... conscious or subconscious, for putting off the decision-making day. (#9)

For Hawkins, framing is not only an interpretive act (in the sense that CRMs must interpret the information provided in an application in order to review it) but it is also a classificatory act. CRMs must classify data and analysis in certain ways so that they are able to present a viable 'case' for a referral or against a referral to other decision-makers, whether that be their supervising commissioner or a 'decision-making committee':

What information suppliers choose to present for decision, and how they choose to present it—what they focus on, emphasize, or omit, for example—frames reality for the ultimate decision-makers. (Hawkins, 2002:56)

This becomes apparent in the detailed information on CRMs review processes as recorded in 'case plans' and, particularly, 'case records'. These records show a full account of all information considered and what was rejected as 'irrelevant' during that process. 'Extant facts can be framed in or out over the career of a case in a serial legal decision-making process' (Hawkins, 2002:57). Of course, this might be most obvious with legal frames, which can help CRMs and commissioners define facts as legally relevant or not, drawing explicitly on their interpretation of the law. However, even here, the legal frame might look very different from the perspective of a lawyer representing an applicant—who may make a generous interpretation of a law or a legal precedent—as opposed to a commissioner who does not want to risk an unsuccessful referral by stretching a legal interpretation to breaking point.

As mentioned above, at the Commission, frames might vary across the organization depending on whether the individual decision-maker is newly in post or has considerable experience, whether they have a background in law or not, whether they are confident in their investigative role or more cautious or anxious, and it is sometimes down to variations in tenacity. One interviewee explained:

There are definitely natural tendencies of those sorts, and every variance in between. And I suppose to some extent that's where the group leader role comes in. Is knowing who's got what tendency, and knowing to try to be the counterbalance to that to some extent. So, in case discussions, you know someone's inclined to keep going, keep going. Perhaps you might challenge that a bit more, try and draw them back, where that's appropriate. And with other people who are perhaps inclined to think 'No, load of nonsense. Not doing anything more, that's the end of it', then you might be trying to challenge a bit more and say, 'What about this, what about that, what about so and so?' (#26)

Other scholars have described decision-making in similar terms, appreciating the interrelationship between social and legal factors. Lacey (1992) notes the importance of context in understanding the nature of discretion, and is concerned, in particular, to highlight the experience of the individual decision-maker's own understanding of their discretionary behaviour. This phenomenological, agent-centred approach has provided insights relating to, for example, 'operational ideologies', 'frames of relevance', or 'assumptive worlds': essentially, value systems which allow individuals to make sense of and impose explanations on the settings in which they work (Lacey, 1992:383). In this sense, her understanding contributes to Hawkins' rich account of frames. Our interviews with caseworkers and commissioners certainly suggested they had somewhat different assumptive worlds. For example, one CRM told us that when he received an application, he:

[W]orked out that, actually, you don't need to know everything about a case in order to be able to review it. If you start from the top down, what am I going to need to know in order to resolve this? ... Every step that I took, I knew why I was doing it. I wasn't just doing it because, well, we've got all this stuff, well, I might as well read it and see if anything occurs to me ... Whereas, I think a lot of other CRMs ... do an almost kind of bottom-up style review, whereby they feel they need to know every single thing about a case. (#63)

Of course, we could draw on the sociology of organizations to explore what Hawkins refers to as the surround and the frame. Indeed, one of the most prominent ontological distinctions made in the sociology of organizations is provided by Weick's (1969, 1995) redirecting of attention from organizations to *organizing*. He (1995) suggested that organizations are not established entities with predefined properties to be discovered by the researcher, as, for example, the distinguished Aston studies had assumed (Pugh, 1981).[19] Rather, organizations are systems of interaction that become organized, and are thus products of sustained human action and interaction (Weick, 1969). Therefore, the researcher's task is to investigate and explain the process of organizing.

For Weick (1995), the environment is, in part, an organizational creation insofar as it is enacted through the organization's actions and interactions; in the case of the Commission, this includes interactions within the organization and beyond—with

---

[19] See Donaldson and Nanfeng (2013) for a review of the relevant literature.

applicants, legal representatives, campaigners, journalists, scientific experts, and so on and so forth. Hence, to understand the organization, it is essential to have one eye on the world it inhabits and interacts with and, occasionally, which it seeks to reform, or which seeks to influence it. In this way, the frame of reference is contextual: an understanding of particular aspects of and processes within the organization is sought as part of a broader exploration of the organizational environments in which they occur (Eldridge and Crombie, 2013). However, such an approach, while helpful, does not give sufficient attention to the 'field'; in this case, it would marginalize the law, both hard and soft.

An analysis of surround, field, and frames allows factors or criteria in decision-making to be given meaning, order, and primacy (Hawkins, 2002). The concepts link micro-level features inherent in a discrete case with broader considerations, such as caseloads, resources, and organizational priorities. These considerations are then set in the organization's and the decision-maker's 'surround', so as to activate the macro-level forces of, for example, politics and economics. The interaction between the concepts of surround, field, and frame thus become explicit and inevitable (Baumgartner, 1992).

In this way, the typology is sensitive to the idea that the actions of a legal bureaucracy are shaped not only by imperatives arising from its legal mandate. Indeed, it shows awareness that decisions are made in rich and complex environments, which act as settings for shifting sets of political, economic, and organizational values. The typology directs attention away from the restrictive, atomistic approach that characterizes much of the legal literature on discretion, instead highlighting the value of understanding decision-making in its broader context (Baumgartner, 1992).

For Hawkins, the practice of discretion is given shape by institutions of law, but more substantially by decision-makers' 'framing behaviour' and interpretive work. The framing behaviour cannot however be understood without reference to the surround and field. Decision-makers make sense of their environment in various ways, and differences in framing behaviour are likely to prompt consideration of how consistently (or otherwise) decisions are made. However, the irony is that discretionary outcomes are, in fact, highly patterned, guided by shared systems of meaning, tacit understandings, organizational routines, and mutually agreed ways of arriving at a decision (Cotterrell, 1998:178). Hence while we saw some differences in framing behaviour, and different approaches to interpreting evidence across many cases, distinct patterns of interpretation emerged. These were the product not of positivist approaches, or of caseworkers blindly following rules within their 'field', but of shared understandings, routines, and working rules, and a shared surround.

A predominant theme in the sociological literature we have reviewed is that discretionary decisions must be viewed from a holistic perspective: they should not be conceived of in wholly individual terms—as only personal, situational, and idiosyncratic (see further, Elks, 2008:336)—but as part of a collective social process. They are likely to be shaped by external social, political, and economic factors, by organizational imperatives and the law, and by non-legally relevant variables that could be cultural or somewhat individualistic.

More broadly, however, we have argued that even when the Commission is interpreting the law, understanding of its analysis and decision-making benefits from a sociological, or perhaps more pertinently, a socio-legal approach as 'the most practical view of legal ideas is one informed by sociological insight. Legal ideas are properly understood sociologically' (Cotterrell, 1998:178).

Our study attempts to bring together both the substantive (the Commission) and the formal or conceptual (decision-making and discretion) in pursuit of a socio-legal contribution to our understanding of the response of the state to claims of wrongful conviction. In this, we draw heavily on Hawkins' (2002) theoretical contribution of 'surround', 'field', and 'frame'. To better understand institutional sense-making and decision-making across these concepts, in Chapter 4 we draw on one study of the sociology of organizations to explore the key stages of decision-making from the receipt of an application to the decision whether or not to refer a case to the Court.

4

Decision-making from Application to Outcome

Introduction

About half of the applications to the Criminal Cases Review Commission ('the Commission') are reviewed over months, and often years—a process which may involve evidence being subjected to forensic tests and expert analysis or even further investigation by an external police force. In other cases, the review is relatively short, comprising little more than consideration of the relevant law and a few key documents from the case files.

In the following chapters, we draw on Hawkins' (2002) notions of surround, field, and frame, as discussed in Chapter 3, to make sense of how individuals make decisions and exercise discretion. Here, we describe the various stages of decision-making—from receipt of application to the decision whether to refer a case to the Court of Appeal ('the Court')—at which the institution produces, organizes, and uses its knowledge for decision-makers to draw on. In doing so, we make use of a theoretical framework derived from Chun Wei Choo's (2006) concept of a 'knowing organization'. We apply Choo's sociology of an organization to our analysis of those institutional forms of knowledge that seek to direct decision-making at the Commission: primarily, the Formal Memoranda and the Casework Guidance Notes. We do this to demonstrate that while these organizational 'guides' may be fairly prescriptive, covering in some detail most decisions that Commission staff will face in reviewing a case, analysis reveals discretion within them, suggesting that decision-makers may interpret their directives somewhat differently.

Variability in its responses to cases causes unease within the Commission. Over the years spent conducting fieldwork, it became clear to us that it is an organization that likes to present itself as consistent in its method and outcomes. Some Commission staff embrace discretion as both inevitable and a strength of the organization. As one interviewee put it:

Clearly, we have to have policies and procedures but there's so much scope for the exercise of discretion ... and a lot of the work is quite subjective ... And we've got a, a sort of bedrock of knowledge and experience and certainly I think many of the practitioners will have that sort of gut feeling that something is wrong with this case, I can't see what it is, but I know. And I know there's disagreements of what the gut feeling is, but as far as I can see that gut feeling isn't anything magical; it's just born from your experience and having people here who've been on the front line and can say, 'There's something wrong with this, I know there's something wrong with this' and start lifting the lid off it so I think that's one of our strengths. (#24)

However, this same interviewee was alarmed when we presented evidence of variability in the screening of applications (see Chapter 6), even suggesting to us that we must have been mistaken in our analysis.

Why someone might be surprised that discretion in an organization would lead to differences in outcome was puzzling to us. However, each time we demonstrated

Reasons to Doubt: Wrongful Convictions and the Criminal Cases Review Commission. © Carolyn Hoyle and Mai Sato 2019. Published 2019 by Oxford University Press.

variability in approach, our data were met with scepticism and defensiveness. Commission staff talking *on behalf of* the Commission, or those talking in the presence of their colleagues, claimed that their decisions are driven by policies and reasonably uniform practices, and by specific case-based factors. However, many admitted to us in interview that they do not always follow internal policies and guidance (Formal Memoranda and Casework Guidance Notes) and their working practices vary from their colleagues. For example, while one told us he would 'almost always ... except in very exceptional circumstances' carry out checks on complainant credibility so as not to 'breach our Formal Memorandum' (#75) (see, in particular, Chapter 8), another readily admitted that:

[Formal Memoranda have] just too much information, and yet even though there is too much information, often it doesn't address the particular thing. So, you have to apply a judgement to it, anyway. And, so I understand that lots of the commissioners barely pay attention to those. (#76)

On the matter of their Casework Guidance Notes, another commissioner observed:

There is even a Casework Guidance Note called 'Gut Instinct' ... You know, I've thought long and hard about this and it strikes me that good instinct is really just a way, it's a phrase for expressing ... a recognition from everything you've taken in about the case that it doesn't sit properly with your experience. (#54)

Interviewees also referred to the policies and guidance as living documents that are regularly edited and so evolve to reflect changing law, and more commonly Court judgments.[1] Hence there will inevitably be some variability in approaches over time, dependent—in part—on the mood music from the Court. This chapter describes the structures in place at the Commission for considering applications and draws on Choo's framework to explain how the organization aims to shape the work of commissioners and case review managers ('CRMs').

The Sociology of an Organization

Choo (2006) integrates organizational theory and information science to understand how organizations process and make sense of information so that they can make informed decisions. He considers how people and groups in organizations work with information, make decisions, and commit resources and capabilities to purposeful action.

Choo's (2006) central thesis is that the three contexts in which information is used and managed—what is described in the wider literature as 'sense-making' (Weick, 1995), 'knowledge-building' (Nonaka and Takeuchi, 1995), and 'decision-making' (Simon, 1976)—are not conceptually distinct, as other sociological commentators have suggested; rather, they are highly interconnected and interactional processes. By analysing how the three processes inform each other, a more comprehensive view of information management in organizations emerges (Choo, 2006).

The interpretation of cues and messages about the environment is the principal information-based activity in *sense-making*. Sense-making is used by the organization to develop shared meaning among members to try to bring about rational and consistent decision-making. Individuals select what information is significant and should

---

[1] In this chapter, we refer to those Casework Guidance Notes and Formal Memoranda in place at the time we conducted our fieldwork. Some Formal Memoranda have been revised in 2017 and 2018.

be attended to, forming possible explanations from experience and institutional knowledge.

The conversion of knowledge is the main activity in *knowledge-creation*. Institutional knowledge is created within the organization by the conversion of tacit knowledge into explicit knowledge. Individuals share their personal knowledge through dialogue and discourse and articulate what they know intuitively, committing it to institutional knowledge.

During *decision-making*, the key information-based activity is the processing of information about all available alternatives to select the option that can successfully achieve desired objectives. That, in turn, refines the institutional knowledge so it can be harnessed for further decisions.

In this chapter, our focus is not on the individual decision-maker, but on how the organization helps to shape and produce decisions. Organizational premises, rules, and routines direct decision-makers; they are valuable in that they structure the search for information and evaluation of alternatives. On this view, all three modes of information use—interpretation, conversion, and processing—are dynamic, social processes that continually constitute and reconstitute meaning, knowledge, and action. Choo's approach helps us to understand organizational continuities or changes, the explicit and implicit organizational pressures and impulses, as well as institutional knowledge that will, in turn, inform the 'field' (Hawkins, 2002; see Chapter 3) that shapes decision-making.

Furthermore, Choo's model allows us to appreciate how organizations aim to control sometimes complex and drawn-out processes by imposing routines and structures, signalling to the outside world that it is an ordered machine, with consistency in its approach. Turning to the Commission, this is clear in the systematic case records and Statements of Reasons produced to account for its decisions during investigation. The thoroughness and consistency of these records speak to a relatively uniform approach to reviewing applications, with decisions influenced by little more than the law and the type of case under consideration. However, as we described in Chapter 3, the positivist assumption that an informed legal actor thoughtfully and rationally weighs up the issues within a legal framework and adjudicates the case with a view to little more than the law is of limited value here. Making sense of applications and deciding what investigations to carry out is a complex process, guided by more than the law; other structural and cultural variables inform the process and introduce inevitable variability across cases. However, this does not happen in a vacuum; the Commission influences decision-making by creating and providing knowledge to draw on. We now describe the various stages in the progress of an application to show the many points at which discretion might be exercised, returning to Choo's thesis at the conclusion.

Categorizing Applications

Before an application is reviewed by the Commission, it must be decided if it is eligible for consideration. This decision is informed by the law. Section 13 of the Criminal Appeal Act 1995 sets out the test the Commission must apply in deciding whether to refer a conviction, verdict, finding, or sentence to the appropriate appellate court. The appropriate court for Crown Court convictions being the Court, and for magistrates court convictions, the Crown Court. There must be a 'real possibility' that a conviction, verdict, finding, or sentence would not be upheld if a reference were to be made (section 13(1)(a)). If the application relates to a conviction, verdict, or finding there must be 'an argument, or evidence' which has not been raised previously (section 13(1) (b)(i)). In other words, the case must pass a threshold; there must be something 'fresh' as well as persuasive. Similarly, if the application relates to a sentence there must be 'an argument on a point of law, or information' which has not been raised previously (section 13(1)(b)(ii).5). In all cases, an appeal should have been determined, or leave to appeal against it refused, before the convicted person applies to the Commission (section 13(1)(c)), though the Commission can consider an application that does not meet this criterion in 'exceptional circumstances' (see below).

Applications received by the Commission are initially sorted by a team of about eight administrators called the Casework Administration Team ('CAT team'). The first responsibility of the CAT team is to decide if a case is eligible for consideration by the Commission. Ordinarily, this will mean establishing that the applicant has already appealed and, if not, the CAT team will alert the screening team to this, with the pre-sumption that the applicant will be told to appeal to the Court directly. Occasionally, applications are ineligible as they fall outside of the jurisdiction of the Commission, either geographically (for example, the offence took place outside England, Wales, or Northern Ireland), or because they relate to a civil matter, or the case is not yet resolved (an applicant may have a case pending before the Court). When in doubt, the CAT team will seek advice from the Commission's legal adviser or a legally trained commis-sioner. If the case is *clearly* ineligible, a letter will be sent to the applicant without fur-ther screening. However, all cases where there has been no appeal but where the case is otherwise eligible will be routed through screening as the decision about whether there are 'exceptional circumstances' is a somewhat complex one requiring the expertise of a commissioner or, latterly, a group leader (see below and Chapter 6).

In most cases, therefore, the CAT team prepares the application for screening by collating relevant supporting documents, many of which are sourced from databases that the Commission has direct access to, noting on the file 'no-appeal' cases or 're-applications' (see below). Clearly, the way that information is gathered by the organ-ization at this early stage has an impact on the approach taken by those responsible for screening cases.

Stage One: Screening Cases

As the Commission's Formal Memorandum on stage 1 decisions makes clear:

> Applications to the Commission are examined to see whether there is a basis for referral, either on issues raised by the applicant or others identified following investigation by the Commission. Screening is the process whereby applications are considered initially, key documents obtained and the need for investigation examined. (Criminal Cases Review Commission, 2013e)

At the start of our fieldwork, the Commission employed only about half of their com-missioners on screening. Over the years, these commissioners developed considerable expertise in efficiently reviewing applications, though we identified some variability in decision-making at this early stage (see Chapter 6). The screening role was then expanded to include all commissioners and the situation was different again in 2018. The CAT team now allocates most cases to group leaders,[2] who screen all 'first-time' applications (as distinct from 're-applications') that have been through the appeals process, which should be a requirement for the Commission to investigate the case.

---

[2] The Commission currently has five 'groups' of CRMs, with a group leader for each.

They also screen reapplications when a first or even a second application has not led to a referral and the applicant feels there is something new for the Commission to consider. Further, they consider 'no-appeal' cases (where the applicant's normal appeal rights remain) if it is thought that the case will require a substantive (stage two) review.

CRMs assist the screening process by examining 'no-appeal' cases to identify any 'exceptional circumstances' that would allow the Commission to review the case even though the applicant has not gone through the regular appeals process. They also screen reapplications for something 'new' that might indicate the need for a further substantive review. In cases where there would seem to be no reviewable grounds, a CRM may be asked to carry out research before the final decision is made. Including group leaders and CRMs in screening allows the Commission to focus its most expensive resource—commissioners—on providing expertise at all stages of the investigation, but it also serves to give group leaders responsibility for the overall decision-making process, from application to referral decisions.

Applicants with legal representation often submit an application that provides detailed information about the case and what might raise fresh evidence or argument to satisfy the real possibility test. Lawyers sometimes append evidence from the case to the application. Otherwise, the CAT team will use the Commission's powers to secure all key documents from public bodies (Criminal Appeal Act 1995, section 17; see below, and further, Chapter 12).[3] For applications concerning conviction at the Crown Court, these include the indictment, summing up, advice and grounds of appeal, the criminal appeal office summary, the single judge's ruling, and the full court judgment. In magistrates' cases, this includes the trial court file and the Crown Court appeal file (Criminal Cases Review Commission, 2013e). There may be further requests for information from the CAT team; for example, if staff involved in screening feel that a case may raise issues of fair process, the CAT team will likely be asked to secure the police file.

When a decision has been made to subject an application to a stage two review, the case goes back to the CAT team to allocate to a group.[4] A group leader will then assign the case to a CRM, usually mindful only of individuals' caseloads but sometimes with a view to identifying a CRM with particular expertise relevant to the case. However, while the case is waiting to be reviewed, the CAT team will continue to locate documents that the person responsible for screening considered relevant to the investigation so that the CRM receives a reasonably complete file.

Exceptional circumstances

Applicants to the Commission are supposed to have exhausted the normal appeals process, and to have new evidence or argument that might challenge their conviction; referrals back to the Court without fresh evidence or argument should be 'particularly rare' (Criminal Cases Review Commission, 2017d). However, applications from persons who have not already appealed are not uncommon, comprising about 40 per cent of total applications each year. Section 13(2) of the Criminal Appeal Act 1995 allows the Commission to review such cases, and to make a reference 'if it appears to the Commission that there are exceptional circumstances which justify making it'. The

---

[3] Section 18A of the Criminal Appeal Act 1995, which was inserted by the Criminal Cases Review Commission (Information) Act 2016, expanded section 17 powers to private bodies and individuals.

[4] This was the practice when we collected our data. Now each group has its own dedicated CAT team and therefore cases are divided between groups before the preliminary data gathering stages.

Formal Memorandum states 'It is vital that the Commission does not, other than for compelling reasons, usurp the conventional appeals process' (Criminal Cases Review Commission, 2017d), in recognition of the impact that will have on those who have already satisfied the previous appeal criterion and will be waiting in the queue. Hence, it claims, 'a decision by the Commission to review or to refer any "no-appeal" case will be unusual' (Criminal Cases Review Commission, 2017d). However, this was not rare, and we witnessed some variability among screening commissioners in how they dealt with such cases (see Chapter 6).

The Formal Memorandum provides considerable discretion on exceptional circumstances, stating explicitly that 'It would be impossible to issue a prescriptive list of circumstances that might be considered exceptional' (Criminal Cases Review Commission, 2017d). Nonetheless, it goes on to provide some illustrative examples, including sensitive information that should only be disclosed in a confidential annex to the Court; evidence of a compelling or compassionate need for the case to be considered quickly by an appellate court; evidence of the applicant suffering from a disability or mental illness that might put him at a significant disadvantage in securing legal representation or in pursuing an application for leave to appeal to the Crown Court or the Court; or that there is new scientific, medical, or expert evidence the applicant could not reasonably be expected to discover. When we began our fieldwork, commissioners involved in screening appeared to interpret these guidelines liberally, but more recently the Commission has become more restrictive in its interpretation of exceptional circumstances, not in small part because of the rising number of applications, limited resources, and concerns about average review times (see Chapter 6).

Clearly, how a case is screened, and who screens it, will have some bearing on the progress of the case and the eventual outcome. The Commission has changed its practice over the years we have conducted our research, and has started to apply more rigorously its statutory powers to refuse to review 'no-appeal' cases, with a shifting interpretation of 'exceptional circumstances'. Hence, the Commission is guiding its staff on how to make sense of applications and, in doing so, shifting the 'field' by creating new knowledge about which cases it is appropriate to allocate scarce resources to, knowledge that will shape individuals' decisions.

Stage Two: Reviewing Cases

The Criminal Appeal Act 1995 allows the Commission to refer to an appropriate appeal court 'any case in which it considers that there is a real possibility that a conviction, verdict, finding or sentence would not be upheld' (Criminal Cases Review Commission, 2015f:para:1). Sections 9–12 of the Criminal Appeal Act 1995 give the Commission the *power* to refer if the case satisfies the section 13 real possibility test, but do not impose a *duty* to do so. There are circumstances under which the Commission will choose not to refer a case back to the Court even if it meets the real possibility test. For example, if an applicant has been convicted on one indictment of fifteen sexual offences against various children and there is evidence that one of the convictions may be unsafe, the Commission might choose not to refer if they consider that these other offences, and the sentence, would not be affected. Commissioners might also be influenced by the age of the case or the fact that the applicant is deceased. Take, for example, the infamous case of *Timothy Evans*. Wrongfully convicted and executed in 1950 for the murder of his daughter, Evans was granted a posthumous free pardon a few years after the publication of Ludovic Kennedy's book, *10 Rillington Place* (1961).

Pardons do not quash convictions and so after Evans' family received substantial ex gratia compensation payments in 2003, they applied to have his case reviewed by the Commission. While the Commission acknowledged that if the case were to be referred there was a real possibility that the conviction would be quashed, it felt that the resource implications of pursuing a reference outweighed the benefits that may ensue from a successful referral, particularly given that Evans had already been pardoned, his family compensated, and Evans was long deceased. The family sought judicial review of this decision but the Administrative Court ruled that the Commission's decision could not be impugned in law, noting that where the convicted person was dead, different standards of fairness applied (*Mary Westlake v Criminal Cases Review Commission*).[5]

Once a case has been allocated for review, it must be decided—if it has not already been decided at screening—if the case should proceed along a regular track, or if it deserves to be 'fast-tracked'.

Deciding how quickly to start and complete an investigation

Given that the Commission has, at any one time, a relatively large volume of cases waiting to be reviewed, it has an automatic system for ordering cases and a discretionary process for deciding whether any particular case should be given priority over others waiting in the queue.

Level 1 cases are allocated as soon as resources permit. The Commission aims to allocate all level 1 cases within a maximum of three months from the decision to prioritize, though it currently misses that target by about a month.[6] Cases referred by the Court under section 15 of the Criminal Appeal Act (see below, and Chapter 11) are automatically prioritized at level 1, as are sentence only cases where the applicant has less than two years to serve his prison sentence. However, there are other cases in which the Commission can exercise discretion in allocating priority level 1. These include: cases where the applicant is very old or unwell and there is a risk that they might die before the case is dealt with; where the applicant (or a close family member) is in serious ill-health which might be directly and significantly aggravated by delay; where the applicant is young and a conviction is likely to have exceptionally adverse impact on their welfare, or educational or career prospects; where there is a risk that the Commission will be unable to secure or obtain relevant information or evidence, or that the evidence might deteriorate should there be delays; where it is in the interests of operational effectiveness; or where the impact of delay on the criminal justice system is likely to be significant. In recent years, newspaper and social media reports have questioned the Commission's prioritization of the application of the footballer, Ched Evans, assuming the decision was influenced by his prominence (Hardman, 2016). However, the Commission insists that 'The public profile of an applicant, or the level of public support for an applicant … will [not usually be taken] into account when responding to a request for prioritisation' (Criminal Cases Review Commission, 2016a).

Applicants waiting in the queue for their cases to be allocated, or whose cases have been allocated to a CRM but feel that the investigation is taking too long, may also be sensitive to the prioritization of government-initiated reviews. In Chapter 7 we discuss the Attorney General's review of cases relating to sudden unexplained infant

---

[5] [2004] EWHC 2779 (Admin).
[6] All information on targets in this chapter is drawn from Criminal Cases Review Commission (Criminal Cases Review Commission, 2016a).

deaths, which led to some cases being expedited, annoying other applicants. As one interviewee explained:

I got a wonderful letter from an applicant complaining about this and saying, you know, 'Next time I'm wrongfully convicted of something I'll be sure I'm wrongfully convicted of something sexy like killing a baby and then perhaps you'll actually take it seriously. I unfortunately was wrongfully convicted of something that is not sexy and which you therefore are not going to expedite.' I thought that was rather a powerful argument actually. (#27)

Where the applicant is in custody and has not previously applied to the Commission, the case will automatically be assigned level 2 priority (unless the applicant can demonstrate any of the criteria that would afford them a level 1 priority). That said, the Commission has discretion to prioritize the case at level 2 (rather than 3) even when the applicant has previously applied if it can be demonstrated that they could not have been expected to raise any new matters relied on in support of the reapplication in a previous application. Furthermore, the organization has discretionary power to allocate the case to level 2 priority even when the applicant is at liberty, where individual factors demonstrate that the conviction has had an exceptionally adverse impact on the applicant or on other individuals. The Commission aims to allocate all level 2 cases within twenty-six weeks of receipt and achieved this target in 2015/16 when cases were allocated within an average of just over nineteen weeks (Criminal Cases Review Commission, 2016a).[7] Finally, all other cases are treated as level 3, which includes most applicants who are at liberty. The Commission aims to allocate these cases within seventy-eight weeks of receipt and achieved this target in 2015/16 when it took an average of just over fifty-five weeks (Criminal Cases Review Commission, 2016a).

Of course, applicants will be keen to have their cases started soon, but also to have them reviewed thoroughly and quickly. As we discuss in Chapter 12, Commission staff are only too aware of the tension between a thorough and an expeditious review. While they will want to subject the application to a detailed investigation, not least to avoid complaints or judicial review (see below), they will also be keen not to keep the applicant waiting too long, particularly if they are in prison and if they have a resolute legal representative fighting their corner. The Commission's Key Performance Indicator for the duration of review is less than twenty-eight weeks from the case being allocated to a CRM to the initial decision whether to refer (the Provisional Statement of Reasons), a target it reached in 2015–16. The Key Performance Indicator for the overall time from application to the final decision (Statement of Reasons) is fifty-six weeks for 'custody' cases, eighty-eight weeks for 'at liberty' cases, and fifteen weeks for 'no-appeal' cases (all targets were reached in 2015–16) (Criminal Cases Review Commission, 2016a). That said, these are average times and there are outliers, cases which take much longer to review, sometimes years, alongside those cases which prove to be quick to process, such as the recent cases concerning the wrongful conviction of asylum seekers (Sato et al., 2017; see also Chapter 10). In other words, there is variation across cases which is, in the main, accounted for by the types of investigations needed or chosen for some cases but not others. Generally, those cases that can be resolved by a review of the case papers and the relevant legal sources, with no other investigation, are far quicker to process than those that depend on expert evidence from outside the Commission. However, as

---

[7] The Commission's current target is to reduce the time to allocate cases to a maximum of three months, and the current duration is five months (Information provided by the Commission, December 2017).

we demonstrate in Chapters 6–13, some variation is not explicable by reference to the complexity of the case or reliance on external actors.

Collecting evidence

CRMs typically start their review of a case by reading all the available papers in the file. This might take weeks in cases where there are considerable data. They will take note of claims made by the applicant and their legal representative, though typically look beyond those as applicants often do not know what went wrong in the investigation that led to their wrongful conviction; which tests were fallible, which experts erred. The CRM then makes a case plan for how to proceed and begins a case record to collate details of each and every part of their investigation; consultations with external stakeholders and with others in the Commission (including decision-making committee members); and investigations carried out by those outside of the Commission and decisions made following those investigations, with the reasoning recorded for those decisions. Records relevant to the case, the applicant, or any witnesses to the crime might already have been retrieved during screening. However, at some stage during the review CRMs are likely to need further information from other public or private bodies.

Powers to collect evidence from public and private bodies and individuals

In most cases, applicants, even those with legal representation, do not have access to all the records from the trial. They are unable to require statutory and other bodies to provide information or other potential evidence in their possession.[8] The Commission has this power under section 17 of the Criminal Appeal Act 1995:

Where the Commission believes that a person serving in a public body has possession or control of a document or other material which may assist the Commission in the exercise of any of its functions. When requested to do so, a public body is under a duty to make such material available to the Commission, providing such a request is reasonable. (Criminal Cases Review Commission, 2016f)[9]

In deciding if a request is 'reasonable' the Commission must consider that evidence from a public body might assist it in determining whether a case should be referred to an appellate court. However, the Formal Memorandum makes clear that material relating directly or indirectly to a case would typically satisfy the requirement of reasonableness (Criminal Cases Review Commission, 2016f).

In sexual offence cases, CRMs might consider medical records—relating to the applicant or to witnesses—to be of interest to the case. Given the sensitivity of medical data, the Commission has a Formal Memorandum on when and how to use medical records, but considerable discretion in deciding when it is appropriate to do so. For example,

---

[8] The refusal of the police to release evidence for further DNA testing to the legal representative of a man wishing to appeal his conviction was challenged in the case of *R v Nunn* [2014] UKSC 37. Here the Court found that there already existed a reliable 'safety net ... in the CCRC ... an independent body specifically skilled in examining the details of evidence and in determining when and if there is a real prospect of material emerging which affects the safety of a conviction' (para:39). Hence the Commission remains, for now, the only reliable route to securing evidence that might challenge the safety of a conviction.

[9] The Commission may require a public body (i) to produce material; (ii) to allow access to it; (iii) to allow the Commission to take it away; (iv) to allow the Commission to make and take away a copy in an appropriate form (Criminal Cases Review Commission, 2016f).

the Memorandum states 'the Commission will seek no more than the level of disclosure necessary in each case' (Criminal Cases Review Commission, 2017g:para:10).

Recently, following the completion of our fieldwork, the Criminal Cases Review Commission (Information) Act 2016 inserted section 18A into the Criminal Appeal Act 1995 to extend the Commission's power to obtain material from private bodies and individuals. This change in the legislation, in force since July 2016, was the result of years of campaigning for change by the Commission, its friends, and even its critics, and came soon after the House of Commons Justice Committee Report on the Commission made clear that:

[T]he extension of the CCRC's section 17 powers to cover private bodies is urgently necessary and commands universal support ... It should be a matter of great urgency and priority for the next Government to bring forward legislation to implement the extension of the CCRC's powers so that it can compel material necessary for it to carry out investigations from private bodies through an application to the courts. No new Criminal Justice Bill should be introduced without the inclusion of such a clause. (House of Commons Justice Committee, 2015:paras:44–5)[10]

Some convictions, particularly for sex offences, are based primarily on the testimony of a witness without corroborating or forensic evidence. In such cases, the Commission must decide whether the credibility of this key witness should be investigated, if it is thought that relevant information has been missed during the investigation, or the trial and appeal process. Furthermore, there are cases where important information about the witness becomes available only after the conviction and appeal. Hence the Commission can use its powers to check for any undisclosed or new information relating to a witness's credibility.[11] Again, sensitivity is needed in such cases, especially where the witness may be vulnerable or where investigations may result in a prosecution of that witness for perverting the course of justice. Hence, in deciding whether to use these powers, the Commission must have regard to witnesses' article 8 rights under the European Convention on Human Rights. Enquires must not be arbitrary, but made only when 'reasonable', 'proportionate', and strictly limited to 'what is required'. Again, these are somewhat flexible and subjective concepts and it should not surprise us if CRMs interpret rights and restrictions differently. However, in all cases, the Commission must record in the case record the reasons for deciding that such enquiries were both reasonable and necessary, a record that could be scrutinized by a group leader, commissioner, or even made disclosable in a judicial review.

Interviews to collect evidence or information

Much of the evidence that will be relevant to many cases can be found within the papers acquired by the Commission's section 17 powers, or in the legal resources available to CRMs. Hence, most reviews involve a considerable amount of 'desktop' investigation. That said, CRMs will identify cases where it would be helpful to their review to interview the applicant, a witness, a criminal justice agent, or an expert, and perhaps conduct other investigatory work. While the Formal Memorandum on interviewing

---

[10] The first author gave evidence to the Justice Committee explaining why this power was essential for the successful review of applications at the Commission.

[11] CRMs have the discretion to scrutinize various records, including: the Police National Computer, Police National Database, Social Services Department Files, Police Child Protection Files, Education Department Files, Criminal Injuries Compensation Authority Files, civil actions, medical records, and any information that points to prior false allegations or retractions previous allegations (Criminal Cases Review Commission, 2017c).

has considerable information on best practice, particularly for interviewing vulnerable people, it says little about the circumstances in which the Commission might decide to conduct an interview, noting only that, 'in most cases there must be a belief that the interviewee is able to provide information or evidence that is material to the case review' (Criminal Cases Review Commission, 2016c:para:4). That leaves considerable discretion in deciding what is likely to be material to the review, and as we discuss in Chapter 12, CRMs vary enormously in the amount and the type of 'non-desktop' investigations they carry out.

Communication with applicants

Just as we have observed some variability in CRMs inclination to conduct interviews with people outside of the Commission, we also found some differences in their approach to maintaining communication with the applicants. The Formal Memorandum on communicating with applicants makes clear that while the Commission aims to be open with applicants, it needs to ensure that cases are reviewed and progressed in a timely fashion (Criminal Cases Review Commission, 2018b). In other words, in this important matter of communication with the very person who is most invested in the case, the Commission aims to balance its own resources with what might be thought of as 'procedural justice' (e.g. Tyler, 2011). We return to this issue in Chapters 12 and 13, but here it is important to note that the Formal Memorandum is clear that in most cases the CRM should study the application before making contact with the applicant.

The first substantive letter to the applicant will typically set out the Commission's understanding of the issues and seek clarification and confirmation of those issues where necessary. It advises that contact with applicants should be maintained by the CRM at least once every three months while the review is in progress. But beyond that, there is almost no direction on the frequency of contact or the level of information to be disclosed. This, we found in our cases, was a cause of distress and frustration to some of the applicants who felt that they were being kept out of the loop. Furthermore, it was clear to us that applicants received dissimilar levels of contact. While this was sometimes a product of the type of investigation ongoing, it was not always apparent why some CRMs maintained more regular contact and provided the applicant with more detail on the progress of the investigation than their colleagues. It seemed that, to some extent, the personality of the CRM was influential as well as the tenacity of the applicant or their legal representative. As one experienced commissioner explained to us:

Part of it is a matter of personality, and part of it, I suspect, would be a question of the issues that are raised and, … by definition, a bit like with different advocates, … someone will notice a point that will go unnoticed [by] another. (#11)

Expert witnesses

As we discuss in Chapter 7, many of the cases considered by the Commission turn on expert evidence. In many, expert evidence, often scientific evidence, will have been crucial to the successful conviction of the applicant. So too will such evidence inform both the review of the conviction and the decision whether to refer it back to the Court, as well as the evidence presented in the Statement of Reasons. When to seek expert testimony, what evidence to acquire, and who to select as an expert witness, will however be largely at the discretion of the CRM and those working with them on the case. Sometimes the applicant, or their legal representative, requests that the Commission instructs an expert. However, the Commission 'will only do so if it considers that it will assist the review' (Criminal Cases Review Commission, 2017e:para:3). It has discretion about whether to seek further evidence, or more up-to-date evidence, from any expert witnesses who testified at trial, as well as evidence from a new expert. As we discuss in Chapter 12, reviewing evidence from expert witnesses can be a time-consuming and expensive process. It can also cause delays in the investigation.[12] Hence decision-makers at the Commission must balance the thoroughness of an investigation with efficiency in making decisions about who they should seek evidence from. As we suggest in Chapters 6–13, this balancing exercise is not entirely driven by the variables in the case; it may be influenced by the CRM's personality and skills but also by the knowledge acquired and retained by the Commission from previous investigations.

Appointing an investigating officer to the case

As we discuss in Chapter 12, section 19 of the Criminal Appeal Act 1995 gives the Commission the power to require the chief officer of the original investigating body to appoint an investigating officer to assist in a review. The Formal Memorandum on section 19 requirements provides a non-exhaustive list of factors which a committee of three commissioners may take into account when deciding whether to appoint an investigating officer, including the scale and nature of the enquiry and if police expertise is considered essential. This will likely be so where there are grounds to suspect that a police officer committed an offence such as perjury or perverting the course of justice, or where another person, not involved in the case in an official capacity, has committed a serious offence that might lead to prosecution; for example, they have lied in their role as a prosecution witness and might be subject to prosecution for perverting the course of justice. There is a further non-exhaustive list of factors that the Commission should consider when deciding whether to appoint an investigating officer from a police force other than the force that was involved in the original investigation: if, for example, there is concern that an investigating officer from the original investigating police force might not be seen to be impartial (see Chapter 11 for more detail). The Formal Memorandum further indicates considerable discretion in deciding how to instruct the investigating officer (Criminal Cases Review Commission, 2015e).

Obligations to investigate on behalf of the Court

Most of the Commission's work is focused on reviewing cases which have already been considered and dismissed by the Court, but section 15 of the Criminal Appeal Act addresses those situations where the Court has directed the Commission to investigate a discrete issue or issues on the Court's behalf.[13] The Court can ask the Commission to carry out investigation during first instance appeals or during applications for leave to appeal, and the Commission prioritizes such investigations (see above). While the remit of the investigation is typically set by the Court, the Commission has some

---

[12] Delays might also be caused by an applicant's legal representative and CRMs have a Formal Memorandum to follow to try to avoid or respond to delays (Criminal Cases Review Commission, 2015c).

[13] The Court has the power to make such directions under section 23A(1) of the Criminal Appeal Act 1968.

discretion in deciding whether to go beyond this narrow remit (Criminal Cases Review Commission, 2015d; examined in Chapter 11).

Our description of the stage two review process has demonstrated that many aspects of individual decision-making is subject to the shifting influence of the organizational imperatives of the Commission. For example, how the Commission responds to the potential for wrongful convictions to have a 'knock-on' effect on other counts in the same conviction is influenced by the Court's evolving jurisprudence in such cases. A shifting culture around resources might impact on prioritization and the speed of reviews, though these too can be influenced by criticisms from beyond the Commission focused on cases reported in the media. Similarly, and more obviously, reviews will have changed in response to the recent extension of the Commission's section 17 powers. These shifts in both knowledge and how the organization makes sense of cases alter the conditions of the field in ways that play out in individual decision-making.

Decision-making

Deciding whether to refer

At a certain stage during each case, the Commission must decide if there are reasons to doubt the safety of the conviction and if therefore they are minded to refer the case back to the Court; and, if so, on what grounds. A decision to refer must be made by a Committee of no fewer than three commissioners (a decision-making committee) (Criminal Appeal Act 1995, sections 9–12). In three other situations, a decision-making committee must deliberate and agree on a course of action: when the Commission reports to the Court (section 15(4); see section15 directions from the Court, above and at Chapter 11); when the Commission is inclined to provide to the Home Secretary a statement in connection with the exercise of the Royal Prerogative of Mercy (section 16(1)(b)); and when the CRM and their supervising commissioner wishes to appoint an investigating officer to the case (section 19; see above and at Chapter 11).

Where the CRM considers that the case does not meet the real possibility test, only one commissioner is required to approve the decision not to make a reference back to the Court ('single commissioner' decision). The assigned commissioner must then be satisfied that: (i) all necessary enquiries have been made; and (ii) on the material currently available there is no real possibility that the conviction, verdict, finding, or sentence would not be upheld (Criminal Cases Review Commission, 2015f). It is then the responsibility of the commissioner to communicate this decision by sending the Provisional Statement of Reasons to the applicant. If the commissioner directs that further work is required before a decision can be reached, the reasons will be set out and that work will be undertaken by the CRM. The case will be returned to the commissioner when the required further work has been completed. The assigned commissioner may at any time decide to refer the case to a decision-making committee.

Decision-making committees

Decision-making committees generally comprise three commissioners including (where practicable) one commissioner who meets the legal qualification requirements set out in section 8(5) of the Criminal Appeal Act 1995 (that is, someone who is legally trained). One of the commissioners will take the role of 'lead' commissioner (where a commissioner has worked on the case, this will usually be that person). Other commissioners are chosen on a 'cab rank' basis. Of course, it is not possible for the committee to see all the papers relating to a case. Oftentimes the material is voluminous, with hard copies of documents and records sometimes running to twenty or more box files. Hence the CRM, along with the supervising commissioner, must select those papers they consider to be relevant to the decision-making process. There is therefore some considerable discretion in deciding what evidence might help to persuade a committee to proceed in the way that the CRM thinks is appropriate. The CRM and the lead commissioner will agree an agenda for the committee and the lead commissioner has the discretion to invite others from the Commission to attend the meeting: for example, the legal adviser or the investigations adviser, as they think appropriate. Requests by applicants to make oral representations to the single commissioner or to the decision-making committee will be considered on a case-by-case basis, with the applicant receiving written reasons for that decision. The CRM's record of the meeting, and the reasons for decisions made, must be approved by the committee.

There are various decisions for a committee to make. It may decide to refer the case back to the Court, in which case the lead commissioner will agree the wording of the Statement of Reasons, though it is signed by all commissioners on the committee. The committee might also decide that the case should not be referred back to the Court, in which event the applicant will be invited to make further written representations (see below). If these are received, the lead commissioner will decide whether to reconvene the committee or to respond individually. Often, the committee decides it has insufficient information upon which to make an informed decision and so directs further investigation by the CRM.

Decision-making committees might be convened at other stages in the case; for example, where the CRM wishes to seek advice or information on particularly complex issues that arise in their review of the case materials. Indeed, in some cases a committee might meet on several occasions. At all stages of decision-making, it is the CRM's responsibility to ensure that the applicant is kept informed of the progress of their case, though there is some discretion about how often the applicant is contacted and how much information is provided (see above) (Criminal Cases Review Commission, 2018c).

Casework documentation

As mentioned above, the Commission receives considerable information on most cases it reviews, often dozens of boxes packed with papers relating to the investigation, the trial, the appeal, and post appeal investigations. The first task for any CRM is to collate and organize all this information so that it is readily accessible, including to others within the Commission. The CRM then collects further information and evidence about the case. Managing information inevitably raises challenges. CRMs must be organized, and record what has been collected and, importantly, why. They must also record decisions made not to pursue lines of investigation or not to collect particular types of evidence. This will be necessary should the investigation be subject to a complaint or judicial review, but also to provide thorough information for the Court in the Statement of Reasons. It is important to show how much time has been spent on the case, what other resources have been devoted to it, and why there have been delays, if applicable.

If a member of staff leaves the Commission, or is asked to turn their attention to another case where their expertise is needed, meticulous case records benefit a new CRM or a new commissioner allocated to the case. All steps taken in the casework process must be recorded in a case record, a living document maintained by the CRM, which develops as the review progresses. Notwithstanding a Formal Memorandum on the recording of the progress of each review, we found some variation in the level of detail in case records that was not always related to the complexities of the case.

'Post-decision' decision-making

Given that most cases are not referred, it is perhaps inevitable that this decision is sometimes contested by the applicant. While the Commission's Formal Memorandum on post-decision activity on cases makes clear that it does not usually receive further contact from the applicant or their representative following a decision not to refer, it states the Commission's policy on information received after a review has been concluded (Criminal Cases Review Commission, 2017h).

A disappointed applicant can make further representations or submissions to the Commission to try to persuade it to reverse its decision not to refer or to continue with the review. Typically, twenty working days are permitted for further submissions, but in more complex cases forty days are allowed. The Formal Memorandum on extensions for further representations and submissions advises commissioners when and how the discretion to permit additional time might be exercised. In this, as with all its decisions, the Commission must balance fairness to the applicant in question with fairness to other applicants waiting in the queue (Criminal Cases Review Commission, 2017f). That said, there are no statutory provisions which set a time limit and so it is entirely at the discretion of those responsible for the review. In several cases, the time has been extended considerably beyond forty days.

Only in those cases where further submissions raise new evidence or argument that has not previously been considered will the Commission consider whether a further review of the case is necessary (Criminal Cases Review Commission, 2017h). Given that this is rare, the Commission allows applicants to reapply. It does not impose a limit on the number of times a person may apply for a review of their conviction, but each subsequent application for the same conviction will be subject to the Commission's existing policy on applications. If an applicant continues to submit applications without raising anything new of relevance, the Director of Casework, in consultation with a commissioner, can decide not to accept any further reapplications (particularly if the applicant is deemed to be a 'persistent applicant') (Criminal Cases Review Commission, 2016e).

Applicants who have not had their case referred to the Court are likely to be disheartened. They will have waited for months, often years, and yet find themselves in the same situation they were on the day they applied. They may believe that the Commission has not dealt with their case appropriately. Hence, a decision not to refer may lead to complaint, other correspondence, and, in some cases, to requests for post-closure disclosure. Applicants can commence proceedings in the Administrative Court for judicial review of an action or decision taken by the Commission in respect of their application. Less typically, proceedings for a judicial review may be issued during the course of the review. If permission is granted by the single judge, the Commission's legal adviser will consider (and advise the Chair of the Commission) whether the claim should be conceded or contested. If conceded, they will decide whether additional work should be undertaken by the Commission, whether the case should be fully reopened and a fresh review commenced, and if so, whether the same CRM and/or commissioners should be involved. In other words, the organization has some considerable discretion in deciding how to respond to judicial review of its prior investigations and decisions (Criminal Cases Review Commission, 2016d).

There has been an increase in judicial reviews of the Commission's investigations or decisions in recent years, with twenty-one challenges in 2015/16 (nineteen of which were started under the 'pre-action protocol' system for judicial review and nine of these went no further). All eleven cases where applicants chose to issue proceedings at the Administrative Court were refused permission to judicially review a Commission decision. However, while the Commission has only ever lost one judicial review, it often conducts further investigations under threat or anticipation of judicial review, as we show in Chapter 13. Indeed, the 2015/16 Annual Report makes clear, 'The Commission would rather spend its resources reviewing cases than contesting expensive litigation' (Criminal Cases Review Commission, 2016a).

Having reviewed the processes through which applications pass when they reach the Commission, we now revisit Choo's (2006) framework for a 'knowing organization' to illuminate how the development of institutional knowledge and culture at the Commission has the capacity to shape the field which, as we explained in Chapter 3, influences individual decision-makers.

Making Sense of Cases

As the discussion above has made clear, the Commission has significant discretion in deciding which applications are eligible for review, which present exceptional circumstances, and which to subject to a full, stage two review. It can also choose how to review its cases; how quickly it will commence investigations, what evidence it will collect, and how it will use its statutory powers. In other words, though there are Formal Memoranda and Casework Guidance Notes, and although the Criminal Appeal Act 1995 provides a legal framework for considering applications, the Commission's structures leave CRMs and commissioners with considerable discretion. In exercising this discretion, they draw on knowledge produced at both the case level and at the organizational level. An example of knowledge produced at the case level might relate to a new forensic procedure or a new expert witness that proved to be advantageous in a certain type of case. Knowledge produced at the organizational level could include the Commission's analysis of Court judgments organized according to the types of issues raised by the applicant and then used to inform their approach to similar cases. Regardless of the genesis of knowledge, once organized—noticed, collated, and recorded in a retrievable fashion—it becomes 'explicit knowledge' (Choo, 2006) for Commission staff to draw on.

Sense-making in an organization, including the Commission, is retrospective; organizations try to interpret what happened in the past, considering both historical and contemporary data. Their challenge is to select a plausible meaning from possibly several alternative meanings to make sense of past events. However, during sense-making, it is not always inevitable what information is needed. It must be decided which data are important and when the information is ambiguous—as it often is—which interpretation is the most plausible. In other words, the process is about the management of ambiguity. For this, decision-makers need values and priorities to clarify what is consequential in the information available, and draw on existing assumptions, beliefs, and expectations rooted within the organizational culture (Choo, 2006:79). The assumptive world that individual decision-makers draw on is created within the organization by processes of identifying and interpreting information that may be useful for members of the organization.

There are three main processes at work in Choo's sense-making: enactment, selection, and retention. In the *enactment* process, information is constructed by selecting, isolating, and highlighting certain information, 'paying attention to some messages and ignoring others' (Choo, 2006:6). In making sense of Court judgments on past cases, certain issues may be dismissed as inconsequential or having no relevance beyond that particular case, while others will be studied in detail. Further information— for example from additional related Court cases—can then be recorded and organized to be readily accessible to others in the institution working on similar cases. The result is a gradual refining of information that remains, nonetheless equivocal as well as a growing set of new data that will also be open to interpretation and re-interpretation in light of the specificities of future cases.

In the *selection* process, those charged with making decisions in specific cases may look at the information already 'enacted' and try to establish what it tells them. In doing so, they draw on past experiences, their own and their colleagues. They overlay 'the new data with interpretations that have worked before in explaining similar or related situations in the past ... Interpretations are selected that provide the best fit with past understandings' (Choo, 2006:6). In other words, in this context, information recorded on the Court's response to past cases, can be used to guide the Commission's response to similar contemporary cases.

Finally, in the *retention* process, products of successful sense-making are retained and stored for further use, for new equivocal situations. Interpretations need to be remembered and made available for future cycles of enactment and selection by members of the organization. Hence a CRM might gravitate towards forensic tests that were proven to be helpful in the past and, indeed, to expert witnesses who have influenced decision-making in previous similar cases. However, this is only possible if the Commission has made accessible its choices and decisions in previous cases and the results of using these data, through the recording of formal and informal data. Hence, retained understandings and meanings become 'the source of organizational culture and strategy' (Choo, 2006:85).

Knowledge Creation

Once members of an organization have interpreted and made sense of ambiguous information and identified what is significant, that knowledge must be converted from individual to institutional knowledge. In the case of the Commission, this is not only so that the process of reviewing cases is transparent and accountable but, importantly, for the development and future recourse to organizational learning. Put simply, data must be shared. It is this process of sharing, formally and informally, that Choo (2006) refers to as 'knowledge creation'.

Choo's (2006) concept of knowledge creation draws on the work of Nonaka and Takeuchi (1995) who explored how organizational knowledge is created. They argued that organizations need to design social processes that generate new knowledge by converting 'tacit knowledge' into 'explicit knowledge'. Tacit knowledge, in this example, is personal knowledge: subjective, culturally and organizationally informed insights and intuitions that come with working in an institution for some time. As such, it is more difficult to share than explicit knowledge which is formal knowledge produced, organized, and circulated within an institution with a particular purpose.

Explicit knowledge is rule-based when knowledge is codified to rules, specifications, standards, systems, and so on (Choo, 2006:141). Hence, memos, Casework Guidance Notes, and Formal Memoranda are all explicit knowledge aimed at influencing tacit knowledge within the Commission, and in some cases, built on tacit knowledge (Choo, 2006:8–9). These organizational manuals provide a 'frame of reference [to set] the boundaries of the scope of' the organizational enquiry and to 'provide the information-organising principles that shape information acquisition and processing patterns' within the Commission (Choo, 2006:107). Organizational memory is also created when CRMs or commissioners save to a case database typical or noteworthy examples of specific types of cases so that others can learn how to approach similar cases: what to look for and what might persuade the Court to overturn a conviction. Hence, a wealth of tacit case-based knowledge develops into a database that can become explicit knowledge.

For Choo, the successful organization must be able to convert tacit knowledge into explicit knowledge and vice versa. This can be achieved through various mechanisms, including socialization, where tacit knowledge can be transferred from an experienced employee to another employee working in the same team or under their supervision or from an expert within the organization, such as a legal adviser or investigations adviser providing relevant information to a CRM. We found variability in CRMs propensity to seek guidance beyond their own commissioner or group leader in their casework.

CRMs may seek advice on relevant case law from legal advisers. Investigations advisers, who are mostly ex-police officers, tend to be good sources of information on the pre-trial process and on the types of investigations that could be done post-conviction, and the risks associated with interviewing the original complainants. While there will always be a commissioner with forensic expertise, the Commission does not have a 'forensics adviser', which can leave CRMs, and even commissioners, feeling anxious. As one explained to us:

> If we were recruiting, I'd certainly be looking at whether we could get somebody who had that sort of skillset. It's always seemed to me odd that we employ a legal adviser, investigations adviser, but we don't, as it were, have a science or a forensics adviser. (#25)

Some case files record the legal adviser advising a CRM to consult with a particular commissioner who is 'our resident expert on [such] matters' (PI1, email quoted in Case Record). However, demand for commissioner expertise inevitably outstrips supply and so, following basic research, CRMs and commissioners must seek advice and information from colleagues and study past cases that would appear to present similar challenges.

Case records often reference other similar ongoing investigations and the Court's response to referral in former comparable cases. For example, in case PI1, a note from the same legal adviser to the CRM reads:

> We have to take each of these applications on a case-by-case basis, but you should also consider the Commission's other unresolved references to date ... I understand that a committee is about to reference one of [another CRMs'] cases on this type of point so you might want to speak to them.

And in case EE15 a decision on whether to refer was delayed while the Commission waited to hear the outcome of a referral in case EE11b (two other cases were also delayed pending this decision). In most cases, the CRM can identify similar applications and seek advice or information from colleagues who worked on those cases:

[We learn how to approach new cases by] sharing information within the Commission; very much that sense of has somebody else recently had a case that's involved this type of issue? What did they find out? What did they discover? Did they have any concerns about it? (#26)

Advice might be sought in formal meetings arranged for that purpose, or in informal chats in the kitchen or the corridor, and information can be drawn from other people's case files.

Explicit knowledge can also be produced by bringing together information from several different sources—including records of meetings, memos on cases, presentations by external and internal speakers, and analysis of legal precedents and Court judgments—and organizing and making accessible that knowledge within the institution's database of records. Choo (2006) refers to this process of developing tacit knowledge from explicit knowledge as 'internalization'.

In addition to tacit and explicit knowledge, organizations have cultural knowledge: the shared assumptions and beliefs about the organization's identity and goals. As Choo (2006) explains, all three categories are engaged simultaneously in organizational work. But while there may be consensus among CRMs about the goals of the organization, as individuals they may respond differently to a culture of openness and accountability. Choo (2006) is clear about the importance of engagement and safety in sharing information, but variances in experience and knowledge—whether legal, organizational, or forensic—can cause anxiety about seeking or sharing knowledge. Investigating possible wrongful convictions in the knowledge that your organization is the last possible option for the applicant is a challenging and stressful business, and the costs of bad decisions only too apparent. There needs to be considerable trust between staff members to facilitate the sharing of information and advice, and even between the Commission and the applicant or their legal representative. A fluid and facilitative sharing of information was apparent in many cases we studied but seemed to be absent in a few.

Decision-making at the Commission

Choo (2006:23) argues that a successful organization will aim to shape decision-making by controlling the 'decision premises' from which decisions are made, rather than controlling the decisions themselves. This is clear at the Commission where there is almost no attempt by the organization to control decisions made by commissioners and CRMs on an individual basis. Although the Commission has moved away from the 'flat' organizational structure of its past[14] to a more hierarchical structure, with group leaders now providing additional 'supervision' to CRMs, and although it has developed a considerable body of 'soft law' by way of guidance manuals, CRMs can proceed with their investigations with relatively minimal oversight. They are, after all, experienced caseworkers used to independent working. Nonetheless, it is clear that 'decision premises' were at work in the form of both 'value premises' and 'factual premises' (Choo, 2006:23). CRMs, like commissioners, are influenced in their work by the cultural values of the organization—the 'value premises'. While two principal values— efficiency and thoroughness—are often in tension, as we discuss in Chapter 12,

---

[14] A few our interviewees referred to the 'flat structure' of the Commission in its early days: 'there was no line management, commissioners were just as important as administrators, everybody was part of one big team. There was no accountability, people were very much put on trust to review cases thoroughly' (#17).

everyone at the Commission is clear that they are both extremely important to the successful operation of the organization and that decision-making should therefore be rational. Choo (2006:11) points out that:

In an ideal world, rational decision-making would require a complete search of available alternatives, reliable information about their consequences, and consistent preferences to evaluate these outcomes. In the real world, such demands on information gathering and processing are unrealistic. Instead of a comprehensive, objective rationality … decision-making in organizations is constrained by the principle of bounded rationality.

This is particularly true at the Commission where the role of decision-maker is explicitly not to reinvestigate the original case in full. In explaining what 'bounds' limit the capacity for rational decision-making, Choo (2006:93–4) considers how the values, indeed the wider culture and goals of the organization, shape decision-making:

A network of shared meanings and interpretations provide the social order, temporal continuity, and contextual clarity for members of an organization to coordinate and relate their actions … Where information is lacking or equivocal, shared beliefs and assumptions can fill in the gap or reduce the ambiguity sufficiently in order for organizations to be able to act.

While there are clear differences in personalities and distinct working practices that can lead to variability across responses at the Commission—as we discussed in Chapter 3—we found certain shared cultural assumptions. Just as analysis of policing has identified 'recipe rules' (Ericson and Haggerty, 1997) or 'working rules' (Hoyle, 1998) to help officers make sense of their everyday experiences and to influence how they behave, such working rules were apparent within the culture of the Commission. There is agreement on the core mission and functions of the organization, but also on the appropriate means to achieve organizational goals as well as the appropriate criteria for measuring success. For example, there was concurrence that CRMs should not go on 'fishing expeditions', with this rather imprecise expression being something of an axiom:

You shouldn't go on fishing expeditions. You know, we're a hard-headed, analytic bunch, and if you want to do something, you've got to analyse very carefully, well, if we did this test, you know, what are the possible outcomes, and, you know, on any of those outcomes, might it help with a reference, and if the answer is no, then why would you do the test, as it were? (#9)

How can you justify putting that exercise which some might describe as a fishing expedition above cases which, when they land on your desk, you yourself would say, 'That needs definite action.' (#33)

There was also some evidence of shared deference to the Court. While this is somewhat inevitable, given the predictive nature of the real possibility test, a point we return to throughout this book (and discuss at some length in Chapter 14), we also discerned a cultural imperative to keep in favour with the Court that seemed to go beyond the legal mandate or matters of efficacy. As one interviewee said of their colleagues:

I think one of the reasons why people here are so wedded to the [real possibility] test and its proper execution is, perhaps not consciously, it but enables them to flatter themselves that they're really getting it right in the way that a Court of Appeal top judge would get it right. So, I think that's what drives it. (#56)

Another interviewee, whose most recent referral had been upheld by the Court, spoke at length about the fact that the Judge had nothing good to say about the Statement of Reasons, concluding:

He didn't quite go to the lengths of saying 'I don't see why the Commission have referred this', but the whole thing just felt very hostile. Not a nice experience … ! (#67)

Another cultural motif is the shared concern that the organization is too cautious. This came out of our interviews and observations. 'I think we could be bolder' (#25) was a constant refrain, though usually followed by a defence of caution or an excuse for it:

I think we're quite a cautious organization and operating within the test is a very safe space in which to operate. There's a statutory test—that's what we're required to do. And going beyond that, I think, requires a degree of ... boldness and imagination, which ... this isn't just true of the Commission, though it certainly is true of the Commission, but I think it's public bodies, by and large, are not set up to be bold and imaginative. They're set up to follow the rules. (#66)

Clearly, despite differences in working styles and personalities across the Commission, there are shared values that—at least to some extent—guide the approach of individual staff to their work.

Decision premises are also influenced by 'factual premises' (Choo, 2006) which determine what a decision-maker perceives as the relevant information in any given decision situation. Hence, at the Commission a decision about referring a case will not be made without a thorough examination of key documents from the trial and any subsequent appeal, or without examination of most of the points raised by the applicant in their application or in correspondence from their legal representative. While decisions are often made on much more information than this, these are the essential factual premises for decision-making and all will be discussed in detail in a highly structured Statement of Reasons.

Decision routines comprise what to search for, what to pay attention to, and what evidence to select as relevant, and the Formal Memorandum and Casework Guidance Notes speak not only to the legal framework and organizational procedures, but to the cultural imperatives of the organization. Hence in reviewing cases, the Commission engages in a series of routines around the collection and management of information as well as ritualized processes for constructing a Statement of Reasons to demonstrate to those outside the organization that it follows fair, consistent, and legitimate procedures.

Drawing on Choo's (2006) model of decision-making to describe the Commission's journey to the final version of the Statement of Reasons should not, however, imply a simple linear sequence. The three processes of sense-making, knowledge creation, and decision-making should be understood as interconnected, with many possible pathways available to decision-makers. Sense-making, knowledge creation, and decision-making continues throughout investigations in the search for the 'right' decision or the 'best' evidence. This search, however, cannot go on indefinitely. An obvious consequence of bounded rationality is that the organization impels decision-makers to satisfice: to select 'a course of action that is satisfactory or good enough rather than seeking the optimal solution' (Choo, 2006:12). In this sense, the institutional value of efficiency can ultimately trump aspirations for thoroughness. This is not only for the benefit of other applicants waiting for their case to be reviewed, but also arguably for the benefit of applicants whose cases are under review. They will not wish to languish in prison while the Commission subjects their case to more and more testing, with little prospect of further clarification, when there may already be sufficient evidence to persuade the Court that there are reasons to doubt the safety of their conviction.

Deciding if, and when, there is sufficient evidence and a real possibility that a conviction would not be upheld if a reference were to be made is clearly a long, challenging, and uncertain journey. Choo's (2006) framework has helped to elucidate the organizational structural and cultural mores that shape this journey. In Chapters 5–13 we consider how the Commission made decisions in those cases that we studied in detail.

5

The Nature of Applications to the Commission

Introduction

The Criminal Cases Review Commission was established following the recommendation of the Royal Commission on Criminal Justice ('the Runciman Commission') that the Home Secretary's power to refer cases to the Court of Appeal ('the Court') should be removed and that a new body be set up to consider alleged miscarriages of justice (see Chapter 1). The Runciman Commission had identified various sources of wrongful conviction revealed by the widely publicized Irish terrorist cases and other convictions, including of Stefan Kiszko, the *Cardiff Three*, and the *Tottenham Three* (Royal Commission on Criminal Justice, 1993:Chapter 1, para:22). It discussed flaws in: police investigations and the prosecution of suspects; the safeguards for suspects; confession evidence, forensic science, and expert evidence; and in the pre-trial, trial, and review procedures in all courts, producing a list of some 352 recommendations for improvements across the system aimed, in part, at reducing wrongful convictions.

There was criticism of the Runciman Commission's scope of enquiry, which—in addition to preventing wrongful convictions—included the effectiveness of the criminal justice system in securing the conviction of the guilty and managing criminal justice resources efficiently. Detractors also took the Runciman Commission to task for its working methods, the data it drew on, and the coverage of the report (e.g. McConville and Bridges, 1994). Inevitably, there followed criticisms of its recommendations, and even a Note of Dissent from one of the commissioners of the Runciman Commission, Professor Michael Zander (Royal Commission on Criminal Justice, 1993:221–35). At the time, practitioners and academics were somewhat pessimistic that while things might have improved, wrongful convictions were not a thing of the past. Defence barrister, Andrew Hall (1994:321) argued:

The inevitable conclusion is that the Commission has failed to address the causes of miscarriages of justice and that its proposals are for the most part cosmetic ... Our criminal justice system is likely to be shaped well into the next century by these flawed and timid proposals. Rather than fewer miscarriages of justice we are likely to see many more, and for many years to come.

Just a few years later, Walker (1999) was a little more optimistic. He cited veteran miscarriages of justice campaigner, Chris Mullin, who had argued that '[i]t would be wrong to pretend that nothing has changed for the better since the great scandals of the early 1990s ... It must be said, however, that progress has been painfully slow' (Walker, 1999:30). Walker (1999:30) then continued:

One might add that change has not been unidirectional, and so progress must also be balanced with retrograde measures ... the hope for the future is not that miscarriages will never occur but that their occurrence will become more evident more quickly than in the very dim but not so distant past.

Reasons to Doubt: Wrongful Convictions and the Criminal Cases Review Commission. © Carolyn Hoyle and Mai Sato 2019. Published 2019 by Oxford University Press.

It is not our job here to decide what impact, if any, the Runciman Commission had on the frequency of wrongful convictions, though there has been no evidence of a diminishing rate. Rather, it is to consider the nature of those wrongful convictions that the Criminal Cases Review Commission ('the Commission') considers, the kinds of issues raised by applicants. We draw for evidence on a brief review of the extant literature on the sources of wrongful conviction, teasing out, towards the end, how these might have shifted over time since the establishment of the Commission.

A Fallible Process

To a greater or lesser extent, all applications to the Commission raise concerns about the reliability of the evidence presented to the trial court or about flaws in criminal procedure. Heaton's (2013:229–32) research on applications to the Commission suggests that the three main issues raised by applicants are concerns about the credibility of the witness or complainant, claims of police or prosecutorial misconduct, and incompetent representation. As the criminal justice process is managed by fallible and sometimes prejudiced individuals, and as criminal trials are examples of 'imperfect procedural justice' (Rawls, 1971:85), it is inevitable that some people will be wrongfully convicted just as it is inevitable that some guilty people will be acquitted.[1] However, notwithstanding their inevitability, several factors make wrongful convictions more likely. A report published by the law reform and human rights organization, JUSTICE (1989) identified five 'common threads' across most known wrongful convictions, including those notorious cases referred to above: wrongful identification, false confessions, perjury by witnesses, police misconduct, and bad trial tactics. However, analysis of sources at that time was limited to consideration of a few, high-profile wrongful convictions. There were no large-scale systematic studies of cases; these came later, primarily in the United States: Zalman (2012:278) estimated the rates of wrongful conviction to be from 0.5–1 per cent, at the low end, to 2–3 per cent, at the high end; more recently, Gross (2013:46) suggested a somewhat broader range of 1–5 per cent of convictions for serious felonies.

While most data on the sources of wrongful conviction has been gathered in the US, these findings seem to be applicable beyond that jurisdiction. Indeed, Roach (2015:385) has argued that though some causes are jurisdiction-specific, the 'basic human psychology that contributes to false confessions, mistaken identifications and police and prosecutorial tunnel vision do not differ from country to country'. Research identifies the same set of likely sources: eyewitness misidentification, false confessions, perjured testimony, forensic error, tunnel vision, prosecutorial misconduct, and ineffective defence (e.g. Davis, 2014; Gould et al., 2013:479; Gould and Leo, 2010:838; Parkes and Cunliffe, 2015:221).

Errors are likely to occur in the investigative phases and tend to escalate, making it less likely that they will be reversed (Gould et al., 2013:504). Rarely does a single piece of evidence *cause* a wrongful conviction; it is likely to be the result of a 'complex interweaving of independent pieces of evidence' (Charman, 2013:56), and the fewer errors present, the less likely a suspect will be wrongfully convicted (Gould et al., 2013:492). Certain sources can shape the outcome of a case but intervening measures can change

---

[1] For a discussion of 'wrongful acquittals', see Slobogin (2014).

the direction and move a case either towards or away from a wrongful conviction, so it is helpful to consider *contributing sources*, rather than exclusive causes (Gould and Leo, 2010:825). Indeed, sources identified as contributing to wrongful convictions will also occur in other cases that result in a rightful acquittal (Gould et al., 2013:480), leading researchers to ask why the system works properly, or at least corrects itself, in some cases but not in others (Gould and Leo, 2010:859).

Gould and his colleagues examined factors present in rightful acquittal cases ('near-misses'[2]) that were not present in wrongful convictions, identifying features that help to explain why innocent defendants are convicted (Gould et al., 2013:480). First is the age of the defendant: young defendants are at an increased risk of wrongful conviction. This may be because young suspects will not always understand the gravity of their situation, be able to provide a credible alibi, or have the knowledge to assist the defence. The criminal history of the defendant can bias the police into narrowing the investigation prematurely and ignoring exculpatory evidence (Gould et al., 2013:477). In focusing on 'the usual suspects', it is prior involvement with the criminal justice system that puts a suspect at risk and not the number of convictions or their similarity to the offence under consideration (Gould et al., 2013:477).

Both a strong defence and a strong prosecution case decrease the probability of a wrongful conviction; while the withholding of evidence, forensic error, and mistaken identification all increase the likelihood of wrongful conviction, with honest mistakes harder to uncover than lies (Gould et al., 2013:499–508). These factors are 'connected and exacerbated' by tunnel vision, which can ensure that initial errors remain undetected or uncorrected (Gould et al., 2013:477), and made more likely by a particularly punitive political climate (Gould et al., 2013:497). Gould and his colleagues claim that this model can predict a wrongful conviction versus a near miss most of the time, with other traditional sources—such as false confessions, official errors or misconduct, and race—appearing to feature in statistically similar rates in both near misses and wrongful convictions, increasing the chance that a suspect will be wrongfully charged and sent to trial but not that he will be convicted (Gould et al., 2013:515).

While it is oftentimes hard to disaggregate the various sources of wrongful conviction in any one case, further consideration of the main broad categories of sources will help the reader to understand the types of issues that are presented by applications to the Commission. These include unreliable witnesses; suspects vulnerable to false confessions; fallible science and expert testimony; and errors in the criminal process, with fear and prejudice about certain offences or suspects sometimes aggravating systemic failings.

As we explained in Chapter 2, our cases were sampled to show how the Commission responds to typical applications. Very crudely, our samples of sexual offence cases and forensic and expert evidence cases tend to concern fresh evidence by way of a new forensic test or a new expert witness, or concerns about the reliability of an expert at trial. These cases can also raise issues about the ability of a vulnerable defendant to present dependable evidence. Hence the following three sections—on the fallibility of witnesses, vulnerable suspects, and the fallibility of science—speak to those cases discussed in Chapters 7 and 8. The final section on due process failures has more relevance for our sample cases analysed in Chapters 9, 10, and 11.

---

[2] Cases that pass through the initial screening and are heading for a prosecution when an officer notices exculpatory evidence and causes the case to be dropped.

The Fallibility of Witnesses

In more than a few of our cases, the reliability of witnesses was subject to critical scrutiny by the Commission, frequently following claims by the applicant that the witness was mistaken or had lied. While this was typically the focus of sexual offence cases, both contemporary and historical (see Chapter 8), it was a feature of other cases that relied on eyewitness testimony. For example, in case EE38c (see Appendix), discussed in Chapter 7, the evidence of the main prosecution witness was subject to critical scrutiny. Here, the witness, Mr P, had described the suspect to the police as 'skinny, with dirty fair hair', 'about 5ft 7in', and 'unshaven'. At the identification parade, the witness identified the appellant who was four inches shorter, 'clean shaven' and dissimilar in other ways. Given that Mr P had claimed to have been face-to-face with the suspect on the street, and that he himself was 5ft 10in, as against the appellant's 5ft 3in, it was of concern to the Commission that he claimed the suspect was just 3 inches shorter, when in fact the height differential was considerable. This 'positive id' was one of two main strands of prosecution evidence at trial, where the witness repeated his assertion that the suspect was about 5ft 7in, and the defence failed to draw the trial court's attention to this anomaly. Meanwhile, an alternative suspect, who was never arrested, bore a close resemblance to the description given by this witness. The Commission referred this case on a range of issues, but focused primarily on the reliability of the key witness and the alternative suspect. Notwithstanding, the Court upheld the conviction.

There has been little research on eyewitness identification in the UK[3] though a recent study demonstrated the fallibility of memory, especially under conditions of stress (Shaw and Wafler, 2016). In the US, empirical studies suggest that eyewitness misidentification is a feature of over three-quarters of known wrongful convictions, most commonly in rape cases (Gould and Leo, 2010:841). Unreliable eyewitness identification is a product of either memory error or of police suggestion and manipulation (Garrett, 2008; Gross et al., 2005; Leo, 2005; Wells and Olson, 2003).

Eyewitness memory is both 'highly malleable and fallible' (Garrett, 2013:73), with natural psychological errors occurring when stress alters a person's perception of an event (Gould and Leo, 2010:841). While witnesses may be sincere, believing that they can remember the crime accurately (Kassin et al., 2013:46), it has been shown that there is little relationship between the certainty of an identification and its accuracy (Garrett, 2013:73; Gould and Leo, 2010:842; Wells and Murray, 1983).

Police behaviour can shape witness testimony. This might happen in rather unsubtle ways, as the case of *Carlos DeLuna* shows. Here, of a potential four witnesses, two refused to try to identify the suspect as they knew they had not had a sufficiently clear view, one tried but failed to identify the suspect, and another was taken directly to the suspect who had been handcuffed into the backseat of a police car. While surrounded by officers the witness was told incriminating information about the suspect and then agreed to identify him. His identification provided the main evidence for the prosecution, resulting in the wrongful conviction and execution of *Carlos DeLuna* in 1989 (Liebman et al., 2014).

However, eyewitnesses can also be influenced by the administrator of the line-up or the identification process itself (Garrett, 2013:74; Gould and Leo, 2010:842). When the line-up administrator is aware of who the suspect is, they can have a strong biasing

---

[3] For a brief review and discussion of recent developments in identification procedures in England and Wales, see Valentine et al. (2007).

effect on the eyewitness (Batts et al., 2014:8). Research suggests various ways in which eyewitnesses can be influenced: by an expectancy effect—when police encourage the results they want (Garrett, 2013:73); by confirmation bias—beliefs concerning the guilt of a suspect influencing eyewitness decision-making (Kassin et al., 2013:45); by police suggestion or overt behaviour confirming and bolstering a witness's identification (for example, by praising the witness or revealing that police suspicions had been confirmed, giving the witness a false sense of confidence (Batts et al., 2014:9; Garrett, 2013:73; Gould and Leo, 2010:842)); or suggestive procedure, one that causes the suspect to stand out (for example, if a suspect in a line-up is the only person of a particular height, build, hair colour, etc., or if one individual looks more like the offender than others (Batts et al., 2014:8; Gould and Leo, 2010:842)). A witness may make a *tentative* ID and the police record it as a *positive* ID (Davis, 2014:4). A mistake may then be influenced by the presence of a confession (Hasel and Kassin, 2009), which in turn enhances the witness' certainty as earlier memories of the real offender may be replaced by images of the individual selected in the identification process (Gould and Leo, 2010:842). Most of the research on the fallibility of line-up procedures has been carried out in the US, but recent research carried out at the Royal Holloway in London suggests that US line-ups are *more* reliable than those in the UK, where false identifications are more likely to occur (Seale-Carlisle and Mickes, 2016).

While many witnesses are mistaken, some knowingly lie to the police and courts and wrongful convictions may occur due to the perjured testimony of police informants who lie for personal gain (Gould and Leo, 2010:851). Indeed, Covey (2013:1160) argues that police perjury is the most prevalent cause of known wrongful convictions, with studies suggesting that between 11 per cent (Huff et al., 1996) and one-fifth of wrongful convictions in the US involved perjured testimony (Gould and Leo, 2010; Scheck et al., 2003). In the case of the *Cardiff Three*, all but one of the witnesses was in custody or had criminal trials pending (O'Brian, 2008:39). Many later retracted their evidence, claiming that police had promised leniency for unrelated criminal charges and threatened and intimidated them into implicating the suspects (O'Brian, 2008:40 and 136–7). This practice was also said to have occurred in the trials of the *Guildford Four* (Hill and Bennett, 1991:129).

Witnesses who lie or manufacture evidence to benefit themselves include 'career informants' who can earn release from prison by falsely testifying against another (Freedman, 2010:739). Such incentivized testimony was a factor in 46 per cent of capital wrongful convictions examined by the Center on Wrongful Convictions (the Center cited in Batts et al., 2014:13). Informants can be rewarded with money, release from prison, or leniency in relation to past or pending criminal activities, without assessment of the reliability and accuracy of their testimony (Batts et al., 2014:13; Davis, 2014:5; Gould and Leo, 2010:851). In the UK, police practices aimed at securing cell confessions are authorized under the Regulation of Investigatory Powers Act 2000. However, the practice has been questioned due to payments and offers of rewards to the inmates providing improper motives, and because witnesses may have numerous previous convictions for dishonesty, perverting the course of justice, and lying under oath (McKay, 2015:2).

Witnesses may lie about sex offences for a range of reasons, from compensation to vengeance or even because they are psychologically unwell (Burnett et al., 2017). We discuss, in both Chapters 7 and 8, cases where witnesses lied about sexual offences and whose credibility the Commission challenged. These are difficult cases, particularly in a time when the mood music is to believe victims' complaints and to take seriously sexual offences, as one commissioner explained to us:

[how we] approached complainant credibility issues, particularly in sex cases, … we were very much swimming against the political tide [that said] you must believe anybody who comes forward, you must believe victims, and it was all very victim-centred justice … but actually we were saying, yeah, that's all very well, but you actually need to be aware that, on rare occasions, … there's somebody who's making an entirely false allegation. (#63)

Unreliable witnesses can do great harm even when a suspect is robust in their defence; they are particularly damaging in cases where the suspect is vulnerable.

Vulnerable Suspects

In some of our cases the Commission considered the vulnerability of the applicant in assessing the possibility of a referral back to the Court. For example, in case EE31 questions were raised about the applicant's capacity to commit the offence. The Commission's Statement of Reasons for a referral to the Court made clear that although the applicant denied the offence when interviewed by the police:

He demonstrated certain personality characteristics of those who make false confessions. His agitated and excited behaviour after the killing, together with his ambivalent remarks to some of the witnesses, can be understood in the terms of his low self-esteem and quest for recognition. (Case EE31, Statement of Reasons)

His demeanour had been a factor in persuading the police that he must be guilty. The Court was provided with evidence that the applicant's disabilities and personality characteristics made him vulnerable to prosecution, though in the event, the case was quashed by the Court on forensic evidence, with little weight being given to vulnerability.

The literature demonstrates that the most typical way that a vulnerable suspect might contribute to their own wrongful conviction is by making a false confession—an admission of guilt and a post-admission narrative that documents relevant details of the crime (Leo, 2009:333). Several cases that led to the establishment of the Runciman Commission were based on false confessions by vulnerable suspects, not least Stefan Kiszko,[4] and, as we discuss in Chapters 7 and 9, the applicant in a few of our cases confessed while in police custody to a crime that they had not committed. In some such cases, the Commission had to establish evidence of the applicant's vulnerability to false confessions.

False confessions are not rare, especially in the most serious of cases (Garrett, 2014:1). Various studies claim that 14–25 per cent of wrongful conviction cases involve false confession; this rises to approximately two-thirds in homicide convictions (Gould and Leo, 2010:844; Leo, 2008, 2009:332; Leo et al., 2013:107; Scheck et al., 2003:361). While most defendants who falsely confess are not convicted because their case does not go to trial (often because prosecutors decline to submit, or dismiss, charges), research suggests that if the case does go to trial, a clear majority of those who falsely confessed are convicted (Leo et al., 2013:27).

A confession is arguably the most damaging piece of evidence that can be presented at trial (Gudjonsson and Pearse, 2011; Ofshe and Leo, 1997:983), often setting in motion an irrefutable presumption of guilt, leading to disadvantage at every stage of the process. Following a confession, officials and jurors tend to interpret all other evidence as inculpatory and corroboratory, even when weak (Leo, 2009; Leo et al., 2013; Ofshe

---

[4] See Rose et al. (1997).

and Leo, 1997:984). Prosecutors tend to charge a suspect who has confessed with the highest number and most serious types of offences (Leo et al., 2013; Ofshe and Leo, 1997:984) and defence lawyers often pressure those who have confessed to plead guilty (Leo, 2009:341; Leo et al., 2013). Almost three-quarters of cases in England and Wales are now resolved through submission of a guilty plea rather than a trial (Fair Trials and Freshfields Bruckhaus Deringer LLP, 2017). With continuing cutbacks to the legal aid budget, and the resulting rise in the number of defendants without adequate legal representation, guilty pleas are likely to rise further, along with the number of those who are wrongfully convicted (Transform Justice, 2016; Chapter 14).

In the courtroom, judges typically do not suppress confessions and instead find them to be voluntary and admissible (Leo et al., 2013). Furthermore, once a confession is introduced to a jury, most jurors tend to assume that the defendant is guilty even when other evidence is presented that raises serious doubts about its reliability; indeed, confessions have more impact on verdicts than any other form of evidence (Garrett, 2014:15; Leo et al., 2013). Prosecution and defence lawyers and judges find it difficult to believe that a person would confess to a crime they had not committed (Garrett, 2014:15; Gould and Leo, 2010:844; Leo, 2009:333–41; Leo et al., 2013), though they should be aware that highly 'suggestible' suspects are vulnerable to wrongful confessions under the coercive conditions of a police interview (Gudjonsson, 2003). Indeed, recent research has shown that in the context of a highly suggestive interview, people can quite readily generate rich false memories of committing a crime (Shaw and Porter, 2015).

Wrongfully accused suspects who confess have typically been subjected to psychologically coercive interrogation methods (Gould and Leo, 2010:846; Leo, 2009:335; Leo et al., 2013). Police investigators may convince the suspect of the benefits of confessing by manipulating the suspect's perceptions of the choices available and the consequences of each; confession emerges as the only rational option (Ofshe and Leo, 1997:984). Interview techniques include pressure, accusation, repetition, false evidence ploys, and attacks on denial, including any inconsistencies, omissions, contradictions, or implausibility in the suspect's account (Gould and Leo, 2010:846; Leo, 2009:335; Ofshe and Leo, 1997:990). Police may also overstate their case—lying about the strength or existence of other evidence, such as from an eyewitness or a co-accused, or from forensic evidence (Leo, 2009:333; Ofshe and Leo, 1997:989–1009). More common are explicit or subtle promises of incentives (emotional benefits, clear conscience, respect, ability to go home, lesser charges, acceptance of a defence, leniency for showing remorse, etc.) or pressures (more serious charges, harsher punishment, arrest of a relative, exploiting fears of prison and losing children, etc.) (Gould and Leo, 2010:846; Leo, 2009:335; Ofshe and Leo, 1997:1053–84).

While coercive physical methods are increasingly rare (Gould and Leo, 2010:846; Leo, 2009:335), tactics designed to break down the suspect's will to resist can include threats, assault, verbal abuse, and the denial of sleep, food, water, and access to a bathroom—factors that impair functioning (Davis, 2014:4; Garrett, 2014:21). Some officers may be insistent, hostile, manipulative, and deceptive (Gould and Leo, 2010:846; Leo, 2009:335), and may subject the suspect to lengthy interrogations (Garrett, 2014:6; Davis, 2014:4), weakening resistance and increasing suggestibility (Leo, 2009:339; Ofshe and Leo, 1997:1061). The physical environment of the police interrogation room can isolate, disempower, and shock the suspect while interrogation methods are stressful, unpleasant, and designed to convince the suspect that his guilt has already been proven and conviction is inevitable, that the evidence against him is overwhelming and his protestations will therefore not be believed. (Batts et al., 2014:11; Gould and Leo, 2010:846–7; Leo, 2009:335–9; Ofshe and Leo, 1997).

Of course, a false confession may not convince a court, unless it is persuasive in its detail and accuracy. It may seem convincing if the police have contaminated or shaped it by disclosing details of the crime to a suspect during the interrogation process, sometimes unintentionally. Feeding of relevant detail can lead to confessions containing 'inside' information that an innocent person could not have known or volunteered (information not in the public domain), including details that are corroborated by crime scene facts (Gould and Leo, 2010:849; Leo, 2009:337).[5] This can lead to false confessions appearing deceptively rich, detailed, and accurate (Garrett, 2015) and the 'coherent and compelling story-line' creates a strong impression that the narrative is true (Leo et al., 2013:776). If the details of constructed confessions are sufficiently graphic and specific police, prosecutors, judges, and juries may overlook inconsistencies or lack of fit with other evidence (Garrett, 2014:15; Gould et al., 2013:13; Leo, 2009:337). While certain procedural protections are in place, including the recording of interviews, relevant details about the crime may be fed to the suspect outside of the main interrogation, such as in police cars, custody suites, or when recorders are turned off (Garrett, 2014:14).

Suspects differ in their ability to withstand interrogation and their vulnerability to falsely confessing. Those who are highly suggestible or compliant are more likely to confess, especially if they do not understand the adversarial nature of the interrogation (Batts et al., 2014:11; Gould and Leo, 2010:847; Leo, 2005, 2009:335; Nobles and Schiff, 2000; Ofshe and Leo, 1997:988). This includes juveniles, who tend to be compliant and trusting towards authoritative figures, submissive, immature, naive, and eager to please. They can be highly suggestible, easily pressured and lack the ability to understand the long-term consequences of their actions. They also have a limited attention span and memory and are less capable of withstanding stress (Garrett, 2014:4; Gould and Leo, 2010:848; Leo, 2009:336).

The developmentally disabled—who tend to have low intelligence and poor understanding, a short attention span, poor memory, and poor communication skills—are vulnerable to manipulation. They look to authority figures for cues for behaviour and are conflict-avoidant and eager to please, responding with an answer they presume to be desired. They also tend to be overwhelmed by stress and lack the ability to withstand pressure (Gould and Leo, 2010:847; Leo, 2009:336). Several high-profile British miscarriages of justice have involved psychologically vulnerable, suggestible, and compliant people, some of whom are unable to distinguish facts from fantasy (Gudjonsson, 2003) (see further, Chapter 7).

The mentally ill may experience guilt, distorted beliefs, an inability to distinguish fact from fiction, severe anxiety, and lack of self-control while being innocent of the offence. They may also have poor attention spans and memory, lack social skills, such as assertiveness, and become easily confused by aggressive questioning (Drizin and Leo, 2004; Gould and Leo, 2010:848; Leo, 2009:33). In the UK, the case of Judith Ward provides a cautionary tale; any statements she made should have been considered unreliable, given her mental illness (Ward, 1993:160–1) and yet she was convicted. In other high-profile cases, incriminating statements were made in interviews where there was no solicitor present (Conlon, 1990:89; O'Brian, 2008:26), with confessions retracted

---

[5] Of the sixty-three false confessions examined by Garrett (2014:13), fifty-nine were contaminated with accurate 'inside information'—crime scene details that an innocent person could not have known.

after the suspect left police custody (Conlon, 1990; Mullin, 1990). Nevertheless, tainted confessions formed a substantial part of the prosecution case, particularly for the *Guildford Four*.

Young suspects and women are vulnerable to false, incriminating testimony (Batts et al., 2014:11; Leo, 2009:335). Women are disproportionately convicted for crimes that probably did not occur (Davis, 2014:1; Gross and Shaffer, 2012:30). Confessions may be produced by 'social or ideological pressures to take responsibility for harms for which one may not be legally responsible, but for which one may feel morally responsible' (Parkes and Cunliffe, 2015:231). Such moral responsibility may be used by investigators to coerce false confessions, particularly in cases of infant death where medical reports are inconclusive and thus reliable evidence is scarce (Parkes and Cunliffe, 2015:231). Indeed, the most common cause of women's wrongful conviction is unethical police and prosecution behaviour, present in 86 per cent of such cases (Ruesink and Marvin, 2007). Cases involving infant deaths, discussed in Chapter 7, demonstrate the vulnerability of some women accused of killing their own babies whose unexplained deaths may have resulted from other non-criminal causes, such as viruses or accidents.

While human error is somewhat predictable, especially in the stressful conditions generated by serious crime, we expect science to be dependable. Applications to the Commission suggest otherwise.

The Fallibility of Science and Expert Testimony

Science is commonly regarded as objective and free of bias, highly reliable and accurate, and embodying clear, rational reasoning—characteristics that appear antithetical to wrongful convictions (Cole, 2012:713–14). Given the recognized limitations in other types of evidence, such as confessions and eyewitness identification, forensic evidence has become accepted as one of the most powerful and compelling sources of evidence (Dror and Bucht, 2012; Laurin, 2013).

Forensic science can identify and exclude suspects with more reliability than traditional forms of evidence gathering (Laurin, 2013). Even forensic techniques that are considered unreliable, such as microscopic hair comparison or serology analysis, may be capable of excluding innocent suspects (Cole, 2012). But some techniques of forensic science relied on by courts, while presented as objective and infallible (Dror and Bucht, 2012), have not been appropriately validated (Laurin, 2013). As one interviewee at the Commission told us:

The dangers of things like facial recognition which I think is a complete non-science, those areas of danger I think are growing increasingly ... I suspect that a lot of miscarriages flow from that kind of thing, perhaps more than they did before. (#27)

The public, jurors, lawyers, and even judges believe that forensic scientists can identify perpetrators with very low error rates (Dror and Bucht, 2012). If evaluated appropriately and objectively, forensic evidence can be a safeguard against the subjective errors of the police, juries, and judges (Kassin et al., 2013:80). However, in practice, it can produce questionable, erroneous, and even fraudulent evidence (Kassin et al., 2013:42). Forensic disciplines are not all underpinned by scientific method; standards are not governed effectively, results can differ considerably, with error-rates unknown, and they rely on subjective, experience-based evaluations, with overstated conclusions appearing in testimonies (Cooper, 2013:254).

In recent years, the reliability of forensic science has been questioned by various people; from individual journalists investigating specific cases, to the US Federal Bureau of Investigations (Robinson, 2015), and even the Executive Office to the President of the US (Executive Office to the President, 2016). A report published by the National Research Council (2009:22) found 'little rigorous systematic research to validate [forensic science's] basic premises and techniques' and blamed the discipline for many wrongful convictions. Other research has pointed to a lack of objective measures and of defined methods, and poor regulation of laboratories (Kassin et al., 2013:42), especially for non-DNA forensic evidence (Cole, 2012:715). Indeed, some now argue that forensic error is one of the major causes of wrongful conviction (Haber and Haber, 2013). In the UK, a study of court judgments over a seven-year period from January 2010 to December 2016 showed that just over a third were argued to be unsafe because they contained misleading evidence. Of those 193 cases where the evidence was misleading, just over a third had faults with forensic evidence as presented to the trial court, or in relation to directions by the judge (Smit et al., 2018:Table 3 and Figure 3).

Forensic science is today considered to be both part of the problem and part of the solution to wrongful convictions (Cole, 2012:715) and growing reliance on forensic evidence is a double-edged sword (Robinson, 2015). Since DNA was first used in the UK to solve the murder of Dawn Ashworth over three decades ago, it has been a powerful resource for the police and the prosecution service. DNA evidence can be reliable, and optimism about ease of access to data and a safer criminal justice system followed the establishment in the UK of the National DNA Database[6] in 1995. DNA profiling has exposed several wrongful convictions and highlighted the lack of oversight in other forensic techniques (Cooper, 2013; Dror and Bucht, 2012; Kassin et al., 2013; Laurin, 2013), but interpretation of DNA evidence remains somewhat subjective, at least in complex situations, and as such is susceptible to bias and contextual influence (Dror and Cole, 2010:163; Dror and Hampikian, 2011:204; Kassin et al., 2013:47). Sometimes DNA evidence available at the time of the trial that could have excluded the defendant is not used (Garrett, 2013:74) and in many cases such evidence does not exist, or may not be available for testing if it has been 'lost' or destroyed (Davis, 2014:2).

DNA has a quantifiable though small error rate (Cooper, 2013:234) and in recent years, more and more cases have come to light—in the UK and the US—that cast doubt on its reliability (e.g. Davis, 2017; Kirchner, 2017). Errors tend to be caused by those who collect, store, or analyse forensic evidence (Kassin et al., 2013:42), and results are not always conclusive. In some applications to the Commission, DNA evidence remained uncertain even after further forensic testing. In case EE23, for example, the applicant had been convicted largely on confession evidence, which he claimed was elicited under coerced conditions, and on DNA evidence, which was unsettled. The Commission refused to refer the case to the Court, arguing that the trial judge and the jury had been aware of the applicant's claims about the confession evidence, and so this was not 'fresh evidence'. Further, while the Commission conceded that the DNA evidence presented at trial would not be admissible by the standards at the time of the review, and while new DNA profiling tests carried out for the Commission remained inconclusive, it was felt that the evidence was still sufficiently robust and that therefore the Court would uphold the conviction. Hardly infallible science.

---

[6] The first of its kind in the world and currently the largest, this database consists of millions of profiles obtained from suspects, victims, volunteers, and crime scene samples, with each new profile routinely checked for matches against others held.

Questions have been raised about the reliability of methods in many forensic science practices (Cooper, 2013). The report of the Runciman Commission (1993) highlighted concerns, including: failure to communicate findings clearly; inequalities between defence and prosecution resources; limited defence access to samples; pro-prosecution bias; 'expert shopping'; and low accuracy of the techniques employed. More recently, it has been revealed that many thousands of forensic tests used to secure criminal convictions for rape and murder, among other crimes, have likely been tampered with and are no longer considered to be reliable (ITV News, 2017).

Further accounts of unreliable forensic testing and storage have emerged since the demise of the national forensic science service. Even a superficial perusal of the news media will indicate a declining faith in forensic science. For example, a recent newspaper investigation suggested that there may be over 500 'doctored' forensic test results produced in England and Wales by 'rogue scientists' working in private laboratories that have replaced the work done by the disbanded government-funded Forensic Science Service (Beckford and Nick, 2017). And the Forensic Science Regulator has warned that the integrity of the criminal justice system is now at risk from poor quality testing (see further, Chapter 14). In the Commission, staff are only too aware of this changing 'surround' (Hawkins, 2002; see Chapter 3); that tests can be, and sometimes are faulty. For this reason, when an applicant has already had evidence tested, the Commission will arrange for further testing by one of its accredited services. That said, nothing is infallible, as an interviewee explained in relation to one of our cases. Here, the accredited service:

had issues replicating the [unaccredited provider's] results ... There were issues about whether [the unaccredited provider] had conducted it properly or whether the [accredited service] had conducted it properly, and actually, it was the [accredited service] that made the mistake. (#55)

Many forensic science techniques involving the analysis of physical evidence have never been validated scientifically (Wells et al., 2013:53). Imprecise method descriptions, and lack of measures, criteria, and quality control, result in considerable variation between analysts and a consequent lack of reliability (Haber and Haber, 2013). Most forensic disciplines do not involve objective judgements and there is thus concern for inter-rater reliability (between experts) and for intra-test reliability (within examiners over time) (Kassin et al., 2013:43). Hence, those investigating possible wrongful convictions based on forensic error must consider if the technique used was reliable and performed properly by a competent analyst (Wells et al., 2013:53).

The National Research Council (2009) concluded that there were problems with standardization, reliability, accuracy, and error and contextual bias in most areas of forensic science, including analysis of firearms, hair, impressions, blood spatter, fibres, handwriting, and fingerprints. It pointed to widespread deficiencies in training, funding, regulation, and standard setting, arguing that courts rely on such evidence without understanding its limitations.

A more recent US report by the Executive Office to the President (2016) concluded that bite mark analysis is unreliable, footwear analysis is not scientifically valid, and that firearms analysis, forensic hair analysis, and latent fingerprint analysis (which once had a reputation for objectivity and accuracy (Dror and Cole, 2010:161–3)) have substantial false positive rates and evidence falls short of the scientific criteria for foundational validity and reliability (Executive Office to the President, 2016).

Forensic science techniques require an analyst to visually examine the evidence from a crime scene and determine whether there is a match to an individual suspect. This is a highly subjective process (Garrett, 2011:86; Kassin et al., 2013:47; Wells et al., 2013:53), too broad to ensure repeatability and reliability, with no guarantee that two analysts following the same method will reach the same conclusions (National Research Council, 2009). Experts present themselves as 'objective and immune to bias' (Kassin et al., 2013:43) and are likely to be viewed by the jury as neutral (Slobogin, 2014:707). However, like others in the criminal process, forensic analysts are vulnerable to contextual bias, influenced by the background of the suspect or other information relating to the case (Charman, 2013:56; Dror and Cole, 2010:161; Wells et al., 2013:53). For example, confessions and other types of evidence can lead to forensic confirmation bias, and forensic scientists may be so certain of a match with one type of evidence, that they ignore discrepancies with others (Gould and Leo, 2010:851; Kassin et al., 2013:42), with bias increasing the likelihood of mistaken judgements (Haber and Haber, 2013).

As we see in Chapter 7, most often, forensic errors involve expert testimony or interpretation of evidence, rather than the testing itself. Errors include failure to inform the jury of key information, overstating inculpatory evidence, misleading and misstating the certainty of results (Gould et al., 2013), and drawing conclusions not supported by the evidence (Davis, 2014:5; Kassin et al., 2013:43; Wells et al., 2013:53). In other words, forensic analysts can offer flawed and invalid conclusions, with hundreds of exonerations having exposed error or fraud among forensic examiners with scientists knowingly providing false results (Laurin, 2013).

An experienced commissioner told us:

You know, we now look back at the *Birmingham Six*, the *Guildford Four*, and we say it was self-evident that they were shocking miscarriages. It is self-evident that the police needed to clean their act up, that we needed to tighten up on PACE and so on and so forth, and it's all so much better now. None of that was self-evident, at least to the establishment, ... before those miscarriages were uncovered and acknowledged. For a very long period of time, intelligent and well-meaning people thought that those were perfectly safe convictions, after the operation of due process by the best criminal justice system in the world ... well-meaning people just not able to see ... what is now ... blindingly obvious. (#9)

It has not yet become 'blindingly obvious' that science is not as reliable as is assumed, though the data we present in Chapter 7 shows confidence in science is diminishing and that flawed expert testimony will persuade the Commission that there are reasons to doubt the safety of some convictions. Furthermore, Chapter 9 will show that when scientists are influenced by flawed police or prosecution evidence, and there are inadequate protections in the criminal process, wrongful convictions are more likely.

Due Process Failures

If forensic scientists can be vulnerable to cognitive bias, it is not surprising that those on the front line of criminal justice—police and prosecutors, who deal with the tragic effects of crime—will be vulnerable to prejudices and preconceptions that challenge their ability to approach serious crimes dispassionately. Weak prosecution cases are more likely to lead to wrongful conviction because if police and prosecutors are sure they have the right suspect but lack proof, not only may they not be dissuaded by exculpatory evidence, but they could be tempted to 'bolster' the case by failing to disclose such evidence to the defence or by relying on 'snitch testimony' (Gould et al., 2013:501).

Some applications to the Commission which focus on scientific evidence also demonstrate police or prosecution malpractice. In case PI2, for example, the Commission's review cast doubt on the veracity of the evidence provided by prosecution witnesses, with one such witness claiming police coercion. While fresh scientific evidence proved to be most persuasive to the Court in quashing this conviction, the fallibility of the witnesses, the police failure to pursue an alternative (and arguably more credible) suspect, and non-disclosure of exculpatory evidence were additional features of the case (see Chapter 9).

Just under one in five of the Commission's referrals to the Court from 1997 to 2011 included police misconduct as a ground for referral (in most it was the principal ground). Just under half were due to direct misconduct, with the others involving an officer who was thought to be sufficiently tainted by association with other cases of proven corruption (Heaton, 2013:150–1).[7]

Police malpractice tends to occur, at least in part, because of tunnel vision—'[t]he premature and exclusive commitment to, and failure to test critically a factual theory' (Doyle, 2010:6). By focusing too readily on one suspect, police may select evidence to build a case while ignoring, disregarding, or suppressing exculpatory evidence (Gould et al., 2013; Gould and Leo, 2010; Kassin et al., 2013). Police may unintentionally focus on the wrong suspect when they feel certain of someone's guilt and 'tweak the evidence in their favour, thinking they are doing good', believing they are doing the right thing; sometimes called noble cause corruption (Davis, 2014:4; see also Parkes and Cunliffe, 2015).[8]

Such cases are more common today than the egregious miscarriages of the past, as one interviewee explained to us:

[T]here's a big difference, I think, between the historic police corruption cases ... and all the recent crime cases ... [In] none of the recent cases ... was there was any mass police corruption, or to frame somebody, or cover up. [But] you still have an element of sort of noble cause corruption, ... perhaps a mind-set is, well, someone's murdered her, we've got a suspect, we can't think of anyone else it could be—it must be him, and then perhaps not doing their jobs as thoroughly as they should. (#40)

Here, the reference is to tunnel vision, which may occur at any stage of the investigation and can sway police, prosecution, and defence counsel, as well as forensic scientists (Gould and Leo, 2010:851). Errors in eyewitness misidentification or forensic analysis may lead the police to ignore relevant exculpatory evidence for the defence (Gould and Leo, 2010:851). As more resources are placed into building a case against a suspect, the actors involved are less willing to accept 'negative feedback' that challenges their arguments (Gould et al., 2013:504), and motivated to seek confirmation of their original beliefs (Ask and Granhag, 2007:565). Time pressure and need for cognitive closure

---

[7] For example, many wrongful convictions flowed from officers active in the now discredited West Midlands Serious Crime squad or the 'Flying squad' at Rigg Approach in London.

[8] The journalist, Raymond Bonner (2012) has penned a particularly vivid account of a case of tunnel vision; the conviction of an African-American man with learning difficulties who was sentenced to death for a crime he did not commit.

can create situations where evidence that is inconsistent with a hypothesis is subject to more scepticism and scrutiny while confirmatory evidence is accepted uncritically (Ask and Granhag, 2007:565).

When there is considerable data, complex information must be processed quickly and efficiently, and people make use of shortcuts to eliminate unnecessary pieces. Although helpful, such shortcuts can lead to 'faulty conclusions' and error (Batts et al., 2014:5–6). Individuals are likely to remain committed to their hypotheses even when faced with contradictory evidence as they are more likely to remember facts consistent with their original hypothesis (Batts et al., 2014:5).

Almost half of all US exonerations involved misconduct by criminal justice officials (Gross and Shaffer, 2012:67), but the most common transgression is failure to disclose exculpatory evidence to the defence (Gould and Leo, 2010:854). In Heaton's (2013:152) study of Court judgments in England and Wales, following Commission referrals, the prosecution failed to comply with disclosure requirements in a fifth of cases. Some such cases are likely to be intentional, but many are accidental; if prosecutors are not provided with such evidence by the police, they may not be aware it exists (Gould and Leo, 2010:855). Like police, prosecutors may suffer from cognitive bias; convinced that a defendant is guilty, they discount evidence that may contradict their conclusions (Batts et al., 2014:5).

Gould and his colleagues found that a strong defence decreased the probability of a wrongful conviction (Gould et al., 2013:508). But while a weak prosecution case can be dismantled by a strong defence, not all defence lawyers have the skills or, more typically, the resources to mount an effective defence. A weak defence and poor representation are highly correlated with a wrongful conviction (Gould et al., 2013:494); as was the case for the *Guildford Four* and the *Birmingham Six* (Mullin, 1990). Examples of inadequate defence representation include: conflicts of interests, lack of expert evidence, acceptance of false confessions, belief in the defendant's guilt (Gould et al., 2013), and defence lawyers encouraging 'dubious plea offers' (Slobogin, 2014:708), with Scheck et al. (2003) finding evidence of inadequate defence in a third of their cases (see also Radelet and Bedau, 1998).

In addition to police and prosecution malpractice, and incompetent counsel, judicial error may play a role in some wrongful convictions. In the cases Gould et al. (2013) examined, many judges lacked training in psychology and forensic science, failed to closely examine the evidence, and failed to level the playing field between prosecution and defence. Not surprisingly, many applications to the Commission suggest that the judge erred in summing up, or at another stage of the trial. Given that judicial error is a common ground of a first appeal, it may be expected that the Commission would rarely refer on this matter, as they need to identify fresh evidence or argument to refer a case. However, Heaton found that in a relatively large number of cases judicial error was at least one of the grounds of appeal in referred cases (Heaton, 2013:151–2).

The Pervasive Influence of Prejudice and Fear

Studies show that certain crimes are more likely to lead to wrongful conviction: for example, rapes and murders. Gross (1996:476–90) argued that the seriousness of the crime is highly correlated with wrongful conviction because police and prosecutors are under pressure to pursue serious crimes even if there is little robust evidence. Phillips and Richardson's (2016:446) research on the US National Registry of Exonerations tested Gross' conclusion that the 'worst crimes produce the worst evidence' and found clear evidence that '[A]s the seriousness of a crime increases, so, too, does the chance of false confession, untruthful snitches, government misconduct, and bad science.' Hence, they show that the relationship between the seriousness of the offence and the likelihood of it resulting in a wrongful conviction is contingent on state actors playing a central role in the production of the evidence. This is not surprising, they argue, when we remember that police officers are most likely to be emotionally affected by rapes and murders which cause such intense distress to all who are aware of the circumstances of the crimes (Phillips and Richardson, 2016:446).

In Heaton's (2015) study of court judgments on Commission referrals from 1997 to 2011, murders and rapes (including other sexual offences) were the two largest categories of cases (133 and 66, respectively, of 374 cases). In sex cases, forensic evidence may be of limited use, but also public fear and revulsion about such offences puts pressure on investigators. Rapes and murders, particularly of children, attract considerable media attention, creating expectations on police and prosecutors to apprehend and convict the offender as soon as possible. This can increase the likelihood of hurried investigations and procedural errors or police and prosecution malpractice (Gould and Leo, 2010:857). Arrests in high-profile cases will likely be greeted with praise and relief within the police service and wider community that may leave the police disinclined to release the suspect at a later stage for fear of embarrassment, even if new evidence suggests they may have prosecuted the wrong person (Gould et al., 2013). Time pressure leads to an 'increased selectivity in information processing' and a reduction in flexibility, limiting the ability to form alternative hypotheses and test them effectively (Ask and Granhag, 2007:563).

Furthermore, judgements about witness reliability can be influenced by 'extra-legal' factors, such as ethnicity and emotional expression. As such, the interpretation of witness information appears to be subjective and influenced by bias (Ask and Granhag, 2007:562). Race seems to be a particularly aggravating feature in cases of eyewitness misidentification (most commonly with a white witness identifying a minority suspect (Gould and Leo, 2010:846–56)) or by introducing bias at trial when all-white juries convict black defendants based on questionable evidence (Gould and Leo, 2010:856).

Changing Nature of Wrongful Convictions

Before we turn in the following chapters to the Commission's response to applications raising the types of concerns we have discussed above, we reflect for a moment on the changing nature of wrongful convictions over the past decade or two.

The Commission is widely acknowledged to be constrained by limited resources, mostly financial but also technical expertise, at a time when the nature of wrongful convictions has shifted somewhat. We produce in Box 5.1 two case summaries from our sample as evidence of changing demands on the Commission. While the first is typical of early cases, the second is typical of current applications, though for ease of comparison, we present cases that were referred to the Court and in which the conviction was quashed.

Box 5.1 Changing demands on the Commission: two cases exemplars

Applicant S

S had been convicted in 1993 of attempted rape, and burglary with intent to rape. The first complainant had provided only a poor description of the assailant; the second complainant told police that a man had broken into her house, just down the street from the site of the first offence, but left without assaulting her. Both witnesses reported that the intruder had a distinctive voice and during house to house enquiries, the police arrested S and interviewed him without a solicitor 'as he had not requested one', though all interviews were taped. S pled guilty to both offences and accompanied police to the location of the offences, showing the officers how he had entered the two premises. He later retracted his confessions, saying they were mere fantasies. He was prosecuted though no forensic evidence linked him to either home or victim and there was no positive identification from either witness. S was convicted on his uncorroborated confession, though it had been retracted long before the trial.

At first appeal, the Court heard that the first victim had subsequently been raped in her home, while S was in prison, and she thought it was the same man, and that this was not S—who she had seen for the first time at the trial. The second offender had been a different build, different age, and had said to her 'It's me again'. Despite this new evidence, the Court was not persuaded that S's conviction was unsafe.

Following an application to the Commission in 2000, expert evidence was sought from a leading forensic psychologist who—following interviews with, and various tests on the applicant—found that the police had engaged in leading questions and prompted S when he was unsure about what he was supposed to have done. S was found to be 'highly suggestible' during police interviews. Initially, he had clearly known little or nothing about the crimes and his self-incrimination came only after the police had fed him information.

Concluding that there were now 'serious reservations about the reliability of the self-incriminating admissions the applicant had made to the police', the case was referred back to the Court in 2001 on grounds of fresh psychological evidence, affording the new evidence about the second intruder 'higher evidential status'. Given that there had been no other evidence against S and very little police investigation into the case (no fingerprint evidence; no police files; no attempt to fully investigate the alternative suspect), there was little else for the Commission to do by way of investigation. The Court quashed the conviction, though the applicant had already served his sentence.

Applicant W

W was convicted of murdering the woman he lived with in 2005. CCTV footage excluded any third-party involvement, but W—who had reported the attack—denied that he was responsible for her death. The trial court heard that W had a history of violence, with evidence given by an ex-partner who had been beaten while pregnant. The police had conducted many interviews with W, but he demonstrated no recollection of harming the victim. The forensic pathologist presented evidence consistent with strangulation, though it was agreed that other injuries on the deceased could have been caused accidentally, from falls while intoxicated (both victim and offender had high levels of alcohol in their blood at the time). The defence argued that another person could have broken into their home and killed the victim or that W had killed her but had not intended to and had no recollection of doing so, due to the high volume of alcohol he had consumed.

W's first appeal against conviction was dismissed and he applied to the Commission in 2008. This first application failed to persuade commissioners that there was any merit in the case, but having received revised submissions from his solicitor, the case was re-opened at the end of 2011.

The Commission's investigation was thorough and wide ranging, including analysis of new medical evidence from MRI and CT scans of W's brain to explore the damage caused by years of alcohol abuse. With this evidence, the Commission was able to challenge the medical evidence at trial and argue that contrary to the prosecution case, W's 'alcohol dependency syndrome'[a] could have caused 'memory blanks' and other cognitive impairments sufficient to establish a defence of diminished responsibility: 'his judgement, ability to reason, understand the consequences of his actions and his ability to control his impulses was seriously and significantly impaired due to the brain damage caused by alcohol dependence and the effects of alcohol consumption itself at the material time'. Scans of other organs confirmed significant alcohol damage.

While this case rested on an understanding of the law of diminished responsibility, and invited meticulous analysis of the relevant case law, the Commission's review led them into an area of relatively new medical science on the effect of alcohol on the brain, including analysis of the results of neuro-psychometric tests. It also required a critical appraisal of the expert evidence presented at trial, something that had not been common in earlier Commission reviews. In this case, new expert witnesses were commissioned to scrutinize the evidence at trial and to demonstrate where it was thought to be flawed. The fresh material was sufficient to persuade the Court to quash the conviction.

[a] A mental disorder under the Mental Health Act 1983 and an abnormality of mind within the remit of the Homicide Act.

While these two cases were not so dissimilar, they presented quite different challenges to the Commission. S was a reasonably easy case to review. There was no science to struggle with, indeed no forensic evidence at all, and it was quite clear that the police investigation had been very poor, providing a clear ground for referral. In contrast, W presented the Commission with various challenges. There seemed to be no alternative suspect. CCTV, rarely found in public places when S was convicted, proved to be inculpatory. Hence, the Commission had to establish how to interpret the complex scientific data on the functioning of the applicant's brain. Scans and their analysis have become much more sophisticated in the past decade and while this provides a potential source of data to help applicants to the Commission, it stretches the Commission's expertise. While many Commission staff are legally trained, most do not have scientific skills to draw on and yet more and more frequently the applications that land on their desks require an understanding of forensic science that would demand a lot of a science graduate. It was within this changing landscape of wrongful convictions—with its decreasing evidence of flagrant police misconduct and increasing scope for forensic science and technology—that we sought to understand how the Commission responds to applications for review. It is the first part in the review process—the screening of applications—that we turn to in Chapter 6.

6

Triage: The Application Screening Process

By definition, screening is at the earliest stage, where sometimes you've hardly got any of the documents, so you might just be guessing . . . it's an inexact science, screening. (#2)[1]

Introduction

We may assume that the most important decision made by the Criminal Cases Review Commission ('the Commission') comes at the end of the review process, when it exercises its discretion to refer a case back to the Court of Appeal ('the Court').[2] If a case is referred, an applicant's search for justice continues to the Court. Otherwise, this decision marks the end of an opportunity to have the conviction quashed.[3] However, many cases come to an end much earlier when the Commission screens out an application without a detailed review. Applications go through two stages: at stage one, cases are screened in or out of the process, and at stage two, decisions on whether to refer cases back to the Court are made after a detailed review. Nearly half (48 per cent) of the applications to the Commission are screened out at stage one, making decisions at this stage just as important as at stage two.[4]

In emergency medicine, triage systems exist to assess the medical needs of patients with criteria to determine treatment under limited resources (Iserson and Moskop, 2007). In a similar way, stage one aims to filter out weak or unsuitable cases and enable the Commission to invest greater resources in meritorious cases. Rejecting apparently weak cases at an early stage can benefit applicants: some can prepare a more persuasive reapplication to the Commission or perhaps achieve finality; as one of our interviewees put it, 'there's . . . a pastoral role in telling people "get on with your lives"' (#19). There is also a danger; unsafe convictions could be screened out erroneously. In this chapter, we seek to understand stage one decision-making.

The Casework Guidance Note on screening states that stage one decision-making is 'done at speed and very often with minimal information' and that it is 'not possible to be 100 per cent accurate all the time' (Criminal Cases Review Commission,

---

[1] All interviews are with Commission staff, including commissioners, case review managers, management staff, and advisers unless we state otherwise.

[2] In some cases, where a conviction was secured in the magistrates' court, a referral is made to the Crown Court.

[3] The option to reapply is open to all applicants (Criminal Cases Review Commission, 2016e); see Chapter 13.

[4] The Commission explains stage one decision-making in the following terms: 'screening is the process whereby applications are considered initially, key documents obtained and the need for investigation examined' (Criminal Cases Review Commission, 2013e). Between 1 January 2005 and 31 December 2014, the Commission received 7,899 cases excluding magistrates court cases, Court Martial cases, and applicants who only wanted their sentence reviewed. Out of a total of 7,899 cases, 3,825 cases were screened out at stage one; these include cases considered to be ineligible by the administrative team.

Reasons to Doubt: Wrongful Convictions and the Criminal Cases Review Commission. © Carolyn Hoyle and Mai Sato 2019. Published 2019 by Oxford University Press.

2011k:para:11).[5] At the same time, it acknowledges that the 'grounds for a referral are frequently not identified by the applicant and only uncovered by the Commission's investigative efforts' (Criminal Cases Review Commission, 2011k:para:6). Here we see a problem: the Commission understands that the sheer number of applications preclude rigorous investigation at stage one, and yet some meritorious applications will contain insufficient information to guide the reviewer. (Chapter 12 discusses the changing organizational demands on the Commission, where efficiency in decision-making is increasingly prioritized.) An interviewee explained to us the difficulty of stage one decision-making as follows:

> You have a relatively brief review of the paperwork that has come in to decide whether it is worrying or complex or messy, in which case it goes for review … I normally always get the summing up and sentencing remarks to give me some background to the case. But you're looking for something new. And usually, the applicant won't give it to you. So you have to use your imagination in looking at the paperwork … But I have a duty to the wider justice system, I have a duty to conserve resources for the organization, so it does mean that you're very focused, and you have to be very fast in dealing with a case. (#19)[6]

This chapter analyses the mechanisms that are in place for stage one decision-making by drawing on Hawkins' (2002) theoretical framework of 'surround', 'field', and 'frame', introduced in Chapter 3. 'Surround' refers to the broad social, political, and economic environments that can shape decision-making, which inevitably change over time. The Commission must respond to shifts in the surround, which are beyond its control. In this chapter, we examine the Commission's response to Court jurisprudence that shapes stage one decision-making.

The Commission's decision 'field' is comprised mainly of law, internal policies, and working rules. We analyse changes to the Commission's policy on screening over the period 2013–17, a transition that continued beyond our fieldwork period. We explore the key decision field that helps Commission staff to identify the factors present in an application that might persuade them to approach their screening decision in one way, rather than another; the 'routine' (Lloyd-Bostock, 1992) ways in which they make sense of the information in the application. The field of screening has evolved to produce shortcuts when such factors are present that facilitate decision-making under time constraints and with limited information (e.g. Gigerenzer, 2008; Lloyd-Bostock, 1992).

In considering the decision field, this and the following empirical chapters draw heavily on our analysis of Casework Guidance Notes as well as all case-specific documents developed on each application under consideration. The various Casework Guidance Notes—not previously the subject of academic enquiry—reveal highly structured mechanisms for shaping decision-making at the Commission. They belie any notion that commissioners and Case Review Managers ('CRMs') have complete discretion to approach their cases in any way they choose; rather, their approach is systematized.

In addition to the surround and field, Hawkins (2002) argues that decision 'frames' allow decision-makers to interpret the world around them. A frame is applied to a case in order to typify and identify the relevant facts that help the decision-maker to reach a decision—in this case whether to screen out an application at stage one, or whether

---

[5] A commissioner informed us that there was a presumption that weak cases should be screened out within six months at stage one decision-making (#7).

[6] This description refers to a screening by a commissioner.

to proceed to a stage two review. We discuss the people—commissioners, CRMs, and group leaders—involved in screening, exploring their background assumptions that lead them towards specific approaches to stage one decision-making.

Stage One Review: Four Types of Applications

When applications first reach the Commission, they are placed into one of four categories (Criminal Cases Review Commission, 2013e):

1. *First-time applications from people who appealed the original verdict before applying to the Commission* (Criminal Cases Review Commission, 2013e). These *post-appeal/first-application* cases are normally screened in to prepare the groundwork for a review by establishing what material needs to be gathered and estimating the amount of work required for stage two review (Criminal Cases Review Commission, 2013b). Before 2013, post-appeal/first applications could have been screened out for having 'no reviewable grounds', but since the introduction of the new screening system, all such cases are screened in.

2. *Applications from people who have not appealed.*[7] For *no-appeal* cases to progress to stage two, *potential exceptional circumstances* need to be identified (Criminal Cases Review Commission, 2013e, 2017d).[8] This is true even if the real possibility test is satisfied.[9] (For definitions of 'exceptional circumstance' and 'real possibility', see Chapter 4.)

3. *Reapplications from people who applied previously to the Commission but were turned down.* The original application may have been in either of the above categories ('post appeal/first application' or 'no-appeal'). These cases are progressed to stage two if the Commission is satisfied that they raise new issues that were not considered at trial, at appeal, or during the Commission's previous review(s) and rejected if they contain no new evidence or argument (Criminal Cases Review Commission, 2013e).

4. *Cases that do not fall under the Commission's mandate.* These are rejected at stage one regardless of their merit. They include cases pending appeal; cautions; fines enforcement; claims for compensation for a wrongful conviction; civil proceedings; County Court proceedings; deportation and asylum issues, excluding criminal convictions arising from such matters; criminal injuries compensation decisions; criminal cases from Scotland, the Channel Islands, or the Isle of Man; and matters in which the applicant was a victim of crime (Criminal Cases Review Commission, 2015g:2).

Thus, applications may be rejected at stage one without further review ('screened out') if they are 'no-appeal' cases but show no potential exceptional circumstances, are reapplications that raise no new issues, or are ineligible for consideration under the Commission's mandate. Applicants still have the option to reapply by submitting a

---

[7] See Chapter 4 on no-appeal cases and exceptional circumstances.

[8] The potential for exceptional circumstances is sufficient at stage one; the existence of actual exceptional circumstances is examined at the end of stage two (Criminal Cases Review Commission, 2017d).

[9] Where there are no potential exceptional circumstances, but a real possibility is apparent, applicants will be advised to apply for leave to appeal, including in cases where the usual time limit for such an application has expired (Criminal Cases Review Commission, 2017d).

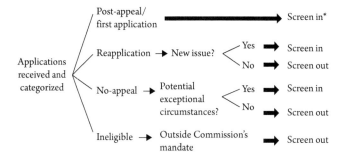

Figure 6.1 Stage one decision-making since 2013

Note: * Before 2013, a single commissioner could screen out a 'post-appeal/first application' case if it was deemed to have no reviewable grounds.

fresh application (Criminal Cases Review Commission, 2016e:para:8).[10] The stage one process is summarized in Figure 6.1.

Individual Commissioners' Decision Frames

Hawkins (2002) argued that substantive law and formal rules may appear to be precise and specific but tend to operate in imprecise ways, and the way in which rules are applied in a particular case is often left to the discretion of the legal actors. In this section, we analyse the individual commissioners' decision frames.[11] We do this by examining commissioners' self-perceptions about screening, colleagues' accounts of commissioner screening, and commissioners' screening record of no-appeal cases.

Commissioners' self-perceptions about screening

We asked commissioners working under the old screening policy about their own approaches to decision-making. First, when asked about their general review style, commissioners tended to refer to the real possibility test, identifying the legal field as guiding decision-making. They acknowledged the influence of individual characteristics in framing decision-making, but assumed that the law was the guiding principle:

We're all independent commissioners from different backgrounds, but there's one job to do: to look to see, on the evidence and facts, if there's anything new to give rise to a real possibility. (#74)

However, when asked about their specific screening style, they acknowledged the importance of non-legal criteria:

You just need to efficiently and effectively look with an open mind, be prepared to make the enquiries that you need to make to reach a reasoned decision, to undertake the investigative steps that may be exculpatory or inculpatory—cost-effective, in the course of that review, to

---

   [10] There is no limit on the number of reapplications, but the Commission may decide not to accept further reapplications if an applicant continues to submit reapplications without raising relevant new evidence or argument (Criminal Cases Review Commission, 2016e:para:8).

   [11] As noted in the introduction, a frame is a structure of experience and values that decision-makers apply in reaching a decision.

have a very analytical mind—and if you do all of those things, then you've got a good chance of reaching the right decision. (#74)

This rational and reasoned, disinterested approach could be thought of as an ideal, but is in sharp contrast to the description of the routine approach of another experienced and rather cynical commissioner who described turning down cases as the norm:

I do what you might call the bargain basement work, which is the no-appeal cases, of which I'm doing about 150 a year, or maybe slightly more than that … I have to be very aware of a kind of 'turn down' attitude that is inherent in the role, sort of 'What rubbish have I got today to deal with?' … I'm desperately looking at the start for something that gives me hope about a case. And when I do that, I transfer it to someone else. I'm such a miserable soul after the years here. You know, that you get into a certain way of thinking about cases, and you get into being cynical … that is the approach I basically use. (#19)

In the past, screening was conducted by individual commissioners with little or no oversight. Hence, whether a commissioner is cynical, superficial, open-minded, or rigorous, can influence the outcome at screening, and lead to inconsistencies in decision-making. At other stages of the review process there can be opportunities for deliberative accountability. For example, at a case committee meeting, three commissioners and a CRM will discuss their views on the merits and weaknesses of a case, and that discussion can, and sometimes does, change the direction of the case. There were few such opportunities in the screening of the cases we studied.

An interviewee described a long-standing quality assurance process used at stage one, in which commissioners 'peer-reviewed' a couple of cases each month and wrote a 'short report', which was 'stored and analysed centrally' (#74).[12] While the robustness of this process was unclear, in particular with respect to making use of the analysis, its existence demonstrates the Commission's awareness of the wide scope for discretion at screening. However, commissioners expressed little concern about substantive inconsistencies in decisions at screening, as long as colleagues were following the right procedures. We enquired whether an interviewee mostly agreed with the screening decisions of other commissioners during the peer-review process, and received the following response:

It's very clearly not about agreeing or disagreeing, because each commissioner will draw their own different conclusions. The two things that you're looking for really are (1) is it Wednesbury-reasonable?,[13] and (2) have the appropriate investigative steps and guidelines and policies and procedures been complied with?; and on the whole, that is the case. I don't think we've identified anything that hasn't been Wednesbury-reasonable, and on the whole, most of the guidelines are complied with. (#74)

In our view, this response raises some concern. Checking for procedural irregularity at screening is of course important, but so is the outcome.[14] When cases go to committee, commissioners robustly discuss the proper outcome—whether or not to refer

[12] The quality assurance process was applied to all commissioners engaged in screening, not restricted to commissioners new to screening. As of January 2017, the quality assurance system has moved from commissioner peer-review to quality assurance review by the Chief Executive or Director of Casework (Email correspondence with the Commission, 4 April 2018). According to the Commission, the new quality assurance system focuses on both quality and consistency.
[13] A decision is considered 'Wednesbury unreasonable' if no reasonable person acting reasonably could have made it (*Associated Provincial Picture Houses Ltd v Wednesbury Corporation* (1948) 1 KB 223).
[14] Three concepts—structure, process, and *outcome* (the Donabedian model)—are often used to draw inferences about the quality of care in health services (Donabedian, 1988).

a case; they do not consider this to be unimportant as long as appropriate investigative steps have been taken. Deliberative accountability at this stage means that if someone on the committee seems to have come to a perverse decision, others will debate the key issues in order to arrive at a defensible position.

The Wednesbury reasonable test should not be of much help here. That is used to assess judicial reviews of a public authority's decision. Therefore, the reference to this test in the quotation above suggests that quality assurance of commissioner's screening practices is primarily intended to defend the Commission against judicial review. It is not used to check whether commissioners interpret the real possibility test similarly in order to ensure a certain level of consistency in outcomes for applicants.

Perceived commissioner variability

Any organization involved with 'diagnostic' processing of cases strives to standardize its procedures so that the outcome of a given case does not depend on who makes the diagnosis. The field of the Commission is comprised of the legal framework for decision-making, notably the real possibility test; the organization's mandate and guidance for achieving it, found in the internal rules and procedures set out in the Casework Guidance Notes and the Formal Memoranda; and informal expectations, notions, and even the ethos of the Commission. This field should minimize variability and inconsistency in decision-making. However, commissioners' individual decision frames—how they understand, interpret, and give meaning to information in each specific case—will inevitably be shaped by personality, predisposition, outlook, and knowledge, and cannot, therefore, be divorced from their legal and organizational approach to decision-making.

[Commissioners] bring a lot of their own previous experience with them, so ... you're going to get different approaches, and that's a good thing, in many respects ... But on the flip side of that, [it] can then lead to, obviously, different approaches and inconsistencies. (#70)

Box 6.1 summarizes sixteen commissioners' decision-making styles and approaches to casework, as well as their attitudes towards applicants, based on information from interviews and fieldwork notes. The box presents interpretations of commissioners' approaches by current and former staff, including commissioners' descriptions of other commissioners.[15] The sixteen commissioners included in Box 6.1 are not the total number of commissioners we approached during fieldwork; they represent just those commissioners who were mentioned (unprompted) at various points during interviews with their colleagues (descriptions are in the interviewees' own words; we did not attempt to interpret or modify what they said). In all categories shown in Box 6.1, descriptions spanned the spectrum from 'inflexible conservative' to 'very liberal'; 'exploratory' to 'decisive' decision-maker; and 'too slow' to 'fast but not rigorous or careful'. Formal rules (e.g. as expressed in Formal Memoranda) and the legislative framework may appear to provide clear guidance on decision-making; however, based on these descriptions of commissioners, it is difficult to identify a clear and cohesive philosophy of the Commission.

Some variability might be more acceptable, or expected, than others. For instance, it is not surprising to find differences in terms of 'other personality traits' (Box 6.1). It would be highly unusual not to see variety in character in any organization, and these

---

[15] We cannot vouch for the accuracy of these judgements.

Box 6.1 Moments of reflection: opinions about commissioners' approach to screening

---

Approach to decision-making: inflexible conservative; conservative; liberal; very liberal; liberal but electrically unsafe … could blow a fuse at any moment; wildcard; found [a] way of dealing with things difficult to stomach sometimes; very summary in his/her instinct; very confident in decision-making; fairly bold decision-maker; decisive; exploratory; not willing to investigate enough; broad-brush approach

Relevance of professional background: too defence-orientated; too academic; legal; too legal; no law degree; Crown Prosecution Service background; lay commissioner; reasonable familiarity with the way criminal justice system/courts operate

Attitudes towards applicants: anti-applicant; judgemental of the applicant; too interested in the stories behind the applications

Speed and thoroughness: too slow; sits on files for months; thorough but slow; extremely efficient; quite fast, too, but not terribly thorough; fast but not rigorous or careful

Other personality traits: extremely acute; extraordinarily bright; very switched on; competent; nightmare; wonderful; lovely person; deeply committed; hardworking; not terribly hardworking

Sources: interviews with commissioners and other Commission staff.

---

perceived differences are not likely to significantly negatively impact the quality or consistency of decision-making.

Variety in commissioners' backgrounds is intentional. Sections 8(5) and 8(6) of the Criminal Appeal Act 1995 require at least one-third of members of the Commission to be legally qualified with more than ten years of experience, and at least two-thirds to have knowledge or experience of an aspect of the criminal justice system. While the proportion of legally qualified commissioners has changed over the years, eight of the fourteen commissioners are not legally qualified (as of September 2017).[16] The Commission's approach to recruitment was therefore motivated in part by a desire for diversity.[17] Some of our interviewees embraced this diversity; one stated that 'it would be wrong if they were nine defence solicitors or nine prosecutors or nine police, ex-police officers, or whatever it is; it's good to have a mix' (#29).[18] Some of the legally qualified commissioners appreciated the special expertise (for example in medicine) of non-legal commissioners (#7). However, legally qualified commissioners expressed the view that all cases—including the ones that benefit from non-legal expertise—need to satisfy the real possibility test, which is a legal framework (#7).

I think the intention was to have a split and I … personally find that very difficult … you've got to know the system, you've got to know what you're looking for on miscarriage,

---

[16] The profile of current commissioners can be found on the Commission's website: https://ccrc. gov.uk/about-us/commissioners/. (Accessed on 26 September 2017.)

[17] The Scottish Commission, which is also required by law (Crime and Punishment (Scotland) Act 1997) to have at least one-third of its members legally qualified, has a mixture of legally qualified and non-qualified board members (equivalent to commissioners), but their legal officers (equivalent to CRMs) are all legally qualified.

[18] An interviewee explained that under the old (commissioner-only) screening process, commissioners would ask for different documents: 'Some commissioners, I think depending on their previous backgrounds … would always ask for CPS file, some would always … look at defence files … different priorities of what they think is important' (#70).

miscarriages don't come stamped, 'This is a miscarriage of justice', you've got to know where to look. (#22)

I used always to defend the system on the basis that ... lawyers are people who'd screwed the whole thing up and what you needed was somebody who was going to be difficult and say 'I don't care what you bloody lawyers say—there has to be a way round this!' ... I'm not sure that really works ... But I think there is a benefit in having ... people from outside, but they have to be quite closely fitted there ... people who have some reasonably close familiarity with the way the criminal justice system [and] courts operate. (#11)

While there may be mixed views on diversity in commissioners' backgrounds, the differences in commissioners' perceived approaches to decision-making provide grounds for concern (see Box 6.1). An applicant would be alarmed to discover his case was assigned to a commissioner described by colleagues as 'anti-applicant', a 'wildcard', or 'very summary in instinct'; no doubt preferring a commissioner described as 'exploratory', 'liberal', and 'thorough'. One interviewee explained that a 'pro-applicant' commissioner would view it as the Commission's mission to 'go out of our way to help people and find things', whereas commissioners with a 'stricter' or 'colder' approach to applicants would consider it applicants' responsibility to properly articulate their arguments, regardless of the safety of their conviction (#72). The Commission articulates a neutral position; not taking sides with the applicant or the criminal justice system (Criminal Cases Review Commission, 2015g). However, at stage one decision-making, when commissioners have limited information, being 'anti-applicant' could militate against spotting a meritorious application, and a certain level of sympathy with the applicant may be necessary to fully appreciate the applicant's argument:

We ought to worry about it ... someone can put their case in a way which looks hopeless and, somehow, you've got to read between the lines and sometimes ... sometimes, the hairs on the back of your neck should stand up, so even though this case looks hopeless, we should do something with it, you know. I think the expeditious screeners are not likely to do it ... I just thought it was dreadful that [name deleted] who were very summary in their instinct were ... screening ... I'm sure that cases slipped through. (#7)

A different interviewee expressed similar concerns:

I get alarmed sometimes by inconsistency. All our commissioners are very individual people and they all have quite strong personalities, but that does lead to a measure of inconsistency of approach ... I think a certain amount of inconsistency is healthy, but if it ever goes too far then I think it's a risk of perhaps doing someone somewhere a disservice. So, I would like to see more consistency, more sharing of information, more consultative decision-making. (#17)

If these descriptions by colleagues are accurate, there are different professional approaches to screening. This means an applicant's experience will be different depending on which commissioner screened the case (which is not a problem in itself), and therefore the chances of getting through screening will also be different depending on the commissioner (which is problematic).[19]

---

[19] In addition to individual variability among commissioners, our interviews also showed cliques among commissioners and conflicts between them (#13; #7; #72). While group and individual differences may balance out by the end of a review, when three commissioners sit on a decision-making committee, at stage one these are more likely to result in different consequences for applicants.

Screening no-appeal cases

Methodologically speaking, it is not easy to differentiate between a decision shaped by the field or the frame, or to pinpoint where the influence of the frame outweighed that of the field, resulting in inconsistencies. Nor can we easily prove whether apparent inconsistencies are a direct result of the unique facts of individual cases or commissioners' decision frames shaping their interpretation of those facts. Nevertheless, our data described above demonstrated different *approaches* to screening and we now turn to data that show differences in *outcome*. We examine commissioners' screening of no-appeal cases quantitatively and qualitatively.

Commissioners' screening record of no-appeal cases

As explained above, section 13(1)(c) of the Criminal Appeal Act 1995 requires that an appeal should have been determined, or leave to appeal refused, before an application is submitted to the Commission. Section 13(2) provides an exception, in that a referral can be made for no-appeal cases 'if it appears to the Commission that there are exceptional circumstances which justify making it'. Table 6.1 summarizes screenings of no-appeal cases between 2005 and 2014 (when commissioners were solely responsible for screening decisions) by fifteen commissioners who had screened twenty or more

Table 6.1 Screening of no-appeal cases by commissioners, 2005–14

Commissioner	% of cases sent for stage two review	Total cases sent for stage two review	Cases with no exceptional circumstances	Total number of no-appeal cases screened
1	4	1	27	28
2	4	51	1,094	1,145
3	5	10	176	186
4	8	18	222	240
5	14	15	92	107
6	20	51	208	259
7	25	17	52	69
8	26	19	55	74
9	26	16	45	61
10	29	69	170	239
11	30	123	282	405
12	39	24	37	61
13	41	13	19	32
14	48	12	13	25
15	50	14	14	28

Source: Micro-level administrative data from the Commission; calculations by the authors.

Notes: Magistrate cases, sentence-only cases, and Martial Court cases were excluded. This table is limited to commissioners who screened twenty or more cases.

no-appeal cases.[20] The data confirm the qualitative findings concerning the variability of screening decisions. For example, Commissioner 1 screened twenty-eight cases and found one case with potential exceptional circumstances. In contrast, Commissioner 15 screened twenty-eight cases between 2010 and 2013 and found fourteen cases with potential exceptional circumstances. No significant differences were found in the profile of cases these two commissioners screened in terms of applicants' gender, custody status, representation, type of offence, or when the applications were received.

Horne (2016:282) argued that the lack of a previous appeal was used to screen out a high proportion of cases with little oversight. Our data show that all but two commissioners were more likely to screen out no-appeal cases than screen them in. Commissioner 2, who screened a total of 1,145 cases, only screened in 4 per cent of them. However, it should be stressed that even among commissioners who were more likely to screen out no-appeal cases there was significant variability.

In aggregated figures for stage one decision-making by year (Figure 6.2), there is a spike in 2012 for the total number of no-appeal cases reaching the commission as well as the proportion of cases sent for stage two review. The increase in no-appeal cases can be explained by the introduction of the simplified application process in the same year (Criminal Cases Review Commission, 2014a). This does not, however, explain the rise in the proportion of no-appeal cases going through to stage two. Between 2005 and 2011, this averaged 11 per cent. It rose sharply in 2012, averaging 22 per cent between 2012 and 2014. There is also considerable variability between 2005 and 2014 in the proportion of no-appeal cases going through to stage two. Between 2005 and 2011, there is a 12-percentage point difference between the lowest proportion of cases sent through in 2006 (5 per cent) and the highest in 2008 (17 per cent).

The sharp increase in the proportion of no-appeal cases going through to stage two may be explained by the number of commissioners who screened stage one cases. Before 2012, three to seven commissioners screened no-appeal cases (Table 6.2). Of

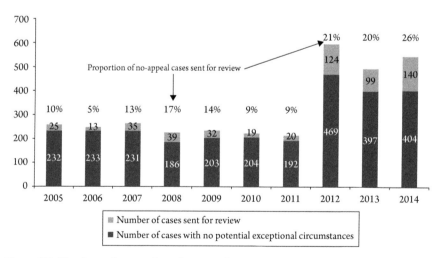

Figure 6.2 Number and proportion of no-appeal cases sent to stage two review, 2005–14

Source: Micro-level administrative data from the Commission; calculations by the authors.

Note: Magistrate cases, sentence-only cases, and Martial Court cases were excluded.

[20] We assigned a number for each commissioner to ensure anonymity.

Table 6.2 Breakdown of no-appeal screening (2005–14), by year and commissioner

Comm-issioner	Cases sent for review/Total number of no-appeal cases										Total
	2005	2006	2007	2008	2009	2010	2011	2012	2013	2014	
1									1/8	0/20	1/27
2	9/70	3/110	1/105	8/125	4/153	3/153	5/124	8/207	10/98		51/1145
3	7/117	3/69									10/186
4	0/54	0/23	4/32	6/35	6/22	0/15	1/32	1/27	4/26	11/65	18/240
5								0/1			15/107
6		3/13	8/33	6/16	4/11	1/14	0/1	10/59	14/58	5/54	51/259
7									7/23	10/46	17/69
8								2/5	10/38	7/31	19/74
9									1/4	15/57	16/61
10		0/5	7/31	4/15	4/10	1/8	3/20	20/58	10/48	20/44	69/239
11		3/11	10/50	8/22	6/24	7/18	9/30	18/84	25/75	37/88	123/405
12		0/5	4/13	3/5	4/9	4/9		9/20			24/61
13								13/32			13/32
14									1/3	11/22	12/25
15								14/28			14/28

Source: Micro-level administrative data from the Commission; calculations by the authors.

Notes: Magistrate cases, sentence-only cases, and Martial Court cases were excluded. This table is limited to commissioners who screened twenty or more cases.

these, two or three handled most of the cases. From 2012 onwards, ten commissioners became involved, with relatively even distribution of caseloads. Not all commissioners who have engaged in screening since 2012 were prone to screen in a no-appeal case. However, the increase in the number of commissioners screening no-appeal cases probably brought in a wider range of approaches to screening, which resulted in an overall increase in the proportion of cases going through to stage two; a finding that confirms variability in screening decisions among commissioners.

Difficulty in identifying exceptional circumstances

Variability in commissioner screening, demonstrated by the quantitative data presented above, speaks to the discretion of individual commissioners when dealing with no-appeal cases. Our qualitative analysis of policy documents and interviews confirms the difficulty in identifying potential exceptional circumstances. The Commission in its Formal Memorandum on Exceptional Circumstances stressed that exceptional circumstances must not be used as grounds for referral unless there are 'compelling reasons' to skip the conventional appeals process (Criminal Cases Review Commission, 2017d).

However, what counts as 'compelling reasons' is open to interpretation. The Formal Memorandum provides guidance on situations that may give rise to exceptional circumstances, but it explicitly states that 'it would be impossible to issue a prescriptive list' (Criminal Cases Review Commission, 2017d; for the Formal Memorandum's illustrative list of exceptional circumstances, see Chapter 4). The Commission's learning process on what may constitute exceptional circumstances is evident in the changing nature of the illustrative list: in the 2015 version, 'applicants who pleaded guilty' was added to the list and 'applicants who are prevented from pursuing an appeal due to threats made against [them or their] family' was deleted (Criminal Cases Review Commission, 2017d).

The difficulty of precisely identifying exceptional circumstances is partly due to the fact that the provision was added as an afterthought, after Parliamentary debate but before the Criminal Appeal Act 1995 was finalized (Criminal Cases Review Commission, 2011f:paras:8–9). The examples of exceptional circumstances were identified and the formal policy within the Commission continued to develop based on lessons learned from no-appeal referrals. The Commission's use of exceptional circumstances was criticized in 2005 by the McKinsey report,[21] which recommended more rigorous filtering of no-appeal cases before accepting them for review. The Commission in 2008 took the view that it would be wrong to automatically reject no-appeal cases but agreed to examine each case in just enough depth to make a decision to review a real possibility (Criminal Cases Review Commission, 2011f:para:16).

The Casework Guidance Note on Exceptional Circumstances published in 2011 attempts to guide screening commissioners on instances where a no-appeal case can be screened in. This may be to obtain sensitive information relating to informants, where there have been significant allegations of malpractice by the police, or where a complainant is alleged to have made subsequent false allegations (Criminal Cases Review Commission, 2011f:para:34). These issues are considered to justify screening in a no-appeal case because applicants and solicitors will generally be unable to make

---

[21] In 2005, McKinsey & Co carried out a review of how the Commission assessed and reviewed cases. It focused on whether investigative processes can be adjusted to improve efficiency and effectiveness. The summary of the report is available from: https://publications.parliament.uk/pa/cm200506/cmselect/cmhaff/1635/1635we10.htm.

appropriate enquiries. This guidance may be helpful in situations where applicants are clear about the need for the Commission's special powers. However, for no-appeal cases where applicants provide very little information in their applications, screening is left to the discretion of the commissioners (Horne, 2016).

The Casework Guidance Note acknowledged that the Commission's approach to exceptional circumstances had been inconsistent (Criminal Cases Review Commission, 2011f:paras:1, 25, 27, 51, and 131). This inconsistency was explained as partly due to the Court's wavering stance on exceptional circumstances. The Commission can use section 17 powers to obtain information that would not be available to applicants and their legal representatives. The Commission can also justify a referral of a no-appeal case if it can show that section 17 powers were necessary to find new information that suggests the conviction is unsafe. In other words, not having appealed is justified because applicants and their legal representatives would not have succeeded in the appeal without section 17 powers.

The use of section 17 powers to refer a no-appeal case was accepted in the case of *Leighton*[22] but not in *Callaghan*.[23] Both cases centred on the reliability of a witness. In *Leighton*, the Court was persuaded that exceptional circumstances existed because fresh evidence concerning the witness would not have been discovered without the Commission's section 17 powers. The applicant's conviction was quashed even though there had been no previous appeal. Similarly, in *Callaghan*, the applicant applied to the Commission without a previous appeal. The Commission used its section 17 powers, which identified information that damaged the credibility of a witness. The Court, however, upheld the conviction in *Callaghan*, and found no exceptional circumstances:

> We are not satisfied that there are any exceptional circumstances. There was no appeal in this case and there is, in our view, nothing in the new material of a compelling nature so as to warrant a reference on the basis of exceptional circumstances ... If we are wrong about that, we are not persuaded that either ground relied upon casts any doubt upon the safety of the conviction. (*Callaghan*, para:22)

The Commission's interpretation of the different Court response to these two cases was that an exceptional-circumstance ruling may be justified if 'the Court likes our reference point' (suggesting that they think the *substance* of the real-possibility test is more important to the Court than finding exceptional circumstances) and that the outcome may simply depend on 'which judges hear the case' (Criminal Cases Review Commission, 2011f:para:79). Here, the Commission is acknowledging discretion and variability in approaches at the Court, and that substance can trump procedure in referrals to the Court.

A commissioner explained that no-appeal cases where the convictions are for sexual offences are more likely to be screened in. Potential exceptional circumstances can be identified quickly at stage one in sexual offence cases, because these cases often turn on complainant credibility and the Commission's unique section 17 powers can be used to obtain sensitive information about complainants (see Chapter 8):

> I have to be able to establish a way of working out that there are exceptional circumstances ... In practice that, in 90 per cent of cases, means cases where our special powers [e.g. section 17 powers] are required to advance the case. And that almost always in turn means sex cases, because in those we can get the [complainant's] social services records, the doctor's records, etc.,

---

[22] [2011] EWCA Crim 311.   [23] [2010] EWCA Crim 2725.

etc.—the compensation claim details that a body with our powers can do, but for example a defence solicitor at this stage simply could not do. So it tends to be those, those sex cases that can show exceptional circumstances. (#19)

Hence, because of the need for the Commission to use its section 17 powers to gain access to information that would not be available to the applicant and their legal representative, and because these powers tend to be used to greatest effect in sexual offence cases, a working assumption within the decision-field has been established that sexual offence cases will likely trigger exceptional circumstances. For other non-sexual offence cases, the screening commissioner could use an exploratory approach and screen in a case to see if investigations lead to a real possibility and an identification of exceptional circumstances. The screening commissioner could also choose to quickly screen out an application because there has been no prior appeal and there is no obvious need for the Commission's special powers. The latter approach has 'enormous efficiency benefits' (Horne, 2016:277) for the Commission because it can facilitate the rapid closing down of a case where there has been no previous appeal. The wide discretion concerning no-appeal cases was captured in an interview with a commissioner in 2014 about finding exceptional circumstances:

It's actually quite difficult ... you'll get rather different answers from all the commissioners ... the way we sort of work away in our little cells, you know, in our individual way ... you kind of wonder whether commissioners are maybe taking different lines on the same ... sort of facts. (#80)

A commissioner with extensive experience in screening no-appeal cases illustrated the somewhat arbitrary nature of exceptional circumstances:

It's very, very rare that you do get exceptional circumstances, and the problem with the law ... is that exceptional circumstances are quite vaguely defined. It is at least arguable. And the people applying to us haven't really got a clue, because they're no longer legally represented because they can't get Legal Aid.... In practice, exceptional circumstances become what *I think* exceptional circumstances are. It's *my interpretation* of the law. Because there's no one bright enough of the people I'm dealing with to actually contradict me. Yeah, that's a horrible thing to say, but it's true.... So I decide what the law is to an extent. (#19, emphasis added)

The Commission's internal documents and our interviews demonstrate the difficulty in providing concrete guidance on what constitutes exceptional circumstances for no-appeal cases. Interviews with decision-makers also highlighted the wide discretion in screening no-appeal cases.

   In summary, our analysis, both qualitative and quantitative, shows variability in commissioners' screening outcomes. *Variability* should not be equated with the *quality* of decision-making. It is not possible to determine from our analysis what approaches are right or wrong, and that was not our intention. Commissioners who screen out most of the no-appeal cases may work quickly, but they may not necessarily screen out meritorious applications. Commissioners who screen in more cases are perhaps more careful and cautious, but that does not mean that all those cases should be subject to a stage two review.

   Good decision-making is often equated with classical rationality, with optimal results thought to be achieved by applying the laws of logic and probability to all the relevant information (Gigerenzer, 2008:25). Decision-making that deviates from classical rationality in various fields, be it economics or medicine, is often discredited as incomplete or irrational (Gigerenzer and Goldstein, 1996:651). In law, Frederick Schauer

(1991) argued that particularistic decision-making ('all things considered' judgements) by ideal judges would yield optimal results. Commissioners who tended to screen in no-appeal cases, or commissioners who were described by colleagues as 'thorough', 'exploratory', 'rigorous', or 'careful' may believe in the 'all things considered' approach to decision-making. Interviewees who were concerned about some commissioners' approach to screening associated quick decisions with poor-quality decisions, and good-quality decisions with thoroughness (Chapter 12 revisits the issue of balancing thoroughness and efficiency).

Research has shown, however, that quick decisions, which deliberately prioritize part of the available information, can enable correct decisions in less time than models that try to examine all information (Gigerenzer, 2008; Gigerenzer and Goldstein, 1996).[24] In other words, decision-making models 'do not have to forsake accuracy for simplicity' (Gigerenzer and Goldstein, 1996:666). It follows therefore that while it is clear that some commissioners are much more willing to screen out a no-appeal case than others, the willingness to make a decision at an earlier stage alone does not necessarily speak to the quality of the decision.

Similarly, to make a normative assessment on acceptable levels of inconsistency or what to do about inconsistency is difficult. When unwanted inconsistencies are detected, we often burden organizations with increased procedural guidance. Consistency, however, is not necessarily achieved by drafting more elaborate rules (Hawkins, 2002). The Commission could tolerate inconsistencies in outcomes as an inevitable consequence of wide discretionary powers and diversity in decision-makers. It might argue that in a highly discretionary system, the differences that we see are within the 'zone of tolerance' (Hawkins, 2002:427). The Commission prides itself on having a variety of decision-makers and reviewers from diverse backgrounds; by design, it celebrates and embraces variability in approach. Overregulating the ways in which individuals review cases may suppress this valued diversity without achieving much by way of consistency in outcome. If this were the justification, it must accept that some meritorious applications may be turned down by one commissioner and not another, or that some commissioners may screen in an unmeritorious application in an excess of caution. In analysing our cases, we found some evidence of this when comparing the Commission's responses to reapplications, following a decision not to review or not to refer a case (see Chapter 13).

However, even recognizing some justifiable defensiveness on variability, there must be a limit to the amount of permissible inconsistency in outcomes. In Chapter 3, we discussed Dworkin's (1977) distinction between 'weak' and 'strong' discretion. He contrasts weak discretion where 'the standards an official must apply cannot be applied mechanically but demand the use of judgement' with a stronger form of discretion, whereby the decision-maker is unbound by any rules or standards set by the authority in question. When there are no rules or criteria for the making of a discretionary decision, decision-makers are not obliged to make a particular decision. In the absence of rules, decision-makers must look

---

[24] Harry Markowitz, recipient of the Nobel Prize in economics for his theoretical work on optimal asset allocation, did not use his award-winning optimization technique for his own retirement investments but relied on a simple heuristic—the 1/N rule (Gigerenzer, 2008:22), which calls for allocating funds equally to the selected investment funds. When the 1/N rule was tested against the optimization models, the models performed better at data fitting for past data but worse at predicting the future.

for principles beyond the law. Dworkin (1977:32–3) argued such strong discretionary judgements can, however, be questioned on the grounds that they are irrational, unfair, or ineffective. The variability that we have found in screening is difficult to explain and would be hard to justify to applicants. While some commissioners were keen to argue that 'each case is individual' (#74) and dismiss any attempt to compare cases, recent changes to screening policy suggest that the Commission was aware of and wanted to minimize this variability.

New Screening Policy

The new screening policy that has been introduced at stage one is less likely—*by design*—to produce substantial inconsistencies in outcomes. Since the screening policy underwent a series of changes both during and after our fieldwork, it was too early to measure whether the new screening process *actually* improved consistency. In our view, it has the potential to minimize idiosyncratic decision-making through a consultative process but does not constrain decision-makers from utilizing their unique decision frames. This section describes the new screening policy, and explores the reactions to it of commissioners and other members of staff during the transition period.

Towards consultative decision-making

At least three revisions to screening policy were published between 2011 and 2017, in the Formal Memorandum on Stage 1 Decisions (Criminal Cases Review Commission, 2013e). Revisions focused on the people—commissioners, group leaders, and CRMs—involved in screening.[25] Since 2013, there has been a clear gradual devolution of power in stage one decision-making, from commissioners with sole responsibility for decisions to more consultative decision-making involving group leaders and CRMs.

Until June 2013, every case was screened in or out by a single commissioner (Criminal Cases Review Commission, 2014a).[26] The Commission was aware of the risks associated with its screening policy; their Casework Guidance Note on Screening stated that a 'Commissioner will need to take great care when finalising a case at Stage 1. Theirs may be the only judgement being applied to the application' (Criminal Cases Review Commission, 2011k:para:6). Since 2011, Commissioners sometimes opted to receive assistance in this process from CRMs (Criminal Cases Review Commission, 2011c, 2011k). This, however, did not change the fact that commissioners were the decision-makers. It was up to a commissioner to decide when CRM support was required and set the boundaries by 'identify[ing] the necessary work to be done' (Criminal Cases Review Commission, 2011c:para:4).

The screening policy changed further in 2013 when group leaders were given responsibility for assisting commissioners. First, they prepared cases by estimating the amount of work required for a stage two review. For example, they decided what material should be preserved or obtained, and provided an advisory note to assist CRMs

---

[25] For applicants, a significant change was made to the application form in January 2011 with the introduction of the Easy Read Form (see the 'Good legal representation' section below for details).

[26] This excluded 'ineligible' cases, some of which were screened out by the administrative team without the approval of a commissioner.

in their reviews (Criminal Cases Review Commission, 2013b). Previously, commissioners carried out this type of preparatory work.

Second, group leaders took over from commissioners the responsibility for screening post-appeal/first application cases (Criminal Cases Review Commission, 2013e). In essence, this took away a commissioner's power to reject these cases at stage one without CRM or group leader involvement. Before 2013, a single commissioner could turn down a case if it was deemed to have no reviewable grounds (Criminal Cases Review Commission, n.d.:paras:6–14). Since then, all post-appeal/first-application cases go to a group leader who estimates the amount of work required. A CRM then carries out the necessary investigation and drafts a statement of reasons. If there is no prospect of a referral, the CRM puts the case before a commissioner for it to be formally turned down (Criminal Cases Review Commission, 2016a). Thus, under the new system, rejection of a post-appeal/first-application case requires review by at least three people rather than a single commissioner.

In 2013, reapplications and no-appeal cases were still exclusively screened by commissioners (Criminal Cases Review Commission, 2013e). Changes in 2015 and 2017 further removed responsibilities from commissioners (Criminal Cases Review Commission, 2013e). The revised Formal Memoranda described the new mechanisms as follows:

No-appeal cases are considered for exceptional circumstances by Case Review Managers. [Where appropriate,] Commissioners make the decisions on cases where no potential exceptional circumstances exist. (Criminal Cases Review Commission, 2013e)

Re-applications are considered for new issues by Case Review Managers. Commissioners make the decisions as to whether the case needs a (further) substantive review. (Criminal Cases Review Commission, 2013e)

Minor revisions to the 2015 guideline were made in 2017. In 2015, after a group leader prepared a no-appeal case, a CRM was given the opportunity to screen, but the final decision rested with the commissioner. In 2017, the phrase 'where appropriate' was inserted, which removed the requirement for a commissioner to make the final decision in all no-appeal cases. Similarly, in 2015 a commissioner still made the final decision on whether a reapplication should be closed or progressed to stage two, assisted by a CRM. By 2017, however, only reapplication cases that were destined to be closed (because they contained no new evidence or argument) required a commissioner's approval (Criminal Cases Review Commission, 2013e).

In summary, the changes to the screening process during 2013–17 demonstrate devolution of power: a move from commissioners single-handedly deciding the fate of all types of applications to a more collaborative decision-making system. Those cases that present prospects for a referral are screened in by group leaders without any commissioner involvement, and under group leader guidance; if a CRM believes that a reapplication presents no new evidence or argument or that a no-appeal case has no exceptional circumstances, it will be passed on for a commissioner to sign-off. Hence, at least three members of staff—a group leader, a CRM, and a commissioner—are involved in decisions to screen out cases, previously made unilaterally. The new screening policy is clearly intended to reduce the risk of rejecting meritorious cases without a stage two review.

The new screening policy could be seen as little more than a slight change if we bear in mind that commissioners remain the final arbiters. However, our interviews, carried out during the transition period, suggest that the new policy allows group leaders and CRMs to challenge and revisit commissioners' screening decisions (#68), and perhaps not surprisingly commissioners were equivocal.[27] One acknowledged that under the new system:

The group leaders are much more sort of strong and involved in things than we had two or three years ago … And if a case review manager thinks I've got it wrong, they will have no hesitation to actually say 'You got it wrong' … here's a potential problem if you have a commissioner with a … very strong personality who doesn't take argument. (#19)

The decision field, including, as it does, the *Casework Guidance Note on Screening* (Criminal Cases Review Commission, 2011k)[28] and the real possibility test under section 13(1) of the Criminal Appeal Act 1995, has shifted because of changing policy on screening. As such, the decision frame—the structure of knowledge, values, experience, and meanings that decision-makers employ in choosing how to respond to applications—has also shifted as it now involves other people, with their unique characteristics, approaches, and backgrounds. There is now scope for negotiation and collaboration, with the inevitable impact on outcomes.

Changes to screening were not only motivated by a desire for increased consistency but also by the need to improve fairness and efficiency. Under the previous system, commissioners could turn down unmeritorious cases quickly because they worked independently. While this may appear to be efficient, in effect it unfairly prioritized unmeritorious cases, because commissioners dealt with these quickly while potentially meritorious cases were put in a queue to be reviewed later (#72, #66, #70, #68). Now, all applications go into the same queue regardless of their potential merit. The need for efficiency became particularly crucial after 2012, when the number of applications to the Commission rose steeply following the introduction of a new, simplified application process.[29] This led to longer waiting times for applicants.[30] It was therefore decided to shift more of the 'valuable' commissioner resource (Criminal Cases Review Commission, 2014a) from stage one decision-making to the important stage two.[31]

Responses to the change in screening policy

While all non-commissioner staff we interviewed were in favour of moving away from commissioner-centred screening, not all commissioners approved of the new policy. One spoke positively about it, citing efficiency and the prior problems with variability in commissioners' screening speed (#77). Others, however, expressed strong objections (#22). There was no doubt that screening had become 'an extremely

[27] When commissioners were still fully in charge of no-appeal and reapplication cases, an interviewee informed us, staff did challenge commissioners on their screening decisions: 'About two-thirds, they agreed to take them back, and a third of them, they dug their heels in and said, "No, I still want it to go through for a review." And that is largely determined by which commissioner it was, not the merits of the argument! Some of them don't like other people marking their homework' (#64).

[28] However, see Chapter 8 on sexual abuse cases where commissioners sometimes did not follow the Casework Guidance Note.

[29] The number of applications increased from around 1,000 a year to 1,470 in 2012/13 and 1,625 in 2013/14 (Criminal Cases Review Commission, 2014a). The new application form (Easy Read Form) is available at https://ccrc.gov.uk/making-application/how-to-apply/.

[30] For applicants at liberty, the time from receipt of the application to allocation to a CRM for review increased from 9 months in 2012/13 to 10.4 months in 2013/14 and 15.3 months in 2014/15, and decreased to 12.7 months in 2015/16 (Criminal Cases Review Commission, 2013a, 2014b, 2015a, 2016a).

[31] The new screening policy was also considered to eliminate duplication of effort by commissioners and group leaders, who both gave directions to CRMs before they commenced their reviews (#66, #70, #68, #64).

sensitive area' (#72), with commissioners split between those who believed that only they should be responsible for stage one decision-making and those who considered it best to devolve this power. The following quote captures the politics behind the new stage one decision-making and the divisions between commissioners and other members of staff:

[Screening] used to be entirely the preserve of the commissioners because ... they had special powers that were granted by the Queen to enable them to do things that mere mortals weren't capable of, but we decided that wasn't the case anymore and that, actually, looking at cases when they first come in is ... something that other people can do as well. (#64)

Most commissioners did not directly express their unease with the change in policy; instead, they emphasized their role as decision-makers.

My own role as a commissioner is as a decision-maker; it's my task to make the decision. (#22)

The commissioners make all decisions, and we make decisions on everything, provisional decisions and final decisions, so who looks at cases to get it to that point is up to the management. (#74)

By contrast, other staff, not in the role of commissioner, who were in favour of the new screening policy were more forthcoming about what they saw as commissioners' reservations:

Some of them are, in my view, overly concerned about their perceived status—[for them] it's not right that somebody else is making important decisions in relation to how a case goes. (#64)

The way it's gone now, you don't have that ability to instantly dispose of a case ... The commissioners before, I think, liked the idea that you could sort of summarily get rid of cases. (#68)

Some of them, I think, still wish that perhaps they were doing it themselves. Perhaps those are commissioners who ... tend more towards the view that commissioner input right at the beginning of the case is really very valuable to forming the route of the review, which actually isn't how it works in practice, in my experience. (#72)

These views on screening are about control. For some commissioners, being a decision-maker means being able to determine which cases are worth reviewing when applications *first* reach the Commission, to determine how cases are investigated *during* the review, and to make the *final* judgement on referrals. However, commissioner input at the beginning of a review is not typical of other organizations within the broader legal system. In the police, border control, and regulatory authorities, junior officials are normally the first point of contact, acting as 'gatekeepers of formal legal process' (Hawkins, 2002:26). In emergency medicine, a triage system relies on nurses or junior doctors to assess the medical needs of patients before a case is referred to specialist doctors. The Commission's old screening policy, by contrast, had its most senior members of staff dealing with incoming cases.

Post 2013, devolved responsibility for preparing a stage one case for a review, from commissioners to group leaders, seemed to result in something of a culture shift across the Commission. In estimating the amount of work required for a CRM, deciding what material should be preserved or obtained, and instructing how a case should be reviewed, commissioners had previously been rather didactic. Group leaders, now tasked with this responsibility, were keen not to impose a direction on the course of the CRM's review, emphasizing that 'advisory notes' (Criminal Cases Review Commission, 2013b) to CRMs were couched in 'fairly neutral language', such as 'here's what I've read; this seems to be the difficulty in what the applicant is saying, but you need to look at it' (#68). Group leaders gave the impression that they did not want to 'tie the CRM's hands with [their] comments' (#70).

Noting that commissioners varied in their approach from providing 'very, very succinct and brief' (#70) advisory notes to writing a document 'a couple of pages [long] that was almost a review in itself' (#68), they described commissioner screening as prescriptive. This included giving instructions on how a CRM should review a case as well as predicting the likely outcome of the case:

Some would really be directing you and saying 'make sure you don't ... go down this blind alley' ... and would try and really kind of control. (#68)

If you're saying ... 'I can't see how there is any merit' you are effectively allocating something for it to be closed. (#68)

Some will take very strong views of the case at the outset and say ... 'I can't see any prospect this is going to be referred.' (#70)

Group leaders' 'more relaxed approach' (#66) to case management was underpinned by their confidence in CRMs as independent investigators ('[they are] recruited for their ability to analyse and to go out and investigate' (#68)). Their reluctance to be prescriptive was also associated with a healthy dose of scepticism about what can be achieved in screening. The following quotes illustrate, again, the difficulty of predicting the outcome of the review at screening.

There's every chance that a CRM is going to, when they do more reading, spot a point that I haven't. (#68)

CRM's knowledge of the case is nearly always going to be better than whoever's screened it because they've just read into it in more detail and spent more time doing it. (#70)

My view is that it's only really when the case gets to the case review manager that ... time is ... really valuably invested, because, otherwise, all you're doing is taking little snapshots of information and working out, well, how much more do I read? ... So, you never get the full picture of the case, so you don't get that overall feel for it. (#72)

The limitation of what can be achieved at screening raises concerns, and justifies the recent policy change from a commissioner-centric process to consultative decision-making involving CRMs and group leaders. It represents a shift from a hierarchical culture, in which a commissioner's decision field was to a large extent unconstrained (especially when closing cases), to a more consultative one where commissioners still made decisions but with the knowledge that those decisions could be challenged.

The next section changes focus from individuals to the impact on decision-making of the field and the surround.

Guilty Pleas: Influence of the Surround

As discussed above, differences in individual frames help us to understand variability in decision-making. Baumgartner (1992), however, argues that discretionary outcomes are in fact highly patterned, guided by shared tacit understandings and organizational routines (Chapter 3). She argues that:

[Exercise of discretion] follows clear and specifiable principles and is remarkably patterned and consistent. The decisions officials make when left to their own devices are not mysteriously rooted in the unknown peculiarities of individual cases, but can be anticipated with considerable accuracy from general formulations. They are not fashioned anew in every encounter, but arise from forces that transcend particular incidents. (Baumgartner, 1992:129–30)

We argue that notwithstanding the different frames observed by those involved in stage one decision-making, there are distinct patterns in the way decision-makers interpret and process cases. In this sense, decision frames must be understood in relation to the surround and field (Hawkins, 2002). Here, and in the following section, we identify practical 'triggers' within the decision field at the individual and organizational level, which are 'rules of thumb to cut down on the amount of processing needed' (Lloyd-Bostock, 1992:48). The triggers operate as shortcuts to carry out effective decision-making at stage one.

The reduction in sentence for a guilty plea is widely used in the criminal justice system in England and Wales and is essential for the efficient processing of cases (Ashworth and Redmayne, 2010:chapt:10; Horne, 2013, 2016; McConville, 1998).[32] Though there are administrative reasons for the system to embrace pleas, and incentives for defendants to accept a deal, courts treat a guilty plea as a confession as well as a sign of remorse, as if only guilty defendants will enter a guilty plea (McConville, 1998; *R v Boal*[33]). However, research has shown that defendants can be pressured into pleading guilty to a lesser charge, typically, to receive a reduction in a sentence if the evidence against them appears to be strong (Baldwin and McConville, 1977; Horne, 2013; McConville et al., 1991; Runciman, 1993).[34] A former commissioner offers the following insights on guilty plea applicants:

[T]here have been numerous cases put to the Commission where the applicant has asserted that his or her determination to fight the case at trial was overborne by his or her solicitors and/or counsel insisting upon a plea of guilty. In many cases, intuition most strongly suggests that the applicant (grudgingly or otherwise) accepted advice to earn a discount from sentence by pleading guilty. (Elks, 2008:326)

Horne (2013:6) expressed discomfort with the 'considerable difficulty' defendants face in appealing against a conviction secured following a guilty plea. It is possible for a conviction by guilty plea in the Crown Court to be quashed by the Court under section 2 of the Criminal Appeal Act 1968; however, the Court has shown itself to be extremely reluctant to do this. The decision in *Kelly and Connolly*,[35] a leading case on guilty pleas, stated that 'the scope for finding that an unequivocal and intentional plea of guilty can lead to an unsafe conviction must be exceptional and rare'. In a more recent case, *R v Asiedu*,[36] the Court also reiterated its position that a defendant who pleads guilty is making a formal admission that he is guilty of the offence:

[O]rdinarily, once he has admitted such facts by an unambiguous and deliberately intended plea of guilt, there cannot be an appeal against his conviction, for the simple reason that there is nothing unsafe about a conviction based on the defendant's own voluntary confession in open court. A defendant will not normally be permitted in this court to say that he has changed his

---

[32] The reduction in sentence following a guilty plea is formally recognized under section 144 of the Criminal Justice Act 2003. In 2014, approximately 90 per cent of defendants pleaded guilty at the Crown Court (Sentencing Council, 2015:6). The Sentencing Council for England and Wales (2017:4) justifies sentencing discount for guilty pleas by reference to the public interest and protection of victims and witnesses, arguing that a guilty plea results in a speedy trial, which in turn saves time and money on investigations and trials. The use of sentence discounts for guilty pleas also spares witnesses and victims the trauma of having to give evidence in court.

[33] [1992] 95 Cr App R 272.

[34] Horn (2013:5) highlighted the pragmatic use of discounts for guilty pleas by explaining the Code of Conduct for Barristers, which allows barristers to continue representing a defendant who 'for reasons of his own' pleads guilty while continuing to tell his lawyers he is innocent. In these situations, defendants can enter a guilty plea as long as they do not argue their innocence in court.

[35] [2002] EWCA Crim 2957.   [36] [2015] EWCA Crim 714.

mind and now wishes to deny what he has previously thus admitted in the Crown Court. (*R v Asiedu*, para:19)

The Court went on to highlight exceptions when a guilty plea does not prevent the Court from quashing a conviction as unsafe. For example, the Court may quash a conviction after a guilty plea if it finds that a defendant has been denied a fair trial (see also footnote 37). In *Asiedu*, counsel argued that non-disclosure was an abuse of process and led to the applicant being misled by the Crown and to pleading guilty. However, the Court stated that non-disclosure is not by itself an abuse of process (para:27), and held that the defendant's guilty plea established his guilt (para:35). This case illustrates the Court's stance; it will not quash a defendant's conviction after a guilty plea unless irregularities at trial amounted to an abuse of process (according to its rather narrow definition).

Here, the Court's responses to cases provides the broad setting in which decision-making takes place; the surround. Not surprisingly, the Commission's approach—developed within its decision field—mirrors the Court's. The Formal Memorandum on Discretion in Referrals justifies turning down a case even when a conviction appears to be unsafe:

There may be rare cases where the Commission considers that an admission is made by an applicant in such circumstances that, *even if there were a real possibility of the convictions being quashed*, it should consider exercising its discretion not to refer in the public interest. (Criminal Cases Review Commission, 2016b:para:8, emphasis added)

The Commission's approach to guilty pleas is clearly influenced by the Court.[37] The Casework Guidance Note on Appeals against Conviction Following a Plea of Guilty provides a review of case law, and, drawing on this, 'considers the approach the Crown Court and Court of Appeal will be likely to adopt' (Criminal Cases Review Commission, 2011p:para:1). The Casework Guidance Note concludes by stating that 'the Court has repeatedly made it clear that only very unusual circumstances will persuade it to quash a conviction following a guilty plea' (Criminal Cases Review Commission, 2011p:para:44).[38]

The Commission's decision field on guilty pleas, articulated in the documents above, is thus shaped by the unwavering stance of the surround—the previous decisions by the Court. The Commission has discretion to refer guilty plea cases to the Court (Elks, 2008:326), but chooses to take a pragmatic approach and to work within the surround on guilty plea cases. It is assumed that unnecessarily challenging the Court, where cases are likely to be dismissed, will not benefit the applicant. An interviewee illustrated this pragmatism regarding stage one decision-making, expressing reluctance to carry out a detailed review if an applicant had pleaded guilty:

Where somebody has pleaded guilty and then comes to us with something that makes you think, well, it's very, very unlikely that the Court of Appeal will vacate the plea, then it seems unreasonable to be doing what are quite intrusive checks [on complainants]. (#77)

---

[37] According to Commission policy, a conviction following a guilty plea may be referred if there is overwhelming new evidence that the conviction is unsafe, the plea was entered under duress, there was erroneous legal advice, there was an equivocal plea, the guilty plea was the result of an erroneous ruling on a point of law by the trial judge, or the guilty plea was entered in ignorance of prosecution malpractice (Criminal Cases Review Commission, 2016g).

[38] An interview conducted in 2011 demonstrates the tightening of standards for screening in guilty plea applications: 'We are now starting to challenge people if they've pleaded guilty to say at an early stage, "Well, you pleaded guilty. What do you say about your guilty plea? Are we going to get over that first before we look at anything else?" So I think we're more astute now, and I think we're more careful in the cases that we let through for review' (#17).

One commissioner's general approach to screening was summarized as:

If the person pleaded guilty, I will get the sentencing remarks and the Crown Court file to give me the background to the case. And if it was a contested trial, I will always get the summing up and the sentencing remarks. So it is reviewed, you know, it's reviewed to that extent. But then it won't be an agonizingly careful review of the summing up—for example, to check that directions were given properly ... I am not looking at discrepancies and points of detail in the trial, as opposed to on a bigger picture—do I think there's something wrong, that went wrong here? (#19)

The quote demonstrates the approach of this commissioner to screening, but it also reveals that guilty pleas are viewed as a distinct category requiring slightly different treatment from other categories of cases. For example, in sexual offence cases, guilty pleas often are used as a justification to circumvent an existing policy to carry out credibility checks on complainants (Chapter 8 discusses sexual offence cases).

You always start with the applicant's application, looking to see what they're saying went wrong. In sex cases, we routinely make wider checks on issues to do with credibility of complainants ... So, our policy is routinely to do that, unless we think it's not necessary. So, for example, if you've got a very young complainant or the applicant has pleaded guilty or various things like that, then you probably wouldn't do it. (#77)

Another commissioner also expressed doubts about conducting a credibility check if an applicant had pleaded guilty:

If you look now at our [Formal] Memorandum on sex cases, ... it is very strongly set out with the presumption that we will always do credibility checks ... and that worries me in the sense of what happens when you, one day, get us doing checks that we shouldn't have done? For example, [if] it was a guilty plea, or there was just such overwhelming evidence against the applicant that the crime, he or she did commit the crime. [If] it's a vulnerable complainant—we carry out credibility tests, they find out about it and kill themselves—it's not that unthinkable a situation. (#36)

These two quotes express the commissioners' understanding of the invasive nature of a credibility check and the impact it may have on a complainant, as well as their view that applicants who pleaded guilty should not be entitled to benefit from such invasive checks on complainants (Chapter 8 discusses the development of Commission policy on carrying out credibility checks in sexual offence cases). The quotes may also be interpreted as expressing general dissatisfaction with the blanket policy on credibility checks in sexual offence cases, but guilty plea cases are clearly considered a category that ought to be exempt from this policy.

Other interviews also shed light on interpretation of guilty pleas in general. One commissioner remarked, in the context of historical sexual abuse investigations: 'Some of them pleaded guilty, so I mean it obviously did happen' (#31). Similarly, a CRM describing the character of a complainant stated:

She sort of stood in the witness box and said, 'I was messed up as a child and as a young person, but now, as an adult, I'm okay ... I don't get in trouble' and actually, she was waiting to plead guilty to some benefit fraud offences. (#5)

These two comments suggest that for some at the Commission—following the approach of the Court—a guilty plea is synonymous with a confession of guilt, rather than a tactical approach to securing a reduced sentence or a product of poor legal advice.

In our purposive sample, excluding asylum cases (where all applicants had pleaded guilty, see Chapter 10), there were just four cases in which the applicant had pleaded guilty that were subject to a stage two full review (cases EE3, EE21, EE8, and CS1).[39] Cases EE3 and EE21 were both referred to the Court; the former was upheld, the latter was quashed. However, these cases were unusual in that bodies external to the Commission had initiated the applications. The Attorney General's Interdepartmental Group approached the Commission regarding case EE3, and the Commission treated it as a priority case even though the applicant had died.[40] In case EE21, the Special Crime Division of the Crown Prosecution Service contacted the Commission and indicated that the Crown would not oppose the appeal if the case was referred.[41] Thus, these were cases brought to the Commission by external bodies rather than being screened in for a review through the internal process. In cases EE3, EE21, and EE8 all applicants were vulnerable—suffering from a severe personality disorder (case EE21), in need of psychiatric treatment (case EE3), or with a low IQ (EE8)—all of which cast doubt on their capacity to fully appreciate the plea they were entering.[42]

These cases show that in certain situations the Commission will refer guilty plea cases, but Horne (2016:282) found that, on the whole, the Commission routinely screened out applicants who had pleaded guilty, for all types of cases, including reapplications, no-appeal cases, and post-appeal/first-application cases.[43] She argued that the Commission chose efficiency over remedying wrongful convictions following a guilty plea, screening out guilty plea cases through 'a highly abbreviated process', thus risking 'overlooking meritorious cases' (Horne, 2016:251). Lloyd-Bostock (1992)—in her analysis concerning the screening of accident reports by British factory inspectors— found that inspectors engaged in routine decision-making categorized cases to achieve 'cognitive economy'. Inspectors have to make decisions on large numbers of accident reports and need to develop strategies for processing them quickly. She found that inspectors achieved cognitive economy by 'using some powerful heuristics or rules of thumb', which reduced the amount of information processing required (Lloyd-Bostock, 1992:48). In this sense, the Commission uses the existence of guilty pleas as a shortcut to achieve cognitive economy at stage one decision-making.

While recognizing the usefulness of, and the need for, shortcuts, Lloyd-Bostock (1992:72) warns that routine decisions tend to miss new trends and that they can be inflexible in adapting to unique cases. The following example from our data demonstrates her point. During 2014–16, the number of referrals where applicants pleaded guilty significantly increased. Between 2010 and 2016, forty-nine guilty plea cases were referred to the Court; of these, thirty-two cases were referred to the Court between 2014 and 2016 (Criminal Cases Review Commission, 2016g). The increase in guilty plea referrals was a direct response to the Commission's growing awareness that refugees and asylum

---

[39] See Chapter 7 for more detail concerning cases EE3, EE21, and EE8.

[40] The Interdepartmental Group was set up, following the decision of *R v Cannings* [2004] EWCA Crim 01, to consider homicide convictions where the victim was less than 2 years old. The applicant (deceased at the time of application) was charged with two offences, infanticide and endeavouring to conceal the birth of her child. She pleaded guilty to infanticide but not guilty to concealing the birth of her child. The Commission argued that the applicant pleaded guilty due to the desire to 'get the matter over with', and that it was in her emotional and psychological best interests to do so. The Court dismissed the appeal.

[41] Without conducting its own analysis of the relevant facts or law, but basing its decision on new DNA evidence provided by the Crown Prosecution Service, the Commission referred the case and the conviction for murder of a young woman was quashed.

[42] Case CS1, a rape and indecent assault case, did not share the characteristics described in the other cases. The screening commissioner, in the case record, simply did what the legal representatives asked for in the application (examined social service and Crown Prosecution files). The case was not referred but was subjected to a stage two review.

[43] Horne's study drew on three sample periods in 2011, 2012, and 2013.

seekers were being wrongfully convicted of entering the country illegally (Sato et al., 2017). These cases relate to people who could not obtain travel documents lawfully and were erroneously advised by defence lawyers that they should plead guilty. These asylum cases comprise three-quarters (twenty-four of thirty-two) of the guilty plea referrals mentioned above (Criminal Cases Review Commission, 2016g).

The Commission, at first, erroneously screened out asylum cases, perhaps due to the internal culture that viewed the existence of guilty pleas as a trigger for closing cases.[44] It did not have an internal policy on asylum cases but realized at around 2011 that these cases were not sporadic but were indicative of a larger cluster of cases of refugees and asylum seekers being erroneously advised by defence lawyers to plead guilty and hence wrongfully convicted. A 2012 internal review of previously rejected cases revealed that cases were screened out at stage one due to applicants' pleading guilty at magistrates' court (Sato et al., 2017; see Chapter 10).[45] While Horne's (2016:256) analysis of guilty plea cases across offences found that there was a 'lack of coherent account of what makes a guilty plea conviction "safe" or "unsafe" ', in asylum cases, the Commission took seriously guilty plea cases, resisting the working assumption of the field (see Chapter 10).

Legal Representation

Impact of legal representation on stage one decisions

An application to the Commission can be assisted by a legal representative (Criminal Cases Review Commission, 2015c).[46] On average, a quarter of applicants are legally represented (Hodgson and Horne, 2009).[47] Legal representatives can influence the decision-making process before a case reaches the Commission and during its investigation. Good legal representation may increase the possibility of an application progressing (appropriately or inappropriately) to stage two review. If an applicant has no legal representation, the Commission (formerly just a single commissioner) is the sole adjudicator.

Studies of the English and Scottish Commissions (Hodgson and Horne, 2009; Scottish Criminal Cases Review Commission, 2010) examined the effect of legal representation on the likelihood of applications being screened in at stage one and referred to the Court at stage two. Both studies found that legally represented applications had a higher chance of being referred at stage two and an even higher chance of being screened in at stage one.[48] These studies show the importance of having legal

---

[44] In Sato et al. (2017) we also argued that the political depiction of migrants as 'deviant' and the legislative discourse of 'crimmigration' (Stumpf, 2006) may have influenced stage one decision-makers to miss these unsafe convictions.

[45] The Commission originally thought that these applicants should appeal their convictions before applying to the Commission. Later, it realized that since the applicants had pleaded guilty in a magistrates' court, rather than in the Crown Court, they were unable to appeal their convictions other than through a referral by the Commission under section 108 of the Magistrates' Court Act 1980.

[46] This assistance can take various forms, including representation by family members, relatives, friends, or advocacy groups.

[47] On average, a third of applicants were legally represented during 2005–7 (Hodgson and Horne, 2009).

[48] For example, the study of the English Commission found that around 20 per cent of legally represented applicants were rejected at stage one, compared with 50 per cent of unrepresented applicants (Hodgson and Horne, 2009). The difference in outcomes between applicants with and without legal representation became narrower at stage two, when 8 per cent of legally represented applicants, but only 2 per cent of applicants without legal representation, had their cases referred (Hodgson and Horne, 2009).

representation, especially at stage one. Hodgson and Horne (2009) attributed the gap in the impact of legal representation between stages one and two to the Commission's reasons for referral being different from those identified by the legal representatives. They argued that by stage two, the Commission relies less on the input from legal representatives and more on their own investigative work:[49]

This demonstrates the importance of the work that the [Commission] carries out on its own initiative and its ability to respond to new information during the course of its review, and the danger of limiting a review to the grounds set out in the application (Hodgson and Horne, 2009).

The report on the study of the English Commission, however, expressed caution about making causal links between legal representation and success as measured by decisions at stages one and two. It argued that lawyers may put more effort into cases that are more likely to be referred, and suggested that lawyers may filter out cases they consider unmeritorious (Hodgson and Horne, 2009). The Scottish study found evidence suggesting that lawyers do indeed filter out unmeritorious cases.[50] A lawyer with extensive experience of applications to the Commission confirmed that lawyers may well cherry pick cases:

We, like many appeal lawyers, are doing our own screening. You know, of every ten letters that might hit my desk, only three, four, five are … proceeding, so, you know, we're doing some screening before we even start. (#12)

The filtering of cases by legal representatives before they reach the Commission should not be a concern if the lawyers are careful and effective and thereby save Commission resources. However, there is a danger of false positives, of lawyers incorrectly identifying a safe conviction as unsafe, and then improving the quality of the application sufficiently to persuade the Commission to screen in an unmeritorious case and even to refer it to the Court. Given the parsimonious approach of the Commission, this should not be a great concern. However, false negatives must: lawyers may incorrectly identify an unsafe conviction as safe and refuse to represent an applicant, resulting in a case not reaching the Commission at all or being submitted without representation and therefore with the evidence and information not presented as powerfully as it might be. Given the considerable reductions to the legal aid budget over the past years, this should be cause for some consternation (see Chapter 14). The Commission can rectify a false positive by closing a case, but it cannot rectify a false negative if an applicant is dissuaded from applying.

'Good' legal representation

The above discussion treats legal representation as if it were a dichotomous variable; applicants either have a lawyer or they do not. However, much depends on the quality of legal representation. The range in the quality of legal representation is clear (Hodgson and Horne, 2009; Maddocks and Tan, 2009; Scottish Criminal Cases Review Commission, 2010). Lawyers can make a positive determinative effect, for

---

[49] In eleven out of seventy-four cases referred in the 2005–7 sampling period, none of the referral issues were identified by applicants or their legal representatives (Hodgson and Horne, 2009).

[50] The Scottish study found that the Scottish Legal Aid Board received 308 applications for advice and assistance between 2007 and 2010, and the Scottish Commission received 200 applications from people with legal representation during the same period (Scottish Criminal Cases Review Commission, 2010).

example by reversing a provisional decision not to refer (Hodgson and Horne, 2009). They sometimes make no difference to an application, serving only as an 'application solicitor'—a named legal representative identified by the applicant, but offering little or no input (Maddocks and Tan, 2009:126).[51] And, according to a few commissioners, lawyers can be 'a nightmare ... they get in the way ... they're unhelpful, they don't let you get on with things ... and you can spend more time managing that relationship than getting [on with the investigation]' (#29).

While there may be some less than perfect legal representatives,[52] the Commission encourages applicants to have legally representation:

Whilst non-assisted applicants will be thoroughly and effectively reviewed, it remains Commission policy to encourage constructive and effective representation in order that applicants may be assisted to put forward their best case. (Criminal Cases Review Commission, 2015c:para:2)

That legal representation is preferred by the Commission, and has been found to have an impact on case outcomes (Hodgson and Horne, 2009), is not surprising given that this is true of other situations in which lay people come into contact with the legal system. In both criminal and civil law, legal representation for defendants and claimants is often considered essential.[53] Article 6 of the European Convention on Human Rights, which protects the right to a fair trial, includes the right to legal assistance and free access to legal aid (section 3c). This right justifies and reaffirms the existence of, and the need for, legal representatives at all stages of the legal process, and the Commission is probably no different—regardless of its neutral, inquisitorial rather than adversarial approach to investigating wrongful convictions.

While recognizing the importance of, and preference for, legally assisted applicants, the Commission is clear that it will not discriminate against unrepresented applicants: 'we welcome all applications, whether or not the applicant is legally represented' (Criminal Cases Review Commission, 2015g:1). The Easy Read application form, introduced in 2012, epitomizes the efforts made by the Commission to be inclusive. It uses 'simple words and pictures to aid understanding by people who struggle with reading and writing' (Criminal Cases Review Commission, 2013a:29). This principled approach is commendable and to some extent necessary, because of cuts to legal aid that mean representation at appeal is hard to secure but also that representation at trial might be weaker (Criminal Cases Review Commission, 2016a). Indeed, experiences of incompetent defence counsel at trial can leave some applicants reluctant to seek legal representation. As one Commission staff member told us:

Many applicants come to us unrepresented and remain unrepresented. Many applicants feel they've been badly let down by the system, including their own lawyers, and the last thing they want is a lawyer, you know, letting them down again. (#24)

Despite the principled approach to the equal treatment of all applicants and the improved access for vulnerable applicants to the Commission, in practice, of course,

---

[51] One interviewee said: 'That's not unusual actually, that the representative does very little more than simply packaging up what the applicant has said and sending it on to us' (#34).

[52] Concerns have been raised that some legal representatives do not understand basic aspects of the Commission's remit and can submit applications that are ineligible or present no reviewable grounds (Hodgson and Horne, 2009; Maddocks and Tan, 2009).

[53] Representing oneself is not encouraged, though it is increasingly common due to cuts to legal aid (see Bar Association website on 'Representing yourself in court', available at http://www.barcouncil. org.uk/using-a-barrister/representing-yourself-in-court/).

there seems to be a limit to what the Commission can do with a weak application. A member of staff mused on the advantages of representation:

you can get more material than you do with ... just on their own. And it will be English and you can understand it, so that saves you having to go back for lots more information. (#19)

Commission staff were in fact unanimous that when legal representation is good, it makes a significant difference to the progress of the case.[54] They were careful, however, to note that the quality of the application does not determine the outcome of the case, and good legal representation itself could not guarantee a referral:

You'll get a lawyer signposting you to what they think the issues are that you need to look at, and that doesn't mean that if they're not signposted we wouldn't find them, because one of the things that we are very cautious about is simply accepting what we see at face value. (#24)

   If I get representations from ... [people] I know, who I have got huge respect for, say, and I know personally, and I just know that this guy or this lady is not going to put in representations unless they believe in them, then clearly it's going to have an impact upon—it's not going to affect my final decision, but it's going to have an impact on what I do with the case. (#35)

The first quote reiterates the position that all applications—good or bad, unrepresented or represented—are treated equally. The challenge of living up to this principled position is illustrated by the second interviewee's reflection about working with well-known and 'respected' lawyers—which, while emphasizing impartiality regarding the final decision, acknowledged taking into account a legal representative's good reputation. The following interviewees similarly conceded the impact of a good lawyer's input on screening decisions:

It was a case that could potentially have been closed down quite quickly. It was a case with fairly high-powered legal representation ... It's harder [to screen out a case] when people have put a lot of effort ... So, I think it would have gone to full review. (#7)

   It has to be a factor influencing your mind that, if a reputable solicitor sends you an application form, on the whole it means they've looked at the case themselves and think it has, it is a runner. That it might go somewhere, and you will take it seriously on that basis ... And obviously there's a tendency to say 'Oh this is hopeless' and just not take it further ... But ... there are a few firms who actively put you off, you know, seeing this is from Mr X, you think 'Oh my god!' (#19)

That said, commission staff were keen to impress upon us the importance of equitable treatment:

If a really good submission is put together ... and it's backed by ... [name of a lawyer] who's got a really good reputation and ... solicitors of repute, ... inevitably I think you have to look at it carefully but I would, I would like to think that ... we would be applying the same sort of logic and reasoning to any case, whether they're represented or not. (#40)

Drivers of Stage One Decision-making

Analysis of screening by commissioners under the previous system demonstrated individualistic decision frames, which were heavily influenced by commissioners' different

---

[54] For example, a member of staff noted: 'It varies, and there's no doubt that a good lawyer will make a difference in that you'll get a very clear set of submissions ... You'll get a lawyer signposting you to what they think the issues are that you need to look at' (#24). In another interview, a CRM talked about experiences with a legal representative: 'Sometimes you'll get a very active lawyer who is ... in contact a lot, not just chasing, but trying to assist, and that's got to be good' (#50).

and sometimes competing outlooks, values, and backgrounds. This led to variability in practice that is hard to justify. The new screening policy changed the decision field from commissioner-centric to consultative, bringing group leaders and CRMs into the decision field. While not all commissioners welcomed the new screening policy, the inclusion of group leaders and CRMs—by design—helps mitigate idiosyncratic decision-making by commissioners. Time will tell if the new screening policy will maintain the benefit of diverse individual decision-making approaches while increasing consistency in outcomes within the 'zone of tolerance' (Hawkins, 2002:427).

In addition to individual frames that shaped stage one decision-making, we also identified practical 'triggers' within the decision field at the individual and organizational level, which operated as shortcuts to effective decision-making. For no-appeal cases, the unpredictable stance of the surround concerning what constitutes exceptional circumstances, as seen by evolving Court jurisprudence, made it difficult for the Commission to develop a definitive decision field on exceptional circumstances. While there seemed to be confusion among decision-makers on what constituted exceptional circumstances, sexual offence cases provided something of an exception to the screening 'rules' in no-appeal cases. Similarly, our research suggests that legal representatives, especially those with a good reputation, provided a shortcut to decisions to screen in applications. Finally, a guilty plea operated within the decision field to prompt commission staff to screen out applicants efficiently.

This decision field—with prompts to trigger screening decisions one way or another—was not informed by the Commission's legislative framework, but developed as a pragmatic approach to accommodate the surround. In this case, the Court has developed positions on guilty pleas and what constitutes exceptional circumstances through its case law (though the Court can be somewhat unpredictable when it comes to no-appeal cases). Decision fields developed by the Commission over time, however, are not error-proof. The practice of screening out applicants who pleaded guilty did not effectively differentiate guilty plea applicants whose convictions were safe or unsafe. On this issue, the Commission eventually identified and corrected the wrongful convictions of refugees and asylum seekers, as clear exceptions to the guilty plea assumption in their decision field. The realization that there was a flaw within the decision field led to modifications, which were later reflected in the Commission's formal policies, thus bringing policy in line with practice.

The use of these practical prompts or triggers within the Commission's decision field—concerning guilty pleas, 'good' legal representation, and exceptional circumstances in sexual offence cases—to guide stage one decision-making, may imply 'quick and dirty' decision-making, inferior to an 'all things considered' approach (Schauer, 1991). However, as discussed above, research has shown that the use of shortcuts, which deliberately prioritize part of the available information, can enable correct (sometimes more correct) decisions in less time than models that try to examine all information (Gigerenzer, 2008; Gigerenzer and Goldstein, 1996). In fact, the use of shortcuts is commonplace in our everyday lives. Stockbrokers need to make fast decisions about which stock to buy or sell when only limited information is available; doctors must decide quickly, without doing all possible tests, whether to diagnose a patient with chest pain as suffering from a heart attack.

At stage one decision-making, the Commission must make inferences about cases in a limited time and with limited knowledge in order to leave time and resources at stage two for a more exploratory and detailed 'all things considered' review. Making correct inferences about cases when they first reach the Commission is important, and the intuitive desire may be to investigate fully at this early stage before deciding. However, time is limited, and acting quickly at stage one, especially considering rising numbers of applications, is crucial. The findings described in this chapter suggest that the Commission, in practice, uses 'triggers' as shortcuts to help guide decision-making at stage one. As long as the Commission can adapt its triggers to the changing surround (as it did in responding to the guilty pleas of asylum seekers), this may well be a sensible and an efficient way to screen. The introduction of a deliberative screening policy involving group leaders and CRMs could also work as a safety net to avoid meritorious cases being screened out where triggers may be used too readily.

7

Managing Uncertainty in Forensic and Expert Evidence Cases

We rely a lot more on science than we did. And I think science comes clothed with a veneer of certainty which it isn't always appropriate to have. So, today's certainty is tomorrow's uncertainty. (#25)[1]

Introduction

In the rising tide of public concern about the risks of wrongful conviction that led to the establishment of the Criminal Cases Review Commission ('the Commission'), the notion that forensic evidence might be unreliable, and hence a significant cause of miscarriages of justice, barely registered. Neither the potential fallibility of such science nor possible flaws in the way it was presented in the courtroom received more than cursory attention, and these issues rarely emerged in the course of appeals. Indeed, Malleson's (1993) study of 300 appeals, conducted for the 1993 Royal Commission on Criminal Justice, found only two appeals based on fresh expert scientific evidence, although the convictions in the *Birmingham Six* and the *Maguire Seven* cases during the 1970s and 1980s had relied on forensic science that was later discredited (see Chapter 1). However, when the Commission inherited the backlog of applications from the Home Office C3 Division (see Chapter 1), it would soon discover widespread problems, some of which became apparent as a result of new scientific research. The revelation that forensic science was neither immutable nor infallible would further undermine confidence in the ability of the criminal justice system to secure safe convictions.

Moreover, the first twenty years of the Commission has seen extensive scientific innovation. The Commission has had to respond to developments in crime scene management and forensic investigation; in the reliability of evidence from fibre analysis, blood and secretions, firearms discharge residue, finger printing, and new print marks (e.g. ears, shoes, etc.); in analysis of materials and substances (e.g. fire accelerants) and of locations (e.g. cell site analysis).

There have also been significant advances in the methodological approaches to the collation, interpretation, and presentation of expert testimony that have challenged certain orthodoxies at the 'front end' of criminal justice—in pre-trial investigations and in the courtroom—and in the post-conviction review process. Forensic analysis is a human endeavour and as such is susceptible to error, bias, and manipulation, which compromise its reliability (Kassin et al., 2013; Laurin, 2013). As we made clear in Chapter 5, recent years have seen growing unease among criminal justice professionals about the forensic science process. This has embraced concerns about fallibilities in the identification and collection of evidence; errors of technique in the examination of

---

[1] All interviews in this chapter are with Commission staff, including commissioners, case review managers, management staff, and advisers, unless we state otherwise.

Reasons to Doubt: Wrongful Convictions and the Criminal Cases Review Commission. © Carolyn Hoyle and Mai Sato 2019. Published 2019 by Oxford University Press.

evidence and in the interpretation of results; and misrepresentation of forensic science as more powerful and convincing than it really is, at both the pre-trial and trial stages (Dror and Bucht, 2012).

Error and fallibility have produced high-profile casualties. The fall from grace of eminent statisticians and forensic scientists has shaken the foundations of some convictions (philosophical and trial). Today, while lay persons still have considerable confidence in science, particularly DNA evidence, professionals working within criminal justice systems in many countries have begun to recognize that science and scientists are fallible. Indeed, a recent news article suggests that poor forensic science standards and a manipulation of evidence might have affected more than 10,000 cases in the UK alone, with experts anticipating that it will take up to five years for all the falsified data to be re-examined, leaving many who may have been wrongfully convicted of serious crimes in prison without recourse to review (Beckford, 2017b).[2] In this climate of growing scepticism, experts are under scrutiny as never before.

Expert evidence is written or oral testimony by someone who has specialized knowledge and qualifications equipping them to provide both facts and opinion on technical or scientific matters of relevance to a case. Hence, unlike other non-expert witnesses, who may only give evidence about what they have seen directly or experienced in the case being tried, they may also be asked about broader, relevant issues on the basis of their knowledge and professional experience. Inevitably, expert testimony is likely to be unfamiliar and sometimes impenetrable to non-experts, creating the risk of erroneous decisions by prosecutors and defence counsel, as well as judges and juries. This risk is far greater if the expert evidence is unreliable, as was acknowledged by Lord Justice Leveson in a speech to the Forensic Science Society in 2010:

it is, in my opinion, perfectly clear that expert evidence of doubtful reliability may be admitted too freely with insufficient explanation of the basis for reaching specific conclusions, be challenged too weakly by the opposing advocate and be accepted too readily by the judge or jury at the end of the trial. (Lord Justice Leveson, 2010:15)

This chapter reviews how the Commission makes decisions in cases that 'turn on' forensic science and expert testimony, where scientific data or expertise were instrumental in securing a conviction, and where that science or expertise is now challenged by those seeking an appeal. In doing so, it considers the influence of developments in the 'surround' of the Commission; the broad setting within which decision-making at the Commission takes place (most notably, evolutions in forensic science and the interpretation of evidence). Developments in the scientific landscape require consequent paradigm shifts both in the 'field', in the policies and guidelines of the Commission, and in the 'frame', how Commission staff make sense of, and respond to, expert evidence. Hence, alongside knowledge of the criminal process, statute, and evolving case law, case review managers ('CRMs') and commissioners must develop sufficient understanding of forensic science, and of how juries make sense of expert evidence, in order to investigate these cases and decide which could sensibly be referred back to the Court of Appeal ('the Court'). As Hawkins (2002:49) put it:

Changes that occur in the surround prompt changes in the particular setting for a decision, the field. Equally, a change in the surround may cause a change in the way certain events are interpreted and classified, the frame.

---

[2] Responding to this crisis in confidence, in October 2017 the government Forensic Science Regulator (2017) issued revised Codes of Practice and Conduct for forensic science providers and practitioners in the criminal justice system.

Hence, we consider how the surround impacts on the decision field in forensic and expert evidence cases, and how Commission staff approach their decision-making, by focusing on the main decision frames.

Our Sample of Forensic and Expert Evidence Cases

As explained in Chapter 2, we selected a sample of sixty-one cases involving forty-two applicants (some were reapplications following an unsuccessful application) that turn on forensic and expert evidence, twenty-five of which were referred back to the Court. This chapter draws primarily on these cases (with applicants in this category referred to by a unique identifier prefixed by 'EE'), but also on two cases from other categories—a sexual offence case (CS14) and a case where a police investigation formed part of the Commission review (PI1)—where there were challenges to forensic and expert evidence. As our Appendix shows, our expert evidence sample comprised convictions for the assault or killing of infants; sexual assaults; cases where DNA evidence was key to the appeal; and a range of other more disparate cases relying on psychiatric or psychological evidence (for example on confessions by highly suggestible and otherwise vulnerable defendants), on evidence on material fibres left at the scene of the crime, on firearms discharge residue found on the defendant, and on other forensic evidence. The applicant in many such cases was convicted for murder, but a significant proportion had convictions for rape or sexual assault (where forensic and expert evidence was considered alongside the issue of complainant credibility in sexual offence cases; see further, Chapter 8).

In nineteen of the twenty-five cases referred by the Commission, new expert testimony was presented to the Court that undermined the evidence presented at trial. In just over half of these cases that testimony explicitly referred to advances in research or scientific consensus since the trial. In just a fifth of referrals new forensic science was the key referral ground.

A brief description of three of our cases in Box 7.1 gives a sense of the types of issues raised in forensic and expert evidence cases.[3]

Box 7.1 Précises of forensic and expert evidence cases

Case EE2: The applicant was convicted on two counts of murder, with expert medical evidence presented at trial that she had smothered her two infant children. Following a post-mortem to consider whether they had died from 'sudden infant death syndrome' (SIDS),[a] the coroner's report had found the cause of the first death to be 'unascertained', though evidence had been presented of frequent admissions to hospital for sleep apnoea. The second child had also experienced episodes of sleep apnoea and other health problems but, when he died, SIDS was ruled out on the basis of medical expert evidence, including on the likelihood of two unexplained infant deaths in one family. This case—along with others—was referred to the Commission following the successful appeal against the conviction of Angela Cannings for killing her two infants. In these cases, the prosecution had relied on the evidence of a paediatrician whose claims that 'one cot death is tragic, two is

---

[3] As elsewhere, we have omitted identifying details even in cases that were referred and quashed by the Court, and are therefore in the public domain, to preserve anonymity for applicants and Commission staff (see further, Chapter 2).

suspicious and three is murder' had persuaded juries that babies in such cases had likely been smothered. His assertion that the chances of two babies in the same family dying of natural causes were one in 73 million was discredited by other expert witnesses, including from the Royal Statistical Society, and he was struck off by the General Medical Council for serious professional misconduct in presenting misleading evidence. The Commission reviewed evidence from these similar cases, but also instructed additional experts to comment on all evidence provided at trial. In doing so, it considered evidence that might distinguish this from the Cannings case, as well as consistent factors. It also sought fresh evidence on medical conditions suffered by each of the children. Ultimately, the main ground for referral back to the Court was that the primary expert medical evidence presented at trial had been significantly undermined since the conviction. The Court quashed the conviction.

Case EE9: The applicant was convicted of manslaughter following the death of his girlfriend's infant child (from cerebral swelling and subdural haematoma) while in the applicant's care. The expert witness for the prosecution had given evidence that the injuries to the brain were non-accidental, while the defence case was that the child died from a head injury sustained from a fall. The conviction was upheld on first appeal although fresh expert evidence was presented to support the defence case and an original expert witness for the prosecution had revised her opinion in light of her own accumulating experience and further developments in research. The Commission reviewed all evidence presented at trial and at appeal and obtained the opinions of additional experts on the likelihood of the injuries having been sustained from a fall. Further expert opinion was commissioned on the bruising to the child's head. Despite somewhat conflicting evidence from a range of experts, the Commission concluded that there remained no credible alternative explanation for the injuries sustained by the victim and declined to refer the case.

Cases EE14a,b,&c:[b] The applicant was convicted of various counts of sexual assault of a young girl who was occasionally in his care. There was some medical evidence of injuries to the girl's genitalia and expert evidence on how this should be interpreted. The first application to the Commission, a few months after leave to appeal was dismissed, focused on inconsistencies in the evidence before the jury, limited non-disclosure of potentially exculpatory evidence, and a refusal by the judge to admit certain expert evidence from the defence. The Commission conducted minimum investigation and the case was not referred back to the Court. A second application made two years later (case EE14b) introduced no new grounds and failed to persuade the Commission to refer (indeed the application was read by a screening commissioner and rejected within one day).

By the time of the third, successful application in 2008 (case EE14c) advances had been made in scientific understanding of how 'injuries' to children's genitalia could be interpreted and while the application included other issues which could be thought to challenge the strength of the prosecution case, the Commission's analysis focused on developments in the medical assessment of signs of sexual abuse in the years following the trial. The Commission considered once again all evidence presented at trial, but the main focus of this investigation was on a report published in 2008 by the Royal College of Paediatrics and Child Health on 'The Physical Signs of Child Sexual Abuse: an evidence-based review and guidance'. This cast doubt on the reliability of previous interpretations of abuse and clarified many findings previously considered diagnostic or suggestive of sexual abuse as non-specific (in other words, they occur equally often in children carefully screened for non-abuse).

This report was the main source of fresh evidence in several referrals from the Commission in the years following its publication, and in the preparation of a Casework Guidance Note on Sexual Offences. One of the experts at the Royal College of Paediatrics and Child Health on child sexual abuse, a Consultant Obstetrician Gynaecologist, was approached by the Commission to prepare a report on whether the medical evidence presented at trial could prove that the complainant had been sexually abused. The expert's report found that the evidence was not diagnostic of sexual abuse. Furthermore, it pointed out that best practice now recommended that at least two experienced doctors conducted joint examination, or one doctor with core skills and with photographs taken during examination. This had not been the practice at the time of the applicant's conviction.

The Commission sought further evidence from various experts who had presented at trial and found that some statements had been exaggerated and partial and, in light of recent developments, unsustainable. In referring the case back to the Court, the SOR made clear that had the medical evidence being presented to the jury as it is now understood, it might reasonably have affected the decision of the jury to convict the applicant. The appeal was successful and the applicant's convictions were quashed.

[a] For reasons often not known, a small proportion of infants die unexpectedly during their first weeks, and—less typically—months of life. This is often referred to as 'sudden infant death syndrome' (SIDS) or 'cot death'.
[b] Case references followed by 'a', 'b', 'c', etc. indicate reapplications following an earlier decision by the Commission not to refer a case or reapplications following a referral where the Court upheld the conviction(s). In this case, the applicant applied to have the same convictions considered three times; with the third application being successful in being referred to the Court and the convictions quashed.

Decision Field in Forensic and Expert Evidence Cases

As we demonstrate below, in most forensic and expert evidence cases, Commission staff assess the relative persuasiveness of the old and new evidence, taking account of evolutions in science, scientific method, and interpretation of data. In considering whether the Court might find a conviction to be unsafe, the Commission is bound to reflect on what the jury would have made of the fresh evidence. If it is thought that fresh expert evidence is not sufficiently different from that presented at trial, that it cannot challenge the prosecution case, or that the new expert evidence was known at trial but a tactical decision was made by the defence not to use it (see Elks, 2008:78), the Commission may be reluctant to refer the case. It must work within its legislative framework and be mindful of existing case law to ensure that the evidence it presents is 'fresh' (not previously presented at trial or appeal), that it meets the real possibility test, and that the Court would not dismiss new witnesses as just 'bigger and better' experts. In this, it is guided by internal policies that reflect the Commission's legislative obligations and limitations as well as evolving court jurisprudence—their decision field.

Internal guidance and policy

In expert evidence cases, policies include a publicly available Formal Memorandum on 'experts' (Criminal Cases Review Commission, 2016); and (for internal use only) Casework Guidance Notes on expert evidence (Criminal Cases Review Commission, 2010), on DNA evidence (Criminal Cases Review Commission, 2009b), and on section 13 of the Criminal Appeal Act 1995 (real possibility test) and section 23 of the Criminal Appeal Act 1968 (fresh evidence) (Criminal Cases Review Commission, 2011l). For example, the Casework Guidance Note on expert evidence provides up-to-date scientific information on expert testimony and describes relevant case law. The Formal Memorandum advises on procedures for instructing an expert, guiding staff about when it might be necessary to obtain updated opinion from the original expert or from a new expert.

Internal policies remind Commission staff that they are bound by a legal framework that proscribes a retrial of the facts. In forensic and expert evidence cases this means they cannot contact everyone who gave evidence at trial and ask them to reinvestigate the case anew; they must have good reason for instructing expert witnesses to conduct forensic tests or produce expert analysis on new or old data. Five of our forensic and expert evidence cases were not referred back to the Court because while there was some fresh evidence, most of the applicant's claims and the Commission's findings that challenged the conviction had already been presented at trial or appeal (EE5, EE6, EE14, EE33b&c, EE35; though one (EE14c) was later referred following a reapplication (see Chapter 13)). For example, in case EE5 the Commission considered the new research by Dr G on non-accidental head injuries (discussed below) but came to the conclusion that the applicant:

… was already able to rely on [Dr G's] hypothesis in his defence at trial.… In those [other similar] appeals the views of [Dr G] were accepted as 'fresh evidence'. At [this applicant's] trial, they had already been deployed, so cannot be presented as such. (EE5, Statement of Reasons)

One of these five cases (EE33) had been referred to the Court at first application and this was thought by the Commission to prevent a further referral on any of the grounds put forward in the referral. That said, some evidence had not been included in that referral because it was not new, 'as it could have been adduced at trial and the defence made a legitimate tactical decision not to do so' (EE33, Statement of Reasons). Other cases mention the failure to adduce evidence at trial as just one of many reasons for not referring the case; for example, the Statement of Reasons ('SOR') in case EE30 states that 'The submissions received from [the applicant's] representatives are essentially an attempt of new evidence available at [the applicant's] appeal that was not admitted'.

Furthermore, decision-makers need to be sure that if investigations established facts in favour of the applicant, it would have an impact on the safety of the conviction (Criminal Cases Review Commission, 2011c:para:11). Internal guidance does not state that reviewers should be mindful of limited resources. Moreover, those in managerial roles at the Commission were keen to impress upon us that 'the funding situation … won't have an impact on the quality [of investigations] because that's something that … [the Commission is] fastidious about' (#24). That said, a few interviewees, particularly commissioners, reflected a concern to consider the likely efficacy of investigations which would, inevitably, be expensive:

[budget cuts have] undoubtedly been part of the pressure to try and weed out, if you like, the weaker or the … less worthwhile cases at the beginning. (#27)

Or, as another interviewee put it, 'If we launched a full review in every single case, it would (a) cost too much and (b) not be desirable' (#8).

However, in only one case record did we find explicit reference to the costs of forensic investigations, against the potential benefits. The applicant in case EE27 had been convicted five years previously for rape and assault. Following an unsuccessful appeal, he applied to the Commission asserting that the forensic evidence presented at trial had been flawed, and requesting further DNA testing. The case record shows the CRM's consideration of the request:

any re-examination of DNA material is likely to be inconclusive, but it is possible to have it done. There are two considerations before we should do that; that it will cost a lot of money and that to challenge the trial ID evidence, [new DNA evidence] a) would need to lead to a profile; b) that profile being identifiable; and c) that person being a realistic suspect. (EE27, Case Record)

The supervising commissioner and the investigations adviser were consulted and agreed that 'it would seem little more than speculative were the Commission to spend many thousands of pounds on further examination … And it would be unlikely to challenge the identification evidence which is what this conviction is based on' (EE27, Case Record). Hence it was decided neither to commission further tests nor to refer the case back to the Court.

Clearly, reviewers feel that they must conduct intelligent investigations of forensic and expect evidence, ever mindful of the costs of a lengthy investigation to the applicant, to the original crime victim (should they be informed of the review), to the other applicants waiting in the queue for the Commission to attend to their cases, and to the reputation of a criminal justice system that is under scrutiny long after it has convicted and punished someone for a crime. Hence, in the interests of the fair and responsible use of limited resources, as well as of the sanctity and finality of the jury's decision, Commission policies guide staff to consider which of the issues raised by the applicant needs to be investigated, and cautions that 'there is often a fine dividing line between speculation, fishing, and pursuing something that may or may not be of assistance' (Criminal Cases Review Commission, 2011n:para:16).

While the Commission guidelines make clear that they should 'take into account' all the material submitted by the applicant and 'identify all the issues raised', CRMs are not required to do each and every investigation requested by the applicant (Criminal Cases Review Commission, 2011g:para:6). They should conduct analyses only if they will assist the review (Criminal Cases Review Commission, 2017e). In most of our forensic and expert evidence cases, the applicant asked the Commission to conduct forensic investigations or to review expert evidence. In only seven cases was the applicant's request for the commissioning of forensic tests declined; in most, because 'no firm conclusions could likely be drawn' (EE33, Case Record); in others because there was already enough evidence for referral (EE29, Case Record). Some forensic tests were not pursued because the case was thought to rest on 'a matter of law and it [was] therefore appropriate for the Commission to exercise its judgement in this area without the need for further scientific opinion' (CS14, Statement of Reasons).

The Commission is an independent organization and certainly not at the beck and call of the applicant, but it has a 'responsibility to the applicant to be on the lookout for issues [not] identified or raised' (Criminal Cases Review Commission, 2011g:para:5), particularly for those without legal representation (see Chapter 6), and it conducted forensic tests in four cases from our sample that had not been requested.[4] As one commissioner explained:

A number of our references have been based on things that have never been raised with us by the applicant at all. It's something we've thought 'Actually, something's not quite right here. We need to have a look at it' … trying to predict what are the weak points of the case. (#26)

Needless to say, this does not always work in the applicant's favour. In cases EE24 and EE25 DNA tests further implicated the applicant rather than proving to be exculpatory, and neither case was referred.

The Commission has a responsibility to government and to the Court to review cases thoroughly, use its resources wisely, and refer only those cases that are likely to

---

[4] At the Scottish Commission, we were told this would not likely happen there (#84).

succeed. Given that it rarely knows who is innocent, this means trying to establish which convictions the Court is likely to regard as unsafe. It does this chiefly by considering how the Court has responded to similar cases in the past.

Influence of evolving jurisprudence

The law, both in statute and in practice, 'determines the contours and reach of the field of a legal bureaucracy' such as the Commission by giving it a mandate (Hawkins, 2002:50). In Chapter 3 we described the *statutory* framework within which the Commission operates, and considered how it limits the criteria on which it can refer a case back to the Court to cases that present fresh evidence, not already considered by the trial or appeal courts and that could not have been adduced at trial. In doing so we laid out a part of the 'field' that shapes decision-making in all our cases. But the field is also influenced by the Court's *practice*. The predictive nature of the real possibility test means that the Commission needs to be mindful of the evolving Court jurisprudence and to reflect that in its internal policies, so as to guide decision-making by showing what has been persuasive to the Court in past similar cases and what the Court will not tolerate.

In some of our cases, the Commission explicitly looked for a precedent, with decisions about referral deferred until similar cases had been decided by the Court. For example, having investigated all available evidence in case EE15, the CRM recorded: 'In essence, I am unpersuaded that the new evidence which nullifies the medical evidence is such as to raise a real possibility. I propose to write this up as a non-referral' (EE15, Case Record). The supervising commissioner suggested the case merited consideration by a committee, but before the committee had met, the case was put 'on hold' pending judgment in a similar case before the Court. Following the Court's decision to quash the conviction in the comparator case, case EE15 went to committee, where it was decided that there was sufficient evidence to refer, and the Court subsequently quashed the conviction.

Similarly, the Commission referred case EE14c because 'new medical evidence suggested that the evidence relied on at trial was flawed' (EE14c, Statement of Reasons). In deciding to refer, the case committee had compared it to case EE11b, which had been referred previously and quashed by the Court, arguing that case EE14c was 'a stronger case' and therefore would likely succeed. This approach is not always effective. The Commission referred case EE17, explicitly drawing the Court's attention to its response to similar recent cases:

The Commission notes that the Court of Appeal has quashed convictions in a series of cases where experts at trial had diagnosed abuse by relying on physical signs found during examination. Subsequent developments in medical knowledge have shown the same signs to be neutral and so incapable of supporting allegations of sexual abuse. The Commission has itself referred some of those cases to the Court of Appeal. (EE17, Statement of Reasons)

Notwithstanding the similarities in the cases, the Court upheld the conviction.

Other cases were not referred because the issues they raised had not been well received by the Court in similar cases. For example, in case EE35b, the case record cites precedents, concluding that the Court is 'unreceptive to appeal arguments based on repudiating tactical decisions that resulted unfavourably after discussion with counsel' and that 'there is no real possibility the [Court] would find [the applicant] was incompetently defended or ill-advised'. In relation to another possible ground for appeal, the case record went on to point out the 'strict criteria the [Court] has for accepting retractions, [suggesting that] this would not raise a real possibility' (EE35b, Case Record).

Considerable focus of internal guidance is directed at the question of how persuasive the Court will find new expert witnesses. The Casework Guidance Note on the relationship between section 13 of the Criminal Appeal Act 1995 and section 23 of the Criminal Appeal Act 1968 makes clear that in general the Court regards experts as being 'interchangeable' (as the Court said in the oft-cited case of *Steven Jones*[5]) and is unenthusiastic about receiving new expert evidence on appeal. Indeed, in certain cases (e.g. *Pendleton*[6]), the Court has reminded the Commission that the criminal justice system does not allow two trials; one by jury with one team of lawyers and the second, some years later, in the Court of Appeal after a new expert has been found to say something different to the one at trial.

The Commission's Casework Guidance Note on 'expert evidence' discusses the implications of *Kai-Whitewind*[7] in which expert testimony was the subject of serious dispute. Here, Lord Justice Judge was keen not to open the floodgates to appeals with new expert witnesses just because a case with similar facts had recently persuaded the Court to quash an unsafe conviction.[8] He sought to dispel any notion that all similar convictions should be quashed just because of disputed expert evidence in one case. The judgment made clear that where expert evidence has been given and apparently rejected by the jury, it could only be in the rarest of circumstances that the Court would permit a repetition, or near repetition of the evidence by *another* expert to provide the basis for a successful appeal. If it were otherwise, the judgment goes on to say, the trial process would represent no more than a 'dry run'[9] for one or more of the experts who might then revisit it in the appeal court. The applicant in case EE5 hoped to benefit from the newly conflicting expert evidence on the science of intentional head injuries, following *Cannings*, but all the Commission could find was a limited retraction of one aspect of one expert witness' account at trial. The supervising commissioner concluded 'Like others, I am troubled by this case but see no very obvious grounds for a challenge' (EE5, Case Record). Here, as in other cases (such as EE6 and EE6b), the Court judgment in *Kai-Whitewind* was relied on to conclude that a dispute between medical experts was not of itself a ground for quashing a conviction.

When determining whether the Court is likely to receive the evidence, the Commission should also be mindful of suggesting that a new expert is *superior* to the person who had given evidence at trial. Court jurisprudence has made the Commission wary of the dangers of presenting 'bigger and better' experts. The Casework Guidance Note refers to *R v Horton*,[10] to show that applicants do not have a right to jettison evidence of an apparently eminent and conscientious expert to search for another who might prove favourable to the defence, quoting Lady Justice Hallett's view that the application before her was:

based on an expert shopping expedition. Expert after expert has been discarded until expert or experts have been found willing to support a new diagnosis. This is a practice which … we deprecate.

The Court in this case not only made clear what it would reject, but enunciated situations where obtaining fresh expert evidence *would* be justifiable, including a developing area of science, where significant pieces of evidence had been withheld

---

[5] [1997] 1 Cr App R 86.   [6] [2000] EWCA Crim 45.
[7] [2005] EWCA Crim 1092.   [8] Lord Justice Judge was referring to *Cannings*.
[9] [2005] EWCA Crim 1092; para 97.   [10] [2007] EWCA Crim 607.

or overlooked or misunderstood, or following a blatant misdiagnosis. The SOR in case EE12, reflects on this distinction: 'it will not generally be open to an appellant, without very good reason, to seek to call on appeal a "bigger and better expert" than was called at trial', but goes on to draw on *Steven Jones* to establish that it *would* be allowed 'if it was expedient, necessary, and in the interests of justice'.

The Casework Guidance Note discusses key judgments where the Court *was* willing to receive fresh expert evidence: cases that could demonstrate that the key expert evidence at trial was fundamentally flawed, inaccurate, or misleading; cases where the relevant fresh evidence had not been available at trial but was now capable of casting doubt on the safety of the verdict. It also makes clear that while the evidence might be new and while there may be good reason for the defence failure to introduce it at trial, it may nonetheless be incapable of giving rise to a real possibility that the Court would quash the conviction. In other words, while the Commission can be led on the circumstances within which a new expert witness might be acceptable to the Court, it must still judge whether the jury *may* have acquitted the applicant if they had heard the new evidence or whether in fact the new evidence has no probative value or might even provide further support to the prosecution case. For example, new evidence could prove to be exculpatory on one issue but inculpatory on another. Or the Commission might consider if by introducing the new evidence the applicant's previous convictions or other evidence of 'bad character' would have been revealed to the jury, and that this might have been particularly damaging to the defence.

The field of the Commission has had to adjust to evolving Court jurisprudence on expert opinion. As we discuss below, in most of the child sexual offence cases in our sample (EE14, EE15, EE19, EE20, PI1), the Commission relied on the same new expert witness, a Dr P. This witness became something of a 'bigger and better' expert than those who had given testimony at trial and so the Commission, in these cases, needed to consider if the Court would accept this new evidence. In the event, it did; the convictions were quashed in all five cases. However, in most, the Commission argued that it was not just presenting a 'different expert providing a different opinion, but rather the enunciation of a substantial altering of scientific understanding' (EE15, Statement of Reasons).

Cases were more likely to be referred when the Commission had additional exculpatory evidence to present alongside their 'bigger and better expert'. Hence the minutes of the committee meeting in case EE12 showed agreement that it could not be referred on 'bigger and better expert' grounds, but that the new expert witness' evidence seriously damaged the credibility of the expert opinion presented to the jury (EE12, Case Record). Similarly, in case EE29, while the Commission noted that 'the Court doesn't like when a number of experts are approached and discarded until a favourable opinion is obtained', this case was thought to be different as developments had been made in this area since the applicant's trial 'so it's not just experts rehashing the same methodology' (EE29, Case Record).

When Commission staff are unclear about whether a case might fall foul of the Court's 'bigger and better' prejudice, they sometimes draw on, and in turn help to develop, institutional knowledge on this matter. For example, the CRM in case EE18—concerning a conviction for a sexual assault on a child—sent an email to fellow caseworkers early in the investigation offering a brief description of the relevant facts and asking for guidance:

I think the Commission has covered this issue in other cases and want to know what assistance those cases might offer to my own. Is this an area where medical science has developed in recent years or is this simply a 'bigger and better expert' case? If you have worked on a case where a similar issue has been considered, please let me know.

The case record for case EE4 similarly chronicles the CRM's deliberation with another CRM and consideration of the very similar facts to a previous case, prior to their decision not to refer the case:

After discussion with [CRM], they're of the opinion that a 'bigger and better expert' placing the cause of death outside the time the applicant had sole care of [victim] will not assist. Only a new cause of death (as in [another high-profile case with similar features]) or a new perpetrator is likely to assist the applicant.

In sum, the Court has adopted something of a default position that experts are interchangeable and they do not appreciate appellants seeking to challenge their convictions with new 'bigger and better' experts. Clearly therefore the Commission's task is to establish that the expert testimony at trial was so flawed that the case may be unsafe and to find new scientific evidence or expertise, that could not have been presented at trial, and that the Court might think sufficiently strong to have persuaded the jury to acquit the defendant if it had been presented at trial. Only in such cases does the Commission have a chance of getting past the Court's disinclination to quash a conviction.

We have seen that the decision field of the Commission—the defined setting within which decisions are made—includes statute and case law, and internal guidelines that draw on both. But the field is influenced by the surround—the broad setting within which the Commission operates, and in forensic and expert evidence cases this means the Commission must be aware of and responsive to evolving forensic science and shifting notions about the reliability of expert opinion.

Surround in Forensic and Expert Evidence Cases

Evolutions in science

Forensic developments have raised expectations that new science will come to the rescue of the wrongfully convicted. As one interviewee told us, 'There are certain cases that you can't find anything now, but should the science change . . . they would be cases that you would want to go back to' (#74). New forensic analysis carried out in our forensic and expert evidence cases included tests on biological samples (DNA) (seven cases), on the likely causes of injuries to infants (x10), on firearms or discharge residue (x2), on fingerprints (x1), and on fibres (x1) left at the scene. In many such cases, the Commission responded directly to the changing surround in forensic evidence.

Developments in the accuracy of DNA evidence assisted the applicant in case EE21, triggered by a police reinvestigation of a previously 'solved' murder when it became possible to extract a partial DNA profile from semen swabs stored since the trial. On account of this new DNA evidence, the Crown Prosecution Service informed the Commission that if minded to refer the case back to the Court, the Crown would not oppose the appeal, notwithstanding the defendant's guilty plea at trial (see Chapter 6). The Commission was keen on an expeditious referral as the applicant had already spent over two decades in prison serving a life sentence. Although the case committee acknowledged that the trial court had heard evidence that could not be refuted by new DNA evidence, it resolved to conduct no investigation of the case:

In the interests of expediting the matter, the Commission has conducted no analysis of the facts or law relating to [X's] case. It has based its decision [to refer] solely on the new DNA evidence which gave rise to the letter from the Crown Prosecution Service. Should the Court of Appeal feel that it is necessary to resolve any of the manifold outstanding factual issues thrown up by the case, the Commission's services are available to the Court through s23a[11] of the Criminal Appeal Act 1968. (EE21, Statement of Reasons)

The Court quashed the conviction and the appellant was subsequently awarded compensation.[12]

News of the referral—and increasingly sophisticated DNA techniques of analysis— persuaded the applicant in EE26c to submit a third application to the Commission in 2010 (following unsuccessful applications in 1998 and 2002). His legal representative had already secured crime scene exhibits from the police and instructed a forensic scientist to analyse clothing for DNA. While there was other fresh evidence (from a neurosurgeon), DNA on the victim's clothing which did not originate from the applicant, but from another unknown male, became the main ground for referral. The Court quashed the conviction, commending the Commission for its work, leaving it to reflect on why it had twice declined to refer this case, and prompting a 'lessons learned review' (see further, Chapter 13).

DNA evidence will occasionally be considered sufficient, even if the rest of the story does not add up. Thus, in case CS14b DNA evidence refuted one of the strands of evidence at trial, but nothing further was found to assist the applicant. While concerned that this was insufficient, the case was referred with the SOR stating that had the jury seen this evidence they might have taken a different view of the credibility of the main prosecution witness. In the event, the Court was unpersuaded and upheld the conviction. However, as we discuss below, the Commission usually avoids referring cases without a plausible narrative.

Referrals solely based on DNA evidence are rare. More typically, it is considered in the round, and other evidence might be inculpatory or exculpatory, leaving decision-makers to assess diverse elements and find a plausible narrative in favour or against a referral. Case PI4 focused on analysis of a cigarette butt found at the scene of a murder. DNA testing could not link the applicant to the cigarette (examination of the cigarette at trial in 1990 could show only that the smoker was a 'non-secretor',[13] demonstrating a 75 per cent chance of the cigarette having been smoked by the applicant). An expert was therefore commissioned to examine fingerprints found at the scene following claims about alternative suspects. Nothing in the fingerprint evidence gave rise to a real possibility that the applicant's conviction would be considered unsafe. Nevertheless, the Commission conducted further investigations, including obtaining expert opinions on the victim's watch to produce a detailed reconstruction of the movements of the watch post-mortem and to estimate more accurately the time of death with a view to establishing if the applicant might have been elsewhere at the time. None proved helpful, but the Commission referred the case on the new DNA evidence and on expert testimony on the time of death. This was insufficiently persuasive to the Court, which upheld the conviction.

[11] Under section 23a of the Criminal Appeal Act 1968, the Court may 'order the production of any document, exhibit or other thing connected with the proceedings, the production of which appears to them necessary for the determination of the case'.

[12] At the time of the conviction (1980s), DNA profiling was unavailable and blood-grouping had been unable to exclude the defendant. Considering scientific progress since, the Commission instigated a project to identify similar cases where a conviction had been secured before 1990.

[13] Someone who does not secrete their blood-type antigens into saliva and other bodily fluids.

While in a few of our cases DNA evidence proved to be highly important, with two forensic and expert evidence cases (EE21 and EE26c) quashed by the Court primarily because of DNA evidence, DNA alone is rarely enough to challenge a conviction just as it is rarely sufficient to convict someone.[14] (An obvious exception is DNA testing that proves someone other than a convicted rapist did not attack a given victim.) In these two cases, the victim and applicant were not known to each other, but oftentimes defendants and victims have been in contact prior to the offence and so evidence of the applicant's DNA on the victim or at the scene of the crime is not inevitably inculpatory, nor can DNA tests that rebut assumptions of contact at the scene be entirely exculpatory in such cases if there is other evidence to put the defendant at the scene at the right time. Hence, most forensic tests are not conclusively exculpatory, but must be interpreted by a range of experts who may not agree on their persuasiveness.

Cracks in the veneer of scientific certainty: interpreting forensic evidence

Most of our forensic and expert evidence cases required critical scrutiny of past (at trial or first appeal) or current (throughout Commission review) interpretations of forensic evidence. As one commissioner told us:

In the mid-nineties, there was a feeling in the courts that DNA was unassailable evidence, the magic bullet, and it's only as the years wear on [we're] saying, well actually, how does that work? Like you stand up in court and say, 'It's a match', and then we go on to talk about the match probability. Well let's take it back a step, what do you mean by, 'It's a match'? ... there's an element of human judgement involved in whether it's a match or not. Perhaps we've been looking at totally the wrong debate; it shouldn't be 'what's the probability when you have a match?', it should be: 'how do you get to that, *who's* doing that, *who's* making that decision?' (#29)

Evolutions in forensic science alone rarely shake the foundations of a conviction; the Court needs to be persuaded that new science is relevant and reliable and that the original evidence is no longer dependable. This will not only require a robust challenge to the veracity of expert trial testimony, but a plausible alternative account for other inculpatory non-forensic evidence. Science must be interpreted and explained for it to be persuasive. This is not always possible where the trial court transcript is not available, having been destroyed in line with the five-year retention period currently in operation in courts in England and Wales. In such cases, information that could be useful may not be available and so it may not be possible to know exactly what was presented at trial and what expert opinion was given.[15]

In many of our cases, the applicant or the CRM had concerns about the interpretation and presentation of scientific data at trial and sought to challenge that

---

[14] For over a decade, the Association of Chief Police Officers (2005:para:7.2) guidance has stated that there must be additional non-DNA evidence to support a charge. However, although there is now growing concern about the fallibility of DNA evidence, a recent Court of Appeal judgment in the case of *R v Tsekiri* [2017] EWCA Crim 40 stated that there is no legal or evidential principle which states that a jury cannot consider a case which depends solely on DNA evidence left on an object by a defendant at the scene of a crime, provided the match probability is very high. This overruled what had been set out as the definitive position by the Court in *Byron* [2015] EWCA Crim 997 (see further, Bentley, 2017).

[15] The Commission will typically have access to the summing up, sentencing remarks, or opening and closing speeches but this could leave gaps in their understanding. While experts' testimony from the trial may be available, in some cases it will not and experts may no longer have copies of their reports.

expert testimony. This led to the commissioning of fresh expert evidence where the Commission was persuaded that it might assist their review:

[If] it's clear that the conviction was resting on a significant piece of forensic evidence, then that would drive me or the case review manager, to start doing a bit of research about that area; to ask, 'Is that an area where there's been a shift in scientific opinion recently, and, if so, is that something that we need to explore further?' And as and when it's appropriate, we'll instruct experts. (#26)

Investigations and new reports are typically evaluated with a view to whether they fatally undermine a conviction or merely present different, but equally plausible accounts of what might have taken place.

A considerable proportion of our forensic and expert evidence cases responded to shifts in the surround; challenges to scientific orthodoxy that cast doubt on convictions for violent crime. One commissioner described this process:

there are experts who come along with pet theories, they want to propound them in court, the court accepts what is said and it's only five years later that a better theory comes along and exposes the earlier one for what it was. (#17)

In thirty-one of our cases, scientific expert opinion was commissioned to draw on advances in scientific knowledge, to challenge the original expert testimony, and sometimes to provide evidence not already tested at trial. Many fell into one of two categories of expert opinion on (1) child sexual abuse; or (2) infant head injuries. We consider each of these in turn.

Changing opinion on sexual abuse of children

Evolution in scientific understanding of what is 'normal' in children's genitals brought about significant change to the surround in the review of convictions for sexual abuse of children. Seven of our cases (PI1, EE11b, EE14c, EE15, EE18, EE19b, EE20) involving convictions for the rape and sexual assault of children were referred back to the Court on the basis of new expert testimony following the publication, in 2008, of a report by the Royal College of Paediatrics and Child Health ('RCPCH Report'). Convictions in all seven cases were quashed.

These trials had taken place in the late 1990s/early 2000s when there was consensus among medical experts that certain 'injuries' to children's genitals were indicative of sexual abuse. The RCPCH Report established that clinical findings which were considered to be representative of, consistent with, or probative of sexual abuse—for example 'attenuation' of a girl's hymen—are no longer necessarily regarded as such. The research now demonstrated that such findings have been observed with comparative frequency in non-abused children, as they have with victims of abuse (see cases EE14a,b,&c in Box 7.1, above). As the CRM in case EE11b noted, following a detailed description of the changing expert opinion:

In 'modern money', what [the expert at trial] viewed as 'inconclusive but suggestive', would now just be 'inconclusive'. What she viewed as 'rare', will now be accepted as occurring naturally in a reasonable number of non-abused children. (EE11b, Case Record)

The RCPCH Report also made clear what was required by way of rigorous scientific methods in examining children to produce reliable evidence (notably, pre-abuse examination evidence or examinations that include photographs taken or the involvement of a second medic).

Dr P, a consultant obstetrician gynaecologist and an RCPCH-recognized 'Child Sexual Abuse expert', was commissioned to provide expert testimony on trial evidence in most of these cases. Because the RCPCH Report had not been published at the time of these trials, the Commission could present this new expert testimony, fresh evidence that could not have been relied on by the defence, thus bypassing the section 23 obstacle to a referral. In these cases, this expert stated that 'the way in which the medical evidence at trial was approached, expressed and interpreted was clearly defective' and would not meet with current professional guidelines (PI1, Statement of Reasons). As the Commission in case EE14c put it:

[expert witness'] opinion provides strong support for the contention that, contrary to the way in which the case was left to the jury, the medical evidence did not prove that the complainant had been sexually abused. (EE14c Statement of Reasons)

In such cases, the Commission could conclude that 'the jury had been left with what is now clear as being misleading medical evidence' (PI1, Statement of Reasons).

The original expert witnesses in most cases were asked to report on their own, and others', trial testimony in light of the RCPCH Report. New expert testimonies were critical of inconsistencies in descriptions of injuries, inaccurate use of anatomical language, and insufficiently rigorous examination procedures, with some trial evidence described as 'overstated, even in the context of the 1997 [pre-RCPCH Report] guidance' (EE14c, Statement of Reasons). Sometimes the Commission considered whether children's injuries may have been caused by the kinds of relatively minor accidents that they can sustain in their normal day-to-day activities (e.g., EE16), or by medical conditions, including, for example, severe constipation (e.g., EE14, EE15, EE17).

All but one (EE11b) of these applications were made within a two-year period, from 2006 to 2008, three before the publication of the RCPCH Report, and three following it; the seventh case (EE11b) reached the Commission in 2002 but the review did not begin until 2005 and was under review when the Report was published (it was referred a few months following publication). The three applications immediately after publication of the RCPCH Report (EE14c, EE18, EE20) were in direct response to it, and focused critically on the expert witnesses' evidence at trial, though applicants raised other issues, not least the credibility of complainants. They explored whether the medical evidence would still be *diagnostic* of abuse, or only *suggestive*. In most cases, newly commissioned paediatricians reported that doctors had failed to provide fair expert testimony at trial. In case EE18, the main prosecution witness was commissioned to re-analyse data from their own original examinations and scrutinize the evidence they presented at trial, taking into consideration the RCPCH Report. They concluded:

In light of developments in this area since 1994, and my current knowledge, my present view would not be as stated in the summing up … [My findings] were not diagnostic of anal intercourse and cannot be described as indicative of abuse. (EE18, Statement of Reasons)

As this expert's testimony had been 'an important—and possibly determinative—aspect of the evidence against' the applicant, it was thought by the Commission to 'raise a real possibility that the evidence is no longer determinative' (EE18, Statement of Reasons).

One applicant had made two prior unsuccessful applications to the Commission, who had identified nothing to suggest that the Court would find the convictions to be unsafe. The Commission felt differently following the publication of the RCPCH Report. The screening commissioner, who had also screened the first application, reviewed the previous two applications and recorded:

this is a cause for concern. I'm reviewing the earlier SOR ... and my own previous decision [in the first application]. I believe that we accepted the medical evidence at trial on signs of sexual abuse without demur. (EE14c, Case Record)

The commissioner went on to note discrepancies in the evidence and, referring to improved scientific knowledge produced by the RCPCH Report, concluded:

if this case had been received for the first time today we would have approached it somewhat differently ... I think this reapplication should be accepted ... I believe an application for priority should be made because of the age of the case and the fact that we did not recognise in 1999 or 2002 potential weakness of the medical evidence. (EE14c, Case Record)

The case was allocated to an experienced CRM in December 2008 and referred back to the Court in July 2009; a remarkably quick, and very thorough review which the case record indicates was heading for a referral from day one. While the publication of the RCPCH Report was of assistance to this investigation, the team were in no doubt that the case could have been referred at the earlier application if a thorough and confident review had been conducted at that stage.

Reviews of the earlier three cases did not initially critically appraise the expert medical testimony presented at trial, focusing instead on complainant credibility and inadequate legal representation at trial. However, once the RCPCH Report was published, the reliability of expert evidence became central to these reviews. As with similar cases, 'injuries' to the anus or genitals of the children had been presented to the jury as 'diagnostic' of abuse, with other possible explanations avowed to be unlikely.

While these cases were successful, the Commission soon learned that the RCPCH Report was not *inevitably* fatal to the safety of child sex abuse convictions. In case EE12, the RCPCH Report and new expert witnesses were relied on to argue that the main prosecution witness had:

lacked key competencies and failed to comply with basic requirements in respect of notes, consistent use of terminology and conducting an examination ... and if the jury had known this [and had the benefit of more recent expert evidence] the [trial] court may have acceded to the submission made by the defence as regards to 'no case to answer', particularly bearing in mind [problems with the police interviews]. (EE12, Statement of Reasons)

Notwithstanding the fresh expert evidence and an attack on the credibility of one of the complainants, the Court upheld the conviction because the substance of the new expert witnesses' evidence did not 'introduce anything that has an important new bearing' on the case, and criticisms of the trial expert had already been considered by the jury at trial and 'dealt with in a full, fair and balanced summing-up' (EE12, Court judgment).[16]

While the surround of medical expertise had altered the focus in the decision field at the Commission, as with many other external paradigm shifts in knowledge, the Court was cautious in weighing up the new evidence with all other features of the case and some cases were considered safe despite new expertise brought about by the RCPCH Report. Hence, in reviewing cases, the Commission had to have one eye on the scientific expertise and another on the evolving case law, and case records and Statements of Reasons in some reviews referred to the Court's reluctance to render a conviction unsafe just because the science has moved on:

---

[16] Case EE17, referred for very similar reasons, was also upheld by the Court.

The Commission is aware that the Court of Appeal has clearly indicated that the mere fact that the understanding of good practice has moved on since a conviction was investigated will not of itself render the conviction unsafe, not least because there is a need for finality in judgments. (EE19b, Statement of Reasons)

It became clear that while the RCPCH Report *undermined* the safety of these convictions, the Commission expected the Court to scrutinize the complainant's credibility and consider all other evidence—including other possible reasons for variations in a child's genitals—before concluding that convictions were unsafe. For example, one CRM noted that despite changes to expert evidence, 'there are some puzzling aspects to this case, and a lot of unanswered questions. To do our best "belt and braces" job there will be quite lot of further work to do'; work beyond analysis of the relevance of the RCPCH Report to the safety of that particular conviction (PI1, Case Record). Indeed, internal guidance following these first few appeals warned Commission staff to be circumspect:

It seems clear that even where there is fresh medical evidence the Court of Appeal will generally scrutinise the complainant's credibility and consider all the evidence in the case in the round before concluding that a conviction is unsafe. It is not possible to discern any general principles, and future Commission references will need to be addressed on a case specific basis. (Criminal Cases Review Commission, 2011d:para:30)

Of course, as with other types of cases, the field of the Commission has to presume that the Court speaks with one voice; that its responses to referrals will be consistent across the Court. However, different panels of judges may take different views of the persuasiveness of fresh scientific testimony. For one panel, the new approach may be almost conclusive; for another, of less significance. It is accepted that the Court sometimes shifts in its responses to evidence and argument, but it is also true that occasionally it is inconsistent. Hence the Commission can never be entirely confident in their predictions about how the Court will receive their referrals.

Changing opinion on infant deaths and head injuries

The RCPCH Report was not the only significant development in the surround of expert evidence cases; the Commission also responded to evolving forensic opinion on injuries to infants' brains. New medical expert testimony was commissioned in ten cases (EE1–EE10) where the applicant had been convicted for the murder, infanticide, manslaughter, or (in case EE10) assault of an infant. Each conviction was based primarily on the testimony of an expert witness who persuaded the jury that death could not have been from an accident or from natural causes (e.g. EE2, Box 7.1). A few cases in our sample concerned infants' deaths which were initially thought to be caused by SIDS, and in two (EE1 and EE2) changing expert opinion on the probability of more than one child dying of SIDS was considered during the review. An expert had asserted in other trials that parents—often mothers—killed their babies as they were suffering from 'Munchausen Syndrome by Proxy'[17] and frequently gave erroneous evidence that while one infant death could not be seen as suspicious, two were and three such deaths could be thought of as sufficient evidence to prosecute for murder.[18] During the first

---

[17] Munchausen syndrome by proxy is a mental illness and a form of child abuse. A child's carer will invent fake symptoms or cause real symptoms so that a child appears to medics to be sick.
[18] See Cunliffe, 2011 for discussion of similar cases, including the Australian case of Kathleen Folbigg.

few years of the new millennium, this expert's credibility was challenged and he was eventually struck off the medical register by the General Medical Council.

In some convictions for murder or manslaughter, when there were no bone fractures, bumps, bruises, or neck injuries, the prosecution had successfully argued that death resulted from a 'non-accidental head injury' (often referred to as 'shaken baby syndrome') caused by the person in whose care the child had been at the time of death, or shortly before death.[19] Expert evidence at trial pointed to a triad of intracranial injuries as proof of violent shaking: retinal haemorrhaging, cerebral haemorrhaging, and encephalopathy (Luttner, 2014:1). At the time, the consensus had been that these symptoms could *only* occur due to shaking and any other explanation offered by parents—such as a fall—was likely to be a lie (Duhaime et al., 1998). Indeed, some doctors came to believe that retinal haemorrhages *only* occurred in cases of abuse (Luttner, 2014:2). Hence, a coincidence of these injuries in infants became the hallmark of non-accidental head injury prosecutions.

During the 2000s, a series of publications disputed the theory of 'shaken baby syndrome', challenging the supposed infallibility of the triad, demonstrating that it was not diagnostic of non-accidental head injury (Geddes et al., 2001) nor did it prove that a child was abused or that the last person with the child was responsible for their death (Bradley et al., 2009). Commission reviews therefore focused on criticisms of original expert evidence presented at trial, with fresh expert testimony commonly concluding that the prosecution's case had been overstated.

In three of our cases (EE8–EE10), the applicant asked the Commission to seek fresh expert evidence to demonstrate that the head injury was accidental, occasioned by a fall. In each case, a range of experts was commissioned to conduct tests, re-examine original evidence, and assess those data considering the recent research. In EE8 and EE9, the best that could be concluded was that it was *possible* that the injuries were sustained by an accidental fall. In neither case was there a 'credible alternative explanation' for the injuries, with experts' reports presenting opinion that was 'purely theoretical and speculative, with no clinical or real-life support' (EE9, Case Record). As the Commission understood that the Court has 'emphasised the need for new evidence [in such cases] to constitute a credible medical alternative explanation', it concluded in both cases that 'there is still no real possibility the Court would find the conviction unsafe' (EE9, Case Record).[20]

A plausible alterative narrative was available in the third 'non-accidental head injury' case (EE10) which challenged the accepted wisdom that 'shaken baby syndrome' depends on findings of a triad of symptoms. New experts, drawing on the absence of retinal haemorrhage, asserted that 'there is no evidence to support shaking either as a sole cause of these injuries, or that it is necessary for it to have taken place'. In this case, the jury had been persuaded by the forceful and unequivocal prosecution evidence provided by Dr S. Since the trial, Dr S had been suspended from clinical duties. Her credibility in child abuse cases had been undermined in another case when the judge had criticized her findings as 'unbalanced, obsessive and lacking in judgement', asserting that she was prepared to throw 'objectivity and scientific rigour to the winds

---

[19] In some such cases, the defence had claimed that the infant was a victim of 'sudden infant death syndrome' (SIDS).

[20] This applicant had previously appealed to the Court having received a 'review letter' sent by the Attorney General following an Interdepartmental Group established in the wake of *R v Cannings* to review 258 'battered baby' convictions recorded in the ten years prior to *Cannings* ([2004], 2Cr App R 7; see Box 7.1, case EE2). His case had been heard alongside three others (two, including Commission referral EE10, were successful).

in a highly emotional misrepresentation of the facts' (quoted in EE10, Case Record). Perhaps more important though was the alternative explanation for the head injury, proffered by this applicant, which the trial court had not been persuaded by but which now seemed plausible given contemporary research that showed that babies could be affected by the 'Moro reflex' from just a few weeks old (the applicant had claimed that the seven-week old baby fell while being held when he suddenly arched his back because of the Moro reflex[21]). Following a referral, the Court quashed the conviction.

New research into the neuropathology of head injuries in infants also challenged the consensus that injuries—even when minor—would be noticed as unusual by the carer at the time of death or just prior to death. Studies suggested that on rare occasions an infant can sustain a fatal head injury and yet spend a period symptom-free and presenting to medics as fully lucid before death. Given that case EE7 concerned an apparent delayed asymptomatic deterioration to death, the Commission asked five medical experts—who had given evidence at trial that they *would* have expected the victim to have displayed obvious symptoms very soon after the infliction of the fatal head injuries—to report on the credibility of these new academic articles and their relevance to this case. While two conceded that the possibility of such a delay could not be excluded, the others did not feel that the evolving science assisted this applicant, leaving the Commission to conclude that:

when the articles are read in conjunction with the opinions of all experts, it appears that far more research will be required before the established wisdom (that young children rapidly deteriorate after they have suffered fatal head injury) were to be viewed as unsatisfactory. In these circumstances the Commission considers that the new medical articles do not raise a real possibility that [the applicant's] conviction would be overturned if the case were referred to the Court of Appeal. (EE7, Statement of Reasons)

This case demonstrates that while changing expert evidence can be sufficient to shake the foundations of some convictions, typically there must be significant consensus in opinions and other evidence which supports the applicant's story.

While the RCPCH Report marked a clear development in scientific understanding, and so assisted clients convicted for sexually assaulting children in cases where there was little or no evidence other than slight 'abnormalities' or 'differences' to the child's genitals, the science on injuries to children's brains and on unexplained deaths of infants was still evolving. Hence the Commission needed to find alternative explanations for injuries or deaths, explanations that seemed credible when all the evidence was considered in the round, and that met the real possibility test.

Decision Frames in Forensic and Expert Evidence Cases

While all decision-makers are influenced by the same surround and field, decision frames allow for the ascription of meaning to information in a reflexive process of understanding and interpretation that is shaped by features particular to that case and to that decision-maker (Hawkins, 2002:48–59). Commission staff interpret case-based information and accord relevance to some features over others, with decision frames at all stages of a review influenced by professional knowledge and experience, values, and

---

[21] The Moro reflex is an involuntary infantile reflex—sometimes called a 'startle reflex'—where the baby feels they are falling and suddenly extends their arms out (and sometimes also their legs), arches their back and then curls the limbs back in.

'working rules'. Ultimately, framing helps commissioners and CRMs decide if a case satisfies the real possibility test.

The real possibility test requires decision-makers to judge if, and when, the evidence is sufficient to refer a conviction back to the Court. For this reason, in all cases at various stages of the review, decision-makers employ a legal frame. This is a mechanism for defining certain facts as legally relevant, as having 'the potential for authoritative consequences' (Hawkins, 2002:57). In other words, CRMs interpret each piece of evidence through the lens of the real possibility test to consider if it would be sufficiently persuasive to other Commission staff—first the supervising commissioner and ultimately, in cases that have the potential to satisfy the test, to the case committee, and subsequently to the Court. However, in many, if not most cases, the data are equivocal and challenges to decision frames can help staff to manage ambiguity in their investigations. Challenges can come from all those that contribute to the decision-making process within the Commission, but also from outside—from the applicant and their legal representative.

Hence, our analysis of decision-making in forensic and expert evidence cases suggests two main decision frames; the first, and most obvious, is the legal frame, though here we present it in its contested state; the second, the narrative frame, typically works alongside the legal frame but is informed by the 'stories' that unfold from analysis of cases and that make some cases more plausible than others. In most forensic and expert evidence cases we found both frames at work.

(Contested) legal frame

Legal framing involves assembling the legally relevant facts and applying them; the frame constructs and selectively integrates knowledge and justifies its presence. The process creates a context for framing by others, shaping the way in which it is presented to colleagues for decision. This is the process of case construction. (Hawkins, 2002:57)

The Commission knows the boundaries of the legal decision field. The evidence must be fresh (new); there must be good reason for it not having been adduced at trial; it must not fall foul of the Court's reluctance to hear from 'bigger and better experts'; but it must also be capable of providing robust challenge to the prosecution case. In other words, the Commission must not only consider that there are reasons to doubt the safety of the conviction but be fairly confident that the Court would think the new evidence sufficiently undermines its safety. Given that the Court will consider what the jury would have made of this new evidence if they had been presented with it, the Commission also considers whether it might have made a difference to the verdict had the jury heard it during the trial. At its most basic, this requires decision-makers at the Commission to establish if the fresh evidence is likely to be thought by the Court to afford a sufficiently robust ground for allowing an appeal. Applying this legal decision field to forensic and expert evidence cases through the process of legal framing is not always easy, and in some of our cases the legal frame was contested by the various people who had the responsibility to decide whether a reference to the Court was justified. At its most basic, a CRM and their supervising commissioner might disagree about whether the fresh evidence gathered is sufficiently strong.

Our analysis shows that decision-makers can be ambivalent about whether new forensic tests or new expert evidence are sufficiently robust. In one case, referred by the Commission but upheld by the Court, the CRM described the challenge posed by conflicting expert evidence:

When we'd referred the case before, that had been on the basis of the opinion of [expert A], and [his] evidence had been disputed by [expert B], and [expert C] had been brought in as a third scientist. Now, the scientists had rated whether the fibres were from the same source, on a scale of one to 7, and [expert A] and [expert B] were at opposite ends of the scale. [Expert C] initially put himself at 4, but moved to 5, and significantly distanced himself from [expert A], but he … wasn't quite as sure as [expert B], but was firmly of the view that [expert A] had applied the wrong technique in coming to his conclusions. So, the Court of Appeal found [expert C] a very credible, persuasive witness, and he tilted the balance in my view. (#48)

Case records demonstrate uncertainty when the evidence is ambiguous, and show that at any one time it may not be clear whether the investigation will end in a referral or not. In case EE34, for example, the case record includes extensive notes by the commissioner which read like a deliberation on the pros and cons of the applicant's case. Here, a commissioner requested that the CRM prepare a report for the committee 'that could be written up either as a referral or as a refusal, as long as the issues are laid out before the committee' (EE34, Case Record), not an uncommon request. The record made clear that the CRM preferred the option of a referral, but following deliberation, the committee decided that it was not minded to refer and asked the CRM to rewrite the SOR.

This equivocation was a feature of other complex cases. In case EE17, the CRM was initially persuaded not to refer, believing that the evidence was not sufficiently strong. A draft SOR was shown to the commissioner to see if it should be signed off or if it needed to be agreed by a case committee. The commissioner was not only inclined to take it to committee, but asked the CRM to redraft the SOR 'into a referral SOR' and to 'reverse the analysis and reasons … which are not referable and promote' the expert evidence that could provide grounds for a referral (EE17, Case Record). Who is to say who was 'right' in this case? The committee agreed to refer the case, but the Court upheld the conviction, suggesting the CRM's reticence may have reflected a clearer understanding of the case. However, who was 'right' is not really the point. These examples show that at any one time it is not entirely clear which direction a case will go, that different people throughout the review will shape the way the case is constructed, that the legal facts sometimes do not speak for themselves.

In case EE9 the applicant presented fresh expert evidence from two medical experts in support of their case, after their conviction had been upheld at direct appeal. In addition to reviewing the expert evidence, the CRM sought permission to commission further reports from experts who had testified for the defence at trial (asking them to examine critically a new 'theory' of how the victim—a child—had died). While the new experts acknowledged that this theory was 'possible', neither felt that it was entirely 'plausible', leaving the CRM anxious that the new evidence was not sufficiently strong to persuade the Court to allow the appeal.

Having evaluated all new information, the CRM remained irresolute and therefore sought further expert testimony, specifically on the bruises to the head of the child—the key issue that remained unsettled. Another new expert witness was commissioned, reporting that the number and nature of the bruises on the victim were outside of the norm for an active toddler and that some were consistent with finger grip marks, noted by the CRM to be 'an additional cause for concern' (EE9, Case Record). Nevertheless, the CRM pushed for a referral, with a draft SOR recording:

Having given anxious consideration to all of the issues set out … above, the Commission has decided that, notwithstanding concerns over the bruising to [the victim's] body, [the applicant's] conviction should be referred to the Court of Appeal. This is because the latest reports … constitute compelling fresh evidence in relation to the core issue in [the] case. There is a real possibility that the Court of Appeal will overturn [the applicant's] conviction on the strength of this fresh evidence; and conclude that the bruising to [the victim's] body is, on its own, an insufficient basis for upholding the conviction. (EE9, Draft Statement of Reasons)

Despite the CRM's belief that the evidence was robust, the committee chose to issue a Provisional SOR not to refer the case as it was thought that the bruises posed an insurmountable problem (EE9, Provisional Statement of Reasons). As is not uncommon, this resulted in further submissions from the applicant, none of which was thought satisfactorily to address the concerns raised by the Commission nor strengthen the applicant's case. Typically, this would have been the stage at which the Commission issued a final SOR against a referral, but—still unsure about the case—the CRM sought additional expert testimony from a further two scientists, neither of whom found the applicant's evidence to be entirely plausible.

Following this, further evidence was sought from another expert who was asked to review *all* the expert testimony collected at trial and during review. Interestingly, this new expert suggested that the Commission was not applying the 'right test'; arguing, 'it should not be about whether the Court of Appeal is "persuaded" by evidence, but so long as evidence is not fanciful or untenable it must give rise to real possibility' (EE9, Statement of Reasons). He advised the Commission not to rely so heavily on the bruising and to consider alternative case law which suggested that the Court might be critical of the Crown's changed account of the nature of the case between trial and appeal. This was dismissed by the supervising commissioner as unlikely to be sufficient to render the conviction unsafe, leaving the CRM determined to find 'new evidence to constitute a credible, medical alternative explanation' for the injuries, believing that only this would persuade the Court to quash the conviction (EE9, Case Record). The legal representative thought this was unnecessary, arguing that an alternative explanation does not have to be 'positively credible' but merely 'deserving of careful attention' to be sufficient for a referral (EE9, Case Record). Many legal minds, but little agreement on the strength of the new evidence in this case.

Meanwhile, a second 'Provisional' SOR was issued a full year after the first explaining why the Commission would not refer the case to the Court. Provisional SORs often prompt further submissions, allowing the key decision-makers at the Commission to consider any new information that has come to light but also to revisit their own prior decisions under critical external scrutiny. As such, they inform the construction of a case. Here, additional submissions followed the second Provisional SOR, including additional medical opinion and other case-based information. Another year passed, while the Commission considered the further submissions, after which a final decision was made not to refer the case back to the Court. Though this review took 'only' two years, less than some similar cases, and by no means as long as others,[22] there were very many tests and many experts. The considerable resources devoted to the case reflect the contested nature of the legal decision frame; at any one time the various parties invested in the case were conflicted about the persuasiveness of the evidence. Ultimately, however, challenges from various sources helped the CRM to construct a case against referral following a process characterised by deep ambivalence.

[22] The Commission's most recent Annual Report details the review of Ms McCarthy-Winzar's conviction for murder, the 'longest case in the Commission's 20-year history'. Her case was referred back to the Court in 2016 following eleven years of investigation during which the Commission 'conducted a wide range of enquiries', 'sought the expert advice of approximately 15 experts', and explored 'the latest developments in the relevant science' (Criminal Cases Review Commission, 2017a:18).

As we see in Chapter 13, persistent applicants can play a significant role in the construction of a case for a referral. The Commission's initial decision in case EE32 had been against a referral, but the applicant had commenced judicial review proceedings and the Commission had agreed, by way of a Consent Order, to quash its initial decision not to refer, and to undertake a fresh review. New commissioners and CRMs were appointed, none of whom had any prior experience of the case. This apparently weak case was referred following considerable pressure from the applicant on the *sole* basis of the trial expert witness' 'inaccurate and apparently unreliable [ballistics] evidence' on the gun used in a fatal shooting, even though the rest of the prosecution evidence remained 'undamaged and in some cases strengthened' following the Commission's review (EE32, Case Record).

The case record, that ran to over a hundred pages, suggested that the CRM considered it unlikely that the Court would quash the conviction. This equivocation is reflected in the SOR:

The Commission is not able to determine the degree to which the inaccurate evidence would have had an impact upon the decision the jury reached but we cannot rule out the possibility that it may have been an important factor leading to the original conviction.... The Commission, while trying to assess what the Court might do once it had new evidence, must not usurp the Court's decision making role. The Commission's task is the need to decide whether there is a 'real possibility'. It does not have to be sure or even reasonably sure that the court would quash the original conviction. (EE32, Statement of Reasons)

The CRM was right; the Court upheld the murder conviction, arguing that:

even if the error had been corrected when the evidence was placed before the jury, it seems to us quite impossible to hold that the totality of the evidence, both old and new, would have led the jury to come to a different verdict. (EE32, Court judgment)

The Court's reference to the 'totality of evidence' speaks to the inability of the Commission to provide a plausible story that could dismantle the other prosecution evidence that persuaded the jury to convict. The legal framing remained contested and narrative framing could not assist.

Narrative frame

When it was not clear if new forensic or expert evidence could satisfy the real possibility test, Commission staff frequently turned to a narrative decision frame. Without a smoking gun, produced early in a review, uncertainty can lead to the commissioning of further expert testimony until there seems to be a preponderance of evidence pointing in one direction. In this process, sense-making (see Choo, 2006; Chapter 4) is driven by plausibility and persuasiveness, rather than pursuit of a truth. The Commission must decide if, considering all evidence *now* available, the jury would likely have found the applicant's account sufficiently persuasive, or, more precisely, if the Court would be liable to believe that the jury would have been persuaded.

The challenge, therefore, is for the CRM, supervising commissioner, and, in some cases, the case committee to select a *plausible* meaning from possibly several alternative meanings to make sense of past events about which they inevitably have only partial information. When there are competing expert testimonies, both concerning evidence presented at trial and new expert evidence, they must judge which is the most persuasive. In making these decisions, they adopt a narrative decision frame: can they carve a plausible narrative out of the sometimes disparate evidence at hand. This can be hard if the applicant cannot provide a credible alternative explanation to that presented by the prosecution. For example, the applicant in case EE4 had consistently denied doing anything harmful to the child in his care, but could provide no plausible (innocent) narrative as to what may have caused the child's death.

The applicant in case EE1 had been convicted of the murder of two infants (see above, and cf. EE2, Box 7.1). New expert evidence on the erroneous nature of the trial expert's statistics on probability had already been presented to the Court on direct appeal, which had acknowledged the misleading nature of his testimony but found the medical evidence to be sufficiently robust, and therefore upheld the conviction. Within the legal decision frame, it was clear that the Commission was restricted by the requirement for 'fresh' evidence and so, following the applicant's advice, examined new medical evidence of a possible natural cause of death provided by two experts commissioned by the applicant's solicitor. Subsequent to further medical reviews, which drew the same conclusions, the Commission's reference back to the Court focused on the microbiological tests as providing plausible explanation for a natural cause of death, and the Court duly quashed the conviction.[23] The SOR referred to: 'the overwhelming significance' of the new information about an infection, but the case record shows that the emerging plausible narrative was assisted by other review findings of a more technical nature, all pointing to the truthfulness and credibility of the applicant.

In case PI5—regarding a conviction for attempted murder and possession of a firearm—new ballistic and medical tests were commissioned but there was thought to be insufficient fresh evidence for a referral. At reapplication (PI5b), two new experts were instructed by the Commission to consider claims made in the application that police officers, rather than the applicant, had shot the victim. While this might seem far-fetched, the applicant's account had some plausibility to it, and so experts were commissioned to conduct a reconstruction at the scene to consider the credibility of the cases put forward by both the prosecution and the defence. Though this proved to be unhelpful, the Commission continued to explore other evidence, finding some limited support for the applicant's account, but ultimately failing to identify fresh evidence sufficient for a referral. The attempt to find support for the alternative narrative had reached a dead-end.

Reviews look beyond the forensic and expert testimony to 'the consistency and credibility (or otherwise) of the defendant's story, the defendant's record ... etc.' (EE5, Case Record). Hence, where there is insufficient evidence for a referral but where a plausible narrative pointing to the guilt of the applicant could not be found, case records included comments such as 'Like others, I am troubled by this case, but see no very obvious grounds for a challenge' (EE5, Case Record).

Case EE30 provides an interesting example of the narrative frame at work. Compared to most Commission cases, this was a relatively minor conviction; a burglary and a theft. Nonetheless, the Commission spent many years reviewing the case. The application was received in 2008, screened by a commissioner in November 2008 and allocated to an experienced CRM in September 2009 (a rather quick allocation for an applicant who was at liberty at the time; see Chapter 4). However, the final SOR was not issued until 2013. The lengthy review may be accounted for by the commissioner and the CRM's shared cognitive dissonance (Festinger, 1957). Both felt that the

---

[23] While the new evidence related to only one of the children, the Commission argued that this evidence was so undermining that it potentially destroyed the similar fact evidence argument that had been central to the conviction for murder in the second case, thus rendering the second conviction unsafe.

inculpatory information did not fit their perceptions of the applicant: that the information they had about the crime and the applicant were inconsistent. While forensic testing of fingerprints at the scene and scrutiny of the expertise presented at trial initially looked promising, ultimately, they could find nothing to assist the applicant. The CRM was reluctant to give up for some time as they could not construct a plausible narrative to explain the applicant's crime; what was known about the applicant did not fit with the evidence against him. The screening commissioner had clearly felt similarly concerned when he initially read the application and recorded:

it is a case of some interest relating to the finding of a fingerprint of this applicant who was a man of good character with a very well paid job and an alibi for the time of the burglary. It appears to be an odd but interesting case that should be looked into. (EE30, Case Record)

The group leader too agreed it was 'an odd ... rather troubling case' and the case record suggests that his mind-set—of not seeing the applicant as a criminal—influenced the review. In the event, there was nothing to refer on and reluctantly the team acknowledged 'it is now time to draw a line under this case' (EE30, Case Record).[24]

In weaving a plausible narrative, the Commission may look beyond the legal frame to inform their approach and their persistence. The applicant in case EE16, convicted for indecent assault of a child had explained the injuries to the child's genitals by reference to a sporting accident. Following a thorough review, the Commission concluded that the accident had been too minor to have caused any significant injury and consequently the research published in the RCPCH Report was inapplicable here. However, evidence about the complainant might also have influenced the CRM's perceptions of the case and yet was not, and could not be used in the SOR:

[the complainant's] disclosures were ruled inadmissible [at trial], and we must therefore be very circumspect about placing any reliance on them ... However, from a lay perspective, it is quite clear that [the complainant] was implicating [the applicant] and did not believe that [an accident] was of any significance. (EE16, Case Record)

The case record went on to point out that 'we are also puzzled by [the applicant's] silence in interview'. Though not mentioned in the SOR, this contextual information discussed in the case record may have militated against the CRM finding the applicant's narrative to be plausible.

Clearly, the narrative frame does not compete with the legal frame. A good story cannot compensate for unconvincing forensic evidence that will not satisfy the real possibility test. However, often evidence is contested, pointing to various credible accounts, and in such cases the narrative frame may help the Commission to present to the Court a plausible account of what might have happened.

More Science, Yet More Uncertainty

This chapter has demonstrated the interconnectedness of the surround, the field, and the decision frame. Within the decision frame, neither the surround nor the field recede to the periphery, both are actively drawn on as the CRM or commissioner makes sense of the case before them. We have seen that the relevant features of the surround,

---

[24] Occasionally, we came across other examples of such cognitive dissonance during our fieldwork. One relatively high-profile case caused discomfort among commissioners: while a thorough review had revealed nothing to challenge the safety of an applicant's conviction, all who dealt with the case were sure the applicant had not committed the crime.

in the forensic and expert evidence cases we examined, included shifting opinion about injuries caused to children's genitalia and evolving neuropathology of infants' head injuries. These influenced understanding of certain expert evidence cases and shaped the approach to referrals.

Expert evidence cases often lead to the collation of enormous amounts of sometimes impenetrable information, including statistical data, from all stages of the case—pretrial, through trial, to post-conviction review. They require from Commission staff attention to fine detail, meticulous analysis, and an understanding of science, risk, and probabilities, and it is hardly surprising that Commission staff concede that much forensic science is 'beyond their knowledge' (#79). It is also at times highly contested, not only between those who gave evidence at trial, but also between those commissioned for the review and those invested in the outcome. What is more, most of these cases concern convictions for murder or rape, with many of the victims being infants. The Commission must therefore be mindful of the implications for both the applicant, typically serving a long prison sentence, and the victim or the family of the victim.

Uncertainty and even anxiety are key features of the Commission's decision frame. As the Chair of the Commission explained at the recent twentieth Anniversary conference: there is 'constant anxiety that we might be missing things in the applications' (Foster, 2017a). To manage the pressure occasioned by the complexity and ambiguity of the data before them, some Commission staff engage in long searches for the conclusive evidence that will verify or rebut the applicant's case. Yet most of the information that comes from these searches remains tentative and inconclusive. Others manage to reach a decision with fewer resources. Most benefit from institutional knowledge and engage—to some extent—in collective learning, but a few seem happier pursuing a lone path.

While the Commission has responsibility for selecting and instructing expert witnesses during reviews, the changing knowledge landscape that experts draw on is, of course, also beyond its control. So too are the occasionally dramatic shifts in perceptions about the reliability of those experts, and some of our cases rested on discredited theories or methodological approaches from discredited witnesses. Sometimes the Court disregards new opinion about old experts unless the Commission can dismantle other aspects of the prosecution case and provide an alternative, plausible narrative, a credible story about what happened. Thus, while the Commission has one eye on the science, the other is on the Court's evolving jurisprudence on new expert evidence. When the Court signals a reluctance to open its doors too wide to changing opinions, the Commission follows suit, typically disinclined to push back, particularly if they cannot dismantle the bulk of the prosecution case.

In an organization where there are clear limits to forensic expertise, and where each case is somewhat unique, it should not be surprising that uncertainty will sometimes result in variability in how to interpret the real possibility test. That said, we identified a clear narrative decision frame at work in most of our cases: the search for a plausible explanation that could assist the applicant seems to be just as important as data provided from 'experts in white coats'.

8

Complainant Credibility in Sexual Offence Cases

All sex offences aren't the same. But ... when you're looking at a sex case, [it] does come down to credibility—effectively one person against another. (#63)[1]

Introduction

In sexual offence cases, the question of guilt or innocence often turns on issues of disputed consent—on whose version of events a court elects to believe, the accused's or the complainant's (Criminal Cases Review Commission, 2013d). In such cases, forensic evidence will usually be unhelpful (Criminal Cases Review Commission, 2013d).[2] The Commission highlighted the difficulty of investigating sexual offence cases as follows:

A high percentage of applications to the Commission involve convictions for sexual offences. Such applications can be among the most difficult to review. Many of them involve the word of the complainant against the word of the defendant, and there may be little prospect of finding independent evidence that could affect the safety of the conviction. (Criminal Cases Review Commission, 2011m)

One recent high-profile example was the case of Chedwyn (Ched) Evans, a professional footballer, who was found guilty of raping a woman and sentenced to five years imprisonment in 2012 (*Evans*).[3] Evans claimed that the complainant consented to sex with him when he entered a hotel room where his friend was engaged in sexual intercourse with her. The complainant maintained that she could not remember what happened that evening, as she was inebriated, with the prosecution arguing that this rendered her incapable of consenting to intercourse. After his appeal was dismissed, Evans persisted in his claims of innocence and applied to the Criminal Cases Review Commission ('the Commission'). A ten-month investigation persuaded the Commission to refer Evans' case to the Court of Appeal ('the Court'), which concluded that his original conviction was unsafe, and ordered a retrial (Criminal Cases Review Commission, 2015b; *Evans*[4]). At this second trial, in 2016, the jury found Evans not guilty of rape (Morris and Topping, 2016). The Commission's reasons for referring the case, the Court's decision to allow the appeal, and the retrial that followed all focused on the admissibility of evidence concerning the complainant's sexual history, which was presented as undermining the prosecution case against Evans.

The law protects complainants from intrusive questioning about their private lives, and evidence about a complainant's sexual history is generally not admissible, according to section 41 of the Youth Justice and Criminal Evidence Act 1999. When introduced,

---

[1] All interviews are with Commission staff, including commissioners, criminal case review managers, management staff, and advisers unless we state otherwise.
[2] Chapter 7 focuses on the use of forensic evidence. [3] [2016] EWCA Crim 452.
[4] [2016] EWCA Crim 452.

Reasons to Doubt: Wrongful Convictions and the Criminal Cases Review Commission. © Carolyn Hoyle and Mai Sato 2019. Published 2019 by Oxford University Press.

section 41 was seen as correcting the myth that 'unchaste' women were more likely to consent to intercourse and were less trustworthy (*Evans*, para:44[5]). The protection of complainants under section 41, however, must be balanced by the pursuit of a fair trial for defendants. The key issue in Evans' case was the admissibility of evidence from third parties: evidence about complainants' sexual history can be admitted if it is 'sufficiently similar [to the alleged offence] that it cannot be explained reasonably as co-incidence' (*Evans*, para:73). In Evans' case, the evidence concerning the complainant's (*consensual*) sexual history with two other men was admitted, and considered to be sufficiently similar to render the conviction unsafe.[6] As Justice Hallett explained:

On each occasion [complainant] had been drinking, she is said to have instigated certain sexual activity, directed her sexual partner into certain positions, and used specific words of encouragement. (*Evans*, para:71[7])

This decision generated indignation in national news media.[8] More than forty Labour MPs demanded a change in the law as they were concerned that the outcome of the Evans case would deter women from reporting rape (Hughes, 2016). Women against Rape[9] lamented that the judgment was 'a throwback to the last century when women who reported rape were assumed to be lying' (Women against Rape quoted in Hughes, 2016). The consensus among these critics was that the judgment reflected sexist assumptions that women's sexual history could reliably speak to their character and the likelihood of them making a false accusation of sexual violence.

Complainants' credibility goes to the heart of Commission's investigations into alleged wrongful convictions for sexual offences. A quarter of applications to the Commission concern sexual offence cases (Commission's administrative data during 2005–14; Elks, 2008:218),[10] a disproportionately higher rate than sexual offences among all offences recorded by the police (Office for National Statistics, 2017:chapt.8).[11] Sexual offence cases therefore make up a large minority of the Commission's workload, but they also pose challenges. Many present nothing more than a claim that the complainant lied, with little prospect of finding independent evidence (Criminal Cases Review Commission, 2011m; Elks, 2008).[12]

This chapter examines the Commission's approach to sexual offence cases, based on our analysis of forty-six cases reviewed by the Commission between 1998 and 2011.[13]

[5] [2016] EWCA Crim 452.
[6] The Court made clear its reluctance to allow the complainant's sexual history with third parties into evidence: 'We have reached this conclusion with a considerable degree of hesitation' (*Evans*, para:74).
[7] [2016] EWCA Crim 452.
[8] *The Independ*ent reported, 'Ched Evans: Scrutinising women's sexual history in rape trial "set us back 30 years"' (England, 2016); a headline in *The Telegraph* read, 'Ched Evans verdict: Why we should all feel anxious about high profile rape cases' (Smith, 2016).
[9] This organization campaigns for and offers support to women and girls who have been raped or sexually assaulted. See http://womenagainstrape.net/homepage.
[10] Sexual offence cases have comprised 18 per cent of referrals to the Court (Criminal Cases Review Commission, 2016a).
[11] Sexual offences comprised 3 per cent of all victim-based crimes recorded by the police in England and Wales for the year ending March 2017 (Office for National Statistics, 2017:chapt.8).
[12] The Casework Guidance Note describes the difficulty of investigating sexual offence cases as follows: 'The credibility of the complainant is likely to be a central issue in any case of sexual abuse. It is a regular feature of sexual offences that there is little or no independent evidence. The jury is required to decide between the account advanced by the complainant and the account advanced by the defendant, who may often be in a position where all he can say is "she made it up"' (Criminal Cases Review Commission, 2011m).
[13] Sexual offence cases are: CS1 to CS15; HIA1 to HIA14; EE11, EE12, EE14, EE15, EE16, EE17, EE18, EE19, EE20, EE25, EE26, EE27, EE34, EE41, PI1, P3, and PI7; see Appendix.

It focuses on investigation of past behaviour of complainants and the sensitivities involved with such an approach. The Commission's 'field', defined by its organizational policies on sexual offence cases, is discussed in relation to the changing environment of the 'surround' (Hawkins, 2002): the Court's narrowing stance on the type of credibility that might persuade it to quash convictions; the police and Crown Prosecution Service's improvements in their treatment of victims; and the wider politics and media contribution to the growing concerns about victims of historical sexual abuse.

Sexual Offence Cases

Establishing complainant credibility

The 'field' defines the setting in which decisions are made (Hawkins, 2002). In sexual offences cases, the Commission's decision field focuses on investigating the credibility of complainants in order to judge if there is a real possibility that the convictions are unsafe.[14] This section focuses on the 2013 Formal Memorandum, as this was the policy in place at the Commission during our fieldwork. Changes made more recently to the Commission's formal policy regarding investigation of complainant credibility are discussed below. The 2013 Formal Memorandum on Sexual Offence Cases states:

The defendant may allege that the abuse simply did not occur or that it was not the defendant who was responsible. Most offences are committed when the victim and offender are alone, and there is rarely any scientific or other corroborative evidence. It follows that a key issue in most applications to the Commission will be the complainant's credibility. (Criminal Cases Review Commission, 2013d)

The Commission is empowered, by section 17 of the Criminal Appeal Act 1995, to request and obtain documents from public bodies (and, as of July 2016, from private bodies and individuals[15]), which allow them to investigate complainants' credibility. These include social services files, Criminal Injuries Compensation Authority ('CICA') files, information concerning civil actions, information held on the Police National Computer ('PNC') and the Police National Database ('PND'),[16] and medical records (Criminal Cases Review Commission, 2013d).[17] These records can discredit the veracity of the original complaint:

First, material obtained from public bodies may contain information that undermines complainants' credibility. Details of false allegations, whether proved or otherwise, can be checked against the PNC, the PND, and social services files. While past false allegations of sexual abuse do not necessarily mean the allegation in question is also false, they are treated as a 'warning sign' (Criminal Cases Review Commission, 2013d) that casts doubt on the overall credibility of the complainant.

---

[14] In four out of thirty-nine sexual offence cases, the complainant did not know the applicant prior to the attack, and the focus was not on whether the assault occurred, but on whether the applicant was the assailant; therefore, the issue of complainant credibility was not relevant (EE26, EE27, EE34, and EE41).

[15] The change was introduced under section 18A of the Criminal Appeal Act 1995, which was inserted by the Criminal Cases Review Commission (Information) Act 2016.

[16] The PNC holds information on individuals who have been subject to a conviction, caution, reprimand, warning, or arrest (Eastern, 2016). The PND holds 'soft' intelligence such as details of allegations and investigations that did not result in an arrest (Eastern, 2016).

[17] In addition, the Commission may request other material such as Education Department files (information concerning the complainant's behaviour at school) and police child protection files (Criminal Cases Review Commission, 2013d).

Second, complainants' credibility could be undermined if they appear to have been motivated by financial gain. The CICA deals with compensation claims from people who have been physically or mentally injured as a 'blameless victim' (Criminal Injuries Compensation Authority, n.d.). The Commission may use its section 17 powers to gain access to the complainant's CICA statement in order to compare it to the account given at trial (Criminal Cases Review Commission, 2013d). Any discrepancies may be considered to undermine the complainant's credibility—raising the possibility that the complainant may have made a false allegation to profit from the compensation scheme. The same principle applies to civil actions brought against local authorities where a child victim was in the care of social services at the time of the alleged sexual abuse (Criminal Cases Review Commission, 2013d).

Third, complainants' medical records could undermine their credibility. For example, if the prosecution had claimed that the complainant was a virgin at the time of the offence, medical records may be sought for evidence of sexual activity prior to the alleged abuse (e.g. presence of a sexually transmitted infection). This occurred, for example, in case HIA11b, where medical records showed that the complainant had asked a doctor for a prescription for contraceptive pills (HIA11b, Memo written on 16 January 2006). The Commission's policy stresses, however, that medical records shall not be examined 'without good reason' (Criminal Cases Review Commission, 2013d) and acknowledges the need for confidentiality in order not to compromise the 'frank and open relationship between patient and doctor' (Criminal Cases Review Commission, 2017g:para:6).[18] The decision to access the complainants' medical records cannot be taken by a single case review manager ('CRM'); guidance should be sought by a legal or investigations adviser and approved by a group leader (Criminal Cases Review Commission, 2013d).

Caution in the use of section 17 powers to acquire medical records is different to the practice of gaining access to other materials, such as social services files, PNC, PND, CICA, and records of civil actions. The Commission adopts a policy of obtaining these other materials by default for sexual offence cases, and approval must be sought to opt out of the routine practice of reviewing these records:

The decision not to view the [social services department] files **must** be endorsed by a commissioner and the reason recorded in the case record. (Criminal Cases Review Commission, 2013d)

The same instruction is repeated for information on CICA claims (Criminal Cases Review Commission, 2013d), civil actions (Criminal Cases Review Commission, 2013d), and data from the PNC (Criminal Cases Review Commission, 2013d), and the PND (Criminal Cases Review Commission, 2013d).

Developments in the field

The field is defined by and acted on by the organization, and it contains 'sets of ideas about how its ends are to be pursued' (Hawkins, 2002:50). Thorough testing of complainants' credibility became a formal policy of the Commission after certain convictions—based on new information that undermined complainant credibility—were quashed

---

[18] For example, in case CS15 (a case that was not referred to the Court), the Commission's decision not to obtain medical records is provided in the Statement of Reasons: 'The Commission regards medical records as highly confidential and considers that a complainant's medical records should not be examined without good reason. The Commission has not identified good reason in this case' (CS15, Statement of Reasons).

by the Court (CS5 and CS2; see also Elks, 2008:221).[19] In case CS5, the applicant, convicted of the rape of his former partner while the two still shared a home, applied to the Commission in July 2003 arguing that the complainant could not be trusted. The key issue was consent. The screening commissioner summarized the applicant's argument as 'a classic case of who the jury believed' and categorized the case as requiring minimum review (CS5, Case Record). Within a month of the case being allocated for a review, a Provisional Statement of Reasons was approved not to refer the conviction back to the Court (CS5, Case Record). Although the applicant had raised concerns about the reliability of the complainant, no public records were sought to explore this issue. The decision not to refer the case back to Court was based only on information in the application, the Court file, and the defence file (CS5, Provisional Statement of Reasons).

The applicant's legal representatives asked the Commission to look into previous false allegations made by the complainant. In further reviewing this case, the Commission recognized that there can be exceptions to the requirement of section 41 of the Youth Justice and Criminal Evidence Act 1999, which makes evidence about the complainants' sexual history inadmissible. The following entry in the case record illustrates the Commission's recognition of the importance of investigating complainant credibility, and how it could form the basis of a referral point:

Having read [the legal adviser's] advice, ... if the dismissal of the section 41 application was erroneous in that the defence were seeking to expose dishonesty on the part of the victim, it is only relevant to a further appeal if there is some substance to it. We should ask the applicant to explain how he knows of the previous alleged withdrawn complaints (are they provable facts or rumour/gossip on which he is relying?). If he asserts the former, we should then follow up by making enquiries of the police to confirm or otherwise. (CS5, Case Record)

In this case, data gathered by the Commission significantly undermined the complainant's credibility, and following a referral, the Court quashed the conviction in 2005. Case CS5 led to modifications in the decision field and the publication of a revised Formal Memorandum on sexual offence cases in 2006.[20] It established an investigation policy that focused on complainant credibility, which continued in subsequent policies published in 2008 and 2013:

Most offences are committed when the victim and the offender are alone, and there is rarely any scientific or other corroborative evidence. It follows that a key issue in most applications to the Commission will be the victim's credibility ... The Commission's powers give it access to materials which the applicant and his representatives would not normally be able to obtain. (Criminal Cases Review Commission, 2006a:paras:2 and 3)

The 2008 policy explains what to look for in a social services file that may undermine complainant credibility:

---

[19] The CRM who worked on case CS2 spoke about the gradual realization that credibility checks could open up possibilities for a referral: 'Hopefully we've got better over time, with sort of more experience of what might lead somewhere ... So, you know, things like credibility checks ... that wouldn't have occurred to us necessarily in the early days. That's something that we discovered over time' (#65).
[20] The 2006 Formal Memorandum on sexual abuse was titled Formal Memorandum on Child Sexual Abuse. The title of the Formal Memorandum—with mostly the same content—was changed in 2008 to Formal Memorandum on Sexual Offence Cases; the memorandum was updated and released again in 2013 under this title with no changes to the way complainant credibility should be investigated.

Primarily you are looking for anything that could affect the credibility of the complainant or the veracity of the complaint itself. For example: any indication that the complainant has made similar allegations in respect of other individuals, or has retracted the allegation against the applicant at some time, or that family members have made statements which cast doubt on the veracity of the original complaint. Additionally, we should consider whether there is evidence of any incentive for the complainant to have made a false allegation. (Criminal Cases Review Commission, 2008:para:3)

Prior to these changes, the Commission had acknowledged that credibility was relevant in sexual offence cases but did not treat credibility checks as compulsory. The use of section 17 powers was stated as optional: 'the Commission does not routinely request access to SSD [social services department] files in all cases' (Criminal Cases Review Commission, 2005b:para:17). It was mostly restricted to instances of uncorroborated evidence or a lapse of time between alleged offence and the complaint.[21] The 2002 and 2005 Formal Memoranda[22] did not mention the CICA, civil actions, or the PNC. While the use of section 17 powers to gather information from social services files is referred to in the 2005 policy, there is no mention of other helpful sources of data for investigating sexual abuse cases. The influence of the Commission's changing policy from 2006—with its new focus on verifying the credibility of complaints through extensive use of section 17 powers—is evident in responses to our sample of forty-six sexual offence cases.

Before 2006

The field and the frame are in mutual interaction, and the field influences 'which frames move from background to foreground' (Hawkins, 2002:52). The early framing of cases makes clear the old decision field; those post-2006 reflect a prescriptive approach to credibility checks. For cases that reached the Commission before 2006, credibility checks were done selectively when applicants or their legal representatives raised the issue directly or indirectly. For example, credibility checks consisted only of investigating CICA claims in cases CS3 and CS4 (both applicants applied in 2002), and the legal representative in both cases was instrumental in the Commission's decision to review the CICA file.

In one pre-2006 case (CS6a), credibility checks were not done even when applicants raised the issue of complainant credibility. In this case, an unrepresented applicant with a previous criminal history applied to the Commission in 2003 arguing that he was wrongfully convicted of raping his wife's granddaughter. His application claimed that the rape allegation was fabricated. The Commission decided not to do any credibility checks on the complainant; the commissioner approved the Provisional Statement of Reasons following just a month of review, and the final decision not to refer was reached after a further two months reviewing the evidence (CS6a, Case Record). The applicant reapplied in the same year—this time, legally represented—with evidence of what appeared to be a retraction of the rape allegation (CS6b). This specific issue prompted the Commission to carry out CICA checks on the complainant

---

[21] The decision to use section 17 powers was left to the discretion of commissioners at the screening stage, or to a CRM after a case had been allocated for a review (Criminal Cases Review Commission, 2005b:paras:18–20).

[22] The 2002 and 2005 Formal Memoranda were titled Formal Memorandum on Family Abuse Cases and had almost identical wording. The title changed in 2006 to Formal Memorandum on Child Sexual Abuse Cases.

(CS6b, Case Record) and the case was referred back to the Court because of inconsistencies between the evidence at trial and the CICA claim; the conviction was quashed (see further below).

Similarly, in an application received in 2005, the screening commissioner (see Chapter 6) did not instruct the CRM to make use of section 17 powers despite the applicant raising the issue of complainant credibility (CS7, Case Record). When the CRM assigned to the case queried this, the screening commissioner responded that the applicant 'raises extremely narrow and specific legal issues' and that it was not necessary to 'go into adventitious investigation such as social services records' (CS7, Case Record). Uneasy about this advice, the CRM consulted with an investigations adviser, and the decision was reached to carry out credibility checks, in part because of the new policy (the 2006 Formal Memorandum) that was about to be introduced. The CRM entered the following note in the case record:

> Explained the history of the trials [to the investigations adviser] … also advised of the applicant's submission to us. [Investigations adviser] confirmed that the new policy about to be issued is we should look at social service and CICA material unless there is a good reason not to. (CS7, Case Record)

In this case, the new decision field allowed the CRM to adopt a different decision frame to the commissioner, using the revised formal policy to ignore the commissioner's steer, unusual within these somewhat hierarchical relationships.

After 2006

To better understand the transition in policy that occurred in 2006, we can consider the differences in the Commission's response to one case between the first application in 2006 (CS14a), and the reapplication in 2009 (CS14b). The applicant—unrepresented at the first application—claimed to be wrongfully convicted of raping a prostitute (CS14a) and suggested that the Commission investigate the complainant's credibility and conduct forensic tests. The Commission refused to refer his case back to the Court, arguing that new forensic tests would not help and that the complainant's credibility had been dealt with at trial, and was therefore not fresh evidence.[23] The screening commissioner failed to recommend credibility checks even though the new policy had been in place for seven months (CS14a, Case Records). Upon reapplication in 2009, the applicant's legal representative presented information about a new expert witness, but did not raise the issue of complainant credibility. A different screening commissioner who considered the reapplication not only reviewed information about the new expert witness, but ordered that the CRM carry out credibility checks on the complainant (CS14b, Case Records). This case was referred to the Court partly based on complainant credibility, though the Court upheld the conviction (see Table 8.1 below).

Cases CS10 and CS11 (both applications received in 2007) demonstrate that by then the new policy on credibility had been integrated into practice among CRMs. However, the same commissioner who screened both cases requested credibility checks in neither: in case CS10 the applicant had not raised this issue, though in case CS11 he had. Even without this request by the applicant, in case CS10, the CRM noted in

---

[23] Section 23 of the Criminal Appeal Act 1968 allows the Court to receive evidence that was not adduced in the proceedings from which the appeal lies, as long as there is a reasonable explanation for the failure to adduce the evidence in prior proceedings. Hence, evidence should be 'fresh', not previously considered by the Appeal or trial courts (see Chapter 7).

Table 8.1 Sexual offence convictions referred to the Court: Commission referral points and the Court's decision

Case	Court's decision	Complainant credibility	Change in law	Missing documents	Forensic/expert evidence	Other referral points
CS2	Quashed	Commission: argued Court: accepted				
CS3 & CS4 *	Upheld	Commission: argued Court: rejected			Commission: argued Court: rejected	Commission: trial judge summing-up (concerning distress) Court: rejected
CS5	Quashed	Commission: argued Court: accepted				
CS6b	Quashed	Commission: argued Court: accepted				
CS9	Quashed	Commission: argued Court: did not address				
CS10	Quashed	Commission: argued Court: accepted				
CS11	Quashed	Commission: argued Court: accepted				
CS12	Quashed	Commission: argued Court: unclear †				
CS13	Upheld	Commission: argued Court: rejected				
CS14b	Upheld	Commission: argued Court: rejected			Commission: argued Court: rejected	

Case	Outcome				
HIA3b	Partially quashed	Commission: argued Court: rejected	Commission: argued Court: accepted	Commission: argued Court: rejected	Commission: 'cumulative effect' Court: rejected
HIA1b	Partially quashed	Commission: argued Court: partly accepted	Commission: argued Court: accepted	Commission: argued Court: rejected	
HIA12 & HIA13 *	Quashed	Commission: argued Court: accepted	Commission: argued Court: accepted	Commission: argued Court: rejected	Commission: trial judge summing-up (concerning delay, case HIA13 only) Court: rejected
EE1b	Quashed				Commission: argued Court: accepted
EE2	Upheld				Commission: argued Court: rejected
EE4	Quashed				Commission: argued Court: rejected
EE5	Quashed				Commission: argued Court: rejected
EE7	Upheld				Commission: argued Court: rejected
EE8	Quashed				Commission: argued Court: rejected
EE9b	Quashed				Commission: argued Court: rejected
EE20	Quashed				Commission: argued Court: rejected

(Continued)

Table 8.1 *Continued*

Case	Court's decision	Complainant credibility	Change in law	Missing documents	Forensic/expert evidence	Other referral points
EE41	Quashed				Commission: argued Court: rejected	
EE26c	Quashed				Commission: argued Court: rejected	
PI1	Quashed	Commission: argued Court: rejected			Commission: argued Court: rejected	
PI3	Upheld	Commission: argued Court: rejected				

Note: The sexual offence cases that the Commission declined to refer are not included in this table.

* Applicants in cases CS3 and CS4 were co-defendants and were reviewed jointly by the Commission and the Court; cases HIA12 and HIA13 are linked cases.

† The case records for case CS12 make clear that the Court quashed the conviction. However, we have been unable to locate the Court's judgment.

the case record 'consult formal memo on child sex abuse cases … the complainant's credibility is critical. I need to see any CICA file to check her account (and perhaps [social services] files)' (CS10, Case Record). Similarly, in case CS11, the CRM wrote:

It is clear that the case against [applicant] depended on [complainant] … It is possible that, if there is any new evidence that we can find that impacts upon [complainant's] credibility, [then] that might be enough to raise a real possibility. There are no grounds, therefore, for not carrying out the *usual* background checks regarding matters that might impact upon [complainant]. (CS11, Case Record, emphasis added)

This shows that by 2007 carrying out credibility checks, at least in the eyes of this CRM, had become the norm, with the decision field—as informed by the 2006 policy—guiding the decision frame of individuals at the Commission.

When credibility is undermined

A range of information is uncovered through credibility checks, but not all of it undermines complainants' credibility, and not all information that does undermine credibility is thought to render a conviction unsafe. Drawing on our sample of cases, this section examines what typically is considered to be sufficiently damaging to complainant credibility to conclude that there is a real possibility that the Court would find a conviction to be unsafe. It also examines how the Court responded to the Commission's referrals in these cases, as Court judgments help to further shape the decision field.

Twenty-seven of our sample of sexual offence cases were referred to the Court. Table 8.1 lists the reasons for referral.[24] It shows that in the majority of cases, complainant credibility was a reason for referral, either solely or in combination with other referral points, though not for the remaining ten cases (EE11b, EE12, EE14, EE15, EE17, EE18, EE19b, EE20, EE26c, and EE41).[25] In two of these ten cases, the complainant did not know the applicant prior to the attack, and the issue turned on whether the applicant was the attacker (EE41 and EE26c). In the remaining eight cases, the Commission examined the complainants' credibility but could find no reasons to doubt the veracity of their accounts or no evidence to prove that they were unreliable (EE11b,[26] EE12,[27] EE14,[28] EE15,[29] EE17,[30] EE18,[31] EE19b,[32] and EE20[33]).

---

[24] The table also shows the Court's acceptance or rejection of the specific referral points made by the Commission.

[25] Other referral points—'change in law' and 'delay'—are examined below in the section on '"Change in law" and "missing documents" arguments'. Referrals based on forensic evidence are not discussed in this chapter other than to point out that in our purposive sample, it was not the more frequently relied-on point of referral. (For discussion of cases that turn on forensic evidence, see Chapter 7.)

[26] The Commission's investigation raised nothing new about the complainant; the issue of whether the complainant fabricated the allegation had been examined at trial and was therefore not fresh evidence.

[27] The Commission investigated social services files and CICA claims for the two complainants but did not mention its findings in the referral Statement of Reasons.

[28] Documents pertaining to the complainant's credibility were lost or destroyed.

[29] Documents pertaining to the complainant's credibility could not be located.

[30] The Commission investigated the complainant's CICA file but found nothing to assist the referral.

[31] The complainant's CICA file had been destroyed.

[32] Documents pertaining to the complainant's retraction were lost.

[33] The Commission's investigation showed that the complainant's credibility had been undermined at trial and was therefore not fresh evidence.

New evidence about complainants' behaviour that undermines their credibility can be related to pre- or post-trial behaviour. Relevant post-trial behaviour often includes false allegations brought by the complainant after the applicant was convicted, and inconsistencies found between statements made at trial and applications for compensation from the CICA and in civil actions initiated after the accused was convicted. Information about pre-trial behaviour that affects complainants' credibility relates to the issue of non-disclosure of material or information about the complainant that— had it been disclosed—might have assisted the defence.[34] The Criminal Procedure and Investigations Act 1996, and its revisions under part 5 of the Criminal Justice Act 2003, governs the rules on disclosure.[35] The prosecution must disclose to the defence any material that might reasonably be considered capable of undermining the prosecution case or of assisting the defence. The prosecution has a continuing duty to disclose beyond conviction. Under the current law on disclosure, the prosecution can decide the scope of disclosure, and the defence cannot review all the material held by the prosecution (Ashworth and Redmayne, 2010; Elks, 2008). It is therefore possible that the use of section 17 powers, or the review of prosecution files, by the Commission could reveal withheld information (perhaps considered by the prosecution to be irrelevant), of which the defence had no knowledge, but which might be capable of assisting the Commission's review (see further Chapter 10).[36]

Case CS2—one of those that led the Commission to revise policy to require credibility checks in all sexual offence cases (see above)—provides a clear example of a conviction being quashed due to non-disclosure by the prosecution. In this case, the applicant had been convicted of an indecent assault outside the venue of a New Year's Eve party. The complainant claimed that the applicant repeatedly punched her and indecently assaulted her. The Commission identified two areas of evidence in which 'the Crown [Prosecution Service] failed to comply with its duty of disclosure' (CS2, Statement of Reasons). First, the Commission found that the prosecution was aware of the complainant's prior conviction for a non-sexual offence, and five previous allegations of physical and sexual abuse. Three allegations were concluded to be false, and it was found that the complainant had inflicted injuries on herself (CS2, Statement of Reasons).[37] Second, medical records revealed that the complainant had a history of self-harm, which had been known to the police. This information was not disclosed because the prosecution had taken the view that the trial was focused on the identity of the assailant, rather than the credibility of the complainant (CS2, Statement

---

[34] This is not always the case, however. Sometimes the information concerns behaviour of which the prosecuting authority was not aware, thus pointing not to non-disclosure but to a potentially faulty investigation by the police and prosecuting agencies.

[35] The 1996 Act limited the obligation to disclose, which had been expanded by case law. In *Ward* ([1993] 1 WLR 619), the Court extended the duty to disclose all potentially undermining material held by the prosecution. The case was criticized for slowing down the trial process as it left no room for judgement by the prosecution on what to disclose, and in turn increased the volume of disclosure material for the defence (Elks, 2008:304–5).

[36] The Formal Memorandum on Sexual Offence Cases mentions non-disclosure of information undermining complainant credibility: 'It is the duty of the prosecution to disclose any information held which may affect complainant's credibility. The police or the prosecuting authority sometimes are reluctant to disclose such information, or fail to make reasonable inquiries when aware that such information might exist' (Criminal Cases Review Commission, 2013d). See Elks (2008:309–10) for a non-exhaustive list of cases he identified in the first ten years of the Commission's work where non-disclosure was a feature of a Commission referral.

[37] In addition to section 17 powers, in this case, the Commission used its section 19 powers to instruct an independent police service to investigate how the police handled the case (see Chapter 11 on the Commission's use of its section 19 powers).

of Reasons).[38] Though an unusual case, the credibility checks gave the Commission reasons to doubt the safety of the conviction:

There is a real possibility that the Court of Appeal would regard the failure to disclose the medical records as being unfair to [applicant], as it prevented his lawyers recognising the existence of this alternative line of defence, and that the unfairness rendered his conviction unsafe. (CS2, Statement of Reasons)

The Commission's referral—based on complainant credibility, and the possibility that the attack may have been self-inflicted—led the prosecution to declare it would not oppose the appeal. The Court quashed the conviction, although the judgment, somewhat disappointingly, expressed no criticism of the Crown Prosecution Service for non-disclosure (CS2, Court judgment).

Other examples of non-disclosure included in Statements of Reasons to refer sexual offence cases (though not necessarily accepted by the Court) were: false allegations to the police later retracted (CS5); an 'untruthful' complainant (HIA3b); and false allegations to the police found to be fabricated (HIA12). Pre-trial information discovered by the Commission but not previously known to the prosecution (hence not examples of non-disclosure, though some amounted to inadequate police investigation) were: school records showing inconsistencies relating to the whereabouts of the complainant (CS10); a mobile phone log showing that the complainant knew the applicant prior to the alleged assault, and therefore undermining the allegation of 'stranger-rape' (CS10); damaging statements from people close to the complainant (CS12 and PI3); false evidence given in a different trial and previous false allegations (CS12);[39] a fraudulent insurance claim and previous allegations of physical assault which were likely to have been false (CS13); a complainant's tendency to dishonesty (CS11); a complainant's dishonesty about her virginity, drug addiction, and use of contraception (HIA11b); five prior sexual assault allegations recorded in social services files which were likely to have been false (HIA11b); and evidence of sexual activity inconsistent with the complainant's account at trial (CS14b).

Grounds of referral concerning post-trial behaviour of complainants mainly drew evidence from compensation claims (e.g. CICA and civil action) after the accused had been convicted (CS3, CS4, CS6b, CS11, HIA12, and HIA13), with the exception of two cases (PI1 and CS9). In case PI1, the complainant retracted the allegation. The other case involved two post-trial allegations of rape, one in which the accused was acquitted and the other later retracted by the complainant, who at that stage asserted that sex had been consensual (CS9). CICA claims were checked by the Commission to look for inconsistencies in statements (changes to this policy are discussed below). In case CS6b, the Commission found significant differences between the complainant's accounts given at trial and in her subsequent CICA application: for example, at trial she had claimed only to have been raped vaginally, while the CICA application stated that she had been raped vaginally and anally and threatened with a gun. Furthermore, she stated that she had become pregnant *as a result of the rape* and undergone a termination, none of which had been mentioned at trial (CS6b, Statement of Reasons).[40]

[38] In addition to these non-disclosures of information undermining the complainant's credibility, the Commission presented damaging statements it took post-trial from the complainant's former husband, mother, daughter, former boyfriend, and fiancé; all referred to the complainant as an accomplished and convincing liar (SC2, Statement of Reasons).

[39] In this case, the Commission's investigation demonstrated inadequate defence work by solicitors rather than non-disclosure by the prosecution.

[40] Cases CS3 and CS4 show that inconsistencies do not necessarily mean a complainant had lied. The Commission's investigation into the CICA claim—which was written in the form of a third-party

Medical records showed that the pregnancy and the termination occurred before the alleged rape. When questioned by Commission staff, the complainant explained that she had been confused, rather than deliberately lying (CS6b, Statement of Reasons). On appeal, the Court accepted the Commission's argument that the complainant's CICA claim had undermined her credibility:

> Part, at least, of the application to the CICA was false. In other respects, it was inconsistent in significant aspects with the evidence before the jury. [The complainant's] credibility is significantly damaged, damage, we emphasise inextricably linked to the complaint, which resulted in the appellant's conviction. (CS6b, Court judgment)

Similarly, discrepancies between CICA applications and statements made to the police and at trial were identified in cases HIA12 and HIA13—two applicants who had been accused by the same complainant. In both cases, the Court accepted that the complainant was unreliable. In case CS11, the complainant's credibility was undermined by lies: at trial when asked if anyone had informed the complainant that compensation could be applied for upon conviction of the accused, the complainant denied knowledge of the compensation scheme, claiming not to be motivated by financial gain (CS11, Statement of Reasons). The Commission's investigation, however, showed that the complainant had received compensation previously against a different offender. The Court accepted the Commission's argument and stated that this further undermined the complainant's credibility, which was 'already fragile' at trial (CS11, Court judgment).

Inconsistent or false CICA claims, or lies about knowledge of compensation schemes, do not necessarily mean that the sexual offence did not occur. They reflect dishonesty and a desire to profit from the (alleged) victimization, but are not proof that it did not take place. In these cases, the Court viewed the post-trial behaviour of complainants as having undermined their general credibility, which in turn affected the safety of a conviction that was based on that credibility.

The above cases illustrate the centrality of complainant credibility in sexual offence cases and the usefulness of the Commission's section 17 powers. However, the surround—in this case the Court's evolving jurisprudence—is not static and can shift over time; the altered condition can trigger a change in the decision field (Hawkins, 2002:49). The Court's judgment in 2010 in case CS13 may be seen to be narrowing its approach to quashing sexual offence convictions based on complainant credibility. The applicant—convicted of indecent assault and rape—applied to the Commission claiming that the complainant had made a fraudulent insurance claim (CS13, Statement of Reasons). The Commission followed up on this point and carried out the standard credibility checks.

The referral of case CS13 was based on two arguments about the credibility of the complainant. First, the complainant made a fraudulent claim about a car accident at the instigation of her partner, the same partner who first contacted the police about the complainant being a victim of sexual abuse. The complainant later admitted to the insurance company that the claim was fraudulent and the 'accident' had been pre-arranged. The Commission argued that this dishonesty showed that the

---

narrative—showed two inconsistencies when compared with the evidence presented at trial. On appeal, the complainant explained that she did not have the opportunity to see the CICA statement typed up by the solicitor's assistant who interviewed her, and could confirm the veracity only of the evidential statement she had made at trial. The Court sided with the complainant and concluded that the inconsistency was now 'disowned by and has never been adopted by the complainant', thus dismissing the Commission's argument (CS3 and CS4, Court judgment).

complainant was prepared 'to make false allegations in order to obtain compensation' and reminded the Court that complainant credibility was 'the only issue' at trial (CS13, Statement of Reasons). Second, new social services evidence, not available at trial, showed that the complainant had made allegations of physical abuse against her father and his partner which she later admitted were untrue.[41]

The case committee reached a 'speedy' and 'unanimous' (#67) decision to refer the case, agreeing that the new evidence undermined the credibility of the complainant and gave rise to a real possibility that the Court would find the conviction to be unsafe (CS13, Case Committee Minutes). In the event, the Court rejected both arguments and was not shy in expressing its frustration with the referral:

> The proposition that where X's credibility is central to the conviction of Y, merely because of the subsequent conviction of X on the grounds of dishonesty, therefore Y's conviction may be unsafe, is startling and would, if correct, have far-reaching consequences ... With great respect to the Statement of Reasons, the notion of admissions in this area strikes us as wishful thinking. (CS13, Court judgment)

With regard to the fraudulent insurance claim, the Court pointed out that the claim was made after the trial had concluded and therefore it 'could not have had any impact on the complainant's state of mind at the time she made her formal complaint' (CS13, Court judgment). It went on to state that the complainant's false insurance claim 'did not mean that her allegations against the appellant must be false' (CS13, Court judgment).

The Court has, however, in previous Commission referrals, found post-trial events that cast doubt on the complainant's integrity to be probative. For example, discrepancies in the facts presented in post-trial CICA claims—as described above—have been thought to sufficiently undermine the credibility of the complainant as to render the conviction unsafe. It might be possible to argue that CICA claims are an exception, as they usually relate directly to the conviction in question.[42] Prior to the 2010 judgment in case CS13, the Court in 2008 (CS9) and in 2006 (HIA12) had quashed convictions based on *other* types of post-trial behaviour. In one case (CS9), two accusations were made post-trial, of which, one was retracted and the other resulted in an acquittal; in the other case (HIA12), police concluded that an accusation made post-trial was fabricated. Both of these cases, however, differed from case CS13 in that they concerned post-trial allegations of *sexual* abuse. Indeed, the Court relied on the distinction between sexual and non-sexual abuse to reject the second referral point in case CS13, which was based on the new information discovered in social service files. It stated that accepting the new information would have the trial 'descending into a morass of side issues as to physical rather than sexual assault and internal family squabbles' (CS13, Court judgment).

After the 2010 judgment in case CS13, the Court continued to apply a strict approach to complainant credibility. In 2014, while the Court accepted some referral points, it rejected the arguments concerning complainant credibility in case HIA3b. One of the Commission's referral points was based on information found in social services files: the complainant's school tutor's statement that she had fabricated events, a psychiatric report casting doubt on the veracity of her statements, and her work as a

---

[41] Minor inconsistencies were found in the complainant's CICA claim, but these were not the basis of the Commission's main referral points (CS13, Statement of Reasons).

[42] The exception in our sample is case CS11 (described earlier), in which the issue was that the complainant had lied about his knowledge of the existence of compensation.

'go-go dancer', suggestive of 'promiscuity' (HIA3b, Statement of Reasons). The Court was unimpressed by these findings, and stated that the new evidence 'reflect[s] no more than opinion and as such would have been inadmissible. Even were some of it factual, in context, it is of little relevance' (HIA3b, Court judgment).

When asked about the judgment in case CS13 in 2010 and case HIA3b in 2014, an interviewee interpreted the Court's dismissal of its referrals as the 'start of a pattern' of clarification on what is considered relevant in relation to the credibility of a complainant (#72).[43] Another interviewee shared this view:

I don't think ... [case CS13] is the high-water mark of Commission errors but ... in recent years, there's been a number of cases where we're getting the message back, you know, be very careful when you're referring, in sex cases, on victim credibility. (#67)

The perceived change in the surround—the narrowing of the criteria on which the Court will quash convictions based on complainant credibility—provided an opportunity for the Commission to reflect on its decision field concerning the investigation of sexual offence cases. One interviewee said, 'I sense that there's a bit of a change in attitude in the Court of Appeal towards credibility issues [relating to] complainants in sex cases. So, I think we just need to realign ourselves, to question "are the standard checks that we tend to make still justified?"' (#72). Similarly, another interviewee stated:

We do a lot of checks and find out ... quite a range of things about complainants in sex cases, but actually, if we analyse which ones have gone to the Court of Appeal and the Court of Appeal has then quashed the conviction, there's actually a really very limited range of things ... there are an awful lot of other things that we've referred cases on in relation to complainant credibility that the Court of Appeal [has] not been interested in at all ... In the last couple of months, they've heard three of these cases where we've referred them in relation to complainant credibility, and all of them, they've upheld the convictions. (#63)

Awareness seems to have emerged that while the standard credibility checks may uncover considerable information, the Court seems inclined to quash convictions primarily where there is evidence that complainants have made other sexual allegations that are found to be false or have been retracted. The development in the Commission's overall approach to complainant credibility in relation to its surround—namely the Court, the political climate, and the media—are revisited in the final section.

Historical Institutional Abuse Cases

Historical sexual abuse cases have received a great deal of attention over the past few years, in part because of high-profile suspects such as Jimmy Savile (Gittos, 2016:198).[44] In such cases, the passage of time—between the alleged abuse and

---

[43] The interviewee gave the following account: 'My overall impression at the moment is that perhaps the Court of Appeal [is] starting to apply some of the principles that have been created over the last few years, with a refinement of bad character for defendants. So, when bad character applications are made before trial to bring in evidence about a defendant ... great care [is] taken there as to whether something is relevant to ... credibility ... What I see is perhaps the Court of Appeal is starting to adopt that same type of approach with information that might also perhaps be regarded as bad-character-type information with complainants as well' (#72).

[44] Operation Yewtree was set up by the Metropolitan Police in 2012 to examine alleged sexual abuse by Jimmy Savile, and also investigated other sexual assault cases involving high-profile 'celebrities', such as Rolf Harris, Gary Glitter, Max Clifford, and Dave Lee Travis.

reporting—poses a challenge to the Commission's investigations because records may have been destroyed, memories may have faded, and witnesses may have disappeared or died (Criminal Cases Review Commission, 2011m). Most applicants in our sample of historical institutional abuse cases were accused of abusing young people in institutions where they were in a position of responsibility for children's welfare, such as children's homes and boarding schools. These cases involve abuse that is alleged to have occurred when complainants were living in or spending time at these institutions. The Commission, as of 2015, had received forty-seven applications concerning historical institutional abuse and referred six cases back to the Court. Our sample includes fourteen of these (HIA1 to HIA14) including four that were referred to the Court.

This section examines two key features that are often present in historical institutional abuse cases: passage of time, and multiple complainants and convictions per case. It also examines three primary reasons for referral of such cases: 'cumulative effect' (the argument that, when a verdict is based on the testimony of multiple complainants, the loss of credibility by *some* complainants should call the safety of the conviction as a whole into question); a change in the law after the verdict was reached; and 'missing documents' (the argument that lost or destroyed documents could have helped to establish whether the allegation occurred, and therefore the lack of such documents should call into question the safety of the conviction).

Passage of time

Sexual abuse cases, as discussed above, pose a special challenge to the Commission since they often involve uncorroborated evidence. Complainant credibility remains the focus of the Commission's investigation in historical abuse cases but the passage of time presents an additional challenge when several years—in some cases, decades—have passed between the commission of the alleged offence and the reporting of the crime. By the time the application reaches the Commission, relevant records may have been destroyed, recollections may have faded, or witnesses may no longer be contactable (Criminal Cases Review Commission, 2009a, 2011m).

In England and Wales, there is no statute of limitations to prevent the prosecution of offences (except for summary offences) that are alleged to have occurred many years go. Victims of historical sexual abuse (sometimes referred to as 'non-recent' abuse) may have suffered continuing abuse during childhood at the hands of family members or institutional care workers; it may take years, often until they reach adulthood, before they feel ready to deal with their victimization through the criminal justice system (Elks, 2008:230). On the other hand, the catastrophic impact on the life of a defendant of being accused and possibly convicted of historical sexual abuse—often in old age—should not be underestimated (Burnett et al., 2017).

Table 8.2 provides information about time between the alleged offence and trial, and the number of complainants, for each case in our sample of historical institutional abuse cases. The shortest timespan was three years and the longest was thirty years; in most cases more than ten years elapsed between the alleged offence and trial. The number of complainants ranged from two to twenty-three.

Multiple complainants, multiple convictions

A key feature of an historical institutional abuse case is that each applicant has multiple complainants and multiple convictions (see Table 8.2). In our sample, there were, on

Table 8.2 Historical institutional abuse cases: number of complainants and years between alleged offences and trial

Case reference	Commission's decision	Years between alleged offences and trial*	Number of complainants	Total number of convictions on application	Nature of convictions at the time of application
HIA1	Not referred	8–21	4	22	Indecent assault × 19, rape × 3
HIA2	Not referred	11–13	4	12	Buggery × 6, indecent assault × 6
HIA3a&b	Partially referred	23–26	4	11	Indecent assault × 9, attempted buggery × 2
HIA4	Not referred	20–30	14	15	Cruelty to a child × 13, buggery × 2
HIA5	Not referred	9–23	11	21	Indecent assault × 17, rape × 3, buggery × 1
HIA6	Not referred	20–27	5	10	Indecent assault × 5, rape × 4, inciting a child to commit gross indecency × 1
HIA7	Not referred	22–39	12	26	Indecent assault, buggery, attempted buggery
HIA8	Not referred	3–14	9	19	Indecent assault, buggery, attempted buggery
HIA9	Not referred	7–25	10	18	Indecent assault × 11, indecency with a child × 2, rape × 2
HIA10a&b	Not referred	19	23	27	Cruelty to a person under 16 years of age × 5, assault occasioning actual bodily harm × 2, indecent assault × 18, attempted buggery × 1, buggery × 1
HIA11a&b	Partially referred	14	6	14	Indecent assault × 11, buggery × 1, rape × 2
HIA12	Referred	14	2	7	Indecent assault × 3, buggery × 1, rape × 3
HIA13	Referred	11–14	2	4	Indecent assault × 3, indecency with a child × 1
HIA14	Not referred	27	6	11	Indecent assault × 9, rape × 2

* The ranges exist due to the number of allegations made (some reported earlier than others).

average, eight complainants for each applicant: the lowest number of complainants was two (HIA12 and HIA13a&b), and the highest was twenty-three (HIA10). The total number of convictions at the time of application to the Commission is also significant.[45] On average, applicants had sixteen convictions, with four being the lowest and twenty-seven the highest number. Offences included indecent assault, indecency with a child, cruelty to a child, inciting a child to commit gross indecency, buggery, and rape (see Table 8.2 for a complete list). The link between multiple complainants and multiple convictions is clear: the more complainants, the more allegations and the more likely it is that there will be multiple convictions

The reason why there are multiple complainants in each case is less easy to answer. One obvious explanation is that abusers within institutions caring for vulnerable people will use their power and privileges over a number of years to harm many people, who may later make complaints independently of each other. Another possible reason may be found in the police practice of 'trawling'—making unsolicited approaches to some or all former residents of an institution to gather information about a suspect. If police working on an institutional abuse case actively searched for victims to make a stronger case against the accused, this could explain the presence of multiple complainants.

The risks of police trawling were first identified following something of a 'moral panic' (Cohen, 1973) about the sexual abuse of children in institutions by care workers in the mid- to late 1990s. The police response led to numerous arrests of care workers across England and Wales with some innocent people caught in the wide net (Webster, 1998).[46] The Home Affairs Committee in 2002 expressed concern that a case put together using trawling methods could produce unreliable evidence, though trawling per se was not prohibited:

Although we hold some reservations about the conduct of police trawls, we do not accept that trawling should be prohibited ... We believe that senior officers should retain their discretion to determine the nature and scale of an investigation, particularly in complex investigations into past institutional abuse. In every case, however, there should be clear justification for the decision to launch a trawl. (Home Affairs Committee, 2002:para:26)

Trawling was thought to be acceptable only if police interviews were conducted with appropriate safeguards. Hence officers should not ask leading questions (for example, revealing to former residents of a children's home the identity of the suspect) and not inform former residents about the possibility of compensation (Home Affairs Committee, 2002:paras:23–61). The Commission has also been clear that evidence of trawling without any other challenges to the safety of the conviction will not constitute a referral point:

The Commission could not make a reference on the basis only that [police force] conducted their investigation in [applicant's] case in a manner which, in some ways may have fallen short of the standards which might be expected by someone having heard the evidence given to the [Home Affairs Committee]. Rather, the Commission would have to be satisfied that if there was any inadequacy and/or misconduct in the investigation its effect impacted upon the safety of [applicant's] conviction ... It follows that the Commission could not make a reference in [applicant's] case only on the basis that so-called 'trawling' techniques were used to gather evidence. (HIA4, Statement of Reasons)

---

[45] This is different from the number of convictions received at trial. For example, case HIA1 had thirty-one convictions, nine of which were quashed on his first appeal, so when he applied to the Commission, he remained convicted on twenty-two counts.

[46] In Cheshire alone, by the end of 1996, 100 care workers had been arrested (Webster, 1998:11).

There were no referrals made on the basis of trawling or improper police investigation technique in our sample of historical institutional abuse cases (though in HIA11b and HIA12, the Commission did identify flaws in the police investigation, which are discussed below).

Most applicants, however, did raise concerns about the police investigation.[47] Across those cases, the Commission carried out three types of investigations. It reviewed police files and databases concerning the police operation in question (e.g. Operation Care, Operation Juno, Operation Goldfinch, and Operation Clyde) and at times conducted interviews with police officers involved with the investigation. It also compared the practices within the investigation to what is recommended in police guidelines. Finally, it looked specifically for possible contamination by checking if the police had used any form of advertisement encouraging potential complainants to come forward, and if so whether these notices stated the nature of allegations or the name of the accused.

In some cases, trawling tactics that were thought to be problematic had been raised at trial or on appeal, providing nothing new for a Commission referral (HIA1, HIA5, HIA7, HIA8). In other cases, the Commission's investigation did not identify any improper police practices (HIA2, HIA3a, HIA4, HIA10a, HIA13). For example, in HIA3a, the Commission interviewed the investigating police force and made the following observation:

The police were careful throughout the investigation not to mention the nature of the allegations to former staff and residents of the care homes or to mention [the applicant's] name. This is reflected in the pro forma which the police worked to when speaking to residents and staff. (HIA3a, Statement of Reasons)

In two of our cases (HIA11b and HIA12), however, the Commission considered that the police investigation methods had been flawed. Both cases were referred to the Court (with some or all of the convictions subsequently quashed), but in neither did due process concerns feature as a ground for referral. In case HIA11b, the Commission discovered inappropriate use of trawling, and in case HIA12, it found other problems with police investigation. Both cases were referred to the Court; case HIA11b's conviction was partially quashed, and case HIA12's was completely quashed.

In case HIA11b, the Commission visited the police force that carried out the investigation to look into their database and to interview an officer about how the investigation was conducted (HIA11b, Statement of Reasons). The Commission was informed that there was no advertisement or appeal for complainants. It discovered later that this information was not true: an article in a local newspaper had given the applicant's name and the number of counts of sexual offences he had been charged with and asked anyone concerned to come forward. An excerpt from the article reads:

Former [care home] manager [applicant] has been charged with 15 counts of sex offences—Police and Social Services jointly appeal for anyone who knew [applicant] in the mid 1980's to come forward. (HIA11b, article quoted in the Statement of Reasons)

The Commission found that one of the complainants had made allegations after the publication of the article. However, it also noted that the police had attempted to contact the complainant independently some time before that, as they were aware that she had been fostered by the applicant (HIA11b, Statement of Reasons). The Commission

---

[47] The exceptions were cases HIA6, HIA9, HIA14, and HIA3b and HIA10b. The latter two cases were reapplications and did not raise concerns about police investigation because they had been examined in cases HIA3a and HIA10a.

mentioned the article in its Statement of Reasons, but decided *not* to include this information as a referral point. It justified its decision by stating that the applicant's trial solicitors 'were in possession of a copy of the press release which informed the [local newspaper] article', and therefore 'those defending [applicant] would have had the opportunity to challenge the decision to issue this press release and the contents thereof' (HIA11b, Statement of Reasons; see above for a discussion on non-disclosure). In other words, the defence had an opportunity to adduce the evidence in prior proceedings.

In case HIA12, the Commission again discovered leading interviews carried out by the police. The following quote from an interview with the investigating CRM explains how the police secured the cooperation of a second complainant against the accused:

The police approached [complainant], no allegations against [complainant] were forthcoming, and then they went back because they only had one complainant against [applicant] and I had a police memo or action document, basically the first one was 'Approach [complainant] and see if she's got anything to say against [applicant].' Result: 'Have seen [applicant], no allegations have been made.' And then later on, when it would appear that the police were actually quite anxious about this, there was another action generated and it was this time more specific: 'Go and see [complainant] and see if [applicant] has ever had anal intercourse with her.' A leading question, they've already seen her twice and, lo and behold, at the third time of asking, yes, it just so happens that [applicant] did have that kind of sexual activity with her and, and that's how it came about. (#33)

The Statement of Reasons for case HIA12 explained that the complainant was interviewed by the police three times, but is silent on the questionable technique used by the police. In this sense, though both cases HIA11b and HIA12 imply criticism of the way investigations were carried out by the police, the Commission took the view that the investigation techniques alone were not sufficiently strong to be a ground for referral, and decided to prioritize other issues, mainly complainant credibility. Another interviewee, experienced in reviewing historical institutional abuse cases, stated that there were no clear-cut cases where the Commission could conclude that improper investigation was carried out:

You have to trust the police to an extent ... From what I remember, I don't think any of the allegations have ever really been that the police had put witnesses up to it, other than perhaps by misleading them. (#2)

Of course, we cannot exclude the possibility that the Commission may have been reluctant to criticize the police. Alternatively, given that trawling per se was considered acceptable by the Home Affairs Committee (2002), it may have made pragmatic decisions not to delve too deeply into the issue of trawling in its referrals. It is not possible, from the examination of institutional historical abuse cases, to draw any firm conclusions on the Commission's willingness (or the lack thereof) to use police misconduct as a basis for referral (see further Chapter 9).[48]

'Cumulative effect' argument

While the Commission did not refer any of our sample of cases back to the Court because of trawling, the safety of convictions can still be affected by its use. Trawling allows the police to gather multiple complainants, which lends strength to a case. To a large extent, a strong case in historical institutional abuse means being able to present

---

[48] The Commission's handling of police misconduct and malpractice is further examined in Chapter 9.

'similar fact' evidence from more than one complainant. Having multiple testimonies does not mean each is true, but it 'passes for corroboration' and each testimony is treated as verification of the others (Burnett, 2016:289). Defence lawyers have described this practice as 'a numbers game' (Barlow and Newby, 2009:2) that creates 'a phantom shared narrative' (Saltrese, 2015). A jury may be impressed with the sheer number of complainants but overlook the quality of each testimony. They may ask 'why would so many complainants come forward if it were not true?' and erroneously see multiple similar accounts as evidence of abuse, ignoring the risk of cross-contamination (Saltrese, 2015). In this way, trawling as an investigative *method* (if used properly) may be legitimate, but the *product* of trawling may make a weak case look significantly stronger than it is.[49]

While a jury may be impressed and influenced by the number of complainants (and the number of allegations), the Commission should not be blinded by the tactic of quantity over quality. In our sample, while the number of complainants across cases ranged from two to twenty-three, the four referrals by the Commission to the Court had relatively few complainants (four each for cases HIA3 and HIA11b, and two each for cases HIA12 and HIA13) (Table 8.2).[50]

The inferred relationship between the number of complainants and the likelihood of a case being referred is not conclusive. The total number of historical institutional abuse cases that the Commission has investigated since its inception in 1997 is not large (estimated at forty-seven), and the inference is drawn from the fourteen cases in our sample. However, what we can say with some confidence is that having more complainants does make the Commission's investigation more arduous and time consuming. A CRM who was working on a case at the time of our interview described the volume of material to review when examining the credibility of 'just' four complainants (HIA1):

Probably equivalent of eight or nine normal archive boxes. Prison file for one of the complainants was in excess of ... a well-stuffed archive box. The social services file that we got electronically was ... I think somewhere in the region of six, seven hundred documents. It is a lot of material, and managing it is a constant kind of challenge because ... you can't just sort of read through it and think, oh right, okay, make a note of that, and then go back to find [it]. You have to index as you go. (#38)

In reviewing material, the Commission may discover new evidence, either undisclosed at trial or relating to post-trial activity, that could undermine the credibility of some complainants but not others:

You very often get several complainants, if not ten. And you might be able to knock two or three out on that ... But that is only three or four charges. And then one of our problems is that ... we've got ten convictions left, even though we can knock out four. (#31)

If the Commission could only find information that undermined the credibility of complainants A and B, but not C, under this hypothetical scenario, it has the following options:

---

[49] The risk was amplified by *DPP v P* [1991] 2AC 447. Previously, for multiple allegations to be considered as mutually corroborative, they had to be 'strikingly similar'. *DPP v P* removed this requirement.

[50] For case HIA11, not all allegations were referred to the Court: the non-referred portion (referred to as case HIA11a) had two complainants whose credibility could not be undermined, and case HIA11b was referred with the remaining four complainants.

1. Decline to refer any convictions, thus exercising the Commission's discretion not to refer even when there is a real possibility (cases HIA6 and HIA8).

2. Refer only convictions relating to A and B, not those relating to C (cases HIA11a&b).

3. Refer all convictions; for convictions related to C, rely on the 'cumulative effect' argument, which asserts that the challenges to convictions A and B have weakened the integrity of the overall case to the extent that the other counts should also be quashed, even though no specific grounds have been found to do so (case HIA3b).

These options are unique to historical institutional abuse cases where multiple complainants are typical.

Under the first option, the Commission has the discretion not to refer a case to the Court 'even where the statutory conditions for referral are satisfied' (Criminal Cases Review Commission, 2016b).[51] It exercises such discretion if a referral would not benefit the applicant:

> Very often we find that … we can often only knock some [convictions] out because there are always so many different complainants. And if we're left with several complainants who still justify the sentence he got on the charges he was convicted of, then we … exercise our discretion not to refer. Because it has to be in the public interest, and it won't be in the public interest if the effect will be of no benefit to the applicant. (#31)

The Commission will take into consideration the seriousness of the offence, the nature and severity of the sentence, the age of the conviction, and its impact on the applicant—such as loss of job opportunities, loss of reputation, personal sense of injustice, and effect on family (Criminal Cases Review Commission, 2016b). The Commission also considers the 'public interest' argument that people should remain convicted only of offences where the conviction is safe (Criminal Cases Review Commission, 2016b). This principle was applied in cases HIA6 and HIA8.

In case HIA6, there were five complainants and the applicant had been convicted of ten counts of sexual offences, from indecent assault to rape (see Table 8.2). The Commission's investigation showed that the two counts of indecent assault could be quashed due to a change in law (discussed in the following section) but that there were no grounds to refer the rape convictions to the Court. The sentence for those assaults was two years' imprisonment to run concurrently with a sentence of twelve years for the rape convictions.[52] Therefore, the Commission argued that the applicant (who was in prison) would not see his total prison time reduced, and that there was no 'public interest' served by making a referral (HIA6, Statement of Reasons).

The applicant in case HIA8 had nineteen convictions for sexual offences against nine complainants. The Commission found new evidence that may render three of the convictions unsafe, but these convictions had also resulted in concurrent sentences, and so his time in custody would not be reduced. The applicant's legal representative argued that the Commission should nevertheless refer, on the basis that the applicant was entitled to the opportunity to clear his name even for a small number of the total counts against him. The Commission rejected this argument, based on the fact that

---

[51] Clark [2001] EWCA Crim 884; Smith (Wallace Duncan) [2004] EWCA Crim 631.

[52] When a defendant is convicted of two or more crimes, a judge may impose sentences to be served consecutively or concurrently, with the longest sentence determining the time served.

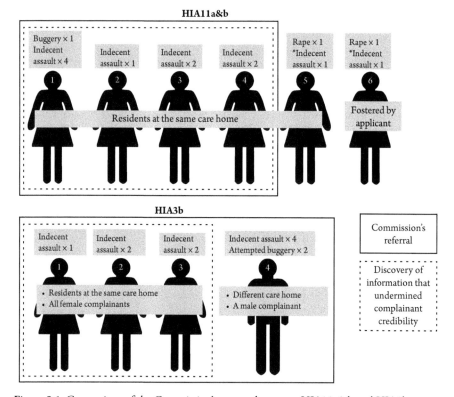

Figure 8.1 Comparison of the Commission's approach to cases HIA11a&b and HIA3b

Note: * Indecent assault convictions for complainants 5 and 6 in cases HIA11a&b were referred to the Court based on the 'change in law' argument, not based on complainant credibility. The remaining two rape charges were not referred.

the applicant would remain convicted on more serious counts (buggery and attempted buggery) and remain a registered sex offender (HIA6, Statement of Reasons).

The second option, to refer some but not all convictions, was adopted in cases HIA11a&b. The applicant was in charge of a children's home during the late 1980s. He was tried on twenty-five counts including rape, buggery, and indecent assault, and convicted of fourteen counts brought by six female complainants. Five of the complainants were at a children's home where the applicant worked, and the other fostered by the applicant and his partner (see Figure 8.1). The Commission's investigation found a real possibility that the convictions relating to four of the five complainants at the children's home could be unsafe, but was unable to find anything new to undermine the safety of the convictions relating to one complainant at the children's home or to the foster child.[53]

The implications were that even if the Court accepted all of the Commission's referral points, the applicant would remain convicted for the two rapes and stay on the sex offender register. Notwithstanding, the Commission referred the case because 'it would still be a tangible benefit to [the applicant] in terms of the totality of his

---

[53] The two indecent assault convictions relating to these two complainants were referred as they were based on a change in law rather than on complainant credibility.

convictions' (HIA11a&b, Case Committee Minutes).[54] The Court accepted some of the Commission's referral points, which resulted in a sentence reduction of two years, though by this point the applicant had already served his sentence.

An interviewee described the choice between referring no convictions (option 1) and referring some convictions (option 2) back to the Court as follows:

If we can knock all the rapes out and he's only convicted of indecent assaults, then we might well refer it, because there is a benefit to him in doing so, because he's not a rapist; he's an indecent assaultist. Which, in theory at least, is a better thing to be if you have to choose about these things. (#31)

In practical terms, in HIA11a&b, after the Commission's referral, the applicant's status changed from being convicted of rape (× 2), buggery (× 1), and indecent assault (× 11), to being convicted of rape (× 2) and indecent assault (× 4). Whether this truly benefitted the applicant is uncertain. What is clear, however, is that in other sexual offence cases where the issue came down to one complainant's word against the applicant, the convictions that were quashed and the discoveries that were made in cases HIA11a&b would have been significant. This brings us back to the point about the difficulty of quashing all convictions in historical institutional abuse cases due to the existence of multiple complainants.

The third and final option for the Commission, when it cannot find new evidence to quash each conviction in a case, is to nonetheless refer all of them based on the 'cumulative effect' argument, as was used in case HIA3b. This applicant was prosecuted on twenty-six counts and was convicted of eleven, including attempted buggery and multiple counts of indecent assault. There were four complainants in total: three female complainants from one children's home, and one male complainant in a separate children's home some distance away (Figure 8.1). The Commission's investigation found new arguments and evidence that raised a real possibility that the convictions for abuse of the three female complainants were unsafe, but nothing new relating to the male complainant.

The Commission used 'change in law', 'missing documents', and 'complainant credibility' arguments to refer five indecent assault convictions relating to the three complainants. It referred the remaining convictions, relating to the last complainant (four for indecent assault and two for attempted buggery), based on 'cumulative effect' (HIA3b, Statement of Reasons).

The Court quashed only two convictions for indecent assault, based on changes in the law (discussed below). It was not persuaded by the Commission's arguments about 'cumulative effect', stating that the remaining complainant's allegations were sufficiently similar to the rest for two reasons. First, the remaining complainant was a male (the others were female) and the alleged abuse occurred at a different children's home (unknown to the three women complainants), so 'contamination' was unlikely. Second, the remaining male complainant admitted to a close friendship with the applicant, who shared a flat with him after discharge from care—unlike the other complainants (HIA3b, Court judgment).

This referral could be seen as a brave move by the Commission, but was also an inconsistent decision, when compared with other cases. There were six convictions in relation to the boy—where no new argument or evidence could be found—and these included the most serious offence. It would have been surprising if the Court had been persuaded to quash these convictions.[55] Indeed, in cases HIA11a&b discussed above, the Commission decided *not* to refer the two remaining rape charges because they were considered to be sufficiently different from the other counts and from each other (Figure 8.1). One of the complainants was also living with the applicant rather than at a children's home, so the risk of contamination between complainants did not exist.

In our view, referrals based on cumulative effect can be justified in historical institutional abuse cases because it can act as a counter-balance to the use of multiple complainants' testimonies to provide similar fact evidence as corroboration. Without this resource, it would be an almost impossible task to quash all convictions based on fresh evidence when the number of complainants strengthens the qualitatively weak trial evidence and where there is a risk of contamination of evidence by police trawling.

The decision field for investigating historical institutional abuse cases was not clearly defined by formal policies, unlike the sexual offence cases examined above that normally involved a relatively quick reporting of abuse and only one complainant. The formal policy treated historical institutional abuse cases as a sub-category of sexual offence cases and mentioned them in passing without any specific guidance on how they should be investigated (Criminal Cases Review Commission, 2013d, 2017c). The inconsistent decisions made in cases HIA3b and HIA11a&b may have been due to the lack of clearly defined policy to guide CRMs and commissioners, which brought different individual decision frames to the foreground (Hawkins, 2002:52).

The CRM assigned to case HIA3b was different to the one assigned to cases HIA11a&b; the six commissioners who sat on two case committees (three in each committee) were different.[56] The commissioner involved in case HIA3b described the CRM who worked on the case as 'very clever' (#31). A different interviewee (who was not involved in case HIA3b), without any prompts from us, described the same CRM as:

I'm utterly in awe of [CRM's] phenomenal skill of dealing not just with a volume of cases but the technical stuff, because [CRM] had the highest number of … referrals, dozens of them, and that does reflect [CRM's] phenomenal ability, but we can't all be [CRM]. You know, the majority of us would say [CRM] was exceptional. (#67)

While we do not have any interview data describing the CRM who worked on cases HIA11a&b, our interview reveals that the CRM in case HIA3b is known to have the highest number of referrals. Taking into consideration that cases are allocated at random, not based on the potential merits of the case, it is possible that the CRM in case HIA3b has a 'pro-applicant' outlook (Chapter 6) to case review and adopts a referral-oriented frame.

A solicitor who represented both applicants in cases HIA3b and HIA11a&b also praised the work of the CRM in case HIA3b:

Now, I can put up a pile of [Commission] refusals on historic care home cases. There's a case of [HIA3b] that's been referred—who knows what the ultimate outcome will be, but it's like

---

[55] The solicitor who represented the applicants in case HIA3b (and cases HIA11a&b)—before learning of the Court's decision on case HIA3b—acknowledged that the referral was ambitious and predicted the Court's decision as: 'Partial win', going on to explain: There's a risk … the problem with [case HIA3b] was that, if it had been a similar fact case, I'd have been pretty confident. The difficulty in the argument being advanced by the Commission—and I'm very grateful they're advancing it, but it is that, effectively, once you've damaged certain aspects of the case, then the rest should fall.' (#12)

[56] The only overlap was the screening commissioner in both cases.

a completely different approach on [HIA3b] and it's because it had a great case review manager … Yeah, someone that was interested … After that referral, we had then further refusals, going back to the same old approach. (#12)

We do not want to suggest that only this CRM could have produced this outcome in these cases, but our interviews demonstrate the impressive reputation of this particular CRM inside and outside the Commission. Furthermore, in our view, the facts of the cases were not sufficiently distinct to account for the difference in outcome. Without a clearly defined field for historical cases to guide CRMs and commissioners' decision-making, it is plausible that this particular CRM was influential in persuading the case committee to use the 'cumulative effect' argument in referring the whole case back to the Court.[57]

'Change in law' and 'missing documents' arguments

The Commission used the 'change in law' and 'missing documents' arguments in two cases to refer convictions back to the Court (Table 8.1). First, evolving case law (*R v J*[58]) on underage consensual sexual intercourse was relied upon to quash a number of indecent assault convictions in case HIA3b (two counts) and case HIA11b (six counts). The Sexual Offences Act 1956 states that consensual sexual intercourse with a child under 16 must be reported within twelve months. In both cases, as the twelve-month period had passed, the prosecution at trial changed the charge from sexual intercourse with a child under 16 to indecent assault, for which both applicants were convicted. This, it seems, was common practice in cases where the twelve-month period had elapsed.

However, the 2005 case of *R v J* confirmed that an indecent assault charge (in lieu of an under-age consensual sex charge) could not be applied due to the passage of time. For example, in case HIA11, the applicant had been charged on indictment with both rape and indecent assault, the latter being framed as an alternative to rape in case the prosecution failed to establish the absence of consent to sexual intercourse (HIA11b, Statement of Reasons). In reference to the change in law under *R v J*, the Court accepted the Commission's referral point and quashed the relevant convictions for cases HIA3b and HIA11b.

For the applicant in case HIA3b, this was a second application to the Commission; he had first applied in 2003 (HIA3a) before *R v J*. However, this was not the only case law of relevance to his case. The Commission was of the view that his reapplication also benefitted from the 2006 *R v Sheikh*[59] judgment concerning missing documents, to which we turn now.[60]

Sheikh provided a tool for lawyers to rebut uncorroborated allegations of historical abuse (Elks, 2008:236). In this case, twenty years had passed between the alleged offence and trial. Not surprisingly, some of the documents that might have been probative had been lost over time and could therefore be of no assistance to the prosecution or the defence. The absence of annual leave records meant the defendant was unable to rebut the allegation that the abuse took place on a particular date. The Court quashed

---

[57] Case committee minutes do not provide any evidence concerning the role CRM played in the Commission's final decision to refer the whole case back to the Court.
[58] *R v J* [2005] 1 Cr App R 277. [59] *R v Sheikh* [2006] EWCA Crim 2625.
[60] The Statement of Reasons in case HIA3b had three referral points: 1) change in law based on *R v V*; 2) 'delay' based on *Sheikh*; and 3) complainant credibility (see above).

the conviction, stating that the missing documents were likely to have included re-cords that could have refuted the allegation, and their absence denied the defendant a fair trial.

The Commission relied on the *Sheikh* judgment in cases HIA3b and HIA11b. However, while the Court accepted the *R v J* change in law argument in both cases, it rejected the *Sheikh* argument concerning missing documents (HIA3b and HIA11b, Statements of Reasons). An interviewee explained to us that the Court rarely accepts the missing document argument:

> If there is a document that is gone, and that document would have shown for sure one way or the other, whether the offence had been committed, then [the Court] will sometimes quash it now. But it's very, very tightly looked at. And it's got to be a document which would have made a huge difference … But they're very tricky about it. (#31)

In case HIA3b, the complainant alleged that the indecent assault by the applicant occurred on a Saturday sometime in August when she was the only girl at the care home. The Commission used available documents to narrow the possibilities down to a Saturday on which the abuse could have taken place, and argued that if records were available, it would be possible to demonstrate whether or not the applicant was at the care home. The Court rejected the argument stating that it was not possible to know the provenance and accuracy of the documents alleged to have existed, but now lost (HIA11b, Statement of Reasons).

In case HIA11b, one of the complainants had made allegations of indecent assault, then retracted them, only to renew them. She explained at trial that she temporarily withdrew her allegations after being pressured and bullied by other residents who had been angered that privileges had been withdrawn from all residents because of her complaint, and not because they were untrue (HIA11b, Statement of Reasons). In its referral, the Commission relied on *Sheikh* claiming that the daily log, now destroyed, would have recorded disciplinary measures such as the withdrawal of privileges and would therefore have demonstrated the veracity of the account on retraction (HIA11b, Statement of Reasons). Rejecting this argument, the Court distinguished case HIA11b from *Sheikh*; it argued that the two counts of indecent assault had been corroborated by statements from police officers, social workers, and employees at the care home at trial. The issue concerning the missing document did not relate to the allegation itself but to an 'ancillary issue' (HIA11b, Court judgment).

Responding to the Surround

The political climate can be an important part of the surround and may shape the field in which specific policies are formulated, and the decisions taken in par-ticular cases by the application of decision frames (Hawkins, 2002). 'The surround is not, however, unchanging' (Hawkins, 2002:49). Over the last fifty years, the treatment of alleged victims of sexual violence has changed—in law and policy—from an assumption that 'complainants may be lying' to 'complainants should be believed'. The environment of the surround—defined by Court judgments, police and prosecution policies, government initiatives, and media reporting—has shifted from a focus on wrongful convictions to wrongful acquittals. This section examines the changing narrative, and the ways that the Commission has responded to this evolving surround.

From doubting to believing the complainant

During the 1950s and the1960s the police had enormous power; most prosecution decisions were made by the police or by lawyers instructed and controlled by the police (Sanders, 2016:83). As discussed in Chapter 1, the case of Maxwell Confait in the 1970s led to the establishment of the Royal Commission on Criminal Procedure. The Royal Commission found that the police had too much power without any checks or controls, and to tackle this problem a state prosecution agency, independent of the police (the Crown Prosecution Service) was formed. In relation to rape cases, the credibility of the police was damaged by transmission of a BBC documentary *Police* (1982) by Roger Graef, which documented the bullying of a rape victim by Thames Valley police.

As concerns for their treatment gathered pace, victims were given much more credence from the 1970s. Section 2 of the Sexual Offences (Amendment) Act 1976 was the first piece of legislation to restrict the use of evidence concerning a complainant's sexual history. As pointed out in the Introduction, section 41 of the Youth Justice and Criminal Evidence Act 1999 further protected complainants' privacy concerning their sexual history (although the *Evans* case demonstrated that such protection needs to be balanced against the pursuit of a fair trial).[61] Other changes have also been made to encourage complainants of sexual abuse to report their experience, such as removing time limits for delayed prosecutions, guaranteeing anonymity to complainants, and providing the option to give evidence via video link or from behind a screen (Burnett, 2016:283).

Article 2(2) of the Sexual Offences Act 1956 provided that someone accused of a sexual offence should not be convicted on the evidence of one witness alone unless that witness testimony was corroborated.[62] Under this Act, juries were warned about the dangers of relying on uncorroborated evidence. The assumption, under the law, was that a complainant's testimony alone should not be trusted, and the hurdle to achieve a conviction was set high. The position of the law changed under the Criminal Justice and Public Order Act 1994. Section 31(1) removed the requirement for a judge to warn the jury about the dangers of convicting the accused on uncorroborated evidence. The Court further clarified the position in *Makanjoula*,[63] stating that corroboration warnings should not be given unless there was evidence to suggest that a complainant was unreliable.

These changes in law and policy, which began in the 1970s, were also influenced by the second wave of feminism (1960s–1980s), which altered the way allegations of sexual abuse were perceived.[64] Susan Brownmiller's (1975) book *Against Our Will: Men, Women and Rape* challenged the belief that women often lied about sexual abuse and prompted a body of similar academic and polemic publications on the sexual abuse and subjugation of women and the failure of the state to respond appropriately. Indeed,

---

[61] Other changes in law include the Criminal Justice and Public Order Act 1994, which made rape within marriage illegal, and the Sexual Offences Act 2003, which removes 'honest but unreasonable belief in consent' as a defence against a rape charge.

[62] Article 2(2) states that 'a person shall not be convicted of an offence under this section on the evidence of one witness only, unless the witness is corroborated in some material particular by evidence implicating the accused'.

[63] *R v Makanjoula* [1995] 3 All ER 730.

[64] The first wave of feminism worked to achieve equality in rights such as the right to vote, whereas the second wave focused more on the sexist power structures that result in discrimination within society.

Rumney (2006:143) argued that Brownmiller's book helped create an 'overwhelming consensus' in the United States and elsewhere that false rape complaints are rare.

In the 2000s, the environment of the surround—which had been moving towards a victim-centred approach more concerned with wrongful acquittals—became, albeit briefly, more focused on false allegations and wrongful convictions. The Home Affairs Committee (2002) examined allegations of child abuse in children's homes and other institutions,[65] and concluded that 'a new genre of miscarriages of justice' had arisen from over-enthusiastic pursuit by the police (Home Affairs Committee, 2002:para:2).[66] It was concerned that 'trawling' caused wrongful convictions of care workers in historical institutional abuse cases. The Home Office, however, expressed dissatisfaction with the Home Affairs Committee's finding, stating that it had overestimated the risk of miscarriage of justice and argued that trawling per se was not problematic (see Birch and Taylor (2003) on the contrasting views of the Home Affairs Committee and the Home Office). This short-lived attention to dangers to the accused was overtaken by victim-centred justice as developed under New Labour, which led to initiatives that expanded the protection for vulnerable groups including complainants and witnesses in sexual offence cases (Gittos, 2016:193).[67]

The current political climate of the surround is firmly committed to improving the experiences of victims and increasing the reporting and conviction rates of sexual abuse cases. Operation Yewtree, established in 2012, investigated alleged sexual abuse, predominantly of children, by Jimmy Savile and others, which led to the publication *Giving Victims a Voice* (Gray and Watt, 2013). This report was critical of police and prosecution inaction, and recorded 214 incidents of abuse as crimes without any criminal proceedings (Gray and Watt, 2013:para:7.3). Since Savile was dead and could not be tried, complainants' allegations were treated as 'proven' (Gittos, 2016:198). The report was sympathetic to alleged victims and provided a platform for speaking out, as the title of the report suggested, but was silent on the possibility of false allegations. It also chose to refer to those making allegations as victims instead of complainants—the term normally used before a conviction is secured (Furedi, 2016:43; Gittos, 2016:198). Keir Starmer, a former director of public prosecutions, celebrated the launch of the report and argued that criminal justice agencies had been overly anxious about people making false allegations, based on perceptions about how victims should present:

For too long, child sexual abuse cases have been plagued by myths about how 'real' victims behave which simply do not withstand scrutiny. The days of the model victim are over. From now

---

[65] All of the allegations related to historical abuse. In Merseyside alone, the police investigated 510 former care workers suspected of child abuse; of those, sixty-seven individuals were charged, resulting in thirty-six convictions and nine acquittals. In the remaining twenty-two cases, the prosecution was either discontinued or dismissed by the judge (Home Affairs Committee, 2002).

[66] The Committee expressed concern that a case put together using trawling methods produced unreliable evidence, and set in the context of a growing compensation culture, the risk of miscarriage of justice was high (Home Affairs Committee, 2002).

[67] Gittos (2016:194–5) stated that government-funded research and official publications on responses to sexual offence cases have focused on increasing conviction rates and improving the experiences of witnesses, rather than on the issue of potential wrongful convictions. Baroness Stern in 2010 reviewed the handling of rape cases and argued that 'attitudes, policies and practices have changed fundamentally and for the better' (Stern, 2010:8). For example, she found that 'achieving best evidence' interviews are now widely used in sexual offence trials for children and vulnerable adults (Ministry of Justice, 2011). While service and provisions are likely to vary somewhat across the forty-three police forces in England and Wales, they each have specially trained officers to deal with rape complaints, the Crown Prosecution Service has appointed specialist rape prosecutors, and only those judges trained in sexual offences can hear rape cases (Stern, 2010:4).

on these cases will be investigated and prosecuted differently, whatever the vulnerabilities of the victim. (Starmer, 2013)

Some have argued that the rebalancing of the system, the shift from a concern for wrongful convictions to wrongful acquittals, has gone too far. Brigham (2016) and Furedi (2016) contend that in challenging the myth of the 'lying woman', the myth of the 'never-lying woman' has been created, in which there is a presumption of victimhood that ignores the protections to which defendants are entitled. In Furedi's (2016:42) view, contemporary media outlets often cover sexual abuse stories extensively but uncritically, displaying a perceived obligation to demonstrate solidarity and to believe the complainant.[68] Rose (2016:32) confirms concern among journalists that publishing information refuting or exposing flaws in investigations or claims of sexual abuse would be damaging to their careers.

Over the last fifty years, the pendulum has swung between two sorts of concerns about the failure of due process: wrongful convictions and wrongful acquittals. The change in the surround was driven by various events not just by a zeitgeist or by pure politics, but by real experience of 'victim bashing' *and* evidence of wrongful convictions.

The Commission's response: field and frame

The Commission is not immune to changes in the surround. The Court's dismissal of cases referred on complainant credibility in cases CS13 and HIA3b (discussed above) demonstrated that the Commission reflects on the changing stance of the Court. It is keenly aware of changes in the surround ('much more focus is placed on victims now' (#75)). Faced with the current climate of 'believe everybody' (#75), and the danger of credibility checks not being done properly, one interviewee stated that what the Commission can do is to 'build safeguards around it' (#75).[69]

We asked interviewees whether the Commission should consider changing its decision field requiring credibility checks, which can be very invasive, as it may be seen as 'swimming against the political tide' (#63).[70] Their responses ranged from the principled to the pragmatic. The following interviewee took a principled position not to be swayed by the current victim-centred approach of the surround and reiterated the aim of the Commission:

The victim agenda is high profile, of course, but we can't be swayed by the political agenda or the [Crown Prosecution Service] changing their practice ... I think as long as you're asking yourself

---

[68] Jemma Beales made false rape and sexual assault claims against fifteen men, and was convicted of four counts of perjury and four counts of perverting the course of justice in August 2017. *The Independent* ran an article titled 'False rape allegations are rare—rape is not. Stop using the case of Jemma Beales to discredit all women' (Glosswitch, 2017). The article expressed concern that the reporting of a false rape allegation could distort the image of rape victims, cast unnecessary doubt on the overall occurrence of sexual abuse, and prevent other genuine victims of sexual abuse coming forward. The cultural unease about doubting complaints of sexual abuse and reporting false allegations may stem from a concern not to undo the work of feminists in dismantling the stereotype of the lying-woman and not to encourage the practice of 'victim bashing'.

[69] Interviewees agreed that it is important 'to make sure that victims are treated properly' (#77). However, they believed that when the issue comes down to uncorroborated allegations, credibility checks should be done at the beginning of the criminal justice process as 'a routine part of the police investigation' (#77).

[70] The question was worded as follows: 'The recent political climate, for example the Crown Prosecution Service's new policy on sexual offence cases, is "let's treat the victim as a whole, including their vulnerability". Are there any pressures on the Commission to reconsider the approach taken, as reflected in the Formal Memorandum?'

[if] there's good reason, and then we're treating all of the checks with respect and the highest degree of confidentiality, then I don't think there's any reason to change, that it would ... we would do our applicants a disservice. (#74)

A similar principled position was echoed in another interview, which touched on the importance of the Commission leading by example:

It's always important that the [Crown Prosecution Service] and police are aware that [carrying out credibility checks] is our standard policy, so if somebody comes to us after a conviction, we will uncover these things, so it's wisest for them to be thinking about them during the course of their own investigation. (#77)

Another interviewee provided a more nuanced response to the same question, reflecting on the current legal position as well as the broader political climate:

The background has changed ... since 2006, in the way the criminal justice system approaches victims ... by the time we were shifting to 'let's look at complainant credibility', the criminal justice system was going the other way ... We've widened out what we're looking for. So, a lot of the time, what we find might not actually be admissible anyway. I mean, it seems to me we need to kind of re-focus on what's actually going to matter, what's going to make a difference. (#63)

This response is pragmatic, implying consideration of what might persuade the Court to quash a conviction, and does not set the Commission against the political climate. Another interviewee agreed that the formal policy on complainant credibility should be changed, but took the view that it should be modified to be more in line with the prosecution—a position not shared by the interviewees quoted above:

Interviewer: Now the [Crown Prosecution Service's] policy on sexual abuse cases is 'let's look at the victim as a whole' ... and I guess the current Formal Memorandum is, in a way, in conflict with that approach.

Interviewee: Yes. Yes, yes, certainly, yes. So I think we ... just need to revisit that and perhaps just adjust a little bit our thinking on all of that. So, yes, that's a pending piece of work at the moment. (#72)

These interviews demonstrate contrasting decision frames: a frame that is sensitive to the changing surround and considers it appropriate to adjust to the victim-centred approach concerned with wrongful acquittals, versus a frame concerned with wrongful convictions.

The Commission's decision field, articulated in the formal policy on investigating sexual offence cases, was modified in 2017 (Criminal Cases Review Commission, 2017c). The section above explored the development of the formal policy leading to the implementation of rigorous investigation of complainant credibility. From 2006, all sexual offence cases were subject to credibility checks, and opting out of doing these checks required commissioner approval. The centrality of complainant credibility was also illustrated by the language used in previous formal policies (e.g. 'a key issue in most applications to the Commission will be the victim's credibility' (Criminal Cases Review Commission, 2006a:para:2); 'primarily you are looking for anything that could affect the credibility of the complainant or the veracity of the complaint itself' (Criminal Cases Review Commission, 2008:para:3)). The 2017 policy moved away from treating credibility checks as standard procedure:

Sex offence convictions are a category of offence where witness credibility will often be of real significance. That will depend, however, on all the evidence and all the circumstances. Cases will be assessed on an individual basis applying the 'necessary and reasonable' test. (Criminal Cases Review Commission, 2017c:para:6)

The policy treats credibility checks as only a *possible* avenue of investigation. It requires the decision of whether or not to carry out the checks to be recorded (Criminal Cases Review Commission, 2017c:para:5), but does not assume that such checks will be made.[71]

One area in which the use of section 17 powers had diminished prior to the introduction of the new policy is the checks carried out on CICA files. Interviews show that the checking of CICA files has 'become of relatively little value' (#63) because the CICA claims are no longer filled in from scratch by the complainant. Copies of previous evidential statements made by the complainant are used, and therefore inconsistencies—which had been used to undermine complainant credibility—are unlikely to emerge (#72; #65). Learning from the changing practice with regards to CICA claims, staff at the Commission started to 'challenge the necessity' of carrying out CICA checks (#67). The 2017 policy reflects changes in the way that CICA claims are made, and advises that CICA enquiries are likely to be useful only when a complainant has claimed not to know that compensation is available but has in fact applied for it (Criminal Cases Review Commission, 2017c:para:19).

As the Commission introduced the new policy in 2017—when our fieldwork had been completed—we have not examined the change in the framing of sexual offence cases. It is possible that the 'necessary and reasonable test' required by the 2017 policy is interpreted and applied differently by various members of the Commission. Individuals at the Commission who adopted a victim centred decision frame concerned with wrongful acquittals may choose not to carry out some, or any credibility checks when reviewing a sexual offence case. By contrast, individuals who adopted a decision frame concerned with wrongful convictions and who preferred to go against the surround, may continue to use section 17 powers routinely.

Shifting Beliefs about Complainant Credibility

In sexual abuse cases—contemporary or historical—complainant credibility is central to the outcome of the trial and the safety of the conviction. The Commission can use section 17 powers to examine whether complainants' pre- or post-trial behaviour has undermined their credibility, or if they were motivated by the prospect of victim compensation. The question for the Commission is how far its powers should be used in each case, from checking CICA claims and social services records to carrying out more invasive checks, such as reviewing complainants' medical records. The Commission's decision field, which has encouraged the regular use of credibility checks in sexual offence cases has proved expedient, as the majority of referrals in sexual offence cases made by the Commission are either solely or partly based on complainant credibility.

For historical institutional abuse cases, 'trawling' was not a ground for referral in the cases we studied. Notwithstanding a widespread tolerance for trawling, we suggest its use could affect the safety of a conviction. Trawling enables the police to identify multiple complainants, and strengthens the prosecution's case by numbers even when the quality of each complainant's allegation is weak. Having multiple complainants

---

[71] While the 2017 policy repeats the phrase 'necessary and reasonable' twelve times in a six-page document as the test to be applied, it does not explain what that test means in practice.

renders the Commission's investigation arduous and time consuming because new arguments or evidence need to be found in respect of all complainants.

The Commission has until recently gone against the political climate of the surround that was primarily concerned with wrongful acquittals. As legislation and policies in the last several decades focused on protecting alleged victims, the Commission's decision field—as reflected in the formal policy on sexual abuse cases—became more focused on undermining complainant credibility. Credibility checks on all sexual offence cases became a standard policy embraced by CRMs and commissioners. With growing enthusiasm for victim-centred justice, however, we found that the Commission was not immune to the influence of the changing surround.

The police and the prosecutors gradually moved away from viewing complainants' vulnerability, such as a troubled upbringing, promiscuity, evidence of intoxication, or factors relating to the late reporting of a crime, as undermining their credibility. The Court started to distinguish between vulnerability and credibility more clearly as society's focus shifted from a concern about wrongful convictions to wrongful acquittals. The Commission too—influenced by the Court's narrowing position on what constitutes credibility—became persuaded to stop relying on complainants' vulnerabilities unrelated to sexual abuse (e.g. previous false allegations of *physical* abuse) to discredit them.

The Commission's 2017 policy on sexual offence cases removed the requirement for credibility checks in all sexual offence cases. Our interviews suggest some differences in opinion within the Commission, with some considering it necessary to adjust to the changing surround thus adopting a decision frame primarily concerned with wrongful convictions, and others who believe it wise to adopt a decision framed more concerned with wrongful acquittals. While there may be practical benefits of carrying out fewer credibility checks in sexual offence cases (e.g. stop checking for inconsistencies in CICA claims), it would be wrong to change or adjust the Commission's approach simply because of the current moral and political climate. Our criminal justice system has come a long way in improving the treatment of complainants and reducing wrongful acquittals, but the Commission must remain cautious about the current environment of the surround, which could lead to further wrongful convictions, in order to fulfil its function as a safety net.

9

Responding to Applicants' Allegations of Policing Without Integrity

Procedural irregularities do have their place in unsafe convictions but, equally, I can see why relevance is the ultimate arbiter. (#1)[1]

Introduction

Wrongful convictions typically result from multiple errors—relating to eyewitness misidentification, false confessions, perjured testimony, and forensic error—that are sequential, build upon each other, and are compounded as the investigation continues (see Chapter 5). But a thorough and transparent police investigation, not hampered by tunnel vision, may identify flaws or gaps in the evidence and more reliable information, or even an alternative suspect. In other words, integrity in policing can militate against the negative effects of fallible witnesses and imperfect forensic expertise (see Hunter et al., 2016). Indeed, American research shows that a strong prosecution case—that does not need to rely on equivocal evidence—can reduce the probability of a wrongful conviction by 25 per cent (Gould et al., 2013:499–508). However, the history of wrongful convictions—and our analysis of cases, as presented in previous chapters—has shown that sometimes the prosecution case is built on errors and lies. Some of those who apply to the Criminal Cases Review Commission ('the Commission') claim that policing without integrity has had an impact on the safety of their conviction and the Commission has to decide if there is sufficient evidence to persuade the Court of Appeal ('the Court') that this rendered the conviction unsafe.

The Court's use of the term 'unsafe' has two distinct, if typically overlapping, meanings: either that a factually innocent person has been wrongfully convicted; or that the pre-trial and/or trial process have been irregular, and hence unfair.[2] Lord Bingham LCJ, in *R v CCRC ex parte Pearson*,[3] put it thus:

The expression 'unsafe' in s 2(1)(a) Criminal Appeal Act 1968 does not lend itself to precise definition. In some cases unsafety will be obvious, as (for example) where it appears that someone other than the appellant committed the crime and the appellant did not, or where the appellant has been convicted of an act that was not in law a crime, or where a conviction is shown to be vitiated by serious unfairness in the conduct of the trial or significant legal misdirection ...

[1] All interviews are with Commission staff, including commissioners, case review managers, management staff, and legal or investigations advisers, unless we state otherwise.

[2] For a helpful discussion of this distinction see Roberts, 2003.

[3] [1999] 3 All ER 498; EWHC Admin 452, [2000]; 1 Cr App R 141. This was the first challenge to a decision by the Commission not to refer a conviction to the Court. While Ms Pearson's application to the Administrative Court for judicial review of the Commission's decision was dismissed, Lord Bingham was aware that the judgment would have an important bearing on the Commission's future response to cases and provided detailed analysis of the Commission and the Court's approach to real possibility, safety, and fresh evidence.

It is this last example of 'unsafe' that we focus on in this and the following chapter. It demonstrates that the test of unsafety is more widely protective than a test of innocence. Equally, this test has the potential to 'police' adherence to the rules of criminal procedure to ensure the integrity of the criminal process, much more effectively than a system requiring proof of factual innocence before a conviction can be quashed.[4]

Recent reports of 'anecdotal evidence from innocence projects in England and Wales [indicate] that the inclusion of allegations of police misconduct can be the kiss of death for an application to the Commission' (Thomas, 2017).[5] In this chapter, we explore the extent to which this is true. We present analysis of the Commission's response to claims that policing without integrity impacted on the safety of the applicant's conviction. Policing without integrity can refer to overzealous, unethical, incompetent, or criminal police behaviour, including non-disclosure of evidence that might assist the defence (Dixon, 2016; McConville et al., 1991; Nobles and Schiff, 2000).[6] We frequently use the term misconduct to distinguish cases where criticisms have been made about the police investigation from those where there has been only a claim of non-disclosure.[7] Chapter 10 considers the Commission's response to claims of incompetence or breaches of procedural rules by the legal representatives who acted for the applicant at trial.

Enduring Misconduct, Innocence, and Safety: Surround

The Commission is a product of a particular time, a time when the state and the public could no longer ignore the truth that the criminal process could err and could err badly (Rose, 1996). The series of high profile, mostly terrorist cases that led to the creation of the 1993 Royal Commission on Criminal Justice ('the Runciman Commission') and, in turn, to the establishment of the Commission, involved police misconduct of varying degrees. Most featured non-disclosure of exculpatory evidence, including the cases of *Judith Ward*, the *Guildford Four*, and the *Cardiff Three* (Conlon, 1990:214; Hill and Bennett, 1991:91; Mullin, 1990; O'Brian, 2008:125; Ward, 1993:160). Extreme physical and verbal assault, sleep and food deprivation, and generally threatening behaviour were police tactics in the cases of *Judith Ward*, the *Guildford Four*, the *Birmingham Six*, the *Maguire Seven*, and the *Cardiff Three* (Conlon, 1990:80; Maguire, 1994:41; Mullin, 1990; O'Brian, 2008:24; Ward, 1993:7). Such tactics are thought to have induced false confessions in all of these cases.[8] Signed statements were often vague, inconsistent with the discovered facts of the crime and contradicted each other. Most commonly, it would appear that police fabricated these accounts based on what they knew of the case, aided by fragments of personal information or names provided by the

---

[4] As Herbert Packer (1968) made clear, appellate bodies are critical to the enforcement of due process values.

[5] Though Thomas concedes that the Commission may be more willing to refer cases if the evidence is of historical misconduct, rather than contemporary abuses of process.

[6] For a thorough review of critical scholarship on police and prosecution misconduct, see Sanders, Young, and Burton (2010) and Ashworth and Redmayne (2010).

[7] We do not focus on judicial errors at trial, though it is reasonably common for applicants to provide evidence of this too. Indeed, research conducted by Malleson for the Runciman Commission shows that misdirection by the trial judge and defects in the summing up were the most common grounds for appeal in the 1990s (Royal Commission on Criminal Justice, 1993:paras:35–9). Such cases are reasonably straightforward for the Commission to respond to, with decision-making guided by the law.

[8] With the exception of the Maguire Seven, where no confessions were made (Kee, 1986).

suspect (Conlon, 1990:82; Hill and Bennett, 1991:57). The Runciman Commission was highly critical of the Court's reluctance to quash convictions in these cases; indeed, reluctance to contemplate that police officers could be involved in gross misconduct (see Chapter 1).

While the Police and Criminal Evidence Act of 1984 ('PACE') may have curbed the excesses of police misuse of their powers,[9] it did not put an end to miscarriages of justice (McConville et al., 1991; McConville and Bridges, 1994; Walker and Starmer, 1993). Many cases considered by the 1993 Runciman Commission were products of pre-PACE investigations, but some—such as the *Cardiff Three*—were not. Similarly, many of the wrongful convictions referred back to the Court in the early years of the Commission—not least, the *Rigg Approach* cases and some *West Midlands Drugs Squad* cases—related to convictions secured post-PACE (from 1989 through to 1995; see Elks, 2008:chapt:10).

Many of the cases that led to a collapse in confidence in British criminal justice, particularly the cases of *Stefan Kiszko* (O'Connell, 2017) and *Anne Maguire* (Maguire, 1994), demonstrated that procedural irregularity and innocence need not be thought of as dichotomous; the one is likely to be a contributing factor in the other. These cases were, first and foremost, 'unsafe' convictions, with defendants convicted after a flawed criminal process. There was evidence of innocence, but their convictions were based on systemic flaws in the criminal process, particularly police misconduct and sometimes legal incompetence, and their initial appeals were rejected by an appeals process that was highly deferential to the lower courts. This implies that their convictions deserved to be overturned even if it had not been possible to show that they were 'factually innocent'.

The question of whether seriously flawed due process should result in the quashing of convictions secured by improper means has posed ethical dilemmas to those responsible for a safe criminal justice system over the past few decades. The Runciman Commission considered that public interest was not served by quashing a conviction where there has been a serious flaw in the pre-trial or trial process when there is strong evidence of the offender's guilt unrelated to breaches of due process (though two members offered a dissenting view; Royal Commission on Criminal Justice, 1993:chapt:10, para:48). However, just a few years later the Court took a divergent view in *R v Mullen*.[10] Nicholas Mullen, a member of the Provisional Irish Republican Army, had been convicted for conspiracy to cause explosions and sentenced to thirty years' imprisonment. However, eight years after his trial, the Court was presented with newly disclosed evidence that the police, MI6, the Security Service, and officials from the Foreign Office and the Home Office had colluded with the authorities in Zimbabwe to procure Mullen's deportation in circumstances which were contrary to both Zimbabwean and international law. This, the Court stated, represented 'a blatant and extremely serious failure to adhere to the rule of law' (*R v Mullen*, para:40). The claimant's conviction was accordingly regarded as 'unsafe', notwithstanding the fact that there was 'no challenge to the propriety of the outcome of the trial itself' (*R v Mullen*, para:68). What

---

[9] PACE provided that police interviews should be tape-recorded, that suspects' rights should include the assistance of a solicitor, and in cases where the suspect is considered to be vulnerable, an appropriate adult. PACE also created a statutory presumption against the admission of evidence that had been obtained by oppression and gave trial judges the discretion to exclude evidence due to considerations of fairness. Hence the conditions of detention in police custody and the rules of procedure changed such that it was less likely that the police could coerce unwilling suspects to confess.

[10] [1999] EWCA Crim 278.

amounted to the illegal abduction of a suspect from abroad was sufficient to quash the conviction of a man who was legally proven guilty as charged.

Similarly, the Court's judgment in *Davis, Johnson and Rowe*,[11] a case that involved significant non-disclosure of relevant evidence to the defendants, showed that the Court could find a conviction to be unsafe even when it claims that the evidence against the appellants is persuasive:

> In our view, the case against all three appellants was formidable ... However, we are bound to follow the approach set out earlier in this judgment, namely assuming the irregularities which we have identified had not occurred would a reasonable jury have been bound to return verdicts of guilty? In all conscience, we cannot say that it would ... Accordingly, we cannot say that any of these convictions is safe. They must be quashed and the appeals allowed ... For the better understanding of those who have listened to this judgment and of those who may report it hereafter this is not a finding of innocence, far from it.[12]

Just a few years after these cases had been heard, in September 2006, the Government issued a consultation paper, *Quashing Convictions* that expressed concern that:

> The dominant and settled legal interpretation of the statutory test in the Criminal Appeal Act 1968 (as amended) appears to mean that the Court of Appeal may quash a conviction if they are dissatisfied with some aspect of the procedure at the original trial, even if the person pleaded guilty or the Court are in no doubt that he committed the offence for which he was convicted. The Government believes that the law should not allow people to go free where they were convicted and the Court are satisfied they committed the offence. (Office for Criminal Justice Reform, 2006:para:31)

The report proposed an amendment to the law to 'ensure that the plainly guilty would not have convictions quashed because of a procedural irregularity, where the Court of Appeal were satisfied that the appellant committed the offence' (Office for Criminal Justice Reform, 2006:para:43).

The report provoked considerable criticism from the judiciary, Law Society, Criminal Appeal Lawyers Association, and the Bar Council (Dyer, 2007), from leading NGOs— JUSTICE and Liberty, and from academic lawyers (e.g. Spencer, 2008).[13] For example, Liberty rejected the argument that section 2 of the Criminal Appeal Act 1968 (as amended by the Criminal Appeal Act 1995) should be amended, concluding:

> We are concerned that, once the Court of Appeal's power to quash a conviction outright where there has been serious malpractice on the part of state authorities is removed, the next step will be to take that power away from the courts of first instance. The power to stay proceedings as an abuse of process is an important constitutional safeguard which should not be restricted or removed. (Liberty, 2006:22)

Importantly, the Commission also objected, like the other organizations, on both practical and principled bases. The Government had drawn for its evidence on notorious cases such as *Mullen*; *Chalkley*; *Smith*; and *Togher*,[14] presenting them as if they were common occurrences, whereas—as the response by the Commission made clear— 'such cases of gross and extremely serious affront are rare and there have been many

[11] [2000] EWCA Crim 109.   [12] *Davis, Johnson and Rowe* [2000] EWCA Crim 109.
[13] The Summary of Responses to the Consultation Paper lists all individuals and organizations who responded; see http://webarchive.nationalarchives.gov.uk/20080610162901/http://www.cjsonline.gov.uk/the_cjs/whats_new/news-3588.html.
[14] *Mullen* [1999] EWCA Crim 278; *Chalkley* [1997] EWCA Crim 3416; *Smith* [1999] 2 Cr App R 238; *Togher* [2001] Cr App R 457. For a detailed discussion of the Court's response to these cases, see Ashworth and Redmayne (2005:354–8).

changes to the criminal justice system in the past 20 years to ensure that this remains the case' (Criminal Cases Review Commission, 2006b:para:31).[15]

The Commission was unpersuaded by the Government's proposals:

The Commission for its part considers that where there has been a departure from proper practice or procedure so fundamental or gross as to undermine the integrity of the criminal process, violate its basic values or constitute an affront to justice, the Court should retain its present discretion to quash the conviction and to decline to order a re-trial … If the legislation were to enshrine the principle that any irregularity could be overlooked—provided that the convicted persons are deemed plainly guilty—this would inevitably cause collateral damage to the criminal justice process by which innocent defendants would be more likely to be convicted. (Criminal Cases Review Commission, 2006b:para:36)

The proposed amendments did not find a place in the *Criminal Justice and Immigration Act 2008* but of note here is the Commission's argument that changes were not needed. First, the Commission rightly pointed out that interpretation of the legislation provides that the Court *may* quash a conviction because of procedural irregularities; it does not have to. Further, that the 1995 amendment[16] of the 1968 Act, which the Government had thought was responsible for more liberal responses by the Court, was not intended to disturb the practice of the Court (as was expressed by the Court in *Davis, Johnson and Rowe*[17]). In other words, the Court has always had the discretion to quash convictions where there is evidence of significant breaches of suspects' due process rights.

The Commission's response reviewed judicial interpretation of the safety test since 1995, and it is here that we see its understanding of what the Court will and will not accept and can assume that this guides its approach to the cases under consideration in this chapter. It contends that far from the Court being more likely to allow appeals on technical grounds, unrelated to the guilt or innocence of the applicant, 'the trend has been strongly towards applying the safety test *against* appeals based on "material irregularities" or other technicalities' (Criminal Cases Review Commission, 2006b:para:18; emphasis added). Having reviewed a number of cases to substantiate this assertion, the Commission asserts that:

the weight of authority to support the Commission's view is so overwhelming that this submission would become overweighed with citations if the Commission were to seek to illustrate this point with more than a fraction of recent cases. (Criminal Cases Review Commission, 2006b:para:18)

The Commission's selective review of evolving jurisprudence suggests a 'sea-change' in approach, to a position whereby the Court seeks to establish whether procedural failures 'caused any prejudice to any of the parties, such as to make it unjust to proceed further' (*Clark and McDaid* Court judgment cited in Criminal Cases Review Commission, 2006b:para:19).[18] In other words, the approach of the Court is not to presume that breaches of due process are determinative in themselves.

This document provides clear evidence of how the Commission judges the Court's receptiveness to referrals based on breaches of due process. The Commission is aware that the Court has for some time been disinclined to quash convictions based solely

---

[15] The response by Liberty concurred: 'The majority of convictions that are quashed on appeal do not involve cases in which the Court of Appeal is satisfied as to the appellant's guilt' (Liberty, 2006:para:4; see also Spencer, 2008).

[16] Criminal Appeal Act 1995.   [17] [2001] 1 Cr App R 115.

[18] [2006] EWCA Crim 1196.

on procedural irregularities and was becoming more so (Criminal Cases Review Commission, 2006b:para:63). It considers that the Court 'routinely applies the safety test in the light of its overall sense of justice and not on the basis of technicalities' (Criminal Cases Review Commission, 2006b:para:25). This trend in the Commission's 'surround' (Hawkins, 2002) inevitably influences its decision field, as the Commission tries to predict which cases may be accepted by the Court and which will be rejected.

Policing Without Integrity and the Safety of Convictions: Field

There is no doubt that the Commission responds to trends in the Court's judgments. As a seasoned appeal lawyer told us:

The Commission has a great reluctance in investigating the police ... [and] the Court of Appeal has got a long track history of being reticent to enter into that territory. The Commission, I think, has reacted to that reticence and adopts the same principles. (#12)

That said, it may be too simple to argue that the Court, and therefore the Commission, are 'reticent' (#12). Rather, we need to consider what types of evidence the Commission considers the Court may be persuaded by, and therefore what types of cases the Commission may be confident to refer.

One source of evidence for this is the Casework Guidance Notes that steer commissioners in their reviews: documents not publicly available but which we analysed alongside the Commission's response to our sample of cases. Drawing on the recent trends in the Court's judgments, as described above, the Casework Guidance Note on 'Misconduct by Investigators' advises Commission staff on responding to cases where the misconduct 'undermines the credibility of an individual officer or officers[19] who gave evidence at trial or whose involvement in the case otherwise makes their credibility relevant', and on cases where misconduct 'results in material non-disclosure and potentially undermines the case to such an extent that it amounts to an abuse of process' (Criminal Cases Review Commission, 2012c:para:2). It makes clear that the primary concern of the Court is how evidence of misconduct might have affected the jury's decision to convict the applicant, or the judge's decision on a legal ruling. In other words, evidence of police misconduct 'should not be viewed as determinative' in itself, but rather, considered in light of the overriding question of how it impacts on the safety of the conviction (Criminal Cases Review Commission, 2012c:para:4), as was made clear by the Court's judgment in *Clarke and McDaid*, mentioned earlier.

The starting point for the Commission's analysis of misconduct cases is Lord Lane's rather restrictive judgment in *R v Edwards*.[20] This defined relevant and admissible evidence to include: convictions of relevant officers for a relevant criminal offence; disciplinary charges found proved against the relevant officers; and other cases where the only logical explanation for an acquittal is that the officer's evidence must have been disbelieved (Criminal Cases Review Commission, 2012c:para:10).

---

[19] While we focus here on police officers, the Casework Guidance Note makes clear that the issue of misconduct can arise in relation to any criminal investigator, or civilian employee of an investigatory agency; for example, customs officers, forensic scientists, or scenes or crime officers (Criminal Cases Review Commission, 2012c:para:6).

[20] [1991] 1 WLR 207.

The Casework Guidance Note discusses cases where the Court quashed convictions on the basis of only *suspicion* of misconduct, where the suspicion had been sufficiently serious.[21] It also reports cases where the Court considered if a conviction remained safe when some of the officers involved in the case, or some of the evidence produced, fell within the ambit of suspicion, but where a separate body of evidence remained untainted. The Court saw many such cases resulting from convictions from the 1980s and 1990s following investigations by the West Midlands serious crime squad, the West Midlands drugs squad, and the Metropolitan police flying squad. As the Court put it in 2000, quashing the case of *Martin, Taylor and Brown* (para:13)[22] referred by the Commission:

[i]n practice the precise surgical division between impugned and unimpugned evidence is seldom possible once the jury have experienced what advocates have called the 'stench of corruption'.

While one or two past convictions were overturned, the Casework Guidance Note is clear that:

in more recent cases the Court has signalled a reluctance to quash convictions on the basis of a 'general taint' attributed to all officers within a squad whose practices have been seriously call into question. (Criminal Cases Review Commission, 2012c:para:28)

As Elks (2008:446) points out, the Court has been wary of the 'bandwagon' effect whereby a person, convicted on ample evidence, will opportunistically use evidence of corruption of an officer, that had subsequently come to light, to dispute the safety of their conviction:

If (i) the officer's transgressions occurred long after trial; (ii) the officer's transgressions were trivial; or (iii) the officer's evidence was undisputed, the conviction may be allowed to stand. (Elks, 2008:250)

While the Casework Guidance Note gives helpful advice to Commission staff on how they should balance close analysis of each case on its own merits, with careful regard to the Court's past judgments, it drives home the point that the Court is 'more reluctant than it once was to routinely quash convictions on the basis of the involvement of a corrupt officer' (Criminal Cases Review Commission, 2012c:para:52).

The Casework Guidance Note on Disclosure by Prosecution and Defence reminds Commission staff of the law on the obligations of disclosure taking the reader from the Attorney General's Guidelines through to the Criminal Procedure and Investigations Act 1996, as amended by the Criminal Justice Act 2003. It makes clear that:

fairness ordinarily requires that any material held by the prosecution which weakens its case or strengthens that of the defendant, if not relied on as part of its formal case against the defendant, should be disclosed to the defence. (*R v H and C* cited in Criminal Cases Review Commission, 2011e:para:4)[23]

However, drawing on the protocol for disclosure, it also points out that the trial process should not be 'overburdened or diverted by erroneous and inappropriate disclosure of unused prosecution material, or by misconceived applications in relation to such material' (Criminal Cases Review Commission, 2011e:para:5). Nondisclosure may have the effect of producing new evidence which the Commission can ask the Court to

---

[21] e.g. *R v Whelan* [1997] Crim LR 353.
[22] [2000] EWCA Crim 104 (the appellants were convicted in 1995); see Elks (2008:245) for a discussion of this case.
[23] [2004] UKHL 3.

receive. Alternatively, the very fact of non-disclosure and the resulting prejudice to the defendant's ability to mount their defence may be sufficiently serious in its own right to render a conviction unsafe (Criminal Cases Review Commission, 2011e:para:81). The thrust of the advice in the Casework Guidance Note is to consider whether the undisclosed evidence may have been material to the issues in the case and seek to understand its significance in the context of the case as a whole. As one interviewee explained to us:

It's not non-disclosure *per se* that makes something meritorious. It's always the sort of back-story as to why it wasn't used before. So, I can see where the Court of Appeal are coming from because it always is based on the significance of the material rather than the mechanics of how or why it didn't come about. (#1)

In summary, the Casework Guidance Notes for police misconduct and for non-disclosure make clear that in most cases the Court, and therefore the Commission, will look for evidence that police officers acting dishonourably has had an impact on the safety of the conviction. Evidence of policing without integrity will not, in and of itself, be determinative; the Commission must seek to establish that had police officers investigated thoroughly and behaved with probity, the jury may not have convicted the applicant.

Finally, it is worth pointing out that the Commission's 'decision field' (Hawkins, 2002) is also, inevitably, influenced by its experiences of reviewing applications. While a few egregious cases of wrongdoing by public servants still come to the attention of the Commission, typical applications do not present compelling evidence of gross violations of pre-trial procedures as was seen in *Mullen*, which demonstrated clear abuse of executive power. Most are much less clear cut; what Elks (2008:33–40) has categorized as 'second order' irregularities. As one of our interviewees put it: 'certainly ... [in] none of the recent cases I dealt with ... was there was any mass police corruption or [attempts] to frame somebody or cover up' (#40). This is not to suggest such cases no longer exist, but that the Commission's usual experiences likely reflect the stage at which it sees potential wrongful convictions. Direct appeals, coming as they do so soon after the trial, rarely present fresh evidence and tend, instead, to be based on irregularities in the trial process. Therefore, gross police or prosecutorial misconduct is likely to overturn a conviction at that stage.[24] If the conviction is upheld, complaints about the police will not be fresh for the purpose of a Commission referral, nor will they usually be extremely serious (see Elks, 2008).

Commission Responses to Policing Without Integrity: Frame

To explore the Commission's response to claims that the police acted without integrity, we draw on ninety-four of our cases: contemporary sexual offence cases, historical institutional abuse cases, and forensic and expert evidence cases (see Chapter 2 regarding our category of cases); the focus of the previous two chapters. This allows us to analyse 'typical' Commission cases, in that sexual offence cases and those that turn on forensic and expert evidence form a significant proportion of applications to the Commission. In these cases, the Commission did not consider that the lack of police integrity was

---

[24] For a discussion of the Court's response to 'due process' cases, see Taylor and Ormerod (2004); Dennis (2003); and Ashworth and Redmayne (2005:355), who consider this question within the context of the European Convention on Human Rights Article 6 guarantee to the right to a fair trial.

sufficiently serious to justify using their 'section 19 powers', as the Commission's criteria for making a section 19 appointment of an independent investigator include where there are grounds to suspect that a police officer involved in the pre-trial investigation was involved in misconduct (see Chapter 11).[25] In other words, it would have skewed our analysis of the Commission's typical response to complaints of police misconduct to have included in this discussion their treatment of those cases that they explicitly identified as raising significant concerns about the police investigation.

Table 9.1 shows that the applicant raised the issue of police acting without integrity in just under half (thirty-nine cases) of these ninety-four cases; including just over a third of the forensic and expert evidence cases (twenty-one of sixty cases) and almost two-thirds of the historical institutional abuse cases within the category of sexual offence cases (eleven of seventeen cases). Table 9.2 shows that of those twenty cases that the Commission referred back to the Court, in under half (nine cases) the Statement of Reasons ('SOR') discussed instances of police misconduct but did not present it as a ground for referral, and in only two cases was police misconduct a main ground of referral. Non-disclosure was discussed in fewer cases—just three—though was a ground for referral in five.

On the face of it, our analysis of what happens to those cases where applicants bring to the Commission claims that the police acted without integrity suggests that 'the

Table 9.1 Applicant claims police acted without integrity

Type of case	Case not referred	Case referred	Total
Forensic and Expert Evidence	10	11	21 of 60
Contemporary Sexual Offence	1	6	7 of 17
Historical Institutional Abuse	8	3	11 of 17
TOTAL	19	20	39 of 94

Table 9.2 Commission responses to failures of the police to act with integrity in twenty referral cases

Type of case	Ground for referral*		Discussed in SOR	
	Misconduct	Non-disclosure	Misconduct	Non-disclosure
Forensic and Expert Evidence (11 cases)	2	1	5	3
Contemporary Sexual Offence (6 cases)	0	3	2	0
Historical Institutional Abuse (3 cases)	0	1	2	0
TOTAL	2 of 20	5 of 20	9 of 20	3 of 20

*In these cases, the failure of the police to act with integrity was one of the referral points.

[25] We also exclude Court-directed (section 15) cases, where the Commission is only obliged to investigate *certain* aspects of a case, and 'asylum cases' which were explicitly about wrongful prosecution and particularly, incompetent defence. Inclusion of these cases would have skewed our analysis; instead, they are discussed in subsequent chapters.

inclusion of allegations of police misconduct' is *not* 'the kiss of death for an application to the Commission' (Thomas, 2017), given that over half (eleven of twenty) of the SORs for cases referred following such a claim discussed police misconduct and eight of twenty discussed non-disclosure (and many cases discussed both). However, in only a handful of cases did these issues feature as a main referral point. In that sense, while the Commission will investigate such claims by applicants, it seems to be restricted by its understanding of the approach of the Court from referring on this issue.

Our analysis shows that the Commission is hesitant to present to the Court anything but robust evidence of policing without integrity and will not refer a case on these grounds unless it can demonstrate that this had an impact on the safety of the conviction. Here, as in cases discussed in earlier chapters where the applicant claimed that the complainant could not be relied upon (Chapter 8) or that the forensic evidence was fallible (Chapter 7), the Commission had to identify 'fresh' arguments or evidence—not raised in prior proceedings—sufficient to give rise to a 'real possibility' that the Court would quash the conviction, with good reason why the defence failed to adduce such evidence at trial. In making these decisions, the Commission draws on its statutory framework and internal guidance; in other words, it assumes a legal decision frame (Hawkins, 2002:57; see Chapter 7 for a detailed discussion of legal framing). Hence our first section below explores decision-making in the majority of our cases as a product of this legal decision frame. However, it is not the only decision frame at work here.

In making those crucial decisions about whether evidence of improper policing is determinative—whether it is sufficiently strong to impact on the safety of the conviction—the Commission must interpret each case, with its unique set of factors, in light of the evolving Court jurisprudence. That is never an easy task, and the Commission notes in its internal guidance that the Court is becoming more restrictive in its decision-making. A few of our cases involved breaches of due process of significant severity and import to justify a referral back to the Court. Here, the Commission was clearly working within its legal decision frame, but also, arguably, within a moral decision frame that has regard to the social construction of blame. Hawkins (2002:333) argues that the 'personal feeling which is most prominent and pervasive in legal decision-making is a desire to blame' and found that inspectors in a regulatory agency interpret features they define as relevant in a case to decide not only which cases to prosecute but *how* to prosecute them: which information to present to a court and how to present it. In other words, prosecution is not only a legal, but a social process. Arguably, the same is true of reviewing possible wrongful convictions. To the extent to which the Commission has the power to hold other agencies to account, providing the Court with robust evidence of significant police misconduct serves a wider moral purpose of attributing blame. When the Commission makes a referral on grounds of the failure of the police to act with integrity, it sends a message to the Court—and, through media reporting, to the general public—that the police must bear some responsibility for a wrongful conviction. In this, it is fulfilling a moral function.

While the Commission has an explicitly legal remit, and while it recognizes its moral function to hold the system to account, it is a pragmatic organization and some of its decisions, as we see below, are instrumental. When the Commission chooses not to muddy the waters of an otherwise strong referral by including weaker evidence of police misconduct, we see an instrumental decision frame at work. To some extent, all referrals, just like all prosecutions, are instrumental. They are explicitly aimed at quashing an unsafe conviction. However, in some of the cases presented below, we see an instrumental purpose in the decision *not* to fulfil a moral function, by alerting the

Court to misconduct, but rather to prepare an SOR most likely to persuade the Court to quash the conviction. In this sense, the moral and the instrumental frames may sometimes be in tension, and it is up to the Commission to decide when the wider principle of holding the criminal justice system to account might be sacrificed to the instrumental goal of doing justice to the applicant in that particular case. Finally, and briefly, we suggest some evidence of an organizational frame at work: The Commission can only do so much in pursuing its investigations within its remit and within its limited resources, and cannot pursue each and every possible route to revelation of injustice suggested by the applicant. But first, we turn to the legal decision frame, as this shaped decision-making in the majority of our cases.

Policing without integrity: legal decision frame in action

Our discussion starts with those seven cases in Table 9.2 that were referred back to the Court with police misconduct and non-disclosure as a ground for referral, cases that indicate a legal decision frame.

Referring cases of police misconduct

Research has shown that vulnerabilities are typical of certain mental disorders and can intensify the effectiveness of police interrogation tactics that produce coerced confessions and considerably increase the risk of eliciting false confessions (Follette et al., 2018; Gudjonsson, 2003). The two cases in Table 9.2 where police misconduct was a main ground for referral—cases EE39 and EE41—are particularly egregious examples of police officers behaving without integrity.

The applicant in case EE41 was convicted of an attempted rape and a burglary with intent to rape in 1993 solely on his false confession, although there was no positive identification from either victim and no forensic evidence linking him to either scene of crime or the victims. Moreover, there was an alternative suspect. Following an application to the Commission in 2000, an experienced forensic psychologist was commissioned to examine the applicant and could demonstrate that he was 'highly suggestible', which cast doubt upon the veracity of the confession (EE41, Case Record). The Commission referred the case back to the Court with this fresh expert evidence, which afforded the information about the alternative suspect higher evidential status, and on the further ground that the police had acted without integrity. The SOR pointed out that the police had done very little investigation into the offences—indeed had failed to do the basics, and that the jury had been provided with an abridged version of the interview transcripts, which would have been misleading. Furthermore, the applicant had not been provided with a lawyer (EE41, Statement of Reasons). The Court quashed the conviction on the basis of the expert witness' 'serious reservations about the reliability of the self-incriminating admissions [the applicant] made to the police' (EE41, Court judgment), despite the initial guilty plea (see Chapter 6 for a discussion of the challenges posed by guilty pleas). It made no comments on the police investigation.

The other case (EE39) was referred to the Court in 1999 following an application to the Commission in 1997.[26] The convictions were for the murders of two women in 1982, with the trial taking place in August 1984, soon before police were trained in

---

[26] The applicant had failed in his application for direct appeal and in an application to the Home Office in 1991.

PACE Codes of Practice in 1985 (the only pre-PACE case in our sub-sample of ninety-four cases). The convictions were based on admissions made in the course of a number of police interviews, with no legal representation; admissions that were quickly retracted by the applicant.

Police investigations prior to PACE cannot be judged through the same critical lens as those that followed this legislation. Hence, the Court has recognized the challenges of considering police conduct on historic cases referred by the Commission. In particular, in the cases of *Bentley*; *Hanratty*; and *Hussain*,[27] the Court signalled to the Commission that there must be some limits to the extent to which very old convictions 'should be adjudged unsafe on the basis of a breach of modern standards of fairness' (Elks, 2008:135). According to Elks' research, most of the pre-PACE cases referred by the Commission and quashed by the Court were substantially or wholly based upon confession evidence.[28] Confessions were often made at the conclusion of intensive police questioning, sometimes lasting for days, often without solicitors or appropriate adults present, even though most of the convicted persons were young or otherwise vulnerable (Elks, 2008:137–8). In deciding such cases, the Commission was obliged to consider not only if modern post-PACE standards of fairness were breached, but also whether the standards *at the time of the conviction* had been breached.

At the start of the trial in case EE39, an application was made to exclude the evidence of the interviews, but the judge ruled that the Crown had established that the admissions were voluntary, even though he accepted that the applicant had deliberately been refused access to a solicitor and that had he been represented it is almost certain that he would have been advised not to confess, and probably not to make a statement at all. The main grounds for the Commission's referral concerned material non-disclosure (primarily about another possible suspect) and psychological evidence of the vulnerability of the applicant (see further, Chapter 7). However, the Commission included criticism of police conduct in the 'other grounds' for a referral; providing details of 'oppressive' interviewing and other behaviour suggestive of misconduct in the period between the applicant being arrested and charged (EE39, Statement of Reasons).

The judgment is clear that to decide whether a conviction is safe or unsafe, the Court must apply the substantive criminal law that was in force at the time of the trial (1984) but judge the conduct of the investigation of the case, as well as the trial, with the standards that the Court now applies; that is, post-PACE standards. Hence the Court considered that with the benefit of the new expert evidence on the vulnerability of the suspect, there would have been strong grounds for seeking the exclusion of the confession evidence under sections 76 and 78 of PACE. Furthermore, the Court was clear that even in the context of a pre-PACE investigation, the police had dealt unfairly with a vulnerable suspect. The Court did 'not think it right to make findings of "oppression" in the sense of misconduct by the police, or of "tricks", insofar as that imputes bad faith on the police who conducted these interviews', nor did it consider that there was any evidence that the police in some way 'misconducted the enquiries' (EE39, Court judgment). However, the decision not to allow the suspect to have access to a solicitor (when he had requested legal assistance on numerous occasions) was

---

[27] *Bentley* [1998] EWCA Crim 2516, [2001] 1 Cr App R 307; *Hanratty* [2002] EWCA Crim 1141; *Hussain* [2005] EWCA Crim 31. For a discussion of the Commission's response to these historic cases see Elks (2008:133–6).

[28] Reviews of investigations by the West Midlands serious crime squad and the Metropolitan police flying squad demonstrated significant police corruption and misconduct, including violence in interrogations and fabricated or planted evidence in order to secure convictions (Elks, 2008:244–59).

thought by the Court to be reprehensible: 'they allowed their quest for a conviction to override their responsibilities to an accused, and particularly to a vulnerable accused' (EE39, Court judgment).[29]

On the other hand, while the Court saw some merit in the claim of non-disclosure, it paid little attention to it as there was sufficient evidence to find the convictions to be unsafe (EE39, Court judgment). In this sense, the Court can be pragmatic; if it has sufficient grounds to quash a conviction, it will not often dwell on other failings in the criminal process even though in this case it seems clear that there were breaches of the Attorney General's guidelines (1982) on disclosure in place at the time of the investigation.

In both cases, there was clear evidence of the police acting without integrity and of the considerable disadvantage this caused to vulnerable suspects who pleaded guilty under coercive conditions. The Commission guidelines and the Court's previous cases made clear that here there was sufficient evidence of misconduct to present a real possibility that the Court would find the convictions to be unsafe. The egregious nature of these cases presented a clear legal mandate—and a strong moral one—for referring the cases back to the Court.

Referring cases of non-disclosure

Very often, we find there is non-disclosure of stuff that should have been disclosed, and that's your starting point—if you can find that, that's one step. But the next step is the crucial one, which is whether … okay, it wasn't disclosed, but would it have made any difference? That is the crucial step … in which case, we would second-guess the Court of Appeal, which is what we're doing all the time, that the Court of Appeal would say, 'Sorry, this was an overwhelmingly strong case, and of course these things should have been disclosed, but what we're saying is that, even if they were, it wouldn't have made a blind bit of difference.' The Court of Appeal are quite good at saying that. (#2)

As our analysis of the Commission's internal guidance makes clear, to refer a case back to the Court, breaches of disclosure rules—like breaches of the police codes of practice—must be sufficiently egregious, or the Commission must be able to demonstrate that had the material been disclosed to the defence, or had the police behaved properly, it would have made a difference to the outcome of the case. Our analysis of references to the Court where non-disclosure is a ground for referral suggest a clear legal decision frame in action.

As Table 9.2 shows, non-disclosure by the prosecution of information that might assist the defence was a ground for referral in five of our cases; three contemporary sexual offence cases, one historical institutional abuse case, and one forensic and expert evidence case (this last case, EE39, is discussed above in relation to police misconduct). In the four sexual offence cases where non-disclosure had been a ground for referral the undisclosed information concerned the reliability or honesty of the complainant (see Chapter 8). For example, case CS7 was referred on complainant credibility and

---

[29] While the Commission had not been confident in its referral, with the minutes of the final committee meeting recording that 'their decision was finely balanced', rather unusually, the Court saw fit to pronounce that the appellant was innocent:

> … the longer we listened to the medical evidence and the longer we reviewed the interviews, the clearer we became that the appellant was entitled to more than a conclusion simply that this verdict is unsafe … we believe *he was innocent of these terrible murders*, and he should be entitled to have us say so. (EE39, Court judgment; emphasis added)

non-disclosure, with the SOR suggesting that 'the complainant's medical records, had they been available at the time of trial, would have been seen by the defence as an important piece of evidence' (CS7, Statement of Reasons).

In case CS5, the prosecution had failed to disclose information about prior similar allegations made by the complainant to the police about sexual assault; allegations that were later withdrawn and, importantly, concluded by the police to be false. The SOR implies that the Commission thought the non-disclosure was not accidental but, given its probative value, intent was not the issue; the impact on the safety of the conviction was the overriding concern:

It is particularly disquieting that the defence received a document containing only half of the information provided to the CPS, especially as it was the significant half that was missing.... However, it is the Commission's position that given the impact of the non-disclosure in this case, it is unnecessary to decide whether or not it arose out of bad faith or otherwise. It is sufficient, for the purposes of determining the safety of the conviction, that the material was not given to the defence. The effect of the non-disclosure was that the defence were prevented from [presenting their case] in the most effective way. (CS5, Statement of Reasons)

The case committee had guided the case review manager ('CRM') and supervising commissioner on this matter:

The committee took the view that, in a case such as this where both the breach of duty of non-disclosure, and the significance of the non-disclosed material, were very clear, they did not have to decide whether the non-disclosure was the result of ignorance, incompetence or bad faith. (CS5, Case Committee Minutes)

Although the non-disclosure in this case seemed to be particularly egregious, the case record suggests that prior to the case committee meeting, the CRM was worried that the Court may not accept non-disclosure as a referral point and sought advice from the legal adviser, who added to the case record:

[CRM] has asked for advice about the relationship between a material non-disclosure and s.23 of the 1968 [Criminal Appeal] Act. I don't think it is possible to conclude that [the Court] will automatically receive fresh evidence just because it is of a kind that was Keane-disclosable[30] ... So, I feel that we still need to satisfy ourselves that undisclosed material is 'receivable' under the four tests in s.23. As a creature of statute, [the Court] could only ignore s.23 if there was some statutory basis for doing so. (CS5, Case Record)

As it happens, not only did the Court accept the evidence and quash the conviction but in doing so was unequivocal about the importance to the safe operation of criminal justice of relevant material being disclosed:

there was a regrettable non-disclosure by the Crown ... the Crown concedes that there was a breakdown in communications within the relevant police force for a reason which cannot be discovered. [and] very properly, expressed substantial regret at what has happened to [the appellant] as a result, and the Court joins in that expression of regret ... This case demonstrates ... the importance of prosecuting authorities adhering fully to the obligations on them, so far as disclosure of relevant material to the defence is concerned. (CS5, Court judgment)

Not all cases are similarly received. The Court did not express regret at the equally improper failure to disclose relevant information in case CS2. As discussed in Chapter 8, the applicant had been convicted of a serious sexual offence in 1999 and imprisoned

[30] In *Keane*, it was argued that material should be disclosed if it 'may prove the defendant's innocence or avoid a miscarriage of justice' [1994] 1 WLR 746, 751–2; see Ashworth and Redmayne (2005:248).

for five years (he served just over three), for an 'offence' that it is now clear never took place. Presuming that the complainant was genuine, the defence case had been one of mistaken identity. If the relevant materials had been disclosed to the defence, the applicant could have argued that there was no case to answer.

This application came to the Commission in late 2002 and was screened and allocated to a CRM within a year. However, the CRM had been reviewing the case for another ten months before a Commission-directed police investigation (under the Commission's section 19 powers; see Chapter 11) found evidence that the prosecution had failed to disclose significant evidence that the complainant was a fantasist, a liar, and suffered serious mental health problems including Munchhausen's Syndrome. The early months of the Commission's review had been spent pursuing a similar line of enquiry to that followed by the defence prior to the trial; in the absence of information to the contrary, the Commission believed that the offence had taken place but that the applicant may not have committed it. Having uncovered the non-disclosure of evidence strongly suggesting the complainant had fabricated the whole case, the Commission made a referral in 2006 and the Court quashed the conviction in the same year: seven years wrongfully convicted on the evidence of a woman the police knew to be a liar and knew to have made other similar false allegations, sometimes for pecuniary gain. As the Commission noted in its SOR, 'the failure to disclose material … might have had a significant impact on the time that [the applicant] spent in prison' (CS2, Statement of Reasons).

A subsequent IPCC[31] report on the case, published in 2010, found that the police had failed to disclose material which undermined the prosecution case and assisted the defence case at the original criminal trial; had failed to disclose vital further facts that had come to light during the appeal processes that spoke directly to the credibility of the complainant; had deliberately provided false and misleading information to officers from another police force investigating another allegation by the complainant; and had failed to conduct a non-biased and objective investigation of the alleged case against the applicant thereby preventing him from having a fair trial. Given this damning indictment, which instigated an apology by the police to the appellant, the Court's quashing of this conviction could be described as rather mealy-mouthed: 'We allow this appeal and his conviction is quashed. That is an end of the criminal proceedings as far as he is concerned' (CS2, Court judgment).

One of the commissioners involved in the case, appalled by the flagrant non-disclosure, wrote to the then Director of Public Prosecutions to insist that lessons must be learned from the case, but was disappointed by the response:

It reached someone at the high level and they … deflected me. They evaded the issue. But, you know, I thought it was utterly appalling. The Court of Appeal fudged the issue and the … and the CPS evaded the issue. (#7)

If the Commission judged success of its referrals only in terms of its legal decision frame, it would have been satisfied with this outcome: the case had been quashed, the defendant was free. However, as we note above, sometimes a moral decision frame overlaps with, or operates alongside the legal frame and in this case the moral mandate was frustrated by a Court apparently reluctant to criticize the police and a prosecution service not inclined towards reflection.

---

[31] The Independent Police Complaints Commission, recently renamed the Independent Office for Police Conduct, investigates serious incidents and complaints involving the police; see https://www.policeconduct.gov.uk/.

Case HIA3b similarly raised the issue of the non-disclosure by the prosecution of information relating to the truthfulness of the complainant (see further, Chapter 8). Here the Court was reluctant to make much of this, arguing that:

we would have been cautious to avoid firm conclusions on non-disclosure. Even after the work of [the Commission] it is impossible confidently or with precision to identify what material was disclosed in respect of [the complainant]. It is for example plausible that counsel representing the Appellant knew of what is now labelled 'undisclosed' but chose not to use it. In light of the Crown's pragmatic approach it is unnecessary for us to reach a conclusion on the point so we say no more. (HIA3b, Court judgment)

Here, as in other cases, we see the Court suggesting that the blame could in fact lie with the defence for failing to pursue evidence that might prove exculpatory. The Court's stance was likely anticipated by the Commission as the case record suggests that neither the CRM nor the supervising commissioner were sure whether they had sufficient evidence to make a referral on non-disclosure. For example, an email sent by the commissioner records 'concern as to whether enough has been done to bottom out a definitive answer on what was disclosed to the defence' (HIA3b, Case Record).

When evidence of improper policing is not enough

The Commission refused to refer some cases where applicants had raised concerns about police misconduct or refused to include this as a referral point in other cases that were destined to return to the Court for reasons clearly derived from a legal decision frame: evidence of misconduct or non-disclosure was not fresh, the defence had failed to adduce it at trial, or the evidence was not determinative. That is, in the cases we turn to here, the evidence of policing without integrity was not enough to persuade the Commission to present it to the Court as a ground for referral.

Sometimes where the Commission declined to refer a case back to the Court following a claim that non-disclosure of material had disadvantaged the applicant and impacted on the safety of their conviction (e.g. CS1, HIA4, and HIA7) the rationale was insufficiently robust evidence of non-disclosure. For example, the applicant in case EE42 made several claims that potentially significant material was not disclosed to the defence and about the late disclosure of material (EE42, Application), but the Commission could find:

no reason whatsoever to conclude that any material of relevance to this trial, which might have been of assistance to the applicant, was left undisclosed. [These arguments] produce nothing which could sustain the submission that the conviction is unsafe. (EE42, Statement of Reasons)

In most of our cases though there was some evidence but it did not satisfy the legal tests.

Evidence of improper policing is not 'fresh'

In some forensic and expert evidence cases that were not referred back to the Court, the applicant claimed that the police did not investigate the case thoroughly, or behaved improperly; in particular, there were claims that alternative suspects were not pursued. These assertions tended not to be the focus of Commission reviews because in almost all cases this had already been dealt with at trial and was not therefore fresh (see e.g. EE27, EE14, and EE26b, discussed above). The applicant in case EE23 claimed that his confession to murder had been induced by oppressive interview techniques which breached PACE Codes of Practice, but this had already been raised at trial and the judge had ruled that the confession was admissible, a ruling which the Court at direct appeal concurred with. The SOR explains:

The assertion that [the applicant] had been subject to police oppression was left to the jury ... The trial judge directed the jury that it was ... for them to decide if [his] confession was true and that if they concluded it was not, then they must not use the confession as evidence of [his] guilt. The Commission can find no error of law in the judge's direction. (EE23, Statement of Reasons)

Notwithstanding, the Commission had asked the police service for any disciplinary records on the officer concerned but there were none, and thus no fresh evidence to suggest police misconduct.

Similar examples can be found in our cases that were referred. The Court at direct appeal, in case EE12, had heard evidence of 'material breaches of the Police and Criminal Evidence Act and exceptional evidential difficulties' (EE12, Statement of Reasons) that—together with other weaknesses in the police investigation—should have substantiated the defence's argument that there was no case to answer. However, the Single Judge dismissed these grounds, concluding that the trial judge 'was entitled to conclude the video interviews should be admitted notwithstanding some breaches of the Memorandum of Good Practice' (EE12, Statement of Reasons) and that it had been dealt with sufficiently in summing up, and so the jury had been fully aware of these breaches. In the absence of new evidence about police misconduct, the Commission focused on the fresh medical evidence. However, it did state clearly in the SOR that the flawed interviews created additional reasons to doubt the safety of the conviction:

Had the judge had before her the [fresh evidence], then there is, in the Commission's view, a real possibility she would have concluded that the jury could not properly convict [the applicant]— *especially in a case where the police interviewing techniques were accepted as flawed*—and that the submission of no case to answer would have been successful. (EE12, Statement of Reasons; emphasis added)

This, it seems to us, provides a good example of alerting the Court to breaches of due process even if they cannot stand alone as a ground for referral. This was a decision led by a legal frame but clearly influenced by a moral impulse. Such examples were not so common.

Failure by the defence to adduce evidence of improper policing at trial

Sometimes cases were not referred as the defence had failed to adduce evidence of improper policing at trial (e.g. EE24). Other cases (e.g. EE33) were referred and police misconduct was discussed in the SOR but not included as a ground for referral because the relevant information had been disclosed to the defence, which failed to adduce it at trial. In this case though, the Court had also considered this evidence at the applicant's first appeal and therefore 'any issue arising ... may not now be considered new' (EE33, Statement of Reasons). While such applicants must be frustrated by the legal catch 22 they find themselves in, the Commission is acting within its statutory framework here.

In another case, the applicant had claimed that the police video interview with the complainant had been highly suggestive and involved inappropriate questioning, but the Commission was clear that the defence had the opportunity to present this at trial, but had failed to do so: 'To the extent that the police interview was considered inappropriate, it was open to the defence to challenge it at trial and/or make points to the jury about it.' In relation to the applicant's broader complaint about the adequacy of the police investigation, the SOR concludes that, 'It was open to the defence to point to the lack of corroboration (or indeed allegations) from the siblings, and/or indeed seek to call them as witnesses, at trial' (EE17, Statement of Reasons).

The historical institutional abuse cases which raised concerns about improper policing focused on the police investigatory tactic of 'trawling'. Trawling involves police searching for further complainants to provide evidence of abuse following an allegation from one or more persons, typically residing in a residential institution, that someone in whose care they were in had abused them in the past. We do not discuss these cases in full here, as they are dealt with in Chapter 8, except to say that in case HIA3b the Commission made clear in the SOR that 'the police had been careful throughout the investigation' and, more to the point, stated that any claims about the fallibility of the police investigation could have been raised at trial (HIA3b, Statement of Reasons).

One of the three cases that mentioned non-disclosure but did not use it as a ground for referral[32] provides something of a counter-case to those discussed above. The applicant in case EE38 and the following reapplications (EE38b and EE38c) claimed that non-disclosure of information about a possible alternative suspect had harmed the defence. However, Commission investigations into the question of non-disclosure over the many years from the first application in 1998 to the referral of the case to the Court in 2011, following the third application, concluded that:

it is not possible to attribute the failure to produce [material on the potential alternative suspect] either to non-disclosure by the police or to inadequate defence preparation. However, whatever investigations the police might have pursued had they considered [the alternative suspect's] possible involvement and whatever questions the defence might, in hindsight, have been expected to ask on the material which was disclosed to them, this is not a case in which the defendant made a decision not to use information which was otherwise available. Rather, so far as the Commission can ascertain, [the applicant] was wholly unaware of the information regarding [the alternative suspect] until made aware of that information by the Commission. In the circumstances, the Commission takes the view that there is a real possibility that the Court of Appeal would conclude that there is a good reason for [the applicant] not having raised the material at his trial or in connection with his first appeal. (EE38c, Statement of Reasons)

Thus, the Commission accepted that some evidence had not been disclosed but pre-empted the objection that the defence could have adduced evidence at trial but failed to do so. In the event, the Court seemed unconcerned about that matter but concluded that in spite of the new, previously undisclosed evidence, the conviction was safe, as other evidence remained intact:

In our view, whilst clearly the evidence in relation to [the alternative suspect] would have been useful information and material that the defence could have deployed at trial, it in no way leads us to have any doubts as to the safety of this conviction. (EE38c, Court judgment)

Police misconduct or non-disclosure is not determinative

In most cases, police misconduct identified by the Commission was not thought to meet the threshold whereby it could be said to impact on the safety of the conviction. As the SOR in case HIA4 put it, an application cannot be referred simply on the basis that the investigation fell short of the standards, but the Commission 'would have to be satisfied that if there was any inadequacy and/or misconduct in the investigation its effect impacted upon the safety of the conviction' (HIA4, Statement of Reasons).

---

[32] All referrals were on grounds relating to fresh forensic or expert evidence.

Similarly, in case EE33b, the applicant's claims of police incompetence were insufficient to justify another attempt to persuade the Court, following an earlier unsuccessful referral:

Investigative failures would not be sufficient in themselves to cause the Court of Appeal to quash the conviction … there would need to be specific matters arising from such failures that affected the trial process to a degree that rendered it unsafe. (EE33b, Statement of Reasons)[33]

This was also true of cases that were referred on other grounds. One of the applicants who impugned police integrity in the two contemporary sexual offence cases submitted numerous claims about an inadequate and biased police investigation, including:

They failed to gather forensic evidence; they failed to interview significant witnesses or waited too long to do so; and they showed bias against [the applicant]. (Applicant quoted in CS12, Statement of Reasons)

While the case was referred on complainant credibility, the SOR deals with each of these points, making clear that none are determinative in themselves:

The Commission does not consider there is a real possibility the Court of Appeal would conclude on the material available that there was police bias against [the applicant] and therefore concludes that the Court would not consider any failure in the police investigation sufficient to render the conviction unsafe. (CS12, Statement of Reasons)

Furthermore, in relation to some claims, the SOR pointed out that the police had in fact tried to gather certain types of evidence but were unable to do so. While acknowledging that 'It is not apparent why this was', the SOR states that 'the Commission does not believe [this issue] by itself, caused any unfairness to [the applicant]' (CS12, Statement of Reasons).

In another of our cases where police misconduct was mentioned in the SOR but did not constitute grounds for referral (EE32), the applicant had already unsuccessfully applied to the Home Office for a review of his conviction on a number of occasions. Initially, the Commission declined to refer his case but following judicial review proceedings, agreed, by way of Consent Order, to undertake a fresh review. At that stage, the Commission investigated thoroughly all of the claims made by the applicant, conducting further forensic tests, examining police files in all, but found no evidence of police misconduct sufficiently robust for a referral. Hence it referred the conviction back to the Court on the sole ground of fresh expert testimony. The Court was unpersuaded by the fresh evidence and upheld the conviction, leading to a further three unsuccessful applications, two of which focused on claims of police misconduct.

As part of its further investigations, the Commission obtained from the investigating police force the complaints and discipline records to see if there was any evidence that the officer in charge of the enquiry had exhibited behaviour during his service which could substantiate the claims made in the application. However, there were no disciplinary records in relation to this officer. The Commission also sought evidence about another two officers in the case but, as they had retired more than ten years ago, their records had been destroyed. In the absence of substantiation regarding the claims of perjury and other misconduct, the Commission concluded that it was 'satisfied that it has no grounds for questioning the integrity of any these officers, based on their disciplinary records' (EE32b, Statement of Reasons).

---

[33] They go on to note that 'the same would be true of any defence failings' (EE32b, Statement of Reasons; see Chapter 10).

The applicant in case EE32 first applied to the Commission in 1997, following a refusal by the Home Office to refer his case back to the Court. He claimed that ten photographs from the crime scene and two statements from experts had not been disclosed to the defence, arguing that this constituted a 'knock-out blow' to the conviction requiring an immediate referral to the Court irrespective of the other issues he had raised. Indeed, he claimed that his case was no different from those of the *Birmingham Six* and the *Guildford Four* where non-disclosure by the prosecutors was sufficient to quash the conviction (EE32, Case Record). In the event, the Commission referred the case on the sole basis of inaccurate expert evidence at trial, finding the assertions about non-disclosure to be 'without substance' (EE32, Statement of Reasons). While the SOR concedes that material was not disclosed to the defence, drawing on advice from counsel, it concludes that 'disclosure … would not have had any great impact on the trial' and that the relevant materials were 'not of any significance':

that statement ought to have been disclosed to the Defence but the effect of the non-disclosure could not be said to have disadvantaged the Defence or materially altered the course of proceedings, or affected the outcome of the case. (EE32, Statement of Reasons)

The Court agreed and on all claims of non-disclosure recorded that 'we do not consider that prejudice in any material respect was occasioned to the appellant as a result of such non-disclosure' (EE32, Court judgment). As it was, the Court was also unpersuaded by the main ground for referral and dismissed the appeal, causing the applicant to re-apply to the Commission another three times, without further success.

Instrumental decision frame at work

The reasons discussed above for not including improper policing as a referral point (because it was not new, because the defence had failed to adduce it at trial, and because there was not sufficiently robust evidence to be determinative), are the same for those cases that were not referred as for those that were referred, but on grounds other than policing without integrity. This section deals only with those cases referred back to the Court, that *discussed* improper policing in the SOR, but did not include it as a ground for referral because there was a stronger point or points to refer on, and the Commission preferred not to muddy the waters with apparently weaker issues. This choice suggests an instrumental decision frame at work.

In case EE31, which was referred—and the conviction quashed—solely on the basis of fresh expert testimony, the Commission's investigation found that psychological reports on the defendant had not been disclosed to the defence, but was not convinced that they would have been of material assistance to the defence at trial. The SOR records:

In the Commission's view, it would have been appropriate and reasonable for the CPS to have disclosed the reports by [medical expert] and [investigating police officer] to the defence or at the very least indicated that such information existed but in the view of the CPS was not required to be disclosed. Such a response would almost certainly have encouraged the defence to pursue the matter and seek a ruling by the judge.

Although the defence counsel from the trial had told the Commission that he could have used the reports in his defence, the SOR goes on to state that 'it is questionable whether that documentation would have assisted the defence and whether the reports would have been admissible as evidence' (EE31, Statement of Reasons). Given the strength of the main referral point, the Commission was not minded to make much of the non-disclosure.

The applicant in case EE38 was serving a life sentence for murder and had been refused leave to appeal when he first applied to the Commission in 1998. He claimed that police procedure in an ID-line-up had been improper and that the police had been inconsistent in presenting the evidence against him, thereby confusing him and indirectly causing him to present unreliable evidence, which harmed his defence. A full investigation by the Commission failed to corroborate either of these points. In the second unsuccessful application in 2005, the focus of the Commission's review was a possible alternative suspect. The Commission carried out extensive scientific testing of forensic evidence to see if it was capable of linking the alternative suspect to the victim, but found no evidence sufficiently robust to refer on. Following the threat of judicial review, the Commission established a new case committee in 2011 to consider afresh whether there was a real possibility that the applicant's conviction would be quashed were a reference to be made in relation to the alternative suspect. This committee found that there was such a real possibility and referred the case.

While the bulk of the thirty-two-page SOR is devoted to evidence that supports the alternative suspect thesis, the Commission made a series of mildly critical points about the police, in passing. For example, the SOR claims that the applicant had been:

placed at a disadvantage by the failure both by the police and his trial representatives to recognise the significance of the evidence concerning [the alternative suspect] at the material time … And the failure to adduce this evidence at trial was as a result of a combination of police and defence shortcomings … The Commission finds it surprising that the attempt to establish the identity of the man who had spoken to [a key witness] was not pursued with more vigour. In the Commission's assessment, anyone who appeared to know at [a particular time] that [the victim] had been [killed] ought properly to have attracted suspicion. (EE38, Statement of Reasons)

It is possible that had the Commission—during its first and second reviews of this case—investigated more thoroughly claims made by the applicant about the police investigation, it may have chosen to refer the case earlier. Notes from the committee meetings show that the investigations adviser had told the committee that the police had been at fault in not investigating the alternative suspect and in pursuing other possible witnesses. The committee had considered a referral on the grounds of abuse of process, and the CRM had planned to interview the police sergeant in charge of the case. This had also been the advice of the screening commissioner. However, the case record suggests that the supervising commissioner decided against this, arguing that after almost a decade following the trial, 'it would be a fruitless exercise which would not assist the committee to reach a decision' (EE38, Case Record). It is worth noting that the case record implies that this was not pursued because it was felt that 'this is more of a "fresh evidence case"' (EE38, Case Record). This comment, and others in the case record, hints at an approach which settles on a main point of referral and consequently may pay insufficient regard to other possible points of referral which could, with further investigation, have proven helpful. As it was, the Court upheld the conviction arguing that:

While clearly the evidence in relation to [the alternative suspect] would have been useful information and material that the defence could have deployed at trial, it in no way leads us to have any doubts as to the safety of this conviction. (EE38, Court judgment)

In case CS10, while the Commission did not find that failures in the police investigation were sufficiently strong to form grounds for referral, the SOR includes critical notes about the police investigation:

the Commission considers that the failure of the police to conduct a full and proper investigation was significant, particularly the failure to fully investigate matters relating to [a witness'] credibility. However, ... the Commission does not consider that this is a case where the failure of the police to comply with their duty to investigate was as a result of bad faith or that it caused such serious prejudice to [the applicant] that it was unfair to have tried him or that it resulted in an unfair trial (abuse of process). Instead, the Commission considers that there were a series of factors which together resulted in a less than satisfactory investigation ... (CS10, Statement of Reasons)

The Commission carried out the investigations that the police had failed to do and found sufficient new evidence to undermine the credibility of the main prosecution witness, and this produced the ground for a referral. The case record shows that the Commission considered whether police misconduct should have constituted a third referral point. The CRM was inclined to include it, but the commissioner made clear his views in a note to the CRM in the case record:

I don't think that the prosecution failure ... in the [circumstances] makes the conviction unsafe. The failure to take a statement from [a witness] and disclose it to the defence did deprive the defence of an opportunity to consider calling him and could make the trial unfair. However, in the fast-moving circumstances of how this emerged whilst [a witness] was giving evidence, I wonder if this is a ground in itself or only grist to the mill. On the balance, I incline to the latter. (CS10, Case Record)

In quashing the conviction on the grounds of the fresh evidence, the Court praised the Commission for its 'conscientious hard work in obtaining evidence which so significantly undermined the safety of the verdict' and went on to offer criticism of both the police and the defence for failings leading up to the trial (CS10, Court judgment). Clearly, in this case, the failure to present the information about the police investigation as a referral point did not deter the Court from noting that the police had not behaved well. We asked the commissioner why he had chosen not to include improper policing as a referral point, especially as the CRM was inclined to do so, and he replied:

if you have a series of good points and you overwhelm them with a number of bad points, it almost puts the good points in the shadow, so you're better off ... keep[ing] it concise and focus[ing] on your good points. (#77)

This, and other similar comments in our interviews, speaks to an instrumental decision frame. It may also suggest an efficient approach to referrals; time spent developing possible secondary issues can delay referrals that might already be sufficiently strong to persuade the Court to quash the conviction.

It is arguable that cases CS10 and EE38 could have made more of improper policing in both the investigation and the SOR and in doing so would have satisfied a moral imperative to hold the justice system to account. However, it seemed that, according to the Courts' jurisprudence, evidence of misconduct was not likely to be determinative in itself, and there was other fresh evidence for a referral that appeared to be more persuasive. The Commission considers that the Court is reluctant to make much of improper policing if it is presented with fresh evidence that shows the conviction to be unsafe. However, some staff seemed to be influenced in what they presented to the Court by a desire not to exasperate appeal judges, worried that expressing strong concerns about police integrity in SORs for the Court might not only be dismissed by the

Court, but may antagonize it, which could be detrimental to the applicant. One of our interviewees explained:

if we have concerns … if there are major issues of misbehaviour … then, to the extent that it's relevant, it should go into a Statement of Reasons … In the early days of the Commission … there were some very aggressive Statements of Reasons … where we were particularly critical of police behaviour and actually sort of went for a bit of a rant in the Statement of Reasons … Where we get really, really worked up about things like police misbehaviour or lack of disclosure by the CPS, etc.… it has the opposite effect, you know. The Judges at the other end, at the Court of Appeal, think, you know, this is unrestrained, it's not … it's not measured, you know, we're actually antagonised against the Commission, and therefore we're antagonised about quashing this conviction. (#37)

Clearly, Commission staff feel that their communications with the Court, through their SORs, should be calm and measured if they are to have the desired effect. While this is evidence of an instrumental decision frame at work, a few of our cases indicate more trust in the police than was perhaps deserved, and a reluctance to point the finger of blame.

Moral decision frame at work

Just as the moral decision frame allows the Commission to construct blame in egregious cases, and importantly, to hold the justice system to account, it also provides the latitude to construct a case that does not explicitly apportion blame to the police or prosecutors involved in the investigation. While we did not identify cases with flagrant breaches of due process that were not referred back to the Court, we did find examples of Commission decision-making, certainly as reflected in the language of the SORs, but also in case records and committee meeting minutes, that demonstrated moderate deference to police and Crown prosecutors. In such cases, we see either a moral decision to trust in the integrity of the pre-trial process, or moral values concerned with fault and deserts being trumped by common-sense understandings of the shortcomings inherent in an overburdened criminal justice system. Hence, a CRM we interviewed explained the failings of the senior investigating police officer in one of his cases in terms of a heavy caseload:

I think it's easy to sit back in our sort of ivory tower here and be hyper-critical. What [the police] were faced with, there, in that investigation [describes the complexity of the investigation] and then you've got the fact that [the senior investigating police officer] was, I think, allocated to 13 or 14 other major incidents at the same time, so didn't necessarily have the time to dedicate to it. Now, you know, what they should have done is made sure it was appropriately dedicated to a Deputy [senior investigating police officer] who was able to give regular updates and had a handle on it himself, and that's where one of the failings came about. But I think [the senior investigating police officer] himself, you know, I do have a lot of sympathy for him because it was a difficult case. (#1)

We saw a few examples of less than thorough investigations by the police dismissed as merely 'mistakes' (EE34, Case Record). In case EE33b, the applicant claimed the police had deliberately covered up evidence that would have been helpful to the defence. The Commission's investigation found that while 'there were *errors* in the way in which a number of exhibits were recorded', 'there is no evidence to support the allegation that police officers did not produce all relevant exhibits at court' (EE33b, Statement of Reasons; emphasis added). And in case EE29, allegations of police misconduct were seen by the Commission as 'shortcomings in the investigation' with '[no] evidence of the police acting in bad faith' (EE29, Statement of Reasons). As the SOR in another case put it, 'Officers are aware of the rules of evidence and they will generally (there are some exceptions) exclude hearsay and inadmissible evidence' (HIA5, Statement of Reasons).

While the Commission may acknowledge that police investigations have been less than perfect, clearly sometimes it is inclined to give the police the benefit of the doubt, trusting that they had not *intended* to do less than a thorough and professional investigation. For example, in some cases relating to historical sexual abuse within residential institutions, allegations from applicants and their legal representatives that police investigation techniques—'trawling' in particular—had strayed from correct procedure were met with a somewhat trusting approach on the part of the Commission. As the SOR in case HIA10b put it, 'the police officers might have *unknowingly* implanted incorrect information in the witnesses' minds' (emphasis added). Similarly, in case HIA13, the Commission noted that it had 'uncovered no evidence of improper behaviour on the part of [the police]' (HIA13, Statement of Reasons) with 'no credible evidence of improper or unlawful actions' identified in case HIA10b, with the SOR adding 'Speculation ... does not amount to wrongdoing' (HIA10b, Statement of Reasons).

We should note here that Commission staff were not of one mind as regards to trawling. One interviewee told us, 'trawling, in its own right, I've always argued is ... nothing wrong with that at all, as long as it's done properly' (#2), while another was more concerned:

police trawling? I think it's hugely dangerous, and it's fraught with difficulties ... if the police are going to people and not taking care, then it has huge dangers, massive dangers, to the process. (#35)

That said, most agreed that while there were inherent risks to trawling, such police operations are typically 'evidence-led, in that somebody has made a complaint' (#5) and they trusted that the police would behave properly:

So, I don't have a problem with ... trawling because, you know, the police are properly investigating what could be quite a widespread series of offences. To suggest that sometimes they might taint the future complaint is more difficult, and I think most police officers would be careful not to do that ... they'd be very, very careful to ... ensure that they're not encouraging somebody to make ... false [allegations]. (#58)

As the Commission acknowledges, trawling is not in itself a breach of the rules of fair process, and indeed over fifteen years ago the Home Affairs Committee (2002:42) report into the conduct of investigations into past cases of abuse in children's homes accepted that trawling should not be prohibited, while expressing some reservations about the conduct of police trawls. In particular, it called for the revision of police guidance to minimize the risks of inducing false or exaggerated allegations (Home Affairs Committee, 2002).[34]

By presenting breaches of procedure as stemming from ignorance or structural conditions such as an overwhelming caseload, the Commission can construct a case that shows the applicant's trial was unfair, without suggesting that police or prosecutors intended it to be so. The desire to do so likely stems from a general perception among those at the Commission that the trend over the past decade has been away from

---

[34] See further, Burnett et al. (2017).

blatant and purposeful failures to disclose exculpatory evidence towards accidental or careless breaches:

It may have moved from deliberate non-disclosure to almost accidental non-disclosure because of the lack of staff, the lack of thought, etc. And a lot of disclosure I dealt with … was probably accidental non-disclosure where they simply forgot about it. (#22)

Does it still arise? Yes, undoubtedly. It does still arise and, you know, not always as a result of corruption but just people not realizing that this might have been important or a failure to join the dots and think, gosh, well I suppose this might be something that would [be relevant]. (#27)

While Commission staff sought to assure us that police misconduct was rare today, they conceded that it was not uncommon for police investigations to be poor:

There's no sense that there's been deliberate, you know, impropriety either on behalf of the police or the prosecution. In my experience, it's just been a cock up, you know, that things have been missed and particularly that police … have just not recognized the significance of a piece of information or material, generally to the case … I think it's just … error, mistake … incompetence … negligence, whatever you want to call it. (#29)

Few wanted to call it misconduct and were arguably, therefore, less likely to see mischief when reviewing police investigations. It is likely that the Commission has been a little too complacent here, in assuming that institutionalized corruption and misconduct by police is rare. We return to this in our final section which suggests that this complacency is likely to have been challenged by recent changes in the surround.

Organizational decision frame at work

Where the applicant *believed* that the police had behaved improperly but could provide little corroboration to assist the CRM, the Commission made clear that it could not investigate speculative allegations; it could only pursue specific issues: 'It's not our job to reinvestigate [the case] … The police did that' (#6). While this arose in only a few of our cases, it suggests an organizational decision frame at work. The organizational culture of the Commission is shaped to a large extent by the pursuit of efficiency, driven in the main by the obligation to use wisely their limited public resources (see Chapter 12). However, it is not only resources but the Commission's remit which guides its response to applicants: the Commission was set up to review evidence of wrongful conviction, not to replicate the mandate of the police and prosecution services. For example, in case EE24, the applicant claimed that there had been a 'police cover-up' but could provide little evidence for this. Noting first that 'the extent of the police investigation into other suspects was well rehearsed at trial', the SOR went on to record:

Whilst the Commission will investigate or cause to be investigated any aspect of a police investigation which it considers may have led to a miscarriage of justice, it is not the function of the Commission to fully investigate every aspect of a police investigation. (EE24, Statement of Reasons)

The applicant in case EE26b indicated that there *may* be some undisclosed material regarding arrest procedures but in the absence of clearer information, the Commission noted that 'it does not investigate matters on the basis of pure speculation' (EE26b, Statement of Reasons). Of course, it is not clear how the applicant might have secured clearer information without the Commission's section 17 investigatory powers. In response, in further submissions, the applicant suggested that there had been a 'police cover-up', to which the Commission repeated that this was mere 'speculation with no evidence to support' it (EE26b, Statement of Reasons). It went on to point out that differences in witnesses written statements and oral testimony in court 'could have various explanations, and do not amount to supporting evidence of improper pressure' (EE26b, Statement of Reasons). The same expression was used in case EE27, where the applicant's claims of police misconduct were dismissed as 'no more than speculation' (EE27, Case Record). One of our interviewees explained to us:

> With a thousand or so applications a year, you haven't got the resources to re-investigate every case, so you're looking for pointers where things may have gone [wrong] ... and the reality is, with limited resources, you're likely to go the extra mile if you ... [only] if you have a bad feeling that things have gone awry. (#40)

In other words, the Commission is keen to impress upon applicants that it is a review body and cannot therefore duplicate the role of the pre-trial investigatory bodies.

Past, Present, and Future Challenges for the Commission

We opened this chapter with a discussion of those egregious cases of wrongful conviction that led to the establishment of two royal commissions on criminal procedure and criminal justice; police misconduct in those cases was sufficient to justify systemic change. Research has demonstrated that the police are more than capable of circumventing the rules aimed at ensuring due process of law (Cape and Young, 2008), and of sustained corruption and gross breaches of the rules of disclosure (see Sanders et al., 2010 for a review of this literature), though this would not be typical. Significant breaches of due process which cast a shadow over the whole case—as was determined in the famous case of *Mullen*, discussed above—are reasonably straightforward for the Commission. We have seen that such cases are likely to be referred, criticism of the police will be robust and the Court can be expected to quash convictions. Commission staff typically approach such cases from a legal decision frame, but we saw evidence too of a moral decision frame at work.

These cases are now fairly unusual, and meanwhile the Court's jurisprudence has evolved. It has made clear over the past decade or so that evidence that was not disclosed at trial must be relevant to the safety of the conviction—material to the issues in the case—to persuade the Court to quash the conviction. Evidence of other forms of misconduct should similarly not be viewed as determinative in itself but, instead, must be considered in light of how it impacts on the issue of the safety of the conviction. There must, in other words, be a nexus between the due process failure and the safety of the conviction, without an assumption that one inevitably undermines the other. That is the challenge that the Commission now faces in reviewing applications that often include claims of policing without integrity. They cannot refer a case if the Court will simply say 'so what?' Nevertheless, it is a position that most in the Commission now agree with; as one experienced CRM explained to us:

> I wouldn't necessarily be entirely comfortable with a criminal justice system that overturns a conviction on the basis of something not being disclosed to the defence which isn't relevant ... (#1)

This is the approach now and will likely remain so for the foreseeable future. However, it is possible that recent changes in the surround may filter through and produce shifts in thinking in the Commission, particularly on the issue of non-disclosure.

The most recent review of the disclosure of unused material in volume crown court cases, published by Her Majesty's Crown Prosecution Service Inspectorate and Her Majesty's Inspectorate of Constabulary (2017), identifies a number of concerns relating to how disclosure is managed. It shows that police scheduling 'is routinely poor', with one in five disclosure schedules being wholly inadequate, while 'revelation by the police to the prosecutor of material that may undermine the prosecution case or assist the defence case is rare' (Her Majesty's Crown Prosecution Service Inspectorate and Her Majesty's Inspectorate of Constabulary, 2017:3). Indeed, it found that neither the police nor prosecutors managed sensitive material effectively and prosecutors failed to manage ongoing disclosure and to challenge police failings.[35] The report concludes that:

there needs to be cultural shift that approaches the concept of disclosure differently, that sees it as key to the prosecution process where both agencies add value, rather than an administrative function. Only then will assurance be provided that prosecution agencies are motivated in their desire for a fair trial, rather than one that focuses on the prosecution case and pays insufficient heed to potential evidence for the defence that lies within the unused material in their possession. (Her Majesty's Crown Prosecution Service Inspectorate and Her Majesty's Inspectorate of Constabulary, 2017:3)

Within the context of the current significantly underfunded criminal justice system, the recommendations of this important report may be unrealistic. However, it is on the Commission's radar and there is evidence that the organization is becoming increasingly concerned about non-disclosure, particularly in light of its relatively recent investigation of the wrongful conviction of Adam Joof and his co-defendants for the 'gangland' murder in 2002 of Kevin Nunes.

The Commission was asked by the Court[36] in 2009 to investigate the case of *Joof* and used its powers[37] to appoint the then Chief Constable of Derbyshire Constabulary to investigate the pre-trial processes and decisions. The trial had taken place in 2008, over two decades after the introduction of PACE, yet this investigation demonstrated systemic corruption in the protected witness unit of Staffordshire police and failure to disclose evidence that would assist the defence (see Rose, 2017b).[38] Indeed, in quashing the convictions against Joof and his four co-defendants, the Court described this as 'a very bad case of non-disclosure' ([2012] EWCA Crim 1475, para:38) and 'a serious perversion of the course of justice' (para:39). The judgment ended with an expression of hope that 'lessons will be learnt from this shocking episode' (para:39). This is perhaps not likely as none of the officers involved were prosecuted (Rose, 2017b). They almost never are.

The Commission's investigation of this case took place while we were conducting our research and we were aware of the buzz it created. Commissioners rightly felt it was significant, that it would likely lead to a successful appeal, and, following the completion of the review for the Court, it was clear that many Commission staff—not just those who worked on the case—were satisfied that significant police misconduct had been uncovered. Before this case was resolved, one experienced commissioner had told us, 'We're past the days of police corruption. And what we're into is disclosure.

[35] The review findings reflected academic research on the problems inherent in the disclosure scheme (e.g. Plotnikoff and Woolfson, 2001). The Criminal Procedure and Investigations Act 1996 was introduced to address concerns that prosecution disclosure had become too generous but it is now argued that the legislation allows prosecutors to apply the disclosure test too strictly (Ashworth and Redmayne, 2005:240).

[36] Pursuant to section 15 of the Criminal Appeal Act 1995; see Chapter 11.

[37] Pursuant to section 19 of the Criminal Appeal Act 1995; see Chapter 11.

[38] And for his discussion of similar misconduct in investigations by Staffordshire police that demonstrate misfeasance and malicious prosecution, see Rose (2017a, 2017c).

And … lack of disclosure … is meaning that people do not have a fair and just trial' (#52). While a few commissioners may have reassessed their views on police corruption since this notorious case, many were already of a mind that non-disclosure remained a significant problem and that it was likely to get worse, not better.

Recent cases, attracting significant media attention as we finish this book in early 2018, demonstrate increasing concern beyond the Commission that police and prosecutors are failing to disclosure relevant information to the defence in a timely fashion. While this seems to be a particular problem with rape prosecutions, raising concerns of 'unconscious bias' against those accused of rape (see, for example, the cases of *Liam Allen*,[39] *Samuel Armstrong, Danny Kay*, and *Isaac Itiary*[40]), most commentators agree that non-disclosure affects all types of offences and is also associated with austerity measures, the proliferation of data, and even persistent police culture which produces tunnel vision. In response to these recent cases, the Metropolitan Police Service has begun a review of thirty rape cases due to go to trial and plans to review many more investigations following this, and the Attorney General has commenced a review of disclosure (BBC News, 2014).

At the recent 20th Anniversary Conference for the Commission, the then Chair, Richard Foster, spoke about the current threats to justice:

Much has improved since the 1970s. And until recently I might have said that the worst excesses have all been curbed. But problems undoubtedly remain and in some cases things have recently got worse again. I would highlight as the biggest single current problem very significant police and prosecution failures to fulfil their obligations of disclosure. (Foster, 2017a:5)

Various other presentations at the Conference alluded to the considerable growth in the volume of material which police and prosecutors need to consider in preparing for full and proper disclosure to the defence. The proliferation of mobile communications data and satellite data,[41] as well as data from the growing trend among police officers to wear body cameras that can record each and every interaction with the public, as well as crime scenes, has added to the problem. We now have the conditions whereby almost unmanageable quantities of data—much of it that could be deleted or made inaccessible at the push of a button—must be reviewed by police officers who do not necessarily have sufficient skills and almost certainly will not have sufficient resources to do the job properly, given the current fiscal climate which has drawn resources away from policing. This makes 'accidental' non-disclosure much more likely in future.

A few weeks later, interviewed by the *Mail on Sunday*, Foster reiterated that 'non-disclosure of material that could prove a suspect's innocence is the "biggest single problem" affecting the right to a fair trial' (Beckford, 2017b). This was not the first time he had raised this issue in a public forum; he has made clear the Commission's concern about non-disclosure in its Annual Reports, most strongly in 2015–16. Furthermore, he has in the past few years written on this matter to the Attorney General and Solicitor General, to the Director of Public Prosecutions, and to the National Police Chiefs'

---

[39] The rape trial of Liam Allan was stopped when prosecutors finally uncovered a disk containing over 40,000 messages showing that his accuser had frequently asked for casual sex.

[40] For a discussion of these cases, see Observer Editorial (2017) which refers to 'atrocious failures' that blight the criminal justice system and raises the question of whether disclosure decisions should be taken away from the police.

[41] In an interview with the Mail on Sunday, Foster explained that there had been an 'explosion' of emails, text messages, social media posts, and CCTV footage that had put increasing demands on detectives while police budget have shrunk (Beckford, 2017a).

Council, urging them to act on the increasing evidence of failures of the police and CPS to adhere to the rules of disclosure (see further Chapter 14).

Foster has made clear that non-disclosure means:

people may be wrongly induced to plead guilty because a full and fair account of the police investigation has been denied them. It means the right to a fair trial may have been denied because evidence which might have assisted the accused person's defence was not made available to them or their lawyers. (Foster, 2017a)

It is remarkable that in 2017 this still needs to be said. We doubt that those responsible for changes to the criminal process in the 1980s and 1990s would have anticipated that some twenty to thirty years later failures of suspects' due process rights would still be of significant concern to public servants. As one of our interviewees said in relation to non-disclosure, 'that should be routine now and shouldn't be happening, but it still is' (#58). Meanwhile, cuts to the legal aid budget have left defence lawyers much less likely to have the resources to put up a competent defence, an issue we turn to in the next chapter.

10

Responding to Applicants' Claims of Inadequate Defence

There's a sense that we sometimes skirt over [defence incompetence] issues . . . Defence incompetence is raised in a huge amount of cases . . . you pick one up and, you know, think, 'oh no', 'not again'. . . (#29)[1]

Introduction

Chapter 9 showed that the Criminal Cases Review Commission ('the Commission') is reluctant to refer cases to the Court of Appeal ('the Court') solely on evidence that there was police misconduct during the pre-trial or trial process, unless it can demonstrate that the misconduct had a direct impact on the safety of the conviction. Here we consider if this is true of the Commission's approach to claims of inadequate or incompetent legal defence. We present analysis of the Commission's response to cases where the applicant claims that there were procedural irregularities or incompetence by their defence solicitor or counsel.

Many applicants and their legal representatives claim that the trial lawyers were inadequate or incompetent, though usually this is one of a number of complaints about unfairness affecting the pre-trial or trial process, and most applicants also present other information that could produce fresh argument or evidence to cast a doubt on the safety of their conviction.

Applicants may believe that the defence team was egregiously poor, but there are few concrete examples provided in applications to the Commission to support these claims.[2] Many suggest that the defence failed to properly scrutinize witnesses' statements for inconsistencies or other evidence of unreliability (e.g. EE15) or failed to call or to cross-examine witnesses that the applicant claims could have been helpful to the defence (e.g. EE19b). Some complaints focus on delays or last-minute changes to counsel (e.g. EE11b), with others more concerned with apparent failures to challenge the prosecution evidence effectively (e.g. EE12). Occasionally, applicants refer to the lack of equality of arms: 'the defence had no access to HOLMES[3] and were under-resourced in comparison with the prosecution' (HIA7, Application).

Alongside concerns that the defence failed to adduce evidence that may have been exculpatory, many applicants offer rather vague complaints that the quality of the legal

---

[1] All interviews in this chapter are with Commission staff, including commissioners, case review managers, management staff, and advisers, unless we state otherwise.

[2] Among vague grievances, some applicants will refer to 'flagrant incompetence' though this test is no longer deployed by the Court when measuring just how poor legal representation has to be. The Casework Guidance Note on 'Inadequate Defence' suggests that the shift away from the flagrant incompetence yardstick came with *R v Clinton* [1993] 2 All ER 998 and was approved in *R v Fergus* [1994] 98 Cr App R 313 (Criminal Cases Review Commission, 2012b).

[3] A national police database of information on major investigations.

Reasons to Doubt: Wrongful Convictions and the Criminal Cases Review Commission. © Carolyn Hoyle and Mai Sato 2019. Published 2019 by Oxford University Press.

representation 'fell short of what was expected' and may have 'materially affected the outcome of the appeal' (EE26, Application), or that the barrister at trial did not do everything that the client asked for or expected in providing a robust defence.

In some cases, it is undoubtedly true that their defence team was less than perfect. In others, there may have been no wrongdoing on the part of the defence; the case was simply weak, with no exculpatory evidence or reliable witnesses to call (see Gould et al., 2013:83). Furthermore, defendants might not understand the strategies adopted by their defence team, who may have sound tactical reasons for being selective about the presentation of evidence.

As with claims of police misconduct or incompetence, the Commission cannot present to the Court evidence that the defence was inadequate or incompetent unless it can demonstrate that this had an impact on the safety of the conviction. Furthermore, if incompetence meant that the defence failed to secure potentially exculpatory evidence, and the Commission's investigation produces this evidence, it must be able to provide a good reason for the failure of the defence to adduce this evidence at trial. As with other concerns raised by applicants, the Commission's decisions in responding to complaints about their defence are shaped by the Commission's 'decision field' (Hawkins, 2002), with its relevant legislation and case law. The following section considers its influence before moving on to show how decisions are framed in specific cases.

Having analysed the Commission's response to 'typical' applications, we then move on to present a case study of the Commission's handling of a particular category of cases: asylum and immigration applicants. Here we show the potential for a more reciprocal relationship between the Commission and its 'decision field' and 'surround' (Hawkins, 2002), with evidence that occasionally the Commission can shift both the field and surround.

Decision Field

[T]he Court of Appeal these days are very reluctant to quash something on the basis of incompetent counsel. (#2)

As we have made clear in previous chapters, the Commission's decision field is shaped by the surround (Hawkins, 2002); in particular by the evolving jurisprudence of the Court. Hence, the Commission's Casework Guidance Note on 'Inadequate Defence' warns commissioners and case review managers ('CRMs') that the Court has taken 'a characteristically robust approach to appeals founded on allegations of incompetence' (Criminal Cases Review Commission, 2012b:para:5). It informs decision-makers that in many cases such a complaint, even if it is accurate, may not be relevant to the fairness of the proceedings and safety of the conviction, citing Lord Justice Dyson in *R v Butt*:[4]

It is no part of the duty of counsel to put every point of the defendant's case (however peripheral) to a witness or to embark on lengthy cross examination on matters which are not really in issue. It is the duty of counsel to discriminate between important and relevant features of a defence case which must be put to a witness and minor and/or unnecessary matters which do not need to be put. (Criminal Cases Review Commission, 2012b:para:16)

---

[4] [2005] EWCA Crim 805.

As we made clear in Chapter 6, applicants who are legally represented typically present a better case to the Commission. However, appeal lawyers might be particularly inclined to look critically on the work of other lawyers at previous stages of the case. They are used to scrutinizing past decisions with the benefit of hindsight and advances in forensic science, shifts in forensic psychology, and changes in the law. From this advantageous position, without the pressure of an impending trial, they may believe they would have made different choices. However, a decision by counsel cannot be presumed to render the conviction unsafe:

> merely because other counsel might not have made that decision ... It remains necessary to identify ... that there has been conduct of such poor quality (irrespective of what it is called) as to possibly render the proceedings unfair and, more importantly, the conviction unsafe. (Criminal Cases Review Commission, 2012b:para:6)

The Commission's guidance reminds decision-makers that just because applicants feel that they did not get a fair trial, because counsel was inadequate, it does not mean the conviction is unsafe. The Court has been clear on this point over the past two decades, which have seen:

> a gradual shift away from labelling poor conduct, and towards ensuring that the relevant provisions of the European Convention on Human Rights (in particular Article 6) are reflected in the UK jurisprudence. Hence, the court has become increasingly concerned to ensure that the proceedings as a whole are examined for any unfairness as opposed to identifying one or more glaring examples of poor conduct or ineptitude. (Criminal Cases Review Commission, 2012b:para:6)

The Casework Guidance Note discusses in particular the Court's single test approach as adopted in *Nangle*[5] and *Thakrar*[6] (meaning that there is only one test for the Court: has the incompetent representation rendered the conviction unsafe). In *Thakrar*, the Court accepted that the appellant's solicitors fell below the level of reasonably competent but asserted that their failure to carry out their duties in a proper manner did not mean that the conviction was automatically unsafe. The main issue was whether such failings meant that the appellant had not received a fair trial, and that this issue could only be determined by considering the proceedings as a whole. The Court reaffirmed this position in its judgment in another case when it declared:

> While incompetent representation is always to be deplored ... it cannot in itself form a ground of appeal or a reason why a conviction should be found unsafe. We accept that, following the decision of this court in Thakrar ... the test is indeed the *single test of safety*, and that the court no longer has to concern itself with intermediate questions such as whether the advocacy has been flagrantly incompetent. But in order to establish lack of safety in an incompetence case the appellant has to go beyond the incompetence and show that the incompetence lead to identifiable errors or irregularities in the trial which themselves rendered the process unfair or unsafe. (*R v Day (Mark Darren)*[7]; emphasis added)

Notwithstanding, the Casework Guidance Note makes clear that there may be extremely rare cases in which counsel's misbehaviour or ineptitude is so extreme that it constitutes a denial of due process to the client, even if it cannot be clearly established that the behaviour had an impact on the safety of the conviction (Criminal Cases Review Commission, 2012b:para:9). Furthermore, that a series of defence failures could have a cumulative effect that might render the conviction unsafe even when

---

[5] *R v Nangle* [2001] Crim LR 506.   [6] *R v Thakrar* [2001] EWCA Crim 1096.
[7] [2003] EWCA Crim 1060.

each error, if considered separately, would not ordinarily be seen as particularly serious (Criminal Cases Review Commission, 2012b:para:10). We had in our sample of Court directed (section 15) cases one such example (JD1). While this case is discussed in Chapter 11, for our purposes here, it is important to note that the cumulative effect of a series of defence failures in this case was such as to render the conviction unsafe. The Court found that the consequences of each separate error was not sufficiently grave to have an impact on the safety of the conviction, but when considered together, the effect was enough to render the conviction unsafe. Hence, the Casework Guidance Note, drawing on a discussion of this case, reminds Commission staff that a Statement of Reasons ('SOR') should reflect consideration of submissions regarding legal incompetence at both the individual and the cumulative level (Criminal Cases Review Commission, 2012b:para:10).

Of course, one result of incompetent representation at trial may be that exculpatory evidence was missed that could now be presented in appeal as fresh evidence that casts doubt on the safety of the conviction. However, as the previous chapters have demonstrated, the Court is reluctant to admit fresh evidence if it was not put forward at trial as a result of a tactical decision, unless it can be shown that the decision was based on incompetent or erroneous advice:

If the reason for a case not being argued or evidence not being adduced at the trial is that the defendant's legal advisers acted in such a way as to deprive the defendant of a fair trial, then that could amount to a reasonable explanation for the failure to adduce the evidence at trial. However, if there was a deliberate, informed decision by the defendant and his advisers not to advance a defence or evidence known to be available and that decision is made for tactical reasons, then that will not amount to a reasonable explanation for the failure to adduce that evidence at trial. (Hooper LJ[8] cited in Criminal Cases Review Commission, 2012:para:17)

As we will see in what follows, very often this distinction goes to the heart of the Commission's review of these applications.

Applicants' claims of inadequate defence

Applicants to the Commission may have had legal representation at trial, at direct appeal, and perhaps at a prior application to the Commission. They may also be represented at their present application to the Commission. Here we focus only on representation at trial, as their claims of legal incompetence at any other stage are irrelevant to the Commission's review of the safety of their conviction. As the Commission stated in the SOR not to refer in case CS8, 'even if counsel representing [the applicant] on appeal was incompetent (which the Commission does not accept), that would not cause [his] conviction to be unsafe, because his conviction resulted from the trial, not from the appeal' (CS8, Statement of Reasons).

As in Chapter 9, to explore the Commission's response to claims of legal incompetence, we draw here on ninety-four of our cases: contemporary sexual offence cases, historical institutional abuse cases, and forensic and expert evidence cases, the focus of the previous three chapters, allowing us to analyse 'typical' Commission cases.

Table 10.1 shows that the applicant raised the issue of inadequate defence in under a quarter (twenty-four cases) of these ninety-four cases; the conviction was referred back to the Court in fourteen of these. All the SORs—both to refer and not to refer the case back to Court—discussed the applicant's concerns about their legal representation at

Table 10.1 Applicants' claims of inadequate defence

Type of case	Case not referred	Case referred	Total
Forensic and Expert Evidence	4	10 (ground for referral in 1)	14 of 60
Contemporary Sex Crimes	0	4	4 of 17
Historical Institutional Abuse	4	0	4 of 17
TOTAL	8	14	22 of 94

trial, but in only one case was this found to be sufficiently persuasive to form a ground for referral (EE38b).

Chapter 9 demonstrated that injustice can occur when the police fail properly to disclose relevant information to the defence. In case EE38b, discussed in Chapters 7 and 9, the police did not disclose important evidence of an alternative suspect, but the defence also failed to consider the possibility that this was a plausible alternative murder suspect. Furthermore, the defence failed to challenge at trial inconsistencies in the prosecution evidence concerning the height of the suspect, which the Commission thought 'might well have been a line of argument that the defence could have used to challenge the identification' (EE38b, Statement of Reasons). While the case was referred on fresh evidence (relating to the alternative suspect), the Commission included non-disclosure by the police and inadequate defence as a further referral point:

The Commission takes the view that [the applicant] was placed at a disadvantage by the failure both by the police and his trial representatives to recognise the significance of the evidence concerning [the alternative suspect] at the material time ... failure to adduce this evidence ... was a result of a combination of police and defence shortcomings. (EE38b, Statement of Reasons)

As we discuss above, most of the applicants who were critical about counsel at trial claimed that their lawyers had been negligent, failed to conduct sufficient research pre-trial, or failed to cross-examine sufficiently robustly the witnesses at trial. In a few cases, the Commission found the claims to be entirely without validity: that the applicant was mistaken about the availability of information, for example. Hence, in case HIA8 the applicant argued that the defence was incompetent for failing to obtain specific records but after investigating the matter, the Commission concluded that:

[The applicant's] defence lawyers were not aware of this new evidence and, in the Commission's opinion, no fault can be attributed to the defence for this. At the time of the trial and appeal this evidence was not known to the Prosecution, or [Police force]. The Commission considers that no criticism can therefore be made of the defence for not utilising the new evidence at the trial or appeal. (HIA8, Statement of Reasons)

Similarly, in case EE19b claims of defence incompetence were thought by the Commission to be unfounded; defence counsel could not have been expected to call expert witnesses to rebut evidence in the case as the forensic science at the time of the trial had not developed sufficiently to challenge the prosecution case. Here, the Commission had fresh evidence sufficient for a referral and so little more was said about the defence case.

Most cases lie somewhere between clear evidence of incompetence—as demonstrated by case EE38b—and complete lack of such evidence, seen in cases HIA8 and EE19b. Therefore, the Commission has to draw on its decision field to judge if the claims of legal incompetence might persuade the Court to quash the conviction. In making such decisions, it typically adopts a legal decision frame.

Legal Decision Frame

In many cases, the Commission draws on evolving jurisprudence that demonstrates that evidence of poor legal representation will not normally be sufficient to challenge the safety of a conviction unless it can be demonstrated that the inadequate defence impacted on the safety of the conviction, as the following excerpt from an SOR not to refer shows:

It used to be the case that appellants would have to show that there had been 'flagrantly incompetent' representation, but the approach of the Court of Appeal has shifted in recent years away from defining the nature and the extent of incompetence, and towards examining its effect on the fairness of the trial and safety of the conviction. It remains the case, however, that an appeal will only be successful if the representative's failings had a particular effect on the conviction so as to render it unsafe. Incompetence alone will not be enough. (HIA4, Statement of Reasons)

In this historical institutional abuse case, the applicant claimed that his trial counsel had advised that they not criticize the police and their investigation, and had failed to question relevant witnesses or to seek disclosure of pertinent records. The Commission explored each complaint but found none to be persuasive. Their review demonstrated that the applicant and his family had been highly involved in the preparation for trial, demanding their lawyers provide justification and thorough explanation for each and every decision made, so that 'keeping the case under control and within realistic boundaries was a task in itself' (HIA4, Case Record).

The SOR records that the Commission accepted that there may now exist differences of view between the applicant and defence counsel about the extent of challenge to details of prosecution evidence.[9] However, it states that it has 'seen no evidence that could demonstrate that such a decision by counsel was taken in defiance of [the applicant's] instructions or when all promptings of good sense pointed the other way', drawing on the judgment in *R v Butt*:[10]

It is not part of the duty of counsel to put every point of the defendant's case (however peripheral) to a witness or to embark on lengthy cross-examination on matters which are not really in issue. It is the duty of counsel to discriminate between important and relevant features of a defence case which must be put to a witness and minor and or unnecessary matters which do not need to be put … (HIA4, Statement of Reasons)

The SOR also drew on *R v Clinton*[11] which argued that decisions made by barristers 'in good faith after proper consideration of the competing arguments' will not on their own render a conviction unsafe, and on *R v Ullah*[12] which established the test for legal incompetence:

Was the decision or action of counsel based on such fundamentally flawed reasons that it may properly be regarded by the Court of Appeal (Criminal Division) as Wednesbury unreasonable. (HIA4, Statement of Reasons)

---

[9] In particular, the Commission felt that the defence strategy of not criticizing the police and their investigation to avoid alienating the jury could now be seen as unhelpful.
[10] [2005] EWCA Crim 805.   [11] [1993] 2 All ER 998.
[12] *R v Ullah (Alaveed)* [2000] 1 Cr App R 351.

The Commission could not find any evidence of such legal incompetence and reminded the applicant that 'it is not the role of the Commission to consider complaints against members of the bar, or against solicitors, beyond any impact their conduct may have on the safety of a conviction' (HIA4, Statement of Reasons). The review concluded that the defence 'did not fall short of the expected professional standards. It appears that witnesses were rigorously questioned, and that [the] defence was put fully and robustly' (HIA4, Case Record).

The Commission refused to refer murder convictions back to the Court following a long and detailed investigation of case EE42. The application had raised significant concerns about the police investigation but also about the defence counsel who had—in the applicant's opinion—failed to draw the jury's attention to key issues that might weaken the prosecution case, had failed to fully understand certain aspects of the defence, and did not cross-examine a witness that the applicant thought would be helpful to his case. The Commission's review found no evidence to support this, demonstrating that the applicant's 'defence was clearly advanced by his representatives' (EE42, Statement of Reasons). Furthermore, in responding to the applicant's assertion that a number of points the applicant wanted to be brought to the attention of the Court were not raised by his defence, the Commission quoted, in the SOR, from the judgment of Sir Igor Judge in *R v Ulcay & Toygyn*:[13]

> Neither the client, nor if the advocate is a barrister, his instructing solicitor, is entitled to direct counsel how the case should be conducted. The advocate is not a tinkling echo, or a mouthpiece, spouting whatever his client 'instructs' him to say ... It is however always improper for the advocate to seek to challenge evidence which is accepted to be true on the basis of the facts agreed or described by the client, merely because the lay-client, or the professional client, wishes him to do so. He may not accept nor act on such instructions. (EE42, Statement of Reasons)

The Commission argued that the Court could not conclude that the standard of representation was such that it could have rendered the trial unfair.

In case HIA3, the applicant expressed concerns about various matters in his application in 2003, many focusing on complainant credibility, but did not criticize his defence. Just over two years later, the applicant's representative raised further issues including defence incompetence. Indeed, he argued that the representation was so negligent and incompetent as to render the trial process and conviction unsafe. Criticism focused on the repercussions of the lawyer's decision not to inform the jury that the defendant had previously been tried for these offences but the jury could not come to an agreed verdict, and that there had been a further aborted trial. The Commission's investigation focused on delays amounting to an abuse of process, police trawling for evidence, and concerns about the credibility of the complainants (see Chapter 8). While the Commission dealt with some of the issues regarding defence incompetence as they related to specific legal arguments—for example around delay—it rejected the claim that the defence had been incompetent in not alerting the jury to the previous trials:

> It was agreed with the prosecution that no reference would be made to the earlier trial ... [as this] would have seriously prejudiced [the applicant] ... The Commission does not consider that any of the directions given or the lack of any particular direction was such as to render [the applicant's] conviction unsafe. (HIA3, Statement of Reasons)

---

[13] [2007] EWCA Crim 2379.

It declined to refer the case at this stage, though referred some of the applicant's convictions back to the Court four years later, following a change of law regarding unlawful sexual intercourse with a child under the age of 16 (see Chapter 8).

In a few cases (e.g. EE17 and EE10), proof of defence incompetence could not meet the Court's requirement for fresh evidence or argument, as an assertion that defence counsel had failed to submit certain evidence at trial—had already been dealt with and rejected by the Court at direct appeal. This was frustrating for the applicants who felt that the Court had not dealt thoroughly or fairly with them. In discussing such cases, one interviewee explained:

The analytical approach is, well, we need something new, and so have you raised it before, well yeah you raised it at appeal so, you know, well, forget it. And it could be the Court of Appeal has just … summarily dismissed it [but] as far as we're concerned it's not new. (#29)

The applicant in case CS12 claimed that that the defence was 'inadequate both in the preparation for trial and the presentation of his case', asserting that 'it was not possible to challenge the credibility of [the complainant] in cross examination because of incomplete investigation and preparation of the defence case' (CS12, Application). While the Commission could find no evidence of incompetence from the defence files (which suggested that correspondence was prompt and that witnesses were identified and interviewed effectively), it invited defence counsel to respond to the claims. Counsel made clear that their aim had been to focus on cross-examination of the complainant, rather than presenting other witnesses; in other words, that their choices had been tactical. In reviewing this response, the Commission formed the view that:

albeit with the benefit of hindsight … with more detailed and persistent enquiries the solicitors might well have been able to obtain much of the information now available and that in those circumstances counsel would have been better equipped to question [the witness'] credibility in cross examination. (CS12, Statement of Reasons)

However, it did not feel that the defence representation 'fell so far short in their investigations … as to justify a referral on the basis of defence incompetence' (CS12, Statement of Reasons). While the Commission's response to the applicant's claims of police and defence incompetence was well rehearsed in the SOR, the case was referred on fresh evidence relating to the credibility of the victim and the Court quashed the conviction.

Referring on the fresh evidence could have posed difficulties for the Commission if the Court felt that the defence had failed to adduce evidence about the witness's credibility at the time of the trial because of a tactical decision. Hence, the Commission had to establish that the evidence casting doubt on the credibility of the main prosecution witness was not and could not have been known at the time of the trial. The CRM—in the review—interviewed a number of witnesses about information that had come to light *since* the trial; for example, showing that the witness had a reputation for lying and, in particular, that she had admitted to lying after the trial. In making clear that this evidence could not have been adduced at trial, the SOR cites case law on a complainant's credibility being found to be fatally flawed following an investigation post trial,[14] showing that this is not unfamiliar to the Court. The careful construction of the case for the Court nicely demonstrates the challenges in responding to claims of legal incompetence.

---

[14] e.g. *R v Carrington-Jones* [2007] EWCA Crim 2551.

Framing decisions as 'tactical'

The Commission understands that in most cases the Court is unlikely to be persuaded that trial lawyers are incompetent, preferring to assume that there were solid, tactical reasons for their handling of a case. Nonetheless, the Commission must make that predictive judgement; it must decide when inadequate or incompetent defence reaches the level required to suggest an impact on the safety of the conviction and it must judge whether accounts of tactical reasoning are plausible. In Chapter 9, we saw that the Commission sometimes adopts a moral framework in interpreting police behaviour and actions rather generously; minor misconduct being interpreted as unintentional errors. We looked for a similar mindset in cases where the Commission described actions or failures to act on the part of defence lawyers as 'tactical' decisions to advance the case, rather than incompetence. Some of our interviews suggested that Commission staff might be rather too forgiving of legal incompetence. As one interviewee put it:

They're not always competent … but it's the easiest accusation in the world, when you've been convicted, to say, 'my barrister didn't do a very good job'. Well, they did the best job they did, in all probability, in the circumstances. Unless you can say, 'look, this is where they went wrong'. (#51)

Reluctance to believe the worst of lawyers could reflect a shared professional perspective, occasioning some deference towards other lawyers' decisions, given that most Commission staff are legally trained, and many have previously been in legal practice. However, we found no clear examples of this among this sample of cases. Indeed, our data suggest that reluctance to refer cases on incompetent defence can be better explained by the restrictive nature of the Court's test, as demonstrated by the case law discussed above. The Court will only consider a conviction to be unsafe if the appellant can demonstrate that not only was there significant legal incompetence but that it made a difference, that it impacted on the safety on the conviction. Otherwise, it is more likely that decisions will be seen as 'reasonable' or 'tactical'. In turn, the Commission will recognize many decisions as such:

I think the difficulty with criticising the defence is, again, you look, with the benefit of hindsight, at decisions that were made at the time, and I remember talking to defence counsel, who, in fairness to him, had said that this was always one of the cases that had troubled him … and we were asking questions along the lines of 'why didn't you question her further about this, that or the other', and he said to us, 'The reason I didn't was because she was so hostile towards [the applicant] and she was so damaging, we just wanted her out the witness box as soon as we could.' (#1)

In some cases, thorough scrutiny of all the evidence gathered by the Commission suggests applicants' claims of incompetence could not be sustained; that, instead, counsel had been tactical. For example, in case EE31 the Commission found that decisions not to advance a particular defence (based on medical evidence) that the applicant had claimed was misguided was in fact a tactical and reasonable decision (based on the fact that it would have enabled the prosecution to introduce material prejudicial to the defence). In the event, the Commission was able to refer the case on other forensic evidence.

Similarly, in case EE26, the applicant's representative questioned why the defence had not produced a particular witness at trial. The Commission—in its Provisional SOR—stated that it *assumed* this was for tactical reasons. Not unsurprisingly, in further submissions, the representative expressed the view that it was premature to decide this without interviewing the defence solicitors to discover why the evidence had not been applied for at the time of the trial, prompting the Commission to conduct further investigation on this point. As it happens, the trial solicitor was able to provide good reasons. He had interviewed the witness on two or three occasions and found him to be unreliable and uncooperative, and was therefore persuaded not to seek to present him at trial. The Commission's suspicion that this had been a sound, tactical decision seemed to be correct, though they might have established this earlier, through proactive investigation, rather than presuming it. In fact, the case was referred by the Commission some years later, in 2010 (EE26c), on fresh DNA evidence, with no discussion of the legal competence, and the applicant's conviction was quashed.

In case HIA7, the applicant claimed that 'counsel's approach at trial was fatally flawed'—that a potential witness for the defence was not confronted, nor were police witnesses questioned regarding unused material (HIA7, Application). In the SOR explaining why it would not refer the case, the Commission argued that the defence had a sound tactical reason for this, as aspects of the witness' evidence 'would have been highly damaging to the defence case' (HIA7, Statement of Reasons) and there was no reason to believe further exploration of this evidence would assist a referral. In support of this position, the Commission drew on the stance taken by the applicant's counsel at direct appeal, stating that if the appellant's representative had thought this would be worthy of submission, he would have included it in the 'very substantial' grounds on appeal (HIA7, Statement of Reasons). This strikes us as a rather clumsy approach: in effect, the Commission tried to persuade the applicant that one lawyer was competent by pointing out that the other lawyer did not say he was incompetent. For applicants who have lost their trust in lawyers, this is not likely to go down well. Rather unusually, the applicant had argued that trial counsel could have taken the 'bold approach' of raising 'lurking doubt'.[15] While the Commission agreed that this was a possible technique that the defence might have drawn on, the approach taken was, in its view, 'entirely reasonable' and 'as the Commission can not speculate as to what might have been the outcome if a drastically different approach had been taken at trial', this could not form a viable ground of appeal (HIA7, Statement of Reasons).

As this case shows, the Commission sometimes must take explanations by legal representatives at face value. It cannot reinvestigate the case fully, and so if lawyers say particular witnesses were uncooperative or even hostile or were likely to introduce evidence that could have been damaging to the defence, in most cases, the Commission must accept their reasoning. Therefore, when the Commission concludes that the defence was 'entirely reasonable', it is categorically not saying it was the best defence anyone could hope for. It is simply saying that it meets the Court's test of reasonable defence and that none of the information available suggests incompetence that might impact on the safety of the conviction. Whether applicants understand it this way—given the oftentimes highly technical language of the SORs produced by the Commission—is a different matter.

---

[15] The origin of the term 'lurking doubt' can be found in *R v Cooper & McMahon* [1969] 1 Q.B. 267, 53 Cr App R 82 where Widgery LJ stated: 'in cases of this kind the Court must in the end ask itself a subjective question, whether we are content to let the matter stand as it is, or whether there is not some lurking doubt in our minds which makes us wonder whether an injustice has been done. This is a reaction which may not be based strictly on the evidence as such: it is a reaction which can be produced by the general feel of the case as the Court experiences it.' The lurking doubt ground of appeal forms a very small number of all appeals and is seen as a 'last resort' in those cases where no criticism can be made of the trial and yet concern about the conviction lingers (Criminal Cases Review Commission, 2011j) (see Chapter 14).

In most cases where the decision is made to refer convictions back to the Court but not to cite defence incompetence as a ground for referral, the discussion of any defence shortcomings is brief. The SOR will describe the applicant's concerns and conclude that the defence had been adequate, even when it records that there may have been room for improvement. In case EE11b, for example, the applicant claimed that defence counsel was 'inept at cross-examination', had failed to instruct a suitable expert, and had failed to follow instructions regarding the calling of character witnesses (EE11b, Application). The case record demonstrates considerable effort on the part of the Commission in obtaining and analysing the defence files. In the end, the case was referred back to the Court on the basis of fresh medical evidence. The SOR discusses at some length the reasons for finding other submissions to be without support though in a document running to forty-eight pages, the section on 'Incompetence of Legal Team' accounts for just one, three-sentence paragraph. Here, the Commission concludes that the defence counsel was:

required to make a range of tactical decisions in respect of which witnesses to call and what questions to ask. [Counsel] was not obliged to follow [the applicant's] instructions on these points. Accordingly, there is nothing in [counsel's] conduct, or that of the solicitors' that, in the opinion of the Commission, could give rise to a real possibility that the Court of Appeal would regard the conviction as unsafe. (EE11b, Statement of Reasons)

However, one case in our sample (EE15) suggests some equivocation on the part of the Commission, though the evidence of incompetence was insufficiently strong to refer on. The applicant, who was convicted on two counts of rape and gross indecency with a child, argued that the defence failure to bring to the attention of the court inconsistencies in the victims' statements, evidence of prompting by the police and confabulation, and evidence pertaining to undue influence on the victims by their parent had been damaging to his case. The Commission's review focused on fresh evidence that suggested there had been no crime though the CRM tried, unsuccessfully, to establish why the defence had apparently failed to pursue certain evidence. The defence counsel told the Commission that he had neither recollection nor notes relating to the case.[16]

The case was referred on fresh medical evidence and the convictions quashed, but the SOR, in the section on 'other issues raised … which do not form the basis of this reference' (EE15, Statement of Reason), discusses at some length claims that the defence was incompetent by failing to fully analyse interviews and witness statements and by failing to call expert evidence. Its conclusion that: 'while, understandably, the cross-examination of the girls was not that robust or confrontational, it was probing and thorough' (EE15, Statement of Reasons) seems a little contradictory. Regarding the defence failure to present to the court a particular letter that might have assisted the applicant, the Commission observed that this evidence *might* have 'carried real risks' and recorded:

The Commission *presumes* that, if [the applicant] provided this [evidence] to his solicitors, the fact that it was not used was a tactical decision on the part of his defence team. In the circumstances of this case, the Commission is unable to conclude that such a decision would be viewed as either unreasonable or incompetent by the Court of Appeal, or such as to render the verdict unsafe … The defence decision not to raise the matter at trial is one which, in reality, *appears* to

---

[16] The trial had taken place ten years before the application, arguably short enough for most people's memories. Furthermore, the absence of records is perhaps surprising.

have been entirely sensible and in [the applicant's] best interests at the time. (EE15, Statement of Reasons; emphasis added)

In the absence of any evidence to the contrary—given that the defence was unable to recall or provide details of his approach in this case—perhaps the Commission could not have gone further with this. That said, we detect some unease in the SOR which was occasionally reflected in our conversations with Commission staff, including this excerpt from an interview about a case that was not included in our sample:

this young man was ... represented by disgraceful solicitors. They were incompetent to an un-believable degree. And they failed to talk about the issues at all and they failed to instruct legal counsel until Friday, on a murder trial starting on Monday. Given the brief he had, it was impos-sible for [name of QC] to fully consider all the issues. It was no disrespect to him. He just hadn't been given the straw to drink with. So, we wrote to [name of QC], in the most respectful terms, saying, you know, we appreciate you raised every point you could possibly have done in the time, but we think that this issue, had statements been taken, is an important point, and ... he could [have said], 'I'm [name of QC] and I'm terribly good but, on reflection, I understand this point, which has only been drawn to me, had I had this, I might have been able to [take a different line of questioning] ... ' Instead of which he said, 'I'm [name of QC], I'm far cleverer than you, a weekend is easily enough for me to deal with a case, and I utterly and totally reject the sugges-tion.' And then it went to Lord Justice [name omitted], who's a CCRC-hater, and it led to the most vituperative judgment ... I came to a view, if legal incompetence was part of the story, you somehow had to tell the story in a way which didn't suggest that we knew better than the learned counsel. Somehow, you had to ... you had to get [the issue in] through the back door. (#7)

Getting the issue in through the back door could be interpreted in a number of ways: it could mean using the SOR to engage in robust criticisms of the defence even when the evidence does not meet the Court's test for incompetence, but if by sug-gesting incompetence the Commission deprives the applicant of persuading the Court that the fresh evidence should be admitted, it could shoot itself in the foot. Thus, it is more likely to mean getting the referral to the Court by another route (e.g. by re-ferring on fresh evidence) and not including defence incompetence as a referral point, and indeed not being too robust in its criticisms of the defence. This may be strategic, though of course it does not take advantage of the Commission's privileged position to hold the system to account for failures of due process. We return to this point later but here we consider the Commission's instrumental approach to referring on the strongest point, without rehearsing criticisms of the defence, an issue we raised in Chapter 9 in relation to police misconduct.

Instrumental decision frame

As we mention above, and discussed in more detail in Chapter 7, the Commission's decision field shapes its approach to fresh evidence in cases where the defence failed to adduce expert evidence at trial that could now cast doubt on the safety of the convic-tion. In case EE34, the applicant alerted the Commission to expert evidence (relating to a cigarette butt[17]) that could have challenged the prosecution evidence at trial but that the defence had failed to adduce. While the Commission sought such evidence and indeed referred the case on it, it argued in the SOR that the counsel's explanation for not adducing an expert at trial was 'reasonable' (EE34, Statement of Reasons). If the Commission had not been able to present a reasonable explanation for this

---

[17] See Chapter 7 for a discussion of this case.

failure, it could not have referred the case on the fresh expert evidence. Hence the justification for counsel's failure to present this evidence at trial runs to almost two pages of the SOR. Indeed, it reproduces further evidence provided by counsel during the Commission's investigation that 'the prosecution evidence relating to the cigarette "strained credulity to such an extent that it would have been unjustifiable to the Legal Services Commission to instruct" an expert' (EE34, Statement of Reasons). Here, in order to present the fresh evidence to the Court, the Commission could not suggest gross legal incompetence, as there was insufficient evidence of that, nor could it suggest that counsel took a tactical decision not to present it, as that would preclude its presentation at this stage (given that the Court does not allow a change in defence tactic at appeal stage; see further Chapter 7). Hence, the Commission had to find the balance between these.

In cases where both the prosecution and defence seem to have been somewhat incompetent, the Commission's decision field may create an incentive to find fault with the former, rather than the latter. As we mention above, if a review identifies fresh evidence, the Commission must consider whether there is a reasonable explanation for the failure to adduce it at trial, and laying blame at the feet of defence counsel can block this route. In case CS10—a rape case—where the Commission had found evidence to challenge the victim's credibility, it argued that it was 'not reasonable to expect the defence' to have produced this evidence at trial as the police had failed to investigate properly and failed to disclose a relevant witness statement to the defence, thus depriving the defence of the ability to adduce relevant material that would have assisted their case (CS10, Statement of Reasons). Focusing on police non-disclosure allowed the presentation of fresh evidence.

In case CS9, there was sufficient evidence to refer the case to the Court based on doubts about the witness' credibility. The applicant had claimed that his defence counsel was inadequate as his daughters were not called to give evidence. The SOR records in the section 'other matters not forming the basis of the decision to refer':

In order for the Commission properly to assess whether there is a real possibility that the Court of Appeal would admit the evidence [that the applicant thought should have been presented], the Commission would have to assess, amongst other matters, whether there was, as [he] alleges, a failure on behalf of his solicitors and whether or not this amounted to a reasonable explanation for the failure to adduce the evidence at the trial. The Commission considers that it would take some time to resolve this issue and that in the light of the existence of grounds for referral, it is not appropriate to delay an appeal by seeking to resolve these matters. (CS9, Statement of Reasons)

The conviction for indecent assault was quashed without the Commission having to resolve the issue of inadequacies in the defence. This clearly instrumental approach produced a good result for the applicant, but choosing not to investigate claims of legal incompetence may not be good for the integrity of the criminal justice system.

The Commission has been subject to some criticism over the past years for failing to raise awareness and contribute valuable insights into the state of British justice. As an under-resourced, casework organization, it has little time to devote to debates about wider justice matters, and yet is well placed to do so. More than any other organization, it sees close-up evidence of misconduct or ineptitude at every stage of the process and the devastating results when the system errs. After years of reticence, it has, in recent years, shone a spotlight on defence incompetence and breaches of prosecutorial rules in a somewhat unusual set of cases: applications from refugees and asylum seekers who claim to have been wrongfully convicted of entering the United Kingdom

('UK') illegally, with a false identification document or no document at all. We reflect on these applications as they provide an atypical case study of a distinct response to legal incompetence.

Inadequate Defence of Refugees and Asylum Seekers

These cases relate to applicants who were wrongfully convicted of criminal offences for entering the UK illegally.[18] They had not been able to obtain travel documents lawfully and were erroneously advised by defence lawyers that they should plead guilty.

Legal protection for refugees and asylum seekers: decision field

The 1951 Refugee Convention provides that refugees should not be returned to a country where they face serious threats to their lives or freedom. Once refugees enter their destination country, Article 31(1) of the Convention protects them from being punished for breaking immigration rules:

> The Contracting States shall not impose penalties, on account of their illegal entry or presence, on refugees who, coming directly from a territory where their life or freedom was threatened in the sense of Article 1, enter or are present in their territory without authorization, provided they present themselves without delay to the authorities and show good cause for their illegal entry or presence.

The Convention therefore guarantees that refugees entering a contracting state will not be returned to their country of origin, nor punished for violating immigration laws upon entry. This protection extends to those with a confirmed refugee status as well as to 'presumptive refugees' (or asylum seekers)—people who have not yet had this status granted by a state but are in the process of seeking it.[19] The protection does not extend to migrants who do not come 'directly' from a persecuting state, fail to present themselves 'without delay' to authorities, or fail to show good cause for illegal entry.

The UK has been a signatory to the Refugee Convention since 1954, and the Convention was incorporated into domestic law under section 31 of the Immigration and Asylum Act 1999, introduced after the landmark case of *Adimi*.[20] In this case, three asylum seekers were convicted of using false documents under the Forgery and Counterfeiting Act 1981 and two with the further offence of attempting to obtain air services by deception, under the Criminal Attempts Act 1981. The court quashed their convictions, concluding that punishing illegal entry goes against the principle of Article 31, which was intended to provide 'immunity for genuine refugees whose quest for asylum reasonably involved them in breaching the law' (*Adimi*, para:15). Section 31(1) of the 1999 Act provides a statutory defence against a list of identity- and immigration-related offences relevant to refugees and asylum seekers, though it does not prohibit the Crown Prosecution Service ('CPS') from starting criminal proceedings against asylum seekers, as long as their cases are not concluded before their refugee status is determined (see Aliverti, 2014).

---

[18] This section draws heavily on a previously published article: Sato et al. (2017).
[19] The term 'presumptive refugees' was used in *R v Uxbridge Magistrates Court ex parte Adimi* [1999] EWHC Admin 765.
[20] *R v Uxbridge Magistrates Court ex parte Adimi* [1999] EWHC Admin 765.

Five years after the Refugee Convention was formally recognized under domestic law in the Immigration and Asylum Act 1999, the Asylum and Immigration (Treatment of Claimants, etc.) Act 2004 was introduced. Section 2 of the 2004 Act created an offence of a person not having an immigration document at a leave or asylum interview upon entering the UK, raising an interesting question as to how the 2004 Act is interpreted in light of Article 31 of the Refugee Convention and section 31 of the Immigration and Asylum Act 1999. In the case of *Kapoor and Ors*,[21] the appeal court held that section 2 of the 2004 Act 'merely controls or regulates the entitlement to be in the UK and therefore cannot be relied upon as the immigration law which has been breached' (Crown Prosecution Service, n.d.). This means Article 31 and section 31 are not applicable to offences under section 2 of the 2004 Act and do not provide a defence (Crown Prosecution Service, n.d.). In other words, a person who has a successful asylum claim can still be found guilty under section 2 of the 2004 Act.

That said, there are separate statutory defences available under the 2004 Act. They include being a European Economic Area national or being a family member of a European Economic Area national; having a reasonable excuse for not being in possession of a document; proving that a false immigration document has been used throughout the journey to the UK; or having travelled to the UK without any immigration documents (sections 2(4) and 2(5) of the 2004 Act). In *Soe Thet v DPP*,[22] the court—extending the reach of the 2004 Act—held that Thet had a reasonable excuse for not being in possession of a genuine travel document because he had been a political prisoner in Burma and had been unable to obtain a passport in his country. Similarly, a lack of issuing facility or not knowing where to go for a genuine passport is also considered a defence under the 2004 Act, according to the case of *Mohammed and Osman*.[23] While there clearly are defences in law, in practice, the past decade or so has demonstrated that when politics take a punitive turn, the rights of the most vulnerable are not adequately protected, even by those whose job it is to defend them.

Unwelcoming stance: surround in refugee and asylum cases

Refugees and asylum seekers arriving at UK borders clearly have some legal protection. However, over the past decades they have entered an environment pervaded by malign anti-immigrant politics that mark a shift towards what David Garland (2001) has called the *Culture of Control*—the increased public desire for more punitive measures met with the expansion of formal social control. The punitive turn, from the late 1990s, under the Labour government, encouraged the prosecution and criminalization of migrants. Between 1997 and 2010, when the Labour government was in power, eighty-four new immigration-related offences were created compared to only seventy offences during the ninety-one years from 1905 to 1996 (Aliverti, 2014). The UK Border Agency was set up in 2008 to enforce these laws and tackle perceived abuses of immigration rules (Christie, 2016). Moving away from the previous practice of dealing with migrants administratively, their increased reliance on criminal law in dealing with migration resulted in a 54 per cent increase in immigration-related charges in the magistrates' courts between 2004 and 2005, most for failing to produce a valid passport upon entry to the UK (Aliverti, 2014:50).

---

[21] *Kapoor and Ors* [2012] EWCA Crim 435.
[22] *Soe Thet v Director of Public Prosecutions* [2006] EWHC 2701 (Admin).
[23] *Mohammed and Osman* [2007] EWCA Crim 2332.

The widespread political and public desire to control and criminalize migration,[24] and the portrayal of migrants as *deviant*, may have operated as 'anchors' (Tversky and Kahneman, 1974), leading criminal justice agencies to overlook their statutory protection and move away from a 'due process' to a 'crime control' model in asylum cases (Packer, 1968). The CPS proceeded with prosecutions where there was no case to answer, and defence lawyers failed to advise their clients of their defence under Article 31 of the 1991 Act and section 2 of the 2004 Act. Many refugees and asylum seekers were prosecuted and convicted under the new laws *even* in cases where they had a statutory defence,[25] causing further harm to these vulnerable people who had typically fled intolerable living conditions in their country of origin.

Asylum and immigration cases began to present challenges for the Commission in the mid-2000s and the steady stream of cases led the organization, in 2012, to express concern that 'hundreds of asylum seekers and refugees' may have been wrongfully convicted after being advised to plead guilty to offences relating to their entry to the UK (Holiday, 2012). Soon these cases accounted for a large proportion of Commission referrals. For example, between April 2015 and March 2016, the Commission reviewed a total of 1,797 cases and referred thirty-three cases (about 1.8 per cent) to the appeal court (Criminal Cases Review Commission, 2016a).[26] Of these, nine were asylum and immigration cases (Criminal Cases Review Commission, 2016a). Unlike other 'categories' of cases, this was a homogeneous group.

Asylum and immigration offences: homogeneous cases

While convictions referred back to the appeal court by the Commission are usually for fairly serious offences, as demonstrated by our review of cases in previous chapters, which include a high proportion of murder and rape convictions,[27] asylum and immigration applications are not so: their convictions relate to the failure to produce proper documents upon entering the UK.[28] Most applicants were therefore convicted in the magistrates' courts and so appealed to the Crown Court, rather than the Court of Appeal.[29] Unlike most other cases in our sample, applicants had pled guilty, which can pose challenges for the Commission (see Chapter 6).

Notwithstanding, more than a quarter of such cases were referred back to an appeal court; which is, of course, most unusual. For this reason, we focused our analysis on referrals and studied how the Commission made its decisions in these cases. Early in our research, we noted two clear patterns; the Commission was extremely quick in

---

[24] What Stumpf (2006) has referred to as 'crimmigration'.

[25] The judgment of *Mateta & Ors* ([2013] EWCA Crim 1372) provides guidance on this defence, and its complexities in applying it in practice. However, in the same judgment, it makes clear that defence lawyers often failed to raise the existence of such a defence due to incorrect assumptions about the nature of the case: 'It is sufficiently clear ... that the availability of the defence under s. 31 was never raised with the applicant, on the basis of the incorrect assumption that there was no potential defence to the charge' (*Mateta*, para:30).

[26] Of the thirty-three cases, seven were referred for a review of sentence only.

[27] See Appendix.

[28] They include: failure to produce a document contrary to section 2 of the Immigration and Asylum (Treatment of Claimants) Act 2004; attempting to obtain air services by deception under the Criminal Attempts Act 1981; using false documents under the Forgery and Counterfeiting Act 1981; and possession of a false identity document with intent, contrary to section 25(1) of the Identity Cards Act 2006.

[29] For this reason, in discussing this case study we refer to 'the appeal court' to mean either the Crown Court or the Court of Appeal, rather than 'the Court' which explicitly refers to the Court of Appeal.

reviewing the applications and the appeal courts were very receptive to them. Hence, in addition to conducting thorough analysis of the Commission's response to twenty-three cases in our purposeful sample (A1–A23), we collected further basic data on all other cases referred until the end of March 2016: forty-three cases in total.

Our analysis demonstrates that these somewhat different applications produced distinctive responses by the Commission. First, the Commission soon learned that these cases have a higher probability of being quashed by the appeal court. By the end of March 2016, a total of forty-three asylum and immigration cases had been referred. Of these, thirty-six convictions were quashed, four upheld, and three abandoned (see Table 10.2). Excluding pending and abandoned cases, the appeal court had quashed thirty-six of forty cases referred by the Commission, some 90 per cent of cases. In comparison, 68 per cent of all other ('non-asylum') convictions referred by the Commission had been quashed (378 of 560) from its establishment in 1997 to August 2016.[30]

Furthermore, we were able to establish that fewer resources were committed by the Commission to reviewing these cases, as demonstrated by the time taken to review applications, both from 'receipt of the application' to 'allocation to a caseworker', and from 'allocation' to the 'decision to refer' the case back to the appeal court. As we discuss in Chapter 2, the Commission has come under sustained criticism over the past decade or so for being too slow in its investigation of applications. Indeed, delays were a source of critique in the House of Commons Justice Committee (2015) review of the Commission. Yet, asylum and immigration cases seem to run counter to this trend. Such cases first reviewed by the Commission in 2002 took on average thirty-two months from application to referral (see Table 10.2), which is not atypical. However, this reduced to an average of twenty-three months between 2003 and 2009,[31] and by 2011 and 2012, when the number of asylum applications rapidly increased, the Commission was able to refer these cases in, on average, nine months—less than half of the time it took in 2003–9.[32] Most of these applicants were 'at liberty', having already served their short sentences, and this nine-month turnaround was considerably quicker than for the majority of other types of cases. During that time, the Commission had an eighteen-month target for allocating 'at liberty' cases to a caseworker, with the time taken for investigating a case typically adding at least another six to twelve months (Criminal Cases Review Commission, 2012a:11).

Needing fewer resources but securing a higher hit rate, these were, to put it crudely, easy wins for the Commission. Before considering decision frames adopted in reviews of these exceptional cases, we present a brief description of the Commission's response to a typical application to provide the reader with a flavour of these rather unusual cases. Taking ten months from application—in 2012—to referral, case A2 was close to the average length of time to review such cases and shows the Commission in its stride.

Case A2: Mr B was at liberty at the time of his application for review of his conviction and 12-month prison sentence for possession of false identity documents contrary to section 25(1) of the Identity Cards Act 2006.

Aged 25, he had fled his home country, Somalia, after his family were detained by a militia group, and he was beaten and forced into labour. His father and brothers were murdered by the militia group; his mother, wife, and sisters were raped.

---

[30] For all cases, as of August 2016, the Commission has referred a total of 603 Commission referrals, of which 410 appeals were allowed (Criminal Cases Review Commission, n.d.). The figures include sentence-only referrals.

[31] The exception is case A9, which took five months.

[32] This calculation excludes case A4 as an outlier (see Table 10.2).

Table 10.2 Refugee and asylum cases referred back to the appeal court

CCRC receipt of application	CCRC referral date	Court of Appeal date	Court of Appeal decision	Purpose-ful sample	Application allocation (months)	Allocation referral (months)	Application referral (months)
2014	28-Jan-16	14-Sep-16	Abandoned				
2014	10-Feb-16	07-Jul-16	Quashed				
2014	10-Feb-16	28-Mar-17	Quashed				
2014	17-Feb-15	07-May-15	Abandoned				
2014	24-Mar-15	07-May-15	Quashed				
2014	24-Mar-15	07-May-15	Quashed				
2014	22-Apr-15	03-Jul-15	Quashed				
2014	24-Mar-15	17-Dec-15	Quashed				
2014	24-Mar-15	17-Dec-15	Quashed				
2013	13-Jul-15	04-May-16	Upheld				
2013	20-Mar-15	14-May-15	Quashed				
2013	15-Oct-15	13-0c-16	Quashed				
2013	15-Sep-14	07-Oct-14	Quashed				
2013	10-Apr-14	18-Jul-14	Quashed				
2013	23-May-14	11-Jul-14	Quashed				
2012	15-Jan-16	19-May-16	Quashed				
2012	17-Mar-15	07-May-15	Quashed				
2012	29-May-15	26-Feb-16	Upheld				
2012	24-Sep-15	26-Feb-16	Upheld				
2012	01-Dec-14	22-Jul-15	Quashed				
2012	14-Oct-14	18-Jun-15	Quashed				
2012	24-Jun-14	17-Dec-14	Quashed	Al 0	12	7	37
2012	26-Nov-13	26-Jun-14	Quashed	Al 1	1.5	14	15.5
2012	12-Jun-13	30-Jul-13	Quashed	Al 2	1.5	6	7.5
2012	17-Apr-13	30-Jul-13	Quashed	Al 3	5	2	7
2012	28-Mar-13	30-Jul-13	Quashed	A2	N/A	N/A	10
2012	28-Mar-13	17-Jun-13	Quashed	A14	2	5	7
2012	28-Mar-13	17-Jun-13	Quashed	Al 5	2.5	4	6.5
2012	12-Jun-13	30-Jul-13	Quashed	Al 6	1.5	6	7.5
2012	12-Apr-13	17-Jun-13	Quashed	Al 7	0.5	6.5	7
2012	28-Mar-13	30-Jul-13	Abandoned	A5	N/A	N/A	7
2012	30-Mar-12	30-Apr-12	Quashed	A4	N/A	N/A	1 day
2011	29-Mar-12	30-Apr-12	Quashed	A3	N/A	N/A	3.5
2011	29-Mar-12	01-Jun-12	Quashed	Al	N/A	N/A	3
2011	20-Mar-12	18-Jun-12	Quashed	A6	N/A	N/A	11.5
2009	21-Mar-11	05-Jun-11	Quashed				
2009	08-May-13	16-Dec-14	Upheld	Al 8	6	42	48
2008	10-Aug-10	14-Dec-10	Quashed	A19	5.5	17	22.5
2008	10-Aug-10	14-Dec-10	Quashed	A20	5.5	17	22.5

(Continued)

Table 10.2 *Continued*

CCRC receipt of application	CCRC referral date	Court of Appeal date	Court of Appeal decision	Purpose-ful sample	Application allocation (months)	Allocation referral (months)	Application referral (months)
2007	18-Jun-07	11-Jul-07	Quashed	A9	N/A	N/A	6
2003	22-Jun-05	28-Oct-05	Quashed	A21	13	10	23
2002	22-Jun-05	28-Oct-05	Quashed	A22	N/A	N/A	32
2002	22-Jun-05	28-Oct-05	Quashed	A23	24	8	32

Sources: Criminal Cases Review Commission, 'Commission Annual Reports and Accounts' 2006/07 through 2016/17; Criminal Cases Review Commission, 'Case Library' (no date) <http://www.Commission.gov.uk/case-library/> accessed 30 August 2016; Elks, 2008:264; fieldwork records.

Notes:
• 'Allocation' refers to the assignment of a case to a CRM.
• Cases A7 and A8 are non-referral cases and therefore not included in this table.

Mr B managed to escape and fled to Kenya with a relative who bribed various checkpoint officers. The same relative arranged for Mr B to meet an Agent and facilitated payment for a false passport and assistance for Mr B to reach a safe country. He travelled to London, via Nairobi, Dubai, and Greece.

Mr B was detained and interviewed at Gatwick airport as he was in possession of a false passport. Through a Somali interpreter, he stated his intention to claim asylum. An Immigration Officer at Crawley Police Station arrested the applicant and interviewed him under caution with a duty solicitor and interpreter present. In interview, he claimed that he had not left the airport in the prior countries on route to London and had not understood that he could claim asylum in those jurisdictions. He was clear that he did not have a Somali passport (or ID documents) as there was no legitimate government and therefore no passport issuing authority in Somalia. He was charged with possession of a false ID document.

Mr B's legal representative made clear that he faced difficulties because of 'country-hopping'—that he could have claimed asylum in Kenya or Greece, and should have done so—and advised him to plead guilty.

After serving his sentence, Mr B applied to the Commission, using an easy read form and without legal representation. In poor English, he made clear that he had not yet appealed his conviction. Typically, at this stage in 'ordinary' cases, the screening commissioner would review the file to establish if the applicant could demonstrate exceptional circumstances to allow the Commission to refer a case when the applicant has not exhausted their rights to direct appeal (see Chapter 6). Here, the commissioner told administrators to 'move the case to stage 2 as it's one of the asylum/immigration cases' (A2, Case Record), suggesting that a cursory review of a brief application form prepared by a man with poor English, was sufficient to establish exceptional circumstances. The minutes of a committee meeting, held soon after, explain that the Commission is confident to decide on exceptional circumstances rather quickly in these cases, if the application is 'linked by a common nexus' of defendants being erroneously advised to plead guilty to offences that have a statutory defence, and that 'the Commission is currently considering a tranche of these cases, and it is desirable that they should be consolidated at court' (A2, Case Committee Minutes). The committee concluded that Mr B had been deprived of an informed choice about his plea, as he had been given no advice about his section 31 defence.

The SOR argues that Mr B was prosecuted in circumstances that deprived him of the defence available under section 31 Immigration and Asylum Act 1999. The legal advice given to him (to plead guilty) 'was incorrect and had such a bearing on his wrongful conviction that there is a real possibility the Court will regard his conviction as a nullity' (A2, Statement of Reasons). It noted that being Somalian, Mr B could not have acquired a passport, and even if he had, it would not be recognized by the UK government. Furthermore, notwithstanding the fact he had not yet appealed the conviction, the SOR cites his guilty plea on advice as an exceptional circumstance.

The committee noted that this was the first of many committee meetings on similar cases, and stressed the importance of consistency in its approach to those that follow. It also noted that the SOR should:

be approaching this [issue] on the basis that one of the Commission's functions is to feed back into the criminal justice system ... We should make clear that the problems are primarily created by the failure of defence representatives to provide ... clear advice on s31. (A2, Case Committee Minutes)

The committee minutes imply three decision frames at work: a legal frame, requiring the application of specific legislation and the development of case law; a moral frame, with commission staff clear that they wished not only to cause the convictions of applicants to be quashed by the appeal court, but to feedback into the system lessons that might prevent other vulnerable people being wrongfully convicted and punished; and an organizational frame, a way of thinking about individual cases within the framework of many other similar applications that could be dealt with in a more routinized fashion than would be possible with most other applications to the Commission.

Not only did the committee review recent comparable cases, but it flagged up similar ones in the pipeline. This case may also have generated further applications either through the media publicity it attracted or directly through the applicant, who said in a telephone conversation with the CRM that the Commission was the only organization to have listened to him and later told the CRM that he would tell his Somali friends in similar situations to apply to the Commission.

Decision Frames in Refugee and Asylum Cases

Efficiency and justice: organizational decision frame

The swifter turnaround of asylum cases since 2011 reflects both earlier allocation of applications to a CRM and a more efficient review process. For example, the Commission established 'Immigration and Asylum case committee meetings', to consider a few similar cases in the round, as opposed to the typical practice of arranging separate committees for each case. The change can be dated back to around 2008–9, when commission staff became keenly aware of the many similarities in asylum and immigration case applications. A commissioner referred to one such case during screening as 'another Thet + Osman type case' (A19, Case Record), suggesting that it could be approached similarly to a previous successful application. In 2011, notes made during screening of another case included the statement: 'it relates to false document offences committed as part of seeking asylum in the UK. [Name of CRM] is our expert in this area' (A3, Case Record). In other words, these cases were starting to be viewed as a distinct category of case, where particular expertise was developing in the organization. The specific CRM referred to in case A3 was assigned to seven out of eleven cases that the Commission received between 2002 and 2011, and continued to be consulted in subsequent cases.

Accumulation and concentration of expertise reduced the time spent preparing a case for referral. By 2011, after six cases had been referred to the appeal court, previous referral documents were used as templates for further reviews. In May 2011, a Commission Casework Guidance Note titled 'Asylum and Immigration Issues in Casework' (written by the experienced CRM mentioned above) provided an overview of relevant laws and advice on how to approach these cases (Criminal Cases Review Commission, 2014c). Once asylum cases had been identified by the Commission as a distinct category, they were processed efficiently, delivering speedy justice for refugees and asylum seekers.

The ability to identify an 'asylum case', however, did not come easily. The Commission had missed several cases before recognizing the pattern. They had initially rejected three cases (A17, A1, and A21) during screening. In two, the applicants reapplied and their case was reviewed and referred; in the other, the Commission proactively subjected the case to a second review and referred it. Case A21 was an application from 2003, before the 2004 Act was in place. It was one of the earliest cases; only two other asylum cases were being reviewed by the Commission at the time, and these had not yet been referred. These cases demonstrate that the Commission—like other key stakeholders such as defence lawyers and the CPS—was at that stage not yet fully familiar with the law, nor with the political and geographical contexts that should inform review of these applications (e.g. they were insufficiently familiar with the conditions in the countries of origin). The Commission had not yet fully realized that these early cases—in which the 1999 Act and the 2004 Act had not provided the protection as intended—were not sporadic, but were indicative of a larger cluster of cases where refugees and asylum seekers had been incorrectly advised by defence lawyers and hence wrongfully convicted.

More puzzling, however, are the two cases that were screened out years later, in 2011, when the Commission was clearly familiar with such asylum cases and had developed some expertise in dealing with them. When case 34 was rejected at screening in March 2011, seven Commission referrals of asylum cases had resulted in quashed convictions and one was pending a decision by the appeal court. It was initially rejected because the applicant had not already appealed his conviction. When the applicant's legal representative reapplied to the Commission, a different commissioner identified the error made in reviewing the first application and prioritized the application for immediate review, noting, 'We ought to have recognized the referral issue when dealing with the previous application and have caused unnecessary delay' (A1, Case Record). The third case that the Commission had erroneously screened out (A17) was identified after an internal review of previously rejected cases conducted in 2012, at a stage when the Commission realized that there were systemic problems behind such applications.

The Commission originally thought that these applicants should appeal against their convictions before applying to the Commission. Later, it was realized that since the applicants had pleaded guilty in a magistrates' court, rather than in the Crown Court, they were unable to appeal their convictions other than through a referral by the Commission. Hence, the initial rejections had been an error in law, but reflected typical organizational practice for a body that is most used to reviewing Crown Court convictions. In other words, a shift was required in the organizational imperative.

Early responses to such applications were influenced by the Commission's decision field concerning guilty pleas. Case law suggests guilty pleas are indicative of guilt and remorse[33] and before the wave of asylum cases reached the Commission, its usual practice was to refer guilty plea cases back to the appeal courts only under limited circumstances: for example, where the plea was entered under duress, where there was erroneous legal advice, or where the guilty plea resulted from an erroneous ruling on a point of law by the trial judge (Criminal Cases Review Commission, 2016g). The Commission had to adjust its approach and recognize that applicants in asylum cases had pleaded guilty because of poor advice from their lawyers who believed—incorrectly—that they had no defence (A1, Statement of Reasons).

In overlooking these three cases, the Commission may have been influenced by what Tversky and Kahneman (1974) called 'reference point bias'. During decision-making, certain information 'anchors' can dominate judgements. An 'anchor' can frame what is relevant and what solutions are worth considering. For example, the existence of guilty pleas triggering the assumption of guilt, rather than poor legal advice (see Chapter 6). This is particularly likely within the political and legislative discourse that has portrayed migrants as 'deviant' since the late 1990s. However, once the error was apparent, the Commission responded with efficiency and integrity. It referred the cases swiftly and was transparent with applicants about mistakes, noting in one referral document, for example, that an applicant 'was informed, incorrectly—for which the Commission apologise' (A1, Statement of Reasons).

Confident and liberal: legal and moral decision frames

As we mention above, in comparison to the total referral rate, the Commission's referral rate for asylum cases is high, at 27 per cent.[34] If these are 'easy' referrals, asylum cases could provide the Commission with welcome relief at a time when it is subject to considerable criticism for its low referral rate, which tends to be explained in terms of it being too 'deferential' to the appeal court, afraid to refer cases that may be rejected (House of Commons Justice Committee, 2015:8; Naughton, 2009; Nobles and Schiff, 2001; see Chapter 14). Analysis of our cases suggest this is not true of asylum cases. Indeed, here we found evidence of a confident Commission making referrals on rather liberal interpretations of the real possibility test, decisions undoubtedly driven in part by moral outrage at applicant's dire circumstances and the inadequate defence they had received in the UK.

Once such applications have progressed—rapidly—through the screening stage, the Commission conducts a detailed review to determine whether the Court is likely to consider the applicant's conviction to be safe. Reviews focus on information about the applicant, country of origin, and the applicant's journey to the UK. In particular, information is sought on the political and human rights situation in that country, and the applicant's reasons for leaving. These data are appraised with reference to statutory defences, available under the Asylum and Immigration (Treatment of Claimants, etc.) Act 2004 and the Immigration and Asylum Act 1999 in particular. The Commission

---

[33] *R v Boal* [1992] 95 Cr App R 272.
[34] According to the Commission, it received between 150 and 170 asylum applications (as of 2017). Twenty-seven per cent is calculated by estimating 160 asylum case applications divided by the total number of referrals.

might, for example, review what constitutes a 'reasonable excuse' for not being in possession of a legitimate travel document under the 2004 Act, as relevant to *Soe Thet v DPP*; or the meaning of 'coming directly' to the UK under the 1999 Act, as relevant to *Adimi* and confirmed in *Asfaw* and *Mateta*.[35] The proportion of cases where convictions were quashed following a Commission referral is testament to the Commission's ability to make a case to the appeal court that a statutory defence exists (Holiday, 2014a, 2014b).

However, when we look at referrals, we see that they challenge the interpretation of section 31 of the 1999 Act and section 2 of the 2004 Act. For example, the Commission attempted, in several referrals (e.g. A12, A16, A3, A6, and A21), to push the 'liberal interpretation' confirmed in *Asfaw* of what constitutes 'coming directly' to the UK (Holiday, 2014a). While Article 31 of the Refugee Convention requires refugees to come 'directly' from their country of origin, the term 'directly' has been interpreted to allow transits to an intermediate country. The elements to consider are the length of the stay in the intermediate country, the reasons for delaying the trip to their final destination, and whether or not the refugee sought or found protection *de jure* or *de facto* from the persecution from which he or she was seeking to escape.

Many of the cases we studied adopted a clear legal decision frame, whereby the CRM and the commissioners that participated in committee meetings—which often discussed a number of similar such cases—grappled with the complex laws pertaining to statutory defences and drew heavily on previous cases that had been successful at the Court. The content, structure, and tone of most SORs is remarkably similar, given the early emergence of a template for these cases. In most SORs, but also case records, facts relating to the applicant's account were construed in relation to the relevant law in order to present as strong a ground for referral as possible. We do not think it is a stretch to interpret the tenor of these documents as pro-referral from very early on, with relatively little attention given to counterarguments. We had not seen this in other categories of cases.

One case stands out—one of the few cases in which the appeal court upheld the conviction (A18)—as demonstrating a rather bold referral. Here, an Ethiopian national had entered Britain using his own passport on a visitor's visa. He later claimed asylum, stating he fled his country due to fear of repercussions from his membership of the Oromo Liberation Front. He did this, however, under a different name and lied during the asylum interview, resulting in his claim being rejected. He was charged with seeking leave to remain in the UK as a refugee by deception.[36] Although the applicant had legally entered and been legally present in the UK, therefore not meeting the definition of a refugee or an asylum seeker, the Commission attempted to push the current interpretation of the law on defence available under section 31 of the 1999 Act. It supplied medical evidence, which was consistent with torture, and highlighted the risks associated with returning the applicant to Ethiopia. This case suggests that the legal frame was stretched in order to satisfy a moral imperative; to use the appeal process to help prevent the deportation of a person vulnerable to further abuse.

---

[35] *Soe Thet v Director of Public Prosecutions* [2006] EWCH 2701 (Admin); *R v Uxbridge Magistrates Court ex parte Adimi* [1999] EWHC Admin 765; *R v Asfaw* [2008] UKHL 31; *R v Mateta & and Ors* [2013] EWCA Crim 1372.

[36] *R v Eyasu Mulugeta, Farhiya Mohamed Issa, Bahram Firouzi* [2015] EWCA Crim 6. Case A18 concerns Eyasu Mulugeta.

If we consider a rare decision not to refer an asylum and immigration case, we find even when the application was apparently weak, the Commission was prepared to conduct a robust investigation. The applicant in case A8 applied to the Commission in 2012. He had been sentenced to three months in prison in 2006 for failing to show a valid immigration document upon entry to the UK contrary to section 2(1) of the Asylum and Immigration (Treatment of Claimants, etc.) 2004 Act, having left Iran and travelled via three other countries. He had pled guilty, upon advice that he did not have a legal defence. In his application, he claimed that he had believed he was in danger in Iran and could not return home. His application presented no exceptional circumstances, but the screening commission put it for review as it appeared to be a 'classic asylum case' (A8, Case Record).

The case appeared to be weak early in the review. Since released from his sentence, the applicant had voluntarily returned to Iran, got a passport and married, alerting the authorities to his presence with no adverse consequences. All legal advice sought by the Commission was clear that there was no defence and that the Court would be highly unlike to find the conviction to be unsafe. The CRM could find nothing to support the applicant's claims to be a refugee and the applicant could provide no account of what might have occurred to make it safe for him to return to Iran at a later date. In the absence of fresh evidence, the Commission declined to refer the case though not before it had explored various potential avenues for referral, done its utmost to find a plausible account for the applicant's unproblematic return to Iran, and conducted research to try to verify his claims about persecution, which included detailed analysis of the politics and criminal sentencing there. Indeed, within the case record, we found notes asking the experienced CRM (mentioned above) if they could 'suggest a legal argument that offers some way round the obstacle presented ... as to status and credibility' of the applicant (A8, Case Record).

While there is a clear legal frame at work in analysis of these applications, we noted in some case records, a moral impulsion to refer which was clearly for the benefit of the applicant, though the concomitant benefit for the organization, in terms of its efficient use of resources and its statistics on referrals, was ever present. In one case, for example, we read an email recorded on the case record from the lead commissioner, circulated with the agenda and papers for a committee meeting that was also to discuss two other similar cases, an excerpt from which read:

I am hoping that we will be able to decide these cases with a minimum of fuss and agree the SORs so that if we refer they can go out before the end of the month ... This is not only important for our stats ... but [it] is also important to [another applicant] who has suffered unreasonable delay at the hands of the Commission which could work substantially to his detriment as his limited leave to remain expires in a month ... and to] [a third applicant] who has been prevented from pursuing his career as a teacher ... the post-Easter period being one where many vacancies in schools for the next school year are being advertised. (A3, Email quoted in Case Record)

We do not recall in other cases a concern for how the referral might impact on the career prospects of applicants. We are not unsympathetic to this perspective, and do not imply that CRMs and commissioners do not care about other applicants, but note it is not typical of other categories of case. Also atypical is what the Commission did alongside its determined effort to refer these cases: it proactively sought to stop lawyers giving incorrect advice and to stop the CPS from prosecuting cases when lawyers had erroneously advised their clients to plead guilty to offences for which there was a defence.

Keeping the System Honest

During our interviews with Commission staff, we heard concerns about the impact of recent cuts to legal aid, under austerity measures, on the safety of all convictions, not just those of asylum seekers. Many thought that wrongful convictions were likely to become increasingly common as lawyers simply had insufficient resources at their disposal to properly investigate cases. As one interviewee put it:

[E]very time judges come to talk to us, they mutter about how bad the quality of advocacy is, and you've got all this stuff going on about legal aid, and I assume, no doubt part of their complaint about advocacy is the usual sort of judicial broad bias against solicitor advocates, but I get it so universally that I have to assume that there is something in this. And, obviously, there are so many defence lawyers complaining about the fact that they just can't get the work now and so on … That, common-sense would seem to suggest that there will be a sort of corresponding increase in miscarriages, and it will be interesting to see whether there is any kind of corresponding shift in the Court of Appeal's attitude to cases based on inadequate defence, whether they start being more indulgent. I can't imagine they will. It's something that was being talked about earlier today in a different context, about the extent to which we can sensibly undertake to try and compensate for cuts in legal aid. (#11)

At the recent conference to celebrate the twentieth Anniversary of the Commission, much discussion centred around the fiscal climate within which criminal justice is delivered, with the representative from the Ministry of Justice reflecting on the damage done by budget cuts (fieldwork notes). Particular attention was paid to the considerable risks for the safety of convictions posed by damaging cuts to the legal aid budget that have reduced the number of solicitors able or willing to offer assistance to criminal defendants under the legal aid system. Those that continue to offer legal aid defence work cannot be as thorough and careful as they could during times of relative plenty (see Chapter 14).[37]

At the same time, as we saw in Chapter 9, cuts to police services and declining funds for forensic expert witnesses, alongside the privatization and under-regulation of forensic services, make it more likely that errors will impact on the safety of convictions and less likely that those wrongfully convicted will be able to mount a strong appeal. When we add to the mix the recent CPS focus on victims, and insistence that all victims are believed, even if unreliable—as we discussed in Chapter 8—we have the necessary ingredients for a perfect storm which will likely increase wrongful convictions (see Chapter 14). While the Commission has, in recent years, become a little more outspoken on such matters, with the Chair, Richard Foster, occasionally engaging with the media on systemic threats to justice,[38] its response to its asylum and immigration applications has been exceptional.

The Commission's vision statement lists three purposes: 'to enhance public confidence in the criminal justice system', 'to give hope and bring justice to those wrongfully convicted', and 'to contribute to reform and improvements in the law based on our experience' (Criminal Cases Review Commission, n.d.). The second point suggests the Commission is a case-based organization, whereas the first and third points

---

[37] See various essays in *The Justice Gap* 'No Defence: lawyers and miscarriages of justice' (2013b), including by Michael Mansfield QC, Campbell Malone, and Corena Platt, Ed Cape, among others.

[38] For example, in response to recent concerns about non-disclosure following the collapse of rape trials, Richard Foster, the then Chair, wrote a letter for *The Guardian* calling for 'much-needed reform' of the system (Foster, 2017b).

indicate a much wider role, highlighting the organization's commitment to improve the justice system as whole. While the Commission has no legal obligation to carry out wider engagement activities under the Criminal Appeal Act 1995, it is better placed than any other body to do so, as it sees failings across the whole criminal process—from the police, through prosecution service, defence counsel, and the courts.

The Commission has been described as a 'reactive' organization (Nobles and Schiff, 2001:292), and the House of Commons Justice Select Committee (2015) recently pointed out that it is not using its unique position sufficiently to feed back into the criminal justice system. If we believed the system was safe, the Commission would have no need to try to correct systemic faults in other criminal justice agencies. However, research conducted since the 1990s has made absolutely clear that wrongful convictions are not rare, nor is there any evidence that they are on the wane.

The Commission has recently revealed an incipient appetite for going beyond its narrow remit. Its 2015/16 Annual Report details plans to design a system to capture lessons learnt from casework and share them with all relevant parts of the justice system, with the sections on '*feeding back to the criminal justice system*' and '*feeding back in the future*' focusing mainly on asylum cases (Criminal Cases Review Commission, 2016a). This has meant a shift away from its traditional reticence to opine on systemic issues towards direct *critical* dialogue with other criminal justice agencies.

In pursuing this wider remit, the Commission asserted that the wrongful convictions of refugees and asylum-seekers represent 'a failure by all of those involved, police, UK [Border Agency], prosecutors, defence lawyers, and the courts, to understand and apply the criminal law correctly' (Criminal Cases Review Commission, 2015a:7–8). It criticized the CPS and defence lawyers in particular. Commission staff, including the Chair, have, since June 2012, written regularly for legal magazines and newspapers. In December 2013, the Commission's press releases about asylum case referrals started to make clear that the Commission was actively trying to raise awareness of the issue (Criminal Cases Review Commission, 2013c).

In addition to utilizing the media, the Commission wrote directly to key stakeholders with the aim of preventing further unsafe convictions. In September 2011, letters were sent to the CPS and the UK Border Agency alerting them to cases reviewed and referred back to the appeal court (Notes from internal Commission correspondence minutes of meetings). The Commission gave presentations to the Criminal Bar Association in April 2012, defence lawyers in September 2012, relevant NGOs in August 2012, and prisons between June and October 2012 (ibid.). It also communicated with the Solicitors Regulation Authority in 2014 and again in 2015 to raise concerns about the conduct of solicitors (Criminal Cases Review Commission, 2016a).

In an article published by *The Guardian* in 2014, the Commission urged defence lawyers not to advise clients to plead guilty 'inappropriately' and the CPS not to 'bring prosecutions unnecessarily or wrongfully' (Foster, 2014). It has also used its SORs to the appeal court to criticize the incompetency of the CPS. For example, in case A1 the SOR criticized the CPS for their decision to prosecute a Somali national who had failed to produce a valid passport upon entry to the UK when there should have been 'no realistic prospect of success', given that Somalia had not had a passport-issuing authority since 1991. It argued that the CPS had taken 'advantage of the error of the defence in advising a guilty plea' (A1, Statement of Reasons).

The CPS was not particularly responsive to the Commission's efforts to hold it to account. It refused to do a retrospective 'trawl' of past cases due to financial constraints, but did, eventually, update its guidance in relation to section 31 of the 1999

Act in February 2013 (#82). The UK Border Agency took some steps to address the problem (#83). In contrast, the legal profession was most inclined to scrutinize its practices and introduce changes and measures of accountability. The Solicitors' Regulation Authority made a commitment to look into the quality of advice given to defendants seeking asylum (Solicitors Regulation Authority, 2014), and in 2016 published a report on current practices concerning asylum-related legal advice (Solicitors Regulation Authority, 2016). The Authority also investigated serious allegations concerning the competency of certain lawyers. The Law Society issued a new practice note in December 2015 entitled 'Statutory Defences Available to Asylum Seekers Charged with Document Offences' (Law Society, 2015).

The increased number of such applications, particularly in 2013/14, provides evidence of the impact of the Commission's wider engagement (Criminal Cases Review Commission, 2015a:13), with applicants and their legal representatives contacting the Commission after reading various articles (#83). More recently, applications to the Commission concerning asylum cases have been in decline, suggesting that either the CPS or defence lawyers, or both, have taken note of the Commission's concerns and responded more appropriately to such cases. That said, the Commission continues to respond to such cases, with seven applicants being referred back to the appeal court in April 2018 (Criminal Cases Review Commission, 2018a). Furthermore, as austerity measures in public services continue to bite, the Commission may need to adopt similar approaches in other categories of cases, and engage critically and proactively with police, prosecutors, and defence lawyers when evidence of incompetence or misconduct is apparent in their caseload.

The Commission's treatment of certain cases has demonstrated that although it has been accused of not caring about the wrongfully convicted, it is alive to the threat of injustice for the most vulnerable in society, non-citizens and citizens who may today be in a more precarious position than for a long time. Perhaps the Commission could do more to apply the lessons learnt from its response to asylum cases to wider categories of cases or issues. In particular, we would like to see wider engagement with other criminal justice agencies and with government to try to reduce police and prosecution misconduct and to contribute to a larger conversation about the costs to defendants of inadequate defence. The Commission has shown itself more than able to do this, and it could and should impact positively on our criminal justice system, holding it to account for its errors and offering advice on best practice to bring about greater integrity. This can be done by increased stakeholder engagement, a less defensive relationship with the media and academia, and a greater willingness to criticize public bodies and the Commission's own paymaster when justice errs. This is an issue we return to in our final chapter.

11

Working Cooperatively with Other Criminal Justice Institutions

Legal decision-making has instead to be seen in a holistic or systemic perspective, so that decisions are not treated as the work of individual legal actors behaving autonomously and independent of others. (Hawkins, 2002:32)

Introduction

Decision-making by the Criminal Cases Review Commission ('the Commission') is almost always dependent on the cooperation of external bodies or persons. Decisions are the result of investigative work by case review managers ('CRMs') and commissioners who sometimes gather further information and evidence from interviewing applicants, police officers, and witnesses (discussed in Chapter 12). However, as we have described in previous chapters, the Commission does not work alone. For cases that turn on expert evidence, the Commission may choose to instruct forensic experts to provide their opinion and to commission forensic tests, to inform decision-making (see Chapter 7). In contemporary sexual offence cases and historical institutional abuse cases, the Commission uses its section 17 powers extensively and relies on external bodies, such as local authorities and the Criminal Injuries Compensation Authority, to provide information that speaks to the credibility of complainants (see Chapter 8). In this chapter, we examine the 'symbiotic' (Hawkins, 2002:44) relationship between the Commission and the police, and between the Commission and the Court of Appeal ('the Court').

In Chapter 9, we examined cases in which applicants raised the issue of police misconduct. The Commission sometimes used its section 17 powers to obtain police files, or interviewed police officers in order to gain a better understanding of the policing methods used. Under section 19 of the Criminal Appeal Act 1995, the Commission can delegate some of its investigation work to the police. Recourse to section 19 powers involves the police in the Commission's decision-making: the Commission hands over part of the investigative work to the police, and its review in turn becomes reliant on the report that the appointed investigating officer produces. Examples of police assistance under section 19 directions range from interviewing under caution a witness who may have lied under oath, to a new police force investigating the original police force that investigated the case for the prosecution for police misconduct.

In 2012, the Court quashed the conviction of Sam Hallam, who spent seven years in prison for murder (*R v Hallam*[1]). Using section 19 powers, the Commission required Thames Valley police service to investigate the handling of the original investigation by the Metropolitan police. The Commission referred the case back to the Court largely based on the findings in the Thames Valley police report. It revealed the unreliability

---

[1] *R v Hallam* [2012] EWCA Crim 1158.

Reasons to Doubt: Wrongful Convictions and the Criminal Cases Review Commission. © Carolyn Hoyle and Mai Sato 2019. Published 2019 by Oxford University Press.

of witness evidence, non-disclosure of evidence concerning an alternative suspect, and the failure to investigate mobile phone evidence that could have provided Hallam with an alibi. The Court in its judgment praised Thames Valley police for their work on the case, expressing some guarded criticism of the defence and of the Metropolitan police for their original investigation:

For reasons which escape us they [Hallam's two mobile phones] do not seem to have been interrogated by either the investigating officers or the defence team … Given the attachment of young and old to their mobile phones, we cannot understand why someone from either the investigating team or the defence team did not think to examine the phones attributable to the appellant. (Lady Justice Hallett, para:65 *R v Hallam*)

Like the Commission, the Court is also helped in its decision-making. The Court takes into consideration the Commission's research and stated grounds for referral in each case that the Commission is persuaded to make a reference back to the Court. Alternatively, the Court can direct the Commission to investigate and report to the Court on any matter that the Court considers relevant in determining an appeal (section 23A(1) Criminal Appeal Act 1968). Section 15 of the Criminal Appeal Act 1995 specifies how the Commission should conduct such investigations. In section 15 investigations, the Commission is working *for* the Court, and the Court is reliant on the Commission to produce the information it requires. The Court has described its relationship with the Commission as follows:

The relationship between the Court and the CCRC is an important one. Not only does the Court deal with cases referred by the CCRC but the Commission also has an essential role as an independent investigatory body for the Court. (Court of Appeal quoted in Criminal Cases Review Commission, 2011a:17)

Section 15 investigations can range from interviewing jurors about alleged jury impropriety to less typical investigations of alternative suspects (Criminal Cases Review Commission, 2012d:paras:27–43). The Commission produces a 'section 15 report', which informs the Court's decision about the safety of the conviction. The case of *Adams*[2] is well known for the wording of the judgment which quashed Andrew Adams' murder conviction, but which also later indirectly deprived him of state compensation. In quashing Adams' conviction, Lord Justice Gage stated: 'We are not to be taken as finding that if there had been no such failures the appellant would inevitably have been acquitted. We are however satisfied for the reasons given that the verdict is unsafe' (*R v Adams*, para:157). Thanks to this statement, Adams was not considered to qualify for state compensation as a victim of a miscarriage of justice as defined by section 133 of the Criminal Justice Act 1988 (Hoyle, 2016).[3] Less well known is the fact that, after the Commission referred the *Adams* case to the Court, the Court asked the Commission to carry out a section 15 investigation of the jury. The Commission's interviews with jurors from Adams' trial showed that one juror had stated several times to others: 'I know these lads [Adams and the co-accused] and they are guilty' (Lord Justice Gage in *R v Adams,* para:173). The Court, however, did not rely on the Commission's section 15 investigation of jury impropriety to quash the conviction of Adams, citing various failures by the defence to use the available evidence, which had 'cumulatively' rendered the conviction unsafe (*R v Adams*, para:156).

---

[2] *R v Adams* [2007] EWCA Crim 1.
[3] Adams lost his case for state compensation in the Supreme Court in 2011 (*R (on the application of Adams) (FC) v Secretary for Justice* [2011 UKSC 18]), and again in the European Court of Human Rights (*Adams v The United Kingdom, application no. 70601/11*).

This chapter examines the Commission's handling of section 19 and section 15 cases. It primarily concerns two relationships: the relationship between the Commission (decision-maker) and the police (information-provider); and the relationship between the Commission (information-provider) and the Court (decision-maker), showing how these institutions can influence each other:

Those supplying information may create a frame for the subsequent exercise of discretion by describing or presenting the case in a particular fashion, thereby setting cases off in a particular direction, and producing clear and specific expectations as to what the 'right' decision should be. (Hawkins, 2002:34)

We focus on how the Commission deals with the investigating officer in section 19 cases and how it frames the investigation findings to reach a decision on whether or not to refer a case back to the Court. We also examine how the Commission handles its section 15 investigations and how the Court responds to these investigations. Decision-makers at different points—the police, the Commission, and the Court—might be expected to have different 'priorities' (Hawkins, 2002:34). The aim of this chapter is to consider the Commission's decision frames when it manages a section 19 investigation and when it works for the Court on section 15 investigations.

Working with the Police: Section 19 Cases

Selective use of section 19 powers

Section 19 of the Criminal Appeal Act 1995 gives the Commission the power to appoint an investigating officer to assist in the Commission's review. The appointed investigating officer does not need to be a police officer, but all appointments to date have been (Criminal Cases Review Commission, 2012f:para:2). The decision to appoint an investigating officer must be agreed by a committee of three commissioners (Criminal Cases Review Commission, 2015e:para:2). The Formal Memorandum on Section 19 Requirements provides a non-exhaustive list of factors to take into account when deciding whether to appoint an investigating officer. Commissioners should consider the scale and nature of the enquiry, and whether police expertise is considered essential (Criminal Cases Review Commission, 2015e:para:4).

Police expertise may be considered necessary where another person, *not* involved in the case in an official capacity, may have committed a serious offence that could lead to prosecution—such as a lying prosecution witness who may be subject to prosecution for perverting the course of justice (Criminal Cases Review Commission, 2015e:para:4). In such circumstances, the Commission has the power to require the chief officer of the original investigating body to appoint an investigating officer to assist in the Commission's review. The Commission should also consider using its section 19 powers where there are grounds to suspect that a police officer, or other person involved in an official capacity in the investigation of offences or the prosecution of offenders, has committed an offence such as perjury or perverting the course of justice (Criminal Cases Review Commission, 2015e:para:4). In such circumstances, the Commission should consider appointing an investigating officer from a police force other than the force that was involved in the original investigation (Criminal Cases Review Commission, 2015e:para:5). This is to ensure the impartiality of the investigation. The investigating officer involved in such an operation may serve two functions: carrying out investigations for the Commission to help determine the safety of a conviction, and contributing to a police misconduct inquiry (Criminal Cases Review Commission, 2012f:para:25).[4]

In Chapter 9, we found that applicants often raise the issue of police misconduct. However, Table 11.1 shows that the Commission is extremely selective in exercising its discretion to use section 19 powers. The table lists finalized cases (as of January 2012), in which the Commission carried out section 19 investigations. Between 1997 (when the Commission was established) and 2012, the Commission appointed an investigating officer in forty-four cases, of which twenty cases required the appointment of an investigating officer from an external police force. This shows that the Commission uses its section 19 powers sparingly (see 1998–2010 in Table 11.1).[5] In total, the Commission referred almost half of the section 19 cases back to the Court (twenty-one out of forty-three cases),[6] and the Court quashed the convictions in half of the referred cases (eleven out of twenty-one cases).[7]

The Commission's 'decision field' (Hawkins, 2002), defined by its Formal Memorandum and Casework Guidance Note on using section 19 powers, is more restrictive than might be expected from a reading of section 19 of the Criminal Appeal Act 1995. The Act merely states that 'where the Commission believe[s] that inquiries should be made for assisting them *in the exercise of any of their functions in relation to any case* they may require the appointment of an investigating officer to carry out the inquiries' (emphasis added). The Casework Guidance Note on section 19 requirements states there have been relatively few cases where it has been 'necessary' to require the appointment of an investigating officer (Criminal Cases Review Commission, 2012f:para:3), and restricts the use of section 19 powers to 'cases where it is clear that it would not be appropriate for an interview(s) to be conducted, other than under caution, and/or the inquiries necessary are beyond the scope of the Commission's resources' (Criminal Cases Review Commission, 2012f:para:3) suggesting that the Commission's 'decision field' is set more narrowly than the legal 'surround' (Hawkins, 2002)—in this case the Criminal Appeal Act 1995. The Commission delegated its investigative work to the police more extensively in 1997, the year it was established (see Table 11.1). Most of these cases are likely to have been passed on from its predecessor—the C3 (Criminal Policy) Division of the Home Office (see Chapter 1). The C3 Division had no significant resources for investigation and therefore relied heavily on the police (Elks, 2008:23). In this sense, the restrictive use of section 19 powers since 1998

---

[4] For example, in case CS2, an external police force was appointed to investigate possible police misconduct involving an identification parade and the performance of officers in the original investigation. The appointed investigating officer was aware from the outset that the investigation 'clearly had the potential to [lead to] disciplinary' action, as well as impacting on the safety of the conviction (CS2, Case Committee Minutes). The investigating officer interviewed the police officers involved in the original investigation, but they gave pre-prepared statements denying any wrongdoing, and refused to comment further (CS2, Statement of Reasons). Therefore, in this case, the alleged misconduct by the police did not lead to any disciplinary action or form the basis of a referral. Other aspects of the investigating officer's investigation that led to the Commission making a reference back to the Court are discussed later.

[5] The Commission issued section 19 investigations more frequently in 1997, the year that it was established, a point to which we return later.

[6] Case 16 in Table 11.1 is excluded from the calculation as the Court instructed the Commission to produce a section 15 report; therefore the Commission was not in a position to decide whether to refer a case.

[7] Elks—a retired commissioner—argued that the high rate of referrals resulting from section 19 investigations demonstrates the competence of the police in investigating cases effectively and without bias, or without any desire to cover up wrong doing by the police in their original investigation (Elks, 2008:23).

Table 11.1 Section 19 cases: 1997–2010

CCRO ref	Case number	Year of application	Months between s.19 issued and report summited	Original investigating body	External force appointed	Commission's decision	Court's decision	Purposeful sample
212/97	1	1997	17	Surrey		Referred	Quashed	
527/97	2	1997	12	North Wales		Referred	Upheld	
464/97	3	1997	9	Devon & Cornwall	Hampshire	Referred	Upheld	
96/97	4	1997	10	South Wales	Thames Valley	Referred	Quashed	
125/97	5	1997	6	Greater Manchester		Referred	Quashed	
310/97	6	1997	11	Royal Ulster	Metropolitan	Referred	Upheld	
303/97	7	1997	14	Metropolitan		Not Referred	N/A	
36/1997	8	1997	5	Thames Valley	West Mercia	Not Referred	N/A	
8-/198-/97	9	1997	9	Metropolitan	Dorset	Referred	Quashed	
421/97	10	1997	5	South Wales		Not Referred	N/A	
169/97	11	1997	9	Metropolitan		Referred	Upheld	
377/97	12	1997	9	Hertfordshire	Norfolk	Not Referred	N/A	
909/97	13	1997	10	Kent	Metropolitan	Not Referred	N/A	
415/97	14	1997	10	Customs and Excise	Surrey/ Metropolitan	Referred	Quashed]	
1058/97	15	1997	70	West Yorkshire	North Yorkshire	Referred	Quashed	
49/98	16	1998	1	Nottinghamshire		s.15 report	Upheld	
283/98	17	1998	4	Humberside	West Yorkshire	Not Referred	N/A	
281/99	18	1999	Missing	Essex	Hertfordshire	Referred	Upheld	

(Continued)

Table 11.1 *Continued*

CCRO ref	Case number	Year of application	Months between s.19 issued and report summited	Original investigating body	External force appointed	Commission's decision	Court's decision	Purposeful sample
9111/99	19	1999	14	Dorset	Wiltshire	Referred	Quashed	
746/99	20	1999	32	Royal Ulster		Referred	Quashed	
190/99	21	1999	9	Metropolitan		Not Referred	N/A	
37/00	22	2000	16	Greater Manchester		Not Referred	N/A	
176/00	23	2000	6	South Yorkshire		Not Referred	N/A	
460/01	24	2001	5	Metropolitan		Not Referred	N/A	
13N01	25	2001	23	Devon and Cornwall		Referred	Upheld	PI4
171/02	26	2002	16	Greater Manchester		Referred	Upheld	
723/02	27	2002	17	Northamptonshire	West Midlands	Referred	Quashed	CS2
416/03	28	2003	9	Metropolitan	Norfolk	Not Referred	N/A	PI5
211/03	29	2003	19	Lancashire		Not Referred	N/A	
438/03	30	2003	13	Northern Ireland	Merseyside	Not Referred	N/A	
442/03	31	2003	21	Sussex	Surrey	Not Referred	N/A	
569/2004	32	2004	29	Northern Ireland	Metropolitan	Referred	Quashed	
212/04	33	2004	18	Merseyside		Not Referred	N/A	
682/04	34	2004	16	West Midlands		Not Referred	N/A	
495/06	35	2006	18	Greater Manchester		Not Referred	N/A	
397/06	36	2006	Missing	Metropolitan		Not Referred	N/A	PI7
321/06	37	2006	25	Cleveland		Not Referred	N/A	
868/2007	38	2007	16	Staffordshire		Referred	Upheld	PI1
243/2007	39	2007	8	Hampshire		Referred	Upheld	PI3

243/2007	40	2007	13	Humberside	South Yorkshire	Not Referred	N/A	P18c/P19b
914/08	41	2008	4	South Yorkshire	West Yorkshire	Not Referred	N/A	PI6
596/2009	42	2009	15	Staffordshire		Not Referred	N/A	
457/2009	43	2009	20	Metropolitan	Thames Valley	Referred	Quashed	PI2
303/2010	44	2010	4	Hampshire		Referred	Upheld	PI10

Source: 'List of section 19 investigations' updated by the Commission on 9 January 2012; fieldwork notes.

Notes: 1) 'External police force appointed' means the 'original investigating body' was investigated by another force. 2) Case 16: 'S.15 report' under 'Commission's decision' means section 19 was issued to carry out investigations for the Court.

probably demonstrates the Commission's willingness to be self-sufficient in carrying out its investigations, marking a clear departure from its much smaller, more dependent, predecessor.

'Supervising' the police

The Commission's internal guidelines are intended to keep a tight rein on the work carried out by the investigating officer:

> The Commission must ensure that by the end of the police inquiry the IO [investigating officer] has satisfactorily addressed the issues set out in its directions.[8] In complex cases regular meetings between the Commission team and the IO and his team will help ensure the inquiry remains 'on track' ... It would not be acceptable to leave the IO and his team to get on with their inquiry and simply wait for their report to see how they have got on. By the time the IO drafts his report the Commission should be aware in general terms of what it is likely to contain. If this is not the case, then the Commission cannot be said to have adequately *supervised* the inquiry. (Criminal Cases Review Commission, 2012f:para:26; emphasis added)

Note the use of the term 'supervise'.[9] The Commission clearly sees the relationship between the investigating officer and the Commission as hierarchical, and feels the need to instruct, guide, and monitor the investigation closely. The above quotation also shows that the Commission considers it helpful to have 'regular meetings' with the investigating officer and his team. This approach is starkly different from the Commission's formal policy in relation to meeting with applicants and their legal representatives. The Commission does not consider it necessary to meet with applicants because 'in most cases we [the Commission] can find out everything we need to in writing, or on the phone' (Criminal Cases Review Commission, n.d.:5).[10]

However, the Commission is mindful that being too close to the police could potentially compromise its investigation: for the investigation to be credible, the investigating officer must remain independent and must act on behalf of the chief officer of the police force and not on behalf of the Commission (Criminal Cases Review Commission, 2012f:Appendix para:12). Section 20(2) of the Criminal Appeal Act 1995 makes this point: 'A person appointed as an investigating officer shall be permitted to act as such by the person who is the appropriate person in relation to the public body in which he is serving.'

Though the Commission may wish to keep a tight rein on the police investigator, it must trust the police to use their competence in the best interests of the investigation. In theory, the investigating officer could conceal mistakes or misconduct by the original investigating body, which is why campaigners (Cardiff Law School Innocence Project, 2017) have voiced concerns about the danger of 'police on police investigation' (Elks, 2008:23). Delegation of responsibility, even where the hierarchical relationship is clear, renders the principal (in this case the Commission) vulnerable as it needs the help of the agent (the police) to achieve its goal (Handler, 1992:344). In our analysis

---

[8] The Commission is specific about the written directions; it must set out the particular issue or issues it wishes to have examined, and 'wherever possible' the directions should be 'phrased as questions' for the investigating officer to report on (Criminal Cases Review Commission, 2012b:para:20).

[9] The term 'supervise' is also used in section 20(4) of the Criminal Appeal Act 1995: 'The Commission *may* take any steps which they consider appropriate for supervising the undertaking of inquiries by an investigating officer' (emphasis added).

[10] Chapter 12 further discusses the Commission's policy on meeting with applicants and their legal representatives.

of section 19 cases, the Commission did not find any evidence of 'police on police' bias. Indeed, one interviewee at the Commission, who was involved in a case where an investigating officer from an external police force was appointed, remarked that the external police force brought an 'independent mind' to the investigation, and was not afraid to voice concerns over how the original investigation was carried out (#1).

Cooperation with other agencies requires effort on both sides. The Commission certainly recognizes the importance of making the investigating officer feel valued and appreciated, just as Hawkins recognized the need for a regulatory agency to have the cooperation of the regulated (i.e. businesses) 'simply to be able to do its job efficiently and effectively' (Hawkins, 2002:44). The Commission's Casework Guidance Note acknowledges that:

Care must be taken to ensure the IO [investigating officer] and his team feel they have been properly consulted. It is important to recognise the value of the contribution the IO and his team can make by virtue of their police expertise. The IO might well propose amendments to the directions. Should any proposed amendments appear acceptable they should be referred to the committee for approval. (Criminal Cases Review Commission, 2012f:para:22)

The following section examines how the Commission manages section 19 investigations and interprets reports drafted by investigating officers.

Negotiating section 19 investigations

We analysed eleven cases from our purposive sample (PI1–PI10, and CS2[11]), in which the Commission used its section 19 powers (see Table 11.1). Our analysis of these cases shows that the Commission instructed investigating officers to carry out three types of investigations. The first type of investigation required the appointment of an investigating officer from an external police force to deal with potential misconduct by the original investigating force (PI2, PI5, PI6, PI8c/PI9b,[12] and CS2). For example, in one case the Commission instructed an investigating officer to examine the handling of witness investigation and management, to review non-disclosure by the police, and to examine whether an officer lied under oath at an abuse of process hearing. One investigating officer was instructed to establish whether to make enquiries concerning the conduct of an identification procedure to establish whether the officers involved followed the Police and Criminal Evidence Act 1984 codes of practice.

The second type of investigation required the investigating officer to examine the truthfulness of evidence given by witnesses (PI1, PI3, PI6, PI7, PI10, and CS2). If an investigation shows that a witness had lied, this could cast doubt on the safety of the conviction but could also incriminate the witness, potentially exposing him or her to charges of perjury. This justifies the use of section 19 powers, as noted in the previous section. In these cases, the delegated investigation ranged from interviewing the complainant of a rape case to establish whether her alleged retraction was true (PI1); liaising with the Indian police to interview a rape complainant's lover—currently living overseas—to establish whether she had committed perjury (PI7); to finding out why a witness in a murder case decided to go on a television programme and provide

---

[11] Case CS2 is classified as a contemporary sexual offence case in our purposive sample as the safety of the conviction turned on the complainant's credibility. This case is re-examined in this chapter because the Commission decided to exercise its section 19 powers during the investigation. For discussions around complainant credibility, and the facts of the case, see Chapter 8.

[12] In cases PI18c and PI9b, applicants were co-defendants. The Commission carried out a joint section 19 investigation into both cases.

a different account of what was stated at trial (PI10). Finally, the Commission can require the investigating officer to look into a possible alternative suspect (PI4 and PI18c/PI19b).[13] Our analysis of these cases shows that the Commission uses its section 19 powers when there is a possibility that persons may be subject to prosecution or disciplinary proceedings as a result of the investigation. This restrictive approach to using section 19 powers identified in our purposive sample mirrors the Commission's narrowly defined 'decision field' discussed in the previous section.

The Commission sometimes struggled with the management of the section 19 investigation. Elks (2008:23), drawing on his experience as a commissioner, described the difficulty of 'maintaining a satisfactory momentum to enquiries', giving examples of investigating officers juggling other cases or being appointed to a large murder enquiry mid-way through a section 19 investigation. We found evidence of this in some of our cases, but not others. For example, one interviewee spoke about an investigating officer who was 'keen' to investigate, where the difficulty was not maintaining the momentum but curbing the officer's enthusiasm and getting him to 'focus on the specific directions' (#1).

Conversely, in case PI5, it took six months for an investigating officer to be appointed (PI5, Case Record). The investigation concerned allegations that an officer had lied on oath at an abuse of process hearing, and non-disclosure. The Commission wanted an investigating officer with experience of dealing with organized crime. First, an officer from Essex police stepped down because of inadequate experience; then an officer from Kent police declined to conduct the investigation as he was due to retire; a Thames Valley police officer declined due to the 'nature of the enquiry'; a Greater Manchester police officer could not be appointed (though the case record states no clear reason); Bedfordshire police claimed they had insufficient resources to assist; but finally Norfolk police was able to appoint an investigating officer (PI5, Case Record).

Even when an investigating officer has been appointed, the Commission needs to keep a close eye on the progress of the investigation. The investigating officer's work was delayed in case PI6 due to an emergency in the force: the officers allocated to the section 19 investigations were deployed to deal with a terrorism incident (PI6, Case Record). Though the investigating officer promised to have a report finished by a certain date, the deadlines were pushed back to allow the officer to complete all of the section 19 directions. When the first full draft was submitted, it arrived without any supporting documents. Furthermore, the CRM and the Commission's in-house investigations adviser had to visit the police force's headquarters to assist in rewriting the section 19 report as the submitted draft—according to the case record—was 'unsuitable in its present form'.

The Commission does not expect section 19 reports to have the investigating officer's subjective views or comments on the overall safety of the conviction. The Casework Guidance Note warns against this:

The IO [investigating officer] should be discouraged from including his personal opinion and views in the final report other than when relevant to the quality of the information or evidence.

---

[13] The Commission referred case PI10 back to the Court based partly on the new evidence relating to an alternative suspect. However, this investigation was carried out by the Commission and not by the investigating officer. In this case, the Commission argued that there was an individual living in the area at the time of the offence, who had been subsequently convicted of murder, and had this information been available at trial it may have formed the basis for the suggestion of an alternative suspect (PI10, Statement of Reason). The Court was not persuaded by this argument and upheld the conviction.

For example, the IO should not give his views on the relevance a piece of evidence may or may not have to the review or to an appeal, which is for the Commission to consider. He/she may, however, comment upon the matters affecting the credibility or integrity of a witness. (Criminal Cases Review Commission, 2012f:para:27)

The quotation shows that the Commission distinguishes between the role of the police—as information-provider—and the Commission, as the decision-maker. Commissioners and CRMs do not appreciate the police blurring these lines. In case PI6, the CRM amended the draft section 19 report heavily as he thought that it was not written in an objective manner (PI6, Case Record). As discussed above, decision-making power is spread across institutions. However, not all institutions share the same decision-making power (Hawkins, 2002:33). The Commission expects the investigating officer to make decisions based on the narrow fact-finding remit of its section 19 directions, as set by the Commission, and not to participate in decisions concerning the safety of the conviction (the real possibility test).

Referral-orientated frame

The Commission considers it its duty alone to decide whether there is a real possibility that the conviction is unsafe. The sequence of decision-making suggests that the Commission can reflect on the section 19 report but reaches its own conclusions about a referral. Nevertheless, though the Commission's decision follows the police investigation, it is not inevitable that the Commission has all the power in determining the fate of the application. Hawkins argues:

A decision made at one point in the system may close off or profoundly restrict the choice open to a later decision-maker … it is often the case that effective power to decide is frequently assumed by actors other than the official allocated formal legal authority to exercise discretion. For example, real power is afforded by the legal system to those who create or assemble material relevant to a decision for those formally allocated authority to decide. (Hawkins, 2002:34)

Some section 19 investigations confirm an initial working hypothesis about a possible avenue for referring a case back to the Court. Others do not.

In case PI3, the investigating officer interviewed a number of witnesses, including the complainant, to examine the truthfulness of her story at trial. The Commission also carried out its usual credibility checks on the complainant using its section 17 powers (see Chapter 8). While these did not disclose any evidence that could present a real possibility that the conviction was unsafe, the findings from the interviews carried out as part of the section 19 investigation provided evidence concerning the complainant's untruthfulness (PI3, Statement of Reasons). Therefore, the Commission's referral relied heavily on the work done by the investigating officer.

In case CS2, the input from the section 19 investigation made a significant difference to the outcome of the case. It also influenced the way that the Commission reviews sexual offence cases today (see Chapter 8 for the facts of the case). In case CS2—concerning a conviction for indecent assault—the Commission appointed an investigating officer to address three issues: to investigate potential misconduct by the police, to interview a potential witness, and to investigate whether there was any new evidence that might support the applicant's assertion that he did not commit the offence. In essence, the direction given to the investigating officer was to explore procedural irregularities in the investigation, and whether a coherent narrative could be constructed to cast doubt on the likelihood that the applicant was the offender.

None of these avenues produced evidence that presented a real possibility that the conviction might be unsafe. However, the investigating officer identified a line of en-quiry 'beyond those stipulated or foreseen by the Commission' (Elks, 2008:23), and found from the files of the original investigating police force that the complainant had made two prior allegations of serious sexual assault, which the police had concluded to be false, with injuries thought to be as a result of self-harm (CS2, Case Record). This revelation led the investigating officer to make broader enquiries in order to establish whether other evidence could be found to support the theory that the assault in case CS2 was also self-inflicted, so that no crime had taken place. These enquiries, arising from the initiative of the investigating officer, provided significant evidence to support the claim by the applicant that he had committed no offence, and indeed, that there had been no crime committed. Furthermore, they led to changes in the Commission's policy such that complainant credibility checks became required in all sexual offence cases (see Chapter 8). The case was referred on the basis of the evidence produced by the section 19 report, and the Court quashed the conviction. Here, the Commission's working hypothesis about the case was not supported by the police investigation; in-stead, the section 19 inquiry produced alternative reasons to doubt the safety of the conviction.

These findings from cases PI3 and CS2 should not be read as implying that most referrals in cases where the Commission makes use of its section 19 powers are as a result only of the work carried out by the investigating officer. Before appointing an investigating officer, the Commission carries out a preliminary review and directs the investigating officer to find information to confirm or deny a possible hypothesis, and to gather sufficient evidence to support a referral back to the Court if the evidence points in that direction. In other words, the Commission does the groundwork, and the investigating officer is there to test its hypothesis and to gather data not easily accessible to the Commission. The Commission will not request a section 19 investi-gation unless it considers it has a potentially 'strong case'[14] (PI1, Case Record). In this sense, once the Commission has committed itself to a section 19 investigation, the 'frame' (Hawkins, 2002) becomes 'referral orientated'; not something we had been aware of in other types of cases where a rather more cautious approach to interpreting the real possibility test was apparent (Chapters 7–10).

In one case (PI1) the Commission interpreted the section 19 report in a way that suited its referral-orientated frame. The applicant was convicted of raping his step-daughter. His application contained a letter written by the complainant apologizing for destroying his life, explaining that she felt remorseful, and that she intended to make amends (PI1, Statement of Reasons). The Commission exercised its section 19 powers to carry out enquiries relating to the assumed retraction by the complainant. The investigating officer interviewed all relevant parties including the complainant, her mother, and other family members. The CRM had thought that the findings of the section 19 report would be crucial in referring the case back to the Court; that the evidence would confirm the working hypothesis that the applicant had been convicted on the evidence of an unreliable witness. A case record entry made prior to the police interviews states that 'if the section 19 report comes back supporting the retraction, the medical evidence point [another possible referral point] ... becomes more of a "make-weight" point' (PI1, Case Record).

---

[14] In case PI1, the screening commissioner made the following comment on the applicant's sub-mission: 'New evidence ... that complainant admits she lied in alleging rape. She has admitted lie to other members of family. This looks like a strong case' (PI1, Case Record).

In interview, however, the complainant retracted her retraction: she confirmed that she wrote the letter, but explained that her mother pressured her into doing so.[15] The investigating officer informed the CRM that the complainant was 'keen to get it off her chest that she was forced to write the letter by her mother', and added that the complainant 'was utterly convincing' and that he had 'no reason to believe she was lying' (PI1, Case Record, CRM's summary of the telephone conversation with the investigating officer).[16] Faced with this damaging information, the CRM may have been persuaded to abandon the referral-orientated frame. However, the CRM kept on working on the case, stating that 'there are still other points that could be investigated' (PI1, Case Record). For the CRM, the 'other points' concerned the medical evidence, though the quotation above makes clear that the medical evidence had previously been considered to be a 'makeweight' point, something of little independent value to challenge the safety of the conviction.

The review of case PI1 and the publication of the 2008 Royal College of Paediatrics and Child Health report on the physical signs of child sexual abuse (discussed in Chapter 7) coincided. In light of the new report, the CRM approached the prosecution's medical expert to ask if she wished to re-evaluate her opinion, as presented at trial, which had confirmed signs of penetration. The expert's response was disappointing for the applicant. She revised her opinion but only went so far as to state that if she was considering the matter today, her findings would not necessarily be *conclusive* of penetration having occurred but maintained that penetration would still not be excluded (PI6, Statement of Reasons).

Though the section 19 report concerning the matter of retraction had proved unhelpful to the applicant, and the slightly revised expert's opinion was not promising, the Commission nonetheless decided to refer the case. The medical evidence, which was considered to be a 'makeweight' point, became the main ground for referral:

On balance, the Commission considers that the new medical evidence when viewed together with the issues now raised in relation to [the complainant's] credibility (which would not on their own give rise to a real possibility) is sufficient to raise a real possibility that the Court of Appeal would find a basis to conclude that [the applicant's] conviction for rape is unsafe. (PI6, Statement of Reasons)

In addition, the Commission gave the complainant's retraction a *new* interpretation, which seemed to deviate from the finding of the section 19 report, with the complainant's possible unreliability presented as supporting evidence:

[The complainant's] post-trial vacillations is clearly a matter for concern as she has shown she is a witness who will amend her evidence, within the context of a complex family dynamic, in order to suit her own ends and those of her family. In short, it impacts upon her credibility as a witness of truth. (PI6, Statement of Reasons)

As discussed above, the decision to use section 19 powers sets the Commission on a referral-orientated path. It was able to stick to its referral-orientated frame in case PI3 (discussed above), where the section 19 investigations confirmed the Commission's hypotheses. In case CS2 (also discussed above), the section 19 investigation provided an alternative reason to refer the case. In case PI1, however, the existing belief that the

---

[15] In a further twist in this rather messy case, the complainant's mother denied asking the complainant to write the letter.

[16] The final section 19 report also highlighted the fact that the complainant was threatened by her mother to write the letter, and experienced frequent verbal and physical threats when her mother was drunk. However, the mother and other family members described the complainant as a liar.

case ought to be referred was challenged with new information, which denied that the complainant retracted the rape allegation. Instead of adjusting the referral-orientated frame, the Commission in this case continued to review the case by obtaining a medical expert's opinion and by *reinterpreting* the retraction interview to justify a referral.

There was a further twist to case PI1. After the committee had decided to refer, the CRM found that probation and prison services files showed that the applicant made various post-conviction admissions to rape or acknowledgements of guilt to officials (PI1, Case Record). Notwithstanding, a second committee referred the case.[17] The Commission focused on the applicant's learning difficulties and questioned his ability to understand fully the questions that were asked about the admission of guilt:

In the Commission's view the strength of this fresh evidence [medical evidence and the complainant's credibility] outweighs the post-conviction admissions or acknowledgments by [the applicant] (PI1, Statement of Reasons).

The Court upheld the conviction in case PI1, finding the fresh medical evidence to be 'neutral', insufficient to undermine the safety of the conviction (PI1, Court of Appeal). Furthermore, it was not persuaded by the material on post-trial retraction, concluding that it was artificial to seek to assess the credibility and the motivation of a 12-year-old (as the complainant was when the rape occurred) by reference to the complainant's actions five years later. The Court concluded:

The [applicant's] confession evidence now received is extremely strong evidence underpinning the safety of this conviction. Set alongside the evidence of the complainant and the medical evidence ... it leaves us in *no doubt that this conviction is anything other than safe.* Accordingly, the appeal must be dismissed. (PI1, Court of Appeal; emphasis added)

In this case, the Commission stuck to its referral-orientated frame despite a section 19 report that contradicted its hypothesis about the retraction, despite the lukewarm revision of the medical expert's opinion, and despite the applicant's repeated post-conviction admissions of guilt. The Commission was able to interpret the section 19 report in a way that supported its referral-orientated frame. However, the Court (the final decision-maker) did not agree and reverted to what the police (the information-provider) had conveyed in the section 19 report, that the conviction was indeed safe.

Of course, the Commission does not always stick to its referral-orientated frame. It was unable to refer some of its section 19 cases because investigations neither confirmed the Commission's hypotheses, nor provided an alternative avenue for a referral, as we saw in the cases discussed above (PI5, PI6, PI7, and PI18c/PI19b). In cases PI8c/PI19b, the Commission directed the investigating officer to look into possible alternative suspects, but—following the section 19 report—decided not to refer, as the investigating officer was able to find no evidence to support the applicant's claims:

The Commission concurs with [investigating officer's] conclusion that the revelations made have failed to establish any new evidence to support the allegation that other persons were responsible for the murder of [victim]. The assertions and allegations made by [applicant] and his family concerning the involvement of [names of alternative suspects] in the shooting of [victim] are not substantiated by evidence and forensic examinations. (PI18c/PI19b, Statement of Reasons)

In case PI7, the investigating officer was unable to carry out the investigation directed by the Commission, and produced an unusually short three-page section 19

---

[17] Bearing in mind that the Commission often turns down applications where applicants pleaded guilty (see Chapter 6), it is surprising that the Commission referred the case.

report explaining that the complainant and her alleged lover refused to be interviewed, and that there was insufficient evidence to arrest either party in order to carry out the interview. Without their evidence, the Commission was unable to refer the case back to the Court.

In another case (PI6), in which the decision was made not to refer, the section 19 report went as far as to cast doubt on the Commission's grounds for requiring the appointment of an investigating officer in the first place. The Commission had directed the investigating officer to interview the complainant following submissions by the applicant's legal representative that the complainant had retracted her allegation against the applicant. The investigating officer wrote:

It is the opinion of the [investigating officer] that this record does not show [applicant's legal representative] in a good light. If it is accepted that [legal representative's] ability to accurately reflect an attendance note into a statement is called into question then the whole premise of the request to the CCRC to investigate this matter would appear to be on shaky ground. However the reliability of this [legal representative's] statement and the circumstances appertaining to it are matters for the CCRC to assess. (PI6, section 19 report cited in the Statement of Reasons)

Again, without confirmation of the alleged retraction by the complainant, the Commission was unable to refer the case back to the Court. In these cases, the police's section 19 report managed to 'restrict the choice open to a later decision-maker' (Hawkins, 2002:34): the section 19 reports by the police set a clear expectation as to what the 'correct' outcome should be.

Working for the Court: Section 15 Cases

Co-dependency between the Commission and the Court

The main role of the Commission is to review the Court's previous decision to uphold a conviction at first appeal, and in some cases refer those convictions back to the Court.[18] In order to perform its role effectively, the Commission must second-guess the Court's judgment should it be minded to refer the case: the Court will assess the safety of any conviction referred to it by the Commission, but the Commission must predict whether there is a real possibility that the Court would find the conviction to be unsafe. As noted in the introduction, a lesser-known relationship between the Commission and the Court is a product of the Court exercising its discretion (under section 23A(1) Criminal Appeal Act 1968 and section 15 of the Criminal Appeal Act 1995) to direct the Commission to investigate and report to the Court on any matter relating to on-going appeals—that is, when it is considering an appeal or an application for leave to appeal (section 23A(1) Criminal Appeal Act 1968). When the Court directs the Commission, the Commission must start work on the section 15 investigation 'immediately', as it will relate to live proceedings (Criminal Cases Review Commission, 2013a).[19]

---

[18] The Commission can refer a conviction back to the Court under exceptional circumstances in cases where an applicant has not previously appealed.

[19] As a general rule, the Commission prioritizes section 15 investigations (Criminal Cases Review Commission, 2015d:para:3). They are treated as a stage two review case and allocated to a CRM to investigate (Criminal Cases Review Commission, 2015d:5). Our analysis of section 15 cases showed that the Commission started working on these cases within a few days.

The Commission has an existing relationship with the Court through its referrals. Here, it tries to do the best for applicants where there are potential grounds for a referral without antagonizing the Court by referring on grounds that the Court has resisted in the past, as one interviewee explained:

[I]f you're trying to do your best for the individual applicant, and you can get the outcome you think is the appropriate outcome without having a battle with the Court and without irritating the Court, and if, on the other hand, by irritating the Court you might not get the right outcome, I think there's that sort of tactical judgement, as it were. (#25)

In light of this, it would not be a stretch to suggest that the Commission is keen to do a 'good job' with section 15 directions in order to maintain a positive relationship with the Court. Certainly, the Court is appreciative of the Commission's work, and the Commission in turn is keen to reinforce the mutual respect that exists. Almost every year, the Commission's Annual Report publishes the Court's positive feedback on the Commission's work in response to section 15 directions. For example, the following passage was published in the 2014/15 Annual Report:

We [The Court] continue to have a strong relationship with the Criminal Cases Review Commission. Directed investigations under section 23A Criminal Appeal Act 1968 into allegations of jury impropriety depend upon them and no one can ever fail to be impressed by the thoroughness and impartiality of their investigations. (The Court quoted in Criminal Cases Review Commission, 2014a)

At the same time, the Court is keen to stress its independence from the Commission when it comes to referred cases:

We continue to be greatly assisted by the CCRC in the essential matter of directed investigations … Where the Commission refers a case it should be emphasised that our Court does not always quash the matter referred. That is as it should be. (The Court quoted in Criminal Cases Review Commission, 2014a)

In turn, the Commission made a similar statement in its 2013/14 Annual Report, stressing that it is 'steadfastly independent' of the Court, but also making the point that it 'enjoys a professional and constructive relationship' with the Court (Criminal Cases Review Commission, 2014a).

The Court has depended on the Commission to conduct investigations every year. Table 11.2 lists the number of section 15 investigations carried out each year by the Commission between 1997 and 2017, showing ninety-five in total. Just under two thirds involved allegations of irregularity or misconduct relating to jurors (Criminal Cases Review Commission, 2014a). A high proportion of section 15 investigations related particularly to allegations about the inappropriate use of the internet by jurors. For example, the Commission investigated a case, in which a juror, after conviction but before sentencing, contacted the defendant via Facebook (Criminal Cases Review Commission, 2016a). The Commission was tasked with investigating whether or not the juror had used the internet to research the defendant *during* trial. The President of the Queen's Bench Division, (the then) Lord Justice Thomas, issued a protocol in 2012 on the handling of jury irregularities in the Crown Court (Thomas, 2012). The Commission attributed the decrease in section 15 investigations directed by the Court in the last few years (see Table 11.2) to the success of this protocol (Criminal Cases Review Commission, 2016a).

Our purposive sample includes ten section 15 investigations (involving 13 appellants; JD1–JD13): six focused on jurors (JD1, JD3/JD4,[20] JD5, JD7, JD8/JD9, and

---

[20] Appellants in cases JD3/JD4 were co-defendants: the Commission was instructed by the Court to produce a single section 15 report. The same applies to cases JD3/JD4, JD8/JD9, JD8/JD9, and JD12/JD13.

Table 11.2 Number of section 15 investigations: 1997–2017

	Number of section 15 investigations
2016/2017	1
2015/2016	2
2014/2015	4
2013/2014	2
2012/2013	9
2011/2012	8
2010/2011	13*
2009/2010	12*
2008/2009	5
2007/2008	11
2006/2007	11
1997–2006	17

Note: *The Commission's Annual Reports for 2010/11 and 2009/10 refer to the number of appellants rather than the number of section 15 directions. One section 15 direction may involve more than one appellant.

Sources: Criminal Cases Review Commission, Annual Report and Accounts 2006–2017. The figure for 1997–2006 is reported in the 2006/07 Annual Report.

JD11) and four cases comprised other varied investigations (JD2, JD6, JD10, and JD12/JD13). The Commission interviewed jurors to shed light on allegations that: a juror shared his prior knowledge and views of defendants with other jurors (JD1); a juror worked at a prison where the defendants were held and should not have served as a juror in that case (JD3/JD4); jurors had not reached unanimous verdicts on several counts when the foreperson (head juror) had stated that they had (JD5); a juror made racist remarks about the defendants (JD7); a juror was texting during the trial (JD8/JD9); and a juror knew one of the defendants (JD11). The other cases included an investigation into an alternative suspect (JD2 and JD6); possible misconduct by the police (JD10); and alleged retractions by witnesses (JD12/JD13). The following sections examine the Commission's handling of these section 15 investigations and the Court's response to them.

Web of decision-making

Hawkins (2002:32) argued that legal decision-making should be viewed as a product of various actors making decisions 'serially'. Trial and appeal processes appear to proceed along a linear path, with a case moving from the police, to prosecution, to trial, and to appeal, with the Commission providing a last chance at appeal. Our analysis of section 15 cases demonstrates, however, that legal decision-making is more complex than this sequential path suggests: a case may reach the Court (the final decision-maker), but bodies that are involved in the construction of a case at an earlier stage could be brought back to work on the case to re-evaluate or gather new information concerning certain aspects of the case. Our analysis of section 19 investigations by the police confirms this.

For example, in case JD10, the applicant, a 'hit man', was convicted and sentenced to life imprisonment for murder. He applied to the Commission three times. His first application to the Commission was turned down partly because he had not appealed his conviction, but also because the Commission's review into alleged police misconduct and non-disclosure did not raise any exceptional circumstances to justify a referral back to the Court. His second application was based on the fact that the police officer who had been involved in the pre-trial investigation was subsequently found guilty of stealing money. The Commission considered how the dishonesty of this police officer could affect the safety of the applicant's conviction, but after analysing the Crown Prosecution Service's review of the officer's charges, decided not to refer the case back to the Court.[21] The applicant twice unsuccessfully challenged the Commission's decision to turn down the case through judicial review. He then applied to the Commission for a third time.[22] Before the Commission reached a decision, the applicant's lawyers launched an application to the Court for leave to appeal, which resulted in the case being closed at the Commission.

Having been dissatisfied with the Commission's reviews, the applicant and his lawyers may have thought that going straight to the Court would be a quicker and a surer way to overturn the conviction. The irony is that the Court, having received the case, directed it back to the Commission to carry out a section 15 investigation. The Commission's task was to investigate the authenticity of papers anonymously submitted to the applicant's legal representatives, which, if genuine, could cast doubt on the safety of the conviction. In its direction, the Court also asked the Commission to provide any facts or material of relevance to the grounds of appeal, to be drawn from the applicant's previous applications to the Commission. The Commission's section 15 investigation showed that the documents were unlikely to be genuine and found no evidence of police misconduct, nor that the apparently corrupt officer affected the safety of the applicant's conviction. The Court upheld the conviction.

While the Court was careful to stress in its direction that the Commission is 'not asked to report to the Court their opinions on the application' (JD10, Directions by the Court), in essence, it was the work of the Commission which underpinned the Court's decision to uphold the conviction. This again supports Hawkins' (2002) theory that often 'real power' is afforded to those who assemble material relevant to a decision rather than those who are formally allocated to decide. The Commission was able to shape the Court's decision, even though this was not what this applicant wanted. This case also demonstrates that decision-making is not linear but multidirectional, moving back and forth between the decision-making bodies.

In cases JD12/JD13,[23] the Commission also reviewed the same cases twice, but these started off as a section 15 investigation. The Commission was asked to investigate

---

[21] During the Commission's review, the applicant attempted to verify claims that the corrupt police officer had used cash bribes. Twenty-two other applications to the Commission implicated this police officer, with various claims attesting to his corrupt investigations. Only one led to a referral.

[22] The Commission originally reached a provisional decision not to refer the case but received lengthy further representations from the applicant's legal representatives. The further representations went beyond responding to the Commission's reasons for not referring the case, and raised new points. The Commission's policy in these circumstances is to ask the applicant to submit a new application. Here, the Commission continued with the review, noting in the case record heightened media interest in the case and that it should take 'a more generous approach' by continuing with the review.

[23] See footnote 20.

whether the alleged witness retractions in a murder trial amounted to full, free, and frank retractions of earlier statements to the police (JD12/JD13, Section 15 Report). In the event, the Court dismissed the appeal because the Commission found that intimidation and other questionable tactics had been used to obtain the retraction statements from witnesses (JD12/JD13, Court judgment). Following this, the appellants applied to the Commission, which twice reviewed their cases but chose not to refer back to the Court.[24]

The web of legal decision-making, involving the Commission at different points, can also raise potential conflicts of interests. In case JD7, family members were convicted of laundering the proceeds of drug dealing and perverting the course of justice. A man phoned the Court claiming to have heard two jurors on a bus making racist remarks who then left on the bus a copy of the 'draft outline of summing-up' (which would have been made available to members of the jury). The man faxed the front page of the copy of the 'draft outline' to the Court, showing the racist remarks written about the defendants. The Commission was directed by the Court to look into an allegation of jury bias.

Originally, the Court was only able to locate eleven copies of the draft outline. In one of its many directions, the Court instructed the Commission to examine the jury papers to ensure there had only been eleven copies. The Commission looked through the crates where jury material is normally kept, and eventually managed to locate the twelfth copy in a separate cardboard box. Later, the defence counsel alleged that the twelfth copy must have been slipped into the rest of the jury papers between the jurors leaving the Court and the Commission informing the Court about the twelfth copy. Therefore, the Commission was implicated in the 'discovery' of the twelfth copy.

The Court further directed the Commission, under section 15, to interview court staff who dealt with jury documents, in this case to investigate the allegation that a twelfth document may have been inserted by court staff. The Commission disagreed with the Court's decision to conduct further investigations because of the allegation made by counsel, and wrote in the case record that 'the new directions do not appear to have been thought through to any degree'. Though the Commission had pointed out to the Court that there was a conflict of interest, the Court directed the Commission to continue with the section 15 investigation (Criminal Cases Review Commission, 2012d:42).[25] Putting aside the issue of whether or not it was right for the Commission to continue with the section 15 investigation, this case highlights the Court's trust in the integrity of the Commission.

Section 15 investigations are 'often complex and demanding cases', which can 'absorb a substantial amount of casework resources' (Criminal Cases Review Commission, 2013a). In our sample of such cases, the Commission describes section 15 investigations as follows:

As is often the case with section 15 directions, the CoA [the Court] give[s] us a fairly simple issue to solve but generally have no idea of the amount of work involved to investigate it properly and thoroughly. (Cases JD3/JD4, Case Record)

[24] The applicants' second application to the Commission involved a section 19 investigation, shown as cases PI18b/PI9b above.

[25] In this case, the police discovered that the person who had contacted the Court claiming to have witnessed the racist jurors on the bus was in fact a close friend of one of the defendants. The Court dismissed the appeal.

They [the Court] simply do not consider the various angles that a section 15 could throw up. (JD8/JD9, Email sent to the case committee)

In case JD7, discussed above, the Court originally instructed the Commission to carry out various investigations in addition to locating the twelfth copy of the 'draft outline' (e.g. to interview jurors, to interview the man who found the 'draft outline', and to obtain copies of all the newspaper reports of the case). However, after locating the twelfth draft outline, the Commission asked the Court if it needed to carry out the remaining investigations. Similarly, in cases JD8/JD9, the Court instructed the Commission to investigate the allegation that a juror was texting during the trial. The Commission's interview with the juror and preliminary analysis of her phone showed that she did not use her phone during the trial proceedings and deliberations. The Court had also instructed the Commission to look into the juror's internet browsing history. The Commission, however, considered it unnecessary to continue with the investigation concerning the juror's internet history, and the Court agreed. These cases demonstrate the Commission's concern about resources in relation to time-consuming section 15 investigations, and its attempts to minimize unnecessary investigations.

In case JD2, however, the Commission went beyond the Court's section 15 directions. Here, the Commission served two functions: to follow the Court's section 15 directions, and to review and refer back convictions previously considered safe by the Court.[26] Often, the Commission does not have to carry out these functions simultaneously, as we observed in case JD7 and cases JD12/JD13 above. However, in case JD2 it did. The applicant was convicted of killing his foster daughter and applied to the Commission to have his conviction reviewed. When discovered, the victim's head was battered, and a corner of a black bin bag had been pushed deep into her nostril. The Commission referred the case back to the Court based on new scientific evidence in relation to bloodstains, evidence gathered from interviews with the applicant's other daughters, and a possible alternative suspect. Before the hearing, the Court directed the Commission to further investigate the alternative suspect.

In this case, unlike the other section 15 investigations in our purposive sample, the Commission went far beyond the directions given by the Court: to 'investigate and report whether, following the arrest and detention of [alternative suspect], he [the alternative suspect] exhibited any unusual behaviour towards, or other interest in, plastic bags, plastic sheets or other plastic objects' (JD2, Directions by the Court). The Commission began its investigation by issuing many far-reaching section 17 notices; for example, the alternative suspect's psychiatric records as well as all police files relating to him.[27] The extensive nature of the Commission's investigation was such that the police, the Forensic Science Service, and the Crown Prosecution Service made complaints against the Commission. They claimed that the Commission was conducting too broad an investigation, requesting documents outside the remit of the Court's direction.

At the directions hearing, the Court agreed that the Commission's section 17 requests were *ultra vires* (beyond its powers), and warned the Commission to stick to the

---

[26] See footnote 18.
[27] The case record entry shows that the Commission was deliberately trying to adopt a wide interpretation of the Court's directions. The CRM who worked on the case noted: '[Commissioner] and I are both of the view that given the content of the hearing itself, we can adopt a wide approach to this order to encompass anything to do with [the alternative suspect] without the need to inform the Court.' The CRM who worked on the section 15 investigation, before going on sick leave, was the same CRM who had worked on the referral of this case.

'deliberately limited' enquiry. Interestingly, the Commission was reluctant to change course. In responding to the Court, it cited section 15(2) of the Criminal Appeal Act 1995, which allows the Commission to carry out investigations into a matter related to the Court's directions. The Commission's letter also reminded the Court that while the Commission is obliged to *notify* the Court of its investigations into any related matter, it is not obliged to seek *approval* for its decision to investigate a related matter. The Court, in response, reiterated that the Commission's section 17 notices 'appear to be far outside the remit' and the alternative suspect's rights may be violated. In the end, the Commission stated that it had misunderstood the directions from the Court. It argued that it interpreted the phrase 'following' the arrest of the alternative suspect to mean 'flowing from' his arrest rather than the literal meaning of 'subsequent to' the arrest. While the Court did not side with the Commission due to the official complaints made against the Commission by various bodies, the comment made by Kay LJ during the directions hearing about the Commission's wide use of section 17 notices encapsulates the inter-dependent relationship between the Court and the Commission: 'the last thing I want to do is to get into a dispute with anyone, particularly the CCRC because we all need their help' (JD2, Directions Hearing).

The final section 15 report submitted to the Court demonstrates that the alternative suspect had a history of engaging in similar behaviour to that of the murderer in this case. However, the examples that linked the alternative suspect to the murder were based mostly on his behaviour prior to the arrest, and so did not pertain to the Court's narrow direction. The Court found the Commission's section 15 report about the alternative suspect implausible. However, it quashed the conviction on the Commission's other two original grounds for referral.[28]

While the Court did not agree with the findings of the Commission's section 15 investigations of the alternative suspect, which was intended to strengthen the Commission's original referral points, of significance in this case is the amount of effort that the Commission put in to carrying out the section 15 investigations. One of the Commission's key performance indicators is the number of referrals quashed by the Court (discussed in Chapter 12). Therefore, in case JD2, the Commission had a particular interest in shaping the section 15 investigation to its advantage. It probably saw the request to carry out a section 15 investigation as a way to strengthen its referral. In section 15 investigations, it is intended that the Commission be an information-provider, just as the Commission expects of the police following its section 19 directions. This case suggests that the Commission's desire that the Court quashes referred cases motivated it to go beyond simply working for the Court.

The jury as a source of miscarriage of justice

The jury system, under which lay juries determine the verdict in Crown Court trials, has existed in England and Wales since the twelfth century (Nobles and Schiff, 2017), and is enacted under the Juries Act 1984. The possibility of restricting trial by jury has been debated. For example, the 1993 Royal Commission on Criminal Justice proposed a reduction in the range of defendants entitled to a jury trial; and, in 2001, the Auld Report proposed that complex fraud cases be tried alone by a judge, though the House of Lords blocked the resultant Fraud (Trials without a Jury) Bill in 2007, and

---

[28] As noted above, the Commission referred case JD2 back to the Court based on new scientific evidence in relation to bloodstains, the interviews with the applicant's other daughters, and a possible alternative suspect.

the jury is still used in almost all such cases.[29] Lay participation in justice remains sacrosanct to most in England and Wales.[30] It has been described as a 'hallowed institution which ... commands much public confidence' (Lord Justice Auld, 2001:para:1), and 'a lamp that shows that freedom lives' (Sir Patrick Devline in 1956 cited in Lord Justice Auld, 2001:para:9). In addition, in England, 'the public's deep-seated belief in the jury system' (Zander, 2005:para:26) is often taken for granted, even though the right to trial by jury is not recognized as a constitutional right.

Nobles and Schiff (2017) have recently argued that any allegation of miscarriages of justice concerning the jury must operate within the widespread faith that a jury can be relied upon to identify guilt in all manner of complex situations. Section 8 of the Contempt of Court Act 1981 prohibits disclosure concerning the deliberation process, meaning that it is impossible to challenge how and why the jury reached a particular verdict. Nobles and Schiff (2017) also argue that by showing deference to the jury, the Court is able to resist appeals based on the grounds that the jury could have reached a different verdict. The effect of the Court announcing a willingness to reconsider a case where a jury could have reached a different verdict would be to open a floodgate for appeals (ibid.). We return to the issue of the Court's deference to the jury in Chapter 14, but here, we examine six of our section 15 investigations that involved alleged juror bias or misconduct.

In four section 15 investigations, the Commission found that there was no evidence of juror bias or misconduct (JD3/JD4, JD7, JD8/JD9, and JD11), and the Court relied on the Commission's findings in determining the appeals. In these cases, there was no conflict between the Court's deference to the jury and the findings of the section 15 reports. Similarly, in cases JD3/JD4,[31] which looked into the presence on the jury of a prison officer serving in the prison where the two defendants were remanded, the Commission found that the juror had no knowledge of the defendants. Therefore, there was no basis for contending that the prison officer serving on the jury was prejudicial to the defendants, and consequentially the Court upheld the conviction. In case JD7, the Commission's section 15 investigation did not find any jury bias, as discussed above, and the Court upheld the conviction. Similarly, in cases JD8/JD9 (discussed above), the Commission investigated the allegation that a juror was texting during the trial. The interview with the juror and the analysis of her phone showed that she did not use her phone during the trial proceedings and deliberations, and the Court rejected the appeal. Finally, in case JD11, the Commission's section 15 investigations also confirmed no juror bias. In these cases, the section 15 directions did not uncover any issues of jury misconduct; therefore, the Court's decision frame—deference to the jury—was not challenged.

---

[29] Prosecutors apply under section 44 of the Criminal Justice Act 2003 for a trial to be conducted without a jury. *R v Twomey, Blake, Hibberd and Cameron* [2011] EWCA Crim is the only case which was heard by a judge without a jury under section 44 (Crown Prosecution Service, n.d.).

[30] A review of criminal justice systems around the world reveals great diversity in forms of judicial decision-making. Systems range from those in which decision-making power is vested in lay citizens to those which entail exclusive decision-making by professional judges. It is striking that matters as critical as determining the guilt of defendants and passing sentence on the guilty are in some jurisdictions considered best placed in the hands of 'the man on the street' and in others are the sole responsibility of legally trained professionals. The lack of consensus on the value of lay participation in justice is evident also from policy changes over time within jurisdictions. For example, the twentieth century witnessed a decline in lay participation in the criminal process in many jurisdictions: initially, France, Germany, and Italy abandoned the all-lay jury, followed later by India and many African Commonwealth countries (Ma, 1998).

[31] See footnote 20.

In two cases, however, the Commission identified potential issues with jury verdicts that could undermine the safety of the conviction. In case JD5, the judge directed the jury to return unanimous verdicts on all five counts of sexual offence, and the defendant was convicted on the basis of a unanimous jury. However, a juror wrote to the Crown Court stating that contrary to the foreman's indication of unanimous verdicts, the jury had not reached unanimous verdicts on five counts. Hence, the Court directed the Commission to interview the jurors. The Commission interviewed all but one juror, who had moved abroad; they all confirmed that they did not reach unanimous verdicts on all five counts. The Court accepted the Commission's findings and quashed the conviction on the basis that the jury had not given a *true* verdict. However, here the Court did not need to abandon its 'deference to jury' frame. In quashing the conviction, it was defending the jury's *true* decision, reinforcing its decision frame.

In case JD1, the Court directed the Commission to investigate an allegation that the jury received inadmissible evidence concerning the appellant's bad character. The Commission's interviews with the jurors produced mixed results; some jurors confirmed juror bias while others expressed no recollection of such behaviour. The Court quashed the conviction of the appellant but it did not accept the section 15 investigation concerning jury bias. Instead of addressing concerns about juror bias, the Court stressed that the conviction was quashed on *other* counts:

> As we have *already concluded that the verdict of the jury is unsafe, it is strictly unnecessary to consider this [the jury point] ground of appeal.* But we have heard full argument on it and it may be of wider interest than to those directly concerned with this appeal. Accordingly we propose briefly to set out the procedure which we adopted in dealing with this ground of appeal and our reasons for concluding, as we have, that it does not succeed. (JD1, Court of Appeal; emphasis added)

Hawkins (2002:56) argues that differences in framing occur in a decision-making system, as findings move up the decision-making chain: 'the higher the level of decision-making in an organization, the more conscious of wider audiences and the outside world decision-makers become'. In case JD1, there were four grounds of appeal, and possible jury bias was one of them.[32] The Commission's section 15 investigation was inconclusive on the issue of jury bias and the Court's reluctance to quash the conviction because of jury bias could demonstrate its deference to jury decision-making.

Working Cooperatively with the Police and the Court

Legal decision-making is a collaborative process. Our analysis of section 15 and section 19 cases demonstrates that the Commission, the police, and the Court may all be involved in determining the safety of criminal convictions. Collaborative decision-making is not only about cases moving up the decision-making chain serially, where the Court acts as the final arbiter. Instead, the Court may ask the Commission to investigate certain aspects of the case in order to determine the outcome of an appeal. The Court may also ask the Commission to carry out further investigations, even for cases that the Commission referred to the Court. Section 15 investigations highlight the interdependency of the Commission and the Court, and show that the decision-making chain can be multi-directional. They also bring to light the dual role of the

---

[32] The remaining three grounds of appeal were: incompetent defence representation depriving the appellant of a fair trial, material non-disclosure by the prosecution, and errors in the summing-up.

Commission, which on the one hand reviews, and in some cases refers convictions back to the Court, and on the other hand works directly for the Court.

Equally, the Commission does not always review applicants' convictions alone. The Commission can require the assistance of the police to conduct further investigations to help determine whether there is a real possibility that the conviction is unsafe. Our analysis showed that the Commission used section 19 powers sparingly. It relied on the police only in cases where it would not have been appropriate for Commission staff to carry out interviews or investigations. The Commission's decision to require the assistance of the police was an indication of the case being viewed as meritorious. Hence, we saw the Commission apply a 'referral-oriented' frame in its section 19 cases. While it was keen to separate the roles of information-provider and decision-maker when working with the police, our cases highlighted that the section 19 reports by the police guided and directed the Commission's decision-making. In this sense, the distinction between the information-provider and decision-maker becomes less clear in collaborative decision-making.

The analysis of section 15 and section 19 cases challenges the idea that effective power to decide is concentrated in the hands of the *formal* decision-maker or the *final* decision-maker. In theory, the Court (as the formal and final decision-maker) has the power to override the decisions of the Commission and of the police. In practice, however, the decision-making power can be somewhat dispersed across organizations. The formal and final decision-makers rely on, and are restricted by, information gathered and evaluated by others—the Commission in section 15 investigations, and the police in section 19 investigations. Viewing through a wider lens, legal decision-making in these cases reminds us that criminal justice bodies are symbiotic, and they must work together effectively to reach the right outcome. The next chapter continues to explore the Commission's relationship with outside organizations through the lens of efficiency.

12

Managing Efficiency and Thoroughness in Case Review

You've got to do it [the review] well and do it thoroughly, but not lose the sense of urgency ... they tend to pull in different directions, but ... there is a sort of balance to strike. (#68)[1]

Introduction

In an ideal world, the Criminal Cases Review Commission ('the Commission') would, for each application, obtain and review all documents available and investigate all alternative hypotheses on what could have gone wrong with the case before reaching an 'all things considered' (Schauer, 1991) decision. However, it cannot and should not exhaust all avenues of investigation in every case. A speedy review benefits applicants whose cases are under review and others waiting for their cases to be reviewed. With roughly 1,400 applications a year, the Commission must review cases reasonably quickly; otherwise the queues will become too long (see Chapter 2). Time is precious, particularly for applicants in custody, and the Commission must find the right balance between conducting further investigations (e.g. using section 17 powers to obtain more information or commissioning forensic tests) and reaching a decision promptly. Cost efficiencies are equally important for the Commission. As a publicly funded body, it has an obligation to use its resources effectively; staff engaged in a long review put a burden on human resources across the organization, and payments for forensic tests and expert opinion or the instruction of an external police force should be limited to those investigations that would assist the Commission in reaching a decision.

The previous chapters have drawn on Hawkins' (2002) theoretical framework to examine the Commission's handling of cases. They demonstrated how case reviews can be influenced and informed by external factors (the surround), defined by the Commission's ethos and policies (the decision field), or shaped by the ways in which decision-makers understand and make sense of a case drawing on their own and their colleagues' knowledge, experience, values, and the meanings they ascribe to information (the decision frame). The balancing of thoroughness and efficiency is influenced by the field, the frame, and the surround. On the latter, the Ministry of Justice sets the Commission's annual budget through a grant-in-aid (see Chapter 2). External consultants (McKinsey) were tasked with advising the Commission on how to improve efficiency in the review process. The 2005 McKinsey report criticized the way the Commission identified exceptional circumstances and recommended more rigorous filtering of cases where the applicant had not already exhausted the direct appeal

---

[1] All interviews in this chapter are with Commission staff, including commissioners, case review managers, management staff, and advisers, unless we state otherwise.

Reasons to Doubt: Wrongful Convictions and the Criminal Cases Review Commission. © Carolyn Hoyle and Mai Sato 2019. Published 2019 by Oxford University Press.

process ('no-appeal' cases) before accepting them for review in order to increase efficiency (see Chapter 6).

One of the organizational aims of the Commission is '[to] investigate cases as quickly as possible and with thoroughness and care' (Criminal Cases Review Commission, n.d.). According to Choo (2006), 'value premises'—the cultural values of a body—guide organizations in reaching their goals.[2] Here, what may appear to be two competing value premises (James, 2000)—efficiency and thoroughness—are intended to guide the Commission in reaching the 'right' decision. This chapter focuses on the Commission's field that sets the boundaries of the scope of organizational enquiry, and explores the decision frames that help individual decision-makers to operationalize the concepts of thoroughness and efficiency. The Commission is often criticized for not doing enough investigation beyond reviewing trial and appeal documents (see Chapter 2). This chapter analyses the amount of 'empirical' investigation beyond 'desktop' reviews carried out by case review managers ('CRMs') and the use of section 17 powers to obtain information not accessible to applicants and their legal representatives. More broadly, it seeks to understand where the Commission draws the line between reaching a 'satisfactory or good enough' decision and an 'optimal' one (Choo, 2006) in order to persuade the Court of Appeal ('the Court') that the conviction is unsafe. It examines the extent to which thoroughness and efficiency can co-exist, and at what point one value premise (efficiency) may trump aspirations for another (thoroughness).

The Story So Far

Previous chapters have considered thoroughness and efficiency in passing, drawing on Hawkins' (2002) theoretical framework of the surround, field, and frame. In this section, we focus explicitly on how the organizational value premises of achieving thoroughness and efficiency operate to guide decision-making.

Sense-making: case prioritization and screening

To achieve efficiency and thoroughness, the Commission categorizes and treats cases differently from the outset. The early 'sense-making' (Choo, 2006) process is about managing ambiguity without having access to all the information that could be obtained. Chapter 4 explained how the Commission prioritizes some cases. With approximately 1,400 applications a year, the Commission allocates priority according to the characteristics of a case. Priority is given to applicants with less than two years remaining of a prison sentence (for 'sentence only' reviews); and to young, old, or unwell applicants.[3] Conversely, the Commission does not prioritize no-appeal cases where applicants approach the Commission without having exhausted all avenues of the appeal process (see Chapter 4).[4] Prioritization aims to provide fair treatment to

---

[2] In Chapter 4, Choo's theoretical framework on how organizations produce, organize, and process information was applied to describe the way that the Commission investigated cases from start to finish.

[3] A case may also be prioritized if the Commission believes that if a case is left in the queue for a long time, it may no longer be able to secure relevant information.

[4] No-appeal cases are no longer prioritized under the more consultative decision-making system, which involves group leaders and CRMs and replaced the commissioner screening system (see Chapter 6).

applicants by ordering cases depending on how urgent the review is, whether the applicant is deserving of an expedited process, and whether the applicant is in some way vulnerable.

While prioritization does not turn on the merits of a case, the screening process described in Chapter 6 showed that the Commission does in fact engage in decision-making during the early sense-making period of investigation. Instead of carrying out a comprehensive 'all things considered' review (Schauer, 1991), the Commission uses certain 'triggers'—such as the existence of guilty pleas, good legal representation, arguments about the credibility of the complainant, and cases where the applicant has not exhausted their direct appeals—as shortcuts to help guide decision-making at stage one without exhausting all possible avenues of investigation. We argued that these shortcuts, which deliberately prioritize some of the available information, are not only efficient, but can facilitate accurate decisions in less time than models that attempt to try to examine all information (Gigerenzer, 2008; Gigerenzer and Goldstein, 1996; Tversky and Kahneman, 1974).

Nearly half (48 per cent) of the applications to the Commission are screened out at stage one (see Chapter 6). Rejecting weak cases at stage one is one of the most efficient methods of handling cases, as this reduces the demands on Commission resources. It takes the responsibility for the case away from the Commission, with applicants or their legal representatives needing to present the Commission with a persuasive re-application, or to treat the rejection as final. For applicants who are unable to secure good legal representation or those who are unable to put together a reapplication, there is a danger that the 'efficient' screening process will screen out unsafe convictions erroneously.

Knowledge-building: expert evidence and complainant credibility

During the 'sense-making' process of gathering and interpreting information (Choo, 2006) CRMs share tacit knowledge; for example, about new forensic procedures or a new expert witness. This knowledge is acquired from recent case reviews and shared through emails, meetings, informal chats, and advice from group leaders. This improves the efficiency of the organization, though not all staff were keen on seeking advice from their colleagues.

During and after reviews of cases, data should be converted from individual (tacit) knowledge to institutional (explicit) knowledge in order that others in the organization may benefit from it in their own casework (see Chapter 4). Explicit knowledge is rule-based and codified, as opposed to 'tacit knowledge' that is personal, subjective, and informal (Choo, 2006; Nonaka and Takeuchi, 1995). While both types of knowledge allow decision-making in future cases to be easier and quicker, it is explicit knowledge that facilitates formal 'knowledge-building' (Choo, 2006) at the organizational level. As we saw in Chapter 7, in response to the changing 'surround'—the advancement in scientific knowledge, methodology, and expertise; discredited trial experts; and evolving Court jurisprudence—the Commission developed its explicit knowledge by regularly updating its internal guidance.

In analysing sexual offence cases that turned on complainant credibility, we saw explicit knowledge being used to achieve consistency in decision-making (see Chapter 8). The development of explicit knowledge communicated through Formal Memoranda and Casework Guidance Notes set the principles that shape information acquisition and the boundaries of the scope of investigation (Choo, 2006). Having rules about when and how to carry out credibility checks on complainants reduced inconsistency and increased efficiency, so that in sexual offence cases certain checks had become the norm:

Rules ... are, on average, more efficient than discretion, for rules are a way of institutionalizing experience ... Decision-makers exercising discretion, unless they consult some rules or guidelines, risk having to go through the entire process for each decision ... Rules also promote efficiency by telling decision-makers which facts and arguments will be relevant, thus allowing them to exclude from their consideration the many arguments and facts that will be irrelevant. (Schneider, 1992:77)

That said, Schneider (1992:78) concedes that explicit knowledge, as conveyed by rules, is not always more efficient than discretion because 'elaborate and cumbersome rules can impose onerous costs on decision-makers'. We saw that the Commission's formal policy of requiring CRMs to use their section 17 powers to obtain wide-ranging information about the credibility of the complainant (e.g. social services files, victim compensation files, and police files) in sexual offence cases produced thorough investigations. However, the sheer volume of information gathered and analysed under the formal policy often resulted in lengthy reviews, and sometimes invasive checks on complainants whose medical files were scrutinized (see Chapter 8). One interviewee expressed concern about the unintended consequence of having a formal policy that was aimed at thoroughly checking complainant credibility:

I think it's helpful to have a standardized approach [but] I think the danger is in saying 'we must do this in every single case' because I think that's one of the things that could slow us up unnecessarily, but also make us go off on what some people term, you know, fishing expeditions, unnecessarily ... For instance, ... social services files ... could have boxes and boxes of stuff, but is there sufficient evidence to support going off and going through all those files? (#67)

As we discuss in Chapter 8, the Commission's most recent (2017) policy on sexual offence cases reduced the requirement for credibility checks, perhaps to adjust the balance between efficiency and thoroughness.

Defining Efficiency and Thoroughness

In addition to tacit and explicit knowledge, organizations have 'cultural knowledge', which consists of shared beliefs about the nature of the organization and its core capabilities, based on individuals' experiences and observations, but also on their reflections about the organization (Choo, 2006). Cultural knowledge guides decision-makers towards certain decision frames, helping them to see how a particular case should be understood and accorded relevance (Hawkins, 2002:52). This section examines the extent to which the Commission's cultural knowledge is aligned with its tacit and explicit knowledge and with the pursuit of its organizational value premises—efficiency and thoroughness.

Examining the Commission's value premises through key performance indicators

Chapter 4 described one of the Commission's key performance indicators—duration of review—reported in its Annual Reports. Key performance indicators ('KPIs') are a form of explicit knowledge produced by the Commission, which informs us about what the organization considers to be important in measuring its success. The adoption of KPIs to measure the 'success' of the Commission reflects a wider trend in the 2000s when the Labour government developed a system of governance through KPIs (Bevan and Hood, 2006). Commission Annual Reports published between 2012 and 2017 contain eight KPIs (Criminal Cases Review Commission, 2013a, 2014a, 2015a, 2016a, 2017a). Five relate to efficiency and three to successful decision-making. Three of the efficiency measures focus on speed. They measure the duration of review from receipt of application to allocation of a case to a CRM (KPI 1); from allocation to decision whether to reject or refer a case back to the Court (KPI 3);[5] and the balance between the number of cases received and closed (KPI 2) (see Chapter 4). The other two efficiency indicators focus on costs: expenditure against the budget (KPI 8); and staff absences (KPI 7).

The three KPIs that measure the Commission's success are: the proportion of referrals that resulted in a conviction being quashed or a sentence varied (KPI 6);[6] the number of complaints and judicial reviews resolved (KPI 4); and quality assurance (KPI 5). The last indicator on quality assurance is described as 'the quality of review work as measured by the Commission's own quality assurance system' (Criminal Cases Review Commission, 2017a), but the system is not clearly defined, other than to say that a sample of cases (no numbers are given) is examined to see if additional work is required. We saw in Chapter 6 that this quality assurance system, when used for stage one decisions, seems to be more concerned with protecting the Commission from judicial review than ensuring consistency in decision-making.[7]

Most of the Commission's KPIs are measures of efficiency. Clearly, explicit knowledge is being built on the method and outcome of measuring efficiency (speed of review, and cost to the organization). Explicit knowledge has not been generated on thoroughness, other than the one KPI mentioned above, which purports to measure the quality of reviews undertaken but is unclear on what constitutes 'quality'. Hawkins (2002:317) argues that organizations tend to use indicators that can be 'counted in aggregate'. Indicators that are 'clear, conspicuous, and apparently decisive' often become evidence of organizational activity as well as effectiveness (Hawkins, 2002:10). Indicators that are easy to measure lead to problems of synecdoche (focusing on a part to stand for a whole) and organizations sometimes 'game' indicators and focus simply on improving KIP scores rather than genuinely working on achieving organizational goals (Bevan and Hood, 2006). One of the two organizational aims—*efficiency* in terms of speed and cost—is easier to measure; the absence of clear indicators for the other organizational aim, *thoroughness*, likely reflects a difficulty with measurement rather than the Commission's lack of commitment to it. The review of KPIs suggests that the Commission has not yet been able to generate explicit knowledge of thoroughness. A possible proxy for thoroughness may be to use the number of reapplications where the Commission changed its decision from a non-referral (in the original application) to a referral (in the reapplication).[8]

---

[5] This KPI was changed to the number of cases running longer than two years in the 2016/17 Annual Report.

[6] This KPI was changed to an indicator for efficiency in speed, which records the average time taken to notify the Court and applicant of a referral from the point of agreement to refer (Criminal Cases Review Commission, 1999:4). This KPI was removed from the 2015/16 Annual Report (note from the Commission, in response to reading a draft of this chapter, March 2018).

[7] As of January 2017, the quality assurance system has moved from commissioner peer review (see Chapter 6) to quality assurance review by the Chief Executive or Director of Casework (Email correspondence with the Commission, 4 April 2018). According to the Commission, the new quality assurance system focuses on quality and consistency.

[8] See Chapter 13 for a discussion of reapplication cases.

Cultural knowledge on efficiency and thoroughness

Hawkins argues that there are two sorts of performance indicators. One measures what is expected from management and gets fed into official KPIs; the other is what employees have 'lodged in their heads' (Hawkins, 2002:317). We now turn to the cultural knowledge of the Commission by analysing interviews with Commission staff about how they interpreted the organizational values of efficiency and thoroughness. The interviews demonstrate that the Commission's organizational pursuit of efficiency, as captured by the KPIs, is aligned with a shared cultural knowledge ('we all have a sense that ... being able to turn [around] a lot of cases is a sign of efficiency' (#67)).

One interviewee, who described their review style as 'meticulous, quite thorough', repeated the organizational aims of the Commission by stating the importance of 'not los[ing] that sense of urgency and get[ting] on with the work, but do[ing] it thoroughly' (#11). Other interviewees focused on efficiency as an essential skill in reviewing cases and tended to view thoroughness as an approach that could get in the way of efficiency. Some identified being 'purposeful' (#64) and 'good at getting to the key issues in the case as quickly as possible' (#70), and considered CRMs should be able to:

Identify the critical things, elements of a particular situation, accurately and very fast. [CRMs should] do 'right, that's what matters, that's what I'm going to follow-up' not 'okay ... I'm going to do everything' ... [Some CRMs] feel they need to know every single thing about a case, and then they can build towards, right, so the answer is here ... And I was considered fairly radical ... by saying, well, yeah, we've got those files, but I don't actually need to read those in order to be able to work out the answer. (#64)

[We need to know] when a case needs or when an issue needs investigating and when it doesn't ... At what point do you draw the line with the investigation and say this issue has no prospect of going anywhere, let's not waste any more time progressing this because it can never make a difference? ... Those sorts of judgement calls really, I would say, make a good CRM in terms of the review process. (#70)

One interviewee also described case reviewers' inclination to err on the side of 'caution' (#72) and to attempt to review all documents in order not to miss an unsafe conviction, suggesting that this was especially true of those who are new to the Commission and therefore less experienced. They explained the difference between a new member of staff and an experienced one as follows:

Someone who's new to case review is much more likely to take the approach of being more cautious, in the sense of 'I just want to have a look at that to make sure there isn't anything that's necessary ...' and then, with experience, confidence comes, and they're more able to say, 'Yeah, I know that's not going to take us anywhere that's going to lead to un-safety—we don't have to go there at all.' (#72)

There was a clear sense from our interviews that being a quick, efficient reviewer was an essential skill that should be mastered with practice. This interviewee, who had more than ten years' experience at the Commission, said:

It has changed in that I ... avoid the temptation to go down too many unnecessary avenues. I've tried to get quicker ... I'm a slow reviewer ... compared to some who can churn out cases. People have different styles, and my style is very analytical, very methodical ... In the early days, I over-researched ... I was very slow to develop a process of being able to go through the boxes without feeling bound to look and read every single page ... When I first came here, there was a sense of I've got to go through everything in case I miss something, and then, you know, when you've got 26 boxes, it's, you know, it's overwhelming! (#67)

Our interviews indicate that efficiency is defined as the ability to identify the key issues quickly, and to take a calculated risk not to analyse in depth each and every submission from applicants. There was one interviewee, however, who took the view that being thorough was essential and, as described, their review style seemed to be counter to what others saw as desirable. After stating 'I'm very thorough, and I'm cautious as well—I don't want to miss anything' (#69), the interviewee explained their approach as follows:

I like to take things incrementally ... I have a structure that I do in relation to how I handle my reviews ... I want to understand the decisions in relation to the points raised at appeal and what wasn't raised ... I want to understand all of those things .... If you've done all of that background work first, to set it up and understand that matrix, by the time you come to look at the issues the applicant is raising, you can almost visibly knock the ones off that aren't new ... So, the way I do that is I get all my files in order. I'm a bit sort of obsessive-compulsive really in getting my files together. (#69)[9]

The shared commitment among most interviewees to value efficiency in review is understandable in light of an internal performance indicator introduced in 2009 (separate from the official KPIs).[10] This measure was to 'assess [CRM] performance in terms of quantity' (#72) by providing points each time a CRM completes the review of a case. Each case is apportioned a different number of points depending on the size of a case, and the accumulated number of points is then used as a measure of the CRM's efficiency (half a point for a very small review case, one point for a small review case, three points for a medium case, and seven points for a large case (Criminal Cases Review Commission, 2013b)). Our interviews suggest the impact of the internal performance indicator has been significant, and that it has helped to foster a shift in staff attitudes as to what constitutes the 'right' way to perform. Where the emphasis was once on providing a thorough, exhaustive review for all *individual* applications, it now tends towards carrying out an efficient review in a timely manner—albeit that this could benefit *all applicants.*

From a pursuit of perfection to a sense of urgency

Our review of Annual Reports since 1998 highlighted a shift in the Commission's values: from rewarding the thoroughness of a review, to pursuing efficiency in processes. The 1998/1999 Annual Report listed five key organizational values of the Commission: 'independent', 'thorough', 'investigative', 'impartial', and 'open' (Criminal Cases Review Commission, 1999:4).[11] There was no mention of efficiency, speed, or cost. This continued until 2004, but in the 2004/2005 Annual Report, the term 'thoroughness' was deleted from the five words that summarized the Commission's

[9] When asked what makes a good CRM, this interviewee answered: 'I think someone who cares passionately about doing the right thing to get to the right decision in the case, whatever that might be, and that means putting in a lot of the spadework' (#69). This CRM's commitment to a thorough review emphasizes achieving the right decision in each case over the possible unfairness caused to other applicants still waiting in the queue.

[10] The interviewee who informed us of the indicator used to measure CRMs' performance emphasized that this was 'only a partial measure of performance' and with some CRMs, it was 'really unpopular ... partly the fear of being measured in that way, but also the fear that they might not measure up to it' (#72).

[11] Under the term 'thorough' the report states that 'the Commission carries out thorough reviews of convictions and sentences in suspected miscarriages of justice' (Criminal Cases Review Commission, 2013e).

organizational values, and the words were changed to 'independence', 'integrity', 'impartiality', 'professionalism', 'accountability', and 'transparency' (Criminal Cases Review Commission, 2005a:2).

The 2004/2005 report also introduced for the first time the current organizational aims of the Commission; that is, 'to investigate cases as *quickly* as possible and with thoroughness and care' (Criminal Cases Review Commission, 2005a:3; emphasis added), and first mentioned the 'queues' of applicants waiting for their cases to be reviewed (Criminal Cases Review Commission, 2005a:22–32), again demonstrating the Commission's increasing concerns about efficiency. Additional changes were found in the 2006/2007 Annual Report, such as the introduction of KPIs, including those measuring the duration of review, as discussed above (Criminal Cases Review Commission, 2007). It is worth noting that the Commission's explicit concerns about efficiency coincided with the McKinsey review, which recommended ways to improve efficiency in case review (see Chapter 6). One of the major changes introduced to enhance organizational efficiency was the creation of the group leader role (see Chapter 6):

The Commission has introduced changes to ensure that casework is carried out more efficiently and effectively ... Case reviewers are now assigned to caseworking groups and Group Leaders have been appointed to monitor the progress of cases and assist case reviewers to achieve the milestones that have been set. (Criminal Cases Review Commission, 2007:12)

One of our interviewees who joined the Commission in early 2000—before the shift towards the pursuit of efficiency took place—described their frustration with the queues, recalling the culture then as 'there's ... a 10 per cent chance that this [investigation] might lead somewhere, so let's just keep zipping along' (#11). Others also described the 'cultural knowledge' (Choo, 2006) in the early 2000s as being 'take as long as it takes' (#67),[12] and to 'investigate all possible avenues' (#7).[13] The idea that a duty towards applicants was served by providing a fastidious 'all things considered' (Schauer, 1991) review changed in around 2006. Continuing to work on cases beyond a point at which there would likely be any useful returns came to be viewed by some within the Commission as 'selfish ... for the next one in the queue' (#11).

The introduction of group leaders to manage a group of CRMs improved organizational efficiency in several ways.[14] Prior to the existence of group leaders, the Commission had a flat structure and CRMs were 'very much left to [their] own devices' (#64). CRMs had their own caseload and did not work on cases together, so it was difficult to get a sense of how other CRMs reviewed cases. Interviews highlight the solitary nature of a CRM's work:

You see your colleagues around you, how they are, and you see them coming in and reading files and so on, but you don't really know how they are working on their cases. (#64)

---

[12] An interviewee's description of the change was that: 'there was a culture of, you know, we have a duty to the applicants to keep getting through the cases, but the balance was tipped more in "you take as long as it takes", whereas now [2014], I think it's tipped the other way—we take a realistic amount of time, rather than just however long it takes, and we, you know, we've had deadlines in place' (#67).

[13] One interviewee, who believed in the importance of thoroughness of review, expressed frustration towards another member of staff for not wanting to carry out further investigations: 'I didn't think we'd necessarily get anywhere with it [securing new expert evidence] but I thought ... we should sort of investigate all possible avenues ... in the end, we didn't find anything and it wasn't the first, but ... I was furious, you know. I just thought that is not what we're here to do' (#7).

[14] It is not possible to determine the impact of group leaders on the queues of cases because the Commission's reporting on the average duration of review commenced after the introduction of the group leader role.

You don't always see what your colleagues are doing. I don't really read a lot of other people's work unless it gets sent round. (#69)

It is very difficult for CRMs to be able to assess their own performance against other CRMs ... because they do work in a relatively isolated way. (#72)

Former and current group leaders recalled their surprise at the variability in approach when they first witnessed the ways in which the different CRMs in their group reviewed cases:

I thought everybody was doing roughly the same thing ... and they really weren't. (#64)

That was a real eye-opener to all of us as group leaders, when we saw other people's work. It was that expectation that everybody was working to a similar level, and then you turned back the lid, oh my goodness! There's a lot of variety. (#72)

Group leaders were able to identify CRMs 'who just weren't up to the job' (#72). One described 'weak' CRMs: 'going off on wild goose chases, utterly irrelevant inquiries, couldn't distinguish relevance from irrelevance' and the 'extremes [in approaches] that existed at that time' (#72). They were able to provide guidance to such staff on how to review a case, guidance appreciated by one CRM who spoke about the benefits of having a group leader to 'touch base with and say ... I'm slowing up, I'm grinding to a halt on this ... [and] bounce ideas around with me' (#67).

The establishment of the group leader system also meant 'tacit knowledge' (Choo, 2006) created by individual CRMs more easily informed 'explicit knowledge', as group leaders could share new approaches and emerging trends. In the words of one interviewee: 'We are ... formally more structured in the sense that we have teams ... we've also become a lot better about promulgating that knowledge across the organization' (#64). Having a managerial structure that promoted some CRMs to group leaders made it easier to collect information from the bottom up, while group leaders could also apply a top-down approach in order to ensure the newly identified organizational value of efficiency was practiced by CRMs:

CRMs, up until we had group leaders, really didn't feel a huge amount of responsibility for the applicants who were waiting in the queue ... You had your cases, your applicants, and they were very much your problem—I'm going to do everything that I need to do for my cases, and the rest of them isn't my problem, that's the organization's problem. (#64)

Hence, there is little doubt that the current 'value premises' (Choo, 2006) of the Commission prioritize efficiency. However, according to our interviewees, improvements in efficiency were yet to be reflected in the volume of paperwork produced by the Commission, such as the number and detail of case record entries, minutes of meetings, and the length of the Statements of Reasons ('SORs'). Several interviewees criticized SORs' length and content: 'I think we are too slow, too ponderous and the SORs are miles too long' (#52); they were 'overly lawyerly' (#13); 'we have, at various stages, been criticized for our Statements of Reasons getting longer and longer' (#34).

A SOR is a document submitted to the Court setting out the reasons why the conviction may be unsafe, or to the applicant explaining why their case is not to be referred. Review of the SORs within our purposive sample indicated that the same structure is used for a referral and a rejection. On average, SORs were thirty-seven pages long, ranging from nine to ninety-nine pages.[15] A typical SOR—whether for referral

---

[15] The figure is based on our review of seventy SORs from our sample of cases. We selected randomly just over half of our sample of 131 cases, ensuring that we had examples from all six of our sample categories (see Chapter 2 for a discussion of our purposeful sample). The average length

or rejection—sets out the trial and its outcome, the appeal and its outcome, and points raised by the applicant, before finally setting out the investigations carried out by the Commission and its final decision. To use the example of the longest ninety-nine-page referral SOR (EE31), the first twenty-eight pages described the trial and appeal; the applicant's submission was summarized in pages 29–30; and the Commission's finding only began a third of the way through the SOR at page 31. The layout and the detail of a typical SOR was described as a 'parade of knowledge' (#69), meaning that SORs do not 'get … to the nub of it for a very long time' (#34) and 'too detailed and too difficult for applicants to make sense of' (#13). Interviewees expressed doubts as to the necessity of setting out the case for prosecution and defence at trial or the details of the appeal, especially for a rejection SOR written only for applicants (#69). The time spent on finalizing the SORs was considered by another interviewee to be driven primarily by the fear of judicial review:

Too much of an air of perfectionism; the challenge for the Commission is to keep a sense of urgency … And sometimes you feel like we could get this decision out right now … But we're more concerned these days by judicial review … so, obviously we're concerned to make sure our decision-making is as watertight and well-reasoned as it can be. But that does mean that you spend that extra time drafting the perfect SOR and making sure it's all just so. (#29)

Indeed, the possibility of being judicially reviewed seemed to be lurking in the background for others drafting SORs:

The bottom line is, it [the SOR] has to thoroughly explain the reasoning and the factual background behind the reasoning of the Commission's decision, always bearing in mind that we might be judicially reviewed. (#43)

Some thought that detailed case records of investigations were similarly aimed at reducing exposure to judicial review:

Some CRMs log every single thought and every single decision … which takes away time from actually investigating effectively the cases. This is because of a fear of judicial review. (#13)

The Commission receives extensive information on most cases it reviews, often dozens of boxes packed with papers relating to the investigation. CRMs must be organized, record what has been collected and, importantly, why it has been collected, what decisions have been made and why. This is crucial to demonstrate to applicants, their lawyers, and to the Court, in cases that are referred, that the application has been reviewed with sufficient thoroughness and care. It is important for applicants to know exactly what has been done and, importantly, what was not done during the review, what is considered to be persuasive evidence and what is not, if they are to put together a reapplication. In other words, keeping accurate and sufficiently extensive records of the investigative process is important for transparency and accountability. However, some within the Commission feel that the SORs—particularly in the majority of cases that are not referred—are overly long and detailed, and that this reflects concerns about being judicially reviewed. We too felt that some SORs could have included all the relevant detail in a simpler language and with fewer words (see Chapter 13 on the Commission's attitudes towards judicial review).

---

differed between a referral and a 'not minded to refer' SOR. Referral SORs are longer (on average, forty-three pages), with 'rejection' SORs being, on average, thirty-two pages. This differential perhaps reflects the Commission's view that a referral SOR needs to be of better quality and more detailed: 'if it's going to be a referral, it needs to be of a standard that can go to the Court of Appeal' (#70).

A thorough 'all things considered' (Schauer, 1991) review was favoured before the introduction of KPIs on efficiency, and the new group leader system, to manage organizational imperatives. Under the new value premises that focus on efficiency, the old approach became regarded as 'too slow' (#52), 'too cautious' (#56), and 'risk-averse' (#11). This gradual shift away from thoroughness towards an increased emphasis on efficiency did not, however, eradicate the Commission's thorough and methodical approach to case review. However, the *driver* for thoroughness may have shifted, from a desire only to do justice for individual applicants to a desire to protect itself against time-consuming judicial reviews. This is not to say that CRMs and group leaders are not concerned about the applicant, far from it, but that a culture of defensiveness has emerged.

Investigation Beyond a 'Desktop' Review

While the Commission's decision field has shifted somewhat, from an emphasis on thoroughness to efficiency, beyond the Commission, there are mixed messages within the surround. Though legal representatives, campaign groups, and academics have expressed concerns about efficiency, in particular criticizing the Commission for being too slow in its reviews, they have also argued that it should be more thorough. One such criticism is that CRMs and other decision-makers do not go beyond the analysis of 'core (legal) documents' (Criminal Cases Review Commission, 2013e),[16] and that the Commission too rarely carries out further investigations such as instructing experts, and meeting with applicants and their legal representatives, witnesses, or jurors.

Poyser (2012:49) argued that as the Commission becomes increasingly under-resourced due to the growing number of applications and real-terms cuts in funding, it takes a 'superficial "paperwork approach" to cases' and does not utilize its 'extensive investigative powers'. Naughton (2012:21) also criticized the Commission for failing to undertake 'thorough inquiries to investigate' and opting for 'desktop reviews'. Naughton's definition of thorough investigations meant conducting inquiries beyond the review of the legal papers, such as deploying new scientific techniques that could prove an applicant's innocence. Campaign groups have made similar criticisms, urging the Commission to undertake more 'fieldwork investigations' (Innocence Network UK, 2013) such as 'interviewing witnesses, reconstructing crime scenes and meeting with applicants' (Centre for Criminal Appeals quoted in Robins, 2013), as well as carrying out more 'crime scene visits and re- interviewing of witnesses' (Innocence Network UK, 2013).[17] A former commissioner concurred that such 'empirical' investigations were crucial:

The answer only rarely lurks in the paperwork. I have always found that whenever you actually meet a prisoner or a witness, or go to the scene of the crime, you discover something new. You are unlikely to get the same result from simply interrogating a database. (Jessel, 2014)

---

[16] To borrow the term used by the Commission, the following legal documents are referred to as 'core documents' for stage one decision-making: (on indictment) summing-up, advice and grounds of appeal, Criminal Appeal Office summary, single judge's ruling, full court judgment; (for summary offences) magistrates' court file, and Crown Court Appeal file (core documents for applicants wanting their sentences reviewed are omitted).

[17] Acknowledging that these investigations would increase pressure on the Commission's resources, Innocence Network UK argued for thorough reviews to be conducted on fewer cases by excluding those based on points of law or legal technicalities that have no bearing on the applicant's possible *innocence* (Criminal Cases Review Commission, 2011n:para:16).

The anxiety he and others expressed is that the Commission may be missing opportunities to identify new evidence, and may therefore fail to refer unsafe convictions to the Court. Faced with these criticisms, while we were conducting our fieldwork, the Chair of the Commission invited us to conduct a supplementary study of the extent to which empirical investigations are carried out, and what factors militate against such investigations. The task was to generate data to test to what extent such criticisms are accurate and fair.

We viewed 'empirical' investigations as any contact with outside agencies or individuals beyond the Commission to help with its decision-making. This was defined as: meeting with applicants or their lay representatives; meeting with applicants' legal representatives; meeting with witnesses or complainants; meeting with police officers; arranging for the collation or testing of forensic evidence; visiting the scene of the crime; meeting, or conducting a telephone interview, with the original trial or appeal lawyers; or meeting, or conducting a telephone interview, with jurors as potential witnesses to inappropriate juror conduct. For the purpose of this study, we did not include the use of section 17 powers to gain access to records held by public or private bodies (examined in the following section) or the use of section 19 powers to instruct a police force to carry out part of the investigation (examined in Chapter 11).

The use of these powers *should* be considered investigations beyond a 'desktop' review, but as the Commission already kept a record of these activities, inclusion in this study was considered unnecessary. Furthermore, as we described in Chapter 8, it was Commission policy (as described in the relevant Casework Guidance Notes) to make full use of section 17 powers in certain cases—most obviously sexual offence cases—and so there was little room for discretion, unlike with the empirical investigations that were the focus of our survey. Likewise, section 19 investigations were very clearly driven by the type of issues apparent in a case and approved by a committee of commissioners and so, again, there was much less scope for individual approaches by different CRMs. We should also stress that in some cases, desktop reviews—for example, the analysis of materials submitted by applicants or the review of legal issues—may be sufficient to make a referral (as seen in asylum and immigration cases, discussed in Chapter 10). The following sections review the Commission's policy on carrying out empirical investigations and present the findings from our anonymous survey of CRMs about the number of empirical investigations they carried out.

Meeting applicants, legal representatives, and witnesses

The Commission has no formal policies specific to empirical investigations, but there are several Formal Memoranda and Casework Guidance Notes of relevance.[18] In this section, we focus on the Commission's decision field that guides staff on when to meet with applicants, legal representatives, and witnesses. The Commission's policy on meeting with legal representatives is made clear in its 'Guide for Legal Representatives', which states: 'We will not usually meet with you unless this is necessary as part of the review' (Criminal Cases Review Commission, 2015g). As for meeting with applicants, the Commission takes the view that 'the applicant's case is generally best put in writing' to avoid 'misunderstanding or doubt' (Criminal Cases Review Commission,

---

[18] There are Formal Memoranda on 'interviewing', 'communicating with applicants', 'expert selection and instruction', and 'interviewing jurors' (see Commission's website: https://ccrc.gov.uk/publications/ccrc-casework-policies/). There are also Casework Guidance Notes on 'interviewing', 'what enquiries do I need to make?', and 'gut instinct as part of the casework tool kit'.

2018b:para:21). The Commission also takes the position that meeting applicants is a task that should not be done on a regular basis, but restricted to circumstances when it can 'advance the objectives of review' (Criminal Cases Review Commission, 2018b:para:22). The same purposeful approach to interviewing applicants is repeated for witnesses: the Formal Memorandum states that witnesses who gave evidence at trial will not normally be interviewed unless there is reason to believe they are in possession of some new information or evidence or their credibility has been called into question (Criminal Cases Review Commission, 2016c:para:9). The policy states:

Just because the applicant says we should interview a witness that does not necessarily mean that we should. We conduct interviews when they are necessary to the progress of the review. (Criminal Cases Review Commission, 2011h:para:28)

The 'field' (Hawkins, 2002) therefore narrowly shapes the scope of empirical investigation when it comes to meeting with applicants, legal representatives, and witnesses. These guidelines discourage exploratory investigation, and the overall message is one of caution: only do interviews when they are likely to be probative; do not, as our interviewees put it, engage in 'fishing expeditions'[19] (#33; #22) to see if anything emerges. The 'explicit knowledge' that is reflected in these policies, and the cultural knowledge that emerges from our interviews, depict empirical investigations as supplementary to regular review, regarding them as potentially useful but time-consuming, costly, and therefore likely to be inefficient.[20] However, it is not certain whether this explicit and cultural knowledge that regards empirical investigation as inefficient is in fact accurate: no data exist. For example, it is possible that meeting with an applicant might make an investigation shorter, by making inquiries more effective.

The pre-2008 Formal Memoranda on sexual offence cases makes clear that the attitude then towards meeting with applicants was different. Instead of the current cautious approach, the formal policy was encouraging: 'Interviews with applicants should always be considered in sexual abuse cases' (Criminal Cases Review Commission, 2013d). This guidance was deleted when the Formal Memorandum was updated in 2013 and remains absent from the latest 2017 version (Criminal Cases Review Commission, 2013d, 2017c). The change was probably the result of an inconclusive pilot scheme to interview all applicants (see Elks, 2008:218)[21] and of the wider shift in the organizational value premises from thoroughness to efficiency.

Our examination of empirical investigation has so far considered its instrumental value: what impact might it have on decision-making during and at the end of the review. Meeting with applicants, however, may have intrinsic value by showing applicants that their cases matter. Some interviewees recognized the pastoral benefits of visiting applicants, especially those in prison:

---

[19] A Casework Guidance Note titled 'What enquiries do I need to make?' cautions that 'there is often a fine dividing line between speculation, fishing and pursuing something that may or may not be of assistance' (Criminal Cases Review Commission, 2011n:para:16).

[20] One interviewee identified cost efficiencies as a barrier to meeting with applicants: '[interviewing applicants] should be done more. If one had the money and the resources, then I would certainly do it. I was a bit shocked again how little we do it' (#27).

[21] The Commission ran a pilot scheme during 2004–6 testing the impact of interviewing applicants convicted for sexual offences against children, comprising twenty interview and twenty control cases (Elks, 2008: 218). Applicants were interviewed irrespective of whether their applications raised any issues giving rise to obvious concern. The Commission wanted to establish whether an interview would provide information helpful to the review of these cases, but the results were inconclusive and the scheme was discontinued.

I think overwhelmingly the benefit [of meeting with applicants] would be a pastoral one rather than a case one but it seems to me the pastoral one is really important; that people should feel they've had a decent shout and that their point has been understood. (#27)

Spending time with the person who is most invested in the case is important in itself, regardless of whether information gathered from the meeting impacts on the outcome of the case. While the formal policy on meeting with applicants does not encourage such an approach, the recent introduction of the simplified application form, which is aimed at reaching out to vulnerable applicants (see Chapter 6), perhaps signifies the Commission's recent commitment to being 'more available' to applicants (#72).[22]

Surveying CRMs

We questioned CRMs anonymously, using an online survey[23] about the number of empirical investigations they carried out over a one-year period (during April 2013–May 2014).[24] The survey was sent to all forty-five CRMs and the results are based on the twenty-two useable returns we received, which relied on the CRMs' memory of the investigative work carried out.[25] The results showed that during the year, these CRMs had reviewed a total of 314 cases, and carried out 109 empirical investigations.[26] Figure 12.1 displays the frequencies of the types of empirical investigative work carried out by CRMs. There is wide disparity in the type of investigation carried out, with CRMs most frequently meeting with applicants or their lay representatives, and with police officers, and rarely meeting with jurors or visiting the scene of the crime.

To explore the reasons why CRMs felt that empirical investigations were necessary, we asked an open-ended question about their most recent case requiring such investigation and two types of motivations emerged: procedural necessity and a search for new evidence (Table 12.1). Meeting with applicants or their representatives was motivated by 'procedural necessity': to seek clarification (e.g. when key documents are missing, or when submissions are insufficiently clear) or to provide a sensitive response to applicants with mental health problems, where a face-to-face meeting was considered more helpful to the Commission and the applicant than written communication. Investigations such as meeting with witnesses or complainants, seeking expert opinion, and visiting the scene of the crime were motivated primarily by the 'quest for new evidence'. It was, however, unclear whether the decision to seek new evidence was a response to a request by the applicant, or proactively initiated by the CRMs.

Interviews with police officers, or with trial or appeal lawyers, were motivated by procedural necessity as well as by the search for new evidence. Such investigations

---

[22] An interviewee described the change in attitudes towards applicants: 'I think also tied up with our changed approach towards the application form, that if we're going to open our doors to make ourselves more available to people who, by our very acknowledgement, aren't so able to express themselves on paper, we ought to be more willing to go out there and talk to them, to really properly understand what their case is about, what their concerns are' (#72).

[23] The design of the questionnaire was a collaborative process with the management team of the Commission.

[24] CRMs that had worked for less than a year were asked to refer to the duration of their time at the Commission.

[25] An online questionnaire went live in July 2014 and was sent to all forty-five CRMs. We received thirty responses in total, but three respondents identified themselves as not being a CRM, and five respondents withdrew from the survey or gave inconsistent answers giving us a total of twenty-two useable returns.

[26] When making inferences from these figures, we should be mindful of the possibility that two or more empirical investigations were carried out in one case.

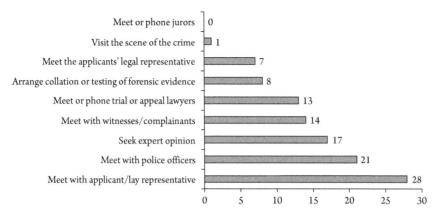

Figure 12.1 Types of 'empirical' investigations

Source: Online survey

Note: The frequencies add up to a total of 109 empirical investigations carried out during April 2013–May 2014.

Table 12.1 Reasons for carrying out empirical investigations

Type of empirical investigations	Procedural necessity	Seek new data
Meet with applicants and/or lay representatives	√	
Meet with applicants' legal representatives	√	
Meet with police officers	√	√
Meet with (or phone) trial or appeal lawyers	√	√
Meet with witnesses/complainants		√
Seek expert opinion		√
Arrange collation or testing of forensic evidence		√
Visit the scene of the crime		√
Meet with (or phone) jurors	n/a	n/a

Source: Online survey

ranged from meeting with police officers to discuss lost or destroyed files, visiting the police to review sensitive material that could not be removed from police premises (procedural necessity), to interviewing police officers about the investigation techniques used, and, more generally, 'to get a better feel for the case' or 'to get background information' (seeking new evidence). An exploratory approach to investigation motivated visits to the scene of the crime; one CRM justified the visit as a way of gaining 'a better understanding of events' (Online survey).

Reporting on their most recent case involving empirical investigation, Figure 12.2 demonstrates that in most cases CRMs take the initiative to conduct investigations. There were two types of investigations: proactive investigations where a CRM took the initiative by suggesting they carry out an empirical investigation, and those proposed by personnel in a senior or specialized role (e.g. investigations adviser, legal adviser, group leaders, or commissioners). CRMs were much more likely to initiate meeting

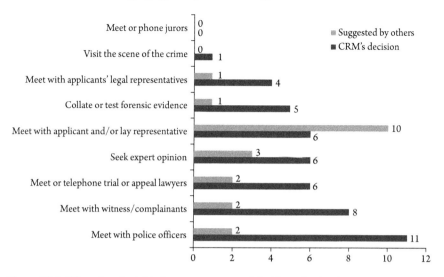

Figure 12.2 Who takes the initiative to carry out empirical investigations?

Source: Online survey

Note: We asked: 'Have you suggested [a type of empirical investigation] between April 2013 and May 2014?' We asked CRMs to focus on their most recent case of investigation; therefore, the figures do not match those in Figure 12.1, which reports the total number of empirical investigations carried out by type.

with police officers, but were less likely to be proactive in meeting with applicants or their lay representatives. The motivation for meeting with applicants was not usually to seek new evidence but rather for reasons of procedural necessity (e.g. managing applicants' expectations and clarifying details of their submissions). Therefore, those in a managerial role—who would be keen to carry out an efficient review—were perhaps more likely to suggest a meeting with applicants to determine the scope of the review and avoid lengthy investigations.

Some CRMs chose not to carry out empirical investigations because they viewed such work as time-consuming and costly. The survey data showed that, in most cases, CRMs were reluctant to do further empirical investigations in cases where the applicant had not raised any issues which would require it. CRMs also made clear that they would avoid investigations if they felt that it would not have changed the outcome of the case one way or another.[27] In this sense, CRMs' investigatory work was largely reactive, so there may be variation in reviews depending on the assertiveness and robustness of the applicant.

There were mixed feelings about the efficacy of meeting with applicants and witnesses. One interviewee expressed scepticism about what can be achieved: 'This idea that you, you know, you can tell a murdering psychopath by sitting opposite them, or you can tell that someone's completely innocent by looking in their eyes, is complete nonsense' (#1). Another, however, described a moment from an interview when a complainant's demeanour had altered the perception of her that had been gained from

---

[27] The Commission turned down a meeting with an applicant in case EE35b, following a request made by the applicant's legal representative and his father. The case record noted: 'There have been two recent requests ... that we interview [applicant]. [Commissioner] and [CRM] considered the Formal Memo on interviewing applicants and agreed that this case did not fall within the criteria for interviewing an applicant, and could not see that interviewing him would advance or assist the review.'

reading the paperwork. This interviewee was investigating a sexual offence case (case SC8, not referred back to the Court) and while carrying out the usual credibility checks on a complainant, inconsistencies in the Criminal Injuries Compensation Authority ('CICA') application were found, leading to a sense that she may be unreliable, an impression that was not confirmed upon meeting her:

It is great to have a referral … when I saw the CICA application form initially and thought, oh, I've got a referral here! … That was a really sobering experience, to meet the complainant, and I think, having met her—and I think this is a reason to be quite cautious about meeting both applicants and victims of crime in the particular case, is … she came across as being such a delicate individual … almost at the point of meeting her, I ended up thinking I hope we can find a good explanation for this inconsistency on the form [laughing] because I feel so sorry for her! (#72)

Face-to-face contact can produce unexpected results. The following three cases resulted in convictions being quashed as a result of empirical investigations. In one case, a CRM wanted to interview an applicant because he had provided two conflicting alibis. It was only when they met in prison that the applicant mentioned evidence to support his story that had not previously been considered, let alone investigated by the defence or prosecution team; evidence that was found to be probative (PI2). A visit to the crime scene in another case revealed a tiny alleyway which had not featured in the prosecution or defence case but which allowed the CRM to understand how the murderer had fled the scene (JD1). In a further case, a visit to the alleged crime scene persuaded the CRM that a woman was highly unlikely to have been raped where she claimed to have been; this led to further enquiries, which demonstrated that the complainant had not in fact been the victim of an offence (CS2). These examples show that empirical investigations can provide unexpected information and point the CRM towards fresh evidence sufficient to convince the Court that the conviction is unsafe.

CRMs were also happy with the Commission's approach to empirical investigations, with only one CRM indicating that 'more investigative work is needed'.[28] The majority of CRMs felt that they had sufficient guidance on when to conduct—and when to stop—empirical investigations,[29] and generally did not feel further guidance was necessary.[30] Open-ended responses suggested CRMs shared 'tacit knowledge' (Choo, 2006) when certain investigations were required and that policies were no substitution for 'common sense' (Online survey):

It is generally clear when investigative work is needed. (Online survey)
We all know when investigative work is appropriate and when it may lead to a real possibility. (Online survey)
Only the CRM can make a sensible decision about this. There is no possibility of having a sensible policy that amounts to saying more than 'use your common sense'. (Online survey)

---

[28] Question: 'Do you think the Commission should encourage its staff to conduct more investigative work?' Responses: 'yes, more investigative work is needed' (one respondent); 'I think the current practice is fine' (fifteen respondents); 'no, less investigative work is needed' (none). The one respondent who felt that the Commission should do further investigative work wrote: 'It can unearth facts that might not be identified through reviewing papers and shows matters are investigated fully' (Online survey).

[29] Question: 'Is it clear when you should pursue/stop investigative work?' Responses: 'it has always been clear' (three respondents); 'generally clear' (eleven respondents); 'sometimes unclear' (two respondents); and 'always unclear' (none).

[30] Question: 'Would you welcome further written guidance which outlines when to conduct—as well as to conclude—investigative work as defined in this survey?' Responses: 'yes' (five respondents); 'no' (eleven respondents).

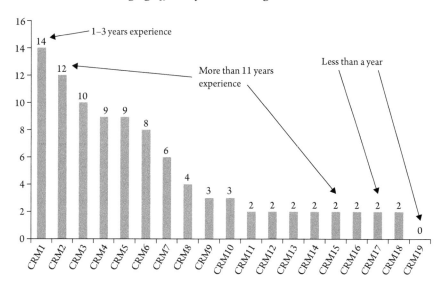

Figure 12.3 Variation in empirical investigations by CRM

Source: Online survey

Notes: Y-axis: the number of investigations carried out. X-axis: CRM by reference number. We received 19 responses for this question.

Bearing in mind that cases are usually allocated randomly and that each CRM is likely to deal with a wide range of applications, we might imagine that over time CRMs would conduct similar amounts of empirical investigations. However, there was considerable variability between CRMs in this respect. In Figure 12.3, the Y-axis shows the number of investigations, and the X-axis shows each CRM by reference number. 'CRM 1' conducted fourteen empirical investigations over the year, whereas 'CRM 19' conducted none. As the cases would not have varied significantly, this finding suggests that CRMs have different views regarding when to investigate and how much investigation is appropriate, despite the assumed shared tacit knowledge.

Based on a suggestion by the Commission that CRMs' experience may explain the variability in the amount of empirical work carried out (fieldwork diary note), we sought to establish whether the amount of investigation conducted was correlated with years of service, as a proxy for experience. It was not. While it makes sense that a CRM who has worked for less than a year at the Commission has done little or no investigation ('CRM 17' and 'CRM 19'), experience often did not equate to more investigation. 'CRM 1', who conducted the greatest number of investigations had only one to three years' experience at the Commission. 'CRM 2' and 'CRM 15' had both worked for more than eleven years at the Commission, but one had conducted twelve investigations ('CRM 2'), while the other had carried out only two ('CRM 15').

Waiting for Information: Section 17 Powers and External Experts

We turn now to the Commission's use of section 17 powers to obtain documents held by external bodies, which was not included in the survey. As discussed in Chapter 8 in relation to complainant credibility, the Commission is empowered by section 17 of the Criminal Appeal Act 1995 to obtain documents that 'may assist the Commission in the exercise of any of [its] functions'. This enables the Commission to request and obtain from public bodies (and, as of July 2016, from private bodies and individuals[31]) materials to which applicants would not normally have access.[32] These include, for example, police files, Crown Prosecution Service files, local authority files (e.g. social services files), court files, prison files, and probation service files (Criminal Cases Review Commission, 2016f).

Section 17(2) of the Criminal Appeal Act 1995 stipulates that the request for material must be 'reasonable'. The Formal Memorandum takes the position that material relating directly or indirectly to a case would typically satisfy the requirement of reasonableness (Criminal Cases Review Commission, 2016f).[33] Public bodies receiving section 17 requests are under a legal duty to comply with the request, and the sensitivity of the material—medical confidentiality, the existence of a court order for public interest immunity, or information protected by Data Protection Acts or the Official Secrets Acts—does not affect the duty placed on the public bodies (Criminal Cases Review Commission, 2016f).

Material secured through the Commission's section 17 requests is essential for conducting thorough reviews. This power differentiates the Commission from applicants and their legal representatives or campaign groups who may have the legal knowledge or the resources to carry out forensic tests, but not access to material that may reveal issues of non-disclosure, police malpractice, or false allegations made by complainants. However, section 17 requests can also cause delays in the investigation, creating inefficiency (Criminal Cases Review Commission, 2012e:para:118). Some organizations issued with a section 17 request argue they are not a public body, some cling onto files claiming that they contain sensitive information, some ignore the Commission's request, while others fail to locate the requested files. When these difficulties arise, if the material is necessary for a thorough review, the Commission has no choice but to 'keep trying, keep trying to persuade [the public body to produce the information], if it's important enough' (#72). While there is a legal duty to obey section 17 orders, there are no consequences for non-compliance, other than judicial review, which can be time-consuming. One interviewee spoke of the Commission's frustrations:

One of the difficulties that we have with section 17 of course is actually the lack of teeth that it has ... Even if an obvious public body, like the CPS, were to say 'We've got this section 17—you know what, we're not complying with it. What are you going to do about it?' ... I think our only option would be to take a judicial review with their decision not to comply with our section 17 notice. (#72)

---

[31] The change was introduced under section 18A of the Criminal Appeal Act 1995, which was inserted by the Criminal Cases Review Commission (Information) Act 2016. The expansion of section 17 powers to private bodies and individuals took place after we completed our fieldwork; therefore, this section deals with the period during which the Commission had access to documents from public bodies only.

[32] The section 17 powers apply to England, Wales, and Northern Ireland, but do not extend to Scotland (Criminal Cases Review Commission, 2012e:para:22).

[33] The Casework Guidance Note explains that the issue of 'reasonable' is for the Commission to assess (Criminal Cases Review Commission, 2012e:paras:23–4). If it were left to the public bodies, then this would require the Commission to provide information about the application that they are not entitled to have. Public bodies may still assert that a section 17 request is unreasonable; in these circumstances, the Commission needs to continue negotiations and attempt to persuade public bodies to hand over the relevant material (2014).

The Commission needs cooperation from public bodies served with section 17 requests to be able to do its job efficiently and effectively but is often thwarted in this process.

Liaising with external bodies and experts

Administratively unavoidable waiting time, caused by actions or inactions outside the Commission, and avoidable delays caused within the Commission, can occur throughout the review. At the beginning, applications join a queue. When a case is allocated for review, CRMs may not be able to start working on a case immediately if they have other case reviews in progress which require their full attention. Illness—or other reasons why a CRM may be temporarily or permanently absent during a review—also creates delays, because any newly allocated CRM needs to go through a process of familiarization with the case. Time will elapse while administrators try to find dates for meetings that are convenient to three busy commissioners and a CRM. Waiting for comments on, and approval of, the SOR by the supervising commissioner can also be time-consuming for the investigating CRM. These are all examples of possible delays that can occur *within* the Commission, delays that are more likely with the increasing number of part-time commissioners.[34] Delays can also be caused by actions or inaction *outside* the Commission. After a section 17 request has been issued, or after an expert has been instructed, external bodies and professionals can cause delays in the review process if they are unresponsive or cannot meet agreed deadlines. Further delays to the progress of a case may occur if the Commission does not communicate effectively with external bodies or experts. These delays account for a significant part of the total length of time reviewing a case.

We turn now to consider how the Commission liaises with external bodies and experts in light of the potential for significant delays to the review process. We analysed administrative data gathered by the Commission on the use of section 17 powers over a period of three years from January 2011 to December 2013, when the Commission received 3,990 applications. During this period, 7,317 section 17 requests were issued in 59 per cent of the cases, with a mean average of 4.9 requests per case. The maximum number of section 17 requests made in one case was 28.

The Commission can request that documents are provided or preserved. (A preservation request is used in cases where the Commission *may* decide to review the material later but does not ask for the documents to be sent to the Commission at the point of request. Instead, the public body is asked to keep the documents safe and not to destroy them.) The Commission was able to preserve or obtain the requested material for over 85 per cent of section 17 requests.[35] The availability of material, however, differed considerably by institution. Courts had the highest positive response rate for providing documents (91 per cent) or preserving them (93 per cent), followed by police forces (85 per cent; 90 per cent for preservation). The lowest positive response rate was for local authorities, such as social services (73 per cent; 62 per cent for preservation).

---

[34] For example, it can be difficult to find a suitable time when all three commissioners can meet for a committee meeting (fieldwork note, November 2017).

[35] Out of the 4,908 requests to *obtain* the material, external bodies responded positively to 4,230; in the remaining requests, the public bodies reported that the material had been destroyed, was missing, or there was no trace of it. In some cases, the public body responded that the request had been sent to the wrong body. Out of a total of 1,735 preservation requests, external bodies responded positively to 1,512; in the remaining requests, the material had been destroyed, was missing, or there was no trace of it, or the external body responded that the request was sent to the wrong public body (this calculation excluded 119 initial requests that were later withdrawn by the Commission).

This ranking of external bodies by positive response rate was correlated with the frequency of the section 17 requests. Courts were most frequently contacted with section 17 requests (38 per cent), followed by police forces (24 per cent), CPS (19 per cent), local authorities (4 per cent), National Health Service bodies (1 per cent), and other agencies (9 per cent). It is not surprising that external bodies that are contacted more frequently tend to have higher positive response rates. Frequently contacted external bodies, such as the courts, are familiar with section 17 requests, understand the purpose, and in some cases offer a named contact, all of which ensures that requests are processed promptly (Criminal Cases Review Commission, 2012e:para:118).

While the above data show that in the majority of cases the Commission manages to obtain or preserve the material it needs, the process is not always smooth. Not all requests are satisfied promptly. As Figure 12.4 shows, the mean average waiting time for section 17 requests (to *obtain* material) is thirty-three days, but the mode average (the most frequent length of waiting period) is six days.[36] The gap between the mean average and the mode tells us that the distribution of waiting time is skewed. The variable waiting time is also apparent from the longest waiting period of 1,000 days.[37]

We reviewed case files to reach a clearer understanding of what was causing the delays. Here we draw on case files that turned on expert evidence (see Chapter 7). Commissioning and obtaining evidence from experts can be a time-consuming and expensive process. It all hinges on effective communication and efficient management of these relationships by CRMs and administrators. Box 12.1 illustrates the reasons for some of the delays in three cases; delays that were caused by internal and external factors. In case EE18, the initial delay was caused by the applicant's legal representative, who responded to the Commission's request some two months after first being contacted. A section 17 request which was sent to the Crown Court was delayed by the Ministry of Justice attempting to locate the file for a whole year before concluding that the file could not be found. The Commission was also inefficient: the first 'chasing' letter was sent to the Ministry of Justice after a three-month period had elapsed following prior contact; the second 'chaser' was sent over five months later. The administrator reported in the case record: 'I'm afraid that I have let my chasing of this case slip.' When the case was ready to be allocated for review, the applicant called to ask for an update and was told by the administrator that the case had 'slipped back significantly'. Though ready to be allocated in May 2009, the case was not actually allocated to a CRM until October 2009.

In the second example (EE12, Box 12.1), the Commission had to approach four experts to obtain a report. At the stage when the third expert could be approached, though the files were ready, the request was delayed by three weeks due to the CRM's annual leave. After the third expert declined to produce a report, the Commission contacted the fourth. This expert did not reply for over a month, during which time the Commission sent two chasers. The expert extended the deadline by two weeks until just prior to Christmas but did not deliver a report until early March (the Commission sent two chasers during this period).

In the final example (EE33c, Box 12.1), the Commission contacted an expert in October 2013. This person responded fairly quickly, asking about the deadline, and explained that he was busy in November, but suggested the second week of December as a feasible deadline for producing a report. The Commission took two weeks to respond

---

[36] The mean average waiting time for section 17 requests to *preserve* the material was forty-five days, but the mode average (the most frequent length of waiting period) was seven days.
[37] The maximum waiting time for a preservation request was 1,088 days.

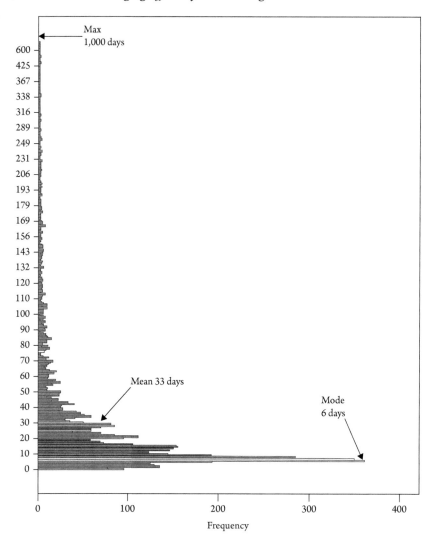

Figure 12.4 Waiting time for section 17 requests

Notes: N = 5,324. Y-axis: the number of days spent waiting for a response. X-axis: frequency of response. This figure presents data for requests to obtain material, and does not include preservation requests.

to this offer; there were two CRMs working on the case and the junior waited for the senior CRM to comment and approve the draft response. In the approved response, the Commission not only expressed no hurry to receive the data, but offered the expert a further five weeks to produce the report:

This is not something that we have a specific deadline for at this stage. As it sounds like the next few months are busy ones for you, would the end of January be a suitable deadline? (Box 12.1)

The above examples suggest that delays are normalized. An interviewee—who was relatively new to the Commission at the time of the interview—described the sometimes slow pace of the Commission:

Box 12.1 Communication between the Commission and external bodies and experts

Section 17 request and other delays (EE18)

04/03/08: Application form received from applicant's legal representative.

31/03/08: Passed to a commissioner for screening.

02/04/08: Commissioner emails applicant's legal representative for missing information.

01/05/08: Chaser sent to the legal representative.

15/05/08: Commissioner screens the case with missing information. Commissioner: 'I regard the lack of response from the solicitor as a lack of professionalism.'

22/05/08: Section 17 request sent to the Ministry of Justice (MoJ) for the Crown Court file.

29/05/08: MoJ informs that the files are not retained after five years from the date of hearing.

30/05/08: MoJ informs that they've located the file, but it is now missing; they will keep looking but are unhopeful it will be found.

03/09/08: MoJ is still looking for the Crown Court file.

23/02/09: Administrator: 'I am afraid that I have let my chasing of this case slip as it wasn't me doing the chasing. Asked [name of another administrator] whether there have been any developments.'

05/05/09: MoJ concludes the search; the file cannot be located. The case becomes ready to be allocated to a CRM.

14/05/09: Call from applicant asking for an update. Administrator: 'I had to tell him that it had been slipped back significantly.'

14/10/09: Case allocated to a CRM.

External expert (EE12)

After going through two experts …

12/05/08: A third expert contacted and the expert agrees to take the case on. Although the file was ready to go, the CRM was on annual leave until 2/06/08.

04/06/08: The file sent to the expert.

13/06/08: An email sent to the expert to confirm the receipt of the file.

16/06/08: The expert raises concerns about not being a registered expert, and asks if this would discredit the expert report if it went to the Court (issue resolved the same day).

24/06/08: The expert raises further concerns.

26/06/08: The expert withdraws.

27/06/08: Other experts contacted.

04/07/08: Speaks to an expert on the phone who is considering assisting. Material sent to the expert for consideration.

22/07/08 & 01/08/08: Chaser emails sent to the expert.

14/08/08: The expert, who had been out of the office on sick leave and then on annual leave, agrees to assist.

17/11/08: The deadline for the report was at the end of November, but the expert emails to say it would be two weeks late (just before Christmas), due to the expert having been injured and the amount of reading required for the report.

09/01/08 & 30/01/09: Chaser emails sent to the expert.

03/03/09: The expert sends the report.

External expert (EE33c)

Two CRMs—one junior CRM and one senior—worked on this case.

10/10/13: Email sent to expert asking for a report.

21/10/13: Email from expert ('Thank you for your request. In principle I would be prepared to supply a report subject to the following: Deadline. How much time do you have? I would struggle to do it before December i.e. November is horrendously busy. Would 2nd week of December be acceptable?')

24/10/13: Draft response written by the junior CRM and sent to the senior CRM for consideration. 04/11/13: Response approved by senior CRM. Email sent to expert ('Thank you for your response and sorry for the delay in getting back to you. Deadline: This is not something that we have a specific deadline for at this stage. As it sounds like the next few months are busy ones for you, would the end of January be a suitable deadline?')

Source: Case records from cases EE18, EE12, and EE33c.

I think that we need to have more of a paced culture. Undoubtedly, you know, everything is a bit sort of slow ... it's quite hard here to set particular deadlines because you're reliant on information coming in and ... everyone's juggling a big caseload ... And I'm very keen that we have much more of a sense of urgency. (#78)

Having examined the Commission's handling of section 17 requests and external experts on the basis of individual case analysis and aggregate data, we now consider the Commission's policy on liaison with external bodies and individuals. The approach of the Commission is examined in relation to compliance theories on securing cooperation from others.

Achieving cooperation without coercion

Comparison of earlier Formal Memoranda on expert selection and instruction with the most recent (2017) shows the Commission's increasing commitment to better control of its relationships with external experts (Criminal Cases Review Commission, 2017e). The original policy states that the scope of the expert's task needs to be agreed in writing but the 2017 policy added the requirement that 'agreed fees' and 'agreed timescale' be included in the expert instruction contract (Criminal Cases Review Commission, 2017e:para:1).

The Casework Guidance Note on Section 17 has a specific section dedicated to non-compliance with section 17 requests, and advises Commission staff on how to deal with delays (Criminal Cases Review Commission, 2012e:paras:116–36). When issuing section 17 requests, the Commission gives public bodies twenty-eight days to respond. If the Commission has not received the material or confirmation that the material has been preserved after a period of twenty-eight days has elapsed, the administrator or the CRM assigned to the case is responsible for following up the request (Criminal Cases Review Commission, 2012e:para:122). Providing public bodies with an extension of a further twenty-eight days is not regarded as 'unreasonable' if the delay is as a result of a short-term absence, caused by sickness or a holiday (Criminal Cases Review Commission, 2012e:para:123). A further ten days will be given for the receipt of a response before the matter is dealt with centrally by management (Criminal Cases Review Commission, 2012e:para:130).

Clearly, the Commission is willing to wait sixty-six days before a matter is taken up by management to decide whether further efforts should be made to pursue the material. The wheels turn more quickly in the Scottish Commission. We were informed that 'we [the Scottish Commission] are not very tolerant of delays', and that their policy gives two weeks for public bodies to respond, with a reminder providing only a one-week extension, before threatening to take them to court (#84).[38]

The Scottish Commission's approach to securing compliance relies on the use of a tighter deadline combined with a threat of legal action. The English Commission does not have recourse to legal coercion, and perhaps because of that, takes a more lenient approach. The Casework Guidance Note instructs administrators and CRMs to 'use the most effective way to monitor and chase those who do not respond' (Criminal Cases Review Commission, 2012e:para:126); however, there is no clear guidance on 'the most effective way' other than 'it will be sensible to use the telephone', rather than written communication (Criminal Cases Review Commission, 2012e:para:128).[39] It would be unfair, however, to depict the Commission as indifferent to delays; it is aware that:

Delays in the provision of section 17 material lead to delays in case review. This is unfair to applicants, particularly to those in custody. It affects case reviewers' individual targets. It affects the Commission's overall performance. (Criminal Cases Review Commission, 2012e:para:131)

The Commission's concern for applicants and the need to protect itself from complaints and judicial review is clear. While the Commission does not provide concrete guidance on how to achieve compliance effectively, it is clear on how progress with section 17 requests should be recorded when delays occur. The Casework Guidance Note instructs staff to 'make a note of the call in the case record' (Criminal Cases Review Commission, 2012e:para:129), and indicates that in the event of non-compliance the Commission 'may need to be able to demonstrate why [it has] been unable to gain access to information needed for our review' (Criminal Cases Review Commission, 2012e:para:136).

There is more than one way for the Commission to manage these sometimes difficult relationships. Securing compliance from organizations and individuals can be broadly divided into instrumental and normative strategies.[40] Instrumental compliance occurs when an individual or an institution offers a reward to encourage others to do (or not to do) something, or threatens punishment to those who do (or fail to do) something. The criminal justice system, by design, operates by deterrent threat, whereby the state punishes those who break the law. Analysing the Health and Safety Executive, Hawkins (2002) found that some inspectors believed that the threat of prosecution can secure compliance of employers. In this sense, the Scottish Commission takes a similar approach, believing that the threat of being taken to court will encourage public bodies to respond (#84).

---

[38] The Scottish Commission has similar powers to the English section 17 powers. Section 194 of the Crime and Punishment (Scotland) Act 1997 empowers the Scottish Commission to request material from a person or public body by applying for a High Court order.

[39] An interviewee explained one of the reasons for delays: '[There is] much more of an emphasis towards don't just keep sending letters, pick the phone up and talk to somebody. Because there are those occasions that we've found that, particularly in the more obscure organizations, the section 17 has been sent … either to the wrong person, it's then been ignored, or the organization has moved or something. We send a chaser, so we lose another month, and that's two months gone, and then perhaps a further month after that, three months gone, you phone up saying "What's happening?" and you [realise that you have the wrong phone number]' (#72).

[40] For a review of literature on instrumental and normative compliance strategies, see Hough and Sato (2014).

Normative compliance, by contrast, is socially motivated behaviour whereby people do what they are required or expected to do because they think it is the 'right thing', and not simply in their own best interests (e.g. Tyler, 2006, 2011). Normative compliance flows from internalized social norms. A moment's thought will tell us that most of us obey the criminal law most of the time, and very rarely, if ever contemplate shoplifting or burgling our neighbours' houses. This reflects the fact that we have well-engrained habits of compliance with the law that originate from a sense that law breaking is *morally* wrong. Despite this—fairly obvious—reality, when we think of securing compliance, we focus almost entirely on instrumental compliance strategies based on coerciveness and deterrent threat. The quotation in the previous section shows that at least some at the English Commission worry about its 'lack of teeth' (#72) in respect of the difficulties in securing compliance.

There are costs to prioritizing instrumental strategies to secure compliance. In crime control policies, an uncompromising and punitive approach can have counterproductive effects in terms of increasing the prison population, which is costly to maintain, alienating segments of the population who are most at risk of involvement in crime, and prompting defiance among the 'over-policed' instead of compliance (e.g. Bowling and Phillips, 2007). Hawkins (2002:45), in his analysis of the Health and Safety Executive, recognized this when he argued that there was a shared understanding that prosecution damages personal relationships and makes the enforcement task more difficult, and that 'informal enforcement techniques should be employed wherever possible'.

Social psychologists provide clues as to how normative compliance can be cultivated and applied in real-life situations. Mechanisms for enhancing normative compliance include the use of descriptive and injunctive norms (Cialdini, 1988; Schultz et al., 2007:430). Injunctive norms describe standards of morally appropriate behaviour: they set out what 'should be done'. By contrast, descriptive norms provide an account of what is normal or widespread behaviour by others. It offers a shortcut to rational thoughtful decision-making when choosing how to behave: if 'everyone else' is doing it, it must be a sensible thing to do.[41] This approach exploits the fact that individuals are social beings and norms 'provide a standard from which people do not want to deviate' (Schultz et al., 2007:430).

The Commission's approach to securing compliance is probably closest to the procedural justice model. It engages in dialogue with external bodies, and listens to their demands and is generous in providing extensions. The Casework Guidance Note specifies that the Commission should engage with external bodies 'as politely as possible' when explaining that compliance with a section 17 request is a statutory requirement (Criminal Cases Review Commission, 2012e:para:129). One of our interviewees explained the Commission's approach to securing compliance as follows:

If you can sort it out by *negotiation* ... that's how we tend to deal with it. It's just through that sheer dogged determination and attempts at *persuading* the organization to offer up the information ... at the same time, to give *reassurance* ... So, lots of reassurance ... to try to make the argument more persuasive. (#72; emphases added)

While the Commission's flexibility may be seen as fair and respectful, it does not seem to utilize the injunctive or the descriptive norms in securing compliance described

---

[41] For example, informing people about the high levels of compliance with tax regulations in order to encourage compliance, or the average energy consumption in that area to encourage reductions in consumption among those who are higher users, are tactics that resort to descriptive norms.

above. Reminding the external bodies of the legal requirement under section 17, or pointing out the agreement between the Commission and external experts, could generate an injunctive norm about providing a just and fair response to applicants and correcting miscarriages of justice. Descriptive norms may also prove to be useful for the Commission in reducing the average waiting time for external bodies and experts. Although we do not have aggregated data for external experts, Figure 12.4 showed that the average (mode) length of time waiting for section 17 requests was six days. This means that in over 7,000 section 17 requests sent in a three-year period, external bodies most frequently replied in a week. There were also significant differences between external bodies that responded before the twenty-eight-day deadline set by the Commission and those that went significantly over. Applying a descriptive norm, the Commission could write to external bodies (and to external experts if data become available) that it *normally* receives a reply from other external bodies within a week, and thereby communicate a standard from which external bodies would not wish to deviate.

The normalization of delays and the 'slow paced culture' (#78) of the Commission may have influenced the creation of the Casework Guidance Note, which allows a generous timeframe and an extension policy more liberal than most external bodies need. While, CRMs and commissioners can work on other cases while they wait for external bodies or experts to respond, time is precious for applicants especially for those who are in custody. These strategies—both injunctive and descriptive—could be an efficient way to minimize delay as they involve minimal resources in comparison with pursuing instrumental approaches, such as judicial review or agitating for changes in the law to introduce enforcement powers, both of which will likely be inefficient in the long run.

Pursuing Efficiency *with* Thoroughness

This chapter has examined the Commission's decision-making process through the lens of efficiency and thoroughness. The Commission's organizational value premises before 2006 prioritized thoroughness, but thereafter became increasingly concerned with tackling the growing queues. Its organizational aim shifted to the current goal: 'to investigate cases as efficiently as possible *with* thoroughness and care' (Criminal Cases Review Commission, 2017a; emphasis added). While the term thoroughness remains, the Commission started to pay more attention to achieving efficiency in case review.

Our survey on the scope of empirical investigations showed that these were narrowly defined and discouraged. Seen as a supplementary to regular review, they were thought to be potentially useful but time-consuming, costly, and therefore likely to be inefficient. Section 17 powers are essential for the Commission in carrying out a thorough review, but they can also cause delays in the investigation and we suggested means for the Commission to secure normative compliance to reduce both internal and external delays.

The shift in the value premise altered the environment of the field as seen in formal policies and 'cultural knowledge' (Choo, 2006). Policies on case prioritization and screening allowed the Commission to achieve efficiency in *all* cases by ranking applications in order of urgency, freeing up resources to be thorough in *some* cases that were screened in. The introduction of the group leader role helped to instil in CRMs a sense of urgency, and provided a management structure to guide the efficient decision-making that had sometimes been lacking. The KPIs—at both organizational and individual levels—helped build 'explicit knowledge' and 'cultural knowledge' about efficiency. The cultural knowledge that emerged from interviews demonstrated that almost all interviewees identified efficiency as a desired skill for a CRM and viewed fastidiousness—an 'all things considered' (Schauer, 1991) approach—as a barrier to reviewing cases effectively. Thoroughness—meandering through all possible avenues of investigation and continuing to work on cases beyond the point at which an informed decision could be formed—became associated with being too cautious, risk-averse, and even careless about applicants waiting in the queue. The Commission's cautious approach to case review and its thoroughness, however, did not disappear altogether. The pursuit of thoroughness continued, albeit with the added motivation of avoiding judicial reviews, an issue we return to in the following chapter.

13

'Post-decision Decision-making'

Finality—sometimes, people say . . . 'some people [applicants to the Commission] need to be told no'. Well, yes, but, you know, finality is not an unassailable virtue. (#69)[1]

Introduction

There is no statutory limitation for criminal proceedings under British criminal law. However, various restrictions provide for *finality* in criminal proceedings.[2] The courts have the power to stay criminal proceedings as an abuse of process if, due to the passage of time, an accused would not be able to have a fair trial.[3] For summary offences, the prosecution cannot accuse a defendant if a written charge is not issued within six months from the date of the commission of the offence (Criminal Procedure Rules 2014). The passage of time is not the only factor in which the idea of finality is upheld over denunciation of crimes committed. Following an acquittal at trial, the prosecution cannot retry the accused even if new evidence is discovered later (the doctrine of *autrefois acquit*, sometimes referred to as the 'double jeopardy' principle).[4] The fundamental question in legal proceedings is 'when is enough, enough?' (Dyson, 2011:3).

Robert Jackson of the US Supreme Court famously stated 'we [the Supreme Court] are not final because we are infallible, but we are infallible only because we are final' (Jackson in *Brown v Allen* 344 US 443). His statement highlights the fact that even though the US Supreme Court has the final say on legal issues, it is not immune from error. In England and Wales, the Criminal Cases Review Commission ('the Commission') is the last resort for those who have exhausted their appeal process but still believe they have been wrongfully convicted and wish to have another hearing at the Court of Appeal ('the Court').[5] Only in a minority of cases—0.8 per cent of cases in 2016/17 (Criminal Cases Review Commission, 2017a:14)—however, does the Commission refer convictions back to the Court so that the Court can judge, once again, if they are safe to be upheld. For applicants whose cases are not referred back, the Commission's decision provides finality in terms of their pursuit of justice. However, as Robert Jackson's quote above illustrates, the Commission, like the Supreme Court, is not immune from error, and neither is the Court of Appeal. Given their fallibility, it would seem unjust if their decisions could not be challenged. The more generous the

---

[1] All interviews are with Commission staff, including commissioners, case review managers, management staff, and advisers unless we state otherwise.

[2] Civil law also provides finality in legal proceedings, and recognizes the need to strike a balance between the interests of claimants and the need to protect defendants from endless litigation (Dyson, 2011).

[3] *Attorney General's Reference (No 1 of 1990)* [1992] Q.B. 630, CA; *Attorney General's Reference (No 2 of 2001)* [2004] 2 AC 72, HL.

[4] One of the exceptions to the doctrine of *autrefois acquit* is for serious offences that carry a maximum sentence of life imprisonment (sections 75–97 of the Criminal Justice Act 2003).

[5] Under exceptional circumstances, applicants to the Commission can have their cases reviewed even when they have not exhausted the appeal process (see Chapters 3 and 6).

Reasons to Doubt: Wrongful Convictions and the Criminal Cases Review Commission. © Carolyn Hoyle and Mai Sato 2019. Published 2019 by Oxford University Press.

scope for challenging decisions made by the Commission, the greater the chance of responding appropriately to wrongful convictions.

Applicants can question the Commission's decision not to refer their cases back to the Court in two ways. They can respond to the Commission's *provisional* decision not to refer their case by providing 'further submissions' (Criminal Cases Review Commission, 2017f). The Commission in certain cases issues a provisional decision not to make a reference before reaching a final decision.[6] If the Commission reaches a final decision not to refer a case, applicants can submit a new application—a 're-application' (Criminal Cases Review Commission, 2013e, 2017h)—to have their case reconsidered.

Repetitive challenges to the Commission's decisions, however, would result in additional burdens on the organization, causing delays for other applicants waiting in the queue to have their cases reviewed. It is therefore reasonable to suggest that there should be a cut-off point at which applicants must accept the Commission's decision in order to 'strike the balance between interests of justice and the need for finality' (Dyson, 2011:8). Zuckerman (1995), in his review of the civil law, provides a justification for 'procedural rationing' of the legal process. He explains that the current system does not guarantee that every litigant must have unimpeded access to full procedural provision. Examples include a presumption in favour of a summary adjudication, by placing the burden on litigants to justify the need for a full procedure if they do not want a summary process (Zuckerman, 1995). In theory at least, the indemnity rule, by which the losing side pays the winner's costs, discourages weak litigations and keeps many disputes out of the court system (Zuckerman, 1995).

These summary procedures are an efficient way of deciding cases and keeping litigation to a minimum. Procedural rationing can remove 'wasteful and unproductive' legal procedures, but it could also 'compromise the standard or accuracy in judgment' (Zuckerman, 1995:169). We cannot deny the possibility that while summary adjudication may produce quick decisions, it may also produce inferior—or in some cases wrong—decisions. Equally, the indemnity rule may aggravate existing economic disadvantage. Instead of discouraging weak litigations, only those who can withstand the financial burden may choose to litigate regardless of the strength of the case. Zuckerman summarizes his argument as follows:

> It would be absurd to say that we are entitled to the best possible legal procedure, however expensive, when we cannot lay a credible claim to the best possible health service or to the best possible transport system. Yet it would be equally absurd to suggest that procedure need not strive to achieve any level of accuracy to satisfy the demands of justice. We are therefore entitled to expect procedures, which strive to provide a reasonable measure of protection of rights, commensurable with the resources that we can afford to spend on the administration of justice. (Zuckerman, 1995:160–1)

The Commission's 'decision field' (Hawkins, 2002)—the requirement that applicants must exhaust their direct appeal rights before applying to the Commission, unless there are exceptional circumstances[7]—creates procedural rationing. The two-stage review process, which screens out what the Commission considers to be unmeritorious

---

[6] The Commission used to offer an opportunity for further submissions in every case. Since 2015, the policy excludes cases where its investigations have revealed nothing other than material which is known about and available in full to the applicant; and cases where it has not found it necessary to make any inquiries at all (Email correspondence with the Commission, 27 March 2018). If there is doubt, the Commission errs on the side of caution in favour of inviting further submissions.

[7] As per section 13(2) of the Criminal Appeal Act 1995; see Chapters 4 and 6.

applications without carrying out a full review, is also an example of procedural rationing (Chapter 6). This policy—not informed by any legal requirement—attempts to strike a balance between the interests of each applicant and all other applicants by reaching a final decision for some *early* in the review process. The Commission also occasionally uses its discretion not to refer a case even when there is a real possibility that the conviction may be unsafe if it is not in the public interest.[8] This does not necessarily minimize the Commission's workload, but saves the Court time and resources.[9] In Chapter 8, we gave examples of cases where decision-makers (informed by the idea of procedural rationing) chose to apply an 'instrumental' decision frame to cases when they considered that a referral would not make a substantial difference to the applicant's reputation or sentence (e.g. a successful referral may result in an applicant being convicted of one account of rape instead of convicted of several counts of rape, but the applicant remains a convicted rapist).

How the Commission utilizes and applies the idea of procedural rationing in further submissions and reapplications is the focus of this chapter. Zuckerman (1995:180) believes judges need to view their role not as 'arbiters of individual disputes' but as 'guardians of scarce judicial resources' and should prioritize the equitable distribution of resources among many actual and potential litigants. By doing so, Zuckerman considers that it is preferable to accept 'some diminution in the level of accuracy in judgments' for the many than to 'dispense higher quality justice to the very few' (ibid.). Any restrictions the Commission may place on applicants, in terms of the number of further submissions or reapplications allowed, may control access to justice and to finality. In the interests of justice, we may want the Commission to allow as many further submissions and reapplication as possible until applicants are satisfied with a decision. However, the Commission's resources are finite, and consideration must also be paid to other applicants in the queue.

The Commission's Policy

Some applicants or their representatives communicate with the Commission throughout the review, providing additional information or making regular enquiries about the progress of their case. Further submissions and reapplications are two post-decision opportunities, which provide applicants with the right to challenge the Commission's provisional and final decisions not to refer their cases back to the Court. This section examines the Commission's 'field' (Hawkins, 2002), which defines the boundaries of the scope of organizational enquiry on further submissions and reapplications, through the lens of 'procedural rationing' (Zuckerman, 1995).

Further submissions

The Commission's Formal Memorandum on further submissions sets out how applicants can respond to a provisional decision not to refer a case back to the Court. It also explains the circumstances in which the Commission allows extensions of time

---

[8] *Clark* [2001] EWCA Crim 884; *Smith (Wallace Duncan)* [2004] EWCA Crim 631.
[9] The Commission can choose not to refer a case back to the Court if it sees no benefit to the applicant or to the criminal justice system. This discretion 'must be exercised in accordance with public law principles: the decision must be lawful, fair and reasonable' (Criminal Cases Review Commission, 2016b:para:4).

for the receipt of further submissions (Criminal Cases Review Commission, 2017f). The Commission's policy is that it 'will always permit' an applicant to respond to its provisional decision not to make a reference (Criminal Cases Review Commission, 2017f:para:2).[10] This is not a statutory requirement under the Criminal Appeal Act 1995,[11] but a product of the Commission's discretionary powers.

The Formal Memorandum offers what may be described as muted support for further submissions for reasons of 'fairness to the applicant in question' (Criminal Cases Review Commission, 2017f:para:7), but indicates concern that the process may go against organizational commitment to efficiency. In the interests of fairness to 'other applicants', it makes clear that applicants should not use the procedure to raise new issues that require the Commission to embark on a different avenue of investigation (Criminal Cases Review Commission, 2017f:para:8).[12] The Formal Memorandum also reiterates the Commission's organizational values by stating that the key objective of the Commission is to deal with cases both 'efficiently and expeditiously' (Criminal Cases Review Commission, 2017f:para:3; Chapter 12).

Further submissions provide an opportunity for individual applicants to ensure that the Commission has correctly understood and reviewed the points raised in the application, and that it has properly investigated the case (e.g. asking the Commission to instruct a different expert, pointing out relevant case law that the Commission failed to consider, or suggesting the Commission take a more robust interpretation of the real possibility test and refer the case). However, as procedures for further submissions and subsequent further review can delay closure of the case, postponing further the pursuit of justice for other applicants waiting in the queue, the Formal Memorandum provides detailed guidance on the circumstances in which the Commission allows extensions of time for the receipt of further submissions.

The length and the number of extensions is entirely at the discretion of the Commission. Typically, the Commission gives twenty working days for further submissions; a case review manager ('CRM') may grant an extension of a further twenty days (Criminal Cases Review Commission, 2017f). Subsequent extensions can be approved only by a group leader, and in 'complex'[13] cases, forty days may be granted (Criminal Cases Review Commission, 2017f).

While the Commission invites further submissions from *all* applicants, it provides extensions of time to only *some* applicants. Rules are in place to 'procedurally ration' (Zuckerman, 1995) applicants from prolonging the duration of the review unnecessarily. The Commission aims to limit extensions only to those who deserve to be given extra time to prepare further submissions, and considers each of the following reasons—in absence of other rationalizations—insufficient to justify an extension:

---

[10] See footnote 6.

[11] While the previous Formal Memorandum stated that providing an opportunity for further submissions is a 'legal requirement' the current version does not confirm this. Before 2015, the Commission took a generous interpretation of *R v Hickey* [1997] EWCA Crim 2028, and every applicant received an opportunity for further submission (Email correspondence with the Commission, 27 March 2018). After 2014, the Commission narrowed the scope for further submissions (see footnote 6).

[12] The Formal Memorandum argues that when applicants raise 'genuine new matters' in further submissions, the Commission has the discretion to ask applicants to submit a new application or to respond to the submissions in the existing case (Criminal Cases Review Commission, 2017f:para:7).

[13] Complex cases are referred to as involving 'the likely difficulty of obtaining or giving necessary instructions or the fact that lengthy documents obtained by the Commission have been disclosed for the first time' (Criminal Cases Review Commission, 2017f:para:6).

(i) the applicant has only recently identified a new issue, argument or matter which, so it is contended, merits consideration and/or investigation by the Commission;

(ii) a change of legal representative, or the initial appointment of a legal representative, by the applicant after the issue of the provisional decision;

(iii) delays by the applicant or his representative in the consideration of the provisional decision. (Criminal Cases Review Commission, 2017f:para:10)

The Commission considers the first reason—the identification of a potentially meritorious new issue—as an insufficient reason, even though the new issue, if the Commission exercises its discretion to investigate, may lead to a discovery of a real possibility that the conviction is unsafe.[14] The second and the third reasons refer to delay caused by applicants or by their representatives. The Commission does not consider it necessary to grant extra time if applicants or their representatives have not been able to prepare a further submission within the given time frame. Again, there is a possibility that an extension would provide an opportunity for applicants or their representatives to identify an issue that could reverse the Commission's decision not to make a reference back to the Court. In these situations, the Commission must decide where to draw the line between offering individualized further reviews to a few against distributing quicker responses to a larger number of applicants, albeit risking the possibility of a compromised review.

Once the Commission has reached a *final* decision not to refer a case, the review process is formally closed (Criminal Cases Review Commission, 2017h). Applicants who feel that there is scope for further review of their case or who believe they have new evidence that casts doubt on the safety of their convictions are left only with the option to 'reapply'; to submit a fresh application. It is to these reapplications that we now turn.

Reapplications

Reapplications are subject to the same two-stage review process as first-time applications (see Chapter 6 for a description of the two-stage review process).[15] While group leaders categorize and allocate first-time applications for CRMs to review (Chapter 6), reapplications are allocated directly to CRMs for screening; they must focus on whether they 'raise new issues not considered at appeal or during the Commission's previous reviews' (Criminal Cases Review Commission, 2013e:para:8). If a CRM finds no new issues, with the approval of a commissioner, the reapplication is screened out and will not be subject to a detailed review (Criminal Cases Review Commission, 2013e).[16]

However, a reapplication turned down at stage one does not automatically bring to an end the legal process for applicants. Instead of 'procedurally rationing' (Zuckerman, 1995) reapplications, the Commission is clear that it 'does not impose a limit on the number of times a person may apply to the Commission' (Criminal Cases Review Commission, 2016e:para:8). Similar to the policy on further submissions, the

[14] See footnote 7.

[15] Here, first-time applications refer to cases where applicants have appealed before applying to the Commission, and do not include 'no appeal' cases (see Chapter 6).

[16] On the other hand, if a CRM considers that the reapplication contains new evidence or argument which might give rise to a real possibility that the conviction is unsafe, the reapplication will be placed in a queue to be allocated for stage two review (Criminal Cases Review Commission, 2013e).

Commission is aware that providing substantial reviews of repeated reapplications would cause delay in reviewing other cases:

> It is clear that official time should not be taken up continuing in correspondence with applicants on the same subject with no new relevant points raised and nothing that can usefully be said in reply. (Criminal Cases Review Commission, 2016e:para:1)

Therefore, the Commission has a policy on 'persistent applicants' to deal with repeated reapplications that it considers to be unmeritorious.[17] It can choose not to acknowledge receipt of, or reply to, submissions from persistent applicants. However, the Commission's policy is clear that being labelled a persistent applicant does not entirely restrict access to the review process because a submission will be 'read, but not replied to, unless it raises fresh and relevant issues' (Criminal Cases Review Commission, 2016e:para:3). In extreme cases, the Commission can decide not to accept any further reapplications from persistent *applicants*. Even when such decisions are made, the Commission's policy is still to accept reapplications from *legal representatives* as long as they identify 'compelling and substantial grounds to justify acceptance of the application' (Criminal Cases Review Commission, 2016e:para:9).

Therefore, while the Commission operates as a last resort for those who have exhausted their appeals, in theory, it could offer an endless opportunity for applicants to have their convictions reviewed. This approach may be justified on the basis of providing justice to individual applicants, but within Zuckerman's (1995:169) framework, this could be seen an as 'wasteful and unproductive'. Whether or not the generous reapplication policy is indeed effective is a matter for empirical enquiry. It depends on how many applicants submit reapplications, and in how many cases the Commission decides to reverse its original decisions and refer them back to the Court as a result of the reapplication.

The Legitimacy of Post-decision Decision-making

Zuckerman (1995) considered that only empirical data can prove as well as justify the legitimacy of procedurally rationed civil law systems. He argued:

> If it is shown that judgments tend to go the same way as the interlocutory decision, one will have established that a move towards summary adjudication would not involve massive sacrifice in accuracy. Equally, if it is shown that in a high proportion of cases a decision to grant or refuse an interlocutory injunction disposes finally of the case, we will have established the legitimacy of this procedure as a method for final adjudication. (Zuckerman, 1995:178–9)

Applying the same logic, if it can be demonstrated that reapplications or further submissions function to reverse the Commission's decision not to refer a case back to the Court, these procedures can be regarded as legitimate. However, this must be weighed against the time and resources committed by the Commission to provide such procedures. Further submissions and reapplications invariably prolong the review process; if empirical evidence suggests that they do not offer any substantial practical benefits, the Commission's current decision field could be called into question.

---

[17] The Commission defines persistent applicants as those 'whose case has been turned down, which raises nothing relevant in addition to the issues that have already been considered by the Commission, or is otherwise inappropriate' (Criminal Cases Review Commission, 2016e:para:3).

Reapplications

Reapplications essentially ask the Commission to reopen cases in which it had reached a final decision not to make a reference to the Court. Exceptions are reapplications after the Commission had originally made a reference to the Court, but the Court upheld the conviction. In these cases, applicants can reapply to the Commission in the hope that the Commission will find further reasons to doubt the safety of their convictions and once again refer their cases back to the Court. In our purposive sample, we found three such examples: cases EE29b,[18] EE32b,[19] and EE33b.[20] The Commission screens in reapplications for a full review when they raise new issues not considered at appeal or during the Commission's previous reviews (Criminal Cases Review Commission, 2013e). Reapplications may relate to a new piece of evidence discovered after the Commission had reached its decision; the publication of a new report, or a change in law that may impact on the safety of the applicant's convictions. The review of reapplications sometimes leads to the discovery of errors by the Commission, or a failure to investigate certain issues during the previous review.

Administrative data from 2005–14 show that the number of reapplications increased dramatically between 2005 and 2007, from 35 to 124.[21] The increase most likely reflects the growing cumulative number of applications reviewed by the Commission since its establishment. The reapplication figures have remained steady since 2007, averaging between 100 and 130 cases per year. Reapplications make up roughly 14 per cent of all applications (2005–14). At stage one, reapplications have approximately a 40 per cent chance of getting through to stage two review (2005–14). In comparison, first time applicants have a 53 per cent chance of getting through to stage two review (2005–14). Therefore, while the Commission's policy does not limit the number of reapplications that applicants can submit (Criminal Cases Review Commission, 2016e:para:8), the majority of reapplication cases are screened out without a full review. In practice, the use of the screening process is an example of 'procedural rationing' (Zuckerman, 1995). Seven per cent of reapplications that reach stage two are referred.[22] In comparison, first-time applications have a 2 per cent referral rate.[23] This means that if reapplication cases are screened in at stage two, they are more than three times as likely as first-time applicants to be referred back to the Court. However, the administrative data does not include information on the proportion of these reapplication-referrals that the Court found to be unsafe.

---

[18] The Commission did not refer the reapplication of case EE29b because while it was reviewing the reapplication, the applicant admitted to the offence and so the case was closed.

[19] Following a judicial review, the Commission referred case EE32a but the Court upheld the conviction. The applicant made three reapplications (EE32b,c,&d) but the Commission did not exercise its discretion to refer the case back to the Court a second time. The subsequent reviews did not find any new argument or evidence that was not deliberated at trial, appeal, or in the previous referral.

[20] The Commission referred case EE33a but exercised its discretion not to refer in two subsequent reapplications (EE33b&c) though it took a considerable amount of time to reach this decision for the final reapplication. Here we saw evidence of a thorough investigation of many of the issues that had been dealt with in the previous applications but also an overly cautious CRM who appeared to be overwhelmed by the responsibility of closing down the case. Indeed, our analysis of the case record suggests an increasingly unconfident CRM at work. This was clearly a borderline case and we believe that had it not already been before the Court, this CRM would have been minded to refer at this stage, suggesting, perhaps, a somewhat deferential approach to the Court.

[21] The administrative data covered the period between 1 January 2005 and 31 December 2014. The following analysis excludes magistrates court cases, Court Martial cases, and applicants who only wanted their sentence reviewed.

[22] This excludes reapplication cases, which were rejected at stage one.

[23] This excludes first-time applications, which were rejected at stage one.

In our purposive sample, there were nineteen applicants who reapplied to the Commission (between them, they submitted forty-five applications in total). One applicant applied to the Commission four times, five applicants applied three times, and the remaining applicants applied twice. The Commission maintained its original decision not to make a reference to the Court in subsequent applications for six of these nineteen applicants.[24] However, it changed its mind in thirteen cases (Table 13.1): in ten cases it changed from a decision not to refer in the first application to a referral in the reapplication;[25] while for three applicants a decision to refer convictions in the first application (which were upheld by the Court) was replaced by a decision not to refer at reapplication.[26] In the former scenario (from a non-referral decision to a referral), the Court quashed the convictions for six applicants, and upheld the convictions for four applicants.

Further submissions

Drawing on the same administrative data analysed in the previous section, we found that for cases where the Commission reached a provisional decision not to refer convictions back to the Court (2,975 cases), approximately half (49 per cent) of applicants or their representatives prepared further submissions (2005–14).[27] However, in only in 0.7 per cent of the cases (ten cases) where the Commission received further submissions did the provisional decision not to refer the case back to the Court change to a final decision to refer. Before we proceed further with our analysis of this significant finding, we must express some caution over the validity of the administrative data. The Commission collects information concerning applicants' or their legal representatives' responses to provisional decisions not to make a reference, but not all responses are entered onto the database.[28]

We decided, therefore, to review our purposive sample to examine whether it revealed a similar pattern for cases that had proceeded to stage two review. In approximately half of our cases, the applicants or their representatives responded with further submissions, a similar proportion to those in the administrative dataset. In six of these cases, the Commission changed the provisional decision *not* to make a reference to a decision to refer the convictions.[29] While this is a much higher rate of cases in which the Commission changed its mind—likely because our purposive sampling method had produced a database of somewhat complex cases—the difference between the

[24] They are cases HIA10a&b, EE35a&b, EE6a&b, PI15a&b, PI18a,b,&c, PI19a&b (Table 13.1).
[25] They are cases HIA3a&b, CS14a&b, CS6a&b, EE22a&b, EE38a,b,&c, EE14a,b,&c, EE26a,b,&c, EE11a&b, EE19a&b, and EE37a&b (Table 13.1).
[26] They are cases EE32a,b,c,&d, EE33a,b,&c, and EE29a&b (Table 13.1).
[27] The 2,975 cases for which the Commission had reached a final decision excludes ineligible cases, and cases where there had been a clear error in data entry.
[28] To complicate matters further, we made certain assumptions about the data that might not be reliable in some cases. In particular, we assumed that in all cases where the Commission had recorded a response to its provisional decision not to make a reference, the applicant or legal representative had responded with further submissions. However, the Commission could not be absolutely sure about the consistency in data entry among administrative staff and suggested that some may have recorded a positive response following *any response* from applicants, including a simple acknowledgement of the Commission's provisional decision not to make a referral.
[29] The six cases are: PI3, CS3, CS4, CS5, EE28, and EE32. Note that CS3 and CS4 are linked cases.

findings are a matter of degree, and in both datasets, the Commission was persuaded to refer, having initially been disinclined, in only a handful of cases.

It appears that legal representatives were instrumental in persuading the Commission to change its final decision in five cases within our purposive sample. In cases CS3 and CS4 ('linked' cases in which the applicants were co-defendants), the legal representative persuaded the Commission to review a particular file that contained damaging information about the complainant's credibility, which led to the cases being referred (see Chapter 8 on cases CS3 and CS4). Before the Commission looked into the complainant's credibility, it treated these cases as borderline cases. The Commission had identified deficiencies in the trial judge's summing up but considered this point did 'not merit a reference on its own' and felt that the case would be strengthened 'if additional grounds were available' (Cases 3 and 4, Case Committee Minutes). These additional grounds were found within the file that the legal representative brought to the attention of the Commission.

Similarly, in case CS5, even though the applicant had raised concerns about the reliability of the complainant, no public records had been sought. The applicant's legal representatives asked the Commission to look into the complainant's previous false allegations, which resulted in the Commission making a referral (see Chapter 8). In case EE28, the legal representative persuaded the Commission that it should refer all of the applicant's convictions, rather than treating them as independent of each other. The Commission took this advice and referred the case:

The Commission has misunderstood the issue in relation to the linkage between counts 1–4 and the potential knock-on effect that an acquittal or quashing on count 1 would have on counts 2–4. (EE28, Statement of Reasons)

In cases EE32a and EE32b, the legal representatives and the applicant both communicated frequently with the Commission throughout the review. When the Commission reached a provisional decision not to make a reference (EE32a), the decision was judicially reviewed. Eventually, the Commission's re-investigation led to a referral (EE32b).

Finally, in case PI3, the applicant was convicted of sexually assaulting his child. While the complainant (the applicant's child) denied retracting her allegation when interviewed, interviews with the complainant's friends and acquaintances portrayed the complainant as a liar. When the Commission reached a provisional decision not to refer, the legal representatives were persuasive in reminding the Commission that it must not usurp the Court's role in determining the safety of the conviction. They argued that only the Court can assess the evidence and that they can only do so having received it. Based on the legal representative's submission, the committee—while noting that 'the decision whether or not to refer this case remains finely balanced' (PI3, Case Committee Minutes)—decided to refer. The case committee minutes state 'looking at the evidence as a whole, and in light of the first set of [further] submissions received, this case should now be referred back to the Court of Appeal'.

Although persuasive further submissions by legal representatives had brought about a different result at the Commission in a minority of cases, the Court quashed the conviction in only one (case CS5) (in case EE28, the Court quashed only some of

Table 13.1 Reapplications: purposive sample

Case reference	Year of application	Commission's final decision	Court's judgment
HIA3a	2003	Non-referral	Upheld
HIA3b	2007	Referral	
CS14a	2006	Non-referral	Upheld
CS14b	2009	Referral	
EE22a	1997	Non-referral	Upheld
EE22b	2007	Referral	
EE38a	1998	Non-referral	Upheld
EE38b	2005	Non-referral	
EE38c	2011	Referral	
CS6a	2003	Non-referral	Quashed
CS6b	2003	Referral	
EE14a	1999	Non-referral	Quashed
EE14b	2002	Non-referral	
EE14c	2008	Referral	
EE26a	1998	Non-referral	Quashed
EE26b	2002	Non-referral	
EE26c	2010	Referral	
EE11a	1999	Non-referral	Quashed
EE11b	2002	Referral	
EE19a	2007	Non-referral	Quashed
EE19b	2008	Referral	
EE37a	2008	Non-referral	Quashed
EE37b	2011	Referral	
EE32a	1997	Referral	Upheld
EE32b	2002	Non-referral	
EE32c	2003	Non-referral	
EE32d	2007	Non-referral	
EE29a	2005	Referral	Upheld
EE29b	2011	Non-referral	
EE33a	1997	Referral	Upheld
EE33b	2003	Non-referral	
EE33c	2010	Non-referral	
HIA10a	2003	Non-referral	
HIA10b	2007	Non-referral	
EE35a	2000	Non-referral	
EE35b	2004	Non-referral	
EE6a	1999	Non-referral	
EE6b	2004	Non-referral	
PI15a	1999	Non-referral	
PI15b	2003	Non-referral	
PI18a	1997	Non-referral	

Table 13.1 *Continued*

Case reference	Year of application	Commission's final decision	Court's judgment
PI18b	2000	Non-referral	
PI18c	2009	Non-referral	
PI19a	2000	Non-referral	
PI19b	2009	Non-referral	

Note: The applicant in the case CS6a applied in 2002 but the Commission closed the case because his appeal was still pending; hence we have not included this case as a reapplication.

the convictions, rejecting the argument that by undermining the safety of some, the Commission had rendered unsafe all convictions). These cases may have been borderline cases that could either have been a referral or a non-referral. The change in the Commission's opinion could suggest that the legal representatives pushed them towards a referral. These cases might also reflect particularly tenacious and skilled legal representatives, appraising the Commission' application of the real possibility test, and causing it to be more liberal in its interpretation.

This finding lends some limited support for the research by Hodgson and Horne (2009), which first showed the positive impact of legal representation on the outcome of applications (see also, Scottish Criminal Cases Review Commission, 2010). While we saw little difference in the proportion of applicants with and without legal representation that submitted further submissions,[30] our findings suggest that the quality of further submissions is key—or that the Commission takes more seriously further submissions from legal representatives.[31]

While we saw examples of effective legal representation, our qualitative analysis showed that occasionally legal representatives served only to prolong the review process. Cases HIA10 and CS15 are two such examples. In HIA10, the legal representative wrote to the Commission shortly after receiving the Provisional Statement of Reasons ('SOR'), and asked for an extension of 3.5 months, suggesting that 'there was much that was wrong' with the Provisional SOR (Box 13.1). The CRM agreed to the extension, but one day before the deadline, the legal representative asked for another two months' extension. The CRM was reluctant but again agreed, recording in the case record that otherwise 'in truth, we could end up with a messy spat' (Box 13.1). Ten days after the second extension had passed, the legal representative wrote to the Commission stating that he would not be sending any further submissions.

The extensions provided in case HIA10 go well beyond what is suggested in the Commission's policy, as explained in the previous section. The current and previous formal policies make clear that delays should not be tolerated as they cause injustice to other applicants. However, the CRM in this case did not frame his response

[30] Legally represented applicants responded to further submission in 51 per cent of provisional decisions not to make a referral in comparison to 48 per cent for applicants with no representation.

[31] Further submissions, and reapplications, work by shifting the onus onto applicants; they must demonstrate that the Commission's provisional or final decisions are wrong. This means that applicants without legal representation could be at a disadvantage, as they may not be able effectively to challenge the Commission's provisional decision not to make a reference to the Court.

Box 13.1 Extension of time on further submissions

HIA10 Case Record

24 Jan 2006: [Provisional SOR] sent out with proposed return date 24/2/06.

 27 Jan 2006: Letter from [legal representative], 26/1/06. **Request extension to 13/4/ 06** … [Legal representative] rang to ask 'who was the author of the report?' … I told [names of commissioners] were involved in the decision/Provisional SOR. [Legal representative] suggested that **there was much that was wrong with the Provisional SOR** and that he needed time. **I agreed to requested extension until 13/4/2006.** Letter of confirmation sent.

 13 April 2006: Letter from [legal representative] 12/4/06. **Extension requested to 16/6/ 06** … [Legal representative] tells me he has commissioned a report from an expert at [name of institution] to challenge [omitted] … He says he will only challenge one other issue, the question of [omitted]. He accepts that if his report is not done by the next deadline he would have to go ahead without it. On this basis, I am inclined to accept his request to extend to June. **In truth, we could end up with a messy spat if we don't and we have waited so long now that another 2 months doesn't really matter.** Reply OK. Letter sent—**extension to 16/6/06 granted.**

 26 June 2006: Letter received from [legal representative] informing us that **he will not be submitting further reps [submissions], dated 22/6/06.**

 28 June 2006: Final SOR sent out to [applicant] and [legal representative].

Note: emphasis added.

(Hawkins, 2002) according to the 'field' as defined by the formal policy on further submissions. A smooth relationship with the legal representative—in the CRM's words, to avoid a 'messy spat' (Box 13.1)—seemed to be more relevant to decision-making. When the legal representative asked for a second extension, the CRM wrote in the case record that 'we have waited so long now that another 2 months doesn't really matter' (Box 13.1). This demonstrates an applicant-centred decision frame that is tolerant and used to delay. In the previous chapter, we illustrated the Commission's cultural shift from thoroughness to efficiency that came around 2006, which puts case HIA10 on the cusp of transition and may explain the decision frame we see here: that is, not yet on board with the Commission's new organizational commitment to efficiency.

In the more recent (2012) case (CS15), the legal representative twice asked for—and was granted—extensions by the Commission, but produced no further submissions (CS15, Case Record). The Commission chased the legal representative after the second deadline had passed. The legal representative contacted the Commission two days after it had sent the final SOR. While the applicant in this case was at liberty, three months had passed during this period. Here, we identified a greater sense of urgency and a clearer organizational decision frame at work; the Commission sent out chasers to the legal representative and decided to send the final SOR without giving further extensions.

Administrative data further suggest a change in the organizational culture away from a rather tolerant approach to further submissions towards a focus on efficiency for the sake of the organization and other applicants waiting for a review. The average number of months spent on further submissions (the period between the Provisional SOR and the final SOR) decreased as the Commission worked to improve efficiency.

In 2005, the mean average time spent on further submissions was 2.9 months, but by 2014, this had almost halved to 1.5 months.

In the previous chapter, we argued that while the culture of the Commission shifted towards a desire for efficiency, with staff being more concerned about delays, the fear of judicial review (discussed in more detail below) militated against the emerging organizational commitment to efficiency. Hence, in many cases, the Commission is generous when legal representatives ask for extensions. Requests for extension of deadlines tend to be made immediately before a deadline expires, as seen in case HIA10 (Table 13.1), and the Commission regularly grants a further twenty working days. We only encountered one instance (EE35a) in our purposive sample when a second extension was refused.

The Commission's refusal to allow a second extension for further submissions led to a reapplication (EE35b), but at that stage the Commission came to the same conclusion that the case should not be referred back to the Court. This time, however, the legal representative became frustrated with the Commission's slow response to their further submissions. When the Commission sent a Provisional SOR in January 2006, the legal representative sent in further submissions in mid-March 2006. The CRM felt that it was not possible to prepare a response to the further submissions by the end of March, when a case committee was scheduled, as this entry in the case record shows:

Owing to pressure of other work and the fact that addressing the further reps will require me to go back through a fairly large amount of material, I have asked [management] if it is possible to put back the final committee by a couple of weeks. Unfortunately, the first available date after 27th March is 9th May. Discussed this with [commissioner] who agreed that the committee could be put back to this date. (EE35b, Case Record)

The legal representative expressed displeasure at the delay in the committee date and pointed out that it was unfair to expect further submissions by a certain date while the Commission had discretion to delay a response to further submissions by a further two months. The Commission disagreed, taking the view that while it was 'unfortunate that there is a delay', the CRM needed 'time to research the further reps', and the Commission 'would have given them [legal representatives] as much time as they needed' (EE35b, Case Record).[32] The legal representative also questioned the Commission on the reasonableness of the delay when the applicant was in custody. The CRM replied that 'it wasn't ideal … [but] it wasn't unusual for people to have to wait until commissioners could be brought together' (EE35b, Case Record).[33] This example again demonstrates the tension played out in the previous chapter between efficiency and thoroughness, and the difficulty in deciding when to conclude post-decision decision-making.

In summary, further submissions have the effect of reversing the Commission's provisional decision not to make a reference to the Court in only a small minority of cases. In our purposive sample, there was only one case in which the Commissions' revised decision to refer, as a result of further submissions, led to the conviction being quashed by the Court. While for that particular applicant, this was, of course, a wonderful outcome, further submissions can prolong the duration of the review, which takes time

[32] The formal policy on further submissions does not allow legal representatives indefinite time to make further submissions.
[33] See also Chapter 12 concerning the difficulty of arranging case committee meetings due to the rise in the number of part-time commissioners.

from other applicants. In this sense, further submissions do not provide convincing evidence to demonstrate empirical legitimacy in Zuckerman's (1995) terms.

Repeated reapplications consume the Commission's time and other resources. The formal policy generously allows multiple reapplications from applicants, but, in practice, the screening process significantly reduces the number of reapplications that are given a full review. However, once the application reaches stage two review, reapplications are more likely to be referred. Our review of reapplications in our purposive sample also showed that in cases where the Commission changed its decision from a non-referral to a referral, the Court quashed the convictions in half of its referrals. In this sense, the evidence supports the empirical legitimacy of the Commission's reapplication system. In the following section, we explore the drivers of the Commission's policy and practice on further submissions and reapplications, and the theoretical justifications for these procedures.

Instrumental Decision-making

So far, we have drawn on Zuckerman's (1995) concept of procedural rationing to determine whether further submissions and reapplications, which invariably interrupt the pursuit of finality, can be justified. Our analysis showed that, in practice, the Commission can be fairly generous in providing extensions of time to receive further submissions from applicants and their legal representatives. From an instrumental approach, our empirical data showed that while reapplications can sometimes be effective, there was little evidence to support the need for further submissions in terms of their impact on case outcome.

Given that we could find little outcome-based legitimacy in providing further submissions, why does the Commission retain such a procedure? Hawkins (2002:32) rejects the claim that cases are purely determined on merit 'independently of wider forces and constraints', and argues that decision-making often results in cases being determined in the context of other decisions or hypothesized issues. In Chapter 12, we found that the possibility of being judicially reviewed may prevent the Commission from becoming a truly efficient organization. It follows that the risk of being judicially reviewed may influence the Commission's generous approach to further submissions and extensions of deadlines, which is a separate matter from any benefits in terms of fair and just outcomes.

Applicants can commence proceedings in the Administrative Court for judicial review of an action or decision taken by the Commission in respect of their application (Criminal Cases Review Commission, 2016d:para:1). Proceedings for a judicial review may be issued during the course of the review, after a final decision has been taken, or on refusal by the Commission to accept a reapplication (Criminal Cases Review Commission, 2016d:para:4). Following a successful judicial review, the Administrative Court can require the Commission to subject the case to a further review. The Commission can avoid litigation by deciding that the challenge should be conceded (Criminal Cases Review Commission, 2016d:para:12). If conceded, the Commission decides the type of additional work it should carry out. It therefore has discretion in deciding how to respond to judicial review.

On average, the Commission receives twenty-seven challenges a year to its investigations or decisions (2007–16).[34] Its policy on judicial review is to try 'wherever

---

[34] According to Annual Reports from 2007 to 2016, the number of challenges has ranged from twenty-one (2008/09, 2010/11, and 2015/16) to thirty-four (2012/13 and 2016/17).

possible to avoid the need for court action' and choose to 'simply concede' whenever a challenge raises a point with sufficient merit (Criminal Cases Review Commission, 2016a). The Commission believes—rightly in our view—that the interest of applicants is served by spending its resources 'reviewing cases [rather] than contesting expensive litigation' (Criminal Cases Review Commission, 2016a).[35] Preventing litigation is also in the Commission's best interest because the costs of judicial reviews are not only financial but also reputational. The Casework Guidance Note on judicial review states that:

A successful judicial review indicates that we [the Commission] got something wrong. This could affect our general reputation and affect our credibility with the judiciary, the media, the public, legal representatives and our applicants. (Criminal Cases Review Commission, 2011i:para:77)

While the majority of applications for judicial review challenge the Commission's final decision not to refer the case back to the Court, the Commission's interim decisions, including how it handles further submissions and the Provisional SOR, have also been subject to judicial review (Criminal Cases Review Commission, 2011i:paras:83–5). Therefore, the Commission's generous approach to further submissions could be one of the various practices that allow for inefficiencies in case review in order to reduce the risk of judicial review.

The example in the previous section (Box 13.1) shows the CRM accepting a second extension for a further submission from the legal representative, a decision that may have been influenced by fear of judicial review, given the case record reference to avoiding 'a messy spat' (HIA10). In another case (EE35a), after having dealt with the legal representative's numerous further submissions and after the final SOR had been sent, the Commission continued to respond to further submissions. A commissioner not directly involved in the case declared this to be 'an illogical decision and a waste of [the Commission's] resources' (EE35a, Case Record). However, the same commissioner made clear that if the Commission had been judicially reviewed, it 'might well have conceded' (EE35a, Case Record).

Furthermore, the fear of judicial review prompted the Commission in case EE35a to invite the applicant to reapply. In the reapplication, the screening commissioner came to the conclusion that 'it is difficult to see much that is new' (EE35b, Case Record), but did not exercise his discretion to screen out the reapplication.[36] Instead, he advised that 'an experienced CRM' should look into the case (EE35b, Case Record). Having familiarized herself with the case, the CRM recorded the following:

The current application is exactly the same as the issues raised previously and also includes criticisms of the way the [Commission] conducted the previous review. It appears that the application was made after [commissioner] suggested (following lengthy post closure correspondences) that they make a fresh application so that a 'fresh pair of eyes' could look at the case—even though the issue they were raising in respect of contacting [expert] had been dealt with numerous times both in the SOR and in correspondence. I was concerned that I was rather backed

---

[35] Even though the Commission has so far only lost one case (*R (on the application of Farnell)* [2003] EWHC 835 Admin), the cost to the Commission was in excess of £75,000 for a one-day hearing (Criminal Cases Review Commission, 2011i:para:78). This is a considerable sum for an increasingly under-resourced organization and most other applicants waiting in the queue would not likely find this to be money well spent.

[36] When case EE35b reached the Commission in 2004, the screening commissioners had discretion to screen out reapplications. Under the current formal policy, a CRM determines whether a reapplication raises new issues. If the CRM does not find anything new, the case will be screened out with the approval of a commissioner (Criminal Cases Review Commission, 2013e).

into a corner in respect of conducting a second review on the same issues after they were effectively invited to make a fresh application. (EE35b, Case Record)

Accommodating the legal representative's demands in cases EE35a&b demonstrates commissioners and CRMs framing their decisions in light of the risk of judicial review, rather than on the merits of the case.[37] In other words, a different type of 'instrumental frame' (Hawkins, 2002) is at work. Adopting Zuckerman's instrumental approach, we may focus on the benefits of identifying a wrongful conviction. According to the screening commissioner's and the CRM's evaluation in case EE35b, there was no instrumental justification for allowing further submissions leading to a reapplication for the purpose of correcting a miscarriage of justice. However, from the perspective of avoiding judicial review, it may have been instrumental to yield to the legal representative's requests in order to protect the Commission's reputation.[38] It is also possible to argue that it was an instrumental decision in the interest of other applicants, as defending a judicial review would have been time-consuming and costly.

As noted above, adopting Zuckerman's instrumental approach to evaluating further submissions and reapplications would lead us to focus on the efficacy of processes and decisions regarding the appropriate referral of cases to the Court (just 0.8 per cent of applications) (Criminal Cases Review Commission, 2017a:14). But this does not speak to the experiences of the overwhelming majority of applicants (99 per cent) whose cases are not referred. Zuckerman's analytical framework does not provide scope for understanding the value of further submissions and reapplications to applicants whose cases are turned down by the Commission. Applicants who have not had their case referred to the Court are likely to be disappointed. They will have waited for months, often years, and yet find themselves in the same situation they were in on the day they applied. They may believe that the Commission has not dealt with their case appropriately or devoted insufficient resources to the review. The Commission tends to interpret applicants' decisions to judicially review as an emotional reaction to their cases being rejected. Indeed, it suggests that 'the majority of applicants for judicial review amount to little more than an attack on our decision not to refer' (Criminal Cases Review Commission, 2011i:para:83).

An undesired outcome, however, may not be the only predictor for judicial review. Procedural justice theory, grounded in social psychology, asserts that perception of *outcome* fairness is not the only determinant of institutional legitimacy. It argues that perceived *procedural* fairness is an important concept in achieving legitimacy, compliance, and cooperation with organizations. There is now a substantial body of research demonstrating that procedural fairness on the part of the police improves citizens' perceptions of legitimacy, and promotes both compliance with the law and cooperation with justice officials (e.g. Jackson et al., 2012; Tyler, 2006, 2011; Tyler and Huo, 2002). Procedural fairness involves: treating people with dignity and respect; listening

---

[37] The Commission agreed to contact the expert who gave evidence at trial, something which the legal representative had been urging the Commission to do since the previous application. The expert stood by his opinion at trial and the other investigations similarly failed to provide sufficient information to raise a real possibility that the Court would quash the applicant's conviction. With a persistent legal representative, and under threat of judicial review, a whole new review had been conducted, repeating much of the work which had already been done. There is probably a fine line between thorough and protracted reviews, with commissioners and legal representatives demarcating the boundary differently. In this case, the legal representative set the boundaries for the review.

[38] While in some cases (such as case EE35a), there may be a conflict between the need to refer genuine miscarriages of justice and the need to avoid judicial review, in other cases the Commission's awareness of judicial review serves to ensure that decision-making is of high quality.

to them and giving them a 'voice' (letting them have their say); and acting legally, sticking to regulations, avoiding corruption. According to this theory, if applicants and their legal representatives see the Commission as procedurally fair, even in cases where the outcome is a decision not to refer, the Commission's perceived legitimacy could remain intact.

In this regard, the opportunity to be able to engage in further submissions or re-applications, even though these procedures may not be of any instrumental benefit to case outcome, could help maintain the perceived legitimacy of the Commission in the eyes of applicants and even their representatives. As a result, the Commission's decisions may be less likely to be contested. If we shift our focus away from the goal of the applicant—to have his or her case referred back to the Court—and towards the bulk of the Commission's cases, we recognize that it is not an organization defined by its ability to refer cases. It is an organization that deals primarily with closure. In this sense, investing time and effort in providing procedural justice to applicants whose cases are turned down could be just as important, if not more so, than investing its resources on successful outcomes for a very few. It should be stressed, however, that this argument assumes that the Commission's current referral rate *accurately* reflects the proportion of cases that present a real possibility that the Court would find the conviction to be unsafe. If the referral rate greatly underrepresents the proportion of possibly unsafe convictions, treating applicants whose cases have been turned down with care may be merely a strategy to make tolerable the Commission's failure to scrutinize and respond effectively to wrongful convictions.

Recognizing the importance of fairness towards applicants whose cases are turned down by the Commission does not change the Commission's existing organizational purposes. Of course, 'bring[ing] justice to the wrongly convicted by referring cases to the appellate courts' (Criminal Cases Review Commission, 2017a) is one of the Commission's stated purposes. Equally, there is a focus on treating *all* applicants 'with courtesy, respect and consideration' and 'inspir[ing] confidence in the integrity of the criminal justice process' (Criminal Cases Review Commission, 2017a). These goals reflect a concern with procedural justice. Indeed, the following quotation suggests that the Commission recognizes that it is able to provide a sense of justice for the many who do not get another chance in Court:

> We do sometimes get letters from applicants whose applications have been refused, thanking us for doing such a thorough job. Sometimes it is the first written explanation they will have received about why they were convicted and why their conviction cannot be challenged. Counsel's advice on appeal can be notoriously brief. (Criminal Cases Review Commission, 2011i:para:54)

As the previous chapter showed, some staff at the Commission felt the statements of reasons were too long and detailed: an anxious 'parade of knowledge' (#69) written for the Court and to protect the Commission from judicial reviews (Chapter 12). However, the quotation above shows that some applicants may benefit from these detailed responses to their applications.

That said, there may be a need to reconsider the way in which current statements of reasons are written. The Commission introduced a simplified application form referred to as the 'Easy Read Form'[39] to reach out to vulnerable applicants (see Chapters 2 and 6). If the Commission considered some applicants unable to complete the previous application form properly, without assistance, it would be wrong to assume that they

---

[39] The Easy Read Form is available from: http://www.ccrc.gov.uk/app/uploads/2015/01/CCRC-Application-form-2016.pdf.

would fully understand the existing statements of reasons. Having widened *access* to the Commission (by way of an 'Easy Read Form'), the Commission now needs to tackle the way that it handles *closure*, if it wants to make sure that applicants who are turned down are satisfied and not further alienated from the criminal justice system. In addition, the legal aid cuts and the difficulty for applicants to secure (good) legal representation mean that the Commission cannot always rely on legal representatives to explain the SOR to applicants. This is not only intrinsically important for applicants but also instrumentally important in order to achieve the above stated organizational purpose of treating all applicants with respect, and to inspire confidence in the criminal justice process.

We do not know whether the current practices around reapplications and further submissions make applicants and their legal representatives feel that they have had a 'voice' in the review process, and that these procedures enhance the perceived legitimacy of the Commission. The formal polices of the Commission reflect some procedural justice ideals, but there is no data, specific to further submissions and reapplications, to demonstrate that these procedures enhance legitimacy. We do not know if the practice of further submissions per se contributes to the perceived legitimacy of the Commission or whether accepting submissions *during* the review and showing that the Commission is willing to communicate with applicants and their legal representatives is enough to maintain its legitimacy. Future research could shed light on this.

Redefining the Relevant Issues

The previous sections examined how the Commission constructs the 'field' (Hawkins, 2002)—the organizationally defined setting in which decisions are made—on further submissions and reapplications. We analysed the empirical and theoretical drivers that underpin the Commission's decision field. In this section, we turn to decision-making at the case level, examining how in certain further submissions and reapplications the cases are redefined, leading the Commission to reach a different outcome. The process of 'framing' (Hawkins, 2002) describes how facts or features in a case are understood and interpreted by decision-makers. Hawkins describes the fluidity of frames as follows:

> Frames are always contingent, and there is always room for negotiation and redefinition within a frame. Once something is keyed, it can be transformed or rekeyed, and new meaning will appear ... Rekeying has fundamental implications for the meaning of the outcome of the dispute, for a change in meaning means a change in locus, scope and consequences, and quite possibly the degree of formality used to produce a decision. (Hawkins, 2002:55)

In some cases, the 'rekeying'—the resultant reinterpretation of existing facts or the selection of different facts—changes the Commission's decision from a non-referral to a referral. We examine the cases in which further submissions or reapplications provided 'a new basis for defining new material as relevant' (Hawkins, 2002:55), and identify the new 'frames' that made the redefining of facts and issues possible.

Developments in the surround

A change in the 'surround' (Hawkins, 2002)—such as a new scientific discovery or a change in law—is beyond the Commission's influence. When events that are outside the control of the Commission take place after a case is turned down, a reapplication provides decision-makers with an opportunity to redefine the relevant facts of, and concerns about the case. In case EE6a, the applicant applied to the Commission without having appealed his conviction to the Court. He had been convicted of murdering his partner's infant child. At trial, seven medical experts agreed that the child's death was not due to sudden infant death syndrome (see Chapter 7) but disagreed as to whether the child's death was caused by injuries as inflicted by the applicant, or by a respiratory infection. The application, in 1999, was 'dealt with summarily' as a no-appeal case and turned down without a full review (EE6b, Case Record). While the Commission can choose to exercise its discretion to make a reference under exceptional circumstances (section 13 of the Criminal Appeal Act 1995; see also Chapter 3), the Commission screens out 'no-appeal' cases regularly without a full review (Chapter 6).

The case was picked up again in 2004 on reapplication. The Commission invited the applicant to reapply (EE6b, Case Record) following the *Cannings* judgment in 2002 and the order from the Attorney General to review all infant death convictions in the last ten years.[40] The *Cannings* judgment argues that if the outcome of the trial depends exclusively or almost exclusively on a serious disagreement between distinguished and reputable experts, it would be unwise and therefore unsafe to proceed. This case provides an example of the change in the 'surround' providing the Commission with a new legal 'frame' to interpret the infant death. However, in the event, the change in the frame did not result in a change in outcome; the Commission's investigation found that the *Cannings* judgment was not applicable to case EE6b, and it decided not to make a reference to the Court.

The Commission screened out case EE11a in 1999, writing to the applicant that it was 'unable to give further consideration to your case as you have not appealed' (EE11b, Statement of Reasons). The applicant reapplied in 2002, following an unsuccessful direct appeal (EE11b) and in 2008, the Commission referred the applicant's convictions for sexual offences[41] on the basis of new medical evidence (EE11b, Statement of Reasons) and the Court quashed his convictions in 2009.

The medical evidence relied on the findings from a report on *The Physical Signs of Child Sexual Abuse* by the Royal College of Paediatrics and Child Health ('RCPCH report'[42]), published in 2008.[43] At the time of the reapplication, case EE11b was prioritized due to the applicant being in custody. However, after the applicant's release from prison in 2003, he no longer met priority criteria; therefore, the CRM did not start work on the case until 2005. The delay was fortuitous as the Commission was able to utilize the findings from the RCPCH report in making a reference to the Court. Once again, the development in the 'surround'—publication of the RCPCH report—provided the Commission with a new scientific 'frame' within which to re-examine the validity of the expert's evidence at trial. What the expert considered as 'signs of anal abuse' was redefined, in light of the new frame, as 'no longer sustainable' (EE11b, Statement of Reasons). The Court in 2009 quashed the applicant's convictions, ten years after the applicant had first applied to the Commission.

However, a careful reading of the Commission's investigation shows that it may have been able to refer the applicant's conviction when he first applied. In his original

[40] *Cannings* [2004] EWCA Crim 1.
[41] The applicant was convicted on seven counts of indecency with a child, two counts of indecent assault, and one count of rape.
[42] The RCPCH report was updated in 2015. The updated report is available from: https://www.rcpch.ac.uk/physical-signs-child-sexual-abuse.
[43] See Chapter 7 regarding the significance of the RCPCH report in other cases.

application in 1999, he had already asked the Commission to examine the medical evidence.[44] The Commission's investigation—in the reapplication—showed that the trial expert's evidence 'was not consistent with mainstream opinion, either *at the time of trial* or now' (EE11b, Case Committee Minutes; emphasis added). In addition, the Commission also found that the expert's evidence presented at trial was 'significantly different from [the expert's] witness statement and capable of misleading the jury' (EE11b, Case Committee Minutes). The publication of the RCPCH report certainly strengthened the Commission's hand in persuading the Court that the trial expert's evidence was unreliable, but our analysis suggests that even without the new report, the Commission might have found a real possibility that the conviction was unsafe. In the first application, there was persuasive evidence to suggest that a referral under the exceptional circumstances was possible. In other words, the applicant presented the Commission with a submission that could have redefined the trial expert's evidence, but the Commission paid more attention to the fact that the applicant had not appealed. Hence, an internal frame, which regularly leads to the rejection of 'no-appeal' cases, was dominant in guiding decision-making in case EE11a. Once the 'no-appeal' frame was no longer in play in the reapplication, the Commission was able to apply a separate frame informed by the development in the surround that led to the applicant's convictions being quashed.

Internal factors: same facts, different decision

While external factors can trigger the redefining of evidence, internal factors—matters within the Commission's control—sometimes have the effect of reversing a previous decision not to make a reference. In these cases, the discovery of the Commission's errors or failures to investigate certain issues may come to light as a result of a new policy on specific cases, or a new pair of eyes.

In case EE14c, a third application from an applicant convicted of anal rape and three counts of indecent assault, the screening commissioner realized that the Commission had made an error in reviewing two previous applications (cases EE14a&b). A letter from the applicant's grandfather in 2008 prompted the screening commissioner to enter the following in the case record:

This case is a cause for concern. On reviewing the earlier [Statement of Reasons] and my own previous decision in 2002, I believe that we accepted the medical evidence at trial on signs of sexual abuse without demur … I believe [the case should be prioritized] because of the age of the case and the fact that we did not recognise in 1999 or 2002 the potential weakness of the medical evidence. (EE14c, Case Record)[45]

In addition to this oversight, by the time of the third application in 2008, the Commission had learnt from its reviews of previous sexual offence cases: a different organizational frame was in place to review such cases (Chapter 8). Hence, the screening commissioner instructed that the 'standard checks' (EE14c, Case Record) be carried out to assess the credibility of the complainant. The development of the new organizational frame is clear from his statement: 'If this case had been received for the first time today we would have approached it somewhat differently' (EE14c, Case Record).

---

[44] The applicant argued in his original no-appeal application (EE11a) that at trial, the rape charge was changed to attempted rape, there was no medical evidence to support a rape charge, and the police were 'corrupt' (EE11b, Statement of Reasons).

[45] While the medical evidence was supportive of buggery, the medical evidence did not support penetrative vaginal intercourse.

While the credibility checks did not redefine the events, the Commission referred the convictions based on the new medical evidence, which suggested that the medical evidence relied on at trial was flawed. The Court quashed the convictions in 2010.

The Court quashed a conviction for rape in case EE26c,[46] based on a referral by the Commission. This was the applicant's third attempt after two unsuccessful applications. In each application, the applicant asked the Commission to conduct forensic testing on the victim's clothing. This was not done at the first and second applications. In the first application, the Commission assumed that any forensic testing would be unable to produce reliable evidence (EE26a, Statement of Reasons).[47] The second application again asked the Commission to carry out forensic testing on further items of clothing (EE26b, Statement of Reasons). The Commission treated this application as a simple rehashing of the issues raised in the first investigation, with the screening commissioner noting in the case record:

Application largely revisits matters raised on previous application with a slightly different spin ... forensic issue dealt with on first application. (EE26b, Case Record)

The CRM who reviewed the reapplication seemed to have followed the screening commissioner's interpretation of case EE26b, and managed to produce, and receive commissioner approval of, a Provisional SOR in just seventeen days. The final SOR concluded:

This was considered in the previous application ... Forensic tests were carried out on all the clothes seized,[48] but no DNA evidence found. The Commission does not arrange for reinvestigations of such matters on a purely speculative basis. (EE26b, Statement of Reasons)

The case seemed to be heading down the same path when a different commissioner screened the third application. This commissioner also considered that the application simply repeated the same grounds:

As with the previous reapplication, this one largely revisits matters raised on the original application with a slightly different spin. Nevertheless—and even though I'm not currently nearly as impressed by the new material as [legal representative] clearly is—the reapplication must be accepted. (EE26c, Case Record)

Despite the pessimistic tone of the screening commissioner in case EE26c, the Commission came to the decision to refer the case to the Court—fourteen years after the first application was received. First, the applicant's legal representative had commissioned forensic testing on the victim's clothing (which the Commission had refused to do in the two previous applications). Therefore, the third application included evidence which established the presence of DNA from an 'unknown male' on the victim's clothing. Second, the CRM allocated to case EE26c conducted a particularly thorough and open-minded review of the case. This led to further forensic testing to eliminate possible sources of the 'unknown male' DNA by excluding the victim's former partner and all the male police officers, witnesses, and scientists who were most likely to have had contact with the victim or her clothing. These two pieces of

---

[46] Case EE26c was also referred to in Chapter 7.
[47] In response to the applicant's request to have forensic testing, the Commission reviewed the medical experts' reports from the trial and responded: 'The Commission does not consider that further medical evidence will alter the position ... which has already been explored by a highly qualified medical professional' (EE26a, Statement of Reasons).
[48] The Commission found out that forensic tests were not carried out on all items of clothing (EE26c, Statement of Reasons).

forensic evidence underpinned the Commission's referral, and the Court quashed the applicant's conviction.

Hawkins (2002:56) argues that certain frames are more 'resistant to negotiation or change' especially if a case has been labelled in a certain way.[49] In cases EE26a,b,&c, we argue that the two screening commissioners (EE26b&c), and the CRM in case EE26b, were 'organizationally located decision-makers' (Hawkins, 2002:57), framing the reapplication from the perspective of pursuing efficiency. They all showed deference to, or complete trust, in previous reviews; and in the case of the CRM in case EE26b, a deference to the hierarchy within the Commission by following the screening commissioner's interpretation of the case. These organizational frames—defined by the pursuit for efficiency and a culture of deference—prevented the reviewers and decision-makers from recognizing the significance of forensic testing.

An interviewee described the review of reapplications in general as 'enormously difficult, people who just keep saying the same thing' (#8), which perhaps reflects how staff, including those involved in case EE26, view reapplications. It suggests pessimism concerning the merits of most reapplications, and trust in the thoroughness and the quality of Commission reviews. Reapplications provide the Commission with an opportunity to revisit cases as fresh applications, sometimes with a new review team, but—as discussed above—the Commission's policy restricts the acceptance of a reapplication to review only when potential new issues are identified. With an organizational frame that focuses on efficiency, any indication of a repeated ground may prevent the decision-maker from looking further. The case record entries of the two screening commissioners above show that they considered cases EE26b&c to be typical reapplications that raise no new issues. The CRM in the second application was deferential to the screening commissioner's analysis and uncritical of the review carried out in the first application, and framed the case as such, producing a SOR demonstrating limited review.

The reframing of the case was only possible because of the work carried out by the legal representatives, independent of the Commission. This work—along with the determination of the CRM in case EE26c not to let the screening commissioners' framing of the case as 'another repeat of points' influence his views—helped redefine the information. The Commission's SOR changed from viewing forensic testing as being unhelpful, to referring the conviction based on those very forensic tests.

The CRM who worked on the third application (EE26c) acknowledged that reviewing reapplications is a 'little uncomfortable' as it could potentially reveal something that may have gone wrong with the original review (Fieldwork Note, 25 May 2014). Case EE26c demonstrates that, even though all CRMs are trained and operate under the same decision field, their individual 'frames'—and differences in approach to case review—can lead to dissimilar conclusions. In fact, the legal representative in case EE26b had specifically requested that a different CRM work on the reapplication (EE26b, Case Record).[50] The Commission often allocates cases subject to judicial review to a different review team (Criminal Cases Review Commission, 2011i), but it does not have any formal policy for the allocation of a different screening commissioner or a different CRM for reapplications. Within our purposive example, we

---

[49] Hawkins (2002:56) argues that 'an event or matter framed by an inspector as "a bad case" is resistant to reframing, and much less likely to be reframed by the [principal investigator] whose task is to approve the recommendation for prosecution'.
[50] In this case, the Commission allocated a different CRM to review EE26b.

found four cases in which the same CRM was allocated to review the reapplication (HIA3a&b, EE38a&b, EE32a,b,&c, and EE29a&b).

Cases EE37b and EE38c provide further examples of a different review team reaching a different conclusion in reapplication cases. In case EE37a, the Commission concluded that 'there is no possibility that the Court of Appeal could be persuaded [by the expert's] new evidence' (EE37a, Statement of Reasons). However, upon reapplication, (EE37b), the same expert's report is used as the main reason for referral: '[new expert's] report provides a compelling evidential basis' (EE37b, Statement of Reasons). In this case, the same evidence and facts reviewed by a separate team brought about a different case outcome. It is possible that the case was borderline, and a different review team was more prepared to take a risk. However, in parallel, there may have been a different decision frame in operation. The fear of judicial review, which was settled in case EE37b, may have pushed the new review team towards a referral. Similarly, in case EE38c, the judicial review of the decision not to make a reference in case EE38b led to the Commission convening a fresh decision-making committee comprising of three commissioners who had not previously dealt with the applicant's case. Again, the new commissioners redefined the same evidence and facts and decided that the case should be referred back to the Court.

Finally, while the risk of judicial review may influence the Commission to refer a case, the Commission is reluctant to '*re*'-refer convictions that the Court had previously upheld. In cases EE32b,c,&d and EE33b&c, the Commission came to the decision not to make a second reference to the Court.[51] In case EE33c, the Court had upheld the conviction in 1995 and then again in 2000 when the Commission referred the applicant's conviction back to the Court. The Case Record highlights the Commission's cautious approach, stating that the case will:

> Need some careful analysis as to what is new and what is not and what extent, if at all, the [Court] can be properly asked to look at an issue again even though they appear to have ruled on it—and indeed whether we have dealt with the issue already in our last SOR. (EE33c, Case Record)

In case EE32d, the Commission was caught between two frames: the fear of judicial review and the fear of losing the Court's trust. The applicant had previously successfully judicially reviewed the Commission's decision not to make a reference, leading to the case later being referred. Perceiving the applicant to be difficult, the Commission agreed to review the application for a fourth time. However, the Commission was also aware that another referral might result in the Court losing trust in the Commission if it challenged the Court's decision again, unless there was a very strong case for a referral. These competing frames led the decision-makers to manage the case delicately: the Commission 'grudgingly' accepted the application with a view to carrying out a 'narrow' and 'concentrated' review based on the points raised by the applicant (EE32d, Case Record).

Second Chance at the 'Last Resort'

Further submissions and reapplications extend the review process, providing applicants with an opportunity to have their cases reconsidered. In theory, this second chance is

---

[51] We have not included case EE29b in this analysis due to the circumstance of this case. See footnote 18.

important. As the quote from the US Supreme Court at the beginning of this chapter illustrates, just because an institution has the final say, does not mean it is free from error. The Commission is intended to act as a safety net for people who have been wrongfully convicted, but it is not immune from error. In this sense, it is reasonable for the 'court of last resort' to ensure there are mechanisms to challenge its decisions.

Quantitative analysis showed that while the Commission's policy did not impose a limit on the number of reapplications an applicant can submit, it applied a rigorous filtering process at screening which significantly reduced the number of reapplications that were given a full review. However, reapplications that were given a full review were more likely to be referred than first-time applications. Our review of reapplications in our purposive sample, also showed that in cases where the Commission changed its decision from a non-referral to a referral, the Court quashed the convictions in half of its referrals. On the other hand, further submissions rarely reversed the Commission's provisional decision not to make a reference. Even when it did, the Court was often not persuaded by the Commission's referrals. In this sense, our evidence supports the empirical legitimacy (Zuckerman, 1995) of the Commission's reapplication system but not of further submissions.

The above analysis, which focuses on the very small percentage of applicants whose cases were referred back to the Court, does not take into consideration the benefits to the overwhelming majority of applicants whose cases are turned down by the Commission. Further submissions and reapplications may be important because they make applicants feel that they have a voice in the review process, and these processes could serve to improve or retain the perceived legitimacy of the Commission. This approach—informed by procedural justice theory—is intrinsically important for applicants so that the Commission can serve as an organization that provides closure in a respectful manner. It is also vital for instrumental reasons if further submissions and reapplications achieve the Commission's organizational purpose of treating all applicants with respect, and inspiring confidence in the criminal justice process. Future research could shed light on whether the Commission can be more robust in declining to accept further submissions without risking damage to its perceived legitimacy, taking into consideration that the reapplication procedure provides a safety net.

Organizational frames—defined by the pursuit of efficiency and a culture of deference—often prevented reviewers and decision-makers from reversing the Commission' original decision not to make a reference. However, when the Commission did reverse its original decision, it applied a different decision frame. Developments in the surround, such as changes in law and new scientific discoveries, provided the Commission with new frames to redefine facts or issues that originally contributed towards the conviction of the applicant. Reapplications, therefore, serve an important function in permitting adaptation to the changes that occur in the surround, which are beyond the Commission's control. Internal factors also shaped the outcome of the case. In some cases, the Commission simply overlooked certain issues or failed to investigate further by taking the judge's summing up at face value or being deferential to the Commission's previous review. However, even when the Commission did not find any errors in its previous review, in some cases it still decided to reverse its decision. In such cases, different CRMs and commissioners had reviewed the reapplication. It is possible that different decision-makers brought their own unique decision frames that viewed some aspects of the case as more salient than did the previous decision-makers. Equally, an organizational frame—defined by fear of judicial review—may have provided the extra push that was needed to persuade the Commission to make a reference to the Court in a few cases.

Either way, these cases demonstrate that even in cases where there are reasons to doubt the safety of a conviction, there can be a fine line between establishing a real possibility that the conviction is unsafe and turning the case down. Reapplications and further submissions can sometimes allow for a new pair of eyes to see something of potential, or reveal information that changes the Commission's mind on difficult cases. An interviewee made the following statement about the difficulty of applying the real possibility test, as well as the difficulty of deciding between finality and continuing with the investigation:

If an organization like … [the Commission] really sets its mind to it, is there any conviction that you couldn't render unsafe? If you really, really threw enough resource over a long enough period … (#25)

In this sense, finality must be provided not because the Commission can at some point be sure of its decision but simply to provide an end to the process.

14

Last Chance for Justice

Introduction

As the Criminal Cases Review Commission ('the Commission') celebrates its twenty-first anniversary, we can be in no doubt that it has come of age. Not only has it grown in confidence, established a stronger organizational structure, and honed its investigative skills since its inception, but it has—somewhat cautiously—begun to assert itself in the wider criminal justice system.

In the late 1990s, a few energetic young lawyers worked with little supervision in a flat organizational structure in this fledgling institution, set up—on the recommendation of the Royal Commission on Criminal Justice ('the Runciman Commission')—in the wake of widespread moral outrage over a series of notorious wrongful convictions that had marred the British justice system in the preceding decades (see Chapters 1 and 2). They set to work on some serious cases inherited from the government review department, the Criminal Case Unit of the C3 (Criminal Policy) Division, which had preceded it. These were cases that campaigners had thought would be the bread and butter of the new Commission's work: notorious wrongful convictions of people who many thought were factually innocent. Some were reasonably easy to refer: the products of appalling breaches of suspects' due process rights from a time when the system had fewer checks and balances. As time moved on, the more egregious cases of police and prosecution misconduct became less common, and instead the Commission was faced with applications from those who felt that lay witnesses had lied, or expert witnesses had been mistaken, basing their testimonies on science that was no longer considered to be reliable. Furthermore, with growing awareness of the Commission among appeal lawyers and lay persons, came increasing numbers of applications from those who had been convicted in the magistrates' courts of less serious offences, and from those who believed that while their conviction was safe, they had been unfairly or wrongfully sentenced. While the number of such applications remains relatively low, critics of the Commission expressed disquiet that the organization was using its valuable resources on cases that had not been a concern for the Runciman Commission.

The Commission evolved in response to increasing demand. Over the past decade, a more hierarchical management and administrative structure was imposed on case review managers ('CRMs'), and with it, increasing guidance for decision-makers with a view to encouraging a more standardized approach to case reviews. Alongside this increasing professionalization of the organization came a greater distance between the Commission and interested persons and bodies beyond its walls. Investigative journalists and human rights NGOs who had moved away from investigating or responding to wrongful convictions—believing that they were now in the safe hands of the Commission[1]—began to express criticism of its cautious approach to reviews and

---

[1] Michael Naughton claimed that when the Commission was established JUSTICE ceased its casework on wrongful convictions precisely on the basis that the Commission was set up to do that work and it was therefore no longer necessary for it to continue (House of Commons Justice Committee, 2014:3).

Reasons to Doubt: Wrongful Convictions and the Criminal Cases Review Commission. © Carolyn Hoyle and Mai Sato 2019. Published 2019 by Oxford University Press.

referrals (see Chapter 2). Innocence projects emerged and assisted some applicants in preparing their submissions to the Commission, presenting something of a confusion of roles and responsibilities that has not yet been resolved.

When we started our research in 2010, we found the Commission to be a thorough, committed, but wary organization, which was working hard at its cases but was also somewhat reticent about engaging with its critics or stakeholders, whether they be applicants, their legal representatives, the media, innocence projects, or others involved in the wider justice system. Since then, we have witnessed further changes to the structure and organization of the Commission as well as its personnel, and changes to the wider 'surround' (Hawkins, 2002) in which the Commission makes its decisions. As we finish this book, it is becoming widely acknowledged that the criminal justice system is once again in crisis, and that errors are likely.

Criminal Justice in Crisis

Throughout our time watching the Commission at work, there were three significant changes to its 'surround' (Hawkins, 2002), all associated with austerity in the public sector: damaging reductions in legal aid for defendants and appellants, increasing evidence of police and prosecution failures to disclose potentially exculpatory evidence, and threats to the reliability of forensic science.

Cuts to legal aid

Brutal cuts to legal aid have left lawyers with insufficient funding to provide a rigorous defence at trial and at appeal. Government funded legal aid has provided legal advice and representation to defendants who have insufficient means to pay for their own lawyer since 1949. Successive governments have sought to limit this resource over the past two decades, with 2008 seeing the introduction of fixed fees in the crown court. However, the series of cuts that started in 2013 attracted the most vehement criticisms within the legal community. Under the Legal Aid, Sentencing and Punishment of Offenders Act, 2013, cuts to family law, welfare, and housing started a trend that soon spread to criminal legal aid. Most recently, in October 2017, the Ministry of Justice reduced the cap on the number of pages of prosecution evidence that criminal legal aid lawyers would automatically be paid to read, from 10,000 to 6,000 (McFadden and Carter, 2018). Coming at a time of rising concern about non-disclosure, it seems remarkable that the government would see fit to reduce funding to the very people who need to sift through voluminous materials in order to challenge the case for the prosecution. As two criminal lawyers put it:

It may well be the case that a 2,000 page expert analysis of a defendant's mobile phone does not contain the key evidence proving the defendant's innocence, but a defence team will not know this unless they consider the report—to refuse to pay them for this time simply makes it more difficult for defence lawyers to represent their clients thoroughly and further restricts access to justice. (McFadden and Carter, 2018)

There is, inevitably, divergence about the precise impact of these cuts, but most recognize that access to legal aid has been increasingly restricted by 'means testing'. While it was once the case that solicitors were paid an hourly rate for most of the work done within the legal aid system, making the more complex cases more profitable, the new fixed fee system means that cases that require much more time, either because of the

nature of the case, or because of vulnerabilities concerning the defendant or the witnesses, are now the least profitable. Some solicitors will therefore decide not to take
them on, leaving the most vulnerable or the most difficult cases at risk of inadequate
legal representation. These are, of course, the cases most likely to lead to a wrongful
conviction, as we described in Chapter 5.

Cuts to legal aid have also impacted on post-conviction justice, and appellants at
direct appeal and applicants to the Commission will find it increasingly difficult to
secure legal advice and effective representation, making it less likely they find themselves before the Court of Appeal ('the Court') (see Chapter 6). This would be objec-
tionable even if we believed the criminal justice system to be impeccable. As it is, the
past few years have demonstrated clearly that certain aspects of pre-trial justice are
nearly as flawed as they were in the decades leading up to the establishment of the
Commission.

Increasing evidence of non-disclosure

Between the end of 2017 and early 2018, barely a week passed without media outrage
over collapsed prosecutions, particularly for rape, following last minute revelations
that the prosecution failed to disclose material to the defence that cast doubt on the
prosecution case, often on the credibility of the victim's account. The government, concerned about the crisis of confidence in the police and the Crown Prosecution Service,
has launched an inquiry into the disclosure of evidence in criminal cases (Commons
Select Committee, 2018), and the Law Society has called on criminal lawyers to provide case studies of failures to disclose unused material that led to, or could have led to,
a miscarriage of justice in order that the Justice Committee fully appreciate the extent
of the problem (The Law Society, 2018). In addition, the Attorney General, who criticized police and the Crown Prosecution Service for not carrying out 'basic' procedure
(Yorke, 2018), has ordered both bodies to review training, develop specialist disclosure
experts in every police force, and provide all multimedia evidence to the defence digi-
tally to tackle 'deep-rooted and systemic' disclosure issues (News, BBC, 2018).

The former Lord Chief Justice, Lord Judge, is concerned that widespread non-
disclosure 'may reduce the prospects of conviction even when the allegation is genuine'
(Lord Judge cited in Gibbs, 2018). It has been suggested that the number of prosecutions to collapse due to disclosure failures had increased by 70 per cent over the past
two years (Gibbs, 2018), but it is not known how many people have been wrongfully
convicted in such circumstances. The then Director of Public Prosecutions, Alison
Saunders expressed irritation at such cases, but affirmed her confidence that no innocent person has been jailed as a result of error (Finkelstein, 2018). Putting aside the
obvious fact that innocent people will have been arrested, sometimes detained, had
their lives subject to close scrutiny for many months and their reputations ruined, even
if they have not then been convicted (Burnett et al., 2017), she simply cannot be confident that innocent people will not have been jailed (Finkelstein, 2018).

Austerity measures in the public sector have created the conditions whereby stretched
police and prosecutors have less time to sift carefully through all of the evidence (Scott,
2018). However, this is not only a resource issue; it is—to some extent—a product of
public institutions failing to adapt to their own changing 'surround' (Hawkins, 2002);
in this case, the exponential rise in use of the internet. Many disclosure errors of the
past few years have arisen in cases where there was a great deal of social media data.
This is likely why rape prosecutions have been at the fore of public concern, given that
most such cases rest on consent, and evidence of a romantic relationship before or after

the alleged rape may speak to this very issue. Today, evidence pertaining to the nature of such relationships is most likely to be available in electronic communications, especially among young people. Social media and other internet traffic create a mass of potentially relevant data, presenting a significant challenge for the prosecution and the defence. As David Ormerod (2017) made clear, science and technology have generated new opportunities for criminal justice, such as providing information through body cameras and police car cameras used by an increasing number of police officers, through images recorded by drones, and data from satellites. But the resulting proliferation of complex data needs to be scrutinized by the police, prosecutors, and defence. It is not surprising that this stretches an under-resourced justice system, and that we are seeing rising disclosure failings in this digital age.

Declining trust in forensic science

The past few years have seen continuing concerns about the reliability and validity of forensic science evidence (see Chapter 7). Indeed, some have suggested that we may be on the cusp of a new rise in wrongful convictions with 'falling forensic science standards making miscarriages of justice inevitable' (e.g. Devlin and Dodd, 2018). In 2012, the government abolished the Forensic Science Service, the primary provider to the police and courts. This led to the establishment of various private providers and the expansion of in-house police forensic services, at a time of cuts to the police budget. Commissioners were perplexed by this short-term strategy to save public funds, and predicted a significant decline in the reliability of forensic data. It seems they were right.

The most recent Forensic Science Regulator's annual report (2018) makes for disturbing reading. It shows that some outsourcing by the police of criminal forensic work to unaccredited private forensic laboratories fails to meet basic quality standards, meaning that innocent people will be convicted, while some guilty people will not. Professor Angela Gallop (2017), one of the UK's most eminent forensic scientists, described the risks arising from rapidly changing technology, an exponential increase in workload, tighter police forensic budgets, lack of accreditation, and conclusions being drawn from fewer samples and tests. She made clear that while wrongful convictions may take time to emerge, when they do, people will look back and see that they started to rise in 2012, when the Forensic Science Service closed.[2] While private labs have been in the news recently, with stories of incompetent work leading to wrongful convictions, Gallop (2017) is adamant that there are similar risks with police in-house forensic services, given that police staff are often at the limits of their expertise and capabilities in such settings. These pitfalls were clear, even to the government, shortly after the Forensic Science Service was closed (House of Commons Science and Technology Select Committee 2013); and certainly by the time of a National Audit Office (2014) investigation, which expressed deep reservations about the lack of accreditation among the various services and argued that the move to free-market forensics was not meeting the justice system's need for high-quality scientific support.

If the courts were very careful about what forensic evidence they would admit, the risks would not be so grave. For example, for over a decade, the Association of Chief Police Officers guidance stated that there must be additional non-DNA evidence to

---

[2] In 2016, the government suggested a return to a national approach to forensic science, though whether that will come about, and what that may look like, is as yet unclear (House of Commons Science and Technology Committee, 2016).

support a charge (Association of Chief Police Officers, 2005:para:7.2). However, although there is now growing concern about the fallibility of DNA evidence, a recent Court judgment (*R v Tsekiri*[3]) stated that there is no legal or evidential principle which states that a jury cannot consider a case which depends solely on DNA evidence left on an object by a defendant at the scene of a crime, provided the match probability is very high.[4]

Threats to access to justice

The declining reliability of forensic science evidence, widespread failures to disclose, and cuts to the legal aid budget have created a new and baleful climate in which wrongful convictions will not be anomalous but the inevitable outcome of a flawed system. This is clear to the Law Society, which has recently issued judicial review proceedings against the ongoing restrictions on access to justice imposed by the Ministry of Justice.[5] It was also clear to participants at the Commission's twentieth Anniversary conference, some of whom argued that under such threats to justice, we need faith in the Commission's ability to provide a safety net. David Ormerod (2017) was confident that 'the CCRC is doing exactly what one would expect to adapt to the future ... rigorously applying independent minds in pursuit of justice'. Similarly, Lord Burnett of Maldon was fulsome in his praise for the Commission:

Since your creation you have put the old system to shame. You have been active in the pursuit of justice, where Home Secretaries were reluctant, understandably reluctant, to act. You have acted consistently with constitutional principle. And, most importantly, you have referred over 630 cases for reconsideration by the courts. An average of 30 a year for the past twenty years. (Lord Burnett of Maldon, 2017:para:12)

At the same event, however, others reiterated concerns and criticisms of the type we described in Chapter 2: primarily, that the Commission's relationship with the Court is too close and comfortable; that the organization is slow and inefficient; that it is insufficiently open to dialogue with its key stakeholders, not least the media; and that its referral rate is too low. We come back these well-rehearsed criticisms in the following sections, but for now we pause to reflect on the last one, as it has become a particular concern among critics but also within the Commission, and if only a handful of cases reaches the Court, by way of the Commission, this raise concerns about access to justice.

As we make clear in Chapter 2, the Commission has over the past two decades been criticized for being risk averse in its referrals to the Court. It had for a long time referred between 3 and 4 percent of its applications—an average of thirty-three referrals a year—and of these between 60 and 70 per cent of convictions were quashed by the Court. However, since the rise in applications—caused in large part by the launch of the 'easy-read' application form and the associated programme of outreach work—the referral rate and the rate at which the Court quashes convictions referred by the Commission have declined. In 2016/17 the referral rate was only 0.8 per cent (twelve of the 1,563 cases concluded, as compared to the historic average of thirty-three referrals a year); with just 46 per cent quashed, as compared to the previous rate which was

[3] [2017] EWCA Crim 40.
[4] This overruled what had been set out as the definitive position by the Court in *Byron* [2015] EWCA Crim 997 (see Bentley, 2017; Chapter 7, footnote 16).
[5] In direct response to the Ministry's decision to reduce the cap on the number of pages of prosecution evidence that criminal legal aid lawyers would automatically be paid to read, discussed above.

close to 70 per cent.[6] Those who contend that too much of the Commission's finite resources is devoted to 'low hanging fruit' (Naughton, 2018) will be concerned to note that of the twelve cases referred in 2016/17 two were for cultivation of cannabis, two for other drug offences, and one for failure to provide information as to the identity of a driver (the other convictions referred were for murder (3), serious assault (1), and sexual offences (3) (Criminal Cases Review Commission, 2017a:78)). While we do not argue that these wrongful convictions had no impact on the lives of those affected, nor do we suggest a blanket ban on convictions from the magistrates' courts, these are not the types of cases that brought about the establishment of the Commission. That said, these less serious cases would be unlikely to provoke reproach if they were among a larger proportion of more serious cases. When the referral rate is just 0.8 per cent, they are rather conspicuous.

The Commission's media spokesperson recently said: 'We don't have a complete answer' as to why the referral rate has dropped; 'they've never dropped this low before'.[7] The Chief Executive's Introduction to the 2016/17 Annual Report, states:

Perhaps the most striking feature about our work this year is that … the number of cases in which we have found a reason to refer a case for appeal has fallen markedly … Another notable feature … has been the number and proportion of cases where applicants won their appeal following a CCRC referral. (Criminal Cases Review Commission, 2017a:6)

The Annual Report suggests that the declining referral rate over the past few years[8] may be accounted for by the fact that there have been no 'batches' of wrongful convictions. In the past, as we saw throughout the preceding chapters, a change in the Commission's surround may have persuaded them to investigate particular cases, often in groups, or to seek out cases proactively, which can sometimes lead to a batch of referrals based on similar grounds or drawing on the same decision field. Such cases create new legal or moral decision frames that allow further similar cases to be dealt with much more efficiently and instigate, in time, adaptations within the decision field.

For example, in Chapter 7 we saw how changing opinion on what is considered to be 'normal' in children's genitals and what may be suggestive of abuse, following a report in 2008 by the Royal College of Paediatrics and Child Health, shaped the Commission's approach to convictions for child sexual abuse. This led to a batch of similar referrals, some of which would not have been reviewed so efficiently or even referred in the absence of a change in this surround. Likewise, changes in the law can result in a series of similar referrals, such as we saw in Chapter 8 in relation to sexual conduct with a minor. Batches of cases also occur when the Commission makes proactive use of its powers to seek out and investigate cases relating to new threats to the safety of convictions; for example, growing awareness that refugees and asylum seekers have been poorly advised, inappropriately prosecuted, and wrongfully convicted of offences relating to their entry to the UK (see Chapter 10). Some 'batch' cases involved more than one applicant in 'multi-handed' cases, further increasing the overall referral rate. In contrast, cases referred during 2016–17 involved single individuals with no apparent 'theme' to link them to other cases (Criminal Cases Review Commission, 2017a:14–15).

---

[6] Over its twenty years (as of April 2017), the Commission had referred 631 cases back to the Court at an average rate of thirty-three cases a year, one in every thirty applications. Of those cases referred, 69 per cent have succeeded on appeal (Criminal Cases Review Commission, 2017a:7).

[7] National Training Conference on Investigating Miscarriages of Justice, 16–17 February 2018, University of Manchester.

[8] In 2014/15 it had reduced to 2.2 per cent and in 2015/16 to 1.8 per cent.

At the twentieth Anniversary conference, commissioners were asked to account for the reduced referral and success rates, and while a couple reiterated the 'batch' thesis, none seemed fully persuaded of this. Indeed, this thesis cannot account for most of the change as the referral rate started to decline while the last main 'batch' of similar cases was ongoing: declining in 2014/15 (to 2.2 per cent) and further still in 2015/16 (to 1.8 per cent) at the very time that a high proportion of the 'asylum and immigration cases' were being referred (twenty-two such cases across these two years; see Table 10.2, Chapter 10). If the batch thesis only explains some of the change, what other causes might reasonably be proposed?

The Chair of the Commission, expressing concern about the declining rate,[9] suggested that it could be partly explained by the reduced rate for legally aided assistance (Foster, 2017a). Time spent by an assiduous lawyer drafting a plausible and persuasive application will make it more likely that a case is fully investigated by the Commission at a 'stage two' review, and therefore, inevitably, create a greater chance of being referred. While it is possible for unrepresented applicants to have their cases referred to the Court, it is less likely that they will be (see Chapter 6). Therefore, the current fiscal climate may have had an impact on the Commission's referral rate.[10]

While some government departments are protected in times of austerity, the Ministry of Justice is not, and it has been estimated that real term cuts since 2011 have been somewhere in the region of between 33 per cent (Brooke, 2017) and 40 per cent (Gibbs quote in McFadden, 2018). Experts have been clear that this will have had a significant impact on the safety of convictions. As the late Sir Henry Brooke (2017) (vice Chair of the Bach Commission) put it, in relation to cuts to, and reforms of, the criminal legal aid system, 'These reforms and cuts have been accompanied by a very distinct deterioration in the quality of criminal justice—with the concomitant risk that innocent people may be convicted of crimes they did not commit'. Similarly, Penelope Gibbs, director of Transform Justice, explains that:

austerity ... definitely has an effect upon miscarriages of justice. Amongst issues such as the low salaries of legal aid lawyers, there are many other examples of where cuts are occurring, which are creating a system in which miscarriages of justice happen with increasing frequency. (Gibbs quoted in McFadden, 2018)

It is clear that cuts to policing, prosecution, and defence services have taken their toll. Fiscal constraints on forensic science services will result in a reduction in the quality of expert reports presented to the courts; as Sir Henry Brooke put it, experts are 'paid peanuts and therefore have to take on lots more work' (Fieldwork notes, Criminal Cases Review Commission twentieth Anniversary conference). Threats to pre-trial justice increase the risk of wrongful convictions at the same time that cuts reduce the chances for those who seek relief in the appeal courts. Recent years have seen a rise in applications for direct appeal without counsel and, as Roberts (2017:321) recently pointed out, it is very difficult for an applicant drafting his or her own grounds

[9] Another Commissioner, David Smith, stated in a tweet following the twentieth Anniversary conference that '[the Commission] shares concerns at the downturn [and] strives to identify referable cases', adding that they were not complacent.
[10] Some commissioners predicted that while the 'easy-read' application form would likely increase the prospects for those vulnerable people with poor literacy skills, it would also attract some who have little prospect of having their case referred to the Court. However, while this would likely have an impact on the *proportion* of applications referred (with a smaller proportion expected in line with an increased application rate), it should not account for the fall in actual number of referred cases.

to succeed at appeal, particularly if the applicant is in custody at the time. It is within this bleak landscape, this changing 'surround' (Hawkins, 2002), that we reflect on our findings and what they tell us about the Commission as a safety net for an ailing criminal justice system.

A Sociological Understanding of Decision-making at the Commission

Drawing on information available at the time, and with guidance from the court, juries make sense of the evidence to come to a reasonable verdict. But, occasionally, verdicts do not seem reasonable. Reading through the extensive case files at the Commission, once or twice we were inclined to believe that the jury got it wrong; that their verdict seemed perverse. The following commissioner thought so too:

I reckon I've seen three or four cases, probably, over my 10 years, where I've been genuinely amazed the jury have convicted, and that I've been really a bit upset that we can't do anything about it. (#2)

Academic research suggests this should not be surprising. Wrongful convictions associated with jury decision-making are well documented: juries often forget what has been said in court, their notes may be less than comprehensive, they are fallible and unreliable arbiters, and even when competent, they can be misled by the judge.[11]

However, believing that the jury made the wrong decision does not get the Commission very far. To remind the reader, section 13 of the Criminal Appeal Act 1995 prevents the Commission from referring a case unless it is satisfied that there is a real possibility that the Court will quash a conviction (or sentence). A conviction can only be referred on the basis of new 'argument' or 'evidence' (section 13(1)), unless there are exceptional circumstances (section 13(2)). Under the Criminal Appeal Act 1968, the Court, in turn, can only allow an appeal if they think the conviction is unsafe (section 2(1)), and will assess the new evidence or argument on the basis of the statutory test for receiving such (section 23). The Commission's 'predictive' real possibility test requires it to try to second guess how the Court may respond, while the Court is expected to imagine how the jury would have acted given different information; something of a two-stage second-guessing process.

The Commission cannot reinvestigate the original case to find new argument or evidence. Decision-making must, instead, be constrained by the principle of bounded rationality and shaped by organizational value premises (Choo, 2006; see Chapter 4). Sense-making is retrospective; decision-makers at the Commission try to interpret what happened years ago in light of historical data (amassed pre-trial and presented at court) and contemporary data (gathered post-conviction). They make sense of this data in the context of the surround, the Commission's own decision field, and commissioners' and CRMs' decision frames.

In the preceding chapters we reviewed how the Commission made decisions in those categories of cases included in our purposeful sample: cases that 'turn on' forensic science and expert testimony (see Chapter 7); sexual offence cases—both historical institutional abuse cases and contemporary sexual offence cases, where the

---

[11] For a review of the empirical evidence on jury fallibility see Forst (2013:32–5).

Commission's main focus of investigation was on the credibility of the complainant (see Chapter 8); cases where the Commission saw fit to delegate its investigation to a police force (see Chapter 11); cases where the Court directed the Commission to investigate an aspect of the case (see Chapter 11); and cases where migrants or asylum seekers were convicted of entering the UK without the appropriate documents (see Chapter 10). Chapters 9 and 10 focused on those cases within our sample which raised questions about a failure of police or prosecution integrity, or of the defence to provide adequate representation.

In examining the Commission's response to these cases, we considered the influence of developments in the 'surround' (Hawkins, 2002) of the Commission; the broad setting within which decision-making at the Commission takes place. We demonstrated that developments in the surround require consequent paradigm shifts in the 'field'—in the policies and guidelines of the Commission—and in the 'frame', how commission staff make sense of information; how they interpret, classify, and respond to evidence in their cases (Hawkins, 2002:49).

The surround

The surround is not static (Hawkins, 2002). It shifts according to wider social and political changes beyond the control of the Commission, and when it does, the Commission must usually move with it. A changing surround is perhaps best understood by considering paradigm shifts in science. Evolutions in forensic science—for example, developments in the accuracy and application of DNA evidence or in the interpretation of expert evidence—were beyond the control of the Commission and yet directly impacted on its reviews (see Chapter 7). For instance, evolving expert opinion on head injuries and deaths among infants shifted the approach of the Commission to these cases.

Shifting value premises as regards to suspects' due process rights happen in the political surround but also in the Court's evolving jurisprudence. More than a decade ago, government attempts to restrict the quashing of convictions based on police or prosecution misconduct—not least failures to disclose unused material to the defence—were resisted by the Commission. Nonetheless, the Commission has had to respond to the Court's increasing reluctance to quash such convictions unless due process failures are determinative in themselves (see Chapter 9). There must, in other words, be a nexus between the due process failure and the safety of the conviction. This shift in the surround presents a challenge to the Commission in reviewing applications based on claims of policing without integrity or incompetent or inadequate defence at trial; referrals now must be able to demonstrate that police misconduct or poor defence rendered the convictions unsafe.

The Commission's approach in sexual offence cases had been firmly rooted in concern for defendants' fair trial rights, following a few key cases which turned on witness credibility. This approach informed the decision field, with the Casework Guidance Notes directing CRMs and commissioners to carry out a series of witness credibility checks. As we explained in Chapter 8, recent shifts in the political climate, with a new commitment to improving the experiences of victims, to believing their testimonies, and to increasing the reporting and conviction rates in sexual abuse cases, created an environment whereby the Commission, in 2017, was persuaded to alter its policy on sexual offence cases by reducing the requirement for credibility checks; a clear example of the surround impacting on the field.

The decision field

Choo's (2006) model considers how organizations aim to control sometimes complex and drawn-out processes by imposing routines and structures, signalling to the outside world that it is an ordered machine, with consistency in its approach (see Chapter 4). However, we found Hawkins' concept of the decision field helpful in exploring *how* the Commission constructs these routines and structures and thereby shapes CRMs' and commissioners' decision-making. Changes to legislation and developments in case law that take place in the surround inevitably impact on the decision field, and Formal Memoranda and Casework Guidance Notes, and other internal guidance, are developed to reflect both the dictates of, but also the latitude within the law. Hence in reviewing cases, the Commission engages in a series of routines around the collection and management of information, as well as ritualized processes for constructing a Statement of Reasons ('SOR'), to demonstrate to those outside the organization that it follows fair, consistent, and legitimate procedures.

The surround provides the Commission with specific powers—for example, to require public (and now private) agencies to disclose data that could assist their investigations (section 17, Criminal Appeal Act 1995)—but the Commission develops internal guidelines to tell decision-makers when and how to use those powers (see Chapter 12). Similarly, legislation has established the real possibility test that must be met before referring a case back to the Court, but internal guidance that draws on the Court's developing response to referrals, and to direct appeals, helps commissioners to decide, in each case, whether and when it has been met, and thereby informs the approach to reviews. Hence, the 'law in books' and the 'law in action' are central features of the decision field, but Formal Memoranda and Casework Guidance Notes provide information about other influences. Decision routines comprise what to search for, what to pay attention to, and what evidence to select as relevant, and the internal guidance speaks not only to the legal framework and legal practice, but also to organizational procedures and the cultural imperatives of the organization.

Chapters 9 and 10 showed us that internal guidance reminds the Commission of the necessity to demonstrate how any misconduct by police or prosecutors, or incompetence by the defence, might impact on the safety of the conviction; that it is not enough to simply demonstrate misconduct or incompetence. That said, it also makes clear that there are some cases that are beyond the pale: extremely rare cases in which counsel's misbehaviour or ineptitude or police misconduct is so extreme that it constitutes a denial of due process to the client, even if it cannot be clearly established that the behaviour had an impact on the safety of the conviction. Similarly, other chapters showed the ways in which internal guidance in the Commission's decision field shapes its approach to fresh evidence in cases where the defence failed to adduce expert evidence at trial that could now cast doubt on the safety of the conviction.

Internal guidance provides 'explicit knowledge', knowledge that is rule-based and codified (Choo, 2006:141), but which is also aimed at influencing tacit knowledge within the Commission, and in some cases, builds on 'tacit knowledge' (Choo, 2006:8–9). By tacit knowledge, we refer to personal, subjective, culturally, and organizationally informed insights and intuitions that come from working in an institution for some time. It includes knowledge about specific types of cases, about what evidence will and will not impress the Court. As such, it is more difficult to share than the more formal, explicit knowledge which is produced, organized, and circulated within an institution with a particular purpose: in our case, by way of internal guidance. However, tacit case-based knowledge can be held within the institutions' mechanisms for knowledge sharing (in this case, the Commission's database of cases and approaches) and can then become explicit knowledge.

For Choo (2006), the successful organization must be able to convert tacit know-ledge into explicit knowledge and vice versa. This can be achieved through various mechanisms, including socialization—where tacit knowledge can be transferred from an experienced employee to another employee working in the same team or under their supervision—or from an expert within the organization, such as a legal adviser or in-vestigations adviser providing relevant information to a CRM. Decision-makers draw on tacit knowledge in order to interpret and apply the information within internal guidelines in individual cases. In doing so, the information in the field is used to make decisions in particular cases. Such processes require fluid communication channels, but these were not always apparent at the Commission and variability led to somewhat different approaches at decision-making, different ways of framing the information available and therefore responding to it, a point to which we return below. Hence, while the field draws on the surround and impacts on decision frames, frames are also products of individual commissioners and CRMs making sense of the oftentimes com-plex data before them.

The decision frame

In all of our chapters, decision-making was shaped by a legal decision frame, with the Commission first and foremost being led by the decision field. For example, being careful not to antagonize the Court by presenting testimony from 'bigger and better' experts (see Chapter 7). However, we also saw evidence of other decision frames at play when there was a clear legal frame, if this was considered to be insufficient to make a successful referral. For example, in Chapter 7 we showed that the Court's scepticism about 'bigger and better' experts caused the Commission to try to dismantle other aspects of the prosecution case and weave an alternative story within a narrative decision frame. In Chapter 10, the legal frame was also shaped by an instrumental purpose: attempts to frame poor defence work as 'tactical' in order to focus on other elements of the case more likely to prove persuasive to the Court.

The Commission choosing not to include weak evidence of police misconduct as a ground for referral when they had other strong grounds was evidence of an instru-mental decision frame at work. And we were aware of an organizational frame at work (keeping a check on its own limited resources) where the Commission decided not to investigate fully apparently weak claims of police misconduct where the applicant had provided no clear evidence to support their claim (see Chapter 9). We also found some evidence of a moral decision frame; cases of particularly egregious police or pros-ecutorial misconduct where commissioners appeared to be driven partly by a desire to blame and to hold to account those in the criminal process who had failed to demon-strate professional integrity. At times, we saw decision framing that brought together the legal and the moral, such as with the Commission's response to asylum cases (see Chapter 10).

Our empirical chapters (Chapters 6–13) demonstrated the interconnectedness of the surround, the field, and the frame. Neither the surround nor the field recede to the periphery of the decision frame, both are actively drawn on as the CRM or com-missioner makes sense of the case before them, albeit in sometimes different ways depending on how each decision-maker manages uncertain data. To manage uncer-tainty and ambiguity, key features of the Commission's decision frame, some staff en-gage in collective learning, drawing on the shared tacit knowledge of the Commission, while others tread a rather more secluded path, quietly progressing with their investigation but sometimes reluctant to draw on institutional learning so that decisions are not always predictable. There is truth in the Commission's claim that each case will be assessed on its merits, and that each case is unique, but while we found much consistency across the Commission in terms of decision frames, our analysis revealed some variability. This was particularly evident when cases were reviewed a second or even a third time following reapplication (see Chapter 13).

Variability in approaches and outcomes

As we made clear in Chapter 4, the Commission is an organization that likes to present itself as consistent in its method and outcomes. But if the same case can be handled differently by different CRMs and commissioners, we must acknowledge variability in the Commission's response to cases. Indeed, we found some variability in CRMs' inclination to conduct empirical investigations in their cases, with some expressing a clear preference for desktop research while others were keen to go out and meet with applicants or witnesses or visit the scene of the crime (processes that help to develop tacit knowledge) (see Chapter 12). Our data showed that CRMs carried out 'empirical' investigations in over a third of their cases. However, it also showed considerable variation across CRMs that could not be fully accounted for by the type of case or by the experience of the CRM. In many cases, much of the investigation can be done by thorough review of the materials submitted by applicants and their legal representatives, and by consideration of case law, legislation, and precedents set by the Court, as well as by issuing requests for data held by public bodies under its section 17 powers (which the Commission does in approximately 60 per cent of its applications according to administrative data collected during 2011–13). It is important to remember that this desk-based work uses investigative as well as legal skills. Furthermore, some cases do not require 'empirical investigation', but simply a close analysis of the documents, case law, and statutes. However, the level of variation we found strongly suggests different personalities and aptitudes shape review work.

Furthermore, our analysis of expert evidence cases in Chapter 7 showed some variability in applying decision frames. This suggests that variables beyond case-based factors can influence a review and the decision whether or not to refer. This is not surprising. Though we write about 'the Commission' making decisions, judgments about whether a case meets the real possibility test are made by a committee of three commissioners (see Chapter 4); in any one case, personalities, professional backgrounds, and experiences shape the proceedings, guiding deliberations towards one outcome rather than another. Choices about how to investigate a case are made by individual CRMs working closely with a commissioner, who can make a decision not to refer a case, thus bringing to an end the hopes of an applicant who may have been waiting for years for this decision. Lawyers who have experience of working with the Commission are critical of variability in approaches to cases, as one explained to us:

I think there's a general inconsistency across the teams and … From my perspective, the CRM is the person in effective power really … they're the ones that do all the legwork and really drive the direction of the case and … therefore, the consistency amongst the, effectively, foot soldiers is absolutely paramount … [but] there is just such great inconsistency. (#12)

Some variability is inevitable in any organization that allows for discretion. Commission staff embrace discretion as a strength of the organization, acknowledging that their working practices vary from their colleagues, with some admitting they do not always follow guidance. But nonetheless, they worried about variability in responses, as one commissioner told us:

I get alarmed sometimes by inconsistency. All our commissioners are very individual people and they all have quite strong personalities but that does lead to a measure of inconsistency of approach. (#17; see further, Chapter 6)

The Commission has, in recent years, made efforts to increase consistency in its reviews; moving away from individualistic decision-making by commissioners to a more consultative decision-making; as well as moving away from a rather flat organizational structure towards greater supervision of CRMs by group leaders (see Chapter 6). Its internal information mechanisms process and build knowledge for its staff to draw on in order to make sense of cases and make informed, consistent decisions. However, not all individual staff draw on or perceive the knowledge base in the same way and will sometimes come to different conclusions in reviewing similar cases. Choo (2006:23) argues that successful organizations shape decision-making by controlling the 'decision premises' from which decisions are made, rather than controlling the decisions themselves. There is little attempt at the Commission to control decisions made by commissioners and CRMs on an individual basis, but they are influenced in their decision-making by the cultural values of the organization, the 'value premises'. That said, oftentimes, these premises are in tension, not least those principal values of efficiency and thoroughness (see Chapter 12), and this can lead to variation in prioritizing behaviour.

Efficiency requires that the Commission screens out nearly half of its applications as it cannot subject all to a full (stage two) review. This is a process that causes some unease within an already anxious organization. As one commissioner put it, in a published article:

Some cases are unlikely to go anywhere and will be rejected more summarily than others. Even that is fraught with obvious dangers, however. How can we be sure that a rejected case is not a hidden miscarriage? There is no easy answer to that question. (Smith, 2017)

In Chapter 6, we argued that the screening process is constrained by the principle of bounded rationality. The Commission uses certain 'triggers'—such as the existence of guilty pleas, good legal representation, arguments about the credibility of the complainant, and failure to exhaust direct appeals—as shortcuts to help guide decision-making at stage one without exhausting all possible avenues of investigation. Rejecting weak cases at an early stage is one of the most efficient methods of handling cases, as this significantly minimizes the use of Commission resources. It effectively takes the responsibility for the case away from the Commission and puts it back in the hands of the applicant, obliging applicants to initiate further action by way of further submissions and reapplications (see Chapter 13).

At that stage, applicants or their legal representatives need to present the Commission with a persuasive reapplication, or to treat the rejection as final. For applicants who are unable to secure good legal representation or those who are unable to put together a reapplication, there is a danger that the 'efficient' screening process will screen out unsafe convictions erroneously. That said, the risk of rejecting unsafe convictions must be balanced against the benefit of being able to focus the Commission's finite resources on providing a thorough review of 'screened-in' cases that are considered to be meritorious.

Of course, staff do not always agree on which cases are meritorious and which can be excluded early on. Analysis of screening by commissioners under the system in operation when we started our fieldwork demonstrated individualistic decision frames, which were heavily influenced by commissioners' different and sometimes competing outlooks, values, and backgrounds (see Chapter 6). The new screening policy—introduced while we were conducting our research—changed the decision field from commissioner-centric to consultative, bringing group leaders and CRMs into the decision-making process. While not all commissioners welcomed the new screening policy, the inclusion of group leaders and CRMs—by design—helped to mitigate idiosyncratic decision-making by commissioners, and enhanced efficiency by using the more expensive resource—commissioners—at the review stage, when their authority and expertise was most effective.

Efficiency is not entirely within the control of the Commission. While avoidable delays can be the product of inefficiencies within the Commission, often in pursuit of thoroughness, delays can be caused by actions or inactions outside the Commission. For example, after a 'section 17' request for data from a public body has been issued or after an expert had been instructed, external bodies and professionals can delay the review process if they are unresponsive or cannot meet agreed deadlines.

Furthermore, often information that would help with an efficient review is not available. For example, it is rare for the Commission to have a full transcript of a trial, as tapes or transcripts of proceedings are often destroyed, in line with the five-year retention period currently operated by court reporters. In many cases, a transcript of *part* of the proceedings is available—for example, summing-up, sentencing remarks, opening or closing speeches, a particular witness's evidence—and the Commission routinely uses its section 17 powers to obtain that. They can sometimes piece together relevant information from the counsel's and judge's notebooks. But while the Commission claims that it very rarely has need of the full transcript of a criminal trial, it believes that recordings from some criminal proceedings should be kept for much longer than five years, and that it may be more appropriate to follow similar guidelines to those in use by the police, the Forensic Archive, or the Crown Prosecution Service, where the length of time that material about a case is kept depends on the seriousness of the offence or length of sentence.[12] Given most of the Commission's cases relate to serious offences, with long prison sentences, this change would be of considerable benefit.

It is sometimes difficult to establish exactly what a key witness said at trial, in either their evidence in chief or under cross-examination, and, therefore, whether an apparently fresh piece of evidence has or has not been previously aired. Judges' summings-up may not be sufficiently detailed, or, in rare cases, may be inaccurate. Barristers' notes may also be inadequate, assuming they can be traced, and in the increasingly large number of serious cases where barristers operate without a junior, may not exist at all. This issue can be particularly acute in dealing with expert or scientific evidence. Now that recordings are, almost invariably, digital, there seems to us to be no reason why they should not be kept indefinitely, or for a minimum period of 100 years. Long-term digital data storage of all Crown court trials could be accomplished with minimal cost. It is notable that in most American states, transcripts of the entirety of trials are both preserved and made freely available in all serious cases. The adoption of a similar policy in England and Wales would, at a minimum, make some Commission reviews speedier and more efficient.

Delays can also result from the Commission failing to communicate effectively with external bodies or experts, and from following slowly and methodically every possible lead in an investigation, with the pursuit of thoroughness hindering the Commission's

---

[12] Email communication with Director of Casework, February 2018.

commitment to efficiency. Prior to 2006, the Commission's organizational value premises prioritized thoroughness, but we noticed a move thereafter towards efficiency: from a focus on reaching the 'right' decisions in individual cases, no matter how long that took, to prioritizing the investigation of cases as efficiently as possible, though still with thoroughness and care. The changed value premise altered the field as seen in formal policies and cultural understanding of the mission and while a concern for thoroughness remained, it seemed now to be motivated more by the desire to protect the Commission against external scrutiny, by way of judicial review (see Chapter 12).

Zuckerman (1995:180) believes judges need to view their role not as 'arbiters of individual disputes' but as 'guardians of scarce judicial resources' and should behave fairly in distributing resources to actual and potential litigants. The same might be said of the Commission. Repetitive challenges to the Commission's decisions not to refer cases back to the Court result in additional burdens on the Commission, causing delays for other applicants waiting in the queue to have their cases reviewed. However, here the fear of judicial review militated against the emerging organizational commitment to efficiency and kept decision-makers sufficiently focused on the pursuit of thoroughness. Hence, in many cases, the Commission is generous when legal representatives ask for extensions of time to submit further material or arguments to the Commission, following a provisional decision not to refer a case. The Commission's policy is similarly liberal when it comes to accepting reapplications, placing no limit on the number of reapplications an applicant can submit.

In a few cases, we saw the threat of judicial review persuade the Commission to revisit a case, or to refer when it had initially been disinclined to do so. For example, following a detailed investigation, case EE29a (discussed in Chapter 7) was clearly heading for a decision not to refer, when a high-profile public figure made comments about the case, causing the legal adviser to warn of a potential for judicial review. In light of this, the commissioner put the case to a committee to reflect on this new public scrutiny, and it was decided to refer the case, on the basis of new forensic evidence and expert opinion. The Court upheld the conviction, but the Commission avoided judicial review.[13] In this case, external forces influenced the process, though it made no difference to the eventual outcome.

The Commission's Relationship with 'Stakeholders'

In considering how the Commission manages its relationships with those bodies who have an interest in specific cases (e.g., lawyers, innocence projects, campaigning organizations), as well as those with an interest in the operation of the Commission more generally, such as politicians and the media, Duff (2009) draws on the systems approach advanced by Nobles and Schiff (1995) in their analysis of the Court. This helps us to understand a challenge for the Commission in communication with those outside of the organization: the language of wrongful convictions. While within the language must be of *safety*, outside it is of *innocence*. A wrongful conviction is one that the Court declares to be unsafe, regardless of what the media or campaigners might think. The Court's pronouncement must be justified only by legal doctrine. However, the Commission is not the same as the Court, and while it must consider its applications within the Court's legal framework, it has a duty to communicate effectively with those beyond the Court. Nobles and Schiff (1995) considered the Runciman Commission

---

[13] In other cases (e.g. EE38c), we saw that a decision to judicially review Commission decisions not to refer can bring about a prompt revision of that decision.

to be something of a 'linkage institution', a body which straddles two different systems (politics and the law) and which must attempt meaningful communication with both. Duff (2009) argues that the same description might be applied to the Scottish and English Commissions, which inevitably have to engage in meaningful communication with the lay world (political actors interested in their work, the media, innocence projects, and of course applicants), as well as with the legal system (primarily the Court but also other criminal justice bodies; see Chapter 11).

As we described in Chapter 2, the tension between lay and legal stakeholders is perhaps most apparent in discussions of innocence. Campaigners, in particular, struggle to understand how evidence which to them seems compelling might be insufficient to persuade the Commission to refer a case, or the Court to overturn a conviction. Similarly, gross procedural impropriety which might give rise to a reference and lead to the quashing of a conviction might dismay the media if it is clear that the applicant is factually guilty (see Chapter 9). Indeed, such cases have been discussed by campaigners and some academics as evidence that the Commission has somehow lost its way:

> [T]he CCRC's reviews are mere safety checks on the lawfulness or otherwise of criminal convictions, as opposed to in-depth inquisitorial investigations that seek the truth of claims of innocence by alleged innocent victims of wrongful convictions. This disconnects the CCRC, entirely, from what the [Runciman Commission] and the public envisaged. This is perhaps most apparent at the extremes of the CCRC's operations when it means assisting the factually guilty to have convictions overturned on points of law and breaches of due process and failing to refer the cases of potentially factually innocent victims of wrongful conviction and imprisonment who are unable to fulfil the 'real possibility test' to the satisfaction of the CCRC, for instance in cases where the CCRC decide that the evidence that undermines the evidence that led to the conviction is not 'fresh' evidence and so not admissible in the [Court]. (Naughton, 2018)

Most Commission reviews are not 'mere safety checks', and it is extremely rare for a conviction of a person who appears unequivocally to be factually guilty to be quashed. However, the fact that informed commentators believe this suggests that the Commission has not been entirely effective in its communication with interested parties.

Engagement with the media and campaigners

Before the Commission was established, investigative journalists had a significant role to play in bringing apparent wrongful convictions to the attention of the Court, and generally raising awareness about injustice among the wider public. As Nobles and Schiff pointed out over two decades ago:

> the history of high profile miscarriages of justice is also a history of the relationship between the press and the legal system. Indeed, the establishment of the Court of Appeal in 1907 was in large part due to media outrage and campaigning about specific wrongful convictions. (Nobles and Schiff, 1995:311)

From its inception, following media concern with egregious wrongful convictions, the Commission has had the unenviable task of responding to the concerns of law, politics, and the media (Nobles and Schiff, 1995:301) and has tried to balance these conflicting interests for the past twenty-one years. Some have argued that its establishment may have led to a reduced interest in wrongful convictions within the media,[14]

---

[14] Michael Zander argued that journalists thought that the Commission now did the job they had once done, and they no longer needed to investigate such cases (Fieldwork note, Commission's twentieth Anniversary conference).

though it is also true that journalists have found it increasingly difficult to work on such stories given the growing reluctance of the prison service to allow them access to prisoners,[15] as well as the demise of the local court reporter (e.g. Thornton, 2017). For whatever reason, there are fewer journalists focused on wrongful convictions, and the two prime-time television strands that were, in the 1990s, devoted to investigating wrongful convictions—*Rough Justice* on BBC 1 and *Trial and Error* on Channel 4— were cancelled many years ago. However, despite this reduction in the level of media interest, the Commission has done little to engage the media proactively, and often appears to respond to media enquiries defensively.

Moreover, while reviews in a handful of our cases started with a thorough examination of materials produced and collated by journalists, and in others the CRM kept in contact with a reporter at regular stages of the review, in most reviews they were kept at arm's length, seen either as irrelevant to the investigation, or even as a distraction. While a few journalists may be inadvertently unconstructive, it seemed to us a shame that their skills and drive were not harnessed by the Commission, either in specific cases or more generally.

The sometimes-distant relationship between the Commission and the media, innocence projects, and legal campaigners surfaced at the twentieth Anniversary conference, not for the first time, with some audience members expressing irritation with the Commission. Remarkably, at this 'stakeholder' event, which could have been a high-profile opportunity to present the best of the Commission's work to a wider audience, the only journalists present were a BBC presenter who had agreed to chair the proceedings, and a print journalist who had performed the same function at the previous Commission conference two years earlier. Other journalists who had learnt about the event and asked to attend were, astonishingly, told they were not welcome, a matter which became a subject of intense discussion at the conference itself. As a direct result of this exchange, just three months later the Commission launched a new 'public engagement initiative': a lecture series, 'to stimulate wider debate about important issues facing the CCRC and the criminal justice system more widely', and a stakeholder forum 'to promote dialogue and understanding between the Commission and a cross-section of its key stakeholders and users'. In a clear shift from its previous cautious approach to engagement, one commissioner stated that he hoped:

this will be the start of a new phase of greater transparency and openness at the CCRC at a critical time for criminal justice. We aim to put the CCRC at the centre of debate about wrongful convictions. CCRC staff and Commissioners are looking forward to engaging with stakeholders and users at the new forum and we are always receptive to ideas for improved ways of working. (Smith cited in Robins, 2018)

If the Commission is true to its word, and we have no reason to believe it will not be, this will be something of a departure from its prior reticence. Though another representative from the Commission has claimed that the organization has 'never shied away from engaging honestly with [its] stakeholders, and even with its most trenchant critics' (Head of Communications cited in Robins, 2018), our experience does not entirely fit with this notion. We found certain commissioners and CRMs rather reluctant

---

[15] Michael O'Hare, denied access to journalists while in prison, successfully challenged the Home Secretary on the rights of prisoners to talk to journalists, though experienced reporters, including David Rose, Brian Thornton, and Louise Shorter, remain frustrated by thwarted access to prisoners (Fieldwork note, Commission's twentieth Anniversary conference).

to engage with stakeholders, particular in relation to specific cases and not always with good reason.

Engagement with other criminal justice institutions

The Commission works closely with other criminal justice institutions in its casework. It makes wide use of its section 17 powers to secure data from public (and now private) bodies (see Chapter 12), works cooperatively with the police and the Court-directing investigations from the former, and doing investigations for the latter (see Chapter 11), and is in regular contact with other bodies through the course of each review. It also occasionally seeks to investigate categories of cases proactively when reviews suggest that science has evolved, and there is potential for identifying other similar wrongful convictions. For example, it reviewed older cases of murder and sexual assault following improvements in DNA testing that became apparent after its referral of Sean Hodgson's conviction for murder. It also invited those convicted of the murder of their own infants to reapply to the Commission in light of the Court's response to the Angela Cannings case (see Chapter 7). However, these were casework focused reviews. Beyond its biennial 'stakeholder conferences', the Commission rarely engages directly with other criminal justice institutions on systemic concerns, preferring to let its thorough and detailed Annual Reports raise issues of concern to all of those working in, or subject to, the criminal process.

A clear exception to the Commission's typical reserve can be seen in its recent approach to the wrongful conviction of asylum seekers and others who have entered the UK without the appropriate documents (see Chapter 10). Here, it engaged robustly and somewhat successfully with defence and prosecution lawyers to respond effectively to those who had been wrongfully convicted but also to try to prevent further miscarriages of justice. The response to the Commission's campaign to raise awareness of 'asylum cases' has been positive, with many criminal justice agencies making changes to reduce the chance of further wrongful convictions, reinforcing the view that the Commission is in a unique position to feed back into the justice system. However, Chapters 9 and 10 suggested that the Commission was less critical than it might have been of inadequate defence or prosecutorial misconduct in other cases. Case law places restrictions on what evidence of non-disclosure of unused material the Court will consider to determine the conviction to be unsafe, leaving the Commission unable, in many cases, to use this as a ground for referral. Hence, for instrumental purposes, the Commission may decide that a full and frank discussion of non-disclosure is not in the best interests of the applicant. However, SORs are not only documents for the Court, they could serve as the Commission's reflections on the health of the criminal justice system and we would therefore encourage the Commission to engage in stronger criticisms of current threats to justice, even when the evidence does not support a referral on that point.

Over the last year or two, the Commission has shown itself rather more willing to engage in critical reflection on the particular issue of non-disclosure, as indicated by a letter sent by the Chair, in 2016, to the Director of Public Prosecutions, Attorney General, the National Police Chief's Council, and others. Published on the Commission's website on 18 January 2018—in the context of a spate of media stories on recent cases where non-disclosure had threatened the integrity of the justice system—the letter states:

During the course of its work, the Commission occasionally encounters themes that occur across a range of case reviews. When these themes give cause for concern, the Commission will seek to draw attention to them in the hope that they can be addressed to the betterment of the wider criminal justice system. (Foster, 2016a)

It then focuses on its main concern:

Regrettably, many of the Commission's referrals are the result of a failure within the [criminal justice system] to disclose relevant information at some point … As a result … the courts may be misled, and the integrity of the justice system potentially called into question … Even when the Commission is of the view that … the evidence does not give rise to a real possibility, it is still a concern that the disclosure protocols have not been observed. (Foster, 2016a)

Shortly after, the Chair reiterated these concerns by focusing on non-disclosure in the 2015–16 Annual Report:

In the past twelve months this Commission has continued to see a steady stream of miscarriages. The single most frequent cause continues to be failure to disclose to the defence information which could have assisted the accused … An individual who perhaps should never have been prosecuted or whose conviction was unsafe suffers unnecessarily because the State did not do a proper job. (Criminal Cases Review Commission, 2016a)

The Report goes on to provide detailed discussion of five of the thirty-three cases referred in 2015–16, four of which involved non-disclosure of evidence that might have assisted the defence.

We applaud this bolder approach to engagement with the wider justice system and to hold to account other agencies that have erred in the pursuit of justice. While the Commission is first and foremost a casework organization, and currently has insufficient resources to do much more than this, it is well placed to provide evidence of failings across the justice system and should not shy away from raising awareness and making recommendations for any changes that it thinks fit, as was recognized by the Runciman Commission (Royal Commission on Criminal Justice, 1993:184–5).

Engagement with applicants and their legal representatives

The Commission operates as an inquisitorial system within an adversarial process, as its guidance for legal representatives makes clear:

The CCRC is inquisitorial rather than adversarial and does not work for either side in a case. It is not uncommon for our enquiries to turn up some new evidence that assists the defence and some that assists the prosecution and all material will be taken into account. We will carry out whatever investigations we consider to be necessary to address an applicant's submissions or any issues in the case that we identify ourselves. (Criminal Cases Review Commission, 2015g:5)

This was intended by Parliament when it was set up as 'a non-adversarial body conducting neutral enquiries' (Home Office, 1994:para:52). We found evidence of this inquisitorial approach when CRMs conducted investigations that the applicant had not requested and when they decided against certain investigations despite the applicant's insistence that they were likely to be probative. Occasionally, of course, case records belie the theory of an inquisitorial approach, suggesting something of an alignment with the applicant or even a referral-oriented decision frame, as we saw in some cases subject to a section 19 investigation when the commissioner decided the case was meritorious (see Chapter 11). Notwithstanding, its engagement with all interested parties should reflect its impartiality. Hence, the Casework Guidance Note on Applicant and Representative Relationships states unequivocally:

The right relationship between a case reviewer and the applicant is one characterised by mutual respect and understanding … they are NOT: your friend; your client; or your cause. If you allow an applicant to become any of these things, or to think that he or she has become any of these things, trouble awaits. (Criminal Cases Review Commission, 2011b:paras:3–5; emphasis in original)

It goes on to advise staff on how to 'maintain a professional, detached relationship' (Criminal Cases Review Commission, 2011b:para:6).

It is no easy task for the Commission to remain unwaveringly disinterested when it is often situated between the interests of the powerful Court and a committed and partial lawyer, who may sometimes be more legally skilled than the CRM or commissioner in the case. As we focus on in Chapters 7–10, the law imposes parameters on the Commission's ability to refer cases back to the Court, the Court regularly reinforces those constraints in its responses to Commission referrals as well as direct appeals, and the Commission is fully cognizant of the limits on its capacity for pushing at the boundaries of the real possibility test. These limits mean that in most cases, a decision is made not to refer a conviction back to the Court, and all communications are with the applicant and his or her legal representative. We have seen in previous chapters that the Commission varies in its commitment to ongoing dialogue with applicants, their families, and their lawyers. A couple of commissioners who had worked as appeal lawyers before joining the Commission expressed some sympathy for frustrated legal representatives whose assistance was needed and yet who were not kept in the loop. One had represented one of the applicants in our sample, before joining the Commission, and the case record records his annoyance at the CRM:

[lawyer] wanted to arrange a meeting … I said I would get in touch about a meeting if it was useful to do so. [lawyer] said that the CCRC could not have it both ways, encouraging solicitors to become involved and then keeping them at arms' length. (EE35, Case Record)

Although the Commission's Formal Memorandum on Communicating with Applicants suggests that the Commission should update applicants regularly—suggesting 'at least every three months', and states that 'it is generally unhelpful … to make piecemeal disclosure of information discovered during the course of a review' (Criminal Cases Review Commission, 2018b:para:24), there is clearly discretion and therefore variation in approach. Some staff assiduously communicate their plans, decisions, and findings with applicants, while others are rather taciturn, rarely seeing the benefit of meeting with the applicant, and though responding in a professional way to enquiries throughout the review, seldom are proactive in their engagement. Inevitably, this leads to frustration among applicants and their representatives, which is all too apparent in communications recorded in the case records. While CRMs in particular often feel that they have good reason for their failures to engage—preferring to wait until they have a result or require further information—this approach is rooted in an understanding of how communication might assist the review, rather than how it might help an anxious applicant who has no idea why the wheels of justice are turning so slowly. Sometimes this could be resolved by a quick chat on the phone or a face-to-face meeting, both to reassure and update the applicant. However, this rarely happens, and is not actively encouraged by the organization. Indeed, the Casework Guidance Note on Applicant and Representative Relationships advises CRMs that letters are more appropriate than telephone calls, while face-to-face meetings are anything but routine and should only be conducted if it will advance the needs of a particular review, and then only following consultation with senior members of staff (Criminal Cases Review Commission, 2011b).[16]

Proof magazine, published by the Justice Gap (January 2017), recently produced 'the Open Justice Charter' on behalf of various wrongful conviction campaigners. This argues that applicants' representatives should be permitted to inspect records obtained by the Commission under its section 17 powers that relate to the applicant's case, at the Commission's premises, with documents not being copied without express permission. It also argues that decisions made by the Commission relating to an applicant's case should be made available, with the applicant's permission, to an applicant's representatives, including case plans, schedules for work, and arrangements to commission experts or test evidence. These measures would inevitably cause delays to the Commission's reviews, and—as we argued in Chapter 12— inefficiencies in one case impact on others in the queue. Nonetheless, these are not unreasonable proposals. Procedural justice demands that applicants know what is happening in their case and why; and why in particular some approaches suggested by the applicant are not being pursued. All the evidence suggests that such knowledge and understanding will help applicants to accept a decision by the Commission not to refer their case (Jackson et al., 2012; Tyler, 2006, 2011). When there has been little ongoing communication throughout the review, a Provisional SOR stating the Commission's intention not to refer the case will likely be a significant blow. Any approach to disclosure must take into consideration other organizations and people affected by a decision to release data to applicants, but perhaps a greater commitment to keeping applicants fully informed during reviews might reduce the need for a formal system.

Whether or not the Commission decides to refer a case back to the Court, it must prepare an SOR, for the Court and the applicant or just for the applicant. Either way, the applicant needs to be able to make sense of the SOR, and this is not likely to be easy. As Duff (2009) pointed out, in relation to referrals, commissioners must present to the Court in the SOR only material that will be persuasive because it fits within the statutory framework and evolving case law, and they must present their evidence in legal terms that are understandable by judges. This may not go down so well with an applicant, particularly one who has no legal representation and might consider the document to be steeped in legalese. We saw in Chapter 12 that cautious Commission staff often spend considerable time drafting SORs and include each and every tiny detail of the investigation and the progress of the case prior to the Commission's review. This was not always an efficient use of the Commission's time and produced protracted and complicated SORs that took rather too long to get to the point. In producing such documents, the Commission may be communicating effectively with the Court, but it forgets the wider audience, most obviously the applicant.

In 2012, the Commission introduced a simplified ('easy read') application form to reach out to vulnerable applicants (e.g. applicants whose first language is not English, those without legal representation, and those with limited literacy skills), which led to a 50 per cent increase in applications (see Chapter 6). Further 'outreach' work included 'surgeries' in prisons to provide pre-application advice and to manage expectations about what might be required for an application to be reviewed to resolve the tension

---

[16] On reading this chapter, the Commission realized that the guidance 'struck the wrong tone' and consequently changed it so that CRMs are not discouraged from conducting face-to-face meetings (note from the Commission after reading this chapter; March 2018).

between encouraging meritorious applications and dealing efficiently with the queues. Having widened access to justice at the point of entry, it now needs to examine how it communicates through its SORs. If vulnerable applicants were not able to complete the old application form properly, it is unlikely that they understand the existing SORs, with their complex legal and forensic language. Cuts to legal aid mean that the Commission cannot necessarily rely on lawyers to explain to applicants the analysis and the conclusions of SORs.

Ensuring that applicants understand why their cases were turned down is important for their peace of mind but also, so they understand what is needed if they are successfully to reapply to the Commission (see Chapter 13). However, it also meets the Commission's stated organizational purpose of treating all applicants with respect, and to 'inspire confidence in the integrity of the criminal justice process' (Criminal Cases Review Commission, 2017a). However, the requirement to produce SORs for only the Court and applicants does little for the confidence of the public more generally. It provides little motivation to make these documents comprehensible to all, nor does it create the opportunity for wider systemic learning. What better incentive could there be for effective communication from the Commission than a requirement that it publish its SORs to a wider readership?

The Commission is currently prohibited from publishing its SORs (section 23, Criminal Appeal Act 1968) so other criminal justice institutions cannot learn the valuable lessons of their investigations. While Court judgments often refer to specific failings in the wider criminal process, if these failings have not directly caused the conviction to be unsafe, they may not be discussed in the published judgment. Furthermore, there are no public documents on the vast majority of cases, as they are not referred to the Court, though these SORs may discuss in detail systemic errors or failings of relevance to the wider justice system.

Of course, SORs contain much information about the applicant and others that applicants would not wish to be in the public domain—especially in cases where the Commission's review found inculpatory evidence—and so applicants' permission would to be needed prior to publication, with opportunities for limited redaction in certain cases. However, publication of SORs would allow journalists, campaigners, or other interested stakeholders to carry out research on what happens within and across Commission reviews. It would make clear the very many cases where there were failures of integrity by the police, prosecution service, or defence lawyers even if these were not sufficiently strong or well evidenced to serve as a ground for referral. They would show the significant amount of investigation done before a decision is made not to refer a case, reassuring some who may be sceptical of the Commission's commitment to justice, but also hold the Commission to account for its approaches across reviews. Individual commissioners told us that they would be pleased to be able to publish their SORs and a recent tweet by the Commission suggested that the organization would welcome a change in this direction.[17] Finally, published SORs would allow interested parties to see which of the Commission's referral points become the focus of the Court's consideration in those cases referred, and which have little traction, thus helping to explicate the rather complex relationship between the two institutions.

---

[17] Referring to criticisms of the Commission's failure to refer the convictions of an applicant represented by the Centre for Criminal Appeals, the Commission tweeted 'It might be an idea for @C4CrimAppeals to publish full @ccrcupdate SORs so that people can decide for themselves' (@ccrcupdate tweet 07/12/2017).

The Commission's Relationship with the Court

In concluding this chapter, and the book, we reflect on the Commission's relationship with the Court. We have discussed at length the real possibility test that restricts the Commission's ability to refer a case back to the Court, and the guidance for the Commission that has come from both the Court of Appeal and the Administrative Court by way of evolving case law. For our purpose here, it is important only to remind ourselves that this test necessarily requires the Commission to decide whether the Court will likely find the conviction to be unsafe. This is why many criticisms of the Commission stem from the nexus created by section 13 of the Criminal Appeal Act 1995: put crudely, if the Court is wrong in its analysis or judgment, the Commission is obliged to sustain erroneous jurisprudence.

While the Commission must second-guess the Court's approach to its own safety test in deciding whether a conviction meets the real possibility test, the Court, in turn, must consider what the jury might have made of the fresh evidence had it been available at trial (the 'jury impact test'). Duff (2009:712) has argued, in relation to the Scottish Commission, that decision-makers cannot easily separate out these decision stages, and commissioners should be open about the fact that in reality they are simply evaluating the evidence themselves. To a point, this is true. Decision-makers do consider whether evidence is persuasive in and of itself, and they do ponder the feasibility of applicants' narratives of events. However, this is only a first stage of 'sense making' (Choo, 2006); following this, they must decide if the evidence would be persuasive to the Court. At this stage, if they could not establish fresh evidence that was likely to be sufficiently robust for the Court, or could not provide good reason why the defence at trial had failed to adduce that fresh evidence, they would decline to refer the case regardless of their own misgivings, sometimes occasioning disquiet within and beyond the Commission.[18] This inevitable 'second-guessing' raises the question of whether the Commission should be regarded as deferential to the Court, and indeed whether the Court is deferential to the jury, given its adherence to the principle of finality.

Court deference to the jury

It was explicitly not our aim to research the Court. We read Court judgments in all our cases that were referred only to complete the applicants' stories and to understand how those judgments then influenced the Commission's response to future similar cases. We have therefore little authority to comment on the matter of the Court's deference to the jury (though see Chapter 11), but we pause to review briefly reliable research on the matter, and arguments that the Court's behaviour must be considered in the context that it sees appeals as a challenge to the principles of judicial finality and 'jury sovereignty' (Malleson, 1994:164). We do so in order to engage with criticisms about the Commission's deference to the Court.

The Court has long harboured a deeply felt reluctance to overturn convictions (Zuckerman, 1991), in part because of its commitment to the supremacy of the jury. As Lord Goddard[19] put it in 1949:

---

[18] As Jessel (2004) has pointed out, this 'lawyerly notion of an "unsafe" conviction [can seem] somewhat anaemic compared with red-blooded innocence'.

[19] *McGrath* [1949] 2 All ER 495.

Where there is evidence on which a jury can act and there has been a proper direction to the jury, this court cannot substitute itself for the jury and re-try the case. This is not our function. If we took any other attitude, it would strike at the very root of trial by jury. (Lord Goddard cited in Nobles and Schiff, 1995:310)[20]

This deference led JUSTICE to criticize the Court's failure to overturn jury verdicts in its 1964 report, stressing 'the fallibility and inexperience of juries whose verdicts do not warrant such reverential treatment by appeal court judges' (JUSTICE cited in Nobles and Schiff, 1995:310). Thirty years later, Malleson (1993) conducted research for the Runciman Commission, reviewing the first 300 appeals against conviction of 1990. She found that in only very limited circumstances was fresh evidence admitted by the Court, and when admitted only rarely did it form the basis of a successful appeal. According to Nobles and Schiff (1995:308), this resistance to fresh evidence was sustained even when the Crown chose not to contest the appeal. The Runciman Commission was clear that this was as a result of the Court's deference to the jury:

Ever since 1907, commentators have detected a reluctance on the part of the Court of Appeal to consider whether a jury has reached a wrong decision ... the Court should be more willing to consider arguments that indicate that a jury might have made a mistake ... [and] more prepared, where appropriate, to admit evidence that might favour the defendant's case even if it was, or could have been, available at the trial. (Royal Commission on Criminal Justice, 1993:Chapt.10, para:3)

Despite evidence that juries can sometimes misunderstand the law as well as the increasingly complex forensic science presented to them (Thomas, 2010), and growing evidence of juries misbehaving (see Chapter 11), deference to the jury may well have increased as confidence in the institution has grown (Roberts and Hough, 2009). Jurors now can sit until they are 75 (older than the judges) and most people can be called for jury service, with a strong expectation that they will serve. Notwithstanding ongoing concerns about their competency to hear complex fraud cases, they remain entrusted with the most difficult and sensitive issues, now hearing evidence of bad character and able to convict on uncorroborated evidence. They have considerable latitude and judges continue to have faith in them (Lady Justice Hallett, 2017). The Court is reluctant to disturb a jury's verdict in part because it has not heard the evidence they heard, nor seen the witnesses. Showing deference to the jury allows the Court to resist appeals based solely on the grounds that the jury could have reached a different verdict (Nobles and Schiff, 2002:676).

New research suggests that the Court today may be more deferential to the jury than ever. Stephanie Roberts (2017)—using the same research method as Malleson (analysing the first 300 available appeals considered in 2016)—found almost double the number of appeals based on fresh evidence, which may hint at a more liberal approach by the Court today. However, in only 19 per cent of her cases did the Court admit the fresh evidence, significantly lower than the 61 per cent in 1990 (Malleson, 1993). This suggests the Court is now more restrictive. Furthermore, of the eight appeals where fresh evidence was admitted in Roberts' (2017) sample, only one was allowed. Her research also found that the most common reason for rejecting fresh evidence under section 23 of the Criminal Appeal Act 1968 was because the evidence had been available at trial and there was no reasonable explanation as to why it was not adduced then (a challenge we saw the Commission grapple with in some of our cases). Those

---

[20] For a discussion of the persistence of this deference in the face of changing statutory formulations of the appeal provisions, see Nobles and Schiff (1996).

Commission staff we spoke with after Robert's (2017) study was published made clear that they were not in the least surprised by her findings; they had noticed that the Court was becoming more reluctant to quash convictions based on fresh evidence. The consistency of data demonstrating the Court's deference to the jury raises the question of what the Commission does about it. Does it fall in line, and select and construct its referrals accordingly, or does it push back and try to shift the Court's behaviour?

Commission deference to the Court?

Regardless of the legislative inevitability of the close predictive nexus between the Commission and the Court, friends and critics of the Commission worry about it being overly submissive. A decade ago, ex-commissioner, Laurie Elks, wrote:

[I]t has been suggested that the Commission has been somewhat intimidated in some cases by the Court's approach ... And has wrongly concluded that the Court would refuse to receive improved expert evidence on the basis of 'finality of trial' considerations. If the Commission has, indeed, adopted that approach—rejecting exposed evidence that significantly improves upon the expert case at trial—that would be a serious criticism. (Elks, 2008:77)

A difficulty with Elks' point is with the notion of 'evidence that significantly improves upon the expert case at trial'. That is a subjective judgement, and the Commission can struggle with it. CRMs and commissioners sometimes await Court judgments in similar cases, or cases that raise analogous issues, before deciding whether new evidence is likely to be seen by the Court to significantly improve on the expert case at trial. In light of those cases, they decide whether to refer and, if so, on what grounds. This is unavoidable deference, but it could also be regarded as a pragmatic use of limited resources; learning from past judgments to identify evidence that is likely to be accepted by the Court, and to play down factors that have not proven to be persuasive in the past. In other words, it is not always clear what is deference and what is pragmatism, and if the Court gets it right, the Commission does too; although, as we say above, if the Court gets it wrong, this approach affords no opportunities for the Commission to correct that.

Concerns about deference continue, and at the Commission's twentieth Anniversary conference, the seasoned miscarriages of justice campaigner and former MP Chris Mullin remarked that the Commission 'gets on a bit too well with the judges in the appeal court', and that it would be preferable if there were a 'healthy tension between the Commission and the Court'. While commissioners argued that recent castigations by the Court for Commission referrals showed that the relationship was not too cosy, others[21] suggested that there should be a slightly lower success rate to demonstrate a sufficiently bold approach to referrals.

The question of an appropriate success rate has troubled the Commission for some time. When we began our research, we put it to commissioners that an almost 70 per cent success rate was perhaps a little too high; that it suggested the Commission was somewhat risk averse in its referrals. Furthermore, its key performance indicators on the proportion of referred convictions quashed by the Court could be seen as providing an institutional incentive to refer cases that are likely to be quashed, rather than those aimed at challenging case law (see Chapter 12).[22] That said, recent data are

---

[21] e.g. Mr Egan, the registrar of criminal appeals.
[22] These particular key performance indicators, relating to the Commission's success rate, were removed in 2015 as it was thought that they were misleading, as they might well create such an

confounding. If the current significantly reduced referral rate were to suggest increasing risk aversion, with the Commission not wishing to be rebuked for audacious referrals based on a more liberal interpretation of the real possibility test, we might expect to see a higher rate of referred cases quashed, regardless of the raw numbers. Instead, the reduced referral rate has coincided with a reduced success rate. It is not clear what we might make of that, but those commissioners and CRMs we have spoken with are concerned about their historically low referral rate and keen to see it increase. They are also troubled by variability in their response to cases. It is far from clear how they might decrease variability and increase their (successful) referral rate within the statutory constraints, but before considering the Commission's appetite for bolder referral decisions, we make one suggestion which might have bearing on both of these issues.

Our empirical chapters have made clear that the Court's evolving jurisprudence directly impacts on the Commission's decision field, which thereafter influences decision frames. Casework Guidance Notes that tell decision-makers at the Commission how to respond to particular types of cases are for the most part shaped by the Court's prior response to Commission referrals and to direct appeals. This, as we have made clear, inevitably locks the Commission into a close, deferential relationship with the Court. It requires the Commission as an institution to accurately interpret the Court's decisions in order to guide decision-makers, and individual CRMs and commissioners to then correctly interpret the guidance and apply it appropriately.

Given that these decision-makers come from a variety of professional backgrounds—not all legal—it would be surprising if there was no variation in this interpretive process. The Commission's guidance is usually prepared by legally trained personnel—often the legal adviser—but the second stage of interpretive work is not always done by those with legal skills, and this is where errors may occur. It is unlikely that many cases will be referred that the Court would not be receptive to because of errors, as each referral must be agreed by a committee of three commissioners and, given the composition of the Commission, it is likely that at least one of them will be legally qualified.[23] But though there is only a small chance of a false positive, there is a greater risk of a false negative: one CRM and one commissioner may fail to refer a case because they erroneously believe that it does not meet the real possibility test. This could explain some of the variance we found; in particular why some cases were referred following scrutiny by a new team at reapplication, having originally been turned down (see Chapter 13).

While some have criticized the Commission for using committees only for referral decisions,[24] resources would likely preclude committee meetings for all decisions. Quite simply, there are too many cases decided each year and too few commissioners (many now working only part time) to form a committee for each decision. However, the Commission could require the legal adviser or a legally trained commissioner to carry out checks on each decision made not to refer by a commissioner without legal training. While this would likely be resisted by such commissioners and seen as an insult to their professionalism, and the Commission would worry about its already stretched resources, if the Commission is committed to 'smarter' (#33) investigations,

institutional incentive (note from the Commission, in response to reading a draft of this chapter, March 2018).

[23] Furthermore, a request can be made for a legally qualified commissioner to be on the committee in cases involving a complex point of law (Criminal Cases Review Commission, 2011d:paras:19–22).

[24] Naughton (2018:para:8) has argued that 'this betrays a structural bias against the referral of cases as the hurdle is higher, which serves to undermine the role of a body set up to assist alleged victims of miscarriages of justice'.

it should use its legal expertise where it counts. The skills of non-lawyers could be more actively drawn on in cases requiring other proficiencies, such as forensic or scientific knowledge to make better use of particular expertise. Furthermore, an investment of resources at this stage might reduce time spent responding to resubmissions and re-applications. It would also create the conditions for more confident referrals that might push at the boundaries of the Court's jurisprudence.

Pushing at the boundaries

Though the Commission is institutionally deferential to the Court, it is not powerless to act in those difficult cases that cause unease. At the risk of a lower success rate, it can choose to be bolder in its referrals, making use of its powers to refer on 'lurking doubt' or bypassing the system and applying for a Royal Prerogative of Mercy. However, the Commission has expressed little appetite for these options.

References to lurking doubt go back some decades. As Lord Justice Widgery explained:

in cases of this kind the Court must in the end ask itself a subjective question, whether we are content to let the matter stand as it is, or whether there is not some lurking doubt in our minds which makes us wonder whether an injustice has been done. This is a reaction which may not be based strictly on the evidence as such: it is a reaction which can be produced by the general feel of the case as the Court experiences it. (Lord Justice Widgery in *R v Cooper and McMahon*)[25]

More recently, Lord Chief Justice Bingham stated:

Cases however arise in which unsafety is much less obvious: cases in which the Court, although by no means persuaded of the appellant's innocence, is subject to some lurking doubt or uneasiness whether an injustice has been done ... If, on consideration of all the facts and circumstances of the case before it, the Court entertains real doubts whether the appellant was guilty ... the court will consider the conviction unsafe. (Lord Chief Justice Bingham in *R v CCRC ex parte Pearson*)[26]

As the Court has been extremely reluctant to entertain appeals on this ground (Roberts, 2004), 'the Commission ... has steered clear of "lurking doubt" as a freestanding ground for any of its references ...' (Elks, 2008:125). Its rather brief Casework Guidance Note on lurking doubt does not encourage its use, asserting that it is:

very much a 'last resort' in those cases where no criticism can be made of the trial and yet concern about the conviction lingers. It tends to be argued when all other grounds have failed and very rarely provides a ground of appeal on its own. (Criminal Cases Review Commission, 2011j:para:2)

One past commissioner expressed his dislike of 'lurking doubt' as a ground of appeal, arguing that the Court should never quash a conviction on 'a mere visceral or inchoate reaction' to the evidence but rather should always base its decision on a careful analysis of the case and a sound legal premise (Leigh, 2006:809). A current commissioner explained his concern for other applicants:

There'll be other cases where it will be quite clear that there are real lines of enquiry that need to be pursued, so you're very conscious that actually there are people in the system whose cases are crying out for some action by the organization for very concrete reasons. The problem you then have is how can you justify as an individual putting a lurking doubt case where you can't

---

[25] [1969] 1 Q.B. 267, 53 Cr App R 82.
[26] [2001] 1 Cr App R 141, [1999] 3 All ER 498, [1999] COD 202.

actually put your finger on anything, you can't really justify it across a table and it's, it's down to your own feeling, it's very subjective, it's a hunch … some might describe as a fishing expedition, above cases which, when they land on your desk, you yourself would say, 'that needs definite action'? (#33)

Given the Commission's approach to lurking doubt is not likely to shift—and if it did, would involve only one or two cases each year—we consider the prospects of the Commission moving towards a bolder approach to its referrals.

A bolder approach to referrals

While it is acknowledged that the Commission is hamstrung by the Court, it has been argued that it could be more proactive in trying to change the Court's jurisprudence. The argument goes that bolder referrals could broaden the Court's remit, given it is obliged to hear all those referrals made by the Commission (e.g. Nobles and Schiff, 2005:189).

The former Chair of the Commission, Graham Zellick, was keen for it to push at the standards of the Court, considering it well placed to develop the law by making a referral when the law is unclear, conflicting, or underdeveloped (Zellick, 2005:950). More recently, a current commissioner argued that:

Our legal analysis must be clever and exact but our investigations must be thorough and unstinting. We must never be so in thrall to the Court of Appeal that we stop making decisions in the best interests of justice. (Smith, 2017)

A commendable aspiration, but as we come to the end of this project, we wonder how attainable it is. Though the Commission can, and does, refer cases at reapplication that it previously considered not to meet the real possibility test (see Chapter 13), it has no appetite to refer a conviction that the Court has upheld following a prior referral. In theory, the Commission can refer a case as many times as it likes, and the Court will be obliged to grant a full appeal in each case, even if it is not impressed by the Commission's obstinacy. However, in practice the Commission does not do so. One of our cases caused us to reflect critically on this reluctance.

The Court upheld a conviction for murder in case EE33a following a referral in 1997, despite expert psychological evidence and other fresh evidence. Two further applications (EE33b&c) committed the Commission to many years of review, further expert witnesses, and considerable expense, but it was decided not to refer the case back to the Court as that 'would simply be asking the Court to reconsider its previous decisions, and there is no real possibility that the conviction would be quashed on this basis' (EE33c, Case Record). While this could be true, there was a substantial body of fresh evidence that had not been considered by the Court and which might have been persuasive to a newly convened Court. In our opinion, this was a case where the Commission might have risked the ire of the Court by asking it to revisit its prior decision. From our position, the evidence, while not the most robust, was sufficiently persuasive. Furthermore, had the Commission referred, and the Court upheld the conviction, there would still be one more option.

If the Court will not quash a conviction following a referral, the Commission can refer a case to the Home Secretary to consider exercising the Royal Prerogative of Mercy (section 16, Criminal Appeal Act 1995). The Runciman Commission recommended this power effectively to bypass the Court for those occasional cases where exculpatory evidence was inadmissible, and the Court would be powerless to act, but where the Commission was convinced of the innocence of an applicant. Duff (2009:722) suggests that this power illustrates 'that the Commissions are not entirely subordinate to the appeal courts, nor were they intended to be'. However, while the English Commission has considered using its section 16 power several times, it has only made one such referral. This was in a case where an applicant provided assistance to the authorities after being sentenced. The Commission made a reference to the Justice Secretary to recommend the use of the Royal Prerogative of Mercy, but the Justice Secretary declined to do so.

Of course, if the Commission regularly referred cases that did not present to the Court evidence of unsafety, the Court would issue rebukes, to the detriment of a good relationship, and would, in any event, uphold the convictions. This raises three related questions: 1) Would there be disadvantages for the Commission from regular rebukes and a damaged relationship? 2) Would there be disadvantages for the applicant of a referral that is not likely to be quashed by the Court? 3) Would there be wider disadvantages to other applications currently being reviewed or other applicants waiting in the queue?

The Commission and the Court must maintain a reasonably harmonious relationship as the success of each requires the cooperation of the other, as we discussed in Chapter 11. However, the relationship could be more challenging and occasionally combative without unduly compromising its symbiotic nature.

There are of course disadvantages for applicants of referrals that have small prospect of success. Raised expectations will be shattered by yet another failure to receive justice. However, as we are considering only a *somewhat* bolder approach, these would be reasonably strong applications and the risk of disappointment for some would need to be balanced by the opportunity for success for a few.

Finally, there is always the risk of depriving others waiting in the queue when CRMs devote more time to the application in hand. However, here we are referring only to those cases where considerable time has already been invested at stage two (see, for example, case EE33c, discussed above and in Chapters 7 and 13).

Balanced against these pitfalls is the potential to shift the Court's thinking in certain borderline cases, which would benefit not only the applicant but other applicants in similar cases. The Commission has an obligation to use its finite resources expeditiously in the interests of justice for all applicants, and not to clog up the system with hopeless cases. However, the line between a bold referral and an unconvincing case—the place at which the real possibility test is met—can be unclear, and it should not be surprising that staff felt conflicted on this matter.

One interviewee clearly struggled to articulate the difficulties posed by borderline cases:

You should be slow to challenge the decision of the jury if it was made on full facts, or nearly full facts. You need something that really is genuinely new and powerful ... your job is to push and, if it's marginal, if you think, we're really not happy here, they really ought to have another look at this, even though we're not terribly optimistic, I think you refer in those cases. If it's ... I don't like this, but ... my long experience tells me that this simply will not get through, then, in those circumstances, I think it is unfair to the applicant to refer, ... to be making a stand. Ugh [sighing], all these things are so difficult, other than in the rare case where you're so sure they're innocent that you have to, you know, you have to refer. (#36)

Another was more adamant:

I think we could be bolder ... the suggestion that you might be bolder is heard [by other commissioners] as, 'this is an attack on my professional integrity. I have looked at a case. I have exercised my professional judgement against a statutory test, and I've come to this view. And that's that.' Whereas my view is, there are cut-and-dried cases, and there's a grey area. And I think in the grey area, we ought to lean more towards referring. (#25)

Beyond pushing through a few more borderline cases, and risking the wrath of the Court, there is not a great deal more that the Commission can do within its legal framework. In light of this, there has been some discussion about whether the real possibility test is the 'right' test (see Chapter 2). It was not our intention to explore this. Our goal was to understand how the Commission makes its decisions based on the legal framework that has been imposed on it. However, it is worth saying as we draw this project to a close that in a few of our cases, we have seen CRMs and commissioners tie themselves up in knots trying to fit their case—which on the face of it seemed meritorious—into the dictates of the fresh evidence requirements.

We do not object to the Commission being somewhat subordinate to the Court; indeed, there seems an inevitability to this given its function as a review body, not a court of law. However, the Court's restrictions on admissibility of evidence (under its section 23 provisions) mean that some potentially unsafe convictions never get through its doors. Some of our cases were not referred because the Commission cannot submit evidence if it had been used at trial or at a prior appeal, or had been available, but not adduced at trial, and there is no adequate explanation for this failure. Though we recognize the importance of the principle of finality, given cuts to legal aid and the failures of the defence, the police, and the prosecution, this restriction leaves us with some unease.

Our experience of watching the Commission making difficult choices about which cases to refer and which to reject, decisions that cause individual CRMs and commissioners considerable anxiety, suggest that analysis of the deference of the Commission to the Court does not get us very far. It is deferential because the legislation has made it so. Those who criticize the real possibility test may actually be criticizing the safety test of the Court, as one commissioner put it:

In terms of our critics, … the issue that the debate is coalescing around at the moment is 'Is the test right?' which in part, if not in whole, is code for 'We don't like what the Court of Appeal does'. Because … at one level, since the Court of Appeal decides, you could have any test, any old test you wanted as the basis for referral, but the only rules that will count will be the rules around safety that the Court applies. So, if you don't like the real possibility test, you're saying I don't like what the Court of Appeal does … in some ways, it's a sort of oblique way of criticizing the Court, in my judgement. And the most … interesting suggestion, … we've made … speculates about the value of our having the power to make … a 'contrarian reference'; that is to say, even if we … don't think that there's a real possibility that the Court would quash, on the basis of the rules, of the game that has got to be played, and we nevertheless have doubts about whether or not there's been a miscarriage, … we ought to have the ability, in exceptional circumstances, to make a contrarian reference, … which then compels the Court to look again and justify the original decision or not. (#9)

If the Commission were prepared to push at the boundaries of the real possibility test, and make bolder, sometimes 'contrarian' referrals, and if the Court were more inclined to be receptive to fresh evidence, and less deferential to the jury and the principle of finality, we suspect few would complain about the real possibility test. In such circumstances, some of those cases that campaigners consider to be meritorious would more likely be referred, and both the referral rate and the rate at which the Court quashed unsafe convictions would increase. Of course, this may not be good for public confidence and trust in the criminal justice system, as people would be aware that pre-trial and trial justice often errs. Then again, newspaper articles investigating instances of non-disclosure (referred to above) published in early 2018 suggest that systemic changes at the front end of the system are needed to increase public trust, and should that happen, there may be fewer cases for the Commission and the Court to judge.

Our research has shown that the Commission is not a perfect organization. It has more variability than most applicants would be happy with, it remains a little more cautious in its referrals than it may need to be, it is sometimes too slow and ponderous, and it has, until recently, been somewhat reluctant to make use of its knowledge of what can and does go wrong in the criminal justice process. However, of one thing we can be sure: it is a whole lot better than its predecessor, C3, and there is no other organization currently in place to take on the Commission's vital work. With increasing evidence of errors in our underfunded criminal justice system, wrongful convictions are set to rise. It would be nothing short of an own goal for critics to fight to remove the Commission from our struggling criminal justice system or for the government to fail to fund it adequately for the task at hand.

APPENDIX

Case ID	Case category	Year of application	Offence(s)	CCRC decision	CA judgment
HIA1	Historical Institutional Abuse	2007	Indecent assault, buggery, rape	Non-referral	n/a
HIA2	Historical Institutional Abuse	2007	Buggery x 6 & indecent assault x 6	Non-referral	n/a
HIA3b	Historical Institutional Abuse	2007	Indecent assault, attempted buggery	Referral	Part quashed
HIA3a		2003	Indecent assault, attempted buggery	Non-referral	n/a
HIA4	Historical Institutional Abuse	2004	Cruelty, buggery	Non-referral	n/a
HIA5	Historical Institutional Abuse	2005	Indecent assault, buggery, rape	Non-referral	n/a
HIA6	Historical Institutional Abuse	2007	Indecent assault, rape, inciting a child	Non-referral	n/a
HIA7	Historical Institutional Abuse	2008	Indecent assault, attempted buggery, buggery	Non-referral	n/a
HIA8	Historical Institutional Abuse	2003	Indecent assault, attempted buggery, buggery	Non-referral	n/a
HIA9	Historical Institutional Abuse	2007	Rape, buggery, indecent assault, indecency with a child	Non-referral	n/a
HIA10b	Historical Institutional Abuse	2007	ABH, indecent assault, attempted buggery, buggery	Non-referral	n/a
HIA10a		2003	ABH, indecent assault, attempted buggery, buggery	Non-referral	n/a
HIA11a	Historical Institutional Abuse	2002	Buggery, indecent assault, rape	Non-referral	n/a
HIA11b	Historical Institutional Abuse	2006	Buggery, indecent assault, rape	Referral	Part quashed
HIA12	Historical Institutional Abuse	2001	Rape, buggery, indecent assault	Referral	Quashed
HIA13	Historical Institutional Abuse	2000	Indecent assault	Referral	Quashed
HIA14	Historical Institutional Abuse	2010	Rape, indecent assault	Non-referral	n/a
CS1	Contemporary Sexual Crimes	2002	Rape	Non-referral	n/a
CS2	Contemporary Sexual Crimes	2002	Indecent assault	Referral	Quashed
CS3	Contemporary Sexual Crimes	2002	Rape	Referral	Upheld

Case ID	Case category	Year of application	Offence(s)	CCRC decision	CA judgment
CS4	Contemporary Sexual Crimes	2002	Rape	Referral	Upheld
CS5	Contemporary Sexual Crimes	2003	Rape	Referral	Quashed
CS6b	Contemporary Sexual Crimes	2003	Rape	Referral	Quashed
CS6a		2003	Rape	Non-referral	n/a
CS7	Contemporary Sexual Crimes	2005	Indecent assault, gross indecency	Non-referral	n/a
CS8	Contemporary Sexual Crimes	2005	Incest	Non-referral	n/a
CS9	Contemporary Sexual Crimes	2006	Indecent assault	Referral	Quashed
CS10	Contemporary Sexual Crimes	2007	Rape	Referral	Quashed
CS11	Contemporary Sexual Crimes	2007	Attempted buggery, indecent assault	Referral	Quashed
CS12	Contemporary Sexual Crimes	2007	Rape	Referral	Quashed
CS13	Contemporary Sexual Crimes	2008	Indecent assault, rape	Referral	Upheld
CS14b	Contemporary Sexual Crimes	2009	Rape, assault occasioning ABH	Referral	Upheld
CS14a		2006	Rape, assault occasioning ABH	Non-referral	n/a
CS15	Contemporary Sexual Crimes	2011	Indecent assault, gross indecency with a child	Non-referral	n/a
EE1	Expert evidence—infant death	2001	Murder x 2	Referral	Quashed
EE2	Expert evidence—infant death	2003	Murder x 2	Referral	Quashed
EE3	Expert evidence—infant death	2004	Infanticide	Referral	Upheld
EE4	Expert evidence—infant death	2002	Manslaughter	Non-referral	n/a
EE5	Expert evidence—infant death	2004	Manslaughter	Non-referral	n/a
EE6b	Expert evidence—infant death	2004	Murder	Non-referral	n/a
EE6a		1999	Murder, cruelty	Non-referral	n/a
EE7	Expert evidence—infant death	2005	Murder	Non-referral	n/a
EE8	Expert evidence—infant death	2002	Murder	Non-referral	n/a
EE9	Expert evidence—infant death	2006	Manslaughter	Non-referral	n/a
EE10	Expert evidence—infant injuries	2000	Assault occasioning GBH	Referral	Quashed

Case ID	Case category	Year of application	Offence(s)	CCRC decision	CA judgment
EE11b	Expert evidence—sexual assault	2002	Rape, indecent assault x7	Referral	Quashed
EE11a		1999	Sexual assault, rape	Non-referral	n/a
EE12	Expert evidence—sexual assault	2006	Rape, indecency with a child, indecent assault	Referral	Upheld
EE13	Expert evidence—sexual assault	2006	GBH with intent	Referral	Upheld
EE14c	Expert evidence—sexual assault	2008	Rape, indecent assault x7	Referral	Quashed
EE14a		1999	Rape, indecent assault	Non-referral	n/a
EE14b		2002	Rape, indecent assault	Non-referral	n/a
EE15	Expert evidence—sexual assault	2006	Rape x 2, attempted rape, gross indecency with a child	Referral	Quashed
EE16	Expert evidence—sexual assault	2007	Indecent assault	Non-referral	n/a
EE17	Expert evidence—sexual assault	2009	Indecent assault	Referral	Upheld
EE18	Expert evidence—sexual assault	2008	Buggery, indecency with a child	Referral	Quashed
EE19b	Expert evidence—sexual assault	2008	Indecent assault of minor	Referral	Quashed
EE19a		2007	Indecent assault of minor	Non-referral	n/a
EE20	Expert evidence—sexual assault	2008	Rape, indecent assault, attempted rape	Referral	Quashed
EE21	Expert evidence—DNA	2009	Murder	Referral	Quashed
EE22b	Expert evidence—DNA	2007	Murder x 2	Referral	Upheld
EE22a		1997	Murder x 2	Non-referral	n/a
EE23	Expert evidence—DNA	2003	Murder	Non-referral	n/a
EE24	Expert evidence—DNA	2001	Murder	Non-referral	n/a
EE25	Expert evidence—DNA	2000	Murder & buggery	Non-referral	n/a
EE26c	Expert evidence—DNA	2010	Attempted rape	Referral	Quashed
EE26a		1998	Attempted rape	Non-referral	n/a
EE26b		2002	Attempted rape	Non-referral	n/a
EE27	Expert evidence—DNA	2009	Rape x 2 & GBH	Non-referral	n/a
EE28	Expert evidence—other	2004	Burglary x 3, attempted burglary	Referral	Part quashed
EE29a	Expert evidence—other	2005	Murder	Referral	Upheld
EE29b	Expert evidence—other	2001	Murder	Application withdrawn	n/a

Case ID	Case category	Year of application	Offence(s)	CCRC decision	CA judgment
EE30	Expert evidence—other	2008	Burglary & theft	Non-referral	n/a
EE31	Expert evidence—other	2002	Murder	Referral	Quashed
EE32d	Expert evidence—other	2007	Murder	Non-referral	n/a
EE32a		1997	Murder	Referral	Upheld
EE32b		2002	Murder	Non-referral	n/a
EE32c		2003	Murder	Non-referral	n/a
EE33c	Expert evidence—other	2010	Murder	Non-referral	n/a
EE33b		2003	Murder	Non-referral	n/a
EE33a		1997	Murder	Referral	Upheld
EE34	Expert evidence—other	2005	Indecent assault	Non-referral	n/a
EE35b	Expert evidence—other	2004	Murder & arson	Non-referral	n/a
EE35a		2000	Murder & arson	Non-referral	n/a
EE36	Expert evidence—other	2009	Robbery	Non-referral	n/a
EE37b	Expert evidence—other	2011	Murder	Referral	Quashed
EE37a		2008	Murder	Non-referral	n/a
EE38c	Expert evidence—other	2011	Murder	Referral	Upheld
EE38b		2005	Murder	Non-referral	n/a
EE38a		1998	Murder	Non-referral	n/a
EE39	Expert evidence—other	1997	Murder x 2	Referral	Quashed
EE40	Expert evidence—other	2011	Murder	Non-referral	n/a
EE41	Expert evidence—other	2000	Attempted rape	Referral	Quashed
EE42b	Expert evidence—other	2014	Murder x 4	Open	n/a
EE42a		2008	Murder x 4	Non-referral	n/a
PI1	Police investigation (s 19)	2007	Rape	Referral	Quashed
PI2	Police investigation (s 19)	2008	Murder, conspiracy to GBH, violent disorder	Referral	Quashed
PI3	Police investigation (s 19)	2007	Assault, rape	Referral	Upheld
PI4	Police investigation (s 19)	2001	Murder	Referral	Upheld
PI5b	Police investigation (s 19)	2003	Attempted murder, possessing firearm	Non-referral	n/a

Case ID	Case category	Year of application	Offence(s)	CCRC decision	CA judgment
PI5a		1999	Attempted murder, possessing firearm	Non-referral	n/a
PI6	Police investigation (s 19)	2008	Murder	Non-referral	n/a
PI7	Police investigation (s 19)	2006	Rape	Non-referral	n/a
PI8c	Police investigation (s 19)	2009	Murder	Non-referral	n/a
PI8b		2000	Murder	Non-referral	n/a
PI8a		1997	Murder	Non-referral	n/a
PI9b	Police investigation (s 19)	2009	Murder	Non-referral	n/a
PI9a		2000	Murder	Non-referral	n/a
PI10	Police investigation (s 19)	2010	Murder	Referral	Upheld
JD1	Jury directed (s 15)	2006	Murder	n/a	n/a
JD2	Jury directed (s 15)	2004	Murder	n/a	n/a
JD3	Jury directed (s 15)	2010	Murder	n/a	n/a
JD4	Jury directed (s 15)	2010	Murder	n/a	n/a
JD5	Jury directed (s 15)	2007	Indecent assault, gross indecency with a child	n/a	n/a
JD6	Jury directed (s 15)	2003	Murder	n/a	n/a
JD7	Jury directed (s 15)	2011	Conspiracy to transfer & remove criminal property	n/a	n/a
JD8	Jury directed (s 15)	2011	Conspiracy to commit blackmail	n/a	n/a
JD9	Jury directed (s 15)	2011	Murder x 4	n/a	n/a
JD10	Jury directed (s 15)	2011	Murder	n/a	n/a
JD11	Jury directed (s 15)	2011	Conspiracy to supply class A drugs	n/a	n/a
JD12	Jury directed (s 15)	1997	Murder	n/a	n/a
JD13	Jury directed (s 15)	1997	Murder	n/a	n/a
A1	Asylum & Immigration	2011	Failure to produce a document contrary to section 2 Immigration and Asylum Act 2004	Referral	Quashed
A2	Asylum & Immigration	2012	Possession of a false identity document	Referral	Quashed
A3	Asylum & Immigration	2011	Possession of a false instrument with intent; attempting to obtain air services by deception	Referral	Quashed
A4	Asylum & Immigration	2012	Possession of a false instrument with intent; attempting to obtain air services by deception	Referral	Quashed

Case ID	Case category	Year of application	Offence(s)	CCRC decision	CA judgment
A5	Asylum & Immigration	2012	Possession of a false identity document with intent, contrary to section 25(1) of the Identity Cards Act 2006	Referral	Abandoned
A6	Asylum & Immigration	2011	Failure to produce a document contrary to section 2 Immigration and Asylum Act 2004	Referral	Quashed
A7	Asylum & Immigration	2012	Possession of false identity document with intent	Non-referral	n/a
A8	Asylum & Immigration	2012	Failure to produce a document contrary to section 2 Immigration and Asylum (Treatment of Claimants) Act 2004	Non-referral	n/a
A9	Asylum & Immigration	2007	Failure to produce an immigration document	Referral	Quashed
A10	Asylum & Immigration	2012	Possession of an identity document with improper intention	Referral	Quashed
A11	Asylum & Immigration	2012	Possession of an improperly obtained identity document	Referral	Quashed
A12	Asylum & Immigration	2012	Possession of an identity document with improper intention	Referral	Quashed
A13	Asylum & Immigration	2012	Possession of another's identity document	Referral	Quashed
A14	Asylum & Immigration	2012	Failure to produce a document contrary to section 2 Immigration and Asylum (Treatment of Claimants) Act 2004	Referral	Quashed
A15	Asylum & Immigration	2012	Using a false instrument with intent; attempting to obtain services by deception	Referral	Quashed
A16	Asylum & Immigration	2012	Possession of an identity document with improper intention	Referral	Quashed
A17	Asylum & Immigration	2012	Attempt to obtain services by deception; possession of a false instrument with intent	Referral	Quashed
A18	Asylum & Immigration	2009	Seeking leave to remain in the United Kingdom as a refugee by deception	Referral	Upheld

Case ID	Case category	Year of application	Offence(s)	CCRC decision	CA judgment
A19	Asylum & Immigration	2008	Failure to produce a document contrary to section 2 Immigration and Asylum (Treatment of Claimants) Act 2004	Referral	Quashed
A20	Asylum & Immigration	2008	Failure to produce a document contrary to section 2 Immigration and Asylum (Treatment of Claimants) Act 2004	Referral	Quashed
A21	Asylum & Immigration	2003	Attempting to obtain services by deception; possession of false instrument	Referral	Quashed
A22	Asylum & Immigration	2002	Attempting to obtain services by deception; possession of false instrument	Referral	Quashed
A23	Asylum & Immigration	2002	Attempting to obtain services by deception; possession of false instrument	Referral	Quashed

References

Aliverti, Ana. 2014. *Crimes of Mobility: Criminal Law and the Regulation of Immigration*. Abingdon: Routledge.

Ashworth, Andrew. 1998. *The Criminal Process*. 2nd ed. Oxford: Oxford University Press.

Ashworth, Andrew and Mike Redmayne. 2005. *The Criminal Process*. 3rd ed. Oxford: Oxford University Press.

Ashworth, Andrew and Mike Redmayne. 2010. *The Criminal Process*. 4th ed. Oxford: Oxford University Press.

Ask, Karl and Pär Anders Granhag. 2007. 'Motivational Bias in Criminal Investigators' Judgments of Witness Reliability'. *Journal of Applied Social Psychology* 37(3):561–91.

Association of Chief Police Officers. 2005. *DNA Good Practice Manual 2nd Edition*.

Baldwin, John and Mike McConville. 1977. *Negotiated Justice: Pressures to Plead Guilty*. London: Martin.

Baldwin, John and Mike McConville. 1979. *Jury Trials*. Oxford: Oxford University Press.

Baldwin, Robert. 1995. *Rules and Government*. Oxford: Clarendon Press.

Barak, Aharon. 1989. *Judicial Discretion*. New Haven and London: Yale University Press.

Barlow, Mark and Mark Newby. 2009. 'The Challenges of Historic Allegations of Past Sexual Abuse'. *The Way Ahead*.

Batts, Anthony W., Maddy DeLone, and Darrel W. Stephens. 2014. 'Policing and Wrongful Convictions'. *New Perspectives in Policing* 1–31.

Baumgartner, Mary P. 1992. 'The Myth of Discretion'. Pp. 129–62 in *The Uses of Discretion*, edited by K. Hawkins. Oxford: Oxford University Press.

BBC News. 2014. 'William Roache Found Not Guilty of Rape and Indecent Assault'. February 6. Retrieved (http://www.bbc.co.uk/news/uk-england-26068034).

Beckford, Martin. 2017a. 'Failure of Police Who Bury Key Evidence Is Britain's Biggest Cause of Miscarriages of Justice, Watchdog Warns'. *Mail on Sunday*, December 24.

Beckford, Martin. 2017b. 'Forensics Scandal Now Hits TEN THOUSAND Cases: Rogue Scientists May Have Tampered with Blood Tests in Suspect Cases Including Murder and Rape'. *Mail on Sunday*, October 15.

Beckford, Martin and Nick Craven. 2017. 'Courts Face Crisis over 500 "Fixed" Forensic Tests: Hundreds May Appeal against Drug and Child Custody Verdicts after Scientists Are Accused of Doctoring Data'. *Mail on Sunday*, February 19. Retrieved (http://www.dailymail.co.uk/news/article-4238578/Courts-face-crisis-500-fixed-forensic-tests.html).

Bell, John. 1992. 'Discretionary Decision-Making: A Jurisprudential View'. Pp. 89–112 in *The Uses of Discretion*, edited by K. Hawkins. Oxford: Oxford University Press.

Bentley, David. 2017. 'DNA—an Unstoppable March'. *The Law Society Gazette*, March.

Bevan, Gwyn and Christopher Hood. 2006. 'What's Measured Is What Matters: Targets and Gaming in the English Public Health Care System'. *Public Administration* 84(3):517–38.

Birch, Di and Claire Taylor. 2003. ' "People Like Us?": Responding to Allegations of Past Abuse in Care'. *Criminal Law Review* 12:823–49.

Birdling, Malcolm. 2011. 'Correction of Miscarriages of Justice in New Zealand and England'. University of Oxford (Unpublished Doctor of Philosophy thesis).

Bonner, Raymond. 2012. *Anatomy of Injustice: A Murder Case Gone Wrong*. New York: Vintage.

Bottomley, Keith. 1973. *Decisions in the Penal Process*. London: Martin Robertson.

Bourdieu, Pierre. 1990. *The Logic of Practice*. Stanford, CA: Stanford University Press.

Bowling, Ben. 1999. *Violent Racism: Victimization, Policing and Social Context*. Oxford: Oxford University Press.

Bowling, Ben and Coretta Phillips. 2007. 'Disproportionate and Discriminatory: Reviewing the Evidence on Police Stop and Search'. *Modern Law Review* 70(6):936–61.

Bradley, Caroline, Alistair Munt, and Grace Hale. 2009. 'Shaken Baby Syndrome and the Imperfect Triad'. *Archbold News* (7):1–2.

Bradney, Anthony G. D. 1992. 'How the Law Thinks about Children: Book Review'. *International Journal of Law, Policy and the Family* 6(3):417–20.

Brigham, John. 2016. ' "Rape Culture" Narrative, State Feminism, and the Presumption of Guilt'. Pp. 66–81 in *Wrongful Allegations of Sexual and Child Abuse*, edited by R. Burnett. Oxford: Oxford University Press.

Brooke, Henry. 2017. 'The Bach Report: (7) Criminal Justice'. *Henry Brooke: Musings, Memories and Miscellanea*, September.

Brownmiller, Susan. 1975. *Against Our Will: Men, Women and Rape*. New York: Simon & Schuster.

Bucks, Jonathan. 2016. 'Fury as Government Body HELPS Immigrants QUASH CONVICTIONS for Illegal Entry to Britain'. *Sunday Express*, January 9.

Bunting, Dan. 2014. 'Criminal Cases Review Commission'. *UK Criminal Law Blog*. Retrieved (http://ukcriminallawblog.com/criminal-cases-review-commission/).

Burnett, Ros. 2016. 'Reducing the Incidence and Harms of Wrongful Allegations of Abuse'. Pp. 282–95 in *Wrongful Allegations of Sexual and Child Abuse*, edited by R. Burnett. Oxford: Oxford University Press.

Burnett, Ros, Carolyn Hoyle, and Naomi-Ellen Speechley. 2017. 'The Context and Impact of Being Wrongly Accused of Abuse in Occupations of Trust'. *The Howard Journal of Crime and Justice* 56(2):176–97.

Campbell, Elaine. 1999. 'Towards a Sociological Theory of Discretion'. *International Journal of the Sociology of Law* 27(1):79–101.

Campbell, Kathryn M. and Myriam Denov. 2012. 'When Justice Fails: Wrongful Convictions in Canada'. Pp. 252–68 in *Criminal Justice in Canada*, edited by J. V. Roberts and M. G. Grossman. Toronto: Nelson Education.

Canadian Department of Justice. 2016. 'Criminal Conviction Review'. *Department of Justice*.

Cape, Ed and Richard Young. 2008. *Regulating Policing: The Police and Criminal Evidence Act 1984—Past, Present and Future*. Oxford: Hart Publishing.

Cardiff Law School Innocence Project. 2017. 'Police Misconduct and the CCRC'. *The Justice Gap*. Retrieved (http://thejusticegap.com/2017/04/ccrc20-police-misconduct-ccrc/).

Charman, Steve D. 2013. 'The Forensic Confirmation Bias: A Problem of Evidence Integration, Not Just Evidence Evaluation'. *Journal of Applied Research in Memory and Cognition* 2(1):56–8.

Choo, Chun Wei. 2006. *The Knowing Organization: How Organizations Use Information to Construct Meaning, Create Knowledge, and Make Decisions*. 2nd ed. New York: Oxford University Press.

Christie, Gary. 2016. *Prosecuting the Persecuted in Scotland: Article 31 (1) of the 1951 Refugee Convention and the Scottish Criminal Justice System*.

Cialdini, Robert B. 1988. *Influence: Science and Practice*. 2nd ed. Glenview, IL: Scott, Foresman.

Cohen, Stanley. 1973. *Folk Devils and Moral Panics: The Creation of the Mods and Rockers*. London: Paladin.

Cole, Simon A. 2012. 'Forensic Science and Wrongful Convictions: From Exposer to Contributor to Corrector'. *New England Law Review* 46:711–36.

Coleman, Clive, David Dixon, and Keith Bottomley. 1993. 'Police Investigative Procedures: Researching the Impact of PACE'. Pp. 17–31 in *Justice in Error*, edited by C. Walker and K. Starmer. London: Blackstone Press.

Commons Select Committee. 2018. *Disclosure of Evidence in Criminal Cases Examined*. Retrieved (https://www.parliament.uk/business/committees/committees-a-z/commons-select/justice-committee/news-parliament-2017/disclosure-evidence-criminal-cases-launch-17-19/).

Conlon, Gerry. 1990. *Proved Innocent: The Story of Gerry Conlon of the Guildford Four.* London: Hamish Hamilton.

Cooper, Sarah. 2013. 'The Collision of Law and Science: American Court Responses to Developments in Forensic Science'. *Pace Law Review* 33(1):234–301.

Cotterrell, Roger. 1998. 'Why Must Legal Ideas Be Interpreted Sociologically?' *Journal of Law and Society* 25(2):171–92.

Covey, Russell. 2013. 'Police Misconduct as a Cause of Wrongful Convictions'. *Washington University Law Review* 90(4):1133–89.

Criminal Cases Review Commission. 1999. *Annual Report 1998/99.*

Criminal Cases Review Commission. 2005a. *Annual Report and Accounts 2004/05.*

Criminal Cases Review Commission. 2005b. *Formal Memorandum Family Abuse Cases.*

Criminal Cases Review Commission. 2006a. *Formal Memorandum Child Sexual Abuse Cases.*

Criminal Cases Review Commission. 2006b. 'Quashing Convictions': The Responses of the Criminal Cases Review Commission (11 December 2006).*

Criminal Cases Review Commission. 2007. *Annual Report and Accounts 2006/07.*

Criminal Cases Review Commission. 2008. *This Document Is Linked to the Commission's Formal Memorandum on Sexual Offences.*

Criminal Cases Review Commission. 2009a. *Casework Guidance Note Delay as an Abuse of Process.*

Criminal Cases Review Commission. 2009b. *Casework Guidance Note DNA Evidence.*

Criminal Cases Review Commission. 2010. *Casework Guidance Note Expert Evidence.*

Criminal Cases Review Commission. 2011a. *Annual Report and Accounts 2010/11.*

Criminal Cases Review Commission. 2011b. *Casework Guidance Note Applicant and Representative Relationships.*

Criminal Cases Review Commission. 2011c. *Casework Guidance Note CRM Work on Stage 1 Cases.*

Criminal Cases Review Commission. 2011d. *Casework Guidance Note Decision-Making Committees.*

Criminal Cases Review Commission. 2011e. *Casework Guidance Note Disclosure by Prosecution & Defence Investigators.*

Criminal Cases Review Commission. 2011f. *Casework Guidance Note Exceptional Circumstances.*

Criminal Cases Review Commission. 2011g. *Casework Guidance Note Identifying the Issues.*

Criminal Cases Review Commission. 2011h. *Casework Guidance Note Interviewing.*

Criminal Cases Review Commission. 2011i. *Casework Guidance Note Judicial Review.*

Criminal Cases Review Commission. 2011j. *Casework Guidance Note Lurking Doubt.*

Criminal Cases Review Commission. 2011k. *Casework Guidance Note Screening.*

Criminal Cases Review Commission. 2011l. *Casework Guidance Note Section 13 and Section 23.*

Criminal Cases Review Commission. 2011m. *Casework Guidance Note Sexual Offences.*

Criminal Cases Review Commission. 2011n. *Casework Guidance Note What Enquiries Do I Need to Make?*

Criminal Cases Review Commission. 2011o. *Casework Guidance Note What Is a Real Possibility?*

Criminal Cases Review Commission. 2011p. *Casework Guidance Note Appeals against Conviction Following a Plea of Guilty.*

Criminal Cases Review Commission. 2012a. *Annual Report and Accounts 2011/12.*

Criminal Cases Review Commission. 2012b. *Casework Guidance Note Inadequate Defence.*

Criminal Cases Review Commission. 2012c. *Casework Guidance Note Misconduct by Investigators.*

Criminal Cases Review Commission. 2012d. *Casework Guidance Note Section 15 Directions from the Court of Appeal.*

Criminal Cases Review Commission. 2012e. *Casework Guidance Note Section 17 Criminal Appeal Act 1995.*

Criminal Cases Review Commission. 2012f. *Casework Guidance Note Section 19 Requirements to Appoint an Investigating Officer.*

Criminal Cases Review Commission. 2013a. *Annual Report and Accounts 2012/13.*

Criminal Cases Review Commission. 2013b. *Casework Guidance Note Stage 1 Process.*

Criminal Cases Review Commission. 2013c. 'Commission Refers the Conviction of Busani Zondo'. *Criminal Cases Review Commission*, December 3. Retrieved (https://ccrc.gov.uk/commission-refers-the-conviction-of-busani-zondo/).

Criminal Cases Review Commission. 2013d. *Formal Memorandum Sexual Offence Cases.*

Criminal Cases Review Commission. 2013e. *Formal Memorandum Stage 1 Decisions (Including Re-Applications).*

Criminal Cases Review Commission. 2014a. *Annual Report and Accounts 2013/14.*

Criminal Cases Review Commission. 2014b. *Annual Report and Accounts 2014/15.*

Criminal Cases Review Commission. 2014c. *Casework Guidance Note Asylum and Immigration Issues in Casework.*

Criminal Cases Review Commission. 2015a. *Annual Report and Accounts 2014/15.*

Criminal Cases Review Commission. 2015b. 'Commission Refers the Rape Conviction of Ched Evans to the Court of Appeal'. Retrieved (https://ccrc.gov.uk/commission-refers-the-rape-conviction-of-ched-evans-to-the-court-of-appeal/).

Criminal Cases Review Commission. 2015c. *Formal Memorandum Applicants' Representatives: Inappropriate Conduct.*

Criminal Cases Review Commission. 2015d. *Formal Memorandum Section 15 Directions from the Court of Appeal.*

Criminal Cases Review Commission. 2015e. *Formal Memorandum Section 19 Requirements to Appoint an Investigating Officer.*

Criminal Cases Review Commission. 2015f. *Formal Memorandum Stage 2 Decision-Making Process.*

Criminal Cases Review Commission. 2015g. *Guidance for Legal Representatives.*

Criminal Cases Review Commission. 2016a. *Annual Report and Accounts 2015/16.*

Criminal Cases Review Commission. 2016b. *Formal Memorandum Discretion in Referrals.*

Criminal Cases Review Commission. 2016c. *Formal Memorandum Interviewing.*

Criminal Cases Review Commission. 2016d. *Formal Memorandum Judicial Review: Policy and Procedure.*

Criminal Cases Review Commission. 2016e. *Formal Memorandum Persistent Applicants.*

Criminal Cases Review Commission. 2016f. *Formal Memorandum The Commission's Power to Obtain Material from Public Bodies under S.17 of the Criminal Appeal Act 1995.*

Criminal Cases Review Commission. 2016g. *Response by the Criminal Cases Review Commission.* Retrieved (http://www.ccrc.gov.uk/wp-content/uploads/2016/06/CCRC-Sentencing-Council-consultation-April-2016.pdf).

Criminal Cases Review Commission. 2017a. *Annual Report and Accounts 2016/17.*

Criminal Cases Review Commission. 2017b. *Business Plan 2016 to 2017.*

Criminal Cases Review Commission. 2017c. *Formal Memorandum Enquiries as to Witness Credibility.*

Criminal Cases Review Commission. 2017d. *Formal Memorandum Exceptional Circumstances.*

Criminal Cases Review Commission. 2017e. *Formal Memorandum Experts Selection and Instruction.*

Criminal Cases Review Commission. 2017f. *Formal Memorandum Extensions for Further Representations/Submissions.*

Criminal Cases Review Commission. 2017g. *Formal Memorandum Medical Records.*

Criminal Cases Review Commission. 2017h. *Formal Memorandum Post-Decision Activity on Cases.*

Criminal Cases Review Commission. 2018a. 'Commission Refers the Convictions of Seven People Convicted of Travel Document Offences'. *Criminal Cases Review Commission.*

Criminal Cases Review Commission. 2018b. *Formal Memorandum Communicating with Applicants.*

Criminal Cases Review Commission. 2018c. *Formal Memorandum Decision-Making Process.*

Criminal Cases Review Commission. n.d. 'Case Statistics'. *n.d.* Retrieved (https://ccrc.gov.uk/case-statistics/).

Criminal Cases Review Commission. n.d. *Formal Memorandum Stage 1 Decisions (Including NRG Cases and Re-Applications).*

Criminal Cases Review Commission. n.d. *Questions and Answers about the CCRC.* Retrieved (https://s3-eu-west-2.amazonaws.com/ccrc-prod-storage-1jdn5d1f6iq1l/uploads/2015/01/CCRC-Useful-information-for-potential-applicants.pdf).

Criminal Cases Review Commission. n.d. 'What We Do'. *Criminal Cases Review Commission.*

Criminal Cases Review Commission. n.d. 'Who We Are'. *Criminal Cases Review Commission.*

Criminal Injuries Compensation Authority. n.d. 'About Us'. *Ministry of Justice.*

Crown Prosecution Service. n.d. 'Legal Guidance—Immigration'. *Crown Prosecution Service.*

Crown Prosecution Service. n.d. 'Non-Jury Trials: Legal Guidance'. *Crown Prosecution Service.*

Curtis, John. 2015. 'Righting Wrongs'. *Counsel.* Retrieved (https://www.counselmagazine.co.uk/articles/righting-wrongs).

Davis, Kenneth C. 1969. *Discretionary Justice: A Preliminary Inquiry.* Baton Rouge: Louisiana State University Press.

Davis, Kevin. 2014. 'Prisoner Exonerations Are at an All-Time High, and It's Not because of DNA Testing'. *ABA Journal.*

Davis, Nicola. 2017. 'DNA in the Dock: How Flawed Techniques Send Innocent People to Prison'. *The Guardian*, October 2.

Dennis, Ian. 2003. 'Fair Trials and Safe Convictions'. *Current Legal Problems* 56(1):211–37.

Devlin, Hannah and Vikram Dodd. 2018. 'Falling Forensic Science Standards "Making Miscarriages of Justice Inevitable"'. *The Guardian*, January 19. Retrieved (https://www.theguardian.com/uk-news/2018/jan/19/uk-police-forces-failing-to-meet-forensic-standards-safe-regulator-miscarriages-justice-outsourcing).

Dioso-Villa, Rachel. 2014. 'Out of Grace: Inequity in Post-Exoneration Remedies for Wrongful Conviction'. *University of New South Wales Law Journal* 37(1):349–75.

Dixon, David. 2016. 'Integrity, Interrogation and Criminal Justice'. Pp. 75–95 in *The Integrity of the Criminal Process*, edited by J. Hunter, P. Roberts, S. N. M. Young, and D. Dixon.

Donabedian, Anaïd. 1988. 'The Quality of Care: How Can It Be Assessed?' *Journal of the American Medical Association* 260(12):1743–8.

Donaldson, Lex and Ben Nanfeng Luo. 2013. 'The Aston Programme Contribution to Organizational Research: A Literature Review'. *International Journal of Management Reviews* 16(1):84–104.

Doward, Jamie. 2011. 'Miscarriages of Justice Are Going Unchallenged by Watchdog, Says QC'. *The Guardian*, May 29.

Doyle, James M. 2010. *From Error Toward Quality: A Federal Role in Support of Criminal Process.* Retrieved (https://www.acslaw.org/sites/default/files/ACS Issue Brief - Doyle - From Error Toward Quality.pdf).

Drizin, Steven and Richard A. Leo. 2004. 'The Problem of False Confessions in the Post-DNA World'. *North Carolina Law Review* 82:891–1007.

Dror, Itiel E. and Rebecca Bucht. 2012. 'Psychological Perspectives on Problems with Forensic Science Evidence'. Pp. 257–76 in *Conviction of the Innocent: Lessons from Psychological Research*, edited by B. L. Cutler. Washington DC: American Psychological Association.

Dror, Itiel E. and Simon A. Cole. 2010. 'The Vision In "Blind" Justice: Expert Perception, Judgment, and Visual Cognition in Forensic Pattern Recognition'. *Psychonomic Bulletin & Review* 17(2):161–7.

Dror, Itiel E. and Greg Hampikian. 2011. 'Subjectivity and Bias in Forensic DNA Mixture Interpretation'. *Science & Justice* 51(4):204–8.

Duff, Peter. 2009. 'Straddling Two Worlds: Reflections of a Retired Criminal Cases Review Commissioner'. *The Modern Law Review* 72(5):693–722.

Duhaime, Ann-Christine, Cindy W. Christian, Lucy Balian Rorke, and Robert A. Zimmerman. 1998. 'Nonaccidental Head Injury in Infants—The "Shaken-Baby Syndrome"'. *New England Journal of Medicine* 338(25):1822–9.

Dworkin, Ronald. 1963. 'Judicial Discretion'. *The Journal of Philosophy* 60(21):624–38.

Dworkin, Ronald. 1977. *Taking Rights Seriously*. Boston: Harvard University Press.

Dyer, Clare. 2007. 'Judges Furious over Plan to Cut Appeal Court's Powers'. *The Guardian*, October 6.

Dyson, John. 2011. *Time to Call It a Day: Some Reflections on Finality and the Law*. Retrieved (https://www.supremecourt.uk/docs/speech_111014.pdf).

Eastern, Richard. 2016. 'Removal of Information Held on the Police National Computer and Police National Database'. *Sonn Macmillan Walker*. Retrieved (https://www.criminalsolicitor.co.uk/legal-guides/removal-of-information-held-on-the-police-national-computer-and-police-national-database/).

Eldridge, John E. T. and Alastair D. Crombie. 2013. *A Sociology of Organisations (Routledge Library Editions: Organizations: Theory & Behaviour)*. Abingdon: Routledge.

Elks, Laurie. 2008. 'Righting Miscarriages of Justice? Ten Years of the Criminal Cases Review Commission'. London: JUSTICE.

Emerson, Robert M. and Blair Paley. 1992. 'Organizational Horizons and Complaint-Filing'. Pp. 231–48 in *The Uses of Discretion*, edited by K. Hawkins. Oxford: Oxford University Press.

England, Charlotte. 2016. 'Ched Evans: Scrutinising Women's Sexual History in Rape Trial "Set Us Back 30 Years"'. *The Independent*, October 15. Retrieved (http://www.independent.co.uk/news/uk/crime/ched-evans-rape-case-cleared-not-guilty-sets-us-back-30-years-vera-baird-solicitor-general-womens-a7363291.html).

Ericson, Richard V. and Kevin D. Haggerty. 1997. *Policing the Risk Society*. Oxford: Oxford University Press.

Evans, Matt. 2012. 'The Dilemma of Maintaining Innocence'. Pp. 61–4 in *Wrongly Accused: Who Is Responsible for Investigating Miscarriages of Justice?*, edited by J. Robins. The Justice Gap and Solicitors Journal.

Executive Office to the President. 2016. *Report to the President: Forensic Science in Criminal Courts: Ensuring Scientific Validity of Feature—Comparison Methods*.

Fair Trials and Freshfields Bruckhaus Deringer LLP. 2017. *The Disappearing Trial: Towards a Rights-Based Approach to Trial Waiver System*. Retrieved (https://www.fairtrials.org/wp-content/uploads/2017/12/Report-The-Disappearing-Trial.pdf).

Feldman, Martha. 1992. 'Social Limits to Discretion: An Organizational Perspective'. Pp. 163–84 in *The Uses of Discretion*, edited by K. Hawkins. Oxford: Oxford University Press.

Festinger, Leon. 1957. *A Theory of Cognitive Dissonance*. Stanford, CA: Stanford University Press. Retrieved 9 February 2018 (http://www.sup.org/books/title/?id=3850#.Wn3rjAFTy0U.mendeley).

Finkelstein, Daniel. 2018. 'Prosecutors Don't Know How Biased They Are'. *The Times*, January 23.

Fisher, Henry. 1977. *Report of an Inquiry by the Honourable Sir Henry Fisher into the Circumstances Leading to the Trial of Three Persons on Charges Arising out of the Death of Maxwell Confait and the Fire at 27 Doggett Road, London SE6*. London.

Follette, William C., Richard A. Leo, and Deborah Davis. 2018. 'Representing People with Mental Disabilities'. In *Mental Health and False Confessions*, edited by E. Kelley. University of San Francisco Law Research Paper No. 2017-16. Retrieved (https://papers.ssrn.com/sol3/papers.cfm?abstract_id=3028918).

Forensic Science Regulator. 2017. *Codes of Practice and Conduct: For Forensic Science Providers and Practitioners in the Criminal Justice System (Issue 4)*.

Forensic Science Regulator. 2018. *Forensic Science Regulator Annual Report 2017*.

Forst, Brian. 2013. 'Wrongful Convictions in a World of Miscarriages of Justice'. Pp. 15–43 in *Wrongful Convictions and Miscarriages of Justice: Causes and Remedies in North American and European Criminal Justice Systems*, edited by R. C. Huff and M. Killias. New York: Routledge.

Foster, Richard. 2014. 'Wrongful Prosecutions Add to Refugee Woe'. *The Guardian*, February 24. Retrieved (https://www.theguardian.com/law/2014/feb/24/wrongful-prosecutions-refugee-woe).

Foster, Richard. 2016a. 'Text of Letter Sent 5 July 2016 from CCRC Chair Richard Foster to DPP, Attorney General and Others'. *Criminal Cases Review Commission*.

Foster, Richard. 2016b. 'We Genuinely Welcome Applications from You'. *The Justice Gap*.

Foster, Richard. 2017a. 'CCRC 20th Anniversary Speech by Richard Foster CBE, Chair of the CCRC'.

Foster, Richard. 2017b. 'Letters: Liam Allan and Isaac Itiary Trial Collapses Should Lead to Much-Needed Reform'. December 22. Retrieved (https://www.theguardian.com/law/2017/dec/22/liam-allan-and-isaac-itiary-trial-collapses-should-lead-to-much-needed-reform).

Freedman, Monroe H. 2010. 'The Cooperating Witness Who Lies—A Challenge to Defense Lawyers, Prosecutors, and Judges'. *Ohio State Journal of Criminal Law* 7(2):739–48.

Furedi, Frank. 2016. 'Moral Crusades, Child Protection, Celebrities, and the Duty to Believe'. Pp. 42–53 in *Wrongful Allegations of Sexual and Child Abuse*, edited by R. Burnett. Oxford.

Galligan, Denis J. 1986. *Discretionary Powers: Legal Study of Official Discretion*. Oxford: Clarendon Press.

Gallop, Angela. 2017. 'Threats to Justice from Forensic Science'. In *CCRC 20th Anniversary Conference presentation*. Criminal Cases Review Commission. Retrieved (https://ccrc.gov.uk/threats-to-justice-from-forensic-science-presentation-for-ccrc-conf-november-2017-ppt/).

Garland, David. 2001. *The Culture of Control: Crime and Social Order in Contemporary Society*. Oxford: Oxford University Press.

Garrett, Brandon L. 2008. 'Judging Innocence'. *Columbia Law Review* 108:55–141.

Garrett, Brandon L. 2011. *Convicting the Innocent: Where Criminal Prosecutions Go Wrong*. Cambridge, MA: Harvard University Press.

Garrett, Brandon L. 2013. 'Trial and Error'. Pp. 77–90 in *Wrongful Convictions and Miscarriages of Justice: Causes and Remedies in North American and European Criminal Justice Systems*. New York: Routledge.

Garrett, Brandon L. 2014. 'Eyewitness Identification and Police Practices: A Virginia Case Study'. *Virginia Journal of Criminal Law* 2(1):1–20.

Garrett, Brandon L. 2015. 'Contaminated Confessions Revisited'. *Virginia Law Review* 101:395–454.

Geddes, J. F., Allan K. Hackshaw, G. H. Vowles, C. D. Nickols, and H. L. Whitewell. 2001. 'Neuropathology of Inflicted Head Injury in Children: I. Patterns of Brain Damage'. *Brain* 124(7):1290–8.

Gibbs, Frances. 2018. 'Rape Trials under Threat'. *The Times*, January 20.

Gifford, Daniel J. 1983. 'Discretionary Decisionmaking in the Regulatory Agencies: A Conceptual Framework'. *University of Minnesota Law School* 57:101–35.

Gigerenzer, Gerd. 2008. 'Why Heuristics Work'. *Perspectives on Psychological Science* 3(1):20–9.

Gigerenzer, Gerd and Daniel G. Goldstein. 1996. 'Reasoning the Fast and Frugal Way: Models of Bounded Rationality.' *Psychological Review* 103(4):650–69.

Gilligan, Andrew. 2016. 'Revealed: Government Body Helps Asylum Seekers Quash Convictions for Illegal Entry to Britain'. *The Telegraph*, January 9. Retrieved (http://www.telegraph.co.uk/news/uknews/immigration/12090822/Revealed-Government-body-helps-asylum-seekers-quash-convictions-for-illegal-entry-to-Britain.html).

Gittos, Luke. 2016. 'Complaints of Sexual Abuse and the Decline of Objective Prosecuting'. Pp. 190–203 in *Wrongful Allegations of Sexual and Child Abuse*, edited by R. Burnett. Oxford: Oxford University Press.

Glosswitch. 2017. 'False Rape Allegations Are Rare—Rape Is Not. Stop Using the Case of Jemma Beale to Discredit All Women'. *The Independent*, August 25. Retrieved (http://www.independent.co.uk/voices/jemma-beale-woman-lie-about-rape-ten-years-in-prison-not-all-woman-liars-not-all-men-rapists-a7912766.html).

Gould, Jon, Julia Carrano, Richard Leo, and Katie Hail-Jares. 2013. 'Predicting Erroneous Convictions'. *Iowa Law Review* 99:471–522.

Gould, Jon and Richard A. Leo. 2010. 'Centennial Symposium: A Century of Criminal Justice: II: "Justice" in Action: One Hundred Years Later: Wrongful Convictions After a Century of Research'. *Journal of Criminal Law and Criminology* 100:825–68.

Gray, David and Peter Watt. 2013. *Giving Victims a Voice: Joint Report into Sexual Allegations Made against Jimmy Savile*. Retrieved (https://www.nspcc.org.uk/globalassets/documents/research-reports/yewtree-report-giving-victims-voice-jimmy-savile.pdf).

Green, Andrew. 2016. 'Investigative Competence: The CCRC and Innocence Projects'. *The Justice Gap*. Retrieved (http://www.thejusticegap.com/2016/04/investigative-competence-ccrc-innocence-projects/).

Greenawalt, Kent. 1975. 'Discretion and Judicial Decision: The Elusive Quest for the Fetters That Bind Judges'. *Columbia Law Review* 75(2):359–99.

Grimshaw, Roger and Tony Jefferson. 1987. *Interpreting Policework: Policy and Practice in Forms of Beat Policing*. London: Allen & Unwin.

Grøndahl, Pål and Ulf Stridbeck. 2016. 'When Insanity Has Gone Undiscovered by the Courts: The Practice of the Norwegian Criminal Cases Review Commission in Cases of Doubts about Insanity'. *Criminal Behaviour and Mental Health* 26(3):212–24.

Gross, Samuel. 2013. 'How Many False Convictions Are There? How Many Exonerations Are There?' Pp. 45–60 in *Wrongful Convictions and Miscarriages of Justice: Causes and Remedies in North American and European Criminal Justice Systems*, edited by R. C. Huff and M. Killias. New York: Routledge.

Gross, Samuel R. 1996. 'The Risks of Death: Why Erroneous Convictions Are Common in Capital Cases'. *Buffalo Law Review* 44:476–81.

Gross, Samuel R., Kristen Jacoby, Daniel J. Matheson, Nicholas Montgomery, and Sujata Patil. 2005. 'Exonerations in the United States 1989 through 2003'. *The Journal of Criminal Law and Criminology* 95(2):523–60.

Gross, Samuel R. and Michael Shaffer. 2012. *Exonerations in the United States, 1989–2012: Report by the National Registry of Exonerations*.

Gudjonsson, Gisli H. 2003. *The Psychology of Interrogations and Confessions*. Chichester: Wiley.

Gudjonsson, Gisli H. and John Pearse. 2011. 'Suspect Interviews and False Confessions'. *Current Directions in Psychological Science* 20(1):33–7.

Haber, Ralph Norman and Lyn Haber. 2013. 'The Culture of Science: Bias and Forensic Evidence'. *Journal of Applied Research in Memory and Cognition* 2(1):65–7.

Hall, Andrew. 1994. 'It Couldn't Happen Today?' Pp. 313–22 in *Criminal Justice in Crisis*, edited by M. McConville and L. Bridges. Aldershot: Edward Elgar Publishing.

Hamer, David and Gary Edmond. 2013. 'Truth or Lies: Overturning Wrongful Convictions'. *The Conversation*.

Handler, Joel. 1992. 'Discretion: Power, Quiescence, and Trust'. Pp. 331–60 in *The Uses of Discretion*, edited by K. Hawkins. Oxford: Oxford University Press.

Hardman, Robert. 2016. 'How Deplorable There's Justice on Tap to Hound Our Soldiers—but with Sgt Blackman, They Just Throw Away the Key'. *Mail on Sunday*, September 20. Retrieved (http://www.dailymail.co.uk/debate/article-3797464/How-deplorable-s-justice-tap-hound-soldiers-Sgt-Blackman-just-throw-away-key-writes-ROBERT-HARDMAN.html).

Hart, H. L. 1961. *The Concept of Law*. Oxford: Clarendon Press.

Hasel, Lisa E. and Saul M. Kassin. 2009. 'On the Presumption of Evidentiary Independence'. *Psychological Science* 20(1):122–6.

Hawkins, Keith. 1986. 'On Legal Decision-Making'. *Lee Law Review* 43(4):1161–242.

Hawkins, Keith. 1992a. 'The Use of Legal Discretion: Perspectives from Law and Social Science'. Pp. 11–46 in *The Uses of Discretion*, edited by K. Hawkins. Oxford: Oxford University Press.

Hawkins, Keith, ed. 1992b. *The Uses of Discretion*. Oxford: Oxford University Press.

Hawkins, Keith. 2002. *Law as Last Resort: Prosecution Decision-Making in a Regulatory Agency*. Oxford: Oxford University Press.

Hawkins, Keith. 2003. 'Order, Rationality and Silence: Some Reflections on Criminal Justice Decision-Making'. Pp. 186–219 in *Exercising Discretion: Decision-Making in the Criminal Justice System and Beyond*, edited by E. Gelsthorpe and N. Padfield. Cullompton: Willan.

Heaton, Stephen. 2013. 'A Critical Evaluation of the Utility of Using Innocence as a Criterion in the Post-Conviction Process, PhD Thesis'. University of East Anglia.

Heaton, Stephen. 2015. 'The CCRC—Is It Fit for Purpose?' *Archbold Review* (5):6–9.

Her Majesty's Crown Prosecution Service Inspectorate and Her Majesty's Inspectorate of Constabulary. 2017. *Making It Fair: A Joint Inspection of the Disclosure of Unused Material in Volume Crown Court Cases*.

Hill, Paul and Ronan Bennett. 1991. *Stolen Years: Before and After Guildford*. TBS, The Book Service.

Hodgson, Jacqueline and Juliet Horne. 2009. *The Extent and Impact of Legal Representation on Applications to the Criminal Cases Review Commission (CCRC): A Report Prepared for the Legal Services Commission*. Retrieved (https://papers.ssrn.com/sol3/papers.cfm?abstract_id=1483721).

Holdaway, Simon. 1983. *Inside the British Police: A Force at Work*. Oxford: Blackwell.

Holdaway, Simon. 1996. *The Racialisation of British Policing*. London: Macmillan.

Holiday, Yewa. 2012. 'CCRC Concern over Advice given to Refugees'. *The Law Society Gazette*, June 14. Retrieved (http://www.lawgazette.co.uk/law/ccrc-concern-over-advice-given-to-refugees/66102.fullarticle).

Holiday, Yewa. 2014a. 'A Place of Greater Safety: The Prosecution of Refugees for Passport Offences'. *Border Criminologies, University of Oxford*, February 26. Retrieved (https://www.law.ox.ac.uk/research-subject-groups/centre-criminology/centreborder-criminologies/blog/2014/02/place-greater).

Holiday, Yewa. 2014b. 'EU Law Analysis: Penalising Refugees: When Should the CJEU Have Jurisdiction to Interpret Article 31 of the Refugee Convention?' *EU Law Analysis*. Retrieved (http://eulawanalysis.blogspot.co.uk/2014/07/penalising-refugees-when-should-cjeu.html).

Home Affairs Committee. 1982. *Miscarriages of Justice: Sixth Report from the Home Affairs Committee, Session 1981–1982, Together with the Proceedings of the Committee, the Minutes of Evidence and Appendix HC421*. London.

Home Affairs Committee. 2002. *The Conduct of Investigations into Past Cases of Abuse in Children's Homes: Fourth Report of Session 2001–2002*. London.

Home Office. 1994. *Criminal Appeals and the Establishment of a Criminal Cases Review Authority: A Discussion Paper*. London.

Hopkins, Nick. 2012. 'Prisoner's 16-Year Fight to Prise Open the Secrets of Operation Cactus'. *The Guardian*. Retrieved (https://www.theguardian.com/uk/2012/sep/02/kevin-lane-murder-conviction-operation-cactus).

Horne, Juliet. 2013. 'Plea Bargains, Guilty Pleas and the Consequence for Appeal in England and Wales'. *Warwick School of Law Research Paper (Special Plea Bargaining Edition, Editor Jackie Hodgson)* No 2013/10:1–11. Retrieved (https://ssrn.com/abstract=2286681 or http://dx.doi.org/10.2139/ssrn.2286681).

Horne, Juliet. 2016. 'A Plea of Convenience: An Examination of the Guilty Plea in England and Wales' (Unpublished PhD Thesis).

Hough, Mike and Mai Sato. 2014. 'Report on the Compliance with the Law: How Normative and Instrumental Compliance Interact'. In *FP7 Research Project for New European Crimes and Trust-Based Policy Vol. 2*.

House of Commons Justice Committee. 2014. *The Work of the Criminal Cases Review Commission: Written Submissions from G Maddocks, M Naughton and M Newby, 14th January 2014*.

House of Commons Justice Committee. 2015. *Justice—12th Report: Criminal Cases Review Commission HC850*. Retrieved (http://www.publications.parliament.uk/pa/cm201415/cmselect/cmjust/850/85002.htm).

House of Commons Science and Technology Committee. 2013. *Forensic Science Changes Could Jeopardise Criminal Justice System*.

House of Commons Science and Technology Committee. 2016. *Forensic Science Strategy: Summary*. Retrieved (https://publications.parliament.uk/pa/cm201617/cmselect/cmsctech/501/50103.htm#_idTextAnchor004).

House of Lords. 1993. *Hansard Debate 26 October 1993, Vol. 549, cc 777–842*. Retrieved (http://hansard.millbanksystems.com/lords/1993/oct/26/criminal-justice-royal-commission-report).

Hoyle, Carolyn. 1998. *Negotiating Domestic Violence*. Oxford: Oxford University Press.

Hoyle, Carolyn. 2016. 'Compensating Injustice: The Perils of the Innocence Discourse'. In *The Integrity of Criminal Process: From Theory into Practice*, edited by S. Young, J. Hunter, P. Roberts, and D. Dixon. Oxford: Hart.

Huff, Ronald, Arye Rattner, and Edward Sagarin. 1996. *Convicted But Innocent: Wrongful Conviction and Public Policy*. Thousand Oaks, CA: Sage.

Hughes, Laura. 2016. 'Law for Rape Victims Could Be Amended after Ched Evans Case, Attorney General Reveals'. *The Telegraph*, October 27. Retrieved (http://www.telegraph.co.uk/news/2016/10/27/law-for-rape-victims-could-be-amended-after-ched-evans-case-atto/).

Hunter, Jill, Paul Roberts, Simon N. M. Young, and David Dixon, eds. 2016. *The Integrity of Criminal Process: From Theory into Practice*. Oxford: Hart.

Innocence Network UK. 2013. 'Innocence Network UK Report on Criminal Cases Review Commission Published'. *University of Bristol Law School*. Retrieved 9 October 2017 (http://www.bristol.ac.uk/law/news/2013/346.html).

Iserson, Kenneth V. and John C. Moskop. 2007. 'Triage in Medicine, Part I: Concept, History, and Types'. *Annals of Emergency Medicine* 49(3):275–81. Retrieved 16 July 2017 (http://linkinghub.elsevier.com/retrieve/pii/S0196064406007049).

ITV News. 2017. 'More Than 6,000 Forensic Tests Used to Secure Criminal Convictions Feared Tampered with'. *ITV*, May.

Jackson, Jon et al. 2012. 'Why Do People Comply with the Law? Legitimacy and the Influence of Legal Institutions'. *British Journal of Criminology* 52(6):1051–71. Retrieved (https://academic.oup.com/bjc/article-lookup/doi/10.1093/bjc/azs032).

James, Annabelle. 2000. 'The Criminal Cases Review Commission: Economy, Effectiveness and Justice'. *Criminal Law Review* 140–53.

Jefferson, Tony and Roger Grimshaw. 1984. *Controlling the Constable: Police Accountability in England and Wales*. London: Frederick Muller in association with The Cobden Trust.

Jessel, David. 2004. 'Turning a Blind Eye'. *The Guardian*, July 13.

Jessel, David. 2012. 'Time to Reconnect'. Pp. 17–19 in *Wrongly Accused: Who Is Responsible for Investigating Miscarriages of Justice?*, edited by J. Robins. The Justice Gap and Solicitors Journal.

Jessel, David. 2014. 'Opening Speech'. In *FACT Spring Conference: Justice for People Falsely Accused of Sexual and Child Abuse*.

JUSTICE. 1989. *Miscarriages of Justice*. London: JUSTICE.

Kassin, Saul M., Itiel E. Dror, and Jeff Kukucka. 2013. 'The Forensic Confirmation Bias: Problems, Perspectives, and Proposed Solutions'. *Journal of Applied Research in Memory and Cognition* 2(1):42–52.

Keat, Russell. 1971. 'Positivism, Naturalism, and Anti-Naturalism in the Social Sciences'. *Journal for the Theory of Social Behaviour* 1(1):3–17.

Kee, Robert. 1986. *Trial and Error: The Maguires, the Guilford Pub Bombings and British Justice*. London: Penguin Books.

Kennedy, Ludovic. 1961. *Ten Rillington Place*. Victor Gollancz Ltd.

Kerrigan, Kevin. 2009. 'Real Possibility or Fat Chance?' Pp. 166–77 in *The Criminal Cases Review Commission: Hope for the Innocent?*, edited by M. Naughton. Basingstoke: Palgrave Macmillan.

King, Michael. 1993. 'The "Truth" about Autopoiesis'. *Journal of Law and Society* 20(2):218–36.

Kirchner, Lauren. 2017. 'Thousands of Criminal Cases in New York Relied on Disputed DNA Testing Techniques'. *ProPublica*, September.

Lacey, Nicola. 1992. 'The Jurisprudence of Discretion: Escaping the Legal Paradigm'. Pp. 361–88 in *The Uses of Discretion*, edited by K. Hawkins. Oxford: Oxford University Press.

Lady Justice Hallett. 2017. 'Trial by Jury—Past and Present'. In *Gladstone Annual Lecture, Pembroke College Oxford*. Judiciary of England and Wales.

Laurin, Jennifer E. 2013. 'Remapping the Path Forward: Toward a Systematic View of Forensic Science Reform and Oversight'. *Texas Law Review* 91:1051–118.

Laville, Sandra. 2012. 'Criminal Cases Review Commission Must Be Reformed, Say Campaigners'. *Guardian*. Retrieved (https://www.theguardian.com/law/2012/mar/27/criminal-cases-review-commission-reform-campaign).

Law Society. 2015. *Statutory Defences Available to Asylum Seekers Charged with Document Offences*. Retrieved (http://www.lawsociety.org.uk/support-services/advice/practice-notes/statutory-defences-available-to-asylum-seekers-charged-with-document-offences/).

Leigh, Leonard. 2006. 'Lurking Doubt and the Safety of Convictions'. *Criminal Law Review* 809–16.

Lempert, Richard O. 1992. 'Discretion in a Behavioral Perspective: The Case of a Public Housing Eviction Board'. Pp. 185–230 in *The Uses of Discretion*, edited by K. Hawkins. Oxford: Oxford University Press.

Leo, Richard A. 2005. 'Rethinking the Study of Miscarriages of Justice'. *Journal of Contemporary Criminal Justice* 21(3):201–23. Retrieved (http://journals.sagepub.com/doi/10.1177/1043986205277477).

Leo, Richard A. 2008. *Police Interrogation and American Justice*. Cambridge, MA: Harvard University Press.

Leo, Richard A. 2009. 'False Confessions: Causes, Consequences, and Implications'. *Journal of the American Academy of Psychiatry and the Law Online* 37(3):332–43.

Leo, Richard A., Peter Neufeld, Steven A. Drizin, and Andrew E. Taslitz. 2013. 'Promoting Accuracy in the Use of Confession Evidence: An Argument for Pretrial Reliability Assessments to Prevent Wrongful Convictions'. *Temple Law Review* 85(4):759–837.

Leverick, Fiona, James Chalmers, Sarah Armstrong, F. McNeil, and Fergus McNeill. 2009. *Scottish Criminal Cases Review Commission 10th Anniversary Research*. Glasgow.

Liberty. 2006. *Liberty's Response to the Office for Criminal Justice Reform: 'Quashing Convictions'*.

Liebman, James S., Shawn Crowley, Andrew Markquart, Lauren Rosenberg, Lauren Gallo White, and Daniel Zharkovsky. 2014. *The Wrong Carlos*. Columbia University Press.

Lloyd-Bostock, Sally. 1992. 'The Psychology of Routine Discretion: Accident Screening by British Factory Inspectors'. *Law & Policy* 14(2):45–76.

Loader, Ian and Neal Walker. 2008. *Civilizing Security*. Cambridge: Cambridge University Press.

Lord Burnett of Maldon. 2017. *Criminal Cases Review Commission*. London. Retrieved (https://www.judiciary.gov.uk/wp-content/uploads/2017/11/lcj-burnett-criminal-cases-review-commission-20171103.pdf).

Lord Justice Auld. 2001. *Review of the Criminal Courts of England and Wales.*

Lord Justice Leveson. 2010. *Forensic Science Society Expert Evidence in Criminal Courts—The Problem, King's College, University of London.* Retrieved (http://webarchive.nationalarchives. gov.uk/20101224091634/http://www.judiciary.gov.uk/Resources/JCO/Documents/ Speeches/speech-by-lj-leveson-kcl-expert-evidence-161110.pdf).

Luhmann, Niklas. 1985. *Sociological Theory of Law.* London: Routledge.

Luhmann, Niklas. 1986. 'The Self-Reproduction of Law and Its Limits'. Pp. 111–27 in *Dilemmas of Law in the Welfare State,* edited by G. Teubner. New York: Walter de Gruyter.

Luttner, Susan E. 2014. 'Shaken Baby Syndrome: Inadequate Logic, Unvalidated Theory, Insufficient Science'. *Argument & Critique* 1–23.

Ma, Yue. 1998. 'Lay Participation in Criminal Trials: A Comparative Perspective'. *International Criminal Justice Review* 8(1):74–94.

MacGregor, Alastair. 2012. 'Unrealistic Expectations'. Pp. 11–16 in *Wrongly Accused: Who Is Responsible for Investigating Miscarriages of Justice?,* edited by J. Robins. The Justice Gap and Solicitors Journal.

Maddocks, Glyn and Gabe Tan. 2009. 'Applicant Solicitors: Friends or Foe'. Pp. 118–33 in *The Criminal Cases Review Commission: Hope for the Innocent?,* edited by M. Naughton. Basingstoke: Palgrave Macmillan.

Maguire, Anne. 1994. *Why Me? One Woman's Fight for Justice and Dignity.* London: HarperCollins.

Malleson, Kate. 1993. 'Review of the Appeal Process, RCCJ Research Study No 17'. London: HMSO.

Malleson, Kate. 1994. 'Appeals against Conviction and the Principle of Finality'. *Journal of Law and Society* 21(1):151.

Malone, Campbell. 2009. 'Only the Freshest Will Do'. Pp. 107–17 in *The Criminal Cases Review Commission: Hope for the Innocent?,* edited by M. Naughton. Basingstoke: Palgrave Macmillan.

Malone, Campbell. 2012. 'Out of Step'. Pp. 23–6 in *Wrongly Accused: Who Is Responsible for Investigating Miscarriages of Justice?,* edited by J. Robins. The Justice Gap and Solicitors Journal.

May, Paul. 2014. 'Why Does It Take So Long?' *Inside Justice.*

May, Paul. 2017. 'Partly Excellent, Partly Abysmal: 20 Years of the CCRC'. *The Justice Gap.*

McBarnet, Doreen J. 1981. *Conviction: Law, the State and the Construction of Justice.* London: Macmillan.

McCartney, Carole and Stephanie Roberts. 2012. 'Building Institutions to Address Miscarriages of Justice in England and Wales: "Mission Accomplished?"' *University of Cincinnati Law Review* 80(4):1333–61.

McConville, Michael. 1998. 'Plea Bargaining: Ethics and Politics'. *Journal of Law and Society* 25(4):562–87.

McConville, Michael and Lee Bridges, eds. 1994. *Criminal Justice in Crisis.* Aldershot: Edward Elgar Publishing.

McConville, Michael, Andrew Sanders, and Roger Leng. 1991. *The Case for the Prosecution.* London: Routledge.

McFadden, Katie. 2018. 'Is Austerity Causing Miscarriages of Justice?' *The Justice Gap,* January. Retrieved (http://www.thejusticegap.com/2018/01/austerity-causing-miscarriages-justice/).

McFadden, Katie and Oliver Carter. 2018. 'MoJ Face Another Challenge to "Catastrophic" Legal Aid Cuts for Defence Firms'. *The Justice Gap,* January. Retrieved (http://www. thejusticegap.com/2018/01/moj-face-another-challenge-catastrophic-legal-aid-cuts-defence-firms/).

McGourlay, Claire, Andrew Green, and James Cairns. 2016. 'An Open Letter to the CCRC—#2'. *The Justice Gap.*

McGuinness, Terry. 2016. *Criminal Cases Review Commission, Briefing Paper 7448*. London. Retrieved (https://www.google.co.uk/url?sa=t&rct=j&q=&esrc=s&source=web&cd=1&ve d=0ahUKEwjO1e394drZAhVrBMAKHbReDzYQFggpMAA&url=http%3A%2F%2Fres earchbriefings.files.parliament.uk%2Fdocuments%2FCBP-7448%2FCBP-7448.pdf&usg =AOvVaw0VotfESSGXSR6M8nIFqQjH).

McKay, Simon. 2015. *Covert Policing*. Oxford: Oxford University Press.

Ministry of Justice. 2011. *Achieving Best Evidence in Criminal Proceedings: Guidance on Interviewing Victims and Witnesses and Guidance on Special Measures*. Retrieved (http:// www.cps.gov.uk/legal/assets/uploads/files/Achieving Best Evidence in Criminal Proceedings. pdf).

Morris, Stephen and Alexandra Topping. 2016. 'Ched Evans: Footballer Found Not Guilty of Rape in Retrial'. *The Guardian*, October 14. Retrieved (https://www.theguardian.com/ football/2016/oct/14/footballer-ched-evans-cleared-of-in-retrial).

Mullin, Chris. 1990. *Error of Judgement: The Truth about the Birmingham Bombings*. Dublin: Poolbeg Press.

National Audit Office. 2014. *The Home Office's Oversight of Forensic Services*. Retrieved (https:// www.nao.org.uk/wp-content/uploads/2015/01/The-Home-Office's-oversight-of-forensic- services.pdf).

National Research Council. 2009. *Strengthening on Identifying the Needs of the Forensic Sciences Community*.

Naughton, Michael. 2004. 'Redefining Miscarriages of Justice: A Revived Human-Rights Approach to Unearth Subjugated Discourses of Wrongful Criminal Conviction'. *British Journal of Criminology* 45(2):165–82.

Naughton, Michael, ed. 2009. *The Criminal Cases Review Commission: Hope for the Innocent?* Basingstoke: Palgrave Macmillan.

Naughton, Michael. 2012. 'No Champion of Justice'. Pp. 20–3 in *Wrongly Accused: Who Is Responsible for Investigating Miscarriages of Justice?*, edited by J. Robins. The Justice Gap and Solicitors Journal.

Naughton, Michael. 2013. *The Innocent and the Criminal Justice System: A Sociological Analysis of Miscarriages of Justice*. Basingstoke: Palgrave Macmillan.

Naughton, Michael. 2014. 'Wrongful Convictions and Innocence Projects in the UK: Help, Hope and Education'. *Innocence Network UK*.

Naughton, Michael. 2018. *Tailored Review of the Criminal Cases Review Commission: Call for Evidence*. Retrieved (http://michaeljnaughton.com/wp-content/uploads/2018/01/MOJ- tailored-review-of-the-CCRC-10-January-2018-my-ID-removed.pdf).

Naughton, Michael with Tan Gabe. 2010. *Claims of Innocence: An Introduction to Wrongful Convictions and How They Might Be Challenged*. Bristol. Retrieved (http://www. innocencenetwork.org.uk/wp-content/uploads/2012/05/Claims-of-Innocence.pdf).

Nelken, David. 1998. 'Blind Insights? The Limits of a Reflexive Sociology of Law'. *Journal of Law and Society* 25(3):407–26.

New Zealand Law Society. 2016. 'Most Convictions Safe, but How to Recognise Those That Aren't: Justice William Young'. *New Zealand Law Society*.

Newby, Mark. 2009. 'Historical Abuse Cases: Why They Expose the Inadequacy of the Real Possibility Test'. Pp. 97–106 in *The Criminal Cases Review Commission: Hope for the Innocent?*, edited by M. Naughton. Basingstoke: Palgrave Macmillan.

News, BBC. 2018. 'All Current Rape Cases to Be "Urgently" Reviewed over Disclosure Fears'. *BBC News*, January 27.

Nobles, Richard. 2012. 'The CCRC in 2012: An Academic's View'. *Queen Mary University of London, School of Law, Legal Studies Research Series* No. 119/20.

Nobles, Richard and David Schiff. 1995. 'Miscarriages of Justice: A Systems Approach'. *The Modern Law Review* 58(3):299–320. Retrieved (http://doi.wiley.com/10.1111/j.1468- 2230.1995.tb02012.x).

Nobles, Richard and David Schiff. 2000. *Understanding Miscarriages of Justice: Law, the Media and the Inevitability of a Crisis*. Oxford: Oxford University Press.

Nobles, Richard and David Schiff. 2001. 'The Criminal Cases Review Commission: Reporting Success?' *The Modern Law Review* 64(2):280–99.

Nobles, Richard and David Schiff. 2002. 'The Right to Appeal and Workable Systems of Justice'. *Modern Law Review* 65(5):676–701.

Nobles, Richard and David Schiff. 2005. 'The Criminal Cases Review Commission: Establishing a Workable Relationship with the Court of Appeal'. *Criminal Law Review* 173–89.

Nobles, Richard and David Schiff. 2009. 'After Ten Years: An Investment in Justice?' Pp. 151–65 in *The Criminal Cases Review Commission: Hope for the Innocent?*, edited by M. Naughton. Basingstoke: Palgrave Macmillan.

Nobles, Richard and David Schiff. 2017. 'Trials and Miscarriages: An Evolutionary Socio-Historical Analysis'. *Criminal Law Forum*.

Nonaka, Ikujiro and Hirotaka Takeuchi. 1995. *The Knowledge-Creating Company: How Japanese Companies Create the Dynamics of Innovation*. New York: Oxford University Press.

O'Brian, Michael. 2008. *The Death of Justice*. Talybont: Y Lolfa.

O'Brian, William E. 2011. 'Fresh Expert Evidence in CCRC Cases'. *King's Law Journal* 22(1):1–26.

Observer editorial. 2017. 'The Observer View on Miscarriages of Justice'. *The Guardian*, December 29. Retrieved (https://www.theguardian.com/commentisfree/2017/dec/29/the-observer-view-on-miscarriages-of-justice).

O'Connell, Michael. 2017. *Delusions of Innocence: The Tragic Case of Stefan Kiszko*. Hook: Waterside Press.

Office for Criminal Justice Reform. 2006. *Quashing Convictions: A Report of a Review by the Home Secretary, Lord Chancellor and Attorney General: A Consultation Paper, Office for Criminal Justice Reform*. London: Home Office, Office for Criminal Justice Reform.

Office for National Statistics. 2017. *Crime in England and Wales: Year Ending March 2017*. London. Retrieved (https://www.ons.gov.uk/peoplepopulationandcommunity/crimeandjustice/bulletins/crimeinenglandandwales/yearendingmar2017#what-types-of-crime-have-changed-in-the-last-year).

Ofshe, Richard and Richard A. Leo. 1997. 'The Decision to Confess Falsely: Rational Choice and Irrational Action'. *Denver University Law Review* 74:979–1122.

Ormerod, David. 2017. 'The Future of the Criminal Justice System and the CCRC'. In *CCRC 20th Anniversary Conference presentation*. Criminal Cases Review Commission.

Packer, Herbert. 1968. *The Limits of the Criminal Sanction*. Stanford: Stanford University Press.

Parkes, Debra and Emma Cunliffe. 2015. 'Women and Wrongful Convictions: Concepts and Challenges'. *International Journal of Law in Context* 11(3):219–44.

Parliament of South Australia Legislative Review Committee. 2012. *Inquiry into Criminal Cases Review Commission Submission by Ms Bibi Sangha and Dr Bob Moles*. Retrieved (http://netk.net.au/CCRC/LRCSubmission.pdf).

Pattenden, Rosemary. 1982. *The Judge, Discretion and the Criminal Trial*. Oxford: Oxford University Press.

Pattenden, Rosemary. 1996. *English Criminal Appeals 1844–1994*. London: Oxford University Press.

Pepinsky, Harold E. 1984. 'Better Living Through Police Discretion'. *Law and Contemporary Problems* 47:249–67.

Phillips, Scott and Jamie Richardson. 2016. 'The Worst of the Worst: Heinous Crimes and Erroneous Evidence'. *Hofstra Law Review* 45:417–49.

Plotnikoff, Joyce and Richard Woolfson. 2001. *A Fair Balance? Evaluation of the Operation of Disclosure Law*. London: Home Office, Research, Development and Statistics Directorate.

Poyser, Sam. 2012. 'Calling for Renewed Media Interest'. Pp. 46–50 in *Wrongly Accused: Who Is Responsible for Investigating Miscarriages of Justice?*, edited by J. Robins. The Justice Gap and Solicitors Journal.

Price, Julie. 2016. 'An Open Letter to the CCRC'. *The Justice Gap*.

Pugh, Derek S. 1981. 'The Aston Program Perspective. The Aston Program of Research: Retrospect and Prospect'. Pp. 135–66 in *Perspectives on Organization Design and Behaviour*, edited by A. H. Van de Ven and W. Joyce. New York: John Willey.

Quirk, Hannah. 2012. 'Governing in Prose'. Pp. 30–3 in *Wrongly Accused: Who Is Responsible for Investigating Miscarriages of Justice?*, edited by J. Robins. The Justice Gap and Solicitors Journal.

Quirk, Hannah. 2013. 'Dealing with the Past in Northern Ireland'. *The Modern Law Review* 76(6):949–80.

Radelet, Michael L. and Hugo A. Bedau. 1998. 'The Execution of the Innocent'. *Law and Contemporary Problems* 61:105–24.

Rawls, John. 1971. *A Theory of Justice*. Cambridge, MA: Harvard University Press.

Roach, Kent. 2012a. 'An Independent Commission to Review Claims of Wrongful Convictions: Lessons from North Carolina?' *Criminal Law Quarterly* 58:283–302.

Roach, Kent. 2012b. 'Wrongful Convictions in Canada'. *University of Cincinnati Law Review* 80(4):1465–526.

Roach, Kent. 2013. 'More Procedure and Concern about Innocence but Less Justice? Remedies for Wrongful Convictions in the United States and Canada'. Pp. 283–308 in *Wrongful Convictions and Miscarriages of Justice: Causes and Remedies in North American and European Criminal Justice Systems*, edited by R. Huff and M. Killias. New York: Routledge.

Roach, Kent. 2015. 'Comparative Reflections on Miscarriages of Justice in Australia and Canada'. *Flinders Law Journal* 17(2):381–432.

Roberts, Julian V. and Mike Hough. 2009. *Public Opinion and the Jury: An International Literature Review*. London.

Roberts, Stephanie. 2004. 'The Royal Commission on Criminal Justice and Factual Innocence: Remedying Wrongful Convictions in the Court of Appeal'. *Justice* 1(2):86–94.

Roberts, Stephanie. 2017. 'Fresh Evidence and Factual Innocence in the Criminal Division of the Court of Appeal'. *The Journal of Criminal Law* 81(4):303–27.

Roberts, Stephanie and Lynne Weathered. 2008. 'Assisting the Factually Innocent: The Contradictions and Compatibility of Innocence Projects and the Criminal Cases Review Commission'. *Oxford Journal of Legal Studies* 29(1):43–70.

Robins, Jon. 2011. 'Miscarriages of Justice Are Slipping off the Public Radar'. *The Guardian*, June 6.

Robins, Jon, ed. 2012. *Wrongly Accused: Who Is Responsible for Investigating Miscarriages of Justice?* The Justice Gap and Solicitors Journal.

Robins, Jon. 2013. 'Criminal Cases Review Commission—Better the Devil You Know?' *Halsbury's Law Exchange*. Retrieved 9 October 2017 (http://www.halsburyslawexchange.co.uk/criminal-cases-review-commission-better-the-devil-you-know/).

Robins, Jon. 2016. 'University Innocence Projects: Where Are They Now?' *The Guardian*. Retrieved (https://www.theguardian.com/law/2016/apr/27/university-innocence-projects-where-are-they-now).

Robins, Jon. 2017. 'Losing Its Appeal? 20 Years of the CCRC'. *The Justice Gap*. Retrieved (http://www.thejusticegap.com/2017/04/losing-appeal-20-years-ccrc/).

Robins, Jon. 2018. 'CCRC Promises "Greater Transparency and Openness" with Launch of New Public Engagement Initiative'. *The Justice Gap*.

Robinson, Nathan J. 2015. 'Forensic Pseudoscience: The Unheralded Crisis of Criminal Justice'. *Boston Review: A Political and Literary Forum*, November. Retrieved (http://bostonreview.net/books-ideas/nathan-robinson-forensic-pseudoscience-criminal-justice).

Rose, David. 1992. *A Climate of Fear*. London: Bloomsbury Publishing.

Rose, David. 1996. *In the Name of the Law: The Collapse of Criminal Justice*. London: Vintage.

Rose, David. 2011. 'If They Didn't Do It, Who Did? Not Everyone Jailed for Murder Actually Committed Crime. Meet the Commission That Helps to Clear Them'. *Mail on Sunday*, October 1. Retrieved (http://www.dailymail.co.uk/home/moslive/article-2042831/Not-jailed-murder-actually-committed-crime--meet-commission-helps-clear-them.html).

Rose, David. 2016. 'To Catch a Sex Offender: Police, Trawls, and Personal Injury Solicitors'. Pp. 155–74 in *Wrongful Allegations of Sexual and Child Abuse*, edited by R. Burnett. Oxford: Oxford University Press.

Rose, David. 2017a. 'A Force in the Dock: Staffordshire Police Is Accused of Bungling Investigations by Losing Vital Evidence and Failing to Interview Witnesses as Widow Calls for Probe into Motorcyclist Husband's Death to Reopen'. *Mail on Sunday*, July 2.

Rose, David. 2017b. 'Exposed: How "Out-of-Control" Police Promised Murder "Witness" £20,000, Let Him Use Drugs . . . and Paid Rail Fares for Safehouse Hookers'. *Mail on Sunday*, September 23.

Rose, David. 2017c. 'Innocent Man Reveals His Five-Year Ordeal at Hands of "Out of Control" Officers after They Launched a Vendetta Which Led to His Loyal Police Wife Being Hounded Out of Her Job'. *Mail on Sunday*, April 1.

Rose, Jonathan, Steve Panter, and Trevor Wilkinson. 1997. *Innocents: How Justice Failed Stefan Kiszko and Lesley Molseed*. London: Sage.

Royal Commission on Criminal Justice. 1993. *Report (Cm 2263)*. London.

Royal Commission on Criminal Procedure. 1981. *Report (Cmnd 8092)*. London. Retrieved (https://www.gov.uk/government/uploads/system/uploads/attachment_data/file/271971/2263.pdf).

Ruesink, Mitch and Free D. Marvin. 2007. 'Wrongful Convictions among Women'. *Women & Criminal Justice* 16(4):1–23.

Rumney, Philip N. S. 2006. 'False Allegations of Rape'. *The Cambridge Law Journal* 65(1):128–58.

Runciman, Walter Garrison. 1993. *Report of the Royal Commission on Criminal Justice*. Retrieved (https://www.gov.uk/government/publications/report-of-the-royal-commission-on-criminal-justice).

Saguil, Paul J. 2007. 'Improving Wrongful Conviction Review: Lessons from a Comparative Analysis of Continental Criminal Procedure'. *Alberta Law Review* 45:117–36.

Saltrese, Chris. 2015. 'CPS Guidelines and the Pinocchio Effect'. *Chris Saltrese Solicitors Blog*. Retrieved 28 September 2017 (http://www.chrissaltrese.co.uk/cps-guidelines-and-the-pinocchio-effect/).

Sanders, Andrew. 2016. 'The CPS—30 Years on'. *Criminal Law Review*. Retrieved (http://login.westlaw.co.uk/maf/wluk/app/document?&amp).

Sanders, Andrew, Richard Young, and Mandy Burton. 2010. *Criminal Justice*. 4th ed. Oxford: Oxford University Press.

Sato, Mai, Carolyn Hoyle, and Naomi Ellen Speechley. 2017. 'Wrongful Convictions of Refugees and Asylum Seekers: Responses by the Criminal Cases Review Commission'. *Criminal Law Review* (2):106–22.

Schauer, Frederick F. 1991. *Playing by the Rules: A Philosophical Examination of Rule-Based Decision Making in Law and in Life*. Clarendon Press.

Scheck, Barry, Peter Neufeld, and Jim Dwyer. 2003. *Actual Innocence: When Justice Goes Wrong and How to Make It Right*. New American Library.

Schehr, Robert C. and Lynne Weathered. 2004. 'Should the United States Establish a Criminal Cases Review Commission?' *Judicature* 88(3):122–45.

Schluchter, Wolfgang. 2003. 'The Sociology of Law as an Empirical Theory of Validity: European Academy of Sociology, Second Annual Lecture, Paris, November 16, 2002'. *European Sociological Review* 19(5):537–49.

Schneider, Carl E. 1992. 'Discretion and Rules: A Lawyer's View'. Pp. 47–88 in *The Uses of Discretion*, edited by K. Hawkins. Oxford: Oxford University Press.

Schultz, P. Wesley, Jessica M. Nolan, Robert B. Cialdini, Noah J. Goldstein, and Vladas Griskevicius. 2007. 'The Constructive, Destructive, and Reconstructive Power of Social Norms'. *Psychological Science* 18(5):429–34.

Scott, Matthew. 2016. 'Why Is It Wrong to Overturn Wrongful Convictions, Mr Bone?' *BarristerBlogger*, January 11. Retrieved (http://barristerblogger.com/2016/01/11/why-is-it-wrong-to-overturn-wrongful-convictions-peter-bone-mp-seems-to-think-that-it-is/).

Scott, Matthew. 2018. 'Wrongful Convictions Are a Terrible Risk in Our Frighteningly Imperfect Justice System'. *BarristerBlogger*, February 2.

Scottish Criminal Cases Review Commission. 2010. *The Impact of Legal Representation on Applicants to the Scottish Criminal Cases Review Commission*. Retrieved (http://www.sccrc.org.uk/cs/Satellite?blobkey=id&blobwhere=1302883537745&blobheader=application%2Fpdf&blobheadername1=Content-Disposition&blobheadervalue1=inline%3B+filename%3Dsccrc-research-report-legal-representation-2010.pdf&blobcol=urldocument&blobtabl).

Scottish Criminal Cases Review Commission. 2017. *Scottish Criminal Cases Review Commission Annual Report 2016/17*. Retrieved (https://irp-cdn.multiscreensite.com/8f56052e/files/uploaded/c-users-mp01211-desktop-amends-30_06-sccrc-2016-17-annual-report.pdf).

Seale-Carlisle, Travis M. and Laura Mickes. 2016. 'US Line-Ups Outperform UK Line-Ups'. *Royal Society Open Science* 3(9):160300. Retrieved (http://rsos.royalsocietypublishing.org/lookup/doi/10.1098/rsos.160300).

Sentencing Council. 2015. *Crown Court Sentencing Survey Annual Publication: January to December 2014 England and Wales*.

Sentencing Council. 2017. *Reduction in Sentence for a Guilty Plea: Definitive Guideline*.

Shapiro, Scott J. 2007. 'The "Hart–Dworkin" Debate: A Short Guide for the Perplexed'. *Public Law and Legal Theory Working Paper Series, Michigan Law School* 77.

Shaw, Julia and Stephen Porter. 2015. 'Constructing Rich False Memories of Committing Crime'. *Psychological Science* 26(3):291–301.

Shaw, Julia and Michael Wafler. 2016. 'Tipping the Scales: How Defendant Body Type May Result in Eyewitness Biases'. *Psychiatry, Psychology and Law* 23(5):676–83. Retrieved (https://www.tandfonline.com/doi/full/10.1080/13218719.2015.1084664).

Simon, Herbert A. 1976. *Administrative Behaviour: A Study of Decision-Making Processes in Administrative Organization*. 3rd ed. London: The Free Press, Collier Macmillan Publisher.

Skolnick, Jerome H. 1966. *Justice without Trial: Law Enforcement in Democratic Society*. New York: John Wiley & Sons.

Slobogin, Christopher. 2014. 'Lessons from Inquisitorialism'. *Southern California Law Review* 87(3):699–731.

Smit, Nadine M., Ruth M. Morgan, and David A. Lagnado. 2018. 'A Systematic Analysis of Misleading Evidence in Unsafe Rulings in England and Wales'. *Science & Justice* 58(2):128–37. Retrieved (http://linkinghub.elsevier.com/retrieve/pii/S1355030617301144).

Smith, David. 2017. 'Truth and Justice—Like Truth and Journalism—Should Be Indivisible'. *The Justice Gap*. Retrieved (http://www.thejusticegap.com/2017/02/proof-magazine-truth-justice-like-truth-journalism-indivisible/).

Smith, Joan. 2016. 'Ched Evans Verdict: Why We Should All Feel Anxious about High Profile Rape Cases'. *The Telegraph*, October 14. Retrieved (http://www.telegraph.co.uk/women/life/ched-evans-verdict-why-we-should-all-feel-anxious-about-high-pro/).

Snow, Amanda. 2013. 'Police Stranglehold on Justice—Victims'. *New Zealand Herald*, September 15. Retrieved (http://www.nzherald.co.nz/nz/news/article.cfm?c_id=1&objcctid=11124832).

Solicitors Regulation Authority. 2014. *Risk Outlook 2014/2015, Autumn 2014 Update*.

Solicitors Regulation Authority. 2016. *Quality of Legal Services for Asylum Seekers.* Retrieved (http://www.sra.org.uk/sra/how-we-work/reports/asylum-report.page#findings).

South Australian Legislative Review Committee. 2012. *Report of the Legislative Review Committee on Its Inquiry into the Criminal Cases Review Commission Bill 2010.*

Spencer, John. R. 2008. 'Quashing Convictions for Procedural Irregularities'. *The Cambridge Law Journal* 67(2):227–30.

Starmer, Keir. 2013. 'CPS Publishes Fundamental New Approach to Prosecuting Cases of Child Sexual Abuse as Local Government and Family Courts Agree to Share Information for Stronger Prosecutions'. *Crown Prosecution Service.*

Stern, Vivien. 2010. *The Stern Review: A Report by Baroness Vivien Stern CBE of an Independent Review into How Rape Complaints Are Handled by Public Authorities in England and Wales.* London. Retrieved (http://webarchive.nationalarchives.gov.uk/20110608162919/http://www.equalities.gov.uk/pdf/Stern_Review_acc_FINAL.pdf).

Stridbeck, Ulf and Svein Magnussen. 2012a. 'Opening Potentially Wrongful Convictions—Look to Norway'. *Criminal Law Quarterly* 58(2):267–82.

Stridbeck, Ulf and Svein Magnussen. 2012b. 'Prevention of Wrongful Convictions: Norwegian Legal Safeguards and the Criminal Cases Review Commission'. *University of Cincinnati Law Review* 80(4):1373–90.

Stumpf, Juliet P. 2006. 'The Crimmigration Crisis: Immigrants, Crime, and Sovereign Power'. *American University Law Review* 56(367):1689–99.

Taylor, Nicholas and Michael Mansfield. 1999. 'Post-Conviction Procedures'. In *Miscarriages of Justice: A Review of Justice in Error*, edited by C. Walker and K. Starmer. London: Oxford University Press.

Taylor, Nick and David Ormerod. 2004. 'Mind the Gaps: Safety, Fairness and Moral Legitimacy'. *Criminal Law Review* 266–83.

Taylor, Phil. 2013. 'Time for Next Move, Says Ex-Judge'. *New Zealand Herald*, September 28. Retrieved (http://www.nzherald.co.nz/nz/news/article.cfm?c_id=1&objectid=11131183).

Teubner, Gunther. 1984. 'Autopoiesis in Law and Society: A Rejoinder to Blankenburg'. *Law & Society Review* 18(2):291.

The Law Society. 2018. 'Failures in Disclosure Leading to Miscarriages of Justice'. *The Law Society.* Retrieved (http://www.lawsociety.org.uk/news/stories/failures-in-disclosure-leading-to-miscarriages-of-justice/).

Thomas, Alex. 2017. 'Police Misconduct and the CCRC'. *The Justice Gap.*

Thomas, Cheryl. 2010. *Are Juries Fair?* London. Retrieved (https://www.justice.gov.uk/downloads/publications/research-and-analysis/moj-research/are-juries-fair-research.pdf).

Thomas, John. 2012. 'Jury Irregularities in the Crown Court: A Protocol Issued by the President of the Queen's Bench Division'. Retrieved (https://www.judiciary.gov.uk/wp-content/uploads/JCO/Documents/Protocols/jury_irregularities_protocol.pdf).

Thornton, Brian. 2017. 'The Mysterious Case of the Vanishing Court Reporter'. *The Justice Gap*, April. Retrieved (http://www.thejusticegap.com/2017/04/mysterious-case-vanishing-court-reporter/).

Transform Justice. 2016. *Justice Denied? The Experience of Unrepresented Defendants in the Criminal Courts.* Retrieved (http://www.transformjustice.org.uk/wp-content/uploads/2016/04/TJ-APRIL_Singles.pdf).

Tversky, Amos and Daniel Kahneman. 1974. 'Judgment under Uncertainty: Heuristics and Biases'. *Science* 185(4157):1124–31. Retrieved (http://science.sciencemag.org/content/185/4157/1124.abstract).

Tyler, Tom R. 2006. *Why People Obey the Law.* Princeton: Princeton University Press.

Tyler, Tom R. 2011. *Why People Cooperate: The Role of Social Motivations.* Princeton: Princeton University Press.

Tyler, Tom R. and Y. J. Huo. 2002. *Trust in the Law: Encouraging Public Cooperation with the Police and Courts.* New York: Russell-Sage Foundation.

Valentine, Tim, Stephen Darling, and Amina Memon. 2007. 'How Can Psychological Science Enhance the Effectiveness of Identification Procedures? An International Comparison'. *Public Interest Law Reporter* 11:21–39.

Walker, Clive. 1993. 'Introduction'. Pp. 1–17 in *Justice in Error*, edited by C. Walker and K. Starmer. London: Blackstone Press.

Walker, Clive. 1999. 'The Agenda of Miscarriages of Justice'. Pp. 3–30 in *Miscarriages of Justice: A Review of Justice in Error*, edited by C. Walker and K. Starmer. Oxford: Oxford University Press.

Walker, Clive and Kathryn Campbell. 2010. 'The CCRC as an Option for Canada: Forwards or Backwards?' Pp. 191–204 in *The Criminal Cases Review Commission: Hope for the Innocent?*, edited by M. Naughton. Basingstoke: Palgrave Macmillan.

Walker, Clive and Carole McCartney. 2008. 'Criminal Justice and Miscarriages of Justice in England and Wales'. In *Wrongful Conviction: International Perspectives on Miscarriages of Justice*, edited by R. C. Huff and M. Killias. Philadelphia: Temple University Press.

Walker, Clive and Keir Starmer, eds. 1993. *Justice in Error*. London: Blackstone Press.

Walton, Kevin. 2015. 'Legal Philosophy and the Social Sciences: The Potential for Complementarity'. *Jurisprudence* 6(2):231–51.

Waluchow, Wilfred J. 1994. *Inclusive Legal Positivism*. Oxford: Oxford University Press.

Ward, Judith. 1993. *Ambushed: My Story*. Vermilion.

Weber, Max. 1968. *Economy and Society Part 2*.

Webster, Richard. 1998. *The Great Children's Home Panic*. Oxford: Orwell Press.

Weick, Karl E. 1969. *The Social Psychology of Organizing*. Reading, MA: Addison-Wesley Publishing.

Weick, Karl E. 1995. *Sensemaking in Organizations*. Thousand Oaks, CA: Sage.

Wells, Gary L. and Donna M. Murray. 1983. 'What Can Psychology Say about the Neil v. Biggers Criteria for Judging Eyewitness Accuracy?' *Journal of Applied Psychology* 68(3):347–62. Retrieved (http://doi.apa.org/getdoi.cfm?doi=10.1037/0021-9010.68.3.347).

Wells, Gary L. and Elizabeth A. Olson. 2003. 'Eyewitness Testimony'. *Annual Review of Psychology* 54(1):277–95. Retrieved (http://www.annualreviews.org/doi/10.1146/annurev.psych.54.101601.145028).

Wells, Gary L., Miko M. Wilford, and Laura Smalarz. 2013. 'Forensic Science Testing: The Forensic Filler-Control Method for Controlling Contextual Bias, Estimating Error Rates, and Calibrating Analysts' Reports'. *Journal of Applied Research in Memory and Cognition* 2(1):53–5.

Woffinden, Bob. 2010. 'The Criminal Cases Review Commission Had Failed'. *The Guardian*, November 30.

Woffinden, Bob. 2015. 'The Criminal Cases Review Commission'. *Bob Woffinden*.

Wolitz, David. 2010. 'Innocence Commissions and the Future of Post-Conviction Review'. *Arizona Law Review* 52(4):1027–82.

Yorke, Harry. 2018. 'Police Forces and Prosecutors Failing to Carry out "Basic" Procedure in Rape Cases, Attorney General Says'. *The Telegraph*, January 27. Retrieved (https://www.telegraph.co.uk/news/2018/01/27/police-forces-prosecutors-failing-carry-basic-procedure-rape/).

Young, Richard and Andrew Sanders. 1994. 'The Royal Commission on Criminal Justice: A Confidence Trick?' *Oxford Journal of Legal Studies* 14(3):435–48.

Zalman, Marvin. 2012. 'Qualitatively Estimating the Incidence of Wrongful Convictions'. *Criminal Law Bulletin* 48(2):221–79.

Zander, Michael. 2005. *A Response to the Department of Constitutional Affairs' Consultation Paper*.

Zander, Michael. 2012. 'Zander on the CCRC'. *The Justice Gap*.

Zander, Michael. 2015. 'The Criminal Cases Review Commission, the Court of Appeal and Jury Decisions: A Better Way Forward'. *Criminal Law & Justice Weekly* 179(4):74–5.

Zander, Michael. 2017. *Presentation to the Criminal Cases Review Commission 20th Anniversary Conference 2 November 2017.*

Zellick, Graham. 2005. 'The Criminal Cases Review Commission and the Court of Appeal'. *Criminal Law Review* 937–50.

Zuckerman, Adrian A. 1991. 'Miscarriage of Justice and Judicial Responsibility'. *Criminal Law Review* 492–500.

Zuckerman, Adrian A. 1995. 'A Reform of Civil Procedure—Rationing Procedure Rather Than Access to Justice'. *Journal of Law and Society* 22(2):155–88.

Index

Tables, figures, and boxes are indicated by an italic *t*, *f*, and *b* after the page number.